WHEN THE
UNITED STATES
SPOKE FRENCH

ALSO BY FRANÇOIS FURSTENBERG

In the Name of the Father

WHEN THE UNITED STATES SPOKE FRENCH

Five Refugees
Who Shaped a Nation

FRANÇOIS FURSTENBERG

THE PENGUIN PRESS
NEW YORK
2014

THE PENGUIN PRESS
Published by the Penguin Group
Penguin Group (USA) LLC
375 Hudson Street
New York, New York 10014

USA · Canada · UK · Ireland · Australia
New Zealand · India · South Africa · China

penguin.com
A Penguin Random House Company

First published by The Penguin Press, a member of Penguin Group (USA) LLC, 2014

Illustration credits appear on pages 478–80.

ISBN 978-1-59420-441-8

Printed in the United States of America
1   3   5   7   9   10   8   6   4   2

DESIGNED BY AMANDA DEWEY
MAPS BY JEFFREY L. WARD

For Yliette,

My spark

CONTENTS

WHEN THE
UNITED STATES
SPOKE FRENCH

STRANGE REUNIONS:
AN INTRODUCTION

For affliction does not come from the dust,
nor does trouble sprout from the ground,
Yet man is born to trouble, as the sparks fly upward.

JOB 5:6–7

REVOLUTIONARY SPARKS, SET OFF BY THE GREAT EXPLOSION IN France, fly upward. Most fall in Europe. Some, carried west by the trade winds, fall in the Caribbean and set off dry kindling. Others land deep in the North American forests. A few, following the gentle breezes drifting along the American coast, float up the Delaware Bay to Philadelphia.

Just past noon on Thursday, May 22, 1794, Médéric-Louis-Élie Moreau de Saint-Méry, a former revolutionary leader of Paris, walks along a Philadelphia street. He recently fled France along with his family, chased out by threats of arrest and imprisonment, and is now on his way to New York to take a job. The trip takes him through Philadelphia, where he lingers a few days to tour the new capital. Leaving the U.S. House of Representatives, he's on his way to see the presidential mansion when a horse-drawn carriage bears down on him, two seemingly agitated men inside. Moreau is nearsighted and can't see who's in the carriage, but the passengers seem to be waving. As the carriage approaches one man jumps out and pulls Moreau into a big hug while the second emerges more gingerly, lifting out his leg.

At last, Moreau recognizes them: Bon-Albert Briois de Beaumetz and Charles-Maurice de Talleyrand-Périgord, two of France's most prominent aristocrats, both from the noblest of French families, and both, like Moreau, former leaders of the French Revolution. All of them had served in the Assemblée constituante, the legislative body that governed France from 1789 to 1791 and drafted the first constitution in French history, replacing the system of royal absolutism with a constitutional monarchy.

"What joy!" Moreau exclaims. "What happiness! What multiplied embraces!"

Upon their "rapturous meeting," the three go to eat. Moreau's enthusiasm is unabated: "What a dinner! How many things to tell one another after two and a half years! What a wealth of detail to hear and to communicate!"

Afterward, they set off to visit other acquaintances, including Louis-Marie, vicomte de Noailles, another aristocratic Frenchman from one of France's great families who had also been an early leader of the French Revolution, a *constituant,* or member of the Constituent Assembly—and who, like them, now found himself a refugee in Philadelphia.[1]

———————

SIX MONTHS LATER, in November 1794, François-Alexandre-Frédéric, duc de La Rochefoucauld-Liancourt, yet another descendant of one of France's noblest families, a leader of the French Revolution, and also a former *constituant,* has just disembarked from the *Pigou,* the ship that carried him across the Atlantic. He is melancholic, "dejected in spirits," depressed from the terrors he's fled and the family left behind. Now safely on land, he has found lodgings at the Philadelphia City Tavern. It's a terrible choice for someone who might wish to remain inconspicuous: the City Tavern's coffeehouse serves as the gathering place and informal stock exchange for the local merchant community; nowhere in Philadelphia does information circulate more rapidly. Soon the word is out. Talleyrand, hearing about his friend's arrival, rushes over to greet Liancourt. They embrace. After a brief chat about their new country, Talleyrand leaves his exhausted friend to a night of rest—his first on land in over two months.

The next morning, after breakfast, Liancourt returns Talleyrand's

The southeast corner of Third and Market Streets, Philadelphia, circa 1800.

Second Street, north of Market Street, Philadelphia, circa 1800.

visit, and the two head off to see Théophile Cazenove, a Franco-Dutch banker with the resources to employ a French chef, with whom Talleyrand eats most of his meals. Later, they meet Noailles before going to find Moreau, who has by now established himself as a bookseller, his shop having become a meeting point for the French community in Philadelphia.[2]

ROUGHLY A year later, in late 1795 or early 1796, Constantin-François de Chasseboeuf, comte de Volney, the Enlightenment author, traveler, philosopher, and politician—yet another former *constituant*—is planning a dinner party. He is expecting twenty guests, including Louis-Philippe, duc d'Orléans, who will become the king of France in 1830, but is for now living in exile with his brothers in a small house just around the corner. In another time, another place, Volney attended the "grand dinner" that Liancourt hosted weekly in apartments in the Tuileries Palace, where dozens of *constituants* would meet to debate politics and reform in those heady days in early 1790. Volney's Philadelphia party will be just a shadow of that former brilliance; still, he would like something a little special for the occasion. He heads to the *pâtisserie* recently established by Marino, a chef formerly employed by a French aristocrat, who shares his former employer's royalist sympathies. Volney, who is considered something of a radical by his friends, places an order for a "*pâté bien soigné*," made of the rarest and most delicate ingredients, the kind of dish that would have been impossible to find in Philadelphia a few years earlier. The food, the price—everything is arranged; the chef just needs a name and an address for delivery. Only then does he discover his customer's identity.

"Volney!" the chef bursts out in anger. "Volney! . . . Volney!"

It is, according to a witness, "superb to see; one could have painted the scene: his cotton cap on his head, his white apron folded over, and a huge knife at his belt. Suddenly leaving his *casserole*, his charcoal oven still burning, he began to shout in a thunderous voice, trembling with indignation: 'Get out of here, *misérable*, get out of my kitchen, damned atheist . . . damned revolutionary.'"

"Thus," concludes the amused witness, "I saw the very famous, too famous, *monsieur* Chasseboeuf de Volney enter and leave the most famous *pâtissier* of Philadelphia."[3]

———————————

ONE EVENING in late 1795 or early 1796, around eight o'clock, Moreau is sitting in the private office in his bookstore on the corner of Front and Walnut Streets, behind the warehouses that line the Delaware River, when Talleyrand wanders in. The two begin to chat. Eventually, inevitably, their thoughts turn to home, and the two old friends discuss "France's past fate, its present state, and finally what we thought of its future." It's a typical *soirée,* and it plays out like many others: "There alone and without interruption (except when Beaumetz, Talon, Blacons, Noailles, Volney, Payen de Boisneuf, Demeunier, Boilandry, were with us all together or separately) we opened our hearts to one another, we poured out our feelings; and each of us knew the other's most intimate thoughts." The night passes "in these delightful confidences" until it's time to eat. Talleyrand is not hungry; he sips Madeira (which he proclaims "excellent") while Moreau sups on rice and milk cooked on the stove in his bookstore. On other nights, they eat with Moreau's family, when Blacons, Beaumetz, and La Colombe often join in: "Gaiety reigned constantly at our reunions, where we often amused ourselves by playing jokes, particularly when Blacons jestingly 'Monseigneured' Talleyrand, who revenged himself by cuffing him." As often happens, the friends don't notice how late it's gotten until Moreau's wife comes in to chase them off. Talleyrand complies, but "having got as far as the little yard at the foot of my stairs," he sneaks back in to continue the party until Madame Moreau, exasperated, comes back to berate him: "Tomorrow you will play the sluggard in your bed until noon; but promptly at seven o'clock in the morning your friend must get up and open his shop." Chastened, Talleyrand finally limps home to bed, letting Moreau get some much-needed sleep.[4]

———————————

THESE MEN, drifting across the Atlantic like so many sparks, had all landed in Philadelphia. They would make the city their home during the mid-1790s, as the fires set off by the great explosion in France burned at their brightest, with French armies pouring across Europe, naval warfare battering the Caribbean, slaves rising up in Haiti, and émigré refugees fleeing the Continent.

Liberal reformers all, these unlikely nomads had grown up in the courts of Versailles and the glamorous salons of Paris's *hôtels particuliers*. The ideas of Enlightenment theorists had fired their imaginations, and as the French Revolution began in that fateful summer of 1789 they launched themselves into the reforms of French *ancien régime* institutions. It was a hopeful time; everything seemed possible. The most powerful and corrupt monarchy of Europe had fallen to its knees before a revolutionary new power. History seemed to have turned a sharp corner. The promises made by the eighteenth century's philosophes were finally at hand: the power of individuals to remake themselves and their world was at last being realized.

Soon, however, events took on a power of their own. Those who had thought to shape not just their own destinies, but the fate of millions, lost control of the world they had made. They fought to stay the course of the Revolution, and, in the inimitable words of Jean-Antoine-Nicolas de Caritat, marquis de Condorcet, "return it to the slow and soft action of the Enlightenment." But their time had passed. And so they were chased off, out of France, out of Europe, and all the way to Philadelphia.[5]

Noailles was, like his brother-in-law, the marquis de Lafayette, a son of the French nobility, and a liberal who had fought in the American Revolution. In 1779 he led a division of soldiers at the Siege of Savannah, at which free colored troops (*gens de couleur*) from the French Caribbean colony of Saint Domingue fought alongside regular American and French forces. At Yorktown in 1781, it was Noailles who represented the French government at Cornwallis's surrender. During the war, he and Alexander Hamilton became fast friends and remained so for many years after. Dashing and handsome, he was a central figure in the court life of the 1780s, and a frequent dance partner of Marie-Antoinette's. When the French Revolution broke out, he served in the French Assemblée constituante, where he became one of the leading liberal voices, serving as its president during the famous days of August 1789. A *maréchal* in the army when war broke out

Gilbert Stuart painted this grand portrait of his friend Noailles while the two lived in Philadelphia in 1798. Noailles is portrayed on the hill in the foreground and also seen riding in the background at the head of a group of soldiers.

between France and Prussia, he fled to England in 1792 before moving to the United States a year later. He remained in the United States for nearly a decade, much longer than most of his compatriots, where he threw himself into Philadelphia society, and into various speculative schemes to rebuild his fortune.

Talleyrand also descended from one of France's noblest families. Only, perhaps, in *ancien régime* France could a person of his temperament and behavior have ascended as high in the hierarchy of the Catholic Church as he did. Irresistibly charming but notoriously venal—Talleyrand "would sell

Portrait of Talleyrand painted during his time in Philadel-phia by James or Ellen Sharples.

his soul for money," the great French politician Honoré-Gabriel Riqueti, comte de Mirabeau, once said, "and he would be right, for he would be exchanging dung for gold"—he served as the bishop of Autun and then *agent général du clergé de France* (administrator of Church finances). He also speculated actively on the Paris *bourse,* or stock exchange, as a disciple of the Anglo-Swiss financier Isaac Panchaud. When the Revolution began in 1789, he became a leading voice of reform in the Assemblée constituante, which elected him president in February 1790. Fleeing Paris in 1792, he spent two years in England before being expelled in 1794, and fleeing again, this time to the United States. He arrived impatient and restless, launching himself into Philadelphia society, exuberant land speculations, and an extended set of travels through the American backcountry.[6]

Liancourt was probably the most eminent of the refugees by the stan-

Charles Willson Peale painted this miniature portrait of Liancourt—who was forty-seven years old when he arrived in the United States—during his stay in Philadelphia.

dards of *ancien régime* France; certainly he'd been the richest. At Versailles, he'd served as master of the *garde-robe* of Louis XVI—among the most envied titles in France. An agricultural reformer in his vast estates, a founder of schools, hospitals, and prisons, and *maréchal de camp* in the French military, Liancourt was elected to the Estates General in 1789, where he sat with the liberal minority. He joined the great constitutional reforms, and rose to become president of the Assemblée constituante on July 18, 1789. In 1792 he fled to England—his cousin, the more famous duc de La Rochefoucauld-d'Enville, chose to stay in France, and died at the hands of Paris mobs that same year—where he remained until the British Aliens Act exiled him again. He arrived in Philadelphia in November 1794, at the age of forty-seven, deeply melancholic from his incessant travels and his persistent exile. "I am sad, and write. Another day gone," he remarked in his diary a few months after his arrival. Although pleased to be reunited with his friends, he bounced around the city numbly, with his adopted dog Cartouche at his side, the days passing as though in a dream: "If I let my disposition drive me, I would not go out for many days. For what purpose? To whom am I useful, or even pleasant?" An inveterate reformer, he occupied his time in Philadelphia studying the prisons, as though previewing Alexis de Tocqueville's journey some forty years later, and published a summary of his observations with Moreau's press. He eventually gathered the energy to travel beyond the confines of Philadelphia, and spent long months touring the American backcountry.[7]

Gilbert Stuart painted this portrait of Volney, represented here in his capacity as writer and backwoods philosopher, while the two of them lived in Philadelphia.

Volney was an Enlightenment philosopher and a traveler. As a twenty-year-old just arrived in Paris from the provinces, he quickly gained a reputation so impressive as to get himself invited to Madame Helvétius's famous salons, where he met Benjamin Franklin and other prominent liberals. In 1782 he left for Syria and Egypt, where he traveled for three years, returning to publish an account, his *Voyage en Syrie et en Égypte,* in 1787. When the Revolution broke out, he was elected a deputy from the Third Estate representing Anjou and sat in the Assemblée constituante. Volney was on the verge of being sent to the United States as consul when a sudden change in the government led instead to his arrest and ten months' imprisonment. Released in 1794, he taught for a year before leaving France in July 1795. While in the United States, he was based in Philadelphia, where locals remembered him as "a man of proud spirit and sour temper . . . lofty and morose nature." Ever the traveler, he soon set off on extensive tours through the continental interior.[8]

Moreau was born in Martinique, studied law in Paris, and then established himself in Saint Domingue, where he married into a planter family and took detailed notes on the geography, life, and slave culture of the island. In 1788 he returned to Paris, where he became a revolutionary leader and, in 1789, president of the electors of Paris, before being elected to the Constituent Assembly. Fleeing in November 1793 with his wife and two children, he endured a four-month transatlantic journey so grueling that the once chubby Moreau lost fifty-two pounds. Finally, blessedly, they landed in Norfolk, Virginia, in March 1794. By October Moreau and his family had established themselves in Philadelphia, where the former lawyer and planter opened a bookstore, selling books, stationery, and supplies, and published French-language books and a newspaper. He became a pillar of the important French-speaking community in Philadelphia, bridging the worlds of French and Saint Domingue refugees, serving as a hub for the circulation of information and various French goods. Moreau used his time in Philadelphia profitably, soliciting comments on his manuscript about Saint Domingue, before publishing the monumental two-volume *Description topographique, physique, civile, politique et historique de la partie française de l'isle de Saint-Domingue* at his own press in 1797. The only

James Sharples painted this pastel portrait of Moreau de Saint-Méry in 1798, shortly before Moreau returned to France.

non-aristocrat of the group, the prickly Moreau seems to have compensated for his lower social status by being, as Liancourt put it in his diary, "boringly vain," speaking about himself "all day, as he does every day"— even at one point taking two pistols from his home and tracking down a French count who had insulted him to threaten him with a duel.[9]

WHEN THE French Revolution broke out, these men had been among its leaders. In the tradition of French lights like Montesquieu and Voltaire, they had been Anglophiles, convinced of the superiority of the British monarchy and balanced constitution. They believed in free trade abroad, education at home, and the promotion of scientific agriculture. When rebellion broke out in Britain's American colonies they threw their support behind the budding revolution; one even traveled across the Atlantic to serve in the war. They were friends and admirers of Franklin and Jefferson, and they socialized in the same Paris circles. They admired the new republic gradually emerging on the Atlantic's western shores, which seemed to them a rough manifestation of the Enlightenment ideals they'd promoted at home—and which, in the late 1780s, seemed poised to regenerate France.

Amid the euphoria that followed the convocation of the Estates General and the fall of the Bastille in July 1789, these men threw themselves behind the Revolution. It was finally happening: all the ideas that had electrified conversations in cafés, salons, Masonic groups, and scientific societies; that had crowded innumerable columns of newspapers, encyclopedias, almanacs, and journals; all that Enlightenment politics had taught the world could now, at last, come to be. They refused to follow the first wave of royalist émigrés like the king's brother, the comte d'Artois, staying instead to dismantle the sclerotic institutions of *ancien régime* France. It was Noailles who presided over the Assemblée constituante on August 4, 1789, when feudal privileges were abolished, bringing down the first pillar of the tottering *ancien régime*. Two months later, it was Talleyrand who pulled down the second pillar, when on October 10 he brought forward a motion to nationalize Church lands in France. And the Old Regime collapsed.

By the time the new constitution took effect in September 1791, however, events had overtaken the *constituants'* vision for their nation. Reactionary aristocrats had established themselves in Prussia, Austria, and various Italian republics, where angry monarchs warned darkly of war against France. King Louis XVI had attempted to flee France that summer, apparently to join the Revolution's enemies abroad. The move was criticized roundly: "the bad proposition to go to Varennes," Noailles would later describe it in his choppy English, "leaving before the National assembly the fatal writing which led to doubt of his faith."[10] France's fragile new institutions could not keep the growing political tensions in check, and the *constituants* found it impossible to reconcile their duty to the king with their liberal values. The center could not hold. By the end of 1791 suspicion reigned on all sides, and French political life was becoming more violent.

As the center of gravity of French politics shifted left, the momentum slipped from the hands of reformers to those of revolutionaries. In mid-1792 King Louis XVI was arrested and later put on trial. In August, crowds in Paris invaded the Tuileries Palace, overthrowing the monarchy. The National Legislative Assembly declared war against Prussia, which responded by invading France in September. When news of the French defeat at Verdun arrived in Paris in early September 1792, the reaction was swift and severe: clerics and aristocrats suspected of loyalty to the king and subversion of the Revolution were executed in what later became known as the "September Massacres." Squeezed from all sides—from radicals on the left and reactionaries on the right—the liberal aristocrats fled.

And so the five Frenchmen—Liancourt, Moreau, Noailles, Talleyrand, and Volney—ended up in Philadelphia. Some, like Moreau, came directly to the United States—though he and his family had to tread carefully, obtaining passports with the help of friends, and posing as foreigners in case a French or British ship should stop them. Others, like Noailles, Talleyrand, and Liancourt, went first to England, where they lived for a few years before the British Aliens Act of 1793 pushed them across the Atlantic. Once they were in the United States, Philadelphia seemed like a natural place to stop: though puny compared with Europe's great cities, it was the closest thing the country had to a European metropolis. It was the nation's capital, the home of the wealthiest merchants and financiers, and the country's principal port, with well-established trading connections to France and French colonies. It was there that they were most likely to feel at home. Neither they nor their new compatriots knew what, exactly, they were doing in the United States. Some thought they were just killing time, others thought they had come to make money, and still others thought they were spying for France as it sought to reestablish an empire in North America.

As we will see, none of those suspicions was wrong.

———————

THE FRENCH émigrés came to America at a time when the United States was nothing like the global power it is today. It takes a leap of imagination to picture the country as it was then: weak and fragile, a collection of thirteen states huddled along the Atlantic coast, riven by internal divisions, continually under siege by Native and foreign powers. Today, the United States is a continental nation; back then, for all practical purposes, its sovereignty extended from the Atlantic coast to the Appalachian Mountains, with a few fingers jutting out into Kentucky and Tennessee. Native Americans controlled most of the area west of the Appalachians, supported by a complicated set of diplomatic and military alliances with the British in the Great Lakes and the Spanish in Louisiana and Florida. Politically, Americans were bitterly divided. Roughly half the population had opposed the new constitutional government, which they perceived as a betrayal of the values for which they had fought a revolution. Socially, the nation was even more split: angry debtors in the backcountry continually threatened rebellion against their creditors among the urban merchant elite, and their debts only seemed to grow with the persistent deflation of the 1780s. Economically, the nation was essentially insolvent, incapable of paying back the European creditors who had financed the Revolution, and unable to raise funds on international capital markets. Revolutionary soldiers paid in Continental currency found themselves with stacks of paper worth pennies on the dollar. The situation, in short, couldn't have been more precarious.

It was in this context that the French Revolution broke out in 1789. It was an explosion of world-historical proportions, shattering social structures, reshaping nations, pulling down empires, and unleashing global warfare on an unprecedented scale. At first, the French Revolution seemed like a validation of the American experiment: Europe's most powerful monarchy had suddenly fallen—manifesting, it seemed to many Americans, the political values they had affirmed a decade earlier. But before long, the French Revolution would pose the most serious challenges to the young United States. Soon after France proclaimed itself a republic in 1792, war broke out across Europe, and then spread to the Americas, where the world's mightiest navies battled one another in the Caribbean and off the coast of the United States. The bitter warfare led to a great slave insurrection in Saint Domingue, followed by the abolition of slavery across France's

Caribbean colonies and the United States' most important Caribbean trading partner. With U.S. commerce imperiled and public opinion firmly on the side of the country's republican ally, government officials faced the danger that their new and fragile nation would be dragged into a global conflict even as, closer to home, the slave regime on which half of the country's economy depended threatened to collapse. The nation was in no condition to survive such seismic shocks.

But the United States did not disintegrate. By the time the Napoleonic Wars ended in 1815 the country not only had emerged whole but was also set firmly on the course to continental and eventually global power. The country controlled two million square miles of land, its sovereignty extending not just to the Mississippi River but clear across the continent to the Rocky Mountains. Neither British, nor Spanish, nor French, nor Native American power threatened its sovereignty. Politically, the country would never be more united. Financially, the United States had established itself as creditworthy, drawing in capital from financial centers across Europe.

These characters and their experiences will offer new insight into some of the elements of that remarkable transformation. On the simplest level, of course, this is a story about a small group of elite men. But one can't understand the lives of these men without taking their world into account, for theirs are lives that take us from the noisy parliamentary halls of revolutionary France, through the neoclassical salons of London, across the Atlantic into the dirty streets of Philadelphia and the elegant parlors of the city's elite *salonnières,* down the coast into sweltering cane fields in Haiti set alight by insurgent slaves, across the Gulf of Mexico and up the muddy waters of the Mississippi River deep into the forests of the Ohio valley controlled by Native Americans—and then back again. By seeing it all through the eyes of our characters, the remarkable transformations of the United States in its early years will emerge in a different light, as will the connections between those transformations and larger events in the Atlantic world. Their stories will show us some of the ways that ideas, cultural influences, politics, and capital all moved across the Atlantic and back again, and how the three great revolutionary movements of the eighteenth century were intertwined.[11]

The émigrés' time in America mostly took place from 1793 to 1798. These were also some of the most momentous years of Atlantic history: when France executed its king, when war between Britain and France broke out, when slaves in Saint Domingue (later Haiti) broke their chains and won their emancipation, when Native Americans won and then lost control of the Ohio valley, when the United States established itself as a neutral power and gained the right to Mississippi River trade. The picture that emerges here is of a country entangled with the French Revolution and the French Atlantic more broadly. We will find an American capital city that might seem unfamiliar: awash with French people, French goods, and French culture. We will see how social and family networks structured the world of the late eighteenth century, and constituted one way the United States connected to the larger Atlantic world. We will encounter European capital flooding into the United States during the wars of the French Revolution, serving a critical role in developing the U.S. backcountry and consolidating the nation's hold on its contested frontiers. And we will see how the United States very nearly lost control of the trans-Appalachian West in the wake of French schemes and ambitions in the Mississippi valley during the 1790s.[12]

This portrait of the early American Republic departs from historical accounts that have too often set U.S. history apart from that of the rest of the world, as though it existed in a cocoon, sheltered by the oceans on either side of the continent. By highlighting the international dimensions of early American history, these émigrés and their stories help deprovincialize the history of the early Republic and connect it to the larger forces reshaping the Atlantic basin—war and revolution, slavery and abolition, trade and commerce. Although the so-called Federalist period is often understood through the lens of nation formation, from the émigrés' perspective it looked quite different. The United States was enmeshed in a multi- or perhaps pre-national world centered around the movement of people, goods, and capital. Despite its political independence, the country turned resolutely outward: toward Europe, toward the Caribbean, and toward the outer edges of its continental frontiers. It was linked to those distant places by financial connections, social networks, and a continuous flow of goods across oceans, seas, lakes, and rivers. From the émigrés' perspective, the early United States looked less like its own country than a far outpost of European empire and European capitalism.

This account would not be possible without the insights offered by an immensely rich and ever-growing body of scholarship that in recent years has transformed the way historians understand the history of early America. During the past generation, many historians have worked to situate the British colonies and the United States in a broader, "Atlantic" context, while others have pushed even further, locating the United States in its broadest global setting. Led by some of the profession's most eminent historians— and no doubt pushed along by the contemporary wave of globalization that has reshaped our own world—a great outpouring of scholarship on Atlantic and global history has reshaped the way scholars think about the seventeenth and eighteenth centuries, when Europe spread across the ocean to dominate the Atlantic littoral and create empires deep in the continental interior.[13]

The chapters that follow engage not just with the most recent scholarship, however, but also with an older historiography, some of which now dates back more than a century, and is too often spurned by historians today. The subject of land speculation and European diplomacy in the Mississippi valley leads back, almost inevitably, to historians like Frederick Jackson Turner, Charles Beard, Thomas Perkins Abernethy, Arthur Preston Whitaker, and Paul Wallace Gates: scholars of the Progressive school who told grand tales of frontier democracy fitfully emerging in the face of Eastern elite hostility and expanding across the continent. They took a keen interest in the interplay between section and nation, geography and politics. They emphasized the importance of migration and trade, empire and warfare. They saw the Old Northwest as a great crossroads, a kind of continental Mediterranean, which had connected peoples and empires throughout the centuries, a region knit together by trade networks among

Americans, French, Spanish, British, and dozens of Native American nations. And ultimately they saw in the great Mississippi valley the linchpin of American history, and recounted a tale of the U.S. conquest of that territory in the face of European and Native American resistance as a critical turning point.

For all their insight, however, the Progressives clung to a Manichaean view of American history. Theirs were stories of virtue against greed, liberty against tyranny, principle against power. Noble settlers battled venal speculators, failed repeatedly, and then rose, phoenix-like, to create new and more egalitarian societies. Liberty and democracy were the stakes of these epic battles, not just for a continent but for the world. Although that scholarship is often set aside today—rightly criticized for its limited conception of democracy, its inattention to Native Americans and slaves, and its naive vision of backcountry egalitarianism—the Progressives nevertheless offer penetrating observations. Inspired by their work, this book sets out to put it in greater dialogue with the newer. In this regard, it may suggest the outlines of a different and possibly darker portrait of the United States than dreamed of in the Progressives' philosophy—which, beneath its depiction of a nation divided by class interests, still conceived of America as a democratic asylum, a land of opportunity for those with the pluck and determination to realize it. Instead, we find here an ultimately ironic story of how brutal warfare and frenzied speculation, migration and mobility, slavery and emancipation all gave birth to the United States we know today.[14]

These themes and more will emerge as we follow Noailles, Talleyrand, Moreau, Liancourt, and Volney across the Atlantic, as they land in Philadelphia, integrate themselves into the city and its elite social networks, begin speculating on backcountry lands, and eventually become enmeshed in Franco-American diplomacy. In the process, we will encounter some of the most famous events in American history in a different light: from the diplomatic struggles of the 1790s, when the United States sought to maintain neutrality in the face of great warring powers, to the Louisiana Purchase, which more than doubled the size of the country in a single treaty, securing the nation's future as a continental power, and once and for all establishing itself against European and Native American powers on its periphery. Following our French émigrés through their travels in America and back will by then, perhaps, have given us a ground-level view of the events that transformed the Atlantic, and eventually the world, at the dawn of the modern era.

Part 1

THE UNITED STATES
SPEAKS FRENCH

Sic itur ad astra.

Mr. BLANCHARD's
FORTY-FIFTH AERIAL FLIGHT.

MR. BLANCHARD, adopted citizen of the principal cities of Europe, pensioner of the French nation, member and correspondent of several academies and literary societies,

On WEDNESDAY, January 9,

At 10 'oclock precisely in the morning, Will rise from the centre of the PRISON COURT, over the city of Philadelphia.

Subscribers are informed that the doors will be open at 8 o'clock precisely.

Persons arriving from the country to witness the experiment may procure tickets of admission by applying at Oelers's hotel until the EIGHTH, at nine in the evening.—— First seats 5 dollars—second seats 2.

If the weather should prove too unfavorable for the experiment, it will be announced by bills put up at an early hour in the morning.

On a chilly morning in January 1793, an unusually distinguished crowd gathered in the courtyard of the Walnut Street Prison, Philadelphia's largest enclosed square. The gathering included George Washington, the president of the United States; John Adams, the vice president; and Thomas Jefferson, the secretary of state. James Madison, the leader of the House of Representatives, was probably there, along with James Monroe—the nation's first five presidents all assembled in this one space along with hundreds of Philadelphians to watch America's first flight, undertaken by a Frenchman, Jean-Pierre Blanchard. Tickets for the event—five dollars for the best spots—had sold at Oeller's Hotel, a bastion of Philadelphia's French community, where supporters of the French Revolution had recently staged what the *Gazette of the United States*

The Walnut Street Prison is the large building in the background. Blanchard lifted off from the inside courtyard, which was then the city's largest enclosed square.

called "a splendid entertainment," in honor of the spectacular French victory at Valmy against Prussian and Austrian armies. But it was not just Philadelphians who were excited that day. Americans up and down the Atlantic seaboard read the details expectantly; New Yorkers even held out a faint hope that, "if the wind should break fair," Blanchard might make it as far as their city.[1]

Cannons began firing at dawn, the great booms echoing through the city's cobbled streets and the forests and farms of the nearby countryside, drawing hundreds more to the courtyard. By nine in the morning, with temperatures slowly rising into the forties, nearly three hundred spectators crowded in to watch Blanchard prepare for his flight. As the balloon inflated, with a band playing music and cannons still booming, its design gradually became clear: blue spangled with stars. At 10:00 a.m., as promised, Blanchard was ready. The crowd fell silent when President Washington stepped forward and handed the Frenchman a passport written up in his own hand—to reassure whomever he might meet at whatever spot he might land that he was no enemy of the state: not the advance guard of an airborne French invasion. The two said a few words in private, Washington towering over the Frenchman, who stood just over five feet tall. At five minutes past the hour, amid shouts and applause and solemn music, Blanchard, dressed in a blue suit with a cocked hat and white feathers, leaped into the basket and threw off the ballast. Waving a flag—American on one side, French on the other—he soared into the air. The president took off his hat and bowed. "It was indeed a spectacle as magnificent as it was new to us, to see this intrepid aeronaut majestically rise from the earth," reported one witness.[2]

And so another spark flew upward.

As BLANCHARD rose, the crowds in nearby streets marveled at the spectacle: "Admiration was painted on every countenance, and many who had not purchased tickets of admission into the prison yard, now regretted, but too late, their having deprived themselves of witnessing the most interesting scene that the human eye ever beheld." Stevedores with their leathery hands paused for a moment at the docks, putting down their barrels and crates to look up. Solemn Quakers turned their heads to the sky, looking beyond the brims of the hats they refused to remove even indoors, to wonder at the sight of a man in flight. Looking down from the stillness of the sky, Blanchard "could not help being surprized and astonished" at the "immense numbers of people, which covered the open places, the roofs of the houses, the steeples, the streets and the roads." All of Philadelphia, it seemed, was looking up at Blanchard as he drifted above the city. *"Bon*

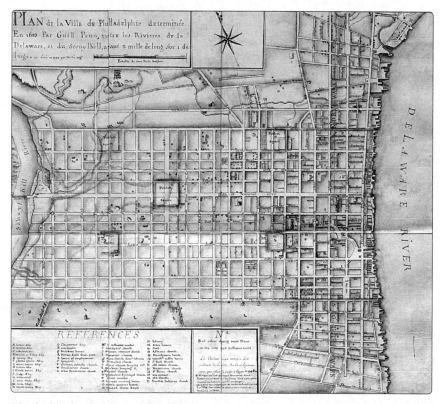

This highly detailed map of Philadelphia, produced by the French engraver Charles Varlé for the Holland Land Company, shows the extent of settlement in the U.S. capital and the location of major landmarks.

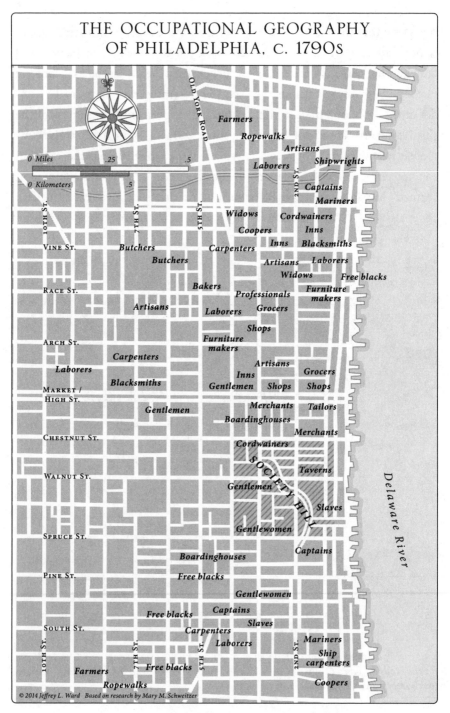

THE OCCUPATIONAL GEOGRAPHY
OF PHILADELPHIA, c. 1790s

Farmers

Ropewalks

Artisans

Laborers   Shipwrights

Captains

Mariners

Widows   Cordwainers

Coopers   Inns

Carpenters   Inns   Blacksmiths

Butchers   Artisans   Laborers

Butchers   Widows   Free blacks

Bakers   Furniture
makers

Professionals

Artisans   Laborers   Grocers

Shops

Furniture
makers

Carpenters   Artisans

Inns   Grocers

Laborers   Blacksmiths   Gentlemen   Shops   Shops

Gentlemen   Merchants   Tailors

Boardinghouses

Merchants

Cordwainers

Taverns

SOCIETY HILL

Gentlemen

Slaves

Gentlewomen

Boardinghouses   Captains

Free blacks

Gentlewomen

Free blacks   Captains

Carpenters   Slaves

Laborers   Mariners

Ship
carpenters

Farmers   Free blacks

Ropewalks   Coopers

OLD YORK ROAD

2ND ST.

5TH ST.

7TH ST.

10TH ST.

VINE ST.

RACE ST.

ARCH ST.

MARKET /
HIGH ST.

CHESTNUT ST.

WALNUT ST.

SPRUCE ST.

PINE ST.

SOUTH ST.

10TH ST.   7TH ST.   5TH ST.   2ND ST.

0 Miles   .25   .5

0 Kilometers   .5

Delaware River

© 2014 Jeffrey L. Ward   Based on research by Mary M. Schweitzer

Notable occupational clusters in 1790s Philadelphia.

Voyage, God bless you, was echoed from every mouth; hats waved, hands lifted up."³

As Blanchard floated twelve hundred feet above the earth, the city of brick and wood stretched out below him, the meandering Schuylkill River off in the west, the majestic Delaware River just to the east. From his perch high above, Blanchard heard echoes of life below: the clatter of a horse's shoes on cobblestone, the bark of a dog prowling the alleys for food, the cries of a baby in a mother's arms, the shout of a young chimney sweep offering his services. As one person after another looked up and gasped, Blanchard listened with quiet satisfaction to "the cries of joy which rent the air."⁴

The soft wind first pushed Blanchard east, across northern Philadelphia, between Market and Race, crossing Fourth, Third, then Second Streets. This was a working-class section of town, and looking down, Blanchard could see the houses of blacksmiths, cordwainers, furniture makers, and other artisans and tradesmen, who worked in their shops on the first floor and lived above with their families. It was Philadelphia's most densely populated neighborhood, the sidewalks filled with servants pushing their way through the crowds on some errand or another, shoppers on their way to the markets, and clerks heading to shops selling goods from all over the world: sugar from the Caribbean, wine from France, cotton from India.

To the south, just below Market Street, lay the city's political and financial center. Rising above the surrounding buildings, Blanchard could easily spot the newly constructed Bank of the United States, conceived by Alex-

The first Bank of the United States, on South Second Street: then and now.

Congress Hall, seat of the U.S. Congress in Philadelphia: then and now.

ander Hamilton to issue government debt and service the nation's payment system. The building would later be acquired by the French merchant Stephen Girard; it still stands today in the heart of Philadelphia.

Blanchard saw just two blocks to the west, and also rising above the neighborhood, the State House, where the Declaration of Independence and the Constitution had been debated and signed, and Congress Hall, where both the House of Representatives and the Senate sat.

These buildings towered above the rest of the city, testifying to Philadelphia's status as the nation's capital city during the 1790s: political capital, cultural capital, and economic capital all rolled into one. It was the only

The Library Company, founded by Benjamin Franklin, which houses the American Philosophical Society: then and now.

time the United States had a single great metropolis the way France has Paris and England has London, and it made Philadelphia by far "the most agreeable city for a foreigner," as Liancourt would write, gathering "more than any other, people who cultivate" literary and scientific inquiry. "It is the seat of a philosophical society, and a large and valuable public library; and of a museum which has an almost complete collection of the minerals and animals of North America."[5]

As Blanchard approached the Delaware River the wind shifted, pushing him south toward Philadelphia's port, the center of the city's commercial life, its raison d'être. Warehouses lined the riverside, and wooden wharves jutted out into the Delaware to welcome ships from the Caribbean and Europe, and even a few from ports as distant as India and China, all of them trading their goods for produce from the fertile Delaware River valley, known as the Atlantic's breadbasket. Hosts of artisans lived and worked

Philadelphia's Arch Street Ferry. The port along the Delaware River was the commercial and economic heart of the U.S. capital.

nearby to service this vast commercial hub: carpenters, joiners, blacksmiths, rope and sail makers, all little cogs in an increasingly complex economic machine moving people and goods from one part of the world to another.

Continuing south, parallel with the Delaware, Blanchard could see the handsome new mansions rising up along Society Hill, above the recently covered Dock Creek, where Philadelphia's merchants, flush from the nation's booming economy, held their elaborate salons and luxurious dinner parties, making Philadelphia's real estate the most expensive in the nation. Perhaps Blanchard even saw a servant carrying a calling card to one of the neighborhood's ornate houses, conveying an invitation to a dinner or tea. Talleyrand, Liancourt, Volney, Noailles, and Moreau would all settle here during their American exile and soon be found strolling these very sidewalks, dropping in on friends, conducting business, and killing time.[6]

Despite its importance to the nation, Philadelphia was still a small city. From his vantage, Blanchard could easily see it in its entirety, beginning at the Delaware River, and running west to Eighth Street—only eight blocks—beyond which the roads were unpaved and the countryside began. On its northern edge the city ended at Vine Street, three blocks north of Market, with the suburb of Northern Liberties just beyond. Just one mile to the south, a mere seven blocks away, the city ended at Cedar (now South) Street, at the suburb of Southwark. In all, Philadelphia totaled less than a square mile. But with a population of over forty thousand in 1790, approaching seventy thousand in 1800, it was densely packed. In Philadelphia's most crowded wards, each building housed, on average, seven to eight people in a total of 1,228 square feet—a figure that included half of the ground floor, typically dedicated to commerce. Many laborers lived with their family in a house containing no more than 500 square feet. Behind the buildings lay outdoor kitchens and washhouses in lots often shared with a horse, pig, or cow. Philadelphia's population density then was far greater than Manhattan's is today. To find a similar density in our day one needs to look all the way to Mumbai.[7]

This intense proximity made it impossible for Blanchard—or any other visitor—to ignore the city's cruel aspects. Some of the faces that turned up to the sky to watch Blanchard that morning belonged to enslaved men and women; although laws for slavery's gradual abolition were on the books, labor was still coerced, not only through slavery but also through the indentured servitude and apprenticeship systems that still prevailed. The divide between rich and poor, already significant, had been widening since the Revolution, as seaboard elites made ever-growing fortunes on trade, commerce, and finance, while farmers and servants struggled under growing debt burdens in a deflationary economy.

The city also stank. In an era before public sewage or public health, rotting animal corpses and every sort of human waste lay putrefying in open sewers, in alleys, or in the streets. When he arrived, Volney was overwhelmed by the "striking odor of marshland, and the smell of oysters." Sewage waste regularly contaminated private wells in the years before Philadelphia's waterworks were established, causing predictable intestinal trouble among residents. Low-lying marshlands abutted the city, causing major health trouble in the summer, when the hot and sticky climate bred mosquitoes carrying yellow fever, driving the wealthy to their summer homes outside the city proper and killing off many poor residents, largely immigrant or African American, who had nowhere to go. Flying high above while others remained stuck below, Blanchard, it might be said, personified the contrasts endemic to eighteenth-century life, when mobility so often meant the difference between life and death.[8]

––––––––––

FLYING UPWARD into the skies, Blanchard seemed to incarnate the wonders of the French Revolution. France's stunning victory at Valmy, which saved the French Revolution, heralded a new age: an age that would be shaped not by kings and noblemen, but by citizens making their own history. France was now a republic. No one exulted at the spectacle more than Americans, they who first proved to the world that humans could carve out their own destiny in pursuit of happiness.

About half after 6 o'clock laſt evening we were happy to meet Mr. Blanchard again in this city going to pay his reſpects to the Preſident of the United Stetes.—He informed us, that his ærial voyage laſted forty-ſix minutes, in which time he ran over a ſpace of more than 15 miles and then deſcended a little to the eaſtward of Woodbury in the ſtate of New-Jerſey—where he took a carriage and returned to Cooper's ferry—and was at the Preſident's, as we have already mentioned at half paſt 6 o'clock laſt evening.

The following lines was addreſſed to Mr. BLAN-CHARD, yeſterday morning.

Grand Blanchard lorſque tu volera dans les air, V'a annonce aux planettes de l' univerſe ; Que les Francois ont vaincu lieurs enemis interieure, Leur intrepidite a expulce les exterieurs: Penetre dans l'olimpe, dis a tous les dieux, Que les Francois ont ete les victorieux : Prie Mars que les armes de la France, Ne laiſſe aux tirants acune eſperance.

Great Blanchard ! as you wing your way toward the heavens ; there announce to all the planets of the univerſe, that Frenchmen have conquered their interior enemies, and that their Exterior Foes have been repulſed by their intrepidity : Dart through Olympus and tell to the gods, that Frenchmen have been victorious. Implore the aid of Mars, that the Arms of France may cruſh the ambitious deſigns of tyrants FOR EVER.

Great Blanchard! as you wing your
way toward the heavens;
There to announce to all the
planets of the universe,
That Frenchmen have conquered
their interior enemies,
And that their Exterior Foes
have been repulsed by their
intrepidity
Dart through Olympus and tell
to the gods,
That Frenchmen have been
victorious.
Implore the aid of Mars, that the
Arms of France
May crush the ambitious designs
of tyrants FOR EVER.

As Blanchard soared above Philadelphia like Icarus, Americans turned up to stare in wonder and pride. A French aeronaut flying through the sky, Blanchard embodied the limitless possibilities promised by the age of Revolutions, this new era of world history. But did anyone notice that Blanchard had lost control of his destiny and could only watch, helpless, as the winds pushed him where they would?

In all, his journey lasted forty-six minutes. He landed about fifteen miles from Philadelphia, just a little east of Woodbury, New Jersey.

BLANCHARD'S VIEW of Philadelphia that morning in 1793, of early America—indeed, of the Atlantic world—was an extraordinarily privileged one. It seemed almost magical. Soaring over the city and looking down, he apprehended Philadelphia's sights and sounds, its objects and people: the city in which the émigré *constituants* would soon arrive. It is a world we today can only reconstruct through the fragments and traces left behind. But looking out, he could see only as far as the distant horizon. Perhaps he saw there the slight bend of the planet, but no more.

Blanchard could not look south and see the island of Saint Domingue, where republicans and royalists, white and colored, slave and free, were just then throwing themselves headlong into a period of vicious warfare that would last another ten years, pulling in the three most powerful empires in the world, killing tens of thousands of soldiers, freeing half a million slaves, and ending with the creation of Haiti. Nor could he see King Louis XVI, then on trial before the French National Assembly, awaiting the verdict that would pronounce his death at the guillotine and launch twenty years of war that would forever change Europe. He probably saw west as far as the Schuylkill River. Beyond that, however, he could not see the rugged Appalachian Mountains dividing Pennsylvania in two, where angry farmers groaned under new taxes slowly pushing them toward rebellion against the new federal government. Nor could his gaze penetrate farther west still, where the Western Confederacy of Native American villages fought American settlers' encroachment into their territory, the U.S. Army mustering for another eighteen months of losing battles in the bitterly contested territory between the Ohio River and the Great Lakes. Most of all, Blanchard could not see the ties that connected all these distant peoples and places to Philadelphia.[9]

No, Blanchard could not possibly understand the forces that shaped the Atlantic world. The frenetic movement that persisted during peace and during war, inside imperial borders and across them, around and around in a continuous flow, following tides and currents and winds, pushing up river valleys, crossing the craggiest mountain passes, and tearing down primeval forests. On and on it beat, the pulse of commodities and people that made up that world, coursing up the American coast, across the North Atlantic to fill the coffers of merchants in London, Amsterdam, Paris, Nantes, and Bordeaux, then south along the European and African coasts, back across the Atlantic to the Caribbean, through the Gulf of Mexico, up the Mississippi, and deep into North America, all the way up the western slopes of the Appalachians. Faster and faster it beat, the centripetal force of it pulling the

Atlantic world ever tighter together—until, suddenly, at the end of the eighteenth century it erupted in a bloody, horrific explosion.

That eruption flung Noailles, Talleyrand, Moreau, Volney, and Liancourt across the Atlantic Ocean. They drifted in, one by one, sparks blown over by the wind. Their individual lives are inseparable from the much larger forces of history. Their stories are, in certain respects, our story.

Chapter 1

FRANCE COMES
TO AMERICA

O
N MAY 3, 1793, LOUIS-MARIE, THE VICOMTE DE NOAILLES, CAME
to America. He had fled France nearly a year earlier, hoping to
return quickly, but European politics were becoming more chaotic. Now he had left the Continent.

Noailles was a dashing soldier and an elegant courtier with the most
polished manners. Like his brother in-law, the marquis de Lafayette, he was
a liberal noble who fought with brio in the American Revolution. After the
Siege of Savannah, in 1779, Noailles' commanding officer praised his "love
for war, for his *métier*," while Admiral d'Estaing himself wrote that he deserved "the king's *grâces*." December 1780 saw Noailles marching with Rochambeau's army through Philadelphia, where he lingered long enough to
dance all night with one of Philadelphia's most beautiful young women at a
ball thrown by the chevalier de La Luzerne. October 1781 found him at
Yorktown, where he repelled the last British attack of the siege, a desperate
sortie Noailles routed as he led a company of his Soissonois Brigade with
the shout "Vive le roi!" When the British at last called for a truce, it was

Noailles who represented the French government in the negotiations for Cornwallis's surrender. And it was Noailles who stood crisply with his brigade, dressed in their ceremonial uniforms adorned with red lapels, light blue collars, and yellow buttons, on the west side of the road to Yorktown, as the British soldiers filed out of the fort, French and American flags already fluttering above, while "universal silence" prevailed below.[1]

Noailles returned to France a hero, his liberal credentials established. In those heady years following France's great victory, he befriended Franklin, worshipped Voltaire, and worked with other liberals to import the best traditions of English political and economic life to France. In 1788 he became a member of the Société des Trente, a collection of liberal notables that included Lafayette, Condorcet, Mirabeau, and the duc de Liancourt. When Louis XVI convened the Estates General in 1789 Noailles jumped into action, taking a leading role in the Assemblée constituante charged with drafting a French constitution. It was he, as much as any single person, who slew France's *ancien régime*: on the night of August 4, 1789, while presiding over the Assemblée constituante, Noailles "sketched a very pathetic and touching scene of the misery of the people, the desolation of the countryside, the horrors of anarchy that reigned in the provinces," as one representative recalled, and proposed in response "not violent means but equality of taxes, the suppression of feudal rights, those of *mainmorte* and other rights of personal servitude." With his speech, Noailles launched what another *constituant* called "a moment of patriotic drunkenness." Over the course of the night, one nobleman after another rose to abandon his special privileges. Aristocratic titles, exemptions from taxes, the clergy's seignorial rights, noble hunting privileges: all were renounced and more. "Let us only regret that we have nothing else left to sacrifice," proclaimed the chevalier de Boufflers after two in the morning. "Let us consider that henceforth the title of 'Frenchman' will be distinction enough for every generous soul." By the time the sun rose on August 5, the legal structure that had underpinned the *ancien régime* for hundreds of years had crumbled.[2]

Noailles had unleashed forces that he and his fellow liberals could not control. A few years later, in April 1792, serving as *maréchal* in the Armée

The French Constituent Assembly on the night of August 4, when feudal privileges were formally abolished. Noailles presided over the assembly that night.

du Nord, on the collapsing front lines of France's war against Prussia and Austria, disgusted by the disorder in the army's ranks, the mutiny, and desertion of soldiers, Noailles resigned his commission. He crossed enemy lines and settled in England, where he found refuge among the community of liberal Whig statesmen he had long admired, with whose politics he felt most at home. It was from England that he learned of the September Massacres in Paris, when—with aristocrats fleeing to enemy lines and murderous Prussian armies closing in on Paris and threatening violent retribution on the population—panicked mobs began attacking those they considered enemies of the Revolution, killing at least eleven hundred, including many of Noailles' friends. The massacres would definitively polarize the growing divide in worldwide opinion about the French Revolution. From Whitehall, the British undersecretary of state James Bland Burges summarized the reports: "Of new massacres; of 160 priests being butchered in a church; of all the prisoners confined in all the prisons having been deliberately and in orderly succession put to death . . . many must have been of high rank and consequence." Burges hoped the Duke of Brunswick's Prussian army would respond without mercy. "Hateful as is the idea of slaughter and devastation, to forbear from inflicting a severe punishment of such shocking crimes will be an offence against mankind," he wrote, hoping that no "weak disinclination" would prevent Brunswick "from annihilating, as far as he can, the theatre of such detestable exploits."[3]

There was no going back; one side or the other was determined to exact bloody revenge: the Paris mobs for the crimes of centuries, the Prussian armies for the crimes of the Paris mobs. The mobs would win the first round. Noailles soon learned the shocking news of the French victory at Valmy—when an army of citizens, many of them armed with nothing more than pitchforks and axes, defeated an army of professional soldiers commanded by aristocratic officers marching under the banner of European monarchs. And then, in late January 1793, Noailles learned that King Louis XVI had been executed and that the French had invaded Belgium, making war between France and Great Britain inevitable. Europe was now careening down a bloody path that would continue through two decades of brutal war.

Despite his political connections, Noailles' situation became precarious. As thousands crossed the English Channel in panic seeking safety, many of them penniless, British authorities grew anxious. "These crowds of *émigrés* add greatly to the uncomfortable circumstances of the time," wrote William Eden, 1st Baron Auckland, the British ambassador to The Hague, in late December 1792. "Though many of the individuals . . . are objects highly worthy both of respect and compassion, it must be allowed that, in general, the levity and dangerous talents of the nation have not been corrected in the school of misfortune." Suspecting that at least some of the new arrivals were "detached and paid by the Jacobin leaders to do mischief and to prepare and promote revolutions," Auckland named Noailles (and Liancourt) among "the exiles who are highly dangerous, and are now said to be in London." No one really knew if England was on the verge of revolution. Certainly many French revolutionaries thought so, and many reactionary Britons, too. In response, British authorities passed the Aliens Act of 1793, sharply restricting the rights of émigrés, including the right of habeas corpus. Thereupon Noailles took matters into his own hands and boarded a ship for the United States in April 1793. It was only a matter of time before Liancourt and Talleyrand would follow.[4]

No doubt as he began the long, uncertain trip across the Atlantic, Noailles thought back to his previous American voyage. In 1780 he had sailed with the comte de Rochambeau and four regiments of French soldiers—fifty-five hundred men in ten ships of war and thirty convoys, along with eight million *livres'* worth of munitions, clothes, tents, and French coin—a conquering army from Europe's greatest continental power. Still in his early twenties, Noailles was the scion of one of France's noblest families. His great-great-grandfather, Antoine de Noailles, had served as the ambassador to England in the middle of the sixteenth century, under King Henri II. Noailles' great-grandfather was one of the most powerful generals under Louis XIV, the Sun King, when France reached its height of power and glory. His grandfather and uncle both attained the rank of *maréchal,* and his father was a distinguished soldier. His mother was Marie-Antoinette's first lady of honor. There were few nobler lineages than this one in the hierarchy of France's *ancien régime,* and the young vicomte was hungry to prove himself fit to inherit his name. "He dreamed of nothing but arms and horses, the school of theory, and German evolutions and discipline," remembered a childhood friend. When war broke out between the American colonies and the British Empire in the 1770s, it struck Noailles—along with his friend and other young, ambitious, liberal aristocrats like them—as a splendid opportunity: "Sanctioned by the authority of long usage, and by the memory of our ancestors, who . . . had often gone forth in search of adventures and military employment, and had displayed their valor, at one time in the Spanish and Italian service against the Saracens, at another, in the armies of Austria, we now eagerly sought the means of transporting ourselves, individually, across the Atlantic, to be ranged under the banners of American freedom." And so Noailles had gone to America, where he fought with valor and returned to France a hero.[5]

But this was a very different trip. No longer posing as a crusader, Noailles now headed to America as a fleeing refugee.

NOAILLES ARRIVED in Philadelphia on May 3, 1793. If he had been hoping to take shelter from the political storms sweeping across Europe, he could hardly have arrived at a worse time. The year was a turning point in the history of the United States and of the Atlantic world. France and Great Britain had just declared war, and the United States that Noailles found was ablaze with French revolutionary fervor, with American leaders desperately seeking to keep the country out of the global warfare. British and French ships were in battle throughout the Atlantic, with some skirmishes so close to the American coast that citizens could watch. "We found the sea so much covered with your vessels that I thought its Empire belonged entirely to Great Britain," Noailles wrote to an English friend shortly after his arrival.[6]

The day before Noailles landed in Philadelphia, the *Embuscade*, a thirty-two-gun French naval frigate, had sailed up the Delaware River, firing fifteen shots in honor of the fifteen states as she approached Philadelphia, a salute answered by two cannons at the Market Street wharf. Philadelphians packed the docks to watch the grand battleship's arrival. Watching a warship sail into port in the eighteenth century was a memorable experience. "One discerns first only the top of the masts. The ship then grows visibly larger; soon she can be seen with her sails filled. She salutes the shore" with the booming crashes of cannon fire. Few by now are unaware that a ship from a distant land is sailing into port. "Coming on them with the swiftness of a bird she comes about, drops anchor, and comes to a standstill. No horseman ever knew better how to handle his horse than these navigators their winged castles."[7]

The excitement grew as the French ship approached. Liberty caps—the great symbol of the French Revolution—adorned each figurehead, another sat on the top gallant mast, and banners fluttered on the other masts. One read, "Enemies of equality, reform or tremble!" Another: "We are armed to defend the rights of man." The *Embuscade* had captured seven prizes, two of which had already preceded the ship to Philadelphia, their flags flying upside down in a signal of submission. "Upon her coming into sight thousands and thousands of the *yeomanry* of the city crowded and covered the wharves," Jefferson reported to James Monroe the next day. "Never before was such a crowd seen there, and when the British colours were seen *reversed*, and the French flag flying above them they burst into peals of exultation." Here was republican France, the country's most important ally, now its sister republic, sailing in triumph over America's former master brought low. Jefferson was thrilled: "All the old spirit of 1776 is rekindling."[8]

The enthusiasm on the streets of Philadelphia had been building for years. Since the calling of the Estates General in 1789 and the fall of the Bastille, the monumental events playing themselves out in Europe had transfixed Americans across geographical and political spectrums. Newspapers reprinted long reports of French politics, speeches in the National Assembly, and, with the outbreak of war between France, Austria, and Prussia, the progress of French armies across the Continent. It seemed to people on both sides of the Atlantic that the republican seed Americans had planted had borne fruit in Europe. And not just anywhere, but in France, the most powerful and corrupt monarchy of the age. All the global hopes that Americans had invested in their revolution were coming true. Paris guards played "Yankee Doodle" just before storming the Bastille, the hated symbol of French tyranny. In 1790 Lafayette sent Washington the key to the demolished prison: "It is a tribute Which I owe as A Son to My Adoptive father," he wrote, "as a Missionary of liberty to its patriarch." The gift was perfectly pitched: Washington, like millions of other Americans, shared the sense that the French and American revolutions were bound together as two manifestations of a single global movement for liberty. "Since the commencement of your revolution our attention has been drawn, with no small anxiety, almost to France alone," Washington later wrote Lafayette. "How great! How important . . . is the part, which the actors in this momentous scene have to perform! Not only the fate of millions of the present day depends upon them, but the happiness of posterity is involved in their decisions." The enthusiasm grew to a climax in late 1792, as word filtered across the Atlantic that an army of French citizen-soldiers had successfully defended the Revolution at Valmy against the forces of monarchy and reaction, and that France had become a republic.[9]

Americans up and down the coast organized celebrations and parades, sang French revolutionary songs, and proudly displayed French patriotic garb. Charlestonians founded the Société patriotique française—later renamed the Société des sans-culottes—to promote solidarity with the French Revolution. It drew the city's republicans, French immigrants, and the French consul to its gatherings. Already, American political life had taken new configurations in response to the French events. A few months later, in May 1793, Philadelphians created their own Democratic-Republican Society, an echo not just of American revolutionary groups like the Sons of Liberty but also of the French Club des Jacobins. At least ten sister organizations sprouted in American cities in 1793, and another twenty-five in 1794, composed of professionals, artisans, tradesmen, craftsmen, and French citizens in support of the French Revolution. Many clubs established connections and correspondence with Jacobin clubs in France. Like their French counterparts, members addressed each other as "Citizen," with some rejecting aristocratic knee breeches in imitation of the French sans-culottes (without breeches). All avowed their solidarity with the French Republic. "Shall we Americans," asked a Virginia Democratic-Republican Society speaker in 1794, "who have kindled the Spark of Liberty stand aloof and see it extinguished when burning a bright flame in France, which hath caught it from us? Do you not see if despots prevail, you must have a despot like the rest of nations? If all tyrants unite against free people, should not all free people unite against tyrants? Yes! Let us unite with France and stand or fall together." "On the accomplishment of the great objects of their Revolution," pronounced members of a Boston Democratic-Republican club that same year, "depends not only the future happiness and prosperity of Frenchmen, but in our opinion of the *whole World of Mankind*."[10]

As the violence in Paris grew, however, with the September Massacres and the execution of Louis XVI in January 1793, American views of the French Revolution began to diverge. The more conservative Federalists, like Alexander Hamilton, John Adams, and George Washington—with their political base in New England, a political culture long imbued with anti-Catholic and anti-French prejudices, joined by established merchants and coastal elites across the country—grew increasingly wary of the events in France. They concluded that the Revolution had spun out of control. What had seemed like a single transatlantic phenomenon now became, in their opinion, separate and divergent movements: the American Revolution standing as the good revolution in contrast to the French. On the other hand, the more radical Democratic-Republicans—often just called Republicans in this period—like Thomas Jefferson and James Madison, took a different view of transatlantic events. With their base of support in the southern states, across the Appalachian backcountry, and among the rural yeomanry, urban artisans, and small merchants, Republicans continued to support the Revolution in spite of the growing violence. Most viewed the bloodshed in France with regret, as the inevitable cost of overthrowing entrenched tyranny. Whatever the excesses, they remained convinced that, as Jefferson famously put it, "the liberty of the whole earth was depending on the issue of the contest." But these diverging opinions did not have a major impact on American politics so long as peace continued between France and England.[11]

Everything changed after February 1793. "The first cannons shot in our climates set fire to all the batteries in America," Voltaire had once complained, and again a familiar dynamic began. War between France, England, and Spain meant war in the Caribbean, right on the United States' doorstep. The Caribbean was the beating heart of the Atlantic economy, sending its vast stores of wealth in the form of sugar, coffee, and other crops coursing through the commercial arteries of the French and British economies. During periods of war, the sugar colonies loomed as ripe fruit to be plucked from the enemy. By the terms of the Treaty of Amity and Commerce of 1778, which the United States had signed with France when it joined the American Revolution, the United States was bound to support France in its Caribbean warfare, receiving French privateers and prizes in its ports, providing naval reinforcement, and furnishing French ships with supplies. And now war had come. How would the United States respond? Would the country risk another war with Britain to uphold its revolutionary alliance, repay the military debt it owed France, and support the cause

Edmond-Charles Genet, the French minister
sent to the United States in April 1793.

of global republicanism? Or would the country play it safe and stay out of the war by reneging on its commitment to France?[12]

French authorities could not be sure, and it was to shore up the support of its ally and organize Caribbean warfare that the new republic sent a young and reckless ambassador with impeccable credentials. He arrived in the United States just a month before Noailles.

EDMOND-CHARLES GENET was only thirty years old when he landed in America. His mission was the result of a series of events that began with the rise of the Girondins to power in France, the execution of King Louis XVI, and the outbreak of war with England—a series of events that too hastily hurled Genet to the United States.

Standing five feet eight inches tall, with chestnut hair creeping down a prominent forehead, piercing blue eyes, an aquiline nose, and a round chin, Genet was in certain respects a doppelgänger of the French émigrés

Genet painted by Adolf Ulrich Wertmüller as a twenty-one-year-old man in 1784, when he worked as a translator at the Versailles Court, nearly a decade before he came to the United States.

who would soon follow him across the Atlantic. Whereas many émigrés descended from the heights of the French aristocracy, Genet had scratched his way up from the midlevel bourgeoisie. Whereas the aristocratic émigrés acted with the refined assurance bred by the Versailles Court and the codes of eighteenth-century European diplomacy, Genet was convinced that the old methods of diplomacy were outdated, and *transparency* was the order of the day. The émigrés' rich endowments of subtlety and finesse were precisely the qualities most lacking in Genet. And yet for all their differences they would all leave a permanent mark on Franco-American relations.[13]

Genet originally sailed for Philadelphia, but his crossing was slower than he hoped. Leaving France too early in the season for an easy passage, he endured a rough crossing through the Bay of Biscay, with its "long swells and its furious waters." It took more than two weeks just to clear Cape Finisterre, on the northwest tip of Spain, before they could head south into the Atlantic to catch the trade winds. As his ship, the *Embuscade,* neared Bermuda, it ran across the *Sally,* an English brig, which the French ship promptly captured. Genet knew he was getting close when the boat ran into large amounts of seaweed and the water changed color: they were entering the Gulf Stream, which would push them north along the coast to their destination. But Genet couldn't wait. By the time the boats reached the Carolinas, the young and impatient minister decided to pull in at Charleston. Thus it was, on the morning of April 8, that Genet's ship, with the *Sally* as its prize, cleared the sandy shoals lying at the southern entrance of Charleston Harbor and came into view. An immense crowd gathered at the docks to welcome the French ship, "drawn by their curiosity and by the desire to know if war was declared." It was from Genet that Charleston learned that war had broken out between France and Great Britain.[14]

Genet immediately met Governor William Moultrie of South Carolina, along with various state senators and representatives, and was repeatedly *fêted* by Charleston's pro-Republican population. Overwhelmed by his reception, he sent the *Embuscade* ahead to Philadelphia without him—where its arrival would throw Philadelphians into those peals of exultation that Jefferson had witnessed—and decided to make his way to the capital by land, stopping, if he could, to see President Washington at Mount Vernon along the way. While in Charleston, Genet launched into his mission, commissioning four corsairs, or privateers, to sail into the Caribbean and attack British merchant ships carrying their stores of sugar, coffee, indigo, and more back to Europe. He even began enlisting American citizens to man the French warships: a clear violation, according to eighteenth-century rules of war, of national sovereignty. By the time he left the city, after ten days of celebration and preparations for war—still unrecognized as France's minister to the U.S. government—Genet had also launched plans for an invasion of Spanish-held Florida and Louisiana in the name of France, and begun to recruit soldiers for that cause as well. It had taken him less than two weeks to set himself on a collision course with the U.S. government.[15]

WHILE GENET was being *fêted* in Charleston and Noailles was sailing toward Philadelphia, President Washington was at home in Mount Vernon, where he received the news of war. Washington immediately recognized the delicate situation in which it placed the country. "War having actually commenced between France and Great Britain," he wrote to his secretary of state, Thomas Jefferson, "it behoves the Government of this Country . . . to maintain a strict neutrality." He asked Jefferson and the rest of his cabinet to begin discussing the issue. There was no time to waste. "I have understood that vessels are already designated privateers, and are preparing accordingly." With that, Washington rushed back to Philadelphia to convene an emergency meeting of his cabinet and formulate an official response. On April 22, just twelve days before Noailles arrived in Philadelphia, while Genet was still fooling around in South Carolina, Washington published his famous Proclamation of Neutrality, a document that would guide U.S. policy for much of the next 120 years. It declared the government's intention to "pursue a conduct friendly and impartial towards the belligerent powers," and warned Americans "to avoid all acts and proceedings whatsoever, which may in any manner tend to contravene such disposition."[16]

This was a clear violation of the U.S. treaty with France. And Genet—who still had not met with government officials to be accredited ambassador—was already working at cross-purposes. Rumors began to sprout. The very day that Washington published his neutrality proclamation in the newspapers, *Dunlap's American Daily Advertiser* of Philadelphia fretted:

A variety of reports still continue to amuse and terrify our citizens, respecting the instructions of the French ambassador, and the part our federal government MUST take in the war entered into between England and France—Were these true, we should inevitably be plunged into the horrors of a destructive and unprofitable

war, almost without end or object—but as these have evidently no
better foundation than the momentary hopes or fears of the re-
porters, we shall not, on such authority, retail the IDLE GOSSIP.

It was a strange notice to publish, denying the truth of the very rumors it
was propagating. But these fears were compelling enough that the same
report was picked up and reprinted by at least seven newspapers in five different states. The country was on edge at the prospect of a war among Europe's great powers in the Caribbean—and perhaps also in the Great Lakes
and along the Mississippi River.[17]

Still unaware of Washington's neutrality proclamation, Genet was
heading toward Virginia, his progress delayed by continual celebrations in
the cities and towns he crossed. For provincial Americans, connected to
the world-historical events in Europe only by distant reports and excited
discussions in taverns, here was a rare chance to witness history in the
flesh, as it practically walked into their parlors. Arriving in Stateburg,
South Carolina, late on the night of April 24, stopping just long enough to
sleep, Genet could not even get into his carriage the next morning without
being accosted by a dozen residents presenting him with "a short, though
warm testimony of American esteem and friendship, in behalf of themselves and their neighbors." After he made a brief reply, Genet headed off,
"accompanied a few miles on the road to Camden by several gentlemen of
the village," a touching collection of farmers on horseback trailing Genet's
carriage along the dusty country roads, catching a last glimpse of this man
connected to the French king's execution, as he made his way to meet President Washington.[18]

When he pulled into Camden, just twenty miles north of Stateburg,
Genet was met by an even larger delegation, which organized a ceremony
to express their citizens' feelings for France.

Your nation has a just claim to our gratitude, for the services rendered us in the hour of our distress, whilst we contended against
tyranny and oppression. But, independent of this tie, we feel our-

selves warmly and zealously attached to her, for the noble example which she now gives to the world.

And so it continued, through South Carolina, North Carolina, Virginia, Maryland, and, eventually, Pennsylvania. The nation was alight with French revolutionary fervor, and everywhere he went, Genet was met with toasts and celebrations. When he at last reached Philadelphia on the early afternoon of May 16, three cannon shots were fired from the *Embuscade* to announce his arrival. A large delegation of some of the nation's most eminent citizens met him at Gray's Ferry, on the outskirts of town, for a brief ceremony before parading into town as church bells tolled and thousands of people, many of them dressed in revolutionary red, white, and blue, flocked from across the city to watch the triumphal arrival of France's new republican minister to the United States.

The next day, "an immense body of citizens" held a town meeting in the backyard of Independence Hall before "walking three abreast" to deliver an address to Genet at the City Tavern, where Genet responded with a speech of such eloquence the crowd demanded that he repeat it to those gathered outside. "It is impossible to describe with adequate energy the scene that succeeded," reported one Philadelphia newspaper. "The house and the streets again resounded with congratulations and applause," commented another. The following day, excited Philadelphians held another dinner for Genet at the city's grandest hotel, featuring a table decorated with a liberty tree and liberty caps and festooned with French and American flags. "The *bonnet rouge* was passed from head to head round the table," one attendee remembered. After fifteen toasts, one hundred prominent Philadelphians joined in a rousing performance of "La Marseillaise," along with "two additional stanzas, composed by Citizen Genet," and sung by the French minister "with truly patriotic and republican sentiments." Genet was beside himself. "My voyage was an uninterrupted succession of civic *fêtes,* and my entry into Philadelphia a triumph for liberty," he exulted in a report to the French foreign minister.[19]

Genet had not yet had his credentials recognized by the American government, which had by now issued Washington's Proclamation of Neutrality. But, overwhelmed by his reception over the previous six weeks, by the evident popularity of the French cause and of republicanism more generally, and by the lingering hatred of Great Britain and its monarchy—and prompted, too, by various Jeffersonian politicians—Genet concluded that Washington's neutrality proclamation could not withstand the explosion of pro-French feeling. "All of America has risen up to recognize me as the Minister of the French Republic," Genet wrote in a dispatch, almost drunk with exuberance. "The voice of the People continues to neutralize President Washington's proclamation of neutrality. I live here in the midst of perpetual *fêtes*."[20]

And still the *fêtes* continued. Through the summer months, thousands of Philadelphians, inspired by the glorious events in France, by the republican armies sweeping across Europe, paraded through the city wearing the French *tricolore* on their lapels and cockades on their hats, and singing French patriotic songs. It was Genet who suggested "democratic" to Philadelphians as the name for their society, in imitation of the Jacobin clubs in France. In sympathy, one tavern was renamed the "Guillotined Queen of France." The Republican *General Advertiser* advertised the "very interesting" reproduction of a guillotine, including a wax victim, its body on the trunk of the machine and its head in a straw basket. The excitement even pervaded the city's musical life. Philadelphia's Southwark Theatre played "La Marseillaise" before each performance, with the audience joining in to sing the famous chorus:

> *Aux armes, citoyens,*
> *Formez vos bataillons,*
> *Marchons, marchons!*[21]

All the enthusiasm convinced Genet of the righteousness of his belligerent diplomacy. "I am supplying the Antilles," he reported to the French foreign minister in June. "I am stirring up the Canadians to emancipate themselves from the yoke of England; I am arming the Kentuckians, and I am preparing by sea an expedition that will support their descent on New

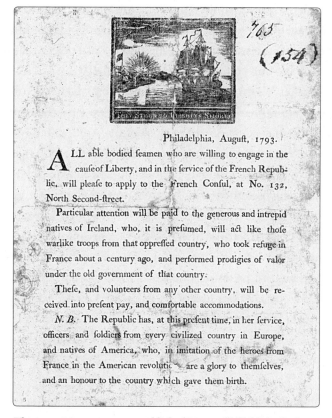

This recruiting poster was published in 1793: "All able bodied seamen who are willing to engage in the cause of Liberty, and in the service of the French Republic, will please to apply to the French Consul, at No. 132, North Second-street."

Orleans." The United States, it appeared, teetered on the verge of war with Great Britain. It was a war that thousands of Americans cheered on: an extension of the American Revolution, as many saw it, that would bring liberty to the world. In July Genet traveled to New York, where the celebrations continued. A month later he was back in Philadelphia recruiting Americans into the French navy. "The Republic has, at this present time, in her service," a recruiting poster announced, "officers and soldiers from every civilized country in Europe," and called for Americans to sign up— "in imitation of the heroes from France in the American revolution." All of this was a flagrant violation of American neutrality, and a direct challenge to the president's power under the Constitution to direct foreign policy. Here was an agent of a foreign nation mobilizing popular opinion to draw the United States into war with Britain. And it wasn't clear that the Washington administration could do much to stop him.[22]

Months after Washington requested his recall, Genet traveled to New York to celebrate Embarkation Day: November 25, 1793, the tenth anniversary of the British evacuation at the close of the American Revolution. Gigantic French warships docked in New York Harbor made their presence known, returning the ceremonial cannon shots fired from the Battery. Did anyone doubt which country was the great power? Genet attended the theater that night with Governor George Clinton and gave a soaring address. "The same all-powerful arm which delivered your country from tyranny is now manifesting itself as the protector of the French people," he gushed. French officers sat in boxes on one side of the theater, American officers just across. "All were in their uniforms, as dressed for the rejoicing day," the theater manager later remembered. French officers and soldiers, along with "many of the New-York militia, artillery, infantry, and dragoons, mingled with the crowd in the pit."

> As soon as the musicians appeared in the orchestra, there was a general call for "Ça ira." The band struck up. The French in the pit joined first, and then the whole audience. Next followed the Marseillois Hymn. The audience stood up. The French took off their hats and sung in a full and solemn chorus. The Americans applauded by gestures and clapping of hands. We can yet recall the figure and voice of one Frenchman, who, standing on a bench in the pit, sung this solemn patriotic song with a clear, loud voice, while his fine manly frame seemed to swell with the enthusiasm of the moment. The hymn ended, shouts of *Vivent les François! Vivent les Americains!* were reiterated until the curtain drew up, and all was silent.

No wonder Genet was so ecstatic: here they were, the popular wills of two republics united in the cause of global freedom. What obstacle would not fall before such assembled righteousness? "It will require all the address, all the temper, and all the firmness of Congress and the States to keep this people out of the war," John Adams wrote his wife that December.[23]

François Barbé-Marbois, who came to America in 1779 during the Revolution, and served as chargé d'affaires in the French mission to the United States in the 1780s, reported that Genet "had secret or avowed followers in several States and up to the heart of Congress." Adams would later recall, albeit with some exaggeration, "the Terrorism, excited by Genet, in 1793, when ten thousand People in the Streets of Philadelphia, day after day, threatened to drag Washington out of his House, and effect a Revolution in the Government, or compel it to declare War in favour of the French Revolution, and against England." Perhaps he can be forgiven his hyperbole; Adams, after all, was hardly the only person who believed that "a total Revolution of Government" was imminent. For Noailles, who knew what Parisian mobs were capable of in the wake of the Tuileries uprising, the massacres of September 1792, and the execution of the king, the events must have seemed like history repeating itself.[24]

ALTHOUGH GENET's mission may seem like the product of one somewhat unhinged ambassador, his diplomacy was planned from France, and he followed instructions almost to the letter. His mission stood as just one pillar of much larger geopolitical objectives then being implemented by France's Girondin leadership—the very people who had chased Noailles, Liancourt, Talleyrand, and the others out of France, and who were now sending French armies across Europe. Several months before Genet left for the United States, the other, considerably more important pillar rose up when Léger-Félicité Sonthonax, another envoy, sailed for the Caribbean colony of Saint Domingue.[25]

The Genet mission may have left its mark on Franco-American relations in the 1790s, but Sonthonax's mission was far more consequential to world history. Sonthonax, like Genet and many others come of age during that stormy time, was young and excitable, convinced that the French Revolution was a moral crusade to regenerate the cause of humanity. Had he

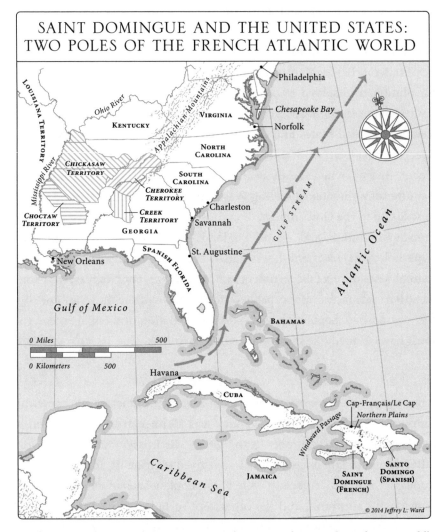

SAINT DOMINGUE AND THE UNITED STATES: TWO POLES OF THE FRENCH ATLANTIC WORLD

In the 1790s, the United States was—at least according to the Atlantic world's geopolitics—an appendage to the Caribbean. America's exports supplied the Caribbean slaves who produced the commodities that powered the global economy; its harbors provided bases for naval operations to the south. With U.S. territory largely limited to the area between the Atlantic Ocean and the Appalachians, the country depended on its trading connections with the sugar islands.

been sent anywhere else, he would no doubt have fallen from the pages of history. Instead, he sailed to Saint Domingue, a colony whose importance to the late eighteenth century is hard to overstate. Over the course of a century, that one French colony—half of a single Caribbean island, with an area one-sixth the size of Virginia—had experienced an economic boom without precedent; by 1789 it was the richest, most productive colony not just of the French Empire, but of any empire. Feeding this economic dynamo with labor, the French slave trade grew so dramatically in the 1780s that it briefly surpassed the British trade for the only time in history, transporting an annual average of 37,000 Africans—a number nearly equivalent to the total population of Philadelphia, greater than that of New York City—from 1783 to 1792. In all, more than 791,000 Africans were taken to Saint Domingue between 1700 and 1789, by which time some 465,000 slaves worked the island's fertile plantations, producing over half the world's coffee, and more sugar than all the British colonies put together. The sum of its trade was staggering. The port of Cap-Français, or Le Cap—a city larger than Boston—was plied by more ships than Marseille, creating vast fortunes for French merchants and bankers, and showering wealth on port cities such as Bordeaux and Nantes—indeed, on French society at large. By 1789 some 218 million *livres'* worth of goods had arrived in France from Saint Domingue, two-thirds of which had been reexported to European markets; an estimated one million of France's twenty-five million inhabitants depended directly on the colonial trade for their livelihoods.[26]

This spectacular growth caused spectacular social tensions: between the thirty thousand *gens de couleur,* or free people of African descent, demanding civil rights and the thirty thousand whites determined to preserve their caste privileges; between wealthy planters itching for freedom from French trade restrictions and a metropolitan government determined to preserve the colony's wealth for France alone; and most of all between the hundreds of thousands of brutally oppressed slaves and the fabulously wealthy planters whose fortunes rested on their exploitation. When the French Revolution broke out in 1789, tensions were already at an all-time high. The Revolution's rhetoric of liberty and equality was, in this context, a match in a tinderbox, providing an opening for the *gens de couleur* to advance their demands for equal rights. There was something unreal about the debates taking place in 1790 and 1791, which saw both *gens de couleur* and whites arguing about liberty and the rights of man while nearly half a million slaves worked under the most grueling conditions imaginable. In 1792 the French National Assembly, under pressure to live up to its rhetoric, proclaimed full equality for the *gens de couleur*. Now the *gens de couleurs* allied with the high-handed French civil commissioners against recalcitrant whites, arresting and deporting those who refused to obey the French law of 1792—amid half a million slaves who looked on.

The inevitable eruption came in August 1791, when some two thousand slaves in the island's rich northern plains—the heart of Saint Domingue's plantation order—rose up and began killing slave owners and their families, and setting fire to the sugar plantations. By September, some fifty thousand slaves were in armed insurrection, a number that may have grown as high as eighty thousand by November. "The noble plain adjoining the Cape was covered with ashes, and the surrounding hills, as far as the eye could reach, and every where presented to us ruins still smoking," wrote a Jamaican planter who sailed into Cap-Français in September. "It was a sight more terrible than the mind of any man, unaccustomed to such a scene, can easily conceive." Smoke and dust blocked out the sky for days. French authorities had sought and failed to restore peace in the island ever since, and as the prospect of war with England loomed in late 1792, they began to fear that France might lose the colony entirely. It was therefore to consolidate French authority on the island that Sonthonax and two fellow commissioners sailed to Saint Domingue, dispatched by the same French administrators who had sent Genet to the United States. They arrived in September 1792 with six thousand soldiers—and a printing press.[27]

The outbreak of war between France, England, and Spain complicated the situation in Saint Domingue, grafting an imperial war onto the existing divisions between royalists and republicans, whites and *gens de couleurs,* free and slave. In late February 1793, a group of French planters in London offered to transfer their allegiance to the British government in exchange for protection and a suspension of debt payments. The planters' turning to England raised the imminent danger that France would lose its most precious colony to its archenemy. It also created an opening for the insurgents, offering the possibility of an alliance between the revolutionary movement in France and insurrectionary slaves in the Caribbean. That same month, the French colonial minister suggested to Sonthonax that he grant legal freedom to insurgents willing to fight for France.[28]

A major element of Genet's mission—and the task that took up the majority of his time in the United States—was to furnish Sonthonax and his allies on the island with logistical and military support. Since the American Revolution, French naval authorities had conceived of the United States largely as an appendage to their Caribbean possessions. Indeed, a significant factor motivating French intervention in the American Revolution was the military and logistical use that a U.S. alliance might serve in the event of a war against Britain in the Caribbean. Through its new ally, France would have a base to provide lumber, tar, and other resources for its navy, provisions for its population, and logistical support for wartime operations. And so Genet was charged with attending to these strategic interests, using the American debt to France to purchase food and military aid for the besieged French forces in Saint Domingue, and ensuring that the United States would open its harbors and ports to French privateers. But matters were moving too fast, even for a diplomat with all of Genet's considerable energy.[29]

A month after Noailles and Genet arrived in Philadelphia, in June 1793, Saint Domingue erupted for the second time. As Sonthonax was beaten back by his political enemies in the streets of Cap-Français, he offered freedom to insurgent slaves willing to defend the island against British and royalist control. Several thousand former slaves descended on the city on June 20. No one will ever know who set the fire, but what is certain is that by the end of the month, much of Le Cap—the most opulent city in the Caribbean, the *perle* of the Antilles—had burned to the ground. Ten thousand people, mostly white, but also many *gens de couleur* and slaves, crowded onto ships in the harbor with whatever possessions they could grab. The first convoy of three hundred ships sailed out of Le Cap with their cargoes

A view of Cap-Français burning in August 1793. It had been the crown jewel of France's almost unimaginably lucrative Caribbean empire. Images such as this—along with reports by the thousands of refugees landing on U.S. shores—produced terror among most slaveholding (and many nonslaveholding) Americans.

of desperate refugees. They made their way northwest along the Cuban coastline, following the established shipping lanes by which so many rich fleets of sugar, coffee, and indigo had traveled, catching the Gulf Stream as it pushed its way out of the Gulf of Mexico and up the Eastern Seaboard. Along the way, British privateers intercepted many of the convoys, making the refugees' misery even worse. The British seized the few possessions the refugees had managed to take with them, in some cases including slaves, claimed as "prizes" and sold into slavery in Jamaica or other British ports. Not surprisingly, the refugees from Saint Domingue arrived in Philadelphia with an intense hatred of Sonthonax's ally Genet and the French revolutionary government they both represented. Back in Saint Domingue, on August 29, with the French Revolution now allied firmly to the insurgent slaves, Sonthonax proclaimed the abolition of slavery in the name of the French Republic.[30]

And that, as the great historian, writer, and activist C. L. R. James put it long ago, "is how white San Domingo destroyed itself."[31]

IN THE midst of all this chaos in the Atlantic world, Noailles landed in Philadelphia. Seventeen ninety-three was an El Niño year, when the ocean's currents brought unusually hot and humid air to North America. That May had been one of the wettest months in years, with storm after storm driving down from the northeast. As rivers and streams overflowed, the city's lowlands turned into marshes, with consequences that would soon prove disastrous as a hot, dry summer began.[32]

Two local newspapers took note of Noailles' arrival. The Republican *General Advertiser* and the Federalist *Gazette* both printed the same notice: "Vicount de Noailles lately arrived here in the Pigou, was a member of the French Constituent Assembly, and left his country after the revolution of the 10th of August," they reported. "He is said to come with the intention of settling here, and brings the means, to the amount of 1,500,000 livres." That equaled roughly $300,000: a vast sum at a time when an unskilled laborer earned a dollar a day. Although the newspapers almost certainly exaggerated the amount of capital Noailles had brought with him, the notices were a clear sign that Noailles was ready to do business.[33]

And do business he did. Soon after his arrival he invested in half a million acres of land in central Pennsylvania along the Susquehanna valley. Still troubled by the September Massacres in Paris, which had seen so many of his friends killed, Noailles imagined himself as the advance guard of a wave of French refugees fleeing Europe. "Since my arrival in this country I have made a purchase of five hundred thousand acres of land," Noailles wrote to a friend in June in his rough English.

> My intention has been to prepare an exile to those of my countrymen who, disgusted of the horrid scene which took place in France,

will forever abandon the theatre which has produced it. My expectation has so well succeeded that now we are settling forty French families in easy circumstances, and fifty German.

There, on the banks of the Susquehanna, they would remake their ideal France in America. "Our manners will be gentle, our conversation animated, our labor act[i]ve," Noailles wrote. "We will be the French people you have known," he added, "and not the present nation."[34]

Noailles was the best connected of the French émigrés. He had fought in the American Revolution and befriended many of its leaders, who now became his friends and business associates. Soon after his arrival, he contacted William Bingham, a Philadelphia merchant who had made his fortune in Martinique during the Revolution. Before long, Noailles made his home in some apartments behind the Binghams' grand mansion on South Third Street. But Bingham was not the only prominent American with whom Noailles established close ties. The day after his arrival, Noailles met with Alexander Hamilton, then secretary of the treasury, with whom he'd developed an intimate friendship during the Revolution. He also sought, through Hamilton, to deliver a letter of introduction to Washington.[35]

Rumors soon began to circulate about Noailles' contact with U.S. administration officials. "Last evening at nine o'clock," read a letter published widely in newspapers around the country, "arrived here from the Court of Ex-Princes at Coblentz, Count de NOAILLES, Ambassador Extraordinary and Plenipotentiary from the Prince Regent of France. At a very late hour he waited on the President with whom he was in private conversation until near morning." A secret meeting carried on through the middle of the night: was it an ominous sign that elements of the *ancien régime* and the Washington administration were conspiring to ally the United States with England against republican France? "M. Genet, Minister from the Republic," added the notice, lest anyone miss the implication, "is on his way from Charleston, S.C. and is daily expected.—The crisis of affairs, it is generally thought, will demand a session of Congress."[36]

Other newspaper accounts refuted these rumors that Noailles had come on an official mission from French royalists. "The artifices which are made use of to excite suspicions against the general government are equally calculated to surprise and disgust," read a letter that circulated widely in newspapers in late June and early July. Calling the accusations against Noailles "a mischievous fabrication," the letter went on to explain that "the Viscount de Noailles is here, as a private gentleman, without any public character whatever, and with views of settlement in this country," and that his politics were hardly those of the reactionary émigrés in Koblenz, as he "differed in his political views with the emigrant nobility, on the one hand; and from the present ruling party on the other." Finally, the letter corrected the account of Noailles' first visit with Washington. "I have learnt," the writer explained,

> that the Viscount de Noailles, on the evening of the day of his arrival . . . called on the President, under whom he had served at the head of a French regiment during the late American war; that there happened to be present, when he came in, Mr. TERNANT, then Minister of *France*; that he staid about fifteen or twenty minutes, conversing on indifferent subjects, and went off either at the same time with, or a little before Mr TERNANT.

(Genet had not yet arrived in Philadelphia to replace Jean-Baptiste Ternant, the previous French ambassador.) Other newspaper accounts reminded readers that Noailles had served in the American Revolution and that it was he who had moved the abolition of feudal titles in the French Constituent Assembly in 1789.[37]

These contradictory reports drew the attention of Genet, who saw dark motives in Noailles' trip. "Noailles and Talon are here," Genet reported to his superiors when he finally arrived in the capital. "Before my arrival, they provided the President of the United States with letters from the pretended Regent, which this old man had the weakness to open, but since the people recognized me, they no longer dare show themselves; if it were worth the trouble, I'd have them chased out." Most historians have regarded Genet's fears as unfounded, the manifestation of his increasing megalomania and paranoia. But there was good reason for Genet to be worried. As he prepared to leave for America, Noailles had suggested to British authorities that he might be useful to them. "Before M. Noailles left England," the British foreign secretary Lord Grenville wrote to the British ambassador to the United States, "he made some offers of service here which were civilly declined on account of his former connections and conduct, and because it was not thought likely that much advantage could be derived from them. He expressed however a desire of being of service to you when he got there, and stated himself to have the means of being so." Although Noailles was not acting as an official agent of the British government, Genet's suspicions were not unfounded. And indeed, Noailles did meet with the British ambassador shortly after he arrived in Philadelphia. What they discussed is unclear, though the minister certainly thought the information was valuable.[38]

Shadowy land deals and shadowy diplomacy in the midst of revolutionary ferment: Noailles had set the pattern for the French émigrés who would follow him. But before their arrival, another ship would pull in from the French Atlantic, docking at Philadelphia some two months after Noailles had landed. Life was about to take a tragic turn.

───────────

THE MATHEMATICIANS tell us that a butterfly flapping its wings can change the course of history. In July 1793 it was not a butterfly but another winged *voyageur* that did. Jet black, with white spots on its thorax, rings on its legs, and lyre-shaped ornamentation on its back, this traveler, like so many others, followed the circuits of Atlantic trade from Africa to the Caribbean and up the North American coast, piercing into the continent along rivers and turnpikes, canals and railroads. Few have had a greater impact on history: this traveler "felled great leaders, decimated armies, and decided the fates of nations."[39]

Not for another century would medical science learn that yellow fever is transmitted by the deadly *Aedes aegypti* mosquito. Only recently has the historian Billy Smith confirmed that the 1793 outbreak began when a colony of British settlers disrupted a monkey habitat in the mangrove swamps on the island of Bolama, off the coast of present-day Guinea-Bissau, Africa, introducing a new and deadly variant of yellow fever into the circuits of

Atlantic trade. When the ship *Hankey* moored off the coast of Bolama for several months in late 1792, the infected mosquitoes laid thousands of eggs in the casks of still water in the ship's hold. As the *Hankey* crossed the Atlantic, its crew and passengers falling sick and dying in catastrophic numbers, the virus reached the Caribbean. Stopping briefly at Grenada, the *Hankey* sailed to the still-smoldering city of Cap-Français in Saint Domingue to pick up desperate refugees fleeing the island. As the "Ship of Death" cruised out of Saint Domingue and north along the North American coast—past the Outer Banks of the Carolinas, past the majestic entrance to the Chesapeake Bay, past Cape Henlopen on the tip of the Delaware River and into the Delaware Bay—the mosquitoes down below continued their deadly work. Finally, the *Hankey* docked along the wharves of Philadelphia's northern reaches, alongside the marshes still damp from the long spring rains, amid weather getting hotter as the summer wore on. The conditions could hardly have been better for a new breed of mosquito to establish itself on the continent.[40]

On August 4, accounts began to circulate about an ominous death. An Englishman by the name of Parkinson, lodging at a boardinghouse on Water Street, adjacent to the pier where the *Hankey* had docked, died suddenly, "the vessels of his brain uncommonly distended and turgid with blood." Something was amiss. An Irish couple and two young Frenchmen who lived at the same boardinghouse were soon infected. One Irish boarder died three days later, followed by one of the French boarders. In short order the owner of the house fell ill and died, along with his wife and then the second French boarder. Only three of the nine people living in the house still lived. A plague was on.[41]

By the end of August, people were fleeing Philadelphia at such rates that "for some weeks . . . almost every hour in the day, carts, waggons, coaches, and chairs, were to be seen transporting families and furniture to the country in every direction. . . . The streets wore the appearance of gloom and melancholy." Estimates of the exodus ranged from seventeen thousand to twenty-three thousand—roughly half the city's population. Wealthy Philadelphians, with access to country houses or friends in nearby towns and states, had the easiest time. The poor were hit worst. Lacking refuge, they remained concentrated in the densest neighborhoods, living in confined courts and crowded alleyways amid animals and pools of dirty, stagnant water. Water Street, the city's narrowest and most densely populated, abutting the Delaware River, was a particular center of death: two-thirds of its residents were killed by the fever. Mathew Carey, the Philadelphia publisher and author of a pamphlet on yellow fever, estimated that seven-eighths of the deaths were among the poor.[42]

But rich neighborhoods were hardly spared. "Fly as soon as you can," cried Noailles to one resident from the steps of William Bingham's mansion, "for pestilence is all around us." Noailles himself eventually fled to Lansdown, the Binghams' country retreat on the site of the current-day Fairmount Park. George Hammond, the British minister in Philadelphia, joined him there. "The disorder now raging in Philadelphia is, I believe, the most malignant in its nature, and the most extensive in its effect, of any with which the human race has ever been afflicted in any country," Hammond reported in terror. "Of my family that remained in town, I have lost my principal servant, and two others are at this moment dead or at the point of death. . . . I hope that the distance (five miles) at which my wife and myself are from Philadelphia will effectually protect us from the danger of the contagion." It was from Lansdown that Noailles updated Hamilton on the situation in Philadelphia: "The epidemic causes awful devastation," Noailles wrote that October. "Until now, the third parallel in front of Valenciennes," he added, referring to a recent siege of the French city that had resulted in nine thousand dead or injured, "would have been less dangerous than a stroll through the streets of Philadelphia."[43]

Yellow fever was a cruel way to die. It started like a simple cold or flu: "The patient first complains of weariness and weakness, which, in a few hours, is succeeded by a sense of chilliness." But soon the pain began, marking the illness as no regular flu: "sharp pains in the eye sockets, feet, loins and stomach." Gradually, the agony grew so intense it felt as if an arm or a leg were breaking; victims' screams could be heard from many houses away. Breathing became shallow and labored. The pulse softened and became irregular. The skin became hot and moist, followed by the "sudden debility in the animal functions of the body": uncontrolled defecation of bloody stool and urine. If the patient did not improve at that point, a gruesome death invariably followed. On the third or fourth day came the terrifying sign: the patient began to vomit "of a matter resembling coffee grounds in colour and consistence." Here it was, the dreaded black vomit, its color due to the hemorrhaging of blood into the stomach. By this time the kidney and liver had failed, and jaundice set in, as skin and fingernails turned "a deep yellow or leaden colour." Blood oozed from the patient's eyes, nose, and mouth. The dying patient "was already a corpse, putrid and horrible." No wonder that flight and panic washed across Philadelphia in that fateful year of 1793.[44]

As the death count grew—from 325 in August to 1,442 in September, reaching a peak of nearly 2,000 in October—the "scenes of distress and misery" accumulated. Bells tolled continuously. Guns fired into the Delaware River; officials hoped the booms would ward off the disorder. Trash lay uncollected in the street. Fires were lit on street corners to protect against the fever, the smoke mingling with the smell of vinegar and camphor wafting across the city. Some people walked through the city with handkerchiefs pressed against their noses, tar in their hands, bags of camphor tied around their necks, while others chewed garlic and carried tarred ropes in their pockets or amulets of dried frogs to keep the disease at bay. Hundreds gathered into churches to pray. "Every body, who can, is flying from the city," Jefferson reported. The government practically disappeared. President Washington fled to Mount Vernon, Secretary of State Jefferson up the Schuylkill River to safety. The Pennsylvania governor left, as did most of the city's magistrates and even the night watchmen. The mail stopped being delivered. "The governor is a stranger to the calamities that oppress Philadelphia," Noailles wrote in early October to Hamilton, who had left for New York after having fallen ill but had recovered from the fever.[45]

Those who remained seemed to experience "a total dissolution of the bonds of society." Mathew Carey reported on a husband deserting his wife of twenty years as she lay on her deathbed, parents forsaking children, and children abandoning parents. He wrote of a pregnant woman, whose husband had just died, left alone in her house as she went into labor and died, and of a servant girl who fell ill and, not finding anyone to take her in, died in a cart. Children orphaned by the death of their parents were left without food or care. Dead bodies lay in the street despite the furious efforts of the city's gravediggers, who buried more than four thousand that summer. Some people were even reported to have been buried alive. Farmers and fishermen refused to bring their goods to the city's markets. Panicked residents of nearby cities and towns stationed guards to prevent arrivals from Philadelphia. Refugees were refused food and shelter, forced out of stagecoaches to die in the woods. One woman arriving in Easton, Maryland, was tarred and feathered. Even Alexander Hamilton was kept in a jail north of New York City when he left Philadelphia. But all the precautions were for naught: "Rain and frost are the only remedies from which we can expect much effect," Noailles wrote.[46]

Finally, in late October, the cold arrived. Winds and rain drove down from the north; the mosquitoes began to die, and the humans to live. On the night of Sunday, October 27, a frost set in. People began to creep back into the city. "Long-absent and welcome faces appear. . . . The stores, so long closed, are opening fast. . . . Market-street is almost as full of waggons as usual. The custom house, for weeks nearly deserted by our mercantile people, is thronged by citizens entering their vessels and goods." By that time, somewhere between four and five thousand people had died—out of a population of slightly more than fifty thousand.[47]

No one at the time knew where the disease had come from. Some people blamed the French arrivals, others immigrants from elsewhere in Europe. Some thought the disease was "a judgment on the [city's] inhabitants for their sins," blaming "the number of sailor taverns and huxter's shops, which are receptacles of all kinds of filth, dirt and nastiness." Others thought the fever came from "the apparel of diseased persons," and still others from "the low and filthy apartments of some of the inhabitants of Water-street." It was not lost on a few observers that the mortality began on Water Street, where "the Sans Culottes lay." Whatever the origin, the death and social disorder in Philadelphia were associated in many minds with the chaos, war, and revolution spreading from France, across Europe, and now to the Americas. "Many believe we have had two disorders in the city, introduced about the same time," Mathew Carey concluded, "the yellow fever, from the West Indies, and a species of pestilence from Marseilles."[48]

But the French Atlantic world had not stopped spewing black vomit to Philadelphia.

CHARLES-MAURICE TALLEYRAND landed in Philadelphia in late April 1794, nearly a year after Noailles. He was just over five feet tall, lean, with blue eyes that took in far more than they revealed, a slightly upturned nose, and a limp in one leg. Of all the émigrés who came to the United States, Talleyrand would leave the greatest mark on the world.[49]

Talleyrand exerts as great a pull on history as he did on the contemporaries who knew him. A man of surpassing talents and epic flaws, he was as admired as he was despised. He was a master of the *bon mot,* and, like Churchill stories in our day, tales of his quips and retorts circulated widely. The historian Albert Sorel wrote that "Talleyrand was an incomparable conversationalist. He had a quick and ready reply. He excelled at summarising a situation in a phrase, a thought in a word." Talleyrand shone—even in late Enlightenment Paris, the city of Voltaire, Mirabeau, and Germaine de Staël, his legendary wit earned him fame and acclamation. He was also licentious—even in late *ancien régime* Paris, the city of the marquis de Sade, and Laclos' marquise de Merteuil and vicomte de Valmont, his debaucheries earned him infamy and condemnation. He was a sensualist in every respect. "He brings with him all the vices of the old regime," Lazare Carnot, a member of the French Directory, later wrote, "without having been able to acquire any of the virtues of the new one." Gouverneur Morris, the American minister in Paris, who shared a lover with Talleyrand in the early 1790s, put it less elegantly: "This man appears to me polished, cold, tricky, ambitious and bad."[50]

Talleyrand descended from one of the oldest families of the French aristocracy. Though he was destined for a career in the army, as the firstborn son of a family from the *noblesse d'épée,* a deformed foot sent him to the Church instead. It was a career for which he was spectacularly unsuited. His rich endowments of intelligence and ambition, however, combined with his family's exalted status, drove him up the ranks of the Church hierarchy. In 1780 he became *agent général du clergé de France,* a position that put him in charge of the Church's finances. During the 1780s, he joined a group of reformers, including Mirabeau, Lafayette, Condorcet, La Rochefoucauld, the theorist Emmanuel-Joseph Sieyès, and the physiocrat Pierre Samuel du Pont de Nemours, who met regularly at the Club de Valois, in Paris's magnificent *Palais Royal.* He was an active participant in the cosmopolitan financial world of prerevolutionary Paris, part of a circle that included Mirabeau, the Swiss financier Étienne Clavière, the Franco-Dutch financier Théophile Cazenove, and that orbited around the Anglo-Swiss Protestant financier Isaac Panchaud, all of them speculating recklessly in the Paris *bourse* as European capital came rushing into France after the peace of 1783. Louis XVI resisted promoting Talleyrand up the Church hierarchy—under, it was said, the curious assumption that a prelate should show minimal evidence of private virtue—but eventually acceded, making him bishop of Autun in 1788.[51]

With the calling of the Estates General, Talleyrand joined with liberals like Noailles, Lafayette, and Liancourt in advocating a constitutional monarchy, reforms of education, and equality of citizenship. It was Bishop Talleyrand who proposed the nationalization of the Catholic Church's vast landholdings. In 1790, he was elected president of the assembly. That same year, he was chosen to celebrate the famous mass at the Fête de la Fédération on Paris's Champ de Mars, which established July 14 as the French national holiday. These were the most exhilarating of times. The liberal project of French constitutional monarchism reached its apogee, and a civil religion was born, secularizing the ancient rituals of religion and fusing them to the new, state-building project. It was Talleyrand who administered the oath of allegiance to the French constitution to King Louis XVI and to Lafayette. And then came the denouement. In 1792 Talleyrand left on a diplomatic mission to England with the object of preserving British neutrality amid France's war with Prussia and Austria. Like many French liberals, Talleyrand had harbored long-standing hopes for a Franco-British alliance; peace between the two great powers, he believed, was the key to European—indeed, world—peace.

Talleyrand's mission to London has been the subject of much speculation: Was he a diplomat? A spy? Did he seek to foment revolution in England? Was he on a financial mission for a coterie of bankers? When he first arrived in London in early 1792, he served as an informal adviser to Bernard-François, marquis de Chauvelin, the young French ambassador. King George III, for one, suspected that Talleyrand was up to no good, writing to his foreign minister, Lord Grenville, that he had "no credence to me," and hoping that he and a colleague might "receive the contempt their characters entitle them to. I know I need not recommend the greatest caution to Lord Grenville in conversing with persons much fitter to be employed with the new club in St. James's Street than with any servants of the Crown." But the king was not the only person to wonder about Talleyrand's activities in London. Beginning with the creation of the French Republic on August 10, 1792, and continuing with the September Massacres, Talleyrand's status became clearer: whatever his situation had been, he was now a private citizen, and no representative of the French government.[52]

Fellow *constituants* soon joined Talleyrand in England, including the duc de Liancourt and Germaine de Staël, the famous author. She and other refugees from Paris's *hôtels particuliers* rented Juniper Hall, a house in Surrey, about twenty miles southwest of London, where they formed a small, tight-knit community. Staël, whose mother, Suzanne Necker, had been one of the great *salonnières* of the eighteenth century, had grown up amid the refined chatter of Paris salons; she now transplanted the institution to suburban London. With Staël serving as the queen bee, a rotating cast of refugees, authors, friends, lovers, and *bons vivants* buzzed around, spending their days reading up on the news pouring out of France, writing letters and essays, and socializing to keep their spirits up. It was a preview of the community that Talleyrand, Noailles, and Liancourt would re-create in Philadelphia. They learned of the king's execution with despair and grief, a sentiment that extended to the tales of murdered royalty and aristocrats but did not encompass the starving peasants or the slaughtered Parisian crowds. Perhaps that would have been expecting too much.[53]

Frances Burney, the British author and a frequent visitor at Juniper Hall, who had spent years at the British court as a keeper of the robes for the queen, had never witnessed anything like the conversation of these veterans of Paris salons and Versailles court life. "*Junipère* society," as she called it, was "of incontestable superiority" to anything she knew. "Ah what days were those of conversational perfection," she later reminisced, "of wit, gaiety, repartee, information, badinage, and eloquence." Burney's reports on her time among the French *constituants* described them as though from a dream. "We dined and stayed till midnight at *Junipère* on Tuesday," she wrote her sister after one party, "and I wish I could recollect but the twentieth part of the excellent things that we said." No doubt some of Burney's fog stemmed from her growing love for General Alexandre d'Arblay, Lafayette's former aide-de-camp, whom she would soon marry, but it also corresponds with other descriptions. Talleyrand excelled in this environment. Although he did not make a good first impression on Burney when they met, Talleyrand eventually won her over, as he did so many others. "It is inconceivable what a convert M. de Talleyrand has made of me," Burney reported to her sister after a few weeks. "I think him now one of the first members, and one of the most charming of this exquisite set.... His powers of entertainment are astonishing, both in information and raillery."[54]

Conversation, for this set, was perhaps the most important talent. ("Our manners will be gentle," Noailles had written of his planned colony in Pennsylvania, "our conversation animated, our labor active.") No one embodied this culture better than Staël, who developed a theory of conversation and its connection to manners and national character. Speech in France, she would later write, "is not just, as it is elsewhere, a means of communicating ideas, sentiments, and practical matters. It is an instrument to be played with love, which revives the mind and soul as music does with some people, or spirits with others." Conversation as performed by the émigrés served to console those who had lost friends and family, fortunes, careers, and country. "The *bon mots* of the French," Staël wrote, recalling, perhaps, her time at Juniper Hall, "have displayed the brilliancy of their merit, and solaced their grief in a lively and piquant manner; at all times they have stood in need of one another, as alternate hearers who mutually encourage each other." Words performed a function; they were al-

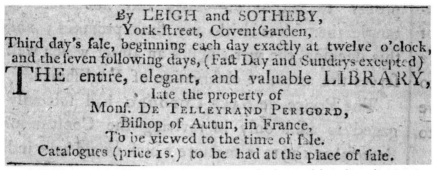

Talleyrand's "entire, elegant, and valuable LIBRARY," *advertised for sale in the* Morning Chronicle *of London, April 13, 1793.*

most alive. They appeased an existential emptiness. They provided the most welcome kind of relief.[55]

For all the solace Talleyrand found in those conversations in Surrey, prosaic concerns eventually intervened. "I'm going to leave my house on Woodstock Street," Talleyrand suddenly announced to his friends in May 1793. "It's too expensive." He was having money problems. Talleyrand raised some funds by selling his library, which he'd had the foresight to bring to England while still on an official diplomatic mission. The sale netted Talleyrand £750, not a terrible sum at a time when Frances Burney lived on an annual pension of £100 per year from the queen. But it was a pittance by the standards of the French aristocracy: "What is this good for?" Talleyrand moaned in a letter to Staël. Such a modest living might be acceptable for a while, but as weeks in exile stretched to months, and then years, it was clear he would need a longer-term solution. "Our role as quiet émigré honestly cannot suit us much longer," Talleyrand wrote in September 1793. "I'll linger until March, either in the city, either in the country, spending as little money as I can," he wrote to Staël in November. "Let me know what the funds of your society are."[56]

The final push came not from his finances but from politics: the anxious British authorities who feared the popular support for the French Revolution among the Irish and the English working classes. Certainly some of the French refugees came to England to foment rebellion, perhaps even

Talleyrand himself. The Aliens Act of 1793 affected Talleyrand as it did Noailles, granting British authorities the right to expel suspect foreigners. The *constituants* were particular targets. Detested by the French royalist refugees who crowded in London's Tory society, and distrusted by the more radical democrats in Britain, they had few defenders. (One might as well try to defend Guy Fawkes as Talleyrand, a friend wrote Burney in 1793.) One Tuesday afternoon in January 1794, the hammer fell. Two men knocked on Talleyrand's door carrying an expulsion order from the king. Talleyrand protested his innocence to anyone who would listen—up to the prime minister and even the king himself—but no one did. So in early March, Talleyrand left for the United States, exiled for the second time in eighteen months. "It's at age 39 that I begin a new life," he wrote to Staël morosely. "America is as good an asylum as any other," he added. "When one has taken courses in political thought, it's a country to see."[57]

"LAND! LAND!" The cry woke Talleyrand as his ship approached the Delaware Bay in late April 1794. Talleyrand climbed to the deck with bleary eyes. It had been thirty-eight days since those aboard had lost sight of England—an easy voyage. But Talleyrand was despondent. He had left his closest friends in Europe and come to America accompanied only by his servant Courtiade and another *constituant,* Bon-Albert Briois de Beaumetz, who was proving a disappointing companion both temperamentally and intellectually.[58]

As the ship had pulled away from England, the other passengers looked longingly back at the land. But not Talleyrand: "Only I felt relief at no longer seeing it. At that time I was strongly charmed by the sea; it provided me with sensations that suited my disposition." Talleyrand gazed at the ocean, preferring its vast emptiness to the company he found on board. He was the only émigré—and surely a rare species of Atlantic traveler—who found the crossing too short. When Talleyrand's ship sat anchored on the headlands of the Delaware waiting for the tide to come in for the journey upriver to Philadelphia, he spied a vessel sailing out. When the pilot told him the ship was sailing for Calcutta—a trip of more than a year—Talleyrand "immediately dispatched a boat to the ship's captain to inquire whether he had room for one more passenger. The ship's destination was of no consequence to me; the trip had to be a long one, and what I wanted was to not leave the sea." But there was no room, so Talleyrand sailed to Philadelphia in spite of himself: "a theoretician without a doctrine," as the great literary scholar Fernand Baldensperger later described him, "a politician without employment, and a libertine without joy." Today we would call him depressed. "I arrived full of repugnance for the novelties that usually interest travelers. I had the greatest trouble rousing in myself the slightest curiosity."[59]

Philadelphia came into view when his ship passed a bend in the river three miles out: a jumble of wooden warehouses crowded on top of each other, wharves jutting chaotically into the river. Talleyrand found the scene no more pleasing on land. Not even the city's architecture, which charmed so many others, held any allure. Low-lying Water Street, onto which passengers debarked, stank from the muck of the street and the deposits rotting in the waste houses. "I can attest that the docks and certain parts of the boulevards exceed in public and private filth anything I saw in Turkey," Volney would later write. Pushing through the crowds greeting his ship, Talleyrand climbed up to Front Street, where he found a city laid out along straight lines, all intersecting at right angles: a monotonous structure of streets that made each one look identical and left newcomers easily confused. The buildings were scarcely more interesting, dull and uniform in their red brick and pale blue marble.[60]

Talleyrand spent his first weeks exploring Philadelphia, meeting old friends and making new ones. Noailles was already well established and introduced Talleyrand to his circle of friends. He ran into Moreau on the streets a month after his arrival. On May 19, Talleyrand swore an oath of allegiance to the state of Pennsylvania and to the United States. The nobleman who, just a few years earlier, administered King Louis XVI's oath to the French constitution as thousands looked on now found himself swearing an oath to a foreign country in front of Mayor Matthew Clarkson.

Despite Talleyrand's intention to escape Atlantic politics, they had followed him to the United States. Philadelphia was still recovering from the yellow fever epidemic, still shaking from the reverberations of the French and Haitian revolutions, and still receiving immigrants from the Caribbean. "American ports are today inundated with Frenchmen," he noted soon after his arrival. The city was tense with diplomatic news: there was, Talleyrand discovered, "an embargo on all vessels in America; for the moment, there is no communication with Europe." Several months earlier, seeking to keep American provisions from France and its colonies, Great Britain had imposed a total blockade of French ports, empowering the British navy to detain neutral ships in the Caribbean and the Atlantic. Armed British privateers seized 250 American ships, treating American seamen and property ruthlessly. It was a brazen violation of the American principle that "free bottoms make free goods": that U.S. neutrality bestowed protection on the country's ships and cargoes. Anti-British sentiment soared across the country. "Partisans of England were tarred and feathered," reported the French minister in May. "In Charleston Pitt and Dumourier were hung in effigy"—William Pitt (the younger), the British prime minister, and Charles-François Dumouriez, the former French general and minister of war who had fled to France's enemies—"along with two Congressmen who are supposed to be partisans of our enemy; in Newport an English vessel was searched despite the *réclamations* of the officers of that nation, and American sailors who had been forced to serve on board were freed." Hammond, the British ambassador, was complaining about all the vigilante activity. A Democratic-Republican society in Charleston, he reported, boarded an English ship "with a party of the militia artillery, carried off the arms, and deposited them in the public stores."[61]

As if the outrages on sea were not enough, thousands of miles inland, just south of the Great Lakes, British forces continued to aid the powerful confederation of Indians resisting U.S. expansion. In February 1794 the governor of British North America denounced American expansion in the Northwest as an aggression against Britain's Indian allies, and urged the Native peoples in Canada to prepare for war against the United States. He directed the governor of Upper Canada (present-day Ontario) to build a new fort in the Ohio valley, to rally the Indians in the region, and to arm British vessels on the Great Lakes. The American population, their anti-

British sentiments still fresh, exploded in anger. Even the pro-British Federalists began to prepare for war. In March, Congress passed a one-month embargo on all trade with Great Britain, which it renewed again in April.[62]

Talleyrand had fled one war-torn continent only to arrive to another on the cusp of war. Conflict with England seemed imminent. In a last, desperate attempt to maintain the peace, Washington appointed John Jay as a special envoy to Great Britain. Jay was a logical pick: he was about as distinguished a statesman as the United States had. He had cowritten the *Federalist Papers* with Alexander Hamilton and James Madison, and served as chief justice of the United States. He was also one of the three signatories—along with Benjamin Franklin and John Adams—of the 1783 Treaty of Paris, which ended the American Revolution. Now he was charged with negotiating what would be, in effect, the sequel. In addition to securing Britain's respect for American shipping, he would try to settle lingering war claims and, perhaps most important, the still unresolved issue of the forts around the Great Lakes from which the British supplied Native Americans.

As it happened, Talleyrand's first letter from the United States made its way to Europe on board the *Ohio,* the very ship carrying Jay to London. It was the only way to get a message across the Atlantic.

UNLIKE TALLEYRAND, Médéric-Louis-Élie Moreau de Saint-Méry arrived in the United States gratefully. Where Talleyrand had hoped to stay at sea and landed "full of repugnance" for his new home, Moreau rejoiced upon his American landfall. "At last I am in this hospitable soil, on this land of freedom," he exclaimed upon arriving in Norfolk, Virginia, in March 1794. He was thankful just to be alive.[63]

Moreau was born not in France but in Martinique, in 1750. As a Creole from the Caribbean bourgeoisie, Moreau stemmed from far more modest roots than the other émigré *constituants:* origins to which his bottomless insecurity would testify. Brilliant and ambitious, he sailed for France at age nineteen to begin his legal training. In a mere three years he had been admitted as an *avocat au Parlement*—analogous to the Superior Court bar.

Moreau returned to the Caribbean, and in 1772 established himself at Cap-Français, Saint Domingue, where he practiced law for several years, married into a planter family, and began to collect data on the history of the French Caribbean legal systems. His research culminated in a six-volume compilation, *Lois et constitutions des colonies françaises de l'Amérique sous le vent,* published from 1784 to 1790. Moreau then determined to write an even more monumental encyclopedia of Saint Domingue and returned to France to complete the manuscript. At the outbreak of the Revolution, Moreau threw himself into the cause and became an *électeur* of Paris. On July 14, 1789, Moreau was serving as president of the *électeurs de Paris;* it was in this capacity that he received a key to the Bastille upon its fall—perhaps the same key Lafayette would later send George Washington. With the established authorities crumbling, Moreau was left practically in charge of Paris for several chaotic days, running the city with what a colleague remembered as remarkable "prudence and *sang-froid.*" He was soon appointed to the governing body of the Paris Commune, serving as secretary and vice president, before being elected to the Assemblée constituante to represent Martinique. By 1792, like many other French liberals, Moreau had become persona non grata. After witnessing the stoning to death of the duc de La Rochefoucauld in Paris that year, he took refuge in Le Havre. Early in the morning of November 9, 1793, he and his family boarded the American ship *Sophie*—just eighteen hours before a warrant for his arrest arrived from Paris.[64]

Winter was a notoriously dangerous time to cross the Atlantic. Only desperation could have driven Moreau and his family to undertake the trip then—and they bore the fullest brunt of the season's fury. Heading south from France to catch the trade winds, the ship ran into strong headwinds after passing the Azores. The passengers suffered terribly from seasickness. The captain's poor planning did little to mitigate these discomforts. "The lack of foresight," Moreau observed in his diary, "seems to be the outstanding characteristic of American sailors." But soon discomfort turned to danger. Rain flooded the hold where Moreau's food was held, killing more than eighty of the chickens his family had planned to consume on the trip. On December 13, just barely a month out to sea, they ate their last bird. The trip was to last three more months. Soon they were down to beets, onion soup, and biscuits. Constipation was followed by diarrhea. For ten terrible days in late January, the ship and crew were "the playthings of a tempest." That was about the time the brandy ran out. Three more storms hit them in February, damaging the masts' supports, breaking the tiller, and leaving the ship, with its rigging weakened and its sails tattered, at the mercy of one more storm.[65]

By the time Moreau mercifully landed in Norfolk, on March 7, 1794, he had lost fifty-two pounds and was commenting mournfully on "the hollowness of my stomach which had replaced its usual rotundity." It would take him several months to recover. (Still weak in May, Moreau consulted a surgeon from Saint Domingue, who criticized his lifelong habit of abstaining from wine, telling him that if he persisted in this dangerous behavior, his life would be at risk. "I took his word for it and began to drink porter," Moreau reported.) But in the scheme of things, Moreau had been lucky. The sight of hundreds of refugees from Saint Domingue, some of whom he knew, gave him another measure by which to gauge his suffering: "Dear God! Their pitiable condition . . . showed me that I had small cause for complaint!"[66]

Wherever Moreau went along the Eastern Seaboard he found French and Saint Domingue refugees pouring in from Europe and the Caribbean. Norfolk was a welcome haven, its residents stridently pro-French: "in their speech, in the affection which leads large numbers to wear the tricolored cockade, and in the eagerness they showed on April 22 to tar and feather an American who had spoken disrespectfully of the French and make him ride an entire day through the streets in a cart." The city was full of refugees from Saint Domingue, great planters brought low, "colonists whose pitiful condition makes our hearts bleed," all of them trying to adjust to their new lives, and to sights as banal but unexpected as the flickering of fireflies at night. All the destitute refugees competed for a limited number of jobs, however, and Moreau was eventually forced to leave in search of employment, sailing north to Baltimore, Philadelphia, and then New York in May 1794.[67]

In an era before industrialization, schedules were eminently flexible, and travel was far riskier and more grueling than it is today. Travelers rode stagecoaches through the night, with drivers doing their best to guide the horses by moonlight; mealtimes came and went; boats got stuck in ice; coaches lost wheels; bags left without their passengers and vice versa. And no European traveler—not one—failed to mention the discomfort of American stagecoaches or the pitiable state of the roads. After passing through Baltimore, Moreau headed for Philadelphia. He first boarded a ship at 8:30 in the morning for a seventeen-hour journey out of Baltimore Harbor and up the Chesapeake Bay, arriving in Frenchtown, at the mouth of the Susquehanna River, at 1:30 in the morning. He stayed on the boat through the night, catching what sleep he could until 4:45, when he and his fellow passengers disembarked to board a stagecoach across the Delmarva Peninsula. A four-hour ride along bumpy roads in a carriage with passengers "crowded in together, unable to stretch their legs because their baggage is placed beneath the benches" brought Moreau to Newcastle, Delaware, where he had lunch and then boarded another boat up the Delaware to Philadelphia, finally docking at 5:00 p.m., as the day was drawing to a close and the oyster vendors began their evening walk through the city hawking the day's catch. He'd left Baltimore some thirty-three hours earlier. And Moreau had it easy: those who traveled between Baltimore and Philadelphia exclusively by coach found the trip even more grueling.[68]

Moreau found Philadelphia, like Norfolk and Baltimore, teeming with Saint Domingue refugees, including friends and acquaintances who updated him with news from the Caribbean. He got a room amid the crowded lodgings and boardinghouses running along North Second Street. It was the next day, May 22, that Moreau ran into Talleyrand and Beaumetz, and had a long, pleasant dinner with them. "After dinner we went together to see Blacons, Count de Noailles, and Talon. Fresh surprise! Fresh pleasures!" On May 25 Moreau reached New York, where he boarded at the inn of a Frenchman. A French merchant house in New York had promised him a job, but when he arrived he found, to his dismay, that it was as a mere clerk hired to stow barrels of flour, pickled pork, rice, salted beef, soda, potash, and other American products for export to the Caribbean. Loading and unloading cargo, crawling into ships' holds to stamp barrels in New York's suffocating summer heat, Moreau suffered physically and emotionally, comparing his work to "galley-slave labor." (Evidently he had never worked as a galley slave in the French navy.) Moreau was almost comically sensitive to slights that seemed to reflect on his social standing. "What an occupation for a man such as I," he exclaimed to his diary, "a member of a sovereign court, high in the public esteem, and almost forty-five years of age!" But he had no choice if he was to support his family. "Oh, my wife and my children! I provided you with bread, but how bitter it was for me!"[69]

Moreau reconnected with Talleyrand as the latter traveled through New York that summer, escaping the Philadelphia heat on his way to explore Maine and upstate New York. The two saw the July Fourth parade in New York along with several other Frenchmen from Talleyrand's lodgings, just across from the Government House, the residence originally built for the president on the north side of Fort George facing Bowling Green.

The Government House, 1797. This house, facing New York's Bowling Green, was originally built for the president of the United States in the hopes that New York would remain the U.S. capital.

From their perch above, the refugees watched New York governor George Clinton parade by, along with a host of pro-French radicals—including Genet, who by now had lost his ambassadorship but remained in the United States.

> The governor and the people who accompanied him in this *fête* were preceded by a long procession of French Jacobins, marching two by two, singing the *Marseillaise* and other republican songs. . . . They interrupted themselves to address invectives to us in the windows where they saw us, Talleyrand, Beaumetz, Cazenove, La Colombe, Baron de la Roche and me. . . . Genêt, brother of Mme. Campan, was in the procession and sang and insulted us like all the others.

Perhaps the scene brought back memories. Did these men who had lost control of a revolution they helped inaugurate, who had been chased out of their country by violent urban mobs, now wonder if the violence had followed them to America? "We wept for our country and for him!" Moreau concluded.[70]

In mid-July 1794 Moreau met with a French baron and Théophile Cazenove, the Dutch banker Talleyrand had already befriended. Together, the three negotiated terms of an agreement to free Moreau from his demeaning job as a shipping clerk and provide him with the capital to launch a more intellectual (if still manual) *métier:* printing. And so, in October 1794, Moreau left New York with his family to open a bookstore and printing operation at the corner of Front and Walnut Streets in Philadelphia. It would become a center of the city's French community.

As GENET, Governor Clinton, and others marched down Broadway singing French revolutionary songs while Talleyrand and Moreau looked on; as French partisans mobilized across the East Coast in Philadelphia, Baltimore, Norfolk, and Charleston, tarring and feathering pro-British elements; as John Jay was getting settled in London, hoping to avert a war between the United States and Great Britain; as the eruptions in France and Haiti showered refugees across the American continent—amid all the turmoil, long-standing political grievances were boiling over along the Appalachian frontier across vast stretches of western Pennsylvania, Maryland, and Virginia.

A whiskey tax was the catalyst. After several years of complaining about the onerous provisions of a new revenue law, tensions exploded in July 1794, when farmers in western Pennsylvania rose up in armed insurrection against the federal government, with the support of two pro-French Democratic-Republican Societies. On July 16, five hundred men attacked the local tax official's house in a battle that killed two insurgents. Two weeks later, on August 1, six thousand men gathered in Braddock's Field, outside of Pittsburgh, to hold a grand review of the rebels. Leaders of the insurrection sent pleas for support to local militias in western Maryland and Virginia. For a brief period in the late summer of 1794, it seemed as though the entire Appalachian backcountry was rising up in an armed rebellion not unlike the American Revolution.

European officials took a keen interest in the events. British officers in Canada and Spanish administrators in New Orleans followed the uprising closely. New Orleans was the outlet for all goods shipped down the Ohio and Mississippi Rivers (including whiskey); Spanish authorities were aware that French agents were prowling the backcountry hoping to mobilize settlers in a war against Spanish possessions, and had made preparations. "From Philadelphia it looked as though Britain and Spain were plotting war," concludes Thomas Slaughter, the foremost historian of the Whiskey Rebellion. "The threat of another international war for the continent seemed imminent to the President, and the outcome by no means assured." In this context, the alliances between the "sans-culottes of Pittsburgh" and foreign officials could hardly have been more alarming to U.S. government officials. It was not clear what connection the émigré *constituants* had to these events, but their sudden arrival on American soil did not reassure American leaders about foreign influences on domestic politics.[71]

PHILADELPHIA WAS abuzz with news about "the expedition from Pittsburgh" when François-Alexandre-Frédéric de La Rochefoucauld, duc de Liancourt, stepped off the *Pigou* onto American shores in late November 1794. Liancourt was unusually tall and stood ramrod straight, with a prominent forehead and piercing blue eyes that did not quite conceal the bookish intelligence that lay behind them. Silent and often brooding, he left a powerful impression on those he met.

> His face, which is very handsome, though not critically so, has rather a haughty expression when left to itself, but becomes soft and spirited in turn, according to whom he speaks, and has great

Liancourt as a deputy to the French Constituent Assembly.

play and variety. His deportment is quite noble, and in a style to announce conscious rank even to the most sedulous equalizer. . . . His manners are such as only admit of comparison with what we have read, not what we have seen; for he has all the air of a man who would wish to lord over men, but to cast himself at the feet of women.

Or so Frances Burney somewhat heatedly described him when she met him in England, just before his exile to the United States. Liancourt impressed Burney not just by his looks but by the eloquence of his speech, the ease of his demeanor, and a playfulness that occasionally poked through. "His first

A print of Liancourt throwing himself at the king's feet, on the night of July 14–15, 1789, when he famously told Louis XVI that a revolution had begun.

address was of the highest style," Burney reported. "I saw here, in the midst of all that at first so powerfully struck me, of dignity, importance, and high-breeding, a true French *polisson*."[72]

Aged forty-seven when he arrived in the United States, Liancourt was the noblest and the richest of all the French aristocrats to come to America during these stormy years. His family had been serving the kings of France for five centuries. One of his ancestors was the author of La Rochefoucauld's *Maximes*. His cousin Louis-Alexandre, duc de La Rochefoucauld, had been one of Franklin's closest friends and one of the United States' most ardent supporters in Paris during the American Revolution. Liancourt's fortune was almost unimaginably vast: at the time of the Revolution, it provided him with an annual income of 446,000 *livres*—in an age when an unskilled laborer earned about 1.5 *livres* per day. Liancourt had served as master of the *garderobe* of Louis XVI, as his father had served Louis XV before him; one of the most eminent and envied titles of *ancien régime* France, it made Liancourt one of the very few people allowed to enter the king's private chambers uninvited. Thus it was he who burst into Louis XVI's bedchambers on the night of July 14, 1789, to inform him of the fall of the Bastille.[73]

"C'est une grande révolte?" the king asked.

"Non, sire!" Liancourt responded. It is one of the most famous retorts in all of French history: "C'est une grande révolution!"[74]

Liancourt's early life was marked by a standard trajectory of a firstborn son of the *noblesse de l'épée*, the nobility of the sword. At age sixteen he was presented as a musketeer, launching the military career into which he'd been born. At seventeen he was married. Despite his exalted lineage, however, Liancourt fit uneasily in the world of eighteenth-century French aristocracy. Born of parents he called "virtuous to the point of severity," Liancourt had a lifelong earnestness that often left him at odds amid the sprightly conversation the French so valued and admired. While still a young man, he regularly attended the famous salons of his aunt Madame d'Enville, the duchess of La Rochefoucauld, and of his friend Julie de Lespinasse. Sitting quietly, too timid to participate in the conversation, Liancourt listened diligently to the raging debates carried on by the great figures of the Physiocratic School, like François Quesnay, Anne-Robert-Jacques Turgot, and Pierre-Samuel du Pont de Nemours, who believed that the wealth of nations derives from agriculture, and who deplored the mercantilist trade restrictions of modern empires. D'Enville's salon also hosted a circle of pro-Americans that included the duc de La Rochefoucauld, her son and Liancourt's cousin; the marquis de Condorcet, who marked Thomas Jefferson's thinking while in Paris; and Lafayette. They all looked to the United States—and to postwar Franco-American commercial relations—as a model for the future global economy. No doubt these circles shaped Liancourt's lifelong interest in agricultural reform, although he never exhibited the theoretical bent of the most eminent Physiocrats, preferring instead more practical reforms. Intimidated by the towering intellects that surrounded him, young Liancourt was determined to improve his knowledge and education. At the age of twenty, he traveled to England "with the affectation," as he later remembered, "of seeking on the other side of the Channel a free government." In England, he met and befriended the agriculturalist Arthur Young, who later visited Liancourt in France for an extended period; Young's published *Travels* would serve as the model for Liancourt's writings on the United States.[75]

In 1789 Liancourt was elected a deputy of the nobility to the Estates General. Like Noailles, Talleyrand, and Moreau, Liancourt took a leading role in the French Revolution, promoting early reforms and advocating for a constitutional monarchy. Like them, he served in the French Assemblée constituante, briefly presiding over that body in July 1789. "He is, undoubtedly, to be esteemed one of those who have had a principal share in the revolution," wrote Arthur Young. "But he has been invariably guided by constitutional motives." For a time, during that hopeful period from 1789 to 1790, Liancourt and his friends succeeded in reconciling their commitments to monarchy and republicanism. They took their seats on the left side of the assembly, against the majority of the nobility. "I attracted blame from all quarters," Liancourt wrote. "While I was treated as tepid, moderate, and suspect by the extremists of the side on which I sat, the extremists on the right side proclaimed me a jacobin, a revolutionary, a traitor to the King, and, which for them was even worse, a traitor to the nobility." Eventually Liancourt realized that the center could not hold: "The excesses and thus the dangers of the revolution were evident to me early on; I soon saw a torrent that would carry away the more moderate."[76]

The summer of 1792 found Liancourt in Rouen, at the head of the French military division of Normandy and Picardy. In July, sensing that matters were spinning out of control, Liancourt urged King Louis XVI to join him there, where he would be better protected and—in the worst case—could be more easily spirited out of the country. When the news of the events of August 10 arrived in Rouen, "in the first impetuosity of rage and despair," Liancourt summoned his officers and troops, took off his hat, and called out: "Vive le roi!" The troops responded with acclamation but the townspeople looked on in ominous silence. Soon after, Liancourt learned that a warrant in Paris had been drawn up for his arrest, as well as for that of his cousin, the duc de La Rochefoucauld: "Less confident, less virtuous than him, I fled the daggers and he succumbed."[77]

Making his way to the coast, Liancourt found a fishing boat to ferry him across the English Channel. Late one August night, Liancourt, his valet, and a friend met the boat, which had two men aboard. One of them took Liancourt for the king of France and refused to ferry the party across. His friend drew a pistol and forced the accuser off the boat. Liancourt and his groom left with the fisherman, hiding under a pile of firewood. Only when they were halfway across the Channel did they feel safe enough to sit up. The fisherman told Liancourt that he knew he was shepherding a *proscrit* to safety, but that such acts always brought luck. (Much later the man would come and eat at Liancourt's table, in his fishing garb, and afterward, according to his son, the two would sit together on the porch and smoke cigars.)

When they landed at Hastings, England, Liancourt and his valet went to the nearest pub. Thirsty and terrified by the ordeal, Liancourt immediately ordered a porter and quaffed it down—then another. Soon he passed out drunk and was carried upstairs to bed. When Liancourt woke up in the empty room, it was the middle of the night; he was alone and had no idea where he was or how he had gotten there. He assumed he must be in prison. He got up, determined to break out. When he crept downstairs, he found himself in the kitchen, as Frances Burney recounted. "He looked round, and the brightness of a shelf of pewter plates struck his eye; under them were pots and kettles shining and polished. '*Ah!*' cried he to himself, '*je suis en Angleterre!*'"[78]

Liancourt fell into a depression. Not even his dog Cartouche, with whom he was soon reunited, could cheer him up. The news kept getting worse. He learned of the death of his cousin and childhood friend, Louis-Alexandre, the duc de La Rochefoucauld. Soon after came the arrest of Louis XVI and his trial for treason. Liancourt wrote a long defense of the king—a defense, really, of the idea that the monarchy and the Revolution could coexist—but it was too late. History had eclipsed them both. Along with the other *constituants* taking refuge in England, he watched the collapse of his dreams as Louis XVI was executed and imperial war began. He was, according to one report, "devoured of a continual sadness." His health declined. Burney recalls him, in these days, visiting at Juniper Hall. "Recollections and sorrow had retaken possession of his mind; and his spirit, his vivacity, his power of rallying, were all at an end. He was strolling about the room with an air the most gloomy, and a face that looked enveloped in clouds of sadness and moroseness. There was a *fierté* almost even fierce in his air and look, as, wrapped in himself, he continued his walk." She didn't want to disturb him, and left him to fight with his inner demons. Eventually he "shook himself and joined us; though he could not bear to sit down, or stand a moment in a place."[79]

Finally, having watched Noailles and Talleyrand leave for America, Liancourt decided to follow. In late September 1794, along with Cartouche, Liancourt boarded the *Pigou* in London. He posed as a Swiss traveler, a prudent measure for such a famous émigré with an outstanding arrest warrant, in the event his ship was stopped by a French vessel. During the trip he kept to himself, occupying his time by writing in his diary, reading, trying to humor the seasick Cartouche, or just looking out to sea. Liancourt had a terrifying few moments when the *Pigou* ran across a thirty-four-cannon French naval vessel posing as a British ship, but the American boat was let go with only a few cursory questions, and Liancourt was left alone. It was late November by the time he saw the lighthouse on Cape Henlopen.

As the ship glided into Delaware Bay, Liancourt could see the coast. The shoreline was low and flat. The trees had not yet lost their foliage; rich reds and yellows from the oaks and poplars blended into darker greens of the great pine trees, reflecting off the glassy blue of the Delaware River.[80]

Liancourt longed for a new start. It was not his choice to come to America; fate had forced his hand, as it had those of his countrymen who, as Talleyrand put it, "escaped from France as one escapes from prison," and who had "not even asked where they would go, but where they could go." Liancourt was determined to make the best of it, however, and hoped the trip would "furnish him with a study . . . which would paint the portrait of a country organized so recently and on such true political principles." He would distract himself by examining the United States—its institutions and its manners. Driven by "a vivid sentiment of patriotism," the investigation might even offer some clues as to how he and his countrymen might rescue their own republican experiment.[81]

"France was trying a new kind of government analogous to that of the United States," Liancourt's son and biographer later mused, "and we can imagine how the portrait of a republican America, surely the wisest of all those that have existed, would have offered the French republic, had it lasted, good examples and useful lessons."[82]

Chapter 2

SETTLING IN AMERICA: PHILADELPHIA SPEAKS FRENCH

*The City Tavern: detail from
a print by William Birch.*

ON THURSDAY, NOVEMBER 27, 1794, LIANCOURT WOKE UP ON THE
third floor of the City Tavern, the grand three-story brick building on the corner of Second and Walnut Streets, two blocks west
of the docks. Built twenty years earlier by Philadelphia's financial and commercial elite, it had become the city's premier space for international merchants, travelers, diplomats, and speculators, who gathered daily on the
first floor to get the latest news, learn about incoming ships sailing up the
Delaware with the next tide, get an early peek at ships' registers, or gather
the prices of commodities and stocks from newspapers from Boston, New
York, Baltimore, and European capitals. Its second floor was divided into
several dining rooms, two of which could be joined to make a large assembly hall fifty feet long: for many years it had been the city's largest in-
door space. The third floor served as a hotel, providing rooms for travelers.
John Adams, fresh out of provincial New England, visited the City Tavern

soon after it opened. After eating a dinner "as elegant as ever was laid upon a table," he pronounced it the "most genteel" tavern in America. Conrad-Alexandre Gérard, France's first ambassador to the United States, threw a grand *fête* for Louis XVI's birthday there during the American Revolution. Banquets were held there for George Washington as he left for Boston in 1775 as the newly appointed commander in chief, as he traveled to Yorktown in 1781, and again in 1789 as he passed through Philadelphia on the way to the first presidential inauguration in New York. It was where foreign eminences such as the journalist and future politician Jacques-Pierre Brissot de Warville and the Mohawk leader Joseph Brant stayed when they visited, where congressmen of all political and regional stripes took their meals; it was where Genet resided when he first arrived in Philadelphia, and where he was *fêted* when he "alighted at the City Tavern" and was given a congratulatory address by local citizens. It was celebrated and gently mocked in a satirical poem about Philadelphia published a few years after the Revolution:

> Exaustless lines could scarce pourtray the group,
> That daily here for news together troop,
> Some good some bad: the English, Irish here
> With French and Dutch familiarly appear;
> The Spaniard, Portuguese and sober Swede,
> Meet India merchants in the course of trade,
> The Russian, Prussian, Turk and Scot & Jew,
> With homebred Yankee here we mixing view.

If Philadelphia's elite community had a hub by which travelers, goods, information, and capital circulated, this was it.[1]

When Liancourt finished his breakfast that morning, he walked past the dining rooms and down to the first floor, where merchants and businessmen were already reading the latest news and trading stocks and notes, and stepped out onto Second Street. As he crossed Walnut Street and headed toward Spruce, he might have been surprised at how French his new city seemed. On the City Tavern's block, where a host of French businesses had established themselves, there was a French hairdresser, a jeweler, a dancing instructor, and a papermaker. Walking to Spruce—just one single block— Liancourt passed a French glass engraver, a French china merchant, a French baker, and a French hatter. He no doubt heard French spoken on the sidewalk. Soon he arrived at Talleyrand's residence on the corner of Second and Spruce, just one block from the tavern.

In the six months since his arrival, Talleyrand had visited large stretches of the northern hinterlands. Drawn in part by his interest in land investments, and chased out in part by Philadelphia's "excessive, suffocating heat," Talleyrand had traveled through New York and Boston and then along the coast of Maine by boat, and into its interior by horseback. Late August and September found Talleyrand back in Boston and New York, before leaving for another trip upstate with some companions. They sailed up the Hudson to Albany, and then proceeded west along the Mohawk valley corridor, the future route of the Erie Canal, through the largely unsettled lands of western New York, traveling amid the fall colors. They visited Niagara Falls before returning to Philadelphia in November, where Talleyrand greeted Liancourt as he arrived in the United States. During those travels, Talleyrand had gained insights into America's manners, its economy, and its citizens' apparent obsession with money, all of which he now shared with Liancourt. After their visit, the two walked over to dine with Théophile Cazenove, the Franco-Dutch banker who was guiding Talleyrand in his land investments and had helped secure financing for Moreau's bookstore. Samuel Richardet—a Frenchman who would soon run the City Tavern—worked as Cazenove's steward, overseeing the kitchen, where a French chef prepared meals for Talleyrand and other visiting Frenchmen. Cazenove's dining room provided a welcome refuge in a city dominated until recently by Quakers and Germans—neither group known for a refined cuisine or discerning palate.[2]

Later that afternoon, Liancourt met with Noailles, who lived in an apartment behind William Bingham's mansion on South Third Street, just a block away from Talleyrand. He then walked two blocks east, dropping into Moreau's bookstore on the corner of Front and Walnut Streets, where the gregarious proprietor immediately began talking about himself, recounting his painful crossing and his humiliating experience working as a shipping clerk in New York. But Liancourt—who would later call Moreau "boringly vain"—was not yet tired of Moreau's favorite topic. "He's a man of character and courage," the exiled duke concluded. Still that same day he met Antoine Omer Talon, a former member of the Constituent Assembly, and Louis-Saint-Ange Morel, chevalier de La Colombe, Lafayette's former aide-de-camp. "All I've seen of the French up to now," he concluded at the end of his first, busy day, "have little liking for America and still less for Americans, whom they paint as miserly, greedy, and occupied solely with cheating in all the transactions they make."[3]

It had been a cruel landing for these *habitués* of Europe's grandest circles, chased first out of France and then, for some, out of England. They had a difficult time getting used to the provincial pride and the sometimes boorish manners of their hosts. The French were hardly alone in their bemusement at Philadelphians' haughtiness about their city—"the *Metropolis* of America these Proud Phylidelphians have publickly named it," Abigail Adams carped when she moved there. But visitors from Europe's capital cities were likelier to see the emptiness of Philadelphians' pretensions, and the ways they papered over a sense of provincial inferiority. "Amongst the uppermost circles in Philadelphia," remarked a British visitor in 1795, "pride, haughtiness, and ostentation are conspicuous." These were not new traits: François-Jean, the marquis de Chastellux, who had visited during the Revolution, had famously mocked the flamboyant humility of Philadelphia's Quakers.[4]

To be sure, those pretensions were not entirely without merit. Philadelphia was grander than any other American city north of Mexico. Its public buildings were among the country's most impressive: Independence Hall, for instance, where the Continental Congress approved the Declaration of Independence in 1776, and where the U.S. Constitution was debated in 1787. Americans today celebrate such buildings as quasi-religious sites. Notable as they were to proud Philadelphians in the eighteenth century—or as they are to Americans today—they were hardly likely to impress the French émigré *constituants*. When Talleyrand sat with the clergy and Liancourt, Volney, and Noailles sat with the aristocracy to debate the French constitu-

The grand portrait of the signing of the Declaration of Independence inside Philadelphia's Independence Hall, painted by John Trumbull in 1818, hangs in the rotunda of the U.S. Capitol. The room—and the event—both look decidedly less epic when compared with the hall in Versailles' Hôtel des Menus Plaisirs, where the Estates General convened in the presence of King Louis XVI on May 5, 1789.

tion, those discussions had taken place in buildings considerably more impressive. Philadelphia was clean, open, and airy, built with straight lines of numbered streets. It had lots of trees. But it was a far cry from the majesty of great European capitals. Over and over again, French visitors complained about the drabness: "nothing is sadder than this uniformity."[5]

Yes, many great minds had gathered in Philadelphia to write a new constitution a few years earlier. Yes, the conversation at Secretary of State Thomas Jefferson's dinner table sparkled. But it was a pale imitation of the debates among the great Physiocrats like Turgot, Quesnay, and du Pont de Nemours that Liancourt had attended in the duchesse d'Enville's salon at the *hôtel* de La Rochefoucauld-Liancourt, one of the most remarkable of Paris's *hôtels particuliers*. Nor did Jefferson's earnest conversation compare to the epic wit and repartee displayed at Madame de Staël's salon, where Talleyrand had been a regular. "Such conversation as was then audible in Paris," one of Talleyrand's biographers wrote, "had never, perhaps, been heard since certain voices in Athens fell silent two thousand years before."[6]

There was no getting around it: the émigrés had landed in the marchlands of European civilization. No wonder they complained.

NOAILLES HAD arrived in May 1793, Talleyrand and Moreau in the spring of 1794, and Liancourt six months after. The winter of 1794–95 was their first together in Philadelphia. Exiled from their homes, families, and country, the émigré *constituants* felt the sting deeply. Their friendship and companionship over the next few months would provide them with some comfort as they began remaking their lives. Slowly regaining their bearings, they would learn about Philadelphia, their new home.

What is so striking about the émigrés' exile in Philadelphia, however, is not how American it was, but rather how *French* it was. The émigrés fled France to a republic whose government and politics they had sought, in large measure, to implement back home in 1789. What they found instead were Americans seeking to live like French aristocrats. The United States was a foreign country, with a different landscape, different language, different manners, and different institutions. And yet here they were, con-

The last page of Benjamin Franklin Bache's General Advertiser, *November 27, 1794—Liancourt's first day in Philadelphia—printed advertisements in both French and English for such goods and services as a fencing academy, French lessons, a French calendar, and a French pocket almanac.*

suming French goods, walking past French stores, and hearing French on the streets. Philadelphia's sights and sounds, its objects and social spaces, all echoed with French intonations.

During the age of the French Revolution, French speakers poured into the city from Europe and the Caribbean. French goods arrived from distant ports. Merchants built grand houses filled with French furniture, French tapestries, and French porcelain that displayed their refined taste and their worldly sophistication. The aromas of French food wafted through the alleys behind South Second Street, while French revolutionary songs, performed almost nightly in the Chestnut Street Theatre, echoed off the cobblestones. This was the material and sensory world by which the émigrés experienced the United States, and it sheds new light on the America they encountered. Seen and heard through the eyes and ears of the émigrés, Philadelphia turns out to be a more cosmopolitan city than previously imagined: not just a city that hosted the debates that forged a constitution and created new political parties, populated by characters like George Washington, John Adams, Thomas Jefferson, and Alexander Hamilton, but also a city that teemed with refugees arguing over the French and Haitian revolutions, with a vibrant French press and thriving French cultural institutions, populated by an unfamiliar cast of characters with intimate links to transatlantic culture. A closer look at this French Philadelphia may give us a new understanding of American culture in the Federalist era.

PHILADELPHIA WAS the U.S. capital, its largest city, and the port with the most trading connections with France and Saint Domingue. It was also the city most transformed by the political, demographic, cultural, and social aftershocks of the French and Haitian revolutions. The French people pouring into Philadelphia would change the city forever, refashioning its trade patterns, its cultural makeup, indeed its very appearance, turning what had been a provincial English, German-inflected town on the fringes of European civilization into a cosmopolitan hub of a kind that had never before existed in North America.[7]

Many of the refugees fleeing the violence in France and the French

Caribbean landed in Philadelphia simply by following the shipping routes. By far the largest number, like Moreau's mother-in-law, came from Saint Domingue. Many others came from France. The exact number of French speakers in Philadelphia in the mid-1790s is hard to determine. The French consul at the time estimated the total number of French people in the city at five thousand—more than 10 percent of the city's 1790 population. The historian Gary Nash examined ships' logs and found that during the peak of the migration, from May 1791 to April 1794, more than three thousand French people—white, free colored, and enslaved—landed in Philadelphia from Saint Domingue alone, though of course not all of them would have stayed in the city. According to another study, the French accounted for 27 percent of immigrants arriving in Philadelphia between 1789 and 1793, second only to the Irish, although that was before the peak of the French refugee migration. In all, 21,405 immigrants remained in Philadelphia by the end of the decade (an additional 17,500 landed at the port of Wilmington and came to Philadelphia by land); if one-quarter of those were French, that amounts to well over 5,000 newly arrived French speakers—this, in a city that began the decade with a total population of slightly more than 40,000, and which by mid-1793 amounted to 51,200. So although we will never know the exact number, it is clear that the French made up a substantial proportion of Philadelphia's population in the 1790s: probably as high as 10 percent, and perhaps even higher.[8]

Even before the new wave of French immigration in the 1790s, the city had experienced major demographic changes. Founded by Quakers, Philadelphia had a political culture that reflected the Society of Friends' understated ethos through most of the colonial era. The arrival of Scottish Presbyterian and German immigrants expanded the city's demographic and linguistic base, but these new immigrants were nearly all Protestant, and the city remained relatively homogeneous through the colonial period; though its population did include people of African descent, Philadelphia was essentially Northern European and Protestant. Even when Irish immigrants started arriving in significant numbers, many were Scots Irish Presbyterian rather than Catholic. It was only in the last years of the eighteenth century that matters began to change.[9]

Philadelphia's economic transformation in this period was even more significant than its demographic evolution. By splitting Great Britain from its colonies, the American Revolution had abruptly cut Philadelphia's merchants off from their established trading partners in Scotland, England, and the British Caribbean, while resentful British policy makers punished the former colonies by excluding them from the empire's Caribbean markets. French merchants jumped into the void, welcoming American partners into their commercial networks as French firms began to penetrate the Philadelphia market in growing numbers. Beginning during the Revolution, when France supplied essential loans and munitions to the embattled American colonists, the United States began trading more intensely with the French mainland and its Caribbean colonies. Meanwhile, French liberals worked to abolish trade barriers in order to further economic liberalization and Franco-American comity. Lafayette, for instance, lobbied at the French court to dismantle tariffs on whale oil and spermaceti—two of New England's most important exports. So grateful were a group of Nantucket fishermen for his efforts that they donated their milk production over a twenty-four-hour period, turned it into a five-hundred-pound cheese, and sent it to Lafayette in France as a gift. Thanks to this new trade, as well as the major French financial commitment to its new ally, by the end of the war, according to the recollections of one old-time Philadelphia immigrant, "French money was almost the only circulating medium." Even American government officials were being paid in French coin.[10]

Trade between the United States and the French Caribbean islands surged after the Revolution, with Philadelphia emerging as a central commercial node thanks to its vibrant port, its access to rich grain-producing hinterlands, its proximity to budding American manufacturers, and its concentration of merchant capital. French travelers to the new nation, like the rising politician Jacques-Pierre Brissot de Warville, paid close attention to data about American exports and the prices of various American commodities. Their interests were not just ideological but also material: fish and lumber from New England; wheat from the Hudson, Delaware, and Susquehanna valleys; rice from the Carolinas—all of these and more poured through the Philadelphia *entrepôt* to feed the Caribbean slaves powering an emergent European-centered global capitalism. Trade to the French sugar islands boomed. During the 1780s, the French Caribbean consumed one-quarter of American flour exports, three-quarters of its salted beef, 73 percent of its livestock, 61 percent of its dried fish, and 80 percent of its pickled fish. The islands, in turn, sent their rich stores of sugar, coffee, rum, molasses, and indigo, much of it then reexported to Europe. By 1790 nearly a third of all U.S. exports went to the West Indies, with the French islands importing more than any others. But no single destination received more American goods than Saint Domingue: 20 percent of all foreign ships arriving from abroad in the late 1780s came from Saint Domingue alone. So intertwined was U.S. and Caribbean trade that even the barrels in which the French colonists packed their goods were made of American wood. By the 1790s the value of American exports to Saint Domingue alone exceeded that to all other Caribbean islands combined. Despite this growing trade, however, and the growing Caribbean reliance on U.S. goods, French navigation laws continued to restrict American ships to a few free ports until 1793.[11]

It is one of the great ironies of the period that American trade—which, according to its most exuberant, Enlightenment-influenced advocates, should have led to universal peace—grew most not from peace but from war, and that insurgent slaves in Saint Domingue succeeded in doing what French liberals had long tried but failed to accomplish. In February 1793, fearful that the British navy would imperil France's ability to supply the sugar colonies, French authorities threw open all of France's colonial ports to American shipping. Genet was partly responsible for this expanded trade, as he frantically purchased goods to ship to the Caribbean islands, paying merchants with the American debt owed to France. Indeed, one of the primary duties of the French ministers in Philadelphia, whatever their political stripes, was to supply French forces in Saint Domingue with provisions; if they neglected this responsibility, reports from French generals in the Caribbean grew frantic. As a result, American exports to the besieged island exploded from $3.2 million in 1790 to $5 million in 1793, reaching $8 million in 1796. By 1796, a few years after France had thrown open its Caribbean colonies to unrestricted trade with the United States, Saint

Ads from Philadelphia newspapers after the American Revolution indicate the growing number of goods imported from France and the French Empire; the United States was slowly being incorporated into French trade networks. From the Pennsylvania Mercury and Universal Daily Advertiser, *June 9, 1786, and the* Philadelphia Gazette and Universal Daily Advertiser, *June 2, 1794.*

Domingue accounted for nearly 35 percent of all foreign ships arriving in Philadelphia. By that time Volney had arrived in the United States and was astounded by the "temporary wealth and the permanent luxury that the European war introduced in this neutral country."[12]

Philadelphia was the principal beneficiary of this expanded trade as its port became the primary U.S. *entrepôt,* with one-fourth of the nation's export trade passing through the harbor. More than a hundred foreign merchants established themselves in the new nation's principal metropolis. Soon imports to Philadelphia from the European mainland, chiefly from France and the Netherlands, nearly equaled those from Great Britain, a dramatic change from the prerevolutionary era. By the middle of the 1780s, merchants like Thomas Willing, Robert Morris, and John Swanwick were importing French coffee, brandy, gloves, calicoes, lace, and more in addition to their familiar stocks of goods. As the eighteenth century drew to a close, Americans thus found themselves linked to French trade networks as never before. But Philadelphia was linked not just to the Caribbean; it also connected to French port cities like Bordeaux and Nantes, and even to French trade outposts as far as Pondicherry, India. Meanwhile, Philadelphia merchants like Robert Morris served as middlemen for the all-important tobacco exports from Virginia—now shipped to France instead of Great Britain. When French refugees began pouring into Philadelphia in the 1790s, in short, the city was ready for them—economically and culturally.[13]

———————————

SINCE THE reign of Louis XIV, France had served as the model of polite society to be emulated throughout Europe and its colonies. French luxury, French goods, French fashion, French gastronomy, and above all French manners had gradually spread across the Continent from the epicenters at Versailles and Paris.

French culture was particularly influential among English elites; by the eighteenth century it was a commonplace that "France," as Edmund Burke put it, "has always more or less influenced manners in England." As Francophobia grew among the popular classes, driven by anti-Catholic sentiment and continual imperial warfare, Francophilia became a way of establishing class markers, and the British gentry and nobility turned more and more toward France. In 1765 twelve thousand Englishmen and Englishwomen visited the Continent—all of them, perhaps needless to say, well off; by 1785 that number had grown to forty thousand. Many of them came back in awe of the manners and food they discovered across the Channel. "In the art of living, the French have generally been esteemed by the rest of Europe, to have made the greatest proficiency," wrote the famed agriculturalist Arthur Young during his travels in the early 1790s. "Their manners have been accordingly more imitated, and their customs more adopted than those of any other nation. Of their cookery, there is but one opinion; for every man in Europe, that can afford a great table, either keeps a French cook, or one instructed in the same manner." And then, of course, there was the French language. Since the seventeenth century, as the historian Marc Fumaroli observes, French "had become the Latin of the Moderns, the international language of diplomacy, of courtly refinement, and more and more of the learned Republic of Letters itself." It was the European elite's lingua franca, spoken from the salons of London to the courts of Saint Petersburg. But it was not just the language that exerted such cultural power:

it was French norms of conversation and sociability. As Immanuel Kant would put it in 1798, "the French nation sets itself apart from all others by its taste for conversation; in that respect France is a model for other nations." If all of elite Europe stood in awe of French manners, taste, and culture, the veneration of polite society was even more acute across the Atlantic, where a sense of cultural inferiority pervaded many circles among the formerly colonial elite.[14]

With the new waves of French refugees pouring into the United States in the 1790s, all the cachet of French refinement and manners now arrived in the American capital. Unlike previous generations of French and Huguenot immigrants to North America, these refugees born of the French and Haitian revolutions were urban rather than rural, artisans and craftsmen rather than farmers and indentured servants. It did not take long for goods and services never before available to appear across the city. French watchmakers began touting their wares, as did French silversmiths—the most famous of whom was Simon Chaudron—goldsmiths, and jewelers. Grocers hawked mustard, wine, and brandy; merchants advertised luxury goods like wigs, pomades, and perfumes. Some of the goods imported had never been seen anywhere in the United States. Moreau claims to have introduced condoms to America: "I carried a complete assortment of them for four years; and while they were primarily intended for the use of French colonials, they were in great demand among Americans," he bragged. "Thus the use of this medium on the vast American continent dates from this time." French bakers introduced new foods to the city, as did French confectioners and pastry chefs. François Faures, formerly a merchant at Le Cap, opened a bakery selling "American and French Bread and Biscuit." One former captain of the French cavalry, an owner of great plantations on Saint Domingue's rich northern plains, who had "lived very sumptuously in Paris," learned how to make ice cream from his *chef d'office* and started a café. "The ice cream he makes," Moreau commented, "would rival those of the *Caveau* of the *Palais Royal* in Paris." Brillat-Savarin, the legendary epicure (a fine cheese named after him is available today), landed in Philadelphia, where he taught French language and violin lessons—and showed

This silver punch pot, made by the French silversmith Simon Chaudron in Philadelphia, is now in possession of New York's Metropolitan Museum of Art.

Americans how to prepare partridge wings *en papillote,* scrambled eggs with cheese, and stewed squirrels in Madeira, all while he tried to figure out how to cook New World game like turkey. When he finally managed, he proclaimed himself a "*dindophile.*"[15]

Drawing on the reputation of French refinement, many French arrivals targeted wealthy Philadelphians, selling their goods and services by trumpeting their connections to the highest levels of French society. Le Breton, a dental surgeon, advertised himself as a "pupil of the celebrated M. Dubois, late dentist to the king and royal family of France, member of the College and Academy of Surgeons of Paris. . . . Keeps a compleat assortment of every thing necessary to be used for the preservation of the mouth and teeth." Madame Mercier, launching herself in the hair and millinery business, announced that she was "a pupil of the Queen's Hair Dresser," adding that her goods and services were "after the most modern taste." George Bartualt, advertising himself as an "upholsterer from Paris," promoted the

Advertisements for some of the French goods and services that flooded Philadelphia in the 1790s.

latest French styles in furniture and decor for Philadelphia's elite. Newspapers abounded with these and many other advertisements for classes in dance, music, art—even manners.[16]

The French refugees were mobilizing their national reputation for culture, fashion, and gentility; they were marketing French refinement. Most of the musicians in Philadelphia's Chestnut Street Theatre were French—probably many of them from Cap-Français in Saint Domingue, where the theater was many times larger than Philadelphia's. Throughout the 1790s, Philadelphia's orchestras performed French revolutionary songs like "La Marseillaise" or "Ça ira"—with audiences threatening violence in case they refused. ("French tunes," Abigail Adams remarked, "have for a long time usurped an uncontrould sway.") Philadelphia theaters began their performances with musical overtures that merged the traditionally American "Yankee Doodle" with the French Revolution's "Marseillaise" into one transnational anthem. But the French cultural influence was hardly limited to music. A building on Walnut Street between Third and Fourth Streets once occupied by a Frenchman named Félix Brunot was turned into an "Académie française," offering language, fencing, and dancing classes, as well as the services of a "perfumer." Mr. Pillet, one of Lafayette's former aides-de-camp, advertised language classes: "having grammatical knowledge of several languages, proposes to teach the French." He added an endorsement by Noailles, who proclaimed himself willing "to give information to any one, of the talents of Mr. Pillet." One refugee from Saint Domingue, who impressed Philadelphians with his dancing skills at an evening ball, was told he would soon be inundated with "more students than he would desire."[17]

These refined French activities found homes in a variety of public spaces in the heart of Philadelphia. Of these, the grandest was Oeller's Hotel. Opened in 1791 on the south side of Chestnut Street, next to Ricketts's Circus, Oeller's replaced the City Tavern as Philadelphia's largest public house. In the 1790s, it was by far the most glorious. "A magnificent building," Moreau called it: "the most beautiful and most comfortable inn in the United States." With a vast assembly room measuring sixty feet square, it served as the site for balls, musical entertainments, and meetings of all kinds. It was also one of the few taverns to invest in an icehouse, serving its famous pineapple-laced punch and crushed ice in cups. It was from Oeller's that B. Quesnest, "dancing master," James Robardet, and Pierre Landrin Duport all taught dance lessons. It was the site for practically every major public event involving the French community. The French Benevolent Society, founded in 1793, held a ball there, and signed up new members every Tuesday. French musicians performed concerts there; crowds celebrated French victories in European warfare there. Joseph Liber, a dental surgeon from Cap-Français, advertised his services at Oeller's Hotel: "he cleans, fills up, files, opens and replaces teeth." When Jean-Pierre Blanchard prepared for his hot-air balloon flight, he made his public announcements at Oeller's. A few months later, it was at Oeller's that Genet held a banquet when he arrived in Philadelphia (tickets sold for four dollars each, this in an age when an unskilled worker earned a dollar a day). As for Oeller himself, he was a pillar of the French community; his name appears as a witness for the naturalization of various French immigrants in Philadelphia.[18]

Although it was Philadelphia's most famous institution, Oeller's was far from unique. Before he went to work for Cazenove, the French refugee Samuel Richardet ran Louth Hall, a tavern on Tenth Street north of Arch. Just outside the city, it hosted all variety of public celebrations in its vast gardens, including a festival to mark the French victory over Holland. A few years later, Richardet brought his French cachet to the City Tavern when he took it over in 1796, promising a public increasingly used to such amenities "Tea, Coffee, Soups, Jellies, Ice Creams, and a variety of French Liquors, together with the usual refreshments." Other sites of French sociability included Epples Tavern, residence of the French surgeon M. Courbe, which also hosted meetings of the French Benevolent Society, as well as a ball sponsored by the French dancing master Monsieur Duport. The Caveau, a café owned by Michel Bossée on Water Street, served a similar function, opening its doors to French residents eager to discuss news and read French newspapers, and also serving as a boardinghouse for French refugees. A variety of French and American bookstores sold French-language books, including Moreau's shop. Another émigré, Joseph E. G. M. De La Grange, ran a French circulating library, and later served as an agent for Saint Domingue refugees making claims against Haiti for compensation on their "lost" property.[19]

In addition to these cultural, commercial, and leisure activities, Philadelphia's taverns and hotels hosted a variety of French political and eleemosynary organizations. Surely the most significant was the French Benevolent Society, which raised money for impoverished Saint Domingue refugees and which still exists today. Established Frenchmen with deep ties to the United States served in its key positions. The secretary was Pierre-Étienne (Peter Stephen) Du Ponceau, a lawyer who came to the United States with the French army during the Revolution and remained in Philadelphia to become one of the city's leading attorneys; a significant part of his practice served French clients, including the French government on matters relating to privateering. (He was also alleged to have been a member of a secret French society that met at Barney McShane's sign of the bunch of grapes, at 23 North Third Street.) Du Ponceau was by now a prominent member of Philadelphia's French community, and with the outbreak of the French Revolution, and war between France and Great Britain, he threw his support behind the French revolutionary cause. Another French organization, the Patriotic French Society of the Friends of Liberty and Equality of Philadelphia, raised money to purchase flour and other provisions to send to the French Republic. On a more purely philanthropic register, Stephen Girard organized a convoy to rescue refugees from Saint Domingue, while on a more social note a local French Masonic chapter, the Loge Française L'Aménité, no. 73, established in Philadelphia in the 1790s, served as a primary locus for French Masons to gather—including Moreau, whose Masonic connections proved invaluable to his integration into Philadelphia life.[20]

The French arrivals also transformed the Catholic Church of Philadelphia. What had been a principally Irish, German, and English congregation suddenly joined with thousands of French-speaking and multiracial parishioners. It has been estimated that refugees from Saint Domingue doubled Baltimore's Catholic population; although estimates for Philadelphia do not exist, given the already significant Catholic population in Maryland, the growth in Philadelphia's population was probably even greater as a percentage. Whites and blacks began attending Philadelphia churches and celebrating marriages and baptisms, serving as godparents and marriage witnesses. In 1794, for instance, Father Cibot of Saint Joseph's Church baptized the daughter of Justina, "a free negress, of the Island of San Domingo." Such events and institutions further reinforced the bonds within the community. Many of the rites were performed by refractory priests, who had refused to swear an oath of allegiance to the French constitution. Over the subsequent decades, these priests would be appointed bishops of newly created dioceses and leave a powerful imprint on American Catholicism. But churches were not the only sites of French sociability: taverns, boardinghouses, shops, and bathhouses became important loci of community for thousands of the new arrivals, both white and black.[21]

The French immigrants vastly enriched Philadelphia's scientific and artistic life. Among the arrivals was Ambroise-Marie-François-Joseph Palisot de Beauvois, a Saint Domingue refugee, a close friend of Moreau's, and a member of the Société royale des sciences et des arts du Cap-Français, also known as the Cercle des Philadelphes. A botanist by training, he had published major works on eighteenth-century entomology. In 1792 he was elected to the American Philosophical Society (APS), and later published a scientific treatise on Charles Willson Peale's museum. In 1796 he would travel through South Carolina and Georgia with Liancourt and help funnel not just natural but also political knowledge back to France on a quasi-official mission for the government. But Palisot was hardly the only French member elected to the APS in the 1790s. The society virtually threw open its doors to French and Saint Domingue refugees, electing Moreau, Liancourt, Talleyrand, and Volney among many others to its ranks. From 1793 to 1798, nearly half the members elected to the APS were foreigners.[22]

Philadelphia also hosted a vibrant Francophone newspaper culture in the 1790s. Several French printers arrived in the wake of the French and Haitian revolutions to a city that had already established itself as the printing capital of the United States. The earliest French newspaper in Philadelphia was the *Courrier de l'Amérique,* published from 1792 to 1793. Moreau published the *Courrier de la France et des colonies* from 1795 to 1796. Louis F. R. A. Gatereau, a refugee from Saint Domingue with an outspokenly royalist and antiabolitionist perspective, published the *Courrier politique,* while another refugee from Saint Domingue, Tanguy de la Boissière, published the *Journal des révolutions de la partie française de Saint-Domingue,* which promoted a broadly similar perspective. Tanguy later edited a bilingual newspaper entitled *Étoile américaine.* Both Tanguy and Gatereau feuded with the French revolutionary ministers in Philadelphia. Other Saint Domingue refugees published yet another newspaper, the *Courrier français,* this one with a more pro-republican outlook, which became the longest-running French newspaper in Philadelphia, often published daily from 1794 to 1798. As multinational crowds paraded the streets singing French revolutionary songs like "La Marseillaise" and "Ça ira," American newspaper editors opened their pages to a French-speaking readership as well. Benjamin Franklin Bache, who was, like his famous grandfather, the editor of a newspaper, and who as a boy had lived and been educated in France and Switzerland, emerged as perhaps Philadelphia's most outspoken supporter of the French Republic. He became a pillar of Philadelphia's French community, using his newspaper to raise money for the Patriotic French Society. The front page of his *Aurora General Advertiser* became, for a time, fully bilingual, running advertisements in French alongside those in English selling goods and services and even land, sometimes in one language and sometimes in both. But Bache was not the only printer to throw his support behind French causes: subscription books for the Patriotic French Society were also kept with the printers Philip Freneau and David Claypoole.[23]

French immigration also transformed Philadelphia's African American community. The historian Gary Nash has identified 848 Philadelphians from Saint Domingue of African descent, both free and enslaved—an influx that increased Philadelphia's black population by at least 25 percent. "They immediately added French to the language of the streets," remarks Nash, "and in a single stroke created biracial congregations at the city's three Catholic churches." Pennsylvania had by this time enacted laws for the gradual emancipation of slaves, which included a provision that any slave imported to Pennsylvania be freed after six months of residence. Because these laws were so often evaded by slave owners, the Pennsylvania Abolition Society regularly intervened to ensure their enforcement, and it recorded manumissions of enslaved immigrants—including 456 manumissions of French slaves between 1793 and 1796. By the end of the eighteenth century, blacks accounted for nearly 10 percent of the city's population, reaching 6,436. "Names such as Félix, Félicité, Zaïre, Alcindor, Calypso, Zephir, Victoire, Laviolet, Figaro, and Jean Baptiste came to be commonly heard throughout the city," Nash writes. The new arrivals taught French to the city's black elite, like the businessman and social reformer James Forten, and furnished hairdressers and skilled workers to what had probably become the most important free black community in the United States.[24]

In short, when the émigré *constituants* arrived in Philadelphia, they found a city as French as any American city could be. "There is," Volney wrote, summing up his impressions of Philadelphia, "a penchant for our arts, our manners, our language." So powerful was this penchant that by the mid-1790s Philadelphia's elite culture, like its popular political culture, had become intensely Gallicized. The borders between French and American culture, politics, identity, and community had grown blurry. "You would be wrong, *monsieur*, to think that a Frenchman would need, among us, to change his *patrie*," said one Philadelphian to a French refugee. "He will never be seen here as a foreigner."[25]

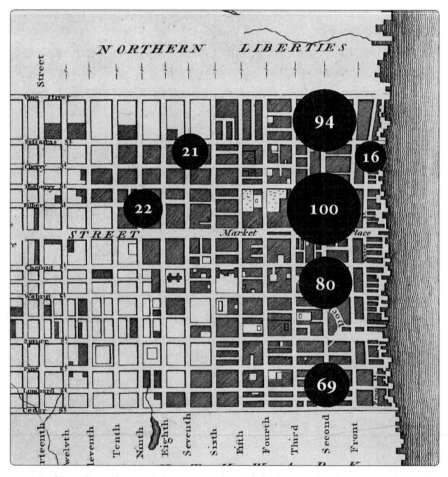

A map of French residences and commercial establishments in the 1790s shows particular concentrations in two parts of the city. The first, north of Market Street along Second and Third Streets between Vine and Mulberry (now Arch), was referred to by some Philadelphians in the 1790s as French-Town. The second, more genteel, south of Market along Second Street, lay near the wealthy neighborhood known as Society Hill.

THE FRENCH MIGRANTS settled unevenly throughout the city. One neighborhood with a particular concentration of French residents lay to the north of Market Street, between Front and Third, Vine and Arch Streets. Known since the mid-eighteenth century as "Helltown," this area, part of Philadelphia's Mulberry Ward, had traditionally served as the city's red-light district, where criminals, alcoholics, vagrants, prostitutes, and escaped slaves and servants all gathered, mingling in the town's roughest taverns to drink, gamble, and watch cockfights or boxing matches. During the 1790s, French and Saint Domingue immigrants poured into the neighborhood. When Moreau passed through Philadelphia in late May 1794, he found hundreds of refugees from Saint Domingue huddling into the inns of North Second Street, like the "miserable haven" where he stayed for two nights, and where he found "a crowd of our unfortunate colonist friends." By 1795 the neighborhood had seen such an influx of French migrants and the establishment of so many French businesses that one city directory referred to it as "French-Town."[26]

The name seems appropriate. A close investigation of various sources, including tax records and city directories, has established the exact location of nearly one thousand French people living in Philadelphia during the 1790s. Charting these on a map of 1790s Philadelphia reveals particular concentrations in specific neighborhoods, including this one. Given the bias of these records—tilted heavily toward elites and those with property who would have figured in city directories and tax records—it is all the more telling to find such a concentration of French residents in the area once known as Helltown, which mostly drew poor people without property.

The map also points to a second area of intense concentration of French residents, this one along Second Street running south of Market. This area was considerably tonier than the neighborhood to the north—the saying among wealthy Philadelphians that "Nobody lives north of Market" was apparently as apt in the 1790s as it would be through the nineteenth and twentieth centuries—with a large number of French residents south of Market identifying themselves simply as "gentleman" or "gentlewoman." In this neighborhood, a wealthy Frenchman could feel right at home. "I was surprised," wrote one former planter from Saint Domingue when he attended a grand ball, "by the beauty of the apartments, the wealth *du monde,* and the *toilette* of the women; I told myself that on this last point all countries were similar." The geographic data are highly illustrative in this regard. A list of French residents on South Second Street, enumerated in the appendix, highlights the concentration of French people in that neighborhood focusing on refined goods and services. It also suggests how various addresses housed different French people over time, with one French renter or boarder replacing another through the 1790s.[27]

It was in this elite neighborhood near South Second Street, known as Society Hill, that Talleyrand, Liancourt, Noailles, Volney, and Moreau all settled. Moreau's bookstore served as an anchor of Philadelphia's French-speaking world. Established on the southwest corner of Front and Walnut Streets, on the edge of Society Hill, it immediately became the premier French-language bookstore in Philadelphia. Moreau hired a clerk who had worked in bookstores in Cap-Français (now Cap-Haïtien) and Geneva. In addition to selling books in French, English, German, Dutch, and Latin, as well as stationery (and condoms), Moreau sold maps, charts, engravings, scientific instruments, and an assortment of other goods. In 1795 he bought a printing press, hired a printer who had worked in Paris and Saint Domingue, and began printing books and a newspaper in both French and English. His shop soon became a hub for the reception and circulation of political, social, economic, and scientific information from points throughout the French Atlantic world to Philadelphia and other parts of the United States. French and Americans often gathered in Moreau's shop to discuss French politics. "Here we know nothing about France," Talleyrand wrote to Moreau while residing in New York. "We get this news from you." Moreau also served as a node for the diffusion of scientific information: he'd been elected a member of the American Philosophical Society back in 1789; he was well connected to the international scientific community, and he published several scientific pamphlets penned by himself and by other members of the APS. His bookstore's customers included not just French people but also prominent Americans like Vice President John Adams, who came from time to time to browse and shop, along with the Philadelphia printer Mathew Carey and others. Moreau also, on occasion, exhibited French artifacts. In the fall of 1795, many Americans came to see the stone from the Bastille that Moreau displayed in his shop.[28]

Moreau's bookstore served as the social center for Philadelphia's tight-knit elite émigré community. "Like Noah's ark," is how one émigré put it: plucked from a drowning world, these men committed to constitutional monarchy gathered together to wait out the storm. By the end of his stay in America, Talleyrand was spending a part of nearly every night at Moreau's, either just the two of them alone or together with other French émigrés. These encounters served not only as a means to exchange news and information but also as a source of friendship and comfort for people who had been torn from their homes and lives across the Atlantic. Moreau's family also provided the émigrés with vicarious links to the families they had left behind in France. Moreau lived above his bookstore with his wife, his daughter, his son, and, for a time, his mother-in-law. In addition, he had a vast extended family in the city: his sister, his first cousin, and his wife's family had also fled Saint Domingue to settle in Philadelphia. The other *constituants,* who came alone, found some comfort in Moreau's family life. Liancourt, who lived nearby in a small apartment, often came over to play with Moreau's son, where they would wrestle "like two schoolboys." On one of his travels, Liancourt picked up an Indian bow and a few arrows that he sent to the boy from New York. Talleyrand, too, grew fond of Moreau's son, even seeking to take him back to Europe with him when he left Philadelphia in 1796.[29]

Théophile Cazenove's house served as another social center for the émigrés. Cazenove descended from an important Huguenot family that fled France after the revocation of the Edict of Nantes to settle in Geneva, and became deeply enmeshed in European commerce. Born in Amsterdam in 1740, Cazenove married into a prominent Dutch merchant family and joined its brokerage and commercial business. After a bankruptcy, he became the agent for a Dutch consortium investing in American securities, which sent him to the United States in 1790. Described by Liancourt as a "gentle, easy, amiable, obliging man," and with the considerable resources

Théophile Cazenove, painted by the French artist Charles B. J. Fevret de Saint Mémin in Philadelphia in 1799.

of Dutch finance at his disposal, he lived a far more comfortable lifestyle than the refugee *constituants*. Talleyrand and Beaumetz, who lived just a few blocks away, ate every day at Cazenove's: "Thus," as Moreau wrote, "the expression 'to dine at our house' [when used by Talleyrand] meant dining at Cazenove's." When Liancourt reported dining "chez les Français" numerous times in February and March 1795, it was almost certainly at Cazenove's that he ate. No doubt the émigrés appreciated Cazenove for his personal qualities, but one suspects the trait they most valued was his taste for refined food. It was a feature he shared with Talleyrand, who was among the most famous epicures of his time. (When Talleyrand returned to France and regained his fortune, he employed Carême, perhaps the greatest French chef of all time, "the King of Chefs and the Chef of Kings.") In Philadelphia Cazenove employed French chefs who, though no Carême, at least helped mitigate the émigrés' brutal encounter with American cooking. "The United States are a country where, if there are thirty-two religions, there is only one dish," observed Talleyrand after his arrival. "And it is a bad one."[30]

THE TWO FRENCH NEIGHBORHOODS—one above Market, more working-class; one below Market, more elite—reflected important cleavages within the French community. It was a large and diverse population, divided by social class, geographic origin, occupation, race, education, and politics. Indeed, given the range of people who made up French Philadelphia, it may be a misnomer even to speak of a "French community" in the singular.

The *constituants* arrived in America seeking refuge from the political conflict tearing Europe apart. Instead, they ran smack into vigorous pro-revolutionary sentiment: French radicals parading in the streets in massive celebrations; French republicans and sailors gathering with Americans in political clubs, coffeehouses, and taverns, giving toasts and speeches, and participating in boisterous, drunken festivals. "No patriotic society gathers without toasting the Republic," wrote France's representatives in the United States. "*Fêtes* are publicly celebrated upon each of our successes as soon as they receive the news." Philadelphia, it seemed, was becoming an American Paris. "I can't give you a clearer idea of the spirit that animates one party or the other," the French minister Joseph Fauchet wrote to his superiors in Paris, "than to compare what is happening here to what happened in France when the Brissotin faction [the Girondins] struggled against the Mountain [the Montagnards]." With imperial warfare in the Caribbean sending the United States careening toward war with England, one Federalist newspaper in Philadelphia feared that "French Republicans" would be "strictly copied in America, and revolutionary tribunals, guillotines, with all other paraphernalia of French liberty, become as common in the one country, as they are now in the other."[31]

The revolutionary enthusiasm of Philadelphia's French and American republicans repelled the *constituants*. "The horrible assassination of the King is today celebrated by a dinner of French patriots," Liancourt wrote in his diary on January 21, 1794, a year after the execution of Louis XVI. "Quelle horreur, quelle barbarie infâme!" As he began traveling through the backcountry, where he continually encountered similar pro-revolutionary sentiment, Liancourt lamented that such radical opinions were not limited to Philadelphia: "These are the sentiments, and such is the language of most Americans; and indeed this must be the opinion of all who do not know the crimes of our revolution." Another French aristocrat who arrived in Boston encountered the pro-revolutionary excitement before she even debarked. The French immigrants on the docks who greeted her ship, "greatly impatient" for news, offered a decidedly hostile welcome. They were "very common: ruined merchants, laborers searching for work. They seemed to us more or less all revolutionaries, and they perceived us, in turn, as aristocrats who had escaped the torments that, according to them, we entirely deserved for our past tyranny." These political divisions were so raw they sometimes spilled over into what could have been unifying celebrations of the Franco-American alliance. In 1793, for instance, Genet declined an invitation to a Fourth of July dinner hosted by the Society of the Cincinnati, the organization of former Revolutionary War officers that included both Americans and Frenchmen. "He could not sit down at table with the Count de Noailles," one Philadelphian remembered. "As the count was a member of the society, such an objection gave great offence to many of the members." And then there was the scene recorded by Moreau, when he, Talleyrand, Beaumetz, and several others watching the Fourth of July parade were jeered by republican crowds. No surprise that Liancourt, at one point during his stay, was led to muse that "in this unhappy time of revolution, a Frenchman is sometimes the worst company that a Frenchman can encounter."[32]

The complex politics of the refugees from the French Caribbean—an estimated 75 percent of whom had been born in France—made the divisions between French radicals and moderate *constituants* even more intractable. Many of the Caribbean refugees were royalists hoping for a reversion to prerevolutionary status quo ante. For years they had conducted their own foreign policy: as early as 1791, Saint Domingue planters had sent commissioners to Philadelphia asking for help battling the *gens de couleur* demanding greater civil rights. They had even proved willing to abandon their loyalties to France, turning to Great Britain for help in fighting the revolutionary authorities led by Sonthonax in the streets of Cap-Français. The French government's 1794 abolitionist policy further frayed the loyalties of the Saint Domingue planters pouring into Philadelphia, who wanted nothing more than to return to their plantations and their slaves.[33]

It did not take long for the bitter politics of Saint Domingue and France to spill over into Philadelphia. With Genet and Fauchet supporting France's Caribbean policy, the Saint Domingue refugees did nothing to hide their hostility to Philadelphia's French authorities—and to the French liberal aristocrats who they believed had naively opened the door to the Jacobins and to the Revolution's excesses. "One doesn't encounter a Frenchman today without having to endure a recounting of his losses, his *malheurs*, of his opinions and hatreds that have resulted," Liancourt reported. The *constituants*, in turn, expressed little sympathy for their compatriots from the Caribbean, referring to Creole planters as "a contemptible race" and "good for nothing." In his journal, Liancourt imagined one Saint Dominguois as "a barbarian without his home, mutilating, beating, assaulting his negroes." Although the *constituants* were not abolitionists, they had long socialized in the same circles as men like Condorcet and Lafayette, who were. And although they never stood up to denounce slavery or joined the French abolitionist Société des amis des noirs, as liberal free trade proponents, they were not likely to embrace slave owners as allies, no matter how much all of them resented the Girondin and Montagnard governments in France.[34]

CHASED FROM their homes, bereft of their fortunes, alienated from other French communities in Philadelphia, the *constituants* fell repeatedly into depression and melancholy, reporting to their friends on the "*ennui* they found in America."[35]

"My dear heart," Liancourt wrote to his wife in France, whom he hadn't seen for three years, and whom he had divorced in order to preserve his property and her safety, "I wish ardently to return to France." The desire lingered continuously: this was what exile meant. They awaited, "suspended," as Talleyrand put it, to find out what fate had in store for their nation. But they intended to return, "as conquerors if the republic succumbs"—so Talleyrand wrote—"as supplicants if it triumphs over its enemies." In the meantime, all fell into periodic depression. Liancourt, more sensitive than the others, felt the pain most keenly: "My isolation is the torment of all my moments, of all my thoughts, torment that leaves me ill-tempered, unpleasant to others no doubt, but still more to myself." To his aunt, the duchesse de La Rochefoucauld-d'Enville, the famous Parisian *salonnière* under whose auspices he had learned so much, and who had lost her son, the cousin with whom he'd grown up, he wrote: "How often have I . . . lamented with painful anxiety, that I was not near you; that I was prevented by cruel circumstances that have separated us . . . in affording you that attention and comfort of which your feeling and afflicted heart stood so much in need!" His inveterate socializing at teas and dinners, the constant invitations he received from the French and Americans alike—none of it could make up for the loss of his family and old friends. In certain respects, they only highlighted his loneliness. "How to believe in friendship, when I am so little known?" he wrote. Liancourt could not reconcile himself to his new situation: "How there are cruel things in my position! . . . I am in a sad mood, that I want to overcome, but that I can scarcely conquer." One gloomy Monday in February 1795, Liancourt visited Talleyrand and Beaumetz before stopping in on Robert Morris and Alexander Hamilton, and then "went home; suffering." A few days later, Liancourt's beloved dog, Cartouche, ran away: "I am sad about it, very sad. I would be made fun of, perhaps, if anyone knew how much I'm preoccupied by it." Never had he felt so alone. "He's the only being who loves me on this continent." By Saturday he was beside himself. "I am sad and I'm not feeling well," he wrote. "Cartouche is lost; it's a true anguish to me." And then, suddenly, the dog came home. "Cartouche is back: I've had great joy about it."[36]

To try to get his mind off his troubles, Liancourt took refuge in hyper-intellectualism; it was an old habit for him. That first winter in Philadelphia, from 1794 to 1795, he focused his attention on Philadelphia's Walnut Street Prison—the very building from which Blanchard had set off on his balloon trip that chilly morning in January 1793. The late eighteenth century was a time when the United States was famous for the humanity of its criminal justice system rather than the reverse, and Philadelphia's prison stood as a great model of civilized incarceration to reformers around the Atlantic world. Europeans in subsequent decades would flock to the United States to study its prisons, but Liancourt may have been the first of these European admirers. He found much to praise in Philadelphia's Walnut Street Prison, founded in "reason and humanity," which had "substituted *la douceur,* firmness, and reason for irons and blows." Liancourt described an institution run on principles of "regularity and order," in which control was achieved through psychological rather than physical means. Prisoners, he wrote, "forgot their ancient habits," and turned instead "to self-reflection." Corporal punishment was forbidden—along with alcohol and even conversation. Prisoners remained in perpetual silence, even at mealtimes, left alone with their thoughts. Any infraction of the rules resulted in solitary confinement, where the isolation was total. The aim of this new method of incarceration was to "soften" the prisoner, "*l'adoucir*," as Liancourt wrote, to "change his nature . . . to make, in some sense, a new being." He did not, however, belittle the psychological toll involved in the system. It was, he concluded, "a prison system severe and terrible, but just and humane."[37]

Even capital punishment, Liancourt presciently observed, "punishes the criminal less severely than long and rigid detentions . . . in separate cells, in which the criminal, left alone with the memories of his crime, stuck in a tormenting disquiet, in long days of *ennui* and desolation, is isolated from all nature, becomes a stranger to the entire world." It is unclear exactly whom Liancourt was describing with this disturbing sketch, which bore a more than passing kinship to his own situation, opposing as it did the executed relatives he'd left behind with his own listless state, full of ennui and isolation, making him a stranger to the world. Like those who invented the Walnut Street Prison, Liancourt and his fellow *constituants* had once sought to "substitute the régime of reason, of justice, for that of irons." Perhaps that is why he grafted here a long digression on the state of politics in France, which, according to Liancourt, "exhibited before the revolution more corruption, perhaps, than many other countries":

If since the revolution it has exhibited more scenes of atrocities and horror than can scarcely be imagined, there have always existed, there still exist now, and there will always exist in the midst of this corruption, and these crimes, men of a pure, enterprising, and courageous virtue, ready to act for the benefit of mankind.

Still, from his exile, Liancourt clung to a faith in the abilities of a few Great Men, pure and enterprising, able to exercise courageous virtue to tame the chaotic forces of history. Nor had he lost all hope in the promise of Enlightened philosophy: "Philanthropy is not found only in the books of those we call the *philosophes;* it is deeply engraved in the hearts of men, and awaits only the establishment of a wise government, which will afford it the means to manifest itself usefully." Through his trials and tribulations, his gloom and his depression, Liancourt had not lost his faith in the possibility of wise government and heroic men. "A slight homage paid to virtue," Liancourt added, with a nod to François, duc de La Rochefoucauld, his renowned ancestor, "will hatch many others." Then, as now, old habits died hard.[38]

MOREAU HAD it both better and worse than Liancourt. His family had fled to safety with him, keeping him from the feelings of loss and isolation that occasionally overcame his friends. On the other hand, a family entailed heavy responsibilities, forcing Moreau to take on demeaning work, first crawling through ships' holds and then opening a bookstore. If one contemporary described Liancourt as "looking more like a worthy tradesman, than a great nobleman," Moreau actually *was* a tradesman and he looked the part. The thought seems to have tortured him. A Frenchman who entered Moreau's bookstore looking for paper and quills was accosted by the owner: "You have no suspicion," he asked with some urgency, "who I am and who I was?"

"*Ma foi, non,*" the customer responded.

"*Eh! bien,*" said Moreau, "I was king of Paris for three days, and today in order to live I am forced to sell ink, quills, and paper in Philadelphia."[39]

Moreau's mother-in-law, whom he called "Maman" and who had known all the luxuries of a wealthy planter in Saint Domingue, felt the sting of exile even more keenly, as she lived out her last days above a bookstore in a foreign land. She "heard the mention of death with sadness, and found the idea of dying on the continent of the United States intolerable." But pass away in Philadelphia she did, unable, despite Moreau's entreaties, to be buried in a Catholic cemetery. The priest was firm: she had died unconfessed.[40]

No one lost more than Noailles, who left his family behind when he fled France. He was despondent about the prospects for his country. "He Seems to despair of Liberty in France," John Adams reported when he saw him in late 1793, "and has lost apparently all hopes of ever living in France." But his personal situation only got worse. We get some sense of his emotional state in the spring of 1794, a year after his arrival, when he shared a letter from his wife with friends, written nearly a year earlier, in which she expressed "the depth of my wounds" at being so far distant, and wondered at the "bitter aggravation of my own anguish." She finished: "Adieu. Adieu. I join my dear children in embracing you; take care of yourself for them and for me. Once more, Adieu." It was probably the last letter Noailles ever received from her: in June 1794, Louise de Noailles met her death at the guillotine along with the vicomte's father. Noailles was devastated when he heard the news several months later. William Bingham, his friend, host, and occasional business partner, sought to provide what comfort he could. But Noailles was inconsolable. "I am touched by your obliging interest," he wrote after Bingham attempted two visits. But "the painful disposition I am in forces me to retire. . . . When I am calmer I will find you to express of my appreciation." Noailles must have felt more cut off from his home than ever. In 1795 he became an American citizen: he was the only émigré of the group to do so. A year later, when John Adams saw the *constituants* at the Binghams' house, he reported that "Noailles declares to them all that he has renounced France forever, that he never will return, in any change of affairs, unless as a Traveller or Visiter."[41]

The émigrés never quite escaped the feeling of existential restlessness that haunted them. "I am already completely bored with *la société*," wrote Liancourt after only four days in Philadelphia, each of them filled with an astonishing regimen of socializing, one dinner party fading into another. "It's not its fault; it's mine. What is all this good for?" This was a new kind of affliction, one whose name had only barely come into existence in

French and did not yet exist in English: expatriation. The word would only be invented during the revolutionary period from 1789 to 1815. "Expatriation from one's *patrie*," Liancourt wrote to his wife, "is a torture that one hides more or less badly, the more or less time one suffers, but whose pain is always deeply felt." Talleyrand, similarly, developed his own theory about exile. "After revolutionary crises," he wrote soon after his return to France, "there are men, grown old under the impression of misfortune, whose souls need in some sense to be made young again. Some would like to cease loving their country, but they must learn to feel that, fortunately, it is impossible." This brand of exile was marked by a sort of agitated listlessness and soul-wrenching unease: "Je m'ennuie à périr dans ce pays" (I am bored to death in this country).[42]

Perhaps the most notable feature of this existential restlessness was a changed sense of time itself. Two months after his arrival, having conversed with Philadelphia's greatest luminaries, visited Wilmington, and toured the great mansions outside of Philadelphia, Liancourt was still in a funk. "Que de jours passés, en *tuant le temps!*" (So many days spent *killing time!*) What did it mean to kill time, exactly? All the émigrés commented on the momentous transformations the French Revolution had unleashed. "Alas! my God!" exclaimed a French count. "In the streets of Philadelphia, I met the greats become small, the ambitious cheated, fools punished, and men of yesterday who were nothing today; parvenus stunned that the wheel of fortune did not stay still for them, when their stars rose to their zenith." These sudden shifts in fortune drew the attention of many observers. "The awful and depressing events of the present age have rendered great changes almost familiar," wrote one contemporary to his brother. "The Duke de Liancourt, who possessed an estate in France of about 25,000 £ sterling a year, now lodges in the House of a Barber in Philadelphia, having saved only as much out of his great fortune, as to keep whole Clothes on his back, and to pay his Board to the Barber. He has no servant, but is obliged to shave and dress himself and to clean his own shoes." It seemed impossible. And yet "we might find many thousands here and many more in England who have experienced the like Changes." Americans marveled at the Orléans children's condition as they traveled the United States. "It was really a curious circumstance for reflection, that three princes, nephews to the first Monarch upon earth, should be driven to the necessity of seeking an asylum in a foreign country," wrote Robert Gilmor, the son of a Baltimore merchant. "Reduced to swim rivers in the wildernesses of America; sleep whole nights upon the earth without any canopy but the heavens, and economise their expenses, when their father had been the richest subject in the universe," he wondered in amazement. These, he concluded, "are thoughts that strike upon the mind with astonishing force and leave lasting impressions of the instability of human greatness and the uncertainty of things in life."[43]

Maybe it was appropriate that they had come to America as this new apprehension of time emerged. Here was a country whose dominant feature—at least according to foreign travelers—was its continuous change and movement. It was where—at least according to some European philosophers—modernity was most conspicuously realized. Liancourt certainly felt a sense of continuous movement as he toured the nation, concluding that the United States was "a country in headlong expansion; that which is true today of its population, its prices, its commerce, was not true six months ago and will not be true six months from now." Time itself was moving forward at an ever-accelerating pace. One expatriate newspaper commented on "events that succeed each other with stunning speed." This new sense of a world in perpetual movement would linger with the émigrés even after their return to Europe. "Revolutions which have shaken up everything," Talleyrand proclaimed in an address given soon after his return, "leave behind them a general restlessness of mind, a necessity for change, an indefinite disposition for hazardous enterprises, and an ambition in the ideas, which tends unceasingly to alter, and to destroy." In this sense of a time fractured by the stunning speed of events—this sense of the uncertainty of life that rendered great changes almost familiar—the émigrés were beginning to apprehend something profoundly new. "The ancients had imagined the river of oblivion, in which, at our exit from life, all our recollections were lost," Talleyrand mused. "The true Lethe at our exit from the revolution is in every thing which opens to men the road of expectation."[44]

Seeking out this oblivion, Liancourt eventually fled, roaming the continent from Maine to South Carolina, the Ohio valley and Canada, taking copious notes that he published upon his return to France in his eight-volume *Voyage dans les États-Unis d'Amérique*. Some of Liancourt's friends found this a futile response. "Running away from what rides behind all of us" is how Théophile Cazenove described Liancourt's travels. "This business of running around through countless tiresome towns strikes me as a miserable remedy against boredom." Talleyrand memorably described Liancourt "taking notes, requesting evidence, writing down observations, and asking a thousand times as many questions as the inquisitive traveler that Sterne talks about." At least some of those he met on his travels found this a tiresome sort of interaction. "For a Frenchman, we all thought him rather dull," one acquaintance reported. "But we considered that out of France he was out of his natural element. Otherwise, there would, I doubt not, have been more good humour." Others were more charitable: "amiable and inoffensive," one witness described Liancourt, "a very plain man." Even Liancourt admitted that he could at times be "inquisitive to the point of indiscretion."[45]

But none of the émigrés was immune to the restlessness, and most went off on similar journeys. Volney spent months wandering the Ohio valley, but to no avail. Talleyrand confessed to feeling the lure of the ocean as he crossed the Atlantic, which offered "sensations suited to my disposition. The sea had great charms for me at that moment; the sensations I received from it correlated to my mood." Before landing in Philadelphia, he'd hoped to remain ship-bound. Once ashore, Talleyrand could hardly sit still, pushing his way through Maine, New York, Niagara Falls, and more: "I wanted to try to tire myself out." And so he wandered, losing himself in the continent as he had hoped to lose himself in the vastness of the oceans: amid "the brute and savage nature; the forests as ancient as the world; debris of plants and trees dead of dilapidation," looking out from high points at "the spires of trees, undulations of the terrain that alone, cut through the regularity of the immense spaces." And still it was hard for Talleyrand to find that pure self-abnegation he sought. "When one has something of an active spirit," he later mused, "losing one's time is not as easy as one would imagine. . . . To wander in the great woods where there is no path, to be on horseback in the middle of the night, to call out to be sure we're together: it all creates sensations I couldn't define." What exactly did it mean to kill time?[46]

Here they were, these men who'd fallen from such exalted heights by seeking and failing to reconcile aristocracy with republicanism. They had served as witnesses, midwives, and victims as a new order was born, and now they hung suspended between two worlds: an old regime that had long structured their existence and a new modernity they could not fully perceive, much less understand. Certainly they were fortunate to have escaped the death that met so many of their friends and family members. But that was only a limited consolation to these men born to the most immense fortunes, who had thought to control not just their own destinies but also the fate of millions around the world, and who now found themselves suddenly struck down to the barest existence. How could such people accept that they were, as one refugee put it, no more than "toy[s] in the hands of a capricious fate"? Liberals in the Age of Revolutions had imagined, perhaps for the first time, that they were in charge of their own destinies—that it was in their power to shape history. And yet they found themselves flung across the ocean by events and circumstances beyond their control. "In the days of my power and affluence, under the ancient *régime* of France, I kept fifty servants," one witness remembered Liancourt saying. "And yet my coat was never as well brushed as it is now, when I brush it myself." Perhaps it was in these oldest and humblest of insights that the greatest truths were to be found.[47]

In part to escape this existential drift, the émigrés turned away from politics and literature and toward the more material and mundane features of their world. "Avant tout," said one émigré, "il fallait vivre." (Before everything, we had to live.) They turned to what they knew best: the world of conversation and salons in the grand, neoclassical *hôtels particuliers* that they'd left behind. They would shake their angst by integrating into Philadelphia's elite world, socializing with its icons, entering into business deals with its shrewdest members. Eventually they would remake their lives, and in the process, they would see America fulfill the hopes they had once harbored for France.[48]

TALLEYRAND, NOAILLES, Liancourt, Volney, and Moreau came to Philadelphia when its elite was in full bloom. It was the age of the great "Republican Court," when the social season featured "a continual succession of balls, dinner-parties, and other scenes of gayety and dissipation," as Philadelphia established the manners and mores for imitators throughout the nation. This world would be long remembered but never recaptured in the centuries to follow, as Philadelphia entered a long and sad decline, falling behind New York and eventually—the greatest ignominy!—Washington society. But in the 1790s, Philadelphia reigned supreme.[49]

The cosmopolitan outlook of Philadelphia's elite was a new phenomenon. Three decades of war and economic expansion beginning in the middle of the eighteenth century toppled the dominance of the Quakers who had once made up Philadelphia's merchant elite. Small merchants climbed to greatness while long-established firms collapsed, and by the end of the century a largely Anglican group with a few streaks of Presbyterianism had risen to prominence. This new elite cast aside the subdued Quaker ethos of the colonial period, and launched the city into the Atlantic world's burgeoning consumer culture. Some of the brightest stars of Philadelphia's new merchant galaxy made their fortunes during the Revolution by trading with France. Robert Morris used his position in the Continental Congress to shower his mercantile firm with government contracts. Morris's agent in Martinique, William Bingham, began a career that by the 1790s would make him, at least according to the British merchant Thomas Twining, "the principal person in Philadelphia, and the wealthiest, probably, in the Union." The shake-up ended when the postwar depression did, in the late 1780s, as the American economy entered a long expansion resulting from the collapse of food production in Europe and the growing demand for wheat and other produce from the Delaware River valley. By the mid-1790s, Philadelphia's new merchant elite was wealthier than ever before, more oriented toward France than ever before, and more engaged in the transatlantic world of luxury consumer goods than ever before.[50]

The new, mostly Anglican merchants who rose to the pinnacles of wealth and power eagerly flaunted their wealth: "They were," observes the historian Thomas Doerflinger, "nouveaux riches." Although they eventually lost their national stature, the great Philadelphia families of the age—the Wharton, Morris, Cadwalader, Biddle, Ingersoll, Coxe, McKean, Hopkinson, Chew, Willing, Rush, and White families—remained at the pinnacle of Philadelphia society for generations to come. As if to mark off this new elite, the city's geographic center began to move west from the waterfront, into the Society Hill neighborhood, from Chestnut to Spruce between First and Fourth Streets. After the enclosure of Dock Creek, which had been an open sewer for decades, this neighborhood emerged as Philadelphia's most fashionable, replacing their former enclave along the Delaware, now squeezed by the growing warehouse district to the north and the sailors' boardinghouses to the south. (The city's elite would continue to push west in the decades to follow: the Civil War era would find them in Rittenhouse Square, then moving north and west to the Main Line suburbs in the twentieth century.) Thus, in the 1790s, a few blocks in Society Hill saw the intense concentration of the city's—indeed, of the nation's—elite, its members knit together by overlapping webs of kinship, friendship, and business partnership.[51]

Anne and William Bingham's mansion was the most imposing of the new houses sprouting up in the neighborhood. It fronted Third Street at the corner of Spruce, and its gardens extended all the way back to Fourth Street. Anne's aunt Elizabeth Powel, widow of the former mayor of Philadelphia Samuel Powel, lived a few doors north of the Binghams on Third Street. Next door to Powel lived Benjamin Chew, president of the Pennsylvania High Court of Errors and Appeals, and next door to him, still along Third, lived Thomas Willing, Anne Bingham's father, William Bingham's father-in-law and business partner, and Elizabeth Powel's brother. On Fourth Street, behind the Binghams' gardens, lived another of Anne Bingham's aunts, Mrs. William Byrd (of Westover); her cousin, Edward Shippen, a member of the Pennsylvania Supreme Court, lived across the street on Fourth. Alexander Hamilton lived one street over, and worked closely

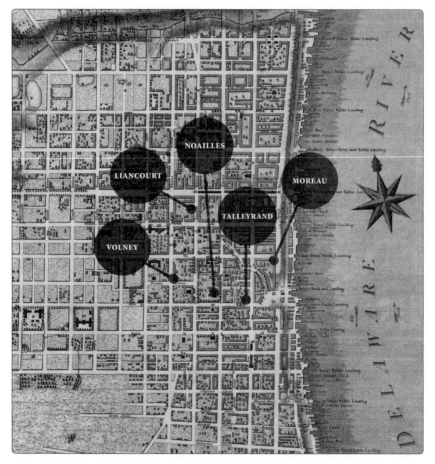

The Society Hill neighborhood, where the French émigré constituants settled, was much airier and greener than the dense working-class neighborhoods to the north. Detail from a 1797 map of Philadelphia.

with Thomas Willing, who was also the president of the Bank of the United States.[52]

The French émigré *constituants* settled in this tightly knit neighborhood. Noailles lived at its social center, in a set of apartments in William and Anne Bingham's mansion. Volney lived two blocks away, at 69 South Fifth Street, just behind the Shippens on Fourth, opposite the African Methodist Episcopal Church, where he could read the inscription on the front: "The people that walked in darkness have seen a great light." ("You'll see," Talleyrand quipped, "he is going to take himself for this light.") Walking one block along Locust Street and turning right on Fourth, Volney could enter the Binghams' house from the back—which would be practical, since he went there not just for dinners and teas but also to teach French to the Bingham daughters. On his way to the Binghams', Volney would have walked by the residence of Louis-Philippe, the duc d'Orléans, at the corner of Fourth and Locust. Talleyrand lived just a block east of the Binghams at Second and Spruce, along with Beaumetz. The duc de La Rochefoucauld-Liancourt lived on a small cul-de-sac running off Fourth Street just below Market, two and a half blocks away from the Binghams, and frequently ate at the City Tavern, just around the corner on Second Street. Moreau established his bookstore at the southwest corner of Front and Walnut, just a block from the City Tavern, and attended Saint Mary's Church, a ten-minute walk away, on Fourth Street between Spruce and Locust.[53]

By the end of 1794, when nearly all the émigré *constituants* had arrived, Philadelphia's elite was no longer just a national elite: it had become an international group, with figures from the highest levels of the European aristocracy living in its midst.

IT AMOUNTED to a lot of change, a cultural and economic reorientation that corresponded with the colossal political and military transformations in the Atlantic world in the 1790s: Philadelphia's surging trade with the French Atlantic; the formation of a large, vibrant, and diverse French community in the heart of Philadelphia; and the emergence of a new economic and social elite in the city. In this context, the arrival of the émigré *constituants* served as a catalyst, accelerating a great cultural reorientation that was already under way.

It had started with the American Revolution. Before, North America's elite had turned to Great Britain as a guide to fashion and manners, and the great ambition of any successful merchant or planter was to re-create the life of the English gentry in the colonies. The social life of elite Philadelphia operated accordingly. The testimony of French-born Peter Stephen Du Ponceau is highly revealing in this regard. Du Ponceau had come to the United States during the American Revolution, when he served with Baron von Steuben. He settled in Philadelphia after the war, and led a distinguished career as a lawyer and linguist. He was, in short, well placed to testify to the remarkable changes in American sociability. Before the war, he wrote:

> There were no French confectioners to supply us with ice creams and *bon bons* of all descriptions. No french cook to stimulate our palates; champaigne and Burgundy wines were unknown. . . . Dinner parties were entirely *à l'Anglaise*. The ladies left early and left the gentlemen at table to indulge in deep potations and in political discussions [which were] the principal topics of conversation at that time.

After the United States broke with England, it set itself on a path toward cultural independence, and Philadelphia's elite began to turn toward its new ally for cultural cues. "The people had forgotten their ancient prejudices and became sincerely attached to their French allies," Du Ponceau continued. "It was truly astonishing. [The] country had become French in many respects. Our ladies dressed in French silks; the gentlemen wore velvet in winter and lighter stuffs in summer, all of French manufacture." When the marquis de Chastellux passed through Philadelphia during the war, the social life already impressed him. "For the first time since my arrival in America, I witnessed music being introduced into society and mingle with its amusements," he wrote after taking tea at the Shippen house with Noailles and Lafayette. "If music and the fine arts prosper in Philadelphia; if society becomes easy and gay, if we learn to accept pleasure when it appears without a formal invitation, then we will be able to enjoy all the advantages peculiar to the manners and the government, without envying anything in Europe." This French influence extended well beyond Philadelphia. The dashing French officers who mingled with wealthy Americans during the Revolution—hosting balls and parties, attending teas and dinners—dazzled the provincial colonists. French manners were the proto-type for the refined English manners the former colonists had sought to emulate; here was a whole new level of refinement, barely before appre-hended. By the time the war ended, Americans on many social levels yearned to speak the language of gentility and culture, the language of their new allies. Increasingly, too, it was the language of trade, the language that ambitious men on the make would want to learn. "Nothing can be of greater advantage to you, than the Frinch Language," wrote one Massachu-setts soldier to his brother in 1782. "I wish I could inflame you with a desire to learn it."[54]

By the mid-1790s, Philadelphia was firmly oriented to French manners, French culture, and French language: all of it enticed an eager population, most particularly the elite. Alexandre Laujon, a young refugee from Saint Domingue, encountered the allure of French culture when he attended a Philadelphia ball, mostly likely in late 1794. He was a talented dancer, and it was not long before others took notice of his skill. Noailles, who had himself been one of the great dancers of the French court at Versailles, ap-proached Laujon and explained that another French dancer, who had been living in Philadelphia for two years, had taken the city by storm; this man was widely regarded as the best in Philadelphia. "But," Noailles continued, "judging that your danse is superior to his, I have undertaken what I be-lieve is an excellent bargain by making a bet on this matter." The details were settled and the two agreed to a dance-off. The entire assembly gath-ered to watch, with people standing on chairs to get a view. Laujon was matched with a partner—one of Thomas Willing's daughters—the orches-tra struck up its music, and off they went. Laujon began slowly, carefully doling out his steps so that he could continually offer new ones, and reserv-ing his best moves for the last *figure*. "I'd requested the one where I could give free rein to the most remarkable steps, and it was then that I revealed my *pirouettes* at eight beats and this famous *pas de Vestris*"—one of the steps recently invented by the famous French dancer Auguste Vestris—"which requires so much lightness, precision, and force in the back of the knee." It was a triumph. As Laujon finished, with applause ringing out in the ballroom, his adversary was the first to congratulate him. Noailles immediately followed and said he was now authorized to introduce the new-comer to "one of the first women of the city": Anne Bingham, who, Laujon reported, "spoke French as well as her own language."[55]

But French influences were not just limited to such dramatic scenes; they insinuated themselves into the quotidian material life of Philadelphia's elite. The French goods shipped over and sold by French merchants had created the supply; French artisans, upholsterers, and designers created the means; and Gallicized Philadelphians created the demand. "Superb Gobelin" adorned the Bingham mansion, for instance: tapestry from the Gobelin factory in Paris's Faubourg Saint-Marcel. The Binghams acquired much of their furniture while they lived in Paris in the 1780s, but they continued their purchases throughout the 1790s. In 1791 Bingham ordered "24 small coffee cups, with a design similar to those used by the Queen & the Duke d'Angouleme," and continued, in subsequent years, to import wines, mocha coffee, vinegar, mustard, dried sweetmeats and fruits, olives, and olive oil—all from France, and all of it to impress and delight the guests at their parties. Robert and Mary Morris—the other great Philadelphia hosts of the period—imported hats from Le Havre, two "sopha's covered with silk Tapestry," and ten armchairs from a Parisian *menuisier*, or cabinetmaker, all the purchases presumably made through their friend and business partner Gouverneur Morris (no relation). But surely the most remarkable piece of furniture in Philadelphia was a clock made in Paris by Herbert Droze, which had once belonged to the queen of France, which the Morrises purchased from Paris for £500: nearly ten times the annual salary of an unskilled worker, more than five times the salary of a typical journeyman. In 1795 they sent it to a French clockmaker in Philadelphia for repairs, where it became a public spectacle. Standing on two large, fluted mahogany pillars, it was said to play twenty different tunes. To cap it all off, the Morrises hired French cooks, a French fencing master for their son, a French dancing master, and a French hairdresser. Despite the effort and expense, none of those teachers seems to have bred in the Morrises the natural refinement of a French aristocrat. In his memoirs, Talleyrand recalled seeing at the Morrises' house an elegant table made from *porcelaine de Sèvres*, bought in Trianon, serving as the resting place for an American hat so simple, Talleyrand scornfully observed, that a European peasant would scarcely have allowed himself to wear it.[56]

BY THE end of the eighteenth century, as the art historian Susan Gray Detweiler observes, "the desire for French luxury furnishings had permeated American mercantile and diplomatic society." What a transformation it was from previous decades.[57]

When the merchant and pillar of Philadelphia society John Cadwalader renovated his house on Second Street in the late 1760s and early 1770s, British fashion dominated. The cooking arrangements were prepared by Peter Biggs, a "marble mason from London, and late mason to the Earl of Essex," and the cooking equipment was purchased from Alexander Smith, "late of London." Hercules Courtenay, a carver and gilder from London, carved the decorations for Cadwalader's famous parlors, among the most ornamented in Philadelphia. The English "stucco worker" James Clow did the plasterwork. If there was a French influence in the house, it is hard to trace. When Robert and Mary Morris decided to build Philadelphia's grandest house in the 1790s, by contrast, they hired the French architect Pierre Charles L'Enfant—the man who laid out Washington, D.C.—to design a structure on the model of a French *hôtel particulier*. A French ironworker built the railings and French-style lanterns for the roof. The French artisan Peter de Beauvais ornamented the interiors. Constructed of red brick adorned with marble pilasters and occupying the entire block between Seventh and Eighth on the east and west, and Chestnut and Walnut on the north and south, the house was such a spectacle that it drew a constant stream of onlookers who came to gawk at the sight.[58]

Given the couple's extravagant tastes, it is probably not surprising that the Morris House—also known as Morris's folly—was still unfinished when Robert Morris, massively overleveraged, landed in debtors' prison in 1798. The house would never be completed. Its furnishings were sold off one by one, even its interior architecture. The semicircular tablets in bas-relief originally designed for the Morris mansion were instead bought by the Chestnut Street Theatre: they represented Comedy and Tragedy.

To be sure, it is hard to draw sharp lines distinguishing French from British styles during this period, when British fashion drew on French models and vice versa. The Queen Anne style of furniture dominant in the early to mid-eighteenth century, for instance, like the popular Chippendale style that followed it, both of them British, were heavily influenced by French fashion and the French turn toward neoclassicism and rococo. English styles, meanwhile, shaped French fashion, particularly among well-heeled liberals like the French *constituants*. Voltaire had spent years in England early in the eighteenth century, and had helped make English fashion and English style all the rage among French aristocrats and intellectuals. The same held true for popular music: the "action music" played in American popular theater descended from British traditions that were themselves appropriated from working-class theaters near Paris. Landscaping followed the pattern, too: Liancourt, like many other French aristocrats of the eighteenth century, added "winding walks, benches, and covered seats, in the English style of gardening," to his estates, as the English agronomist Arthur Young described it when he saw the remarkable gardens at Liancourt. So the two national styles clearly merged. Nevertheless, it is possible to discern a decisive if subtle turn by the Philadelphia elite of the 1790s from London to Paris for its social and stylistic cues.[59]

French influence stretched right through Jefferson's house—he shipped his entire household from Paris to his new house in Philadelphia—to the most symbolically important household of all: George Washington's. Soon after Washington was inaugurated president in 1789, he set himself to acquiring furniture that would "fix the taste of our Country properly," as Gouverneur Morris wrote to Washington. He rented a house to host official events in New York, at that time the nation's capital. Washington's first residence quickly proved too small for his needs, however, and when the comte de Moustier, the French minister to the United States, was called home, Washington moved into his house and bought Moustier's French furniture. The collection included twelve damask upholstered armchairs, six smaller chairs, a sofa, as well as a 309-piece table service, which would be used for official state dinners. Washington took these furnishings with him when the capital moved to Philadelphia, where he hosted his famous levees, or recep-

Side chair manufactured in Paris and porcelain serving dish manufactured at Angoulême, France. Both were among the objects Washington purchased from the departing French minister to the United States, the comte de Moustier.

tions open to the public. Upon his arrival, Washington sent his secretary to scour "the French Stores" of Philadelphia for a set of "waiters, salvers, or whatever they are called. . . . Mr. Morris & Mr. Bingham have them, and the French & Spanish Ministers here," he added. To round out the presidential furniture collection, Washington asked the ubiquitous Gouverneur Morris, whom he would later appoint the American minister to France, to find him some appropriate decorative furniture. Morris sent a beautiful porcelain ornament from Angoulême and various ornate French pieces for the table, including a wine cooler. In addition, Washington hired a French upholsterer in Philadelphia to complete the decor. Thus did the first U.S. state dinners take place with guests seated on French chairs around a French table, and eating off French china. It was in this material world that Washington's beloved stepgranddaughter Eleanor Parke Custis socialized with the French émigrés, wore French fashions, and signed off her letters in French. "The *Sunny* moments of My Life," she later wrote, looking back on that period, "are those which I have the good fortune to pass in Phi[ladelphi]a."[60]

The arrival of the émigré French *constituants* thus corresponded with the peak American enthusiasm for French styles, fashion, architecture,

Angoulême figurine of Venus and cupids, along with an ornamental wine cooler, both bought in Paris by Gouverneur Morris and sent to Washington to decorate the presidential mansion. Both are now at Mount Vernon.

people, politics, trade, and material life. French objects had become incorporated in the daily life and the ritual world of elite Philadelphia, displayed at Philadelphia's levees, in drawing rooms, and in salons—themselves modeled on French forms of sociability. Even as the presidency shifted from Federalist to Republican control in 1800, French material culture continued to dominate. Jefferson furnished the presidential mansion, by then relocated to Washington, D.C., with the objects he'd bought while in Paris, and he employed French chefs throughout his term as secretary of state and as president. (He'd gone to great expense to teach James Hemings, Sally's brother, the art of French cooking while in Paris.) In 1802, when Samuel Richardet, the French chef who had worked for Cazenove and run the City Tavern, where he had regularly served food to Talleyrand, Liancourt, Moreau, and the other émigrés, was looking for work, he wrote to President Jefferson in his heavily accented English: "Having the Honneur of Knowing the President of the U:S: at the time I lived with Theos: Cazenove's Esqr. as is Steward till I want in business, my wiches is to devote my self to the management of some Gentelman family."[61]

Indeed, so much had the French influence transformed the nation's capital in the 1790s, it may be *à propos* to conclude by wondering if Philadelphia and even perhaps the United States in this period should not be considered as much a part of the French Atlantic world as it was an emerging American nation.

Chapter 3

FRANCO-AMERICAN NETWORKS AND POLITE ATLANTIC SPACES

I F YOU WERE A TRAVELER IN THE EIGHTEENTH CENTURY, YOU WOULD want to set out with a stack of letters from friends at home to their friends, family members, or acquaintances abroad. Your best bet would be to pick a friend with an extensive family. If she had a brother or a cousin or an in-law abroad—perfect. You'd have a friend in a foreign place to introduce you to local acquaintances, you would probably have an invitation to dinner, and you might even have a place to stay. If not, another approach would be to track down a nearby diplomat—an ambassador or a consul would be ideal, but a secretary to the legation or some other minor figure could work as well. Bankers or merchants were also good bets. The best of these had correspondents in port cities around the world, with a business relationship often built on a family connection or a friendship. Failing all that, you would at least ask for letters from a local personage— the more eminent the better. He might at least have friends or correspondents abroad to whom he could introduce you.

Travel was difficult in this age, when you couldn't know how long it would take a letter to cross the Atlantic or if it would even reach its destination. A Parisian could only imagine what Philadelphia looked like: no reliable photos circulated to prepare her for the sights, no radio or television or movies for the sounds. Even passports didn't contain pictures; only written descriptions of a traveler's features and distinguishing characteristics. It was a supremely anonymous age, when entirely new identities could be created by moving a mere hundred miles—never mind across an ocean. In this context, letter writing helped overcome anonymity; it forged a personal connection, however tenuous or tentative.

This was the world of the French émigré *constituants.* They had crossed the ocean, sometimes in grueling conditions, with little idea what awaited them at the end. They had read about America from books and heard about it from friends and talked about it in Paris salons and at dinner tables, but mostly America had been an ideological weapon for them to deploy in their war against French absolutism. It was an idea rather than a place. And yet here they were. They had all settled in Philadelphia, which they found awash with French people, French business, and French goods. They had established a tight-knit community in the heart of the city, which provided support and orientation amid difficult emotional times. And they discovered an elite society grown wealthy on trade increasingly turned toward France and the French colonies, their salons filled with French furniture, their sociability patterned on French manners. Eventually the émigré *constituants* began to turn outward, toward the American community.

A dense web of networks made the émigrés' integration into American life possible: knit together by letters of introduction, transatlantic friendships, and commercial relationships. These networks facilitated the émigrés' arrival in the United States. They were the means by which friendships and families were forged and business was conducted, the paths through which goods, capital, and people moved across the Atlantic world. They were the links that connected salon life in Paris with Philadelphia dinner parties, extending across the Atlantic from major European centers through the principal American port cities and deep into the American backcountry. They were an essential part of the infrastructure of transatlantic life in the eighteenth century. Understanding how they worked helps us to see how the United States connected to Europe and the Caribbean during the Age of Atlantic Revolutions.

WHEN TALLEYRAND arrived in Philadelphia in April 1794, he carried no fewer than six letters of introduction to major Philadelphia figures. The most notable was a letter to George Washington from William Petty, the Marquis of Lansdowne and 2nd Earl of Shelburne, who had long defended the American cause; he had served as Britain's prime minister after the British defeat at Yorktown, presiding over the peace settlement with the United States. He had since become a correspondent of President Washington's. Wishing to "do justice to a most respectable Individual, suffering under a great deal of combin'd persecution," Lansdowne introduced Talleyrand: "Mr Taillerand is the eldest of one of the first Familys of France," he wrote. Sacrificing "ambition to public principle," he remained a political moderate—a profile dear to Washington's heart—so "as never to pass the line of a constitutionalist, which exposes him to the hatred of the violent party now predominating. . . . In the present situation of Europe he has no where to look for an asylum, except to that Country, which is happy enough to preserve it's peace and it's happiness under your Auspices."[1]

Talleyrand also carried two letters to Dr. Benjamin Rush, a signer of the Declaration of Independence, an eminent physician, and one of Philadelphia's most prominent citizens. The pro-American diplomat and politician Benjamin Vaughan wrote from London on Talleyrand's behalf to his brother John, who had recently moved to Maine, and sent what he called "short circular letters" to other Philadelphia elites. "Our loss will be the gain of America," he averred. "You will be much pleased with his maners & instructed by his conversation." But Talleyrand's most useful letter came from Angelica Church, an American living in London. Church was the daughter of General Philip Schuyler, who laid the groundwork for the defeat of the British general John Burgoyne at the battles of Saratoga, which brought the French into the war and changed the course of history. Her mother was a Van Rensselaer, one of New York's great landowning families; her father descended from the Van Cortlandt clan. Her sister had married Alexander Hamilton. She was friends with Thomas Jefferson, with whom she had carried on a flirtatious correspondence while the two lived in Paris. Church was enmeshed in a web of family and social connections at the highest level of American politics and society, a network she mobilized on behalf of the French *constituants*. "I recommend to your most particular care and attention . . . my friends Messieurs de Talleyrand and de Beaumais," Church wrote to her sister Elizabeth—Hamilton's wife. "Make our Country agreeable to them as far as it is in your power. . . . I have for these persons the most sincere friendship."[2]

These letters had their intended effect, facilitating Talleyrand's integration into Philadelphia's most elite circles. Hamilton immediately became a friend. Having grown up with a mother of Huguenot descent, Hamilton spoke excellent French—"he spoke our language like a Frenchman," according to one French refugee. The two were similarly hardheaded about politics and human motivation, and similarly indifferent to their culture's sexual mores. They hit it off famously, developing "the most intimate liaison," as Talleyrand later described it, drinking and eating together, and spending long evenings under the starry skies during the hot summer of 1795 talking about the American and French revolutions, free trade, and economic development, sometimes until midnight, sometimes even later. "No one has aided me more in gaining my information quickly and surely than Mr. Hamilton," wrote Talleyrand soon after arriving in the United States. "I have found the greatest advantage in forming an intimate liaison with him and every day I have reason to felicitate myself on it." Talleyrand's admiration of Hamilton only grew as their friendship developed. He once even sat in the visitors' gallery of the Supreme Court to hear Hamilton defend Congress's right to establish an excise tax. "He triumphed, and was greatly admired of Talleyrand," wrote one witness. Back in London, Angelica Church received glowing reports about their welcome: "Talleyrand and Beaumetz write in raptures to all their friends of your kindness, and Colonel Hamilton's abilities and manners, and I receive innumerable compliments on his & your account." By the time he left America, Talleyrand considered Hamilton "one of the finest men in America, at least of those I have seen," and—fine praise this!—"at the height of the most distinguished

European statesmen." He would later extend the praise further: "I consider Napoleon, Fox, and Hamilton the three greatest men of our epoch, and if I were forced to decide between the three, I would give without hesitation the first place to Hamilton." Many years after Talleyrand had gone on to climb the greatest heights of European diplomacy, Aaron Burr called on him in Paris, hoping to visit, and left his card. The next day, when he returned, the butler had been instructed to coldly inform Burr that a portrait of Hamilton hung over the mantelpiece in Talleyrand's home. Burr would get no visit.[3]

Surely the letter that most underscores the importance of letters of introduction was one that Talleyrand did not get. As he was leaving Europe, Talleyrand's ship ran into a storm in the English Channel and put into Falmouth for repairs. Talleyrand heard that an American general was in town. Tracking the American down, he peppered him with questions about the United States, but to little avail. After trying and failing several times to strike up conversation, he asked if the general would at least write a few letters of introduction. "No," the American responded. After a few moments of awkward silence, during which the American general evidently saw Talleyrand's astonishment, he added: "I am perhaps the only American who can't give letters for his country.... All my relationships are cut off.... I can never return."

He never did tell Talleyrand his name: it was Benedict Arnold.[4]

WHEN LIANCOURT landed in Philadelphia in November 1794, he, too, came armed with multiple letters of recommendation. Three days after he arrived, time enough to get his bearings, he began to distribute them. "Went to visit all the people for whom I had letters," he noted in his diary. They included Vice President John Adams, Secretary of War Henry Knox, William Bingham, soon to be a U.S. senator, and Pennsylvania High Court judge Benjamin Chew. His letters secured Liancourt an invitation to dine at Knox's house that very day, where he sat next to Alexander Hamilton, for whom he also had a letter. "My Dear Brother," wrote the ubiquitous Angelica Church, "I have very particular and very good motives to ask your kindness for the Duke de Liancourt . . . [who] goes to America, and goes there without a friend, unless my dear Brother, who is always so good, will extend to Monsieur de Liancourt his care—besides many good qualities, this gentleman is the friend of the Marquis de LaFayette." And then, as though for good measure, Church added: "Adieu my dear friend, remember me to Beaumetz and Monsieur de Talleyrand."[5]

Like Talleyrand, Liancourt came to enjoy Hamilton's company. "A man of great genius and great talent," Liancourt reported, adding, "extraordinary for a man who never left America." The two dined together at least five times in December 1794 and four times in January 1795. Passing through New York a few months later, Liancourt renewed the praise, characterizing Hamilton as a man with an "expansive spirit, genius even, clear in his thought, eloquent in his turn of phrase, with knowledge of all sorts, lively sensibility, good character, and great amiability." When he saw Hamilton again a year later in New York, he couldn't resist commenting on his "*moeurs douces* and infinitely agreeable," which is perhaps why Liancourt considered him "in many respects a European." Liancourt made himself such a trusted friend, he even succeeded in wheedling Hamilton's private opinion of George Washington:

> He has little spirit, little knowledge, little instruction, but good judgment, great wisdom, and prudence that seems to be his principal character trait and the guide to his political and private actions. Dissimulated without falsehood, disposed to get carried away, but master of himself, devoted to the good and the glory of his country, faithful republican in all his ventures, but not by reflection or by the opinion that it is the best government for America; persuaded, to the contrary, with many wise men of America, including Mr. Ham[ilton], Mr. Jay, etc., that the government is not strong enough to govern the United States.

The French all seemed fascinated by George Washington, a modern-day Cincinnatus, whose leadership successfully balanced the often conflicting principles of liberty and order, succeeding where the *constituants* had failed.[6]

Liancourt and Talleyrand were not the only émigrés to hold Hamilton in high esteem. Noailles had known Hamilton the longest, having fought with him in the Revolution, when Hamilton served on Washington's staff as liaison to the French officer corps. "Esteem for your talents and acquirements, is a sentiment which from my earliest acquaintances with you, my dear viscount, I have shared in common with all those who have the happiness of knowing you," Hamilton wrote to Noailles in a somewhat breathless 1782 letter, after Noailles had returned to France in the wake of the victory at Yorktown. "A better knowledge of your character has given it in my eyes a more intrinsic merit, and has attached me to you by a friendship founded upon qualities as rare as they are estimable." When Noailles arrived in the United States as a refugee he carried a letter to George Washington from Thomas Pinckney, the U.S. ambassador to Great Britain, as well as at least two letters from Angelica Church, one to Jefferson and a second to Hamilton. "My dear Brother," wrote Church. "You will receive this from a friend of mine and an admirer of your virtues and your talents. He goes to America to partake of that Liberty for which he has often exposed his life, and to render it all the services his knowledge of Europe and of the emigration about to take place to America, give the opportunity of doing." Both letters had their intended effect. "Monsr. de Noailles has been so kind as to deliver me your letter," Jefferson wrote to Church after Noailles had called. "It fills up the measure of his titles to any services I can render him." As for Hamilton, two days after arriving in the United States, Noailles visited his old friend. Within a few weeks, his former impressions had been reconfirmed: "a man of great understanding, fine talents, a communicative genius, an untainted probity, an absolute disinterestedness," Noailles wrote to a correspondent in England.[7]

Letters continued to shape the émigrés' experiences as they left Philadelphia to travel through the American backcountry. Talleyrand's friendship with Hamilton facilitated his travels in the summer and fall of 1794, providing him with letters of recommendation to prominent figures all along his route up the East Coast, through Maine, across upstate New York, and back down the Hudson valley to New York City. Liancourt also traveled with a hefty pack of letters. One of these, from William Bingham, introduced Liancourt as a person for "whom I entertain a great share of Friendship & Esteem," and explained his "desire of forming a more accurate opinion of Pennsylvania, its Society & Improvements." In "requesting your Civilities" of his correspondent, Bingham did not fail to heap praise on Liancourt's "amiable deportment—the integrity of his Conduct in political & private life—the Reverses of Fortune he has met . . . with heroic Fortitude," all of which "have gained him universal Esteem & Consideration." These letters greatly aided Liancourt's travels. Arriving in Reading, Pennsylvania, Liancourt reported having letters for several local notables, "and cannot speak with sufficient praise of the handsome reception we experienced from these gentlemen." These men, in turn, furnished Liancourt with more letters: "They also offered us letters for Lancaster, and for a good part of our route, which, though we were already provided with an abundance, we accepted with the same grace with which they were offered." One American living in central Pennsylvania, recalling the time Liancourt came to his house, testified to the ways that letters could ease a traveler's arrival. "My respect for the writer of the letter would have induced me to avail myself of the honor it offered me," he reported. "But being indisposed and depressed by a domestic affliction, I did not go out." Though it seemed that these Frenchmen were aimlessly wandering the American hinterland, their trips were highly structured by the letters they carried, connecting them from one acquaintance to another in a chain that tied the backcountry together.[8]

Such letters linked not just the major port cities around the Atlantic Seaboard; they permeated the hinterland, crossed the Appalachians, and penetrated deep into the American frontier. When Volney traveled through the backcountry, he did so with no fewer than six letters of introduction from Jefferson to his correspondents in the West, including the governor of Kentucky. Writing to one of these connections a few years later, Jefferson recalled that "Mr. Volney on his return spoke with great acknoledgments of your kind civilities." While in Virginia, Volney also visited George Washington at Mount Vernon, where he spent several days and asked for a few letters from the great man himself. Washington, who was always more circumspect than Jefferson, and who may well have taken a disliking to Volney, wrote a letter notable mostly for its reserve. "Dear Sir," Washington wrote to his former secretary Tobias Lear, then living in Washington. "This letter will be put into your hands by Mr. Volney, who proposes to visit the Federal City. If you are not acquainted with him personally, I am sure you must have a knowledge of his character, his travels and works; I therefore recommend him to your civilities while he remains in the Federal City." Volney found the letter offensive, according to the recollections of one acquaintance, "consider[ing it] to be only equivocal praise, and too feebly expressed to satisfy the expectations of a man of his exalted merit." Most likely inspired by Volney's indignation, the story about Washington's lukewarm introduction persisted, gathering further deformation with each repetition, until the letter Washington supposedly wrote read in its entirety:

C. Volney needs no recommendation from

—George Washington.[9]

———————

THESE LETTERS of introduction structured travelers' lives, connecting Europe's capitals through American port cities to the U.S. backcountry. Few experiences highlight their importance better than those of another émigré to the United States, Henriette Lucie Dillon, marquise de La Tour du Pin-Gouvernet.

Like the émigré *constituants,* La Tour du Pin had grown up in the most exalted circles of France's aristocracy. Her father, Arthur Dillon, son of the 11th Viscount Dillon, fought in the American Revolution, serving with French forces in the Caribbean and at the Siege of Savannah alongside Noailles; in the 1780s, he became the governor of the French colony of Tobago. Her mother, Lucie-Thérèse, was Marie-Antoinette's lady-in-waiting. Her uncle was, like Talleyrand, an archbishop in the French Church. In 1787, at the age of seventeen, she married Frédéric-Séraphin de La Tour du Pin-Gouvernet, a liberal French nobleman and son of the French minister of war, who had fought in the American Revolution as an aide-de-camp to Lafayette. As colonel of the Royal Vaisseaux, it was he who was left in charge when Louis XVI fled Versailles in October 1789. Lucie had been a regular guest at the salons of Madame de Genlis and Suzanne Necker, the most Enlightened gatherings of prerevolutionary Paris, where she discussed French politics and society with Talleyrand and others. Having launched themselves, like Liancourt, Talleyrand, Noailles, and Beaumetz, behind the constitutional reforms of the early stages of the French Revolution, she and her husband had become anathema to the ruling Girondin party by 1793. They tried keeping their heads low, hoping the storm would blow over. Hiding in Bordeaux in 1794, Lucie listened to the drums roll as enemies of the state were brought to the scaffold on the Place nationale, and heard the crash of the guillotine blade that followed. It seemed only a matter of time until she and her family would be counted among the victims of the Terror.[10]

Learning about an American ship, the *Diana,* leaving for Boston, La Tour du Pin jumped to action. She surreptitiously obtained passports through the help of an old friend and had her husband spirited into the city in time to get aboard, just as a new revolutionary agent arrived in Bordeaux determined to hunt down the nobles hiding in attics and cellars across the city. They sailed out into the treacherous waters of the Bay of Biscay ahead of a French naval ship that fired a cannon shot across the *Diana's* bow in a vain attempt to arrest the passengers. Their transatlantic journey was arduous: sixty long days in the face of strong headwinds, their supply of food dwindling to alarming levels. Eventually they arrived in Boston. For La Tour du Pin, the months of accumulated stress seemed suddenly to lift:

> One has to have been exposed to all the suffering to which we were subjected for two months, to the constraints that I had previously endured, to the worries provoked by the situation of my husband and those that I'd had for my own security, to the anxiety caused by the prolonged fear of an always imminent death that would lead to the abandonment, without help or support, of my

two poor children, to be able to appreciate the feeling of joy with which I put my foot on this friendly land.

Relieved as she was to find shelter in America, however, La Tour du Pin now came face-to-face with her new reality. She lacked any acquaintances and found herself entirely dependent on the ship captain's goodwill to get her family oriented in Boston. So unwelcoming did Boston seem, their first night in the New World found them still on board the *Diana,* on which they'd just spent two miserable, hungry months. Though safely arrived on land, the family felt abandoned and adrift.[11]

But all was not as it appeared. Two months earlier, while her ship languished along the French coast waiting for the trade winds, it had encountered a boat headed for England. La Tour du Pin took advantage of the opportunity to send letters to her husband's aunt, the famed *salonnière* Princess d'Hénin, then in London. While La Tour du Pin's ship fought the headwinds across the Atlantic, her letter was wending its way through the parlors of London, where Hénin passed it to her friend Angelica Church, who promptly wrote a letter to her family in Albany, which she dispatched on another ship from England to New York. Church's networks moved faster than the ship slowly carrying La Tour du Pin across the Atlantic, and by the time she arrived in Boston with her family, various letters of introduction had preceded them. Shortly after her landing, La Tour du Pin received "very pressing letters" from General Schuyler, urging her to come to Albany "without delay." He assured her that her family would have no trouble establishing itself in the area and "offered us all of his support." This invitation proved to be a turning point in the family's American stay. Selling the goods they'd shipped over with them "that might have monetary value"—clothes, porcelain, and a piano, which she only now realized would be difficult to transport across the rugged American backcountry—the family was soon making its way through the Massachusetts forest. Arriving in Albany, La Tour du Pin found the Schuylers exceedingly welcoming: "Now I shall have a sixth daughter!" exclaimed General Schuyler when they met. While her husband looked for a farm to buy, the family boarded at the home of a local family, the Van Burens, who employed the marquise as a cleaning lady and seamstress, where she served the future president of the United States, then just a twelve-year-old boy. Eventually, with the Schuylers' help, she and her husband bought a 206-acre farm five miles north of Albany, where they spent several years living a life of yeoman simplicity.[12]

It was on that farm that Talleyrand found her early one afternoon in October 1794, as he toured upstate New York with his traveling companions, guided through the country by his letters of introduction. La Tour du Pin stood in her farmyard with a small axe in her hand, wrestling with a mutton leg for that afternoon's dinner, when she heard a booming voice say in French: "On ne peut embrocher un gigot avec plus de majesté." (One could hardly skewer a leg with more majesty.) Turning around, she saw an incongruous sight: Talleyrand—the former bishop of Autun, a descendant of one of France's noblest families, the man who had celebrated the Mass on the Champ de Mars in Paris on July 14, 1790, and administered the oath of Louis XVI to the French constitution—dressed in the rifle shirt of a backwoods hunter, dismounting his horse, a big smile on his face.[13]

However delightful it was to find friends from home here in the American backcountry, the reunion was nonetheless bittersweet, as they recalled friends and family executed in France. Talleyrand spent several days on La Tour du Pin's farm, along with his traveling companions Beaumetz and Thomas Law, an Englishman who'd recently returned from India and would soon settle in Washington, D.C., and marry into George Washington's family. All were moved by the sight of this former *grande dame* of the French aristocracy serving them milk drawn from a cow by her hands and washing her guests' dishes. Liancourt would visit the following summer on his journey through the American backcountry, carrying letters of introduction from Talleyrand to various local notables, and express similar emotions when he saw Lucie making cream and yellow butter—stamped "La Tour du Pin," sold in Albany markets, apparently excellent and quite in vogue.[14]

LA TOUR du Pin's apparently fortuitous encounter with Talleyrand and Liancourt on the American frontier, former *habitués* of corrupt French court life now embodying the savage nobility of the American, evokes the most romantic sensibilities. Her narrative draws on proto-romantic images of Europeans living a more natural existence, popularizing the ideas of theorists like Jean-Jacques Rousseau and writers like J. Hector St. John de Crèvecoeur. But the truth was far more complicated. When Talleyrand found La Tour du Pin, there was nothing accidental about their encounter: each had been led to the same place by the Schuylers—La Tour du Pin via Church and Talleyrand via Hamilton. A complex web of social, familial, and professional relationships structured their encounter, composed of letters from England and France, visits from old friends, and introductions to new acquaintances.[15]

Of course, La Tour du Pin, Talleyrand, and Liancourt were hardly the typical transatlantic travelers. They were among the most elite figures in the Atlantic world; their likes had rarely been seen in North America, and we should be wary of generalizing from their histories. Most of the people who crossed the Atlantic in the eighteenth century were ship hands, crewmen, officers, sailors—and, vastly outnumbering them all, slaves. Their lives could not have been more different from those of these descendants of France's great aristocratic families. But if their connections were less exalted, other travelers also lived, traveled, and communicated through their own networks—be they free and enslaved black communities in port cities and plantations, radical revolutionary networks spanning the Atlantic, or commercial networks linking planters and merchants. Indeed, what else was the Underground Railroad, through which so many slaves escaped from the South into freedom in the North or in Canada, if not an extended network created by letters and personal acquaintance that facilitated the movement of otherwise anonymous people across vast distances? Obviously the experiences of men like Talleyrand, Beaumetz, and Liancourt fleeing the court life of Paris bore little relation to the experience of Frederick Douglass fleeing Baltimore slavery. But that does not mean that analogies cannot be drawn between them, one story helping us understand the other, both of them pulling life in the eighteenth and nineteenth centuries just a little bit further out from the shadows. By understanding how one particular network operated, far greater phenomena may gradually come into view.[16]

LETTERS OF introduction were not merely private tools with which the French integrated themselves into American social circles or facilitated their travels through the backcountry. They could also have considerable political valence. Their political nature became obvious, and sometimes problematic, when they were addressed to government officials.

Hamilton did not seem to mind receiving the émigrés in his office at the Treasury Department. Washington, on the other hand, was more cautious. Talleyrand had a letter of introduction from Lord Lansdowne, the former British prime minister who had signed the preliminary Treaty of Paris, recognizing American independence. Noailles was a former officer in the French army who had fought in the American Revolution, a friend of Secretary of the Treasury Hamilton and Secretary of War Knox. Was Washington to receive these men privately? Or should he do so at his biweekly levees, where the president, dressed in his court finest—his hair powdered, cocked hat in hand, silver buckles on his shoes, and a sword at his side—received all "respectable citizens and strangers, properly introduced," every other Tuesday from three to four in the afternoon? Although stiff and formal affairs, the levees were public appearances. What impact would a meeting with such men have on Washington's diplomacy? Might they affect his policy of strict neutrality in European affairs? Could Washington risk dragging the United States into war?[17]

It was not rare for private individuals to carry diplomatic messages. Talleyrand claimed his trip from France to England in 1792 had been undertaken as an informal diplomatic mission. Washington similarly used Gouverneur Morris at the start of his presidency as his informal eyes and ears in Paris, before appointing him the official U.S. minister. Later, when Morris proved too unpopular in Paris, William Stephens Smith returned from a trip to Europe with letters to President Washington from the French minister of foreign affairs. So it would hardly have been odd for Washington to wonder whether a meeting with these well-connected Frenchmen, formerly of Louis XVI's court, all of them *constituants* with unknown ties to British politicians and royalist émigrés across Europe, might have some official if back-channel purposes. Washington approached the matter with caution. "In the conversation you may have with a certain Gentleman to-day," he wrote to Hamilton, referring to Noailles,

> I pray you to intimate to him gently, and delicately, that if the letters, or papers wch. he has to present, are (knowingly to him) of a nature which relates to public matters . . . I had rather they should come through the proper channel.
>
> Add thereto, generally that the peculiar situation of European Affairs at this moment[,] my good wishes for his Nation aggregately, my regard for those of it in particular with whom I have had the honor of an acquaintance; My anxious desire to keep this Country in Peace; and the delicacy of my situation renders a circumspect conduct indispensably necessary on my part.

Despite these precautions—and perhaps because of his old friendships—Noailles succeeded in gaining privileged access to Washington. And as Washington had suspected, the meeting did have an unofficial diplomatic purpose. "In private conversation," Noailles wrote in a long report to Lord Windham, soon to be named the British secretary at war, following his meeting, "I was confirmed in my opinion that the President . . . disliked the System of New Republicains as much as might be expected from a man of the true principles of a good government and anxious for the happiness of mankind." Noailles continued with an astute analysis of the state of U.S. politics: how the French Revolution had sown divisions throughout the United States; the sectional character of political opinion ("it is very remarkable that the states which admit slavery were all more in favour of equality and licentiousness"); his opinion of the leadership and direction of the Federalist and Republican Parties; and his assessment of Washington's neutrality proclamation. He also gave Windham several suggestions on maintaining peace with the United States. There is no doubt, in short, that letters of introduction—and the personal encounters they engendered—could conflate the boundaries between the political, diplomatic, and social spheres.[18]

Jean-Antoine Joseph Fauchet, the French minister who had succeeded Genet, saw dangerous political implications in the émigrés' sociability. Their reception by Washington and members of his cabinet caused him real concern: Secretary of War Henry Knox, in particular, seemed "very connected to Noailles." Worried about the evident sympathy between these aristocratic expatriates and the "British Party" in Philadelphia, convinced they were trying to push the United States into a grand alliance against France, Fauchet kept a close eye on their activities and waged a campaign to ban them from Washington's receptions. Each time he spotted an émigré at Washington's receptions he walked out in a huff. Fauchet eventually approached Secretary of State Jefferson about the matter. "Que voulez vous," Jefferson responded. "The audiences of the President are public and anyone has the right to appear." Fauchet was not impressed. "Under the *ancien régime*," he replied, "audiences with the late King of France were public too, and certainly during your war with England we didn't allow the *Tories* and *Arnolds* of your country to appear with Franklin."[19]

Fauchet's objections troubled Washington, who could see that admitting the émigrés to his receptions was "driving the French Minister from them. His visits are much less frequent than they were—and . . . [he] has left no doubt as to the cause." Washington was walking a fine line. He tried conducting his communications with the émigrés in public spaces through intermediaries—as when Liancourt reported that Knox had spoken to him at a ball "on behalf of the President." But this became more difficult as more refugees of various political views filled Philadelphia. Fauchet suspected the worst about the *constituants*. The émigrés, he wrote, "have not abandoned the hope of influencing the government." He believed the social gatherings in Philadelphia that included Talleyrand, Beaumetz, Hamilton, and Knox, along with the English and Dutch ambassadors to the United States, made up a massive transatlantic political conspiracy, "perhaps the most widespread and most skillfully planned of any ever organized against liberty." His suspicions could not have been allayed by the association between Moreau and the arch-Federalist immigrant William Cobbett, who was then translating Moreau's two-volume work on the geography and laws of Saint Domingue.[20]

In fact, the émigrés were not spying for any country—although, as we shall see, Fauchet could be forgiven for thinking they were—but facts were not the point. The highly charged political atmosphere of Philadelphia sociability was. After Talleyrand's arrival in the United States it became clear that more and more distinguished émigrés would be seeking refuge in the young Republic; Washington recognized the difficulty of drawing sharp distinctions between social and political encounters. Prompted by Fauchet's frustrations, he decided that "principles should be adopted in these cases (not only for the President, but the Executive Officers also) by which evils may be avoided and uniformity observed." Fauchet had won his battle. Talleyrand would never get to meet Washington—a great humiliation for a man used to his easy acceptance in Europe's most exalted circles, and an experience that may well have soured him on the U.S. government and its leadership. Nor would Liancourt. "When he came to this country," Washington explained to a group of friends at dinner a few years later, "he brought letters of introduction from the most distinguished persons in England; he had no need of them. In the light of what M. de Lafayette had told me of him, as well as his reputation and conduct, I knew the respect that I owed him." But Washington would not allow these letters to jeopardize his delicate diplomacy of neutrality:

> I could not, however, receive him at my house. . . . I had made a rule not to admit to my house any Frenchman who was regarded as an emigree and who could not be presented by his Minister. I informed M. de Liancourt through my friends of the motives that obliged me to deprive myself of the advantage of seeing him, an advantage which otherwise I would have so much wished, and as soon as I should be out of the administration, I would hope to see him.

As all the discussion and concern about the matter suggested, this was not a minor issue. At a time in the nation's political life when politics and diplomacy were so often conducted through interpersonal networks, the presence or absence of these émigrés at certain social functions had real political implications.[21]

PRESIDENTIAL MANSIONS and diplomatic gatherings were obvious sites of political power. But they were not the only places where politics happened, nor were they the only ways the United States was connected to the world. Focusing on transatlantic networks helps to shine a light on the often hidden aspects of politics, economics, and diplomacy.

Recently, historians have shown how much of the United States' early political life was conducted in coffeehouses, taverns, and parlors—sites traditionally deemed nonpolitical—and at dinner parties or through private correspondence. In this work, they follow a broader political and philosophical reexamination of the very concepts of "public" and "private" to shed rich insight into the formation of politics, revolution, and what used to be called the Enlightenment. In light of that scholarship, it becomes possible to expand our definition of the political realm, and to see how the French émigrés' participation in certain social networks could take on a political cast. When Liancourt reported that he ate at William Bingham's "with the universe," or that he "dined at Mr. Nicklin's with many people, Americans, English merchants established in this country, several members of Congress, all in the best spirit, the most wise, and the best friends of order," these events seem not just social but also political.[22]

If it is something of a truism to state that the American and French Republics each influenced the other, these networks help explain more precisely how they did so. Transatlantic revolutionary influences operated not just through books and newspapers crossing the Atlantic, or from diplomacy developed in government ministries, but also through more informal ways: via friendship and conversation, at coffeehouses and in parlors, across dinner tables and in salons, between everyday people in everyday settings in everyday life. As the *constituants* integrated themselves into Philadelphia's elite social networks, they shared their experiences and their ideas, exercising a subtle influence on their hosts. Volney, for one, recognized the importance of such connections when he called on the French government to cultivate cultural ties in order to advance the Franco-American diplomatic alliance. "Have here artists, distinguished men of letters, a French newspaper, a French school, a library," he urged. "Support a performance, a fine concert and make the embassy mansion a *rendez-vous* for the *bonne société*." Today, it seems like a strikingly modern way of thinking about diplomacy. "We spend millions to kill people and conquer them," Volney added. "*Eh bien,* one-hundredth of that amount employed in entertaining them would make surer conquests." Moreau, too, observed the powerful effect of sociability on international relations. He had watched Genet alienate the Washington administration with his behavior, and also recalled how a previous ambassador attended dinners at Alexander Hamilton's house "with two or three dishes cooked in the French fashion on the pretext of being on a diet." It was no way to make friends. "In brief," Moreau concluded, an ambassador "must use his dinner table for diplomatic purposes."[23]

These international networks of sociability had a subtle but important influence on early American political culture. Consider the Federalists' hostile response to the emerging world of political clubs and newspaper politics. Why did they call them "Jacobin"? Philadelphia, after all, was hardly a stranger to revolutionary movements; they certainly had closer examples at hand. Could their thoughts have been shaped by the experiences of French expatriates fleeing the political turmoil generated by French political clubs and the activities of the Parisian sans-culottes? The French émigrés' stories of revolutionary Paris told at dinner tables and parlors throughout Philadelphia made a powerful impression on their American hosts. Reinforcing this influence was the political outlook the French émigrés shared with American Federalists. Devoted to constitutional republicanism, wary of excessive popular rule, firm believers in the importance of a strong central government and a powerful executive, they shared a transatlantic vision of the ideal political system grounded in Montesquieu's political theory and tempered by a strong dose of skepticism about what they perceived as the democratic excesses of the French Revolution. It is no wonder the French émigrés slipped so easily into the Federalists' social world.[24]

Can we take this line of reflection on the importance of social networks to the early Republic's political life even further? Before the emergence of formal political parties that would organize political debates and create an institutional framework for dissent, these social parties—dinners, balls, salons—served as scaffolding, shaping and perhaps even holding up the Republic during a very fragile time. Congress appropriated an astounding $25,000 per year for George Washington's dinner parties: a vast sum at a time when an unskilled worker earned one dollar per day. It was no accident that some of the most important political landmarks of the period were settled in social arenas—most famously, the "dinner table" bargain between Jefferson, Madison, and Hamilton, in which the Southern states agreed to the federal assumption of state debts in exchange for the relocation of the U.S. capital to the banks of the Potomac River. Social events played a prominent role in politics and diplomacy during the Federalist era. And so they would continue, long after the Federalists, with their famously vilified aristocratic manners, had lost power. When Jefferson became president his dinner table became a central arena of political activity. After that, Dolley Madison's salons and dinner table became among the most important sites for Washington politicking during the Madison administration. The social, in other words, was never separate from the political.[25]

THE ÉMIGRÉS' social networks in Philadelphia revolved around several key points—or nodes, as they are sometimes called. The most central was Anne Bingham, who reigned supreme over what one contemporary called "the highest social circle of Philadelphia."[26]

The first of Thomas Willing's thirteen children, Anne descended from one of Philadelphia's great merchant families. Three of her relatives, including her father, had been mayors of Philadelphia; her family embodied the rising Anglican merchant class that took the reins of economic power from the Quakers after the Seven Years' War. In 1754 her father joined with Robert Morris to establish what became the premier commercial house in Philadelphia. Willing served as a delegate to the Constitutional Convention, where he voted against independence in 1776 on the grounds, he later said, that he did not think the country was ready, and that he had not in any case been authorized to vote in favor. This vote, along with his decision to remain in Philadelphia during the British occupation, called his patriotism into question and rendered him more or less ineligible for elective office after the war. No matter: like other wealthy figures who'd hedged their bets during the Revolution, he turned to unelected public offices, eventually being appointed the first president of the Bank of the United States founded by Alexander Hamilton in the 1790s. Moving seamlessly from trade to government service to finance, Willing understood himself to be a merchant above all, as his portrait by Charles Willson Peale testified. It shows him seated with great self-confidence, his brow slightly furrowed, as though peering forward to view the price of grain futures, with Delaware Bay in the background, the lighthouse at Cape Henlopen in full view.[27]

It was in Willing's firm that the young merchant William Bingham

Thomas Willing, painted by Charles Willson Peale in 1782.

spent the revolutionary years. Stationed in Martinique, he commissioned privateers to harass British shipping in the Caribbean and contracted with French merchants to supply the American war effort—earning lucrative commissions on both. He returned triumphantly to Philadelphia in 1780, a very wealthy man. Anne Willing had just reached sixteen and was already turning heads as one of Philadelphia's most beautiful women, drawing the attention of dashing French officers like Noailles as they passed through the city on their way to Yorktown. William's fortune and Anne's beauty made just the right match, and the couple was wed in October of that year. In May 1783, as the peace negotiations ending the war entered their final stretch in Paris, they left for Europe with a sixteen-month-old daughter. Anne, only eighteen years old, was eager to see the wider world; William, thirty-one and fiercely ambitious, was hoping for an appointment to a diplomatic post. And thus began what Liancourt, when he heard about the trip after arriving in Philadelphia a few years later, called "*la jolie histoire de Mde Bingham à Paris.*"[28]

THE BINGHAMS' first stop was London, where they rented a fashionable house on Cavendish Square that became a gathering place for expatriate Americans. When John Jay arrived in London after signing the peace treaty in Paris, he lodged with the Binghams. John Adams, bouncing around Europe on his various diplomatic missions, was a frequent dinner guest. The Binghams soon befriended Benjamin Vaughan, a Jamaica-born diplomat and politician with extensive American ties, whose friendship with Franklin had helped initiate the negotiations that ended the Revolution. Vaughan was well connected to London's liberal set; he introduced the Binghams to his friend the Marquis of Lansdowne, and to Sir Francis Baring, a liberal member of Parliament and perhaps the country's greatest financier. Lansdowne had just resigned as prime minister of England, after bringing the war to a close with liberal territorial concessions in the Ohio valley, and continued to promote Anglo-American rapprochement. After Lansdowne read a pamphlet that Bingham penned in London outlining the features of a postwar commercial relationship (one that would largely come to pass a decade later with the Jay Treaty), the two struck up a friendship, and the Binghams became regular guests at Lansdowne's monumental house on Berkeley Square, probably the premier gathering place for London's Whig society. Before long, the Binghams had integrated themselves into the circles that encompassed leading members of Britain's liberal intelligentsia, important merchants like Baring, and prominent foreigners as well. It was an astonishingly cosmopolitan milieu: Lansdowne opened his doors to French liberal free-trade reformers in the 1780s, when figures like Honoré de Mirabeau visited London. They were heady times. It was the high-water mark of Franco-British comity, when liberal imaginations on both sides of the Channel were fired with dreams of European peace knit together by free trade and commercial prosperity.[29]

The ambitious William collected famous acquaintances with an eye to impressing his less-traveled American friends. "He will make you believe he was on the most intimate footing with the first characters in Europe and versed in the secrets of every cabinet," Jefferson warned James Madison after he had gotten to know the Binghams. William was particularly eager to meet royalty in Europe's capital cities. When the couple traveled to The Hague, John Adams reported that he "introduced them to the Princess of Orange." Shortly after his arrival in Paris, William went "flourishing out in the morning to accompany papa to Versailles," reported John Adams's daughter, "to be presented to his most Christian majesty, the King of France, with his four horses and three servants, all in the pomp of an American merchant." Bingham was disappointed that day—there was no court—but did not give up, and a few weeks later succeeded in seeing Louis XVI in the flesh. His "ambition promoted it," young Abigail Adams wryly remarked. "What it will promote him to I know not."[30]

William seems to have been quite blind to the ways that others perceived his too-naked ambition. In London, upon learning that etiquette would prevent him from being present at the Court of St. James's for the king's birthday, Bingham kicked up a fuss, writing to John Adams "that his anxiety was so great to pay his respects to the King that he begd he might be presented to day at the levee insted of Thursday at the drawing room," according to a report by Adams's daughter. "In this way it is that he forces

This miniature portrait of William Bingham, painted by Charles Willson Peale in the early 1780s, shows the successful young merchant a few years before his trip to Paris.

himself upon People—ridiculous being," she tartly concluded. Her opinion seems to have been widely shared. "He had a rage for being presented to great men and had no modesty in the methods by which he could effect it," Jefferson opined. "If he obtained access afterwards, it was with such as who were susceptible of impression from the beauty of his wife." William bragged about his successful access to Europe's elite—although he gave it a slightly different slant. "She has seen the best of company," he wrote to Thomas Willing, "which it was my pride and pleasure to have her introduced into." Looking back, one wonders whose ambition it was that drove William to such heights of indelicacy.[31]

Whatever political use he made of Anne, or she of him, William was clearly a doting husband. "If the world was universally as good as her," he wrote to Willing in a touching letter from London, "there would be no occasion for a Heaven hereafter, to reward the virtuous. I sincerely wish, that you may be equally blessed with all your children, and I am confident that you will be the happiest father in the Universe." His solicitous behavior continued throughout the trip, described by one witness as "delicately attentive." In June 1784 William wrote to inform the family that the couple would not be coming home that year. They had spent a year in Europe, but had yet to see Paris. Willing did not complain. "It was very natural for Nancy to wish to gratify her curiosity fully, by staying another year," he wrote back, referring to his daughter by her nickname. "She had cross'd the Ocean already, & had an indulgent friend in you, ready and able to gratify her—I am contented." In the middle of 1784, the Binghams traveled to the Netherlands and then to Paris, where they rented a suite of rooms at the Grand Hotel Muscovite, on the Quai des Augustins in the heart of Paris: the very hotel where the preliminary peace treaty between Britain and the United States had been signed in November 1782. Perhaps Jay had recommended it.[32]

VOLTAIRE ONCE called the *hôtels particuliers* of the Parisian nobility "*des écoles de politesse*"—schools of politeness. During the eighteenth century, gentlemen from England and the colonies were expected to conduct a "Grand Tour" through Europe, with France and Italy the most important sites, to round off the educations then offered at Oxford, Cambridge, and universities throughout the empire. As it had been for the French nobility under Louis XV and for the English aristocracy in the eighteenth century, so it would be for Anne Bingham in the 1780s: Paris's salons would serve as her school, teaching Bingham the refined manners that governed social life in Paris and shaped a nation's politics.[33]

If all of Europe looked to France with some awe as a model of refinement and polite manners, for former colonists from the far side of the Atlantic Ocean, France was particularly strange, exotic, and intimidating. "Their Manners are totally different from those of our own Country," Abigail Adams reported soon after arriving in Paris to join her husband. "It is a matter of great Speculation to me, when these People labour." This was a standard complaint about French society, then as now; and women figured prominently in the neo-Puritan critique of the French as a frivolous people. What it missed was the seriousness that lay just alongside the playfulness of salon life, and the possibilities it opened for elite women of the age. "The salon," as the historian Dena Goodman remarks, "was a socially acceptable substitute for the formal education denied" many aristocratic women. Almost immediately, Anne dedicated herself to learning the polite manners, the conversational skills, and the playful sociability of her new home. Soon after she arrived, Anne met Abigail (Nabby) Adams, daughter of Abigail and John, who had also just come to France. Abigail and Anne were nearly the same age: Abigail was nineteen and Anne twenty when the two met. Both were from American families thrust to great prominence by the Revolution, both preparing to launch careers as their famous relatives had—on the model of Abigail's eponymous mother and Anne's aunt Elizabeth Powel—and both were young and impressionable. And both became attentive students of the manners and behavior of Frenchwomen.[34]

"The women universally in this country, and the ladies of education in particular," Abigail wrote in her diary, "have an ease and softness in their manners, that is not found in any other country perhaps in the world." She repeatedly wondered at the remarkable qualities she found in French-women: "ease and affability, sprightliness, attention, and apparent solicitude to please." Taken together, these made "a real French girl." One day, she found herself seated next to Benjamin Franklin at dinner and raised the subject with him. "French manners," Franklin told her—and he had more experience with Frenchwomen than she, to say the least—"were to be gained no where but at Paris—that was the centre, and there they were all collected and resided." Abigail could not help but agree: "I believe he was here right; there is a something not to be defined, that the French women possess, which, when it ornaments and adorns an English lady, forms something irresistibly charming." These qualities, moreover, compared favorably with the manners of Americans. "I have often complained of a stiffness and reserve in our circles in America, that was disagreeable." What could be better than to import such codes of behavior and politeness to the new nation? "A little French ease adopted would be an improvement."[35]

Bingham was even more impressed. Frenchwomen, she wrote to Thomas Jefferson after her education in Paris, "are more accomplished, and understand the Intercourse of society better than in any other Country. We are irresistibly pleased with them, because they possess the happy Art of making us pleased with ourselves." These were qualities she was eager to learn. "The Arts of Elegance are there considered essential, and are carried to a state of Perfection; the Mind is continually gratified with the admiration of Works of Taste." It all resulted, as Anne saw it, from systematic training: "Their education is of a higher Cast, and by great cultivation they procure a happy variety of Genius, which forms their Conversation." What most impressed Anne were the political opportunities French sociability gave women. "The Women of France interfere in the political of the Country, and often give a decided Turn to the Fate of Empires," she observed. "Either by the gentle Arts of persuasion, or by the commanding force of superior Attractions and Address, they have obtained that Rank and Consideration in society, which the Sex are intitled to, and which they in vain contend for in other Countries. We are therefore bound in Gratitude to admire and revere them, for asserting our Privileges," she concluded, with a final poke at Jefferson: "as much as the Friends of the Liberties of Mankind reverence the successfull Struggles of the American Patriots." She was right to tweak Jefferson, who grumbled while he was in France about "the influence of women in the government." "The manners of the nation," he harrumphed in a 1788 letter to George Washington, "allow them to visit, alone, all persons in office, to sollicit the affairs of the husband, family, or friends, and their sollicitations bid defiance to laws and regulations." What Jefferson derided, Anne admired.[36]

Anne set about cultivating the talents and manners of Frenchwomen. "She loved the French," one Frenchman who later met her reported, "and told me one day that we could pass for the premier nation in spirit and gallantry." She and Abigail met occasionally in the months they spent in Paris, and Abigail's diary reads as a sort of progress report on Anne's *éducation de politesse*. Her ambitions had been laid even before she left Philadelphia; one witness had described Anne and William as engaged in "awkward imitation of the French." During her stay in France, Anne would work her way through that awkwardness. Progress was slow at first. "She has not been long enough in this country," wrote Abigail, shortly after the Binghams arrived, "to have gained that ease of air and manner which is peculiar to the women here." But clearly the raw materials were present. A few French liberals had already heard of her: the marquis de Chastellux had written of Anne's beauty in his *Voyages*, a text circulating in manuscript form in a few

Galleries and gardens of the Palais Royal, *Paris's most fashionable neighborhood in the last days of the* ancien régime.

Parisian salons. She had more than just physical beauty, however; Anne possessed social skills that, with a bit of study, might well turn her into a star of Paris society: "a most pleasing address, and a very happy turn of expression, with a good deal of politeness," as Abigail wrote a few days later, predicting, "She will not fail to please." Abigail watched with no little awe as Anne's social talents developed. "Mrs. B. gains my love and admiration, more and more every time I see her," she reported after dining with the Binghams in late October. "She is possessed of more ease and politeness of behaviour, than any person I have seen." And by this time, she had seen some of France's most eminent women.[37]

Sometime in late 1784 or early 1785, the Binghams moved from the Grand Hotel Muscovite to a set of apartments at the *Palais Royal*, the Parisian quarter recently refurbished by the duc d'Orléans. It was the heart of Paris's commerce, fashion, and high society: "Of all the promenades in Paris," one contemporary guide claimed, it was "the most celebrated and the most frequented." The *Palais Royal* complex was constructed around a series of long, narrow gardens, surrounded by colonnaded walkways and flanked by a vast array of shops: jewelers, tobacconists, dressmakers, clock merchants, drapers, furniture stores, perfumers, silk merchants, and many more, all of them importing the finest consumer goods from across Europe's growing empires. "Countless shops glittered treasures from around the world," wrote one Russian traveler, "riches from India and America, emeralds and diamonds, silver and gold; everything that Nature and Art have produced." Under the protection of the duc d'Orléans, the *Palais Royal* boasted four theaters, including an opera, museums where audiences heard lectures and attended readings, private clubs, lending libraries, and restaurants, all providing spaces of the most sophisticated and fashionable sociability and conversation in Paris. Its cafés were legendary: the café de Foy, the café Corazza, and the café Mécanique, where orders were submitted by acoustic tubes and the drinks served by automated dumbwaiters located within the columns that supported the tables. Buzzing with talk of politics, the cafés of the *Palais Royal* would, in a few years, be the site of intense revolutionary ferment. But for now, liberal politics dominated: with the Club de Valois holding its meetings, which included Talleyrand and Liancourt's cousin among its members, and which eventually evolved into the Société de 1789. It was above all these shops, theaters, and cafés—just above all this excitement and ferment—that the Binghams rented one of the elegant apartments that overlooked the colonnaded gardens.[38]

By January 1785, the Binghams had lived in Paris for slightly more than four months, and Anne had become adept at the most sophisticated forms of polite sociability. She was at home in the *Palais Royal* and known at Versailles as "la belle Américaine." "I was quite as much pleased with her as ever," wrote Adams when he next saw her, "and must confess that she has excellencies that overbalance every want of judgment, or that love for gay life, which is very conspicuous in her, but which I do not wonder at, at all. It is united with so many agreeable and amiable qualities, that it is impossible not to admire her."[39]

The pleasures for which Paris was so notorious fascinated Anne. In early February 1785, she attended a Carnival ball that began at one in the morning and lasted nearly until sunrise. The next day, she reported to Ab-

Abigail (Nabby) Adams, painted by Mather Brown in London in late July 1785, just a few months after she and Anne Bingham socialized together in Paris.

igail that she was "so delighted with Paris, that she says she shall never go to America with her own consent." Abigail, who was a New Englander in her bones, did not share her more exuberant friend's view of the city. Only a descendant of good Puritan stock could attend a play at the Comédie Française in the 1780s and conclude: "I am not fond of comedy in general; I had rather be improved than amused." As for Anne's increasingly gay lifestyle: "I confess I cannot form an idea of this disposition. She has, I believe, by this time, laid the foundation of a future life of unhappiness." The hard living was evidently taking its toll. A month later, Abigail reported—perhaps with a dose of wishful thinking—that "the bloom of the rose is fading—dissipation will blast the fairest flower that ever bloomed; in her it is verified; 'tis a pity so much delicacy and beauty should be sacrificed to a few weeks of pleasure." It is hard to know how accurate these reports were, however, and how much they merely reflected Abigail's prudishness. According to her brother, who agreed that Anne looked "very unwell," the problem was a toothache.[40]

By now, word was beginning to filter back to the United States about Anne's social life. "Her constant intercourse with the fashionable world," William warned his father-in-law with no little understatement, "may have polished her manners." Even Robert Morris, William's former patron and Willing's partner, who had extensive business dealings in France, had gotten wind of her growing love for Paris: "Dont suffer her to become so much attached to Europe as to neglect her native country," he gruffly warned from Philadelphia. Questions about the length of their stay were apparently causing tension between Anne and William. As the time for their return approached, William assured the Adamses that Anne "was perfectly sattisfied with going, indeed she would not stay if she were to follow her own wishes, that all her ideas were American." That does not appear to have been Anne's understanding, however. "This Morning we congratulated her upon, the change of her inclination from last year, but she, denied it all, and declared that necessity was her only motive." She was by all appearances being dragged back to Philadelphia.[41]

In April 1785 the couple left Paris to begin the last stage of their Grand Tour. June found them in Holland, where they again met John Adams, then negotiating an American loan. Adams reported that a "Supper was given, in a great Measure, for Mrs. Bingham." She was a hit. "Much Admiration expressed by all who had seen her, of her Beauty." The Spanish minister to Holland, who was also in attendance, remarked that "she would form herself at Paris." Adams replied "very quick but smiling"—and in his somewhat broken French—"J'espere qu'elle ne se formera a Paris qu'elle est deja formée." (I hope she won't form herself in Paris; that she is already formed.) Adams, like Jefferson, did not approve of Parisian women, or of the ways that European manners shaped their behavior—although, he acknowledged to the Princess of Orange, "there was something there [in Paris] for every Taste." He added in the margin of his diary: "Great Cities as Paris and

London were not good Schools for American young Ladies at present."
After leaving Holland, the Binghams traveled to Switzerland and Italy,
where, like so many other wealthy tourists, they visited the great Roman
ruins, wandering among the evocative traces of the ancient world, pondering the meaning of one empire's fall as a new one in the West began its
rise.[42]

By late 1785 they were back in London, where they spent the final
months of their remarkable European travels. Anne had mastered the
norms of courtly, polite society. As Abigail Adams (Nabby's mother) now
assessed, "Taken all together [she] is the finest woman I ever saw. The intelligence of her countanance, or rather I ought to say animation, the Elegance
of her form, and the affability of her Manners, converts you into admiration." As Anne showed off her talents to London society, the reviews began
pouring in. "Mrs B. is comeing quite into fashion here," young Abigail reported. "The Hair dresser who dresses us upon Court days, inquired of
Mamma whether she knew the Lady so much talkd of here from America—
Mrs Bingham. He had heard of her from a Lady who saw her at Lord Lu-
cans, where she was much admired." Abigail was herself dazzled by her
friend's glamour. "Madame B. shone away in all her splendor," she wrote to
her brother John Quincy after dining with her in London. "Her dress was
that she wore last Winter black and Pink, and I have not seen so elegant a
Woman, since I have been in England." So great was Nabby's fascination, it
drew amused remarks from witnesses. "A Gentlem[an] who sat next [to] me
at table Told me I was in Love with her. O it is true that I never see her
without admiration in the highest degree," Abigail rhapsodized.[43]

Finally, Bingham attended the Court of St. James's, where she was presented by Abigail Adams, playing her role as the wife of the American ambassador. Escorting Anne toward King George III and Queen Charlotte,
Adams "never saw any one so much stared at." Bingham was dressed in one
of the sumptuous gowns she'd bought in Paris and endowed with the per-
fected manners she'd acquired there. "She had prepaird herself in France
for this occasion," Adams wrote. "She is concequently handsomer than
ever." It was a triumph not just for Anne but for America. "I own I felt not

Anne Bingham, from a portrait by Gilbert Stuart.

a little proud of her. St James's did not, and could not produce an other so fine woman," Adams reported with some glee. "She Shone a Goddess, and She moved a Queen."[44]

Crowds gathered to stare. "The various whispers which I heard round me, and the pressing of the Ladies to get a sight of her, was really curious, and must have added an *attom* to the old *score*." People pushed forward to get a sight. "Is she an American, is she an American?" they asked. "Even the *Ladies* were *obliged to confess* that she was truly an elegant woman. You have, said an English Lord to me, but whose name I knew not, one of the finest Ladies to present, that I ever saw. The Emperers Ambassador Whisperd your Pappa, sir your Country produces exceeding fine women."[45]

A few weeks later, the Binghams returned to the United States.

IN 1786 Bingham returned with her husband to Philadelphia with plans for a new mansion in hand, a boatload of goods to furnish it, and the determination to re-create a Parisian salon in Philadelphia.

The Binghams had by now visited the great European capitals and seen Rome's ancient ruins. They had socialized in the neoclassical mansions of the pro-French liberal aristocracy in London and in the *hôtels particuliers* of the pro-British aristocracy in Paris. Having examined the best of Paris and London architecture, they chose as their model the Duke of Manchester's London mansion—the building that now houses the Wallace Collection—and, like the good Americans they were, had "the dimensions of the original . . . somewhat enlarged in the copy." An English architect drafted the plans while they were still in London. Construction began even before their return to Philadelphia and was completed in 1788. Three stories tall, containing an estimated eighteen thousand square feet of interior space, it was by far the largest house in Philadelphia. Like so many other people returning from their Grand Tours, the Binghams had learned to admire the neoclassical style, which prized straight lines and simplicity over the rococo forms in vogue earlier in the eighteenth century. Either directly or indirectly, the neoclassical was heavily influenced by Robert Adam, the great Scottish architect who designed many of the grand English houses of the period; indeed, the Binghams brought back stone ornamentation from the very same English mason who supplied Robert Adam. Endowed with Palladian touches, including a large Venetian window on the front, the Binghams' new mansion, concludes the historian Amy Henderson in her superb study of Philadelphia's material culture, "proclaimed their taste in neoclassicism and a preference for the delicate surface treatment of the Adam style."[46]

The grounds were equally remarkable. Stretching between Third and Fourth Streets on the east and west, Willing's Alley and Pine Street on the north and south, they extended over three acres, interspersed by walks, statuary, shade, and parterres, and were described by one English traveler as "in the best English style." The garden "abounds with the choicest fruit,

The mansion originally built for the Duke of Manchester in London, top, served as the model for the Binghams' Philadelphia mansion. The London house is painted here in the early nineteenth century, after the addition of a neoclassical portico in the front; before that addition, the two mansions would have been nearly identical. A visitor to the Wallace Collection, now housed in the London building, can get a sense of the grandeur of the Binghams' mansion, which burned in 1847 and was torn down.

perhaps unequalled here," stated a Philadelphia directory. "The green-house contains very nearly 500 exotic plants." It grew flowers throughout the year. Tubbed lemon and orange trees and other exotic plants grew in the greenhouse during cold weather, and were brought out to the gardens in the summer. But the greenhouse was only the beginning. "The building is finished in the most superb manner, and annexed to it is every convenience for a family, viz., an ice-house, milk-house, stables, &c." Two fawns given by a friend in South Carolina roamed the gardens. In the spring of 1796, an Englishman on his way home from India stopped to visit Philadel-phia and left the sheep he'd brought from India as well as a Santiapore cow grazing in the Binghams' gardens. The word spread, and Philadelphians came in "considerable numbers" to gawk at the exotic animals. That event was an exception, however; a large wooden fence usually kept local residents out, relegating them to peeking through knotholes to catch a glimpse of the splendid gardens.[47]

The mansion's interior was breathtaking. Gilbert Stuart's portrait of William Bingham gives some indication of its scale and its design, even as it suggests the importance of neoclassicism to the couple's aesthetic sensibility. The hallway in the background of this portrait, with its Corinthian pilasters, bas-reliefs, dentil molding, arched clerestory windows, and extensive use of marble, was said to have been drawn from the mansion's interior. To furnish these grand spaces the Binghams spared no expense, returning from their Grand Tour with a vast array of luxury goods. As a relative of Anne's later remembered, they "had brought from Europe every thing for the house and table which the taste and luxury of the times had invented." In France they bought carpets, textiles, Gobelin tapestry to drape their sofa, a 350-piece set of Sèvres china, 200 pieces of silver tableware, 206 drinking glasses, and busts of Voltaire, Rousseau, and Franklin, the greatest of France's Enlightenment heroes. In England they bought mirrors, armchairs, and fashionable Seddon chairs in the form of a lyre. A harpsichord and a pianoforte returned with them, of unknown provenance. Paintings and busts came from Italy. All of these objects went to furnish the house according to the most refined tastes. The furniture was, according to an English visitor, "elegant and even superb." The principal

William Bingham, painted by Gilbert Stuart in 1797, at the height of his wealth and fame. The setting for this portrait was said to be the interior of the Binghams' grand Philadelphia mansion.

rooms upstairs were adorned with painted ceilings, brilliant silk curtains, and French arabesque wallpaper by the famous Jean-Baptiste Réveillon in bright red, blue, yellow, and green. The parlor contained a sculptured fireplace, rugs, armchairs, and French Gobelin sofas. The Binghams also imported servants, including a butler, a gardener, a confectioner, and a French cook. The result was exactly what the couple intended. "In a word," wrote a Polish nobleman after visiting the mansion, "I thought myself in Europe."[48]

Anne was probably the guiding force driving the purchase of these luxury goods, as suggested by an amusing exchange with Thomas Jefferson, who was still in Paris when the Binghams began to furnish their mansion in Philadelphia. "Commission me to have you a Phaeton made," he playfully wrote to Anne a year after her return. "Shall I fill the box with caps, bonnets &c?" They were two peas in a pod, Jefferson and Anne: it is hard to know who loved shopping more. "They shall be chosen then by whom you please," he added, or "we will call an assembleé des Notables to help you out of the difficulty, as is now the fashion. In short, honour me with your commands of any kind, and they shall be faithfully executed." A few years later, as he was preparing to return to the United States, Jefferson wrote to William to warn him: "I have not yet been honored with the commands of Mrs. Bingham announced in your letter." Evidently the objects Anne selected and the means by which she displayed them served as the subject of much thought, correspondence, and conversation.[49]

These objects and this architecture were not merely intended to dazzle visitors; they had a very specific purpose: to promote a particular kind of elevated sociability. "I have never seen any private house more admirably adapted for the reception of company," a relative of Anne's later remembered. Like a Parisian *hôtel particulier* or a grand London mansion, the Binghams' house created a site in which Philadelphia's social, political, and intellectual elite could engage in polite conversation. A staircase of Italian marble wide enough for plants and flowers on either side curved up from the vestibule on the ground floor to the upstairs rooms, "into saloons decorated with goblin tapestry and reflecting mirrors." Downstairs was the dining room, "papered in the French taste," which followed the best practices of both French and English architecture by encouraging elevated conversation. Parisian salons in the last third of the eighteenth century often took place in dining rooms designed for extended sociability. The Scottish architect Adam similarly believed that "the eating rooms are considered as the apartments of conversation, in which we are to pass a great part of our time," and urged that they be "fitted up with elegance and splendor . . . finished with stucco, and adorned with statues and paintings." Was it in their grand dining room, as Adam suggested, that the Binghams displayed the busts of Franklin, Voltaire, and Rousseau that they brought back from France? Surely it was highly revealing that one foreign visitor took the time to note that "the food is served in silver dishes, the dessert on Sevres porcelain." Whether downstairs in the dining room or upstairs in the spectacu-

Lord Lansdowne's grand dining room, where Bingham socialized when he lived in London. This room, designed by the Scottish architect Robert Adam, is now in the Metropolitan Museum of Art.

lar drawing room, one can imagine the chatter at a Bingham dinner or tea party, as the French *constituants* mixed with the Philadelphia elite, re-creating the soft and easy conversation that Anne Bingham had so admired in France. Like the Lansdowne House in London's Berkeley Square, the Binghams' mansion would serve as the gathering place for eminent foreign travelers to meet prominent local figures. Just as Lansdowne's mansion had become a center for the French *constituants* when they took refuge in England, the Binghams' house now became one of their primary gathering places in the United States: "the meeting point," as one Frenchman recalled, "for all those who came to Philadelphia with a notable name."[50]

In surrounding themselves with grand European objects, refined portraiture, and magnificent neoclassical spaces for importing European forms of sociability, the Binghams created an exclusive space that posed particular challenges in a nation ostensibly dedicated to republican values.

"Wealth," Liancourt observed, "creates in Philadelphia more than else-where distinctions among the different classes of society." One of its primary functions was to erect class barriers, excluding those who could not afford the proper dress or had not learned the proper forms of behavior from European models. More than a few observers disapproved. The Quaker Ann Warder, for instance, called the Binghams' house "ungenteel"; it was certainly un-Quakerly. The French traveler and future revolutionary Jacques-Pierre Brissot, when he traveled in Philadelphia in the late 1780s, denounced Anne Bingham for contributing "more than anyone to promote the taste for luxury." For some, their excess turned the Binghams into subjects of mockery. In their "vanity and nonsense," snorted Arthur Lee of Virginia, "they are more fit subjects of ridicule than admiration." This criticism drew on older republican critiques of luxury that had long peppered assessments of elite salon life. One European visitor saw the Binghams' mansion as an assault on "the spirit of equality" that prevailed in the United States. The Binghams' house, he concluded, "attracts attention, criticism, and envy; and woe for the country if it ceases to astonish." (On the other hand, the always dyspeptic William Maclay, who saw monarchical plots everywhere, and even criticized Washington's levees, praised the Bingham house: "There is a propriety a neatness a Cleanliness that adds to the Splendor of his costly furniture, and elegant Apartments.")[51]

For still others, the mansion stood as a monument to the ill-gotten gains of Bingham's war profiteering, and revealed the ways in which the Revolution had benefited the rich while leaving so many others behind. One satirical poem circulated about the Bingham house, with angry references to Bingham's rise as Robert Morris's agent in Martinique during the war, from which both had profited so handsomely:

Tho' to thy mansion wits and fops repair,
    To game, to feast, to flatter and to stare.
But say, from what bright deeds dost thou derive
    That wealth which bids thee rival British Clive?
Wrung from the hardy sons of toil and war,
    By arts, which petty scoundrels would abhor.[52]

GILBERT STUART's portrait of William Bingham reveals a merchant at the height of his power and wealth: dressed in a rich, black velvet suit, standing at the entrance hall of a glorious mansion, and resting his hand on a table covered with books and papers. Painted by the most sought-after artist of the time at a probable cost of $250, the portrait itself marked Bingham not just as a member of the American elite but also as a member of a well-integrated transatlantic salon culture.[53]

By the mid-1790s, the Binghams had known Stuart for more than a decade. They first met when the Binghams rented a house in London in 1783; the American-born Stuart, who had gone to England to train at Benjamin West's studio, began a family portrait. Stuart also painted John Jay's portrait after he returned from negotiating the Treaty of Paris: Jay had intended to give it to Anne and William as a gift for their hospitality, but it was left incomplete until the 1790s. Having risen to prominence in Great Britain, Stuart returned to the United States in March 1793, arriving in New York just two months before Noailles landed in Philadelphia, with the express purpose of painting the famous president: "There I expect to make a fortune by Washington alone," he crowed. Stuart moved to Philadelphia in November 1794, armed with a letter of introduction that Jay wrote on his behalf before leaving for England to seek a diplomatic rapprochement with England.[54]

Stuart's first portrait of Washington has probably disappeared. A replica, however, was commissioned by the merchant John Vaughan, brother of Benjamin Vaughan—the diplomat and politician who had introduced the Binghams to the Marquis of Lansdowne in London a decade earlier, and who wrote several letters of introduction for Talleyrand when he came to the United States. Today, it is known as the Vaughan Portrait. William Bingham, too, commissioned a replica, which he hung in his mansion and which now sits in the collections of the Winterthur Museum in Delaware. Stuart's portraits so impressed Martha Washington that she commissioned a second type—the iconic and forever unfinished Athenaeum portrait, whose head now stares out from the dollar bill.[55]

Gilbert Stuart, George Washington *(the Vaughan type), 1795.*

Then in early 1796, Stuart received a commission for a third type of Washington portrait, a full-length for the Marquis of Lansdowne. The Binghams insisted on paying the cost ($1,000) and making it their gift to the pro-American lord who had done so much to support the cause of Anglo-American rapprochement. It would be a token of their friendship for Lansdowne, and also of their membership in the most exalted circles of European society. "Mrs. Bingham who received many attentions from Lord Lansdowne when in England has determined to make his Lordship a present of a very fine full length portrait of the President," wrote Alexander Baring to his father, Sir Francis, who had known the Binghams at Lansdowne's mansion a decade earlier. Thanks to Anne's intervention, Stuart succeeded in persuading Washington—who was tired of painters and their constant requests—to sit one more time. Evidently Anne's charms could outmatch even the most stubborn resistance. "Sir," Washington wrote Stuart in April 1796, "I am under promise to Mrs. Bingham, to sit for you tomorrow at nine oclock." It would be Stuart's last sitting with his famous subject, made possible only by Anne's importuning. "It is notorious," Washington's adopted grandson later recalled, that "it was only by hard begging that Mrs. Bingham obtained the sittings for the marquis of Lansdowne's picture."[56]

The Lansdowne portrait would become one of the most famous paintings in the history of American art. It depicted Washington as king of the Republican court, dressed in the clothes he wore to his levees, with a sword at his side, and his right arm stretched out in an oratorical pose as though addressing an audience. On the table covered with red drapery are two books: the *Federalist Papers* and the *Journals of Congress,* both of them meant to remind audiences of Washington's role in forging the nation's Constitution, which is the label on the spine of a richly bound book resting under the table. He had guided the country through the stormy years of his presidency, as the world collapsed into apocalyptic warfare, without sacrificing its republican character. The clouds are now glowing behind him. A rainbow appears. The future of his nation looks bright. "It is the strongest likeness I ever saw and painted by Stewart," Baring reported to his father, before asking for the legendary banker's help in facilitating the painting's international transit. "Pray assist him in having it got through the Custom House and presented at Lansd[owne] house where I am sure it will be a welcome guest."[57]

Baring was right: Lansdowne was delighted with the result. "I have received the picture, which is in every respect worthy of the original," the marquis wrote to William Jackson, Anne's brother-in-law, a few months later. "I consider it as a very magnificent compliment, and the respect I have for both Mr. and Mrs. Bingham will always enhance the value of it to me and my family. I have just had the honor of writing to Mrs. Bingham my acknowledgments." Lansdowne probably hung the portrait in the library of his mansion, a long, grand room with domes at both ends originally designed by Adam to serve as a statue gallery, where it could be seen

Gilbert Stuart, George Washington
(the Lansdowne portrait), 1796.

alongside "exquisite statues" of ancient figures, including Cincinnatus, as
well as a portrait by Rubens, a landscape by Poussin, and busts of Oliver
Cromwell and Isaac Newton, among figures ancient and modern. The portrait garnered rave reviews as Lansdowne's friends and acquaintances came
to admire both the artist and the subject. Lansdowne wrote to Anne that
Stuart's painting "is universally approv'd and admire'd, and I see with satisfaction that there is no one who does not turn away from every thing else,
to pay their homage to General Washington." By that time, the president
had retired from office, perhaps the grandest sign of his republican virtue.
"General Washington's conduct is above all praise," Lansdowne added. "If
I was not too old, I would go to Virginia to do him homage."[58]

The library gallery of the Lansdowne House, where it is likely that Washington's portrait was first displayed, from a photograph taken in 1921.

Lansdowne did not go to Virginia, but he nevertheless paid tribute to the former president in England by hanging Stuart's portrait in his mansion, just as the Binghams hosted the real Washington in theirs. This was an ironic mimicry: the Binghams had self-consciously modeled their home on Lansdowne's, as both a physical space and a social space, seeking to emulate the polished sociability of the liberal European aristocracy. And yet here was a European aristocrat displaying America's greatest republican icon in London! All the symbolism of the republican statecraft Washington had forged was now ensconced in the bosom of one of Europe's most refined aristocratic houses. Philadelphia's Republican Court had extended its fingers all the way back to London. In recognizing the personal relationship that connected the Philadelphia-London hosts, Lansdowne must have gratified the Binghams' deepest yearnings: "Among many circumstances which contribute to enhance the value of it, I shall always consider the quarter from whence it comes as most flattering, & I look forward with the greatest pleasure to the time of shewing you and Mr. Bingham where I have plac'd it."[59]

By this time, William Bingham had already commissioned a replica from Stuart. In the summer of 1797, one visitor managed to see the replica in Stuart's studio, gaining access thanks to a letter of introduction from Noailles, "who was intimate with him & for whom Stewart entertained a great respect." Inside, the traveler found "the first copy he [Stuart] had made of the celebrated full length which he had painted for Mrs. Bingham intended as a present to the Marquis of Lansdown. . . . This copy was for Mr Binghams own use." Bingham's copy of the Washington portrait hung in his country house outside Philadelphia—the Italian-style mansion on a two-hundred-acre estate known as Lansdown, formerly owned by the Penn family—as the original hung in Lansdowne's London mansion. Thus did the two Washingtons stare down at the guests of the transatlantic salon culture, just as the real Washington had presided in his public levees, often dressed in the same kind of outfit he wore in the paintings, complete with a ceremonial sword.[60]

The Lansdowne portrait opens a window into the political and even diplomatic influence of the culture of liberal transatlantic salons. The portrait was painted by Stuart in the wake of the 1794 Jay Treaty, as the United States was engaged in its controversial postwar rapprochement with Great Britain. Washington had staked all his political clout on pushing the treaty through the Senate, at great cost to his reputation and to the Franco-American alliance. The portrait itself—a picture of the American head of state, given as a gift to a former British head of state—may well fall into the tradition of diplomatic exchange that followed the signature of treaties of peace and alliance. Certainly the commission from the Binghams as a gift to Lansdowne suggests as much, since the two men first became friends by their shared commitment to Anglo-American trade and cooperation, as articulated in William Bingham's 1784 pamphlet on the subject, which in many ways sketched the outlines of the relationship forged in the 1794 Jay Treaty. One British newspaper understood the portrait this way, claiming that the painting hanging in Lansdowne's mansion symbolized "the inviolable union between America and Great Britain." Lansdowne had served as the British prime minister who oversaw the negotiations ending the

Revolution; it was he who was responsible for the treaty's generous settlement, and in particular its cession of the Ohio valley to the United States, which aimed to detach the United States from a French diplomatic orbit and establish the basis for a postwar Anglo-American relationship. But its generous terms had permanently cost Lansdowne his political reputation, as well as his post as prime minister. Lansdowne had reminded Washington of these details in a 1791 letter introducing his son, who visited the president in Mount Vernon: "I had the good Fortune to have it in my power to be of some little use in fixing the Boundary between the respective Dominions in a manner," Lansdowne wrote, "which tho' not desir'd by the Alliance must I trust and hope in the end lay the Foundation of cordial Friendship and good understanding." Washington needed no reminder. "This Country has a grateful recollection of the agency your Lordship had in settling the dispute between Great Britain and it," he wrote to Lansdowne after his son's visit, "and fixing the boundary between them."[61]

But it was not just an Anglo-American world of politics, statecraft, and sociability portrayed here; various elements of the Lansdowne portrait symbolized the subtle French influence on this transatlantic salon culture. The portrait's setting—with the neoclassical column, the windswept curtains, and the sky in the background—was copied almost exactly from a French engraving of a seventeenth-century French bishop and another of King Louis XVI; it stands, in this regard, as a pictorial repository of French sources. In keeping with the paradoxical notion of a Republican Court, the Lansdowne portrait combined the French tradition of monarchical portraiture with newer American republican conventions. The sword Washington wears on his hip in Stuart's version is a dress sword rather than a military one. Like so many other elements in the painting—the books on the table, the black velvet suit to signify Washington's civilian rather than military dress—the sword symbolizes the republican character of America's politics, and the supremacy of civilian authority at a highly charged time when Washington had just announced his resignation from the presidency. And this was not just any sword. According to Stuart's daughter, the painter "wanted to introduce a dress-sword, and the Comte de Noailles

Left: Jacques-Bénigne Bossuet *by Hyacinthe Rigaud; right:* Louis XVI *by Antoine-François Callet, both of them models for Gilbert Stuart's Lansdowne portrait.*

kindly furnished a superb silver-mounted rapier, which he brought himself, and presented it to Stuart, saying that it might be useful in painting other portraits of Washington."[62]

Various rumors have since circulated that Noailles, who was friends with Stuart, became even more integral to a later variant of the Lansdowne portrait. According to Washington's grandson, in the original portrait and its replica in the Bingham mansion, Stuart had done a remarkable job in portraying Washington's head, but as for the body, the artist "failed entirely." The president himself sat for the head, but Stuart's model for the body turned out to be too short and fleshy, all out of proportion to the face. Its pose, moreover, lacked Washington's physical grace. That is why, for another version of the portrait, Stuart found a different model: a more elegant and polished one than the stubbier figure he'd used for the original portrait, one who was familiar with the most refined swordsman's poses and gentlemanly stances. That model was none other than Noailles—one of the finest dancers at Marie-Antoinette's court. "That the Viscount de

Gilbert Stuart, George Washington
(the Munro-Lenox portrait), circa 1800.

Noailles actually stood as model seems proven by the pose," writes the art historian Gustavus Eisen. "It is the first or preliminary [fencing] pose immediately before the defensive guard, according to the French school." A descendant of Bingham's agreed. The evidence, she wrote, "was conclusive." The sword and body in this version were Noailles'. Only the head was Washington's.[63]

In this age before photography, having one's picture taken meant having an artist paint or draw a portrait. Portraits were among the most important vehicles for preserving familial and indeed national memories. "Our Children may like to look upon our Likeness when the originals are no more seen," Abigail Adams once wrote to her son about the portrait

Stuart painted of her. And so it is highly symbolic that the likeness upon which millions of Americans would look as they imagined the father of their country was set in a French portrait painting, featuring the body of a French liberal aristocrat wearing a French sword: a perfect representation, if one were needed, of the hybrid nature of this transatlantic liberal salon culture.[64]

THESE WERE the spaces of elite sociability, where Franco-American Atlantic networks materialized. They were not public spaces, but they were not exactly private, either. They were very clearly demarcated by their class associations—they distinguished the elite from everyone else—but beyond that, they functioned as spaces where the political and the private overlapped. And in these spaces, Philadelphia's elite women took on the primary roles.

Anne Bingham had returned from France inspired by the ways that women's sociability influenced that country's politics. Back in the United States, she set about creating the institutions she had found there. She organized *soirées* every week, "which," according to one French visitor, "the beautiful youth attended and where there was frequent dancing." As Bingham clearly realized, polite forms of sociability opened spaces for elite women to participate in political and intellectual life. "What distinguished France from other nations was its extreme sociability," writes the historian Dena Goodman; "what distinguished French sociability from its English form in particular was the role women played in it." French theorists viewed their country as the most civilized because it was the most sociable and the most polite. The greatest of *salonnières,* such as Marie-Thérèse Geoffrin, Julie de Lespinasse, Marie du Deffand, and Suzanne Necker—in whose domains men such as Talleyrand, Noailles, Lafayette, and Liancourt discussed politics, modern philosophy, literature, and more—governed their salons as mini-republics. "The Ladies [in France] are, in a Manner, the Sovereigns of the *learned* World, as well as of the *conversible,*" David Hume had observed in 1742, "and no polite Writer pretends to venture upon the Public without the Approbation of some celebrated Judges of that Sex."

The ideal salon hostess was the linchpin of civility, culture, politics, and refinement—indeed, of the Enlightenment itself. In this world, "society," as Voltaire succinctly put it, "depends on women."[65]

With her manners polished in the salons of Paris and displayed in the physical spaces she had designed, Anne Bingham re-created the French salon in Philadelphia. Like the greatest French *salonnières*, she possessed all the qualities necessary to launch herself "unquestionably"—according to Rufus Griswold, a chronicler of the Republican Court—"at the head of American society." Her beauty was legendary, spoken of in London and Paris, written about in the marquis de Chastellux's now-published travel account, and seen every day on the streets of Philadelphia. "Her manners were a gift," Griswold rhapsodized. She has "copied the tone and carriage of a European lady," wrote a Polish exile. Visitors to her salon would later remember her "conversational cleverness in French and English, graceful manners and polite tact." She was widely renowned for "a combination of expression, grace and figure. . . . She was not witty, but bright, always at ease and kind and courteous to all." She was a masterful conversationalist, making each person the center of her attention. "She joins in every conversation in company; and when engaged herself in conversing with you, she will, by joining directly in another chit chat with another party, convince you, that she was all attention to every one." All who knew her testified to her social graces. "Mrs Bingham stood above competition in her day," recalled one prominent Philadelphian many years later. "Nor has any one of equal refinement in address, or social stateliness, and graceful superintendance of a splendid establishment, been produced since in any Circle of our City." When Abigail Adams, now the vice president's wife, saw Anne again in Philadelphia, she took pleasure in reacquainting herself with "the dazzling Mrs. Bingham," and testified to her role in the capital's social life: "Mrs. Bingham has certainly given the laws to the ladies here, in fashion and elegance; their manners and appearance are superior to what I have seen." Clearly she reigned in Philadelphia's most fashionable circles.[66]

It is no coincidence that these descriptions bore striking similarities to those of the greatest of the French *salonnières*. Like them, Anne created a space for elite women to participate in the nation's politics. "I Yesterday

The portrait of Anne Bingham on the left, with her finger marking the page of a book, emphasizes her intellectual curiosity. The portrait on the right suggests a more pastoral Bingham; it was painted by William Russell Birch, whose first work in Philadelphia was this portrait commissioned by William Bingham. Birch also gave drawing lessons to the Bingham daughters.

dined at Mr Binghams and Sitting next to Madam at Table, had Something like a political Conversation with her," John Adams wrote to his wife in a tone of amused condescension. "She has more ideas of the Subject than I Suspected: and a corrector Judgment." By shaping Philadelphia society, Bingham facilitated—or forestalled—the sorts of diplomatic and political conversation that so frequently took place in these polite spaces. One Frenchman who received an invitation to Anne's weekly *soirées* was quickly congratulated on his success and informed it would make him "promptly known to *le monde*." Such references to *"le monde"*—or *"l'univers,"* by which Liancourt referred to Bingham's dinner guests—helped to define the contours of a certain kind of politics in the early Republic.[67]

But Anne's social world was not just earnest and serious; it was as playful and flirtatious as that of the great French salons. Her playfulness was most evident in her wardrobe. Her dresses, many of them imported from Paris, were legendary. "She blaz'd upon a large party at Mr. Morris's in a

In this Gilbert Stuart portrait, Anne Bingham holds a copy of Volney's Voyage en Syrie et en Egypte. *Volney was a regular guest at the Binghams' dinner parties and gave French lessons to the Bingham daughters.*

dress which eclips'd any that has yet been seen," wrote one contemporary. "A Robe a la Turke of black Velvet, Rich White Sattin Peticoat, body and sleeves . . . Her Head ornamented with Diamond Sprigs interspers'd with artificial flowers, above all, wav'd a towering plume of snow white feathers. Can you imagine a dress more strikingly beautiful?" Even when they were offended by Bingham's outfits, visitors could not help noticing them. "Mrs. Bingham is a very elegant woman who dresses at the height of fashion," wrote John Marshall, the legendary chief justice of the Supreme Court, when he saw her in 1797. "I do not however like that fashion. The sleeve [does] not reach the elbow or the glove come quite to it. There is a vacancy of three or four inches & just [above] the naked elbow is a good clasp." Marshall's description of her dress bears a striking resemblance to the clothing in her portrait by Gilbert Stuart. Whether Stuart's portrait was a faithful guide to the original, or a statement by Bingham about how she wanted to be perceived, the result highlighted her direct, fearless gaze, the luxuriant style of her hair, the low-cut neckline flirtatiously revealing her *décolletage,* and the plush, even sensual, velvet of her robe.[68]

Stuart's portrait did more than portray a woman driving Philadelphia fashion; it also emphasized Anne's intellectual curiosity: the book she holds in her hands, one finger marking a page, is Volney's *Voyage en Syrie et en Egypte,* in its original French. If his portrait emphasized Bingham's interest in literature—and in neoclassical dress—that was in keeping with her interest in and promotion of the arts in Philadelphia. Like her aunt Elizabeth Willing Powel, Bingham actively involved herself in the intellectual life of Philadelphia. She took a keen interest in the Chestnut Street Theatre and served as patron to the Anglo-American actress, author, and educator Susanna Rowson, who promoted a greater role for women in early American letters and culture. In gratitude for Bingham's patronage, Rowson dedicated her first American novel to the Philadelphia *salonnière.* "Under the protecting sanction of your name," she wrote, "I do not fear its meeting a favorable reception from the public in general. For however trifling its merits, your patronage will stamp a value on it, and raise it into that consequence, it otherwise could never attain."[69]

Anne's entertainment was in keeping with her style and ambition. Reporting on one memorable *soirée,* Rebecca Lowndes Stoddert, the navy secretary's wife, described arriving at the Binghams' at about 7:30 in the evening, to find Anne seated "at the head of the drawing-room" to the side of the chimney: carefully positioned to establish her as the evening's presiding authority, much as the French *salonnières* governed their realms. Around 9:00, however, the rigid order began to soften. Dancing began. Punch and lemonade started circulating soon after, followed by "the best ice-cream, as well as the prettiest, that I ever saw . . . carried around in beautiful china cups and gilt spoons." Supper was served around 11:00. "In the middle was an orange-tree with ripe fruit; and where a common spectator might imagine the root was covered with evergreens, some natural and some artificial flowers. . . . The girondole, which hangs immediately over the table, was let down just to reach the top of the tree. You can't think how beautiful it looked. . . . The only meats I saw or heard of were a turkey,

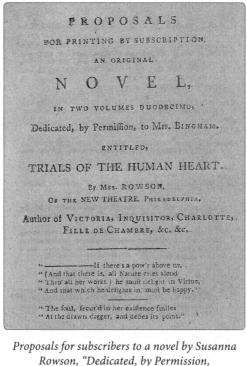

PROPOSALS

FOR PRINTING BY SUBSCRIPTION,

AN ORIGINAL

N O V E L,

IN TWO VOLUMES DUODECIMO,

Dedicated, by Permiſſion, to Mrs. BINGHAM,

ENTITLED,

TRIALS OF THE HUMAN HEART.

By Mrs. ROWSON,

OF THE NEW THEATRE, PHILADELPHIA,

Author of VICTORIA, INQUISITOR, CHARLOTTE,
FILLE DE CHAMBRE, &c. &c.

———————If there's a pow'r above us,
"(And that there is, all Nature cries aloud
"Thro' all her works,) he muſt delight in Virtue,
"And that which he delights in, muſt be happy,"

"The ſoul, ſecur'd in her exiſtence ſmiles
"At the drawn dagger, and defies its point."

*Proposals for subscribers to a novel by Susanna
Rowson, "Dedicated, by Permission,
to Mrs. Bingham."*

fowls, pheasants, and tongues, the latter the best that I ever tasted, which was the only meat I ate. The dessert (all was on the table) consisted of everything that one could conceive of. . . . I never ate better. . . . Near me were three different sorts of cake; I tasted all, but could eat of only one." When Stoddert left at midnight, the party was still going. The noise of music, laughter, and the clinking of French porcelain gradually faded as she made her way home through the dark streets, with the night watchmen's doleful cries echoing on the cobblestone.[70]

ANNE BINGHAM was not the only "node" in the dense social network connecting elite French and American life. Hot on the Binghams' heels were Robert and Mary Morris. Born in England in 1734, Robert Morris had launched his career in the Willing firm, then run by Thomas Willing's

Robert Morris *by Charles Willson Peale, and* Mary Morris *by John Singleton Copley.*

father, Charles. In 1757 Thomas and Robert established the firm of Willing and Morris, developing a rich web of mercantile connections in Britain, Spain, and the West Indies. Morris signed the Declaration of Independence, and his wealth soared during the war, thanks in part to his role on Congress's Secret Committee of Trade, through which his firm secured lucrative contracts to supply the American insurgency. But the relationship was not one-sided; later, during the nadir of U.S. finances, Morris's credit was so great that he used it to shore up the nation's finances! As superintendent of finance in the 1780s, Morris guided the nation through that difficult period, and was in large part responsible for inventing the financial system that Hamilton would later implement. During the 1780s Morris ex-

This image graphically represents the social networks that linked the French émigrés to the American political and economic elite. Letters of introduction and transatlantic friendships served as the means by which the émigrés established American connections that led to social, financial, and diplomatic opportunities. By their extensive social connections, Anne and William Bingham lay at the center of this elaborate web. Other figures, like Théophile Cazenove and Alexander Baring, who moved back and forth between Europe and the United States, also played critical roles.

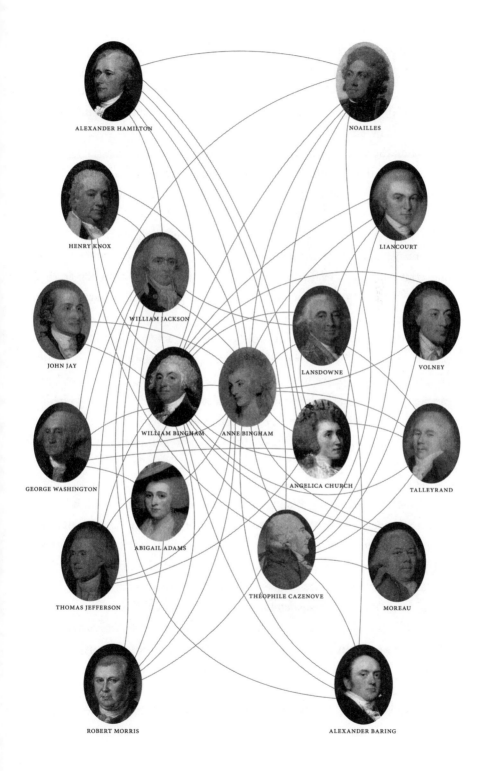

ALEXANDER HAMILTON

NOAILLES

HENRY KNOX

LIANCOURT

WILLIAM JACKSON

JOHN JAY

LANSDOWNE

VOLNEY

WILLIAM BINGHAM   ANNE BINGHAM

GEORGE WASHINGTON

ANGELICA CHURCH

TALLEYRAND

ABIGAIL ADAMS

THÉOPHILE CAZENOVE

THOMAS JEFFERSON

MOREAU

ROBERT MORRIS

ALEXANDER BARING

tended his commercial relations with French merchants; his firm secured the contract to supply Chesapeake tobacco to the Farmers General of France in what was alleged to have been the largest private contract ever signed in the *ancien régime*. By the 1790s Morris had left government service and was focusing his energies on land speculation.[71]

When the U.S. capital moved from New York to Philadelphia, the Morrises took on their exalted roles in Philadelphia society. They rented their house to George Washington—making it the presidential mansion—and moved just next door. It is hard to imagine better-located social real estate. Mary Morris was among the ablest hostesses of Philadelphia society, "suited in all respects for the centre of the fashionable circle in which she moved," one contemporary recalled. "No badly-cooked or cold dinners at their table; no pinched fires upon their hearths; no paucity of waiters; no awkward loons in their drawing-rooms." The Washingtons were frequent visitors at the Morrises' house, adding an extra touch of glamour to Mary Morris's salons. The Morrises, too, socialized regularly with the French émigrés, though the reports were not always favorable. Talleyrand had mocked Robert's hat, while Liancourt called Mary a "*femme à présentation,* without spirit, who imagines herself queen of America because she is in a beautiful salon, she has a beautiful dress, and her husband . . . is building her a beautiful house."[72]

These women—and to the list one would add Angelica Church, daughter of the Revolutionary War general and wealthy New York landowner Philip Schuyler, who provided introductions for Talleyrand, Liancourt, and other French émigrés from London—all had several features in common. All were possessed of great fortunes and numbered among the wealthiest families in the United States. All had extensive kinship connections throughout Philadelphia society, with links to elite families across the United States and, in some cases, across the Atlantic. Stemming from these nodes were extraordinarily elaborate networks, composed of overlapping social, political, familial, and economic ties. Anne Bingham's vast kinship network extended through much of Philadelphia society and even, through her uncle William Byrd, to the Virginia aristocracy. She was the daughter of Thomas Willing, the most respected of Philadelphia's merchants and the president of the First Bank of the United States, who was in business with Robert Morris and her husband. Robert Morris's wife, Mary, was the sister of Bishop William White, head of the recently formed Episcopal Church and a frequent guest at elite Philadelphia's teas and salons; it was he who had married Anne and William Bingham. One of Anne Bingham's aunts was Elizabeth Powel, the famed hostess whose house remains preserved to this day in Philadelphia, whose husband had served as mayor of the city, and who was described by the marquis de Chastellux as *"la prima figura,* as the Italians say." "What most characterizes her," he reported, "is the taste she has for conversation, & the genuinely European use she makes of her spirit & her knowledge." But Powel was appreciated not only by French aristocrats; Benjamin Rush dedicated his *Thoughts upon Female Education* to her.[73]

"GENTEEL BEHAVIOR," writes the historian Richard Bushman, "always reflected the belief that somewhere a glorious circle existed where life was lived at the highest and best, where fashions were set, where true gentility was achieved, where perfect harmony, grace, and beauty could be found." The allure of this mythical world only grew with the ruptures of the French Revolution, adding a temporal dimension to the ideal of perfect gentility, permanently separating the *ancien régime* from the modern present. "Celui qui n'a pas vécu avant 1789 ne connaît pas la douceur de vivre," Talleyrand would one day quip (He who did not live before 1789 does not know the gentle way of life). The remark captured the powerful lure of an imaginary, lost world, that glorious circle somewhere out there, where true harmony, grace, and beauty had existed in all their magnificence. Some Americans, like the Binghams, had traveled to that place and could report back on its wonders. Hard as they worked to build a replica, it nevertheless remained an imitation: just the play of shadows on a wall.[74]

Now, suddenly, this place no longer needed to be imagined: it materialized in Philadelphia salons, in the form of these Frenchmen descended from the summit of French nobility. They were as conversant with the social norms of Versailles court life as they were with the sparkling conversation in the most legendary Parisian salons. It took little time for them to be incorporated into the webs spun by the likes of Anne Bingham and Mary Morris. The émigré *constituants* found themselves entering Philadelphia's refined social spaces, which were adorned with French furniture and wallpaper, and peopled by women dressed in the latest French fashion who expressed themselves in the soft and gentle notes of French sociability. It was as though the set had been created for them.

True gentility now emerged from the shadow world to come into full view. For Philadelphians, it seemed almost like a dream. "Yesterday Philadelphia was honored with nothing less than the arrival of a *Prince*," exulted Lucy Breck, the daughter of a Philadelphian with extensive French connections, upon hearing that the duc d'Orléans had arrived. "[I] am in hourly expectation of a visit from this great personage. Are you not surprised that I write with *so much composure!*" The French aristocrats were bombarded with invitations to teas, suppers, dinners, balls—any social event where they could spice up an evening. Philadelphians "fawn over" Talleyrand and Beaumetz, wrote Liancourt. They were, the French minister in Philadelphia reported, met by Hamilton and "fêted, introduced to his friends; they are invited to dinner at all the houses *comme il faut*." As for Liancourt, he was "fêted, caressed by what is called *la bonne Société*." Lucy Breck's brother recalled seeing "assembled at my father's of an evening in a social way, the 3 princes of Orléans, Talleyrand and his inseparable companion, Beaumetz, Volney and I think the duke of Liancourt; together with many other distinguished emigrant French noblemen." The *constituants* were poised to enchant Philadelphia society, letting elite Philadelphians, however briefly, connect their provincial salons and teas to the glitter of European aristocracy.[75]

The émigrés all orbited around the Bingham mansion. Liancourt regularly attended the Binghams' dinners and teas; his diary is littered with references to their gatherings. Volney was at their house even more frequently, tutoring the Bingham daughters in French. Having a famous Enlightenment philosopher give their daughters private lessons was not just a feather in the Binghams' cap; it also spiced up the conversations at Anne's social gatherings, just as figures like Montesquieu had done with Claudine-

Alexandrine Guérin de Tencin's salons in Paris a half century earlier. As for Volney, he earned "liberal pay [that] contributed materially towards his support." When the Binghams spent the summer at their house outside Philadelphia, Volney lived nearby in Germantown and "used to walk over daily to Landsdown where he taught Mr Bingham's daughters French." He must have taught the daughters well: one witness who spent several days with the Bingham daughters in 1797 reported that "French is almost as natural a language to them as their mother tongue."[76]

But no one was a more familiar presence at the Binghams' than Noailles. Noailles lived inside the Bingham compound, entertaining guests in his third-story room at the end of the garden, borrowing the servants when necessary to have his food prepared in their backyard kitchen. When Thomas Twining, the great-grandson of the tea company's founder, arrived in Philadelphia in April 1796 on his way home from India, he found at the Binghams' "a large party. Besides Mr. and Mrs. Bingham and their two daughters, were Count de Noailles, Count Tilley, Mr. Alexander Baring and others." A few days later Twining returned to the Binghams' for tea,

Lansdown, the Binghams' country house, painted by William Birch.

where he again found Noailles, along with Baring, several senators and congressmen, and "the celebrated Monsr. Volney," who peppered him with questions about India. Noailles became particularly close with Anne. On one occasion, when a young French traveler met Noailles at a Philadelphia ball, the former vicomte encouraged the new arrival to "assiduously follow *madame* Beng[ham]'s society, which he much frequented himself." So much of a part of the family did Noailles become, he casually invited guests to Lansdown, the Bingham country mansion. He also accompanied the Bingham family when they traveled up the East Coast, through Boston, to the Knoxes' grand country mansion, named Montpelier, in Thomaston, Maine, where they were lavishly entertained.[77]

As they penetrated the most intimate social circles of elite Philadelphia, the émigrés charmed their hosts with their courtly French manners, establishing the ideal standards of behavior. There could be few better teachers. Talleyrand, a favorite among the highest ranks of French writers and poets, was possessed of legendary social talents. "Attempts to arm oneself against his faults were in vain," La Tour du Pin wrote about Talleyrand. "His charm always penetrated the armour and left one like a bird fascinated by a serpent's gaze." The dashing duc de Noailles had been Marie-Antoinette's frequent dance partner at Versailles balls—"no amateur in Paris danced so perfectly as he did"—and taught the young Bingham daughters the latest dance steps. Louis-Philippe, duc d'Orléans, now in the line of succession to the French throne, had been tutored by the greatest Enlightenment educator, Madame de Genlis, whose books were read around the Atlantic world and served as the basis for new pedagogical systems in France, Great Britain, and North America.[78]

And what manners they had! One Pennsylvanian later recalled Omer Talon traveling through his town and vividly described his demeanor, which lived up to his idea of French aristocracy: "I have seldom seen a gentleman with whose manners I was more pleased." As for Noailles, he was "remarkable for his figure, his height, and his noble air." To Philadelphians, he may as well have been Lord Chesterfield himself: his "form was perfect; a fine face; tall, graceful, the first amateur dancer of the age, and possessed of very pleasing manners, he was a general favorite." True, not all the French émigrés measured up. Louis-Philippe left the excitable Lucy Breck "extremely disappointed in his person," lacking "that commanding dignity—or even ease of manner—which is generally looked for (and I believe very frequently sought in vain) in so distinguished a rank." Still, Breck admitted that he had certain charms. "There was however a degree of modesty—united with the appearance of a good understanding—discovered in his countenance—and his conversation (from the little I could judge of it, in the space of a quarter of an hour) was pleasing—in short, he is said to be a young man of a most amiable character."[79]

THE ÉMIGRÉS' impact on Philadelphia's sociability built on previous developments, including the Franco-American alliance, the Binghams' influence, and the arrival of thousands of French people in the 1790s, as well as the growing trade with France and its colonies. Collectively, they oriented the cultural life of elite Philadelphia toward France as the eighteenth century drew to a close.

During the war, according to the French-born lawyer Peter Stephen Du Ponceau, "French gentlemen" had introduced a new style of hospitality: "the fashion of evening visits to the ladies. . . . Every evening the ladies were ready to receive visits at their tea-tables where nothing was offered but a dish of tea, and a few cakes, a slice of toast, or bread and butter. There was no company invited, the ladies had with them two or three of their female relations or intimate friends, and the gentlemen came in or walked out as they pleased." His description bears a striking resemblance to the one that young Abigail (Nabby) Adams gave of sociability in Paris. "In company here, every one consults his own pleasure," she reported, contrasting French ease with American stiffness. "The ladies walk about, view the pictures if there are any, chat with any one who pleases them, talk of general subjects, such as the spectacles." The compact life of Philadelphia particularly suited this form of entertainment, where the wealthy all lived within a few blocks of one another, and often on the very same street, making even dozens of visits in a single day possible.[80]

Philadelphia's salons were designed around light refreshments rather than heavy meals. Dinner was the main meal of the day, served in the early afternoon, usually around one or two, though it could be later when Congress was in session. The meal might last several hours, depending on the host. This would be followed by a few hours of work, and then back to the business of socializing. Philadelphia's salons took place in the evening, with visitors calling on their hosts between six and seven. Tea was served "with much form," as one European who toured Philadelphia in 1795 recalled. Conversation, music, card games, and dancing would fill the evening until about ten, when guests began to leave. Some salons—the more official ones—occurred on a regular schedule. Martha Washington held her receptions every Friday from seven to ten (a tradition she'd begun when the capital was still in New York), where she served coffee, tea, cakes, fruits, ices, lemonade, and wines. The British ambassador's wife received company every Monday night from seven until nine or ten for coffee, tea, and cards. "Publick tea parties seem to be an amusement of which the Ladies in this Country are particularly fond," she observed. Very often, evenings were taken up by the French game lottery. As for the conversation, it was "serious or lively according to the humour of the hostess and of the company, but always agreeable and interesting. Sometimes music was introduced, and sometimes feats of drollery, in which the French gentlemen excelled. In some houses the conversation was often literary, in others of a gayer turn." It all resembled the most famous Parisian salons: Julie de Lespinasse opened her doors every day from five to nine in the evening, while Madame Geoffrin held her salons starting at 1:00 p.m. on Mondays for artists and Wednesdays for men of letters.[81]

Liancourt's diary vividly describes this tightly knit social world; it is by far the most detailed account of Franco-American sociability in 1790s Philadelphia. A typical day saw Liancourt conducting business in the morning, or simply resting or writing at home. He usually "dined" in the early afternoon, often with men but not only, and often with a group he referred to as *les Français,* which probably involved Talleyrand and Beaumetz at Théophile Cazenove's house. He then spent his evenings dropping by from house to house socializing, mostly with women. One afternoon in January 1795, for instance, began with tea at a Mr. Strikland's, followed by visits to

Mrs. Lucy Knox and then to Anne Bingham's, where he reported: "Conversation *française* avec elle; je me suis amusé" (*French* conversation with her; I had fun). These visits consisted largely of men dropping by women's parlors throughout the evening and rarely seem to have been prearranged. On another January evening Liancourt visited with Madame Renaud and Madame Maulde de Blacons, two French émigrées in Philadelphia, followed by tea at Mrs. Chew's. "*Voilà* the true state of Philadelphia society," he concluded: "great dinners, grand teas, for all who arrive from Europe—English, French, inhabitants of every country." The intense proximity of Philadelphia's elite social world facilitated this regimen of multiple visits. Liancourt's visits varied from day to day, but his favorites were Judge Benjamin Chew and his family, who lived on Third Street just next door to Elizabeth Powel, two houses down from the Binghams, a mere two blocks from Liancourt's residence. His diary is peppered with compliments extolling the family. "Là seulement," he concluded one evening, "je me trouve à mon aise et presque *at home*" (Only there do I find myself at ease and almost *at home*). That ease must have been in part because Benjamin Chew lived up to the French ideal of polite behavior, uniting "to a natural, penetrating, and lively spirit, great knowledge, an amiable temper, unfailing goodness, a perfect simplicity of manners, and all the virtues."[82]

In these intensely intimate settings in the heart of Philadelphia, amid these close personal relationships, the networks that helped tie the United States to the Atlantic world gradually took shape. They had begun with letters that procured invitations to events guided by the refined norms of Franco-American sociability, and held in spaces designed according to the latest European fashion. From there they gradually turned into friendship and even, at times, kinship.

———

MARRIAGE, AND occasionally love, were key elements forging these networks. That was true on a national scale—the scholars David Shields and Fredrika Teute have called the Republican Court the "republic's prime marriage mart"—as well as an international one. William Bingham had married the daughter of the merchant Thomas Willing, who was Robert

Morris's senior partner in Willing, Morris, and Company, the firm at which Bingham made his fortune while acting as its agent (and the agent of the U.S. Congress) in Martinique during the Revolution. The Binghams' daughter Ann Louisa, in turn, married Alexander Baring, scion of the British banking family that invested in lands with William Bingham. Ann's sister Maria Matilda would later marry Alexander's brother Henry, solidifying the bonds between one of the most important firms in America and the rising mercantile star in the British financial galaxy.[83]

The French émigrés entered these circles in much the same way. Talleyrand's companion Beaumetz married Henry Knox's sister-in-law. Knox, a pillar of Federalist social life, was partnered with Bingham in a major financial investment in lands in the province of Maine. Beaumetz's friends warned him about what they considered to be an ill-advised marriage: "We tried to advise him against this union with a widow who has many children and no fortune, but he was in no mood to listen to our arguments," Moreau reported. "He got married and for his sake we agreed that his future wife should have our interest and affection." Louis-Philippe, duc d'Orléans, who was now in the line of succession to the French throne, fell in love with Thomas Willing's daughter Abigail (Anne Bingham's sister). One Philadelphian recalled seeing "a fine miniature likeness" that Orléans had drawn of Abigail placed on the mantel in the Binghams' reception room: "The Prince was said to be fascinated by her handsome person, polished and graceful deportment." After a public courtship, the duc asked Thomas Willing, the conservative banker sometimes referred to as "Old Square Toes," for his daughter's hand in marriage. Willing refused; he allegedly told Orléans— then a penniless exile—that he was "no match for my daughter." However, Willing is supposed to have added, "If you ever become King, she will be no match for you."[84]

Some relationships were more hidden than others; of a few, one gets only tantalizing glimpses. Alexander Baring, for instance, reported to his father that Noailles' "very great influence in the Bingham family [stems] from certain female reasons you will easily understand." If Sir Francis Baring easily understood these "female reasons," they remain more oblique to posterity. Other relationships became embarrassingly public, as happened after Noailles introduced his friend and business associate comte Alexandre de Tilly to the Binghams. Tilly had landed in Philadelphia penniless, like many others, and as he sank under a mountain of debt he was determined to get back on his feet. A frequent guest at the Binghams' mansion, he drew the notice and then the affections of Maria Bingham, Anne and William's youngest daughter; the love-struck fifteen-year-old sent him chocolates and fruit from her parents' garden. Late one April night the two ran off and were married. Her parents were frantic: Anne was said to be "very ill" and William to have "lost his senses." They sent a series of overwrought letters to Maria urging her to come home—just to talk, they claimed, though when she complied they promptly whisked her out of town. Lawyers were mustered, legal suits threatened. Then the merchants jumped in. Negotiations ensued. Through the mediation of some of the great bankers of the age, including Alexander Baring and Thomas Willing, Tilly named his price. For £5,000 cash plus an annual pension of £500 (and an apology from Baring, who had struck him), he would agree to a divorce and leave the country. And so the deal was done. Poor Anne Bingham: the episode became the talk of elite Philadelphia. "Now you see my dear," Robert Morris wrote to his daughter from debtors' prison, where he remained in the wake of his spectacular financial collapse, "large fortunes do not always give happiness."[85]

The more we examine such relationships, the more it becomes clear that these marriages played a subtle but significant economic role in the United States and the Atlantic world. One of the great themes of this period is of young ambitious men marrying into wealth and launching illustrious careers. William Bingham's marriage into the Willing family, Alexander Baring's into the Bingham family, and Alexander Hamilton's into New York's Schuyler family are all different expressions of the same basic phenomenon. Marriage was the way two less eminent figures—William Stephens Smith and William Jackson—made their entrée into these exalted transatlantic networks: by marrying Abigail (Nabby) Adams, Smith became John Adams's son-in-law; Jackson married Anne's sister Elizabeth, becoming Willing's son-in-law. The young men had much in common. Both had served on George Washington's staff during the Revolution. Both were dashing, polite, and endowed with fine manners, possessing little family wealth but well educated and highly ambitious. Both served in a series of appointed offices in the years after the war: in Europe as minor figures in U.S. foreign missions, as secretaries to more distinguished figures—Jackson under John Laurens during the Revolution, and Smith under John Adams after. Both later used the international contacts they had forged in these diplomatic missions to advance their business interests and their family prospects. And both proved to be disappointments to their relatives. Smith's marriage and career were notorious failures. As for Jackson, if his marriage—at a wedding attended by Washington and Jefferson, among others—brought him obvious financial advantages, the benefits for the Willing clan were less apparent. "The Major in general did not please," one witness reported. "It is whispered in the Court of Scandal that family circumstances rendered the event necessary."[86]

Certainly no case of marriage into a prominent family was more dramatic, or brought more financial rewards, than that of the young banker Pierre-César Labouchère. Born in The Hague in 1772 to a French Protestant family that had fled France after the revocation of the Edict of Nantes, Labouchère was sent to his uncle's firm in Nantes at the age of thirteen, where he was trained in finance. In 1790 he began work as a clerk with the Hope firm of Amsterdam, then the Netherlands' most important merchant bankers and financiers. At the age of twenty-two, already chafing under the restraints of his lowly position, Labouchère traveled to London, where he began to court Dorothy Baring, the daughter of Sir Francis Baring, the Hopes' British associate. According to family lore, it was then that he asked Sir Francis for permission to marry his daughter. Not surprisingly, Baring refused, on the grounds that a mere clerk was no match for his daughter. "Would it make any difference to your decision if you knew that Mr. Hope was about to take me into partnership?" Labouchère asked. Sir Francis admitted it would. Pierre-César then rushed back to Holland, where he demanded that Henry Hope make him a partner. Of course, the powerful banker had no intention of promoting a mere clerk to the partnership. But now Labouchère had a trump card up his sleeve: "Would it make any difference to your decision if you knew that I was engaged to the daughter of Sir Francis Baring?" he asked.[87]

And that was how young Pierre-César Labouchère became a partner at Amsterdam's most important firm and married into one of the most illustrious banking families in history.

WHEN ONE begins to see how marriage and kinship facilitated upward mobility and forged mercantile connections, the centrality of women's roles in these networks becomes ever more interesting. Success was as much a function of kin and social networks as it was a matter of individual uplift or hard work. The émigré *constituants* were, with only one exception, single men traveling across the Atlantic. But the world they encountered in Philadelphia, which opened up all kinds of social and economic opportunities, was shaped by women and their elaborate family networks.

Trust means everything in long-distance trade and finance. That is why personal, social, religious, and familial networks have played a crucial role since the earliest days of capitalism. Without trust, capitalism breaks down. This was true for fourteenth-century Italian city-states like Florence or Genoa and eighteenth-century merchants and bankers, and it is still true for modern financial actors. Just as politics worked through personal relationships before the infrastructure of political parties had fully developed, so did business work through personal networks of trust in an era before the infrastructure of the capitalist economy (rapid communication, credit reports, etc.) had fully developed. Friends and political associates became business partners; business partners became family by marriage. The letters of introduction that circulated across the Atlantic, allowing émigrés to penetrate the social networks of American life, paralleled the letters of credit and bills of exchange transmitted through the same channels, making it possible to conduct business in far-flung places at a time when ensuring the reliability of information across the vast distances of the Atlantic world was perhaps the most pressing issue for international merchants and speculators. Indeed, letters of introduction were carried by the same networks of circulation that tied the Atlantic economy together. "You will have many ways to correspond by the route of commerce," Talleyrand wrote to his friend Madame de Staël, "which I prefer to the means of ambassadors."[88]

The importance of social networks to transatlantic finance was plainly evident to Alexander Baring, scion of the rising Baring Bank, when he landed in the United States in 1795. "I have been introduced . . . to most of the respectable characters in town much to my satisfaction & information," he wrote to his Dutch business partner John Williams Hope shortly after his arrival in Boston. "I am constantly out in some company & . . . am always collecting information of [a] different kind." Alexander Baring's future brother-in-law, Pierre-César Labouchère, would make the connection between sociability and economic interest even more explicit a few years later. "Nothing can be done here without mixing as much as possible in the world," he wrote to Francis Baring from Paris. "It is even at the theaters that one derives information, and Coffee House clerks are as the lowest Ebb." Much of this information was spread through rumor and seemingly idle talk—Baring's letters are littered with phrases like "it is here said," or "it is considered here," or, best of all, "it is whispered." In such a context, one's social connections, one's reputation, and one's access to timely and reliable information could easily mean the difference between fabulous wealth and devastating bankruptcy.[89]

Credit was the key term. "Credit in this country is a delicate subject," Alexander Baring wrote to his father, as he traveled down the East Coast checking in on his family's business relationships and exploring investment opportunities. Some partners, like Thomas Willing, he found trustworthy, and by broadcasting his confidence to associates and acquaintances, he could actually increase the value of Willing's bills of exchange. "The uniform support you have given to Willings," Baring wrote to his father, "the footing I am on with them, and the positive manner I speak to my friends here of them has placed their paper in the very first rank and they have made and can still constantly make a higher exchange than their neighbours whose bills are occasionally disgraced." On the other hand, the consequences of Baring's disapproval could be disastrous. "You may easily conceive," Baring continued in the same letter, "that . . . dishonour to their signatures on a very small sum would totally incapacitate them for drawing sixpence."[90]

The merchant John Swanwick was a case in point. Swanwick had risen to prominence through Robert Morris, becoming a partner in the firm renamed Morris, Willing, and Swanwick in 1783, and then serving as cashier of the United States under Morris. A leading stockholder in the Bank of the United States, Swanwick acted as a principal broker for major American and Dutch investors. In 1796 his fortune was estimated at nearly $650,000. By the time Baring arrived in Philadelphia in the mid-1790s, Swanwick had entered politics and joined the Democratic-Republican Party as a vocal supporter of Genet and an organizer of various pro-French political events. Now separated from the Willing firm, he nevertheless continued to do substantial business with the Barings. But Alexander Baring quickly became critical of Swanwick, calling him a "Jacobin," "a rascal," and a "*brouillon*" on various occasions. He urged his father to end their connection—but only after having settled accounts. "You should I think liquidate his account," Alexander wrote to Francis in late 1796, "and send it to him as soon as possible and when the ballance is setled tell him plainly that you withdraw all credit which will of course close your connection." To cut him off too soon would have left the Barings stuck with Swanwick's notes, which would rapidly depreciate when the word spread. But once they balanced the account, they could withdraw their credit and notify the merchant community.[91]

And that is exactly what happened: Swanwick blamed his collapse in 1797 "on the secret rejection of his bills of exchange on the Baring Brothers." Crushed financially, Swanwick was forced to auction off his possessions, including his library of thirteen hundred volumes. He was bankrupt and depressed, and one observer thought he would die of a "broken heart." It was not his heart, however, but yellow fever that killed him some months later, at the age of thirty-nine. Swanwick had seemingly forgotten—or ignored—the importance of social networks to his financial and indeed physical well-being, and it had cost him dearly.[92]

THE ÉMIGRÉ *constituants* integrated themselves into these elaborate networks that facilitated transatlantic sociability, politics, diplomacy, and finance. The complex web of relationships—social, political, familial—would shape the *constituants'* experiences in the United States. It might not be an exaggeration to say that they would shape the future of the United States itself.

Théophile Cazenove—the banker at whose house Talleyrand regularly ate—was the key "node" connecting the French *constituants* to the American financial world. Like so many other bankers of Huguenot descent, Cazenove had tentacles that extended deep into financial communities on both sides of the Atlantic. In the 1780s he formed part of the circle that orbited around the Swiss financier Isaac Panchaud in Paris, and had later teamed up with the French politician Jacques-Pierre Brissot and the American businessman and politician William Duer in the consortium led by the Swiss financier Étienne Clavière, who speculated on American debt. His brother was a banker in London and later became Talleyrand's private banker. A cousin, Anthony Charles Cazenove, would emigrate from Switzerland to the United States, partner in a land venture with the Swiss-born congressman and future treasury secretary Albert Gallatin, marry into the Lee family of Virginia, and eventually become a Swiss consul to the United States. When Théophile arrived in New York in 1790, he came armed with a letter of introduction from Brissot to Duer, who was then assistant secretary of the treasury. Soon enough, however, he decided Philadelphia was where he needed to base himself. Making large profits by buying up depreciated securities, Cazenove expanded his investments to land, buying up vast tracts in Ohio and western New York (hence the town of Cazenovia) from Robert Morris. Cazenove would direct a great deal of European investment into the United States, creating a wealth of business opportunities for his émigré friends, including securing the capital for Moreau's bookstore.[93]

Talleyrand also had extensive experience in finance, having served as *agent général du clergé* in France, a position that put him in charge of

Church funds. It also connected him to the Caisse d'escompte, an institution founded in 1776 to discount bills of exchange and commercial paper that is often considered the precursor to the Bank of France. In the 1780s he too had been a disciple of the Swiss financier Isaac Panchaud—founder of the Caisse d'escompte—which involved him in circles that included Swiss, Dutch, and Genoan bankers. Few people were more conversant with the complexities of eighteenth-century finance. In the Assemblée constituante he took an active role in state finance and in nationalizing the Church's vast landholdings, which became the basis for the new French currency, or *assignat*. His eye wandered far abroad: like Panchaud, he had immersed himself in projects for financing the French India trade. He also had a long-standing interest in American business opportunities, having discussed possible investments with Gouverneur Morris, the American minister in Paris who had been, like Talleyrand, a lover of Adélaïde de Flahaut. Business was to become his most insistent focus during his American stay. "There are many ways here of making money without a great deal of trouble," he wrote to an associate in London shortly after arriving in Philadelphia. He would continue to urge his friends back in Europe to invest. "There are here more ways of re-making a fortune than in any other place," he wrote to his former lover Germaine de Staël two months later. "In a short time one can make a lot of money." Making the rounds after he arrived in the United States, Talleyrand soon concluded that the best person to do business with was Cazenove.⁹⁴

But Talleyrand was not the only *constituant* to throw himself into business. Noailles also jumped right into a major land scheme in Pennsylvania. Liancourt, too: after learning about his friends' affairs during his first week in Philadelphia, he met with Cazenove to "discuss my business." The following week, Liancourt reported receiving a "proposal of Mr. de Noailles on the . . . lands of Mr B. [Bingham] in the province of Maine." Two days later, he was again meeting with Cazenove "for business," and the day after had "completed my business with Mr Cazenove," deposited a note with a French banker in Philadelphia, and met with Knox and Bingham about their land scheme in Maine. Talleyrand also helped Moreau on several occasions, once inviting him to dine at Cazenove's with Henry Knox, who had begun his illustrious career as a bookseller and who Talleyrand thought could offer advice: "Knox has long had business dealings here with bookshops and is interested in your success," Talleyrand wrote. "He told me a fortnight ago he wished to talk to you to tell you how he thinks you can best prosper." Nor did it take long for Volney to get involved in land speculation. Making contact with Jefferson shortly after his arrival, Volney declined an invitation to visit Monticello: "Already some business has tied me to Philadelphia, and I will endure the yoke with all the more willingness, since it may prepare a future emancipation and an indefinite liberty." Volney later bought lands in New York with the French investor J. D. Le Ray de Chaumont and Moreau.[95]

These complex networks, it turns out, were not just social. They also served as the channels through which major capital investments into the United States would begin to flow. In a manner almost analogous to rivers, these flows would shape the geography of an emerging capitalism in the United States, with webs extending from across the Atlantic through Philadelphia and deep into the continent. And they would lead the French émigrés deep into the continental interior: back behind the already settled coastal plain into the valleys and mountains of the Appalachian region. Although distant from the centers of political and economic power, these were nevertheless some of the most consequential areas of the Atlantic world. Through these relationships, through these investments and flows, the émigrés—who had sought refuge from the revolutionary storms sweeping the Atlantic world—were about to enter some of the world's most hotly disputed territories.

Part 2

THE FRENCH REVOLUTION IN THE WEST

L'histoire événementielle . . . une agitation de surface, les vagues que les marées soulèvent sur leur puissant mouvement . . . c'est la plus passionnante, la plus riche en humanité, la plus dangereuse aussi. Méfions-nous de cette histoire brûlante encore, telle que les contemporains l'ont sentie, décrite, vécue, au rythme de leur vie, brève comme la nôtre. Elle a la dimension de leurs colères, de leurs rêves et de leurs illusions.

The history of events . . . surface agitations, the waves that the tides raise up by their powerful motion . . . it is the most passionate, the richest in humanity, and also the most dangerous. Beware of this still-burning history, as contemporaries felt it, described it, and experienced it by the rhythm of their lives, short as our own. It has the size of their furies, their dreams, and their illusions.

—FERNAND BRAUDEL[1]

Four hundred and eighty million years ago the Atlantic Ocean did not exist. Africa, Europe, and North America were all connected. North America straddled the equator, and what is now the Atlantic coast lay underwater. As the earth's tectonic plates collided in this period of intense geological activity, the African plate slamming into the North American plate, the ocean floor buckled, and great sheets of bedrock began slowly rising up in the air. Humans would one day call these the Appalachian Mountains. Over the millions of years that followed—a time scale so deep, so vast, and so long we can hardly fathom it—slices of rock crumpled and were thrust miles into the sky as the Appalachians reached exalted heights, nearly as tall as the present-day Himalayas. Eventually the continents began to separate. Vast plains and mountain chains were torn asunder, and water poured into the breach. Thus, some 220 million years ago, the Atlantic Ocean was formed, connecting what the earth had divided.

The new ocean linked not just the new continents but the already ancient Appalachian Mountains themselves. Most of the Appalachians drifted west with the American plate, while the remainder stretched across the ever-growing Atlantic, from Norway to the Scottish highlands, across Ireland and Newfoundland, extending to the Atlas Mountains in northern Africa. Over the thousands of millennia that followed, landmasses broke apart and reformed, continental shelves rose and fell, oceans flooded and then dried up, and great sheets of ice conquered the earth's surface and then retreated, only to return again. And through it all, the Appalachian Mountains perdured.[2]

Now weathered far down from their once-lofty heights, the Appalachians today rise gently above a network of waterways that border and intersect North America. To the east, the continent's edge is marked by a series of splendid bays and gulfs, and punctuated by several broad, placid rivers that ebb and flow to the recurring rhythm of the tides. Tidal waters push their way deep into North America, up the waterways that cut through the rich coastal plain—as much as 150 miles up the Hudson River. From the Hudson River running all the way to the Chattahoochee River in present-day Georgia, a long fall line stretches across the East Coast, dividing the coastal plain from the more rugged *piedmont* (French for foothill), where the Appalachians begin. For all of human time, the fall line has divided the continent's interior from the wider world: it is where all waterborne transportation halted. A string of Native American villages once dotted the fall line, as European settlements did later, and as East Coast cities do today, from Paterson, New Jersey, through Trenton and Philadelphia, Baltimore and Washington, down through Richmond, Virginia, Raleigh, North Carolina, all the way to Columbus, Georgia. Everywhere that water flows across that nine-hundred-mile span it becomes either rapids or falls: above, the water runs swiftly; plunging down to the plain below, the rivers drift lazily, thrust back and forth by the Atlantic's tides. For hundreds of years, those falls provided power for humans.[3]

The rivers that connect the Appalachians to the coast only begin to cover the Atlantic's continental hinterland, however. Stretching deep into North America, the Atlantic's drainage basin extends over twice as much of the continent as the Pacific's. "By the gigantic tendrils of its rivers," the Atlantic "lays hold upon the Rockies and the Andes." North of the Appalachians, the Saint Lawrence River descends from the Great Lakes to its mouth in the frigid North Atlantic, watered by several river systems that stretch hundreds of miles into Canada. It was formed when the colossal Laurentide Ice Sheet retreated some ten thousand years ago, scarring the land, leaving vast deposits of boulder and clay behind, and wrenching the Great Lakes' drainage system toward the Gulf of Saint Lawrence. The Laurentian waterways once served as the transportation routes for the millions of furs pulled out of the continent every year by Native American hunters and shipped across the Atlantic by French, English, and Dutch merchants. Today it drains more than 25 percent of the earth's freshwater reserves. "This drainage system, driving seaward in a great, proud arc from Lake Superior to the City of Quebec, was the fact of all facts in the history of the northern half of the continent," writes the historian Donald Creighton. "It commanded an imperial domain."

At the top of the Saint Lawrence lie the Great Lakes. The world's largest body of freshwater, they are the continent's heart, where its two principal arteries meet. The Mississippi and Saint Lawrence watersheds are most accessible in several places: the first, near present-day Chicago, some half-dozen miles from Lake Michigan, is no more than a low wet ridge rising barely fifteen feet above the lake; during the wet season it could be crossed by canoe. A second, slightly longer portage begins at Lake Erie and connects the upper reaches of the Ohio River to the Saint Lawrence waterway. A third passes from the Maumee to the Wabash River, and served as the most direct route connecting Quebec to New Orleans.

All these routes lead to the broad and fertile Mississippi River valley: the largest watershed in North America and the fourth largest in the world. Draining nearly 40 percent of the landmass of today's United States, it stretches west from the Appalachians all the way to the Rocky Mountains, south from Canada to the Gulf of Mexico. Extending up to the western slopes of the Appalachians, the Mississippi River serves as the principal artery for the continent's transportation and commerce. Goods or people traveling down its waterways arrive by necessity in the Gulf of Mexico. That is why North America's vast continental interior has always been, geographically speaking, more connected to the Caribbean than to the Atlantic coast.[4]

After humans migrated to North America, the largest numbers eventually settled in the Mississippi valley. During the warm period from 900 to 1350, at roughly the same time the Vikings from Scandinavia pushed south toward the Mediterranean, Mississippian societies flourished. People and agriculture spread across the continent, linked together by a dense network of trade routes that followed the continent's waterways. The city of Cahokia, established just below the confluence of the Missouri and Missis-

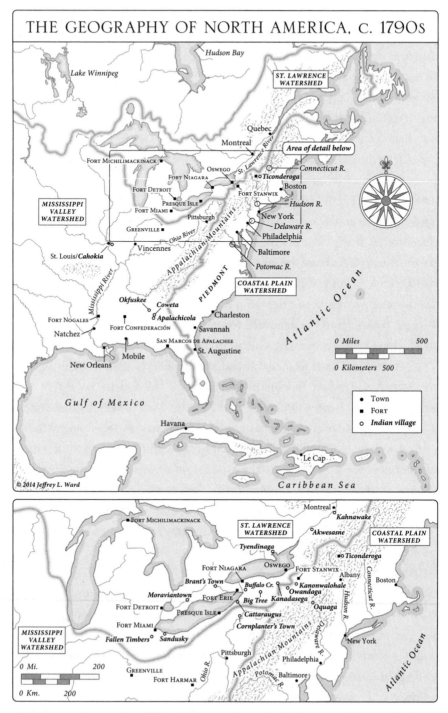

THE GEOGRAPHY OF NORTH AMERICA, c. 1790s

Hudson Bay

Lake Winnipeg

ST. LAWRENCE WATERSHED

Quebec

Montreal

St. Lawrence River

Area of detail below

Fort Michilimackinack ■

Oswego ○ — Connecticut R.

Fort Niagara ■ ○ ■ Ticonderoga

Fort Detroit ■ Boston

Presque Isle ■ Fort Stanwix ■

MISSISSIPPI VALLEY WATERSHED

Fort Miami ■ ○ Hudson R.

Pittsburgh ○ New York

Greenville ■ Delaware R.

Ohio River Philadelphia

Appalachian Mountains

Vincennes Baltimore

St. Louis/*Cahokia* Potomac R.

Mississippi River

PIEDMONT

COASTAL PLAIN WATERSHED

Okfuskee *Coweta* Charleston

Fort Nogales ■ ○ *Apalachicola*

Natchez Fort Confederación ■ Savannah

San Marcos de Apalachee

Mobile St. Augustine

New Orleans

Atlantic Ocean

0 Miles 500

0 Kilometers 500

Gulf of Mexico

● Town
■ Fort
○ *Indian village*

Havana

Le Cap

Caribbean Sea

© 2014 Jeffrey L. Ward

Montreal ●
Kahnawake

■ Fort Michilimackinack

ST. LAWRENCE WATERSHED ○*Akwesasne* **COASTAL PLAIN WATERSHED**

Tyendinaga ○ ■ Ticonderoga

Fort Niagara ■ Oswego ■ Fort Stanwix Albany

Brant's Town ○ *Buffalo Cr.* ○ ○ *Kanonwalohale* Boston

Moraviantown Fort Erie ■ ○ *Owandaga*

Fort Detroit ■ *Big Tree* *Kanadasega* ○

Presque Isle ■ ○ *Cattaraugus* ○*Oquaga*

Fort Miami ■ *Cornplanter's Town* New York

MISSISSIPPI VALLEY WATERSHED *Fallen Timbers* ○ Sandusky *Appalachian Mountains*

Pittsburgh ● *Atlantic Ocean*

0 Mi. 200 Greenville ■ Philadelphia

Fort Harmar ■ Baltimore

0 Km. 200

The contested geography of North America, from the St. Lawrence River to the Great Lakes, the Mississippi Valley, and into the Caribbean.

sippi Rivers, was North America's urban center, the largest city north of
Mexico until the late eighteenth century. The French, when they arrived,
settled the same location and renamed the town after Louis IX, the only
canonized king of France. When it became part of the United States, the
Americans kept the name Saint Louis.

Back in the East, the Appalachian Mountains continued to divide peoples just as they had long divided the continent's waterways. Iroquoian
speakers settled the hills and mountains—Cherokees in the South and Iroquois and Susquehannocks in the North, across what is now Pennsylvania
and New York, up the Appalachians to Lakes Erie and Ontario. Up in the
piedmont and Appalachian highlands, they held a formidable military
position, among the most strategic in North America. In the lowlands
around them, in a vast inverted U stretching across the Atlantic coastal
plain, up through New England and Maine to the Saint Lawrence valley
and around the Appalachians to the Ohio valley and Great Lakes, lived
their bitter enemies and rivals for the fur trade, the Algonquian-speaking
peoples. Under economic, demographic, and climatic pressures in the seventeenth century, the Iroquois struck out with ferocious "hammer blows"
against the Algonquians living to their west, shattering those communities
into hundreds of fragments. This region—the Ohio valley, west of the Appalachians, south of the Great Lakes, and east of the Mississippi—largely
emptied by the Indian wars of the seventeenth century, would be the site
of the most vicious contests between French and English settlers in the
eighteenth.[5]

Just as the Appalachian Mountains divided Native peoples, so they divided European settlers. To the east, the English colonized the coastal tidewater, pushing their way up along the rivers and waterways of the coastal
plain. To the north, the French roamed up the Saint Lawrence valley to the
Great Lakes and down the Mississippi River. They had found the key gateway to the continent's interior; their empire would be defined by water and
bound by alliances with Native American peoples in the west. The English,
by contrast, established an empire of settlement, conquest, and agriculture,
driving Native peoples west. As they filled up the coastal plain, fingers of
British settlement began to jut into the rugged Appalachian Mountains,

Scots Irish and Germans wending their way up the Susquehanna and Potomac Rivers into the Appalachian backcountry, and spreading across the valleys of Pennsylvania, Maryland, Virginia, and North Carolina. Pushing ever farther west across the mountains and into the upper reaches of the Mississippi valley, they inevitably ran into the French and their Algonquian allies.

There it was, at the confluence of three rivers just west of the Appalachian Mountains, on the future site of Pittsburgh, at the northeastern edge of the Mississippi valley, that the French built a fort they named after the governor of Canada, Ange Duquesne de Menneville, the marquis de Duquesne. And there it was that George Washington, a young and inexperienced soldier and surveyor, and Tanaghrisson, an Iroquois leader, were headed to chase them out when, early one morning in 1754, they ambushed a party of sleeping French soldiers, unleashing a chain of events that led to worldwide warfare, the reconfiguration of Europe's global empires, and, twenty-two turbulent years later, the creation of the United States.

THE NEW nation that emerged from the rubble of thirty years of global conflict was ostensibly sovereign across the Appalachian Mountains. That was a novelty in human history: no political entity, Native or European, had ever controlled both sides of the Appalachians without rapidly disintegrating. Unlike the Atlantic Ocean, which served as both barrier and bridge between Europe and America, the Appalachian Mountains unambiguously divided the East from the West. "Nowhere," Henry Adams once observed, "did the eastern settlements touch the western. At least one hundred miles of mountainous country held the two regions everywhere apart." Also unlike the ocean, the Appalachians could be crossed in only a few places. The two most important passages were along the Mohawk River in New York—dominated by the Iroquois—and, some seven hundred miles of rugged terrain to the southwest, the Cumberland Gap, the old Indian trail converted into a wagon road through which thousands of settlers would travel west. By the last third of the eighteenth century, only two other roads crossed the Appalachians. Travel along these routes was grueling and expensive, however, and eastern and western settlements were accessible to each other only with great difficulty.[6]

The separation was not simply one of distance, however; it was more fundamentally one of geographic orientation, founded in the diverging paths of North American waterways. In the original thirteen states, where most settlement lay within fifty miles of the tidewater, the economy and society naturally faced out toward the Atlantic. The western slopes of the Appalachians, by contrast, faced west and south toward the Mississippi River. "All the territory of the United States from the sea to the Mississippi is cut from North to South by long mountain ranges, which contain the sources of an infinity of rivers," read one French report, "some of which run toward the Mississippi, others toward the sea." Waterways remained the determinant feature of American life, as they had for centuries. Through them, nature had decreed that the trans-Appalachian West would be more connected to New Orleans, Havana, and Cap-Français than to Philadelphia, New York, or Boston. Residents on the western side of the Appalachians "will direct all their speculation toward New Orleans, which is the only outlet; the others toward the established cities along the Atlantic Sea." For it was not from any eastern port, but down the Mississippi, via New Orleans and into the Caribbean, that all commerce from the vast region would eventually pass. "In the style of road building in the Roman Empire," a historian once observed, "the watercourses of the West all led to New Orleans." As a strategic site without equal, New Orleans secured control of the entire Mississippi River valley. It was, as another French government report put it, "the key to the West."[7]

French, British, and Spanish officials had thought hard about these geographic features. Even after they had been chased from the mainland, French diplomats continued to view North America through the waterways that accessed the interior, peering up at the Mississippi River from their base in the Caribbean, where the French Empire had retrenched in the wake of its catastrophic defeat against Britain in 1763. From their perspective, Saint Domingue connected naturally to the Gulf of Mexico, up the Mississippi River, and deep into the continental interior. Barges and boats from the upper reaches of the Ohio valley floated goods down to New

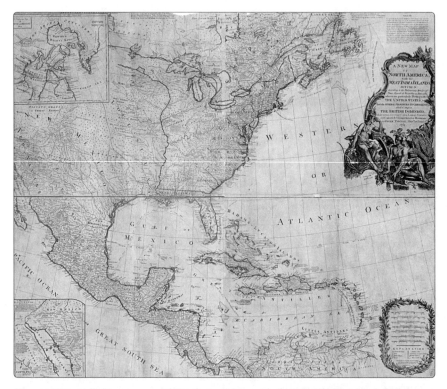

Thomas Pownall, "A new map of North America, with the West India Islands." This map of North America, based on the territorial cessions negotiated in the 1783 Peace of Paris, highlights the waterways of North America, suggesting how imperial policy makers understood the connections between the continent and the Caribbean through the Gulf of Mexico as a single unit.

Orleans, where international merchants awaited. By the turn of the nineteenth century, residents of the Ohio valley were building ships large enough to sail down the Ohio and Mississippi and straight into the Caribbean: landlocked Marietta, Ohio (named for Marie-Antoinette), on the western foot of the Appalachians, had become a shipbuilding center. French naval planners looked on the Mississippi valley as "the nursing mother of our Antilles." For the more far-seeing, the region would connect to the Caribbean not just by the goods it could furnish but also by the market it offered for French exports. "The Mississippi River," Liancourt would write after his travels out west, "can be ascended as far as Kentucky, all the way to Illinois, and in consequence further still, and carry European goods in the same boats that bring the products of these countries to New Orleans."[8]

British diplomats, meanwhile, eyed the Mississippi valley from their perch in the Great Lakes above. They hoped to link the great Mississippi valley through trade and migration to the Great Lakes and Saint Lawrence River throughway. "In a word," as Frederick Jackson Turner observed long ago, "the English government attempted to adopt the western policy of the French." Through Quebec and Montreal, British merchants penetrated the continental interior, channeling capital and goods through the region's waterways and deep into North America. This was a primary purpose behind the Quebec Act of 1774, which joined the Ohio valley to the province of Quebec, attempting thereby to overcome the geographical orientation of the Ohio's waterways by pulling its trade northeast into the Saint Lawrence River rather than southwest to the Mississippi. Despite losing their thirteen seaboard colonies in the Revolution, British officials continued to pursue that ambition, retaining the key strategic forts along the Great Lakes—notwithstanding their promise to cede them to the United States. Given just a little bit of time, British officials hoped, new facts on the ground might overcome the commitments made abroad. "The rapid progress in improvement and population of the settlements formed along the banks of the Mississippi undoubtedly renders the free navigation of that river an object highly desirable," wrote the British minister to the United States in 1792. "It will open a new, extensive, and unrivalled market for British manufactures, with which the inhabitants of those settlements can be more reasonably and plentifully supplied by the means of the water-communications of Canada than through the United States."[9]

Confronting these continental ambitions of Europe's most powerful empires, the United States was left to accomplish what nature had made so difficult: the unification of the East Coast with the trans-Appalachian West.

NATIVE PEOPLES in the West were not going to let that happen without a fight. For Native Americans in the Ohio and Mississippi valleys, the second half of the eighteenth century was an extended period of struggle to maintain control of traditional homelands. They carried out that struggle through a complex system of shifting alliances with rival European powers, playing a decentralized game of balance-of-power politics in areas where European power was weak and dependent. This system had endured with remarkable resilience in the Ohio valley and Great Lakes region, where Native-French alliances long limited British settlement to the Appalachian border.[10]

The collapse of the French Empire during the Seven Years' War posed an existential threat to this continental system. But Native Americans nevertheless fought on. "Although you have conquered the French," said an Ojibwa chief to a British trader after the British victory in 1759, summing up the common sentiment, "you have not yet conquered us!" Continued Native resistance ultimately convinced British authorities to limit colonial settlement beyond the Appalachian Mountains. By the Royal Proclamation of 1763, British authorities reaffirmed Native sovereignty in the territory west of the Appalachians—but at the cost of infuriating settlers and land speculators. None other than Lord Shelburne, later the Marquis of Lansdowne and George Washington's admirer, then the president of the Board of Trade, drafted the proclamation.[11]

Native warfare continued after the American Revolution as it had after the Seven Years' War. In the Treaty of 1783, Lansdowne once again strode across the diplomatic stage—and this time betrayed Britain's Native allies by ceding all the lands between the Ohio River and the Great Lakes to the United States. The same man who, in 1763, had treated the demands of American settlers with indifference when they had been his countrymen, while treating his Native enemies with liberality, now treated the American settlers who were his enemies with liberality, while treating his Native allies with indifference. Native Americans were aghast when they learned the news. One British general reported that the Iroquois "never could believe that our King could pretend to cede to America what was not his own to give." It is no surprise that Native villages in the Ohio valley continued fighting American forces. They did so with the support of British officials on the ground, who viewed the 1783 peace as an "Infamous treaty," and knew how difficult it would be to maintain their reduced empire and their commercial networks without the active support of Native peoples in the West. "The Indians, who had loudly and Justly complained of a treaty in which they were sacrificed by a cession of their country contrary to repeated promises, were with difficulty appeased," wrote one British official to his superiors in London. "However finding the Posts retained and some Assurances given they ceased to murmur and resolved to defend their country extending from the Ohio Northward to the Great Lakes and westward to the Mississippi." With the British supplying their Native allies with gifts and gunpowder as the French had once done, Native Americans successfully defended their territory through the 1780s and into the 1790s, winning spectacular victories against General Josiah Harmar in 1790 and General Arthur St. Clair in 1791. For the fragile American army these defeats could hardly have been more devastating—St. Clair's remains among the worst losses in the history of the U.S. Army—and their strategic consequences more consequential. "As long as Britain is suffered to retain these posts," bemoaned a U.S. congressman in 1792, "we can never hope to succeed against the Indians."[12]

If Native Americans posed an immediate military danger to U.S. sovereignty in the West, the tenuous loyalties of settlers posed a longer-term existential threat. "Mountains, as a rule, are a world apart from civilisations, which are an urban and lowland creation," the historian Fernand Braudel once observed, unwittingly echoing the Progressive historians of the early-twentieth-century United States. "They are a refuge of liberty, democracy and peasant 'republics.'" If this was true of Mediterranean regions like Corsica and the Atlas Mountains, so was it true of the Appalachians, where the rugged landscape seemed to breed a continuous resistance to state power. Since the seventeenth century, backcountry politics had been marked by strong traditions of localism and distrust of centralized authority. Those traditions had drawn many settlers to support the American rebellion in 1776, creating a powerful alliance with coastal merchants and planters. But there was little reason to think that such an alliance was more than temporary: from a cultural perspective, those western-facing backcountry regions were farther from the polished salons of Philadelphia than eastern-facing coastal elites were from London or Paris. Resistance to the new authority rising up on the Eastern Seaboard and dominated by those elites was possible at any time. "The Western settlers," George Washington wrote to Benjamin Harrison, the governor of Virginia, in 1784, "stand as it were upon a pivot—the touch of a feather, would turn them any way—They have look'd down the Mississippi . . . & they looked that way for no other reason, than because they could glide gently down the stream."[13]

The establishment of U.S. sovereignty in the West—and, as it were, the triumph of politics over geography—thus depended on securing the loyalty of these independent-minded settlers. Early reports were not auspicious. "The inhabitants of the Atlantic coast give [to the West] the name *Back-Country*," Volney observed when he crossed the Appalachians in 1796, "indicating by this term their moral attitude, constantly turned toward Europe." Not so in the western settlements: "Scarcely had I crossed the Alleghanys, before I heard [the residents] . . . call the Atlantic coast the *Back-Country*; which proved that their geographic situation has given their views and their interests a new direction, in conformity with that of the waters that serve as roads and doors toward the Gulf of Mexico." All those roads and doors led away from Philadelphia, right into the arms of Spanish officials ensconced, at least for the time being, in New Orleans. "Their sole . . . market was New Orleans by the rivers Ohio and Mississippi," read a report submitted to French authorities. "Without that market, they must labour in vain & Starve." Backcountry settlers were already issuing warnings. "Choose lands for a settlement that are near those of the navigable waters that *run towards* the Atlantick ocean," read one piece of advice for prospective settlers published in various newspapers in 1789, adding ominously, "and which are within the jurisdiction of the U. States." Many people suspected that western settlers might break away from the United States to make a separate peace with a European power that would prove more solicitous to their interests. A national "separation," Thomas Jefferson had warned as early as 1787, "was possible at every moment."[14]

As American settlers poured into western lands, provoking Native reprisals, it was becoming imperative for the U.S. government to assert its sovereignty—or risk losing the region entirely. The quickest way to gain westerners' loyalty was to support their demands for access to Mississippi River trade. "The inhabitants of Kentucky, of Cumberland, and of all the settlements established west of the Appalachian Mountains," read one French government report, "desire nothing more than to . . . obtain for themselves the free navigation of the Mississippi River." And yet American officials seemed deaf to those wishes: in 1786 John Jay, then secretary of foreign affairs, even offered to relinquish U.S. rights to Mississippi River trade to Spain in exchange for commercial benefits favoring the eastern states. British officials sought to exploit westerners' anger, making overtures to prominent landowners, who, ever more disenchanted with their government's policies, began to wonder if their former empire might prove more attentive. "The politics of the western country are verging fast to a crisis," the Canadian governor general Lord Dorchester wrote to his superiors in London in 1789, "and must speedily eventuate in an appeal to the patronage of Spain or Britain." It was the first thing Noailles noted when he arrived in the United States: "The division between the Eastern and Western States of America," he observed, "form two *partis* in the *union.*" French authorities agreed. "Nature has traced future revolutions of North America," one report predicted in 1792. "By the progressive increase of this population" in the West, "a scission between the Atlantic States and those of the West will be inevitable."[15]

Partisan divisions only exacerbated these sectional tensions. In unguarded moments, Federalists could be caught referring to westerners as "a parcel of banditti, who will bid defiance to all authority," as George Washington once put it—"our *own* white Indians," in the words of a Connecticut man. In a 1793 address, members of a Kentucky Democratic-Republican Society complained about the federal government's "neglect bordering on contempt." "Our brethren, on the Eastern Waters," it charged—in a most suggestive formulation—"possess every advantage." "Patriotism, like every other thing, has its bounds," warned a Republican club in western Pennsylvania (part of the Ohio River valley and a hotbed of Republican partisanship). "If the general government will not procure [the right of navigation on the Mississippi] for us, we shall hold ourselves not answerable for any consequences that may result from our own procurement of it." Just what those consequences might be was suggested by William Blount, a territorial governor in the West, a senator from Tennessee, and a major investor in western lands. Worried that France would gain control of the Mississippi, Blount plotted in the late 1790s to seize parts of Louisiana by sailing down the Mississippi with an army of frontiersmen in cooperation with a British fleet. His plan to detach portions of the West from the United States to form an alliance with Great Britain became infamous as the Blount Conspiracy. Blount's scheming forced him out of the Senate; back in Tennessee, he earned "a hero's welcome" and was elected speaker of the state senate.[16]

BY THE 1790s the United States found itself confronting a treacherous continental geography, assaults on its trade at sea, a hostile British Empire to its north, a hostile Spanish Empire to its south, hostile Indian nations to its west, and defiant settlers across the Appalachian country. The idea that the United States would emerge from this mix as a continental power verged on the absurd. No wonder the British politician Lord Sheffield had quipped, "We might as reasonably dread the effects of combinations among the German as among the American states."[17]

Securing American sovereignty in the U.S. backcountry was probably the most pressing existential challenge for the new nation. The solution, in the end, would come from some very unlikely sources, from a few sparks flung across the Atlantic Ocean by the French Revolution. The American backcountry, it turns out, was as bound up with the events in France as was the coast.

Chapter 4

TRANSATLANTIC
LAND SPECULATION

I T WAS LATE IN THE DAY WHEN THREE MEN STRAGGLED INTO TOWN ON horses, a fourth horse loaded with bags just behind, and a big shaggy dog panting alongside. They were speaking French, but that wasn't strange here in Asylum, a small settlement on a horseshoe bend along the Susquehanna River in northern Pennsylvania, near the New York border. The party had been traveling for only sixteen days, and the tall man sitting ramrod straight on his horse hadn't yet taken on the appearance he would by the time he floated down the Mohawk River into Albany some two months later, "his clothes covered in mud and dust, and ripped in several places," looking not "like a first gentleman of the King's Chamber," but rather "like a drowning man escaped from pirates." For now, the duc de La Rochefoucauld-Liancourt still retained some of his polish.[1]

He had arrived in Philadelphia as the fall of 1794 drew to a close, joining the other émigré *constituants,* and spent the winter getting his bearings amid the vast and diverse French community in Philadelphia. Over the course of that winter, he and the other émigrés had enmeshed themselves

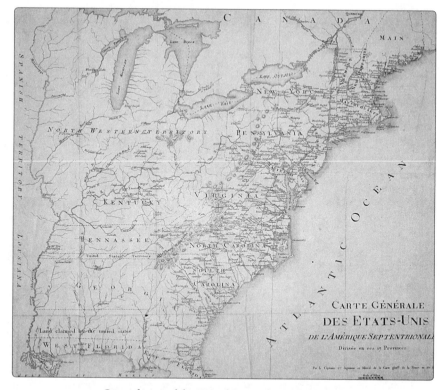

General map of the United States, from Liancourt's
Voyage dans les États-Unis d'Amérique, fait en 1795, 1796 et 1797.

in Philadelphia's elite social networks. Winter was Philadelphia's high social season, when Congress sat in session and the climate was safe from
yellow fever. Socializing in the salons of elite Philadelphia, sharing the gentle conversation and easy manners of the French aristocracy with Philadelphia's elite, Liancourt had slowly settled into his new home. But he had
also, over that time, grown dissatisfied with the company and the conversation. It too often revolved around stocks, land, money, brokers—"small
and disgusting," he once scribbled in his journal—and his spirits kept sinking. In the early spring, one of his closest friends and most frequent dinner
partners, Talleyrand, left for New York, where he planned to spend the
summer. Philadelphia was notoriously dangerous at that time of year, with
its outbreaks of disease amid the stifling heat. ("With each breath of air,"
Talleyrand quipped, "one worries about the one that must follow.") What a

fate that would be: to have escaped the guillotine in France and exile in England only to die of yellow fever in the United States! No, it was time to get away, and to begin exploring his new country. And so the next several months of 1795 would see Liancourt and most of the émigrés away from Philadelphia, exploring the American backcountry and gaining valuable information that would help restore their finances.[2]

Liancourt's traveling party included John Guillemard, an Englishman of French Huguenot descent he'd met in Philadelphia; Joseph, Guillemard's British servant (Americans were famously reluctant to work as servants, and did a poor job at it anyway); three horses for the men and one for the baggage; and Liancourt's dog, Cartouche, a Barbet (water dog) that had been his only constant companion over the last six turbulent years. On May 5, they all headed north out of Philadelphia along the Ridge Road—struck, as all foreign travelers were, by how abruptly the city turned into the country. They cut across the Schuylkill River at the fall line, which was already buzzing with the activity of paper mills and other signs of early American industry, and turned onto the dusty granite road that paralleled the Schuylkill River as it ran northwest through the gently rolling countryside of the Philadelphia hinterland. Spring had begun. The peach and apple trees in the orchards were blooming with flowers, the more intrepid maples and spruces at the edge of the meadows starting to show their leaves. Passing through Norristown to Reading, they cut southwest to Lancaster, leaving the Schuylkill to join the Susquehanna valley, and then began heading north, deep into the Pennsylvania backcountry.[3]

The Susquehanna is one of the oldest rivers in the world; its western branch offers the best path across the Pennsylvania Appalachians, or Alleghenies. As Liancourt followed the river to its fork at Northumberland he did not turn west into the Appalachians, however, but followed the northern branch toward New York, passing through Wilkes-Barre and coming, a day later, to the town of Asylum. Much of this land was owned by two of Pennsylvania's most aggressive speculators: Robert Morris, the Philadelphia merchant and financier, and John Nicholson, the comptroller general of Pennsylvania, who owned or held the rights to some 3.7 million acres of Pennsylvania land—roughly one-seventh of the state. Their landholdings

Le Grand Barbet, the breed of Liancourt's dog, Cartouche, which accompanied him during his American travels. From Georges-Louis Leclerc, comte de Buffon, Histoire naturelle *(1755).*

were princely, even by the standards of French aristocrats, but both men were wildly overleveraged and looking for investors to share the financial burdens. When Noailles had arrived in Philadelphia some two years earlier, it was a perfect match. Morris and Nicholson persuaded him to partner with them, and together they organized the colony of Asylum as a refuge for French émigrés.[4]

Liancourt found a thriving village. More than four hundred lots were laid out in good neoclassical style around a central marketplace, which already contained some fifty houses, several taverns, two stores, a bakery, and a theater. Nearby fields had been cleared for agriculture and were under cultivation. Several houses had risen up near the center of town, impressively large by the standards of the Pennsylvania backcountry. Where frontier settlers typically lived in rough log houses measuring roughly sixteen feet by sixteen feet, Asylum's two-story houses measured thirty by sixty feet and were covered with shingles. By far the most arresting was the

"Grande Maison": three stories high, eighty-four feet long and sixty feet wide, with French windows and eight large fireplaces. It had been built, or so the residents said, for Marie-Antoinette.

As he visited the settlement over the next twelve days, Liancourt reacquainted himself with Henri-François-Lucrecius-Armand de Forest, the marquis de Blacons, another former *constituant* who now ran a store with his wife. He met a former captain in the French cavalry, who had married a refugee from Saint Domingue and settled here on the banks of the Susquehanna along with his cousin, a wealthy widow from Saint Domingue. The cousin had one of the larger houses in the town, with wallpaper and finely crafted furniture in the interior, two small outbuildings joined by a piazza, a garden with fruit trees, poplars, and weeping willows, and a nursery with nine hundred apple trees. Many other residents from France and Saint Domingue had settled here, along with laborers and workers, as well as a few (probably former) slaves from the Caribbean. All sought to create a French colony in the heart of rural Pennsylvania with French people, French clothes, and French manners—and archaeological evidence sug-

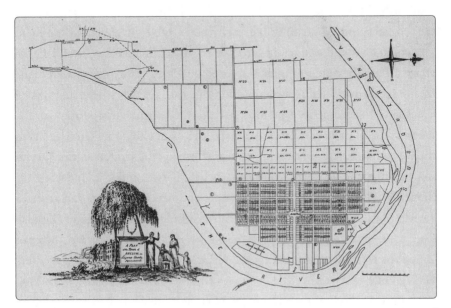

Louise Welles Murray, "A Plan of the Town of Asylum in Luzerne County, Pennsylvania."

gests they succeeded. One family even brought a piano. It would be, as Liancourt reported, a "safe asylum, tranquil, happy."[5]

Asylum fired liberal imaginations across the Atlantic world. In 1794 the young English poets Samuel Taylor Coleridge and Robert Southey imagined a "Pantisocracy," or government by all, to be located in the Susquehanna valley. "When Coleridge and I are sawing down a tree we shall discuss metaphysics," Southey wrote, "criticise poetry when hunting a buffalo, and write sonnets whilst following the plough." From Switzerland, Madame de Staël dreamed of running there with her lover, the former French minister of war Louis Marie Jacques Amalric, the comte de Narbonne. Picturesque and fantastical as this image struck observers—these scattered shards of Enlightened *ancien régime* nobility washed up on the banks of the Susquehanna—there was much more going on here than Coleridge, Southey, Staël, or Liancourt could see.[6]

In Asylum, Liancourt had stumbled on the advance guard of a great incursion into the American hinterland: the flow of European capital into the U.S. continental interior. That capital had built the roads on which Liancourt traveled, the houses he visited, and the taverns where he ate his food. It had built the flour mills and lumber mills that processed the settlers' wheat and wood to make them marketable. It extended credit to settlers to buy land and begin farms, built the churches they attended, the stores where they bought their imported goods, and the bakery that made their bread. But Asylum was not alone in this regard: it was just one of a series of settlements that dotted the American backcountry in the 1790s, some of them successes, others failures, but altogether a testimony to the ways that European capital was transforming the United States. Traveling through the western and northern U.S. backcountry, a landscape reshaped by this foreign capital, Liancourt and his compatriots ran across a variety of other such colonies. West of Asylum, deep in the Ohio valley, lay Gallipolis—the city of Gauls—on the banks of the Ohio River. Northeast of Gallipolis was Castorland, along the Black River in western New York, bordering Lake Ontario. A little to the south of Castorland lay the 3.5 million acres in western New York along Lake Erie and Lake Ontario purchased by the Holland Land Company. Farther east Liancourt found 2 million acres in Maine in which Dutch and English financiers had invested. The French émigrés and other Europeans in their circle funneled much of the capital that created these settlements.

These capital flows were a transformative development. They helped develop the U.S. backcountry, attract settlers, and integrate the region into Atlantic trade networks—all at a time when wobbly state and federal governments risked losing large parts of the territory that Britain had ceded to them at the close of the Revolution, and which Native American nations continued to contest.

———————

By mid-1795 Noailles, Moreau, Talleyrand, and Liancourt had all lived in the United States long enough to become familiar with its social mores and social networks. Having found shelter from the dangers they'd fled in Europe, they had begun to think ahead to a future they hoped would lead them back to France but that risked stranding them abroad. As their exile grew longer, their material constraints began to weigh on them ever more heavily.

"I suffer a great deal," Liancourt wrote to his wife from Philadelphia, "of this obligation to trivial thrift that leads me to watch out not to spend an écu." It was a new experience for him to contemplate "the extreme mediocrity of my fortune." As a foreigner in a strange land, Liancourt was continually receiving favors he was unable to return. It was "in the end a tiresome life . . . fraught with melancholy reflections." The others found themselves in similar circumstances. Noailles lived in an apartment in the Binghams' house. Cazenove reported that Talleyrand had saved of his patrimony "only enough to exist on very economically." It was a humiliating experience for a man who felt more comfortable giving than receiving favors, and the ungenerous description he left of Cazenove in his memoirs— "a man of a fairly enlightened spirit, but slow and timid, of a very *insouciant* character . . . useful for his qualities as much as his flaws"—probably reflects the lingering resentment he still felt at his dependence on a person he considered his social and intellectual inferior. In retrospect, it seems unlikely that these down-and-out aristocrats, failed in revolution and now failed economically, could tell us much about capitalism in the United States. But they do.[7]

Born in the Old World but living in the New, committed to monarchy but admirers of republican virtues, raised in the *ancien régime* and cast into a modernity they could neither fully perceive nor fully comprehend, these erstwhile *constituants* straddled many worlds. Like so many Benjamin Franklins arriving in Philadelphia, they would scrape their way back up the economic ladder by embracing a new spirit. "This country offers rather occasion to reestablish some broken fortune, than to make people in general happy," Noailles wrote to a correspondent in London in his choppy English. Perhaps he had not yet realized that in America fortune and happiness were the same thing. "It was amusing to see the spirit with which he embraced this new avocation," recalled one witness who watched Noailles speculate on stocks and government debt in Philadelphia. "Every day at the coffee-house, or exchange, where the merchants met, that ex-nobleman was the busiest of the busy, holding his bank-book in one hand, while he drove his bargains as earnestly as any regular-bred son of a counting-house." Regular-bred or not, Noailles learned enough to get himself on sound financial footing. "He had nothing on arriving in Philadelphia," Liancourt reported, "and his intelligence and good fortune have gained him perhaps forty to fifty thousand dollars." The émigrés would channel the hunger of gamblers who had suddenly lost their winnings, and remake their lives and sacred fortunes on these new shores. By rebuilding their finances, they would in some measure remake themselves. "I promise myself the restoration of my fortune," Talleyrand vowed, "which will be more precious to me than the one I lost, which I did not owe to my own efforts."[8]

Those with families scattered about, like Liancourt, had even greater motivations. The "principal object" of Liancourt's investment strategy was "to pull funds out of France, in quantities great enough to allow us to live in a sort of comfort and to ensure after me, if my son and myself were to be destined to live in exile forever, to have enough to support him and his family," he wrote to his wife from Philadelphia. "For, even were we happy enough to see ourselves return to France, it would be good and always good to have some money well invested outside." Even the unmarried Talleyrand agreed with this assessment. "My reason tells me that I have to remake a bit of my fortune, so as not to be a burden and continually dependent as I grow older. This idea preoccupies me," he wrote to Madame de Staël.[9]

To begin, they would need capital. "There is a lot of money to earn here," Talleyrand observed, "but it's for those who already have some." If they lacked money, however, the émigrés possessed several important assets: they had experience; they had social connections; and thanks to both, they had access to credit. Liancourt was a disciple of the Physiocrats, or *Économistes,* as they called themselves. He had listened to some of the greatest theorists of the eighteenth century—Turgot, Quesnay, du Pont de Nemours—argue about the relationship between agriculture, commerce, and economic growth. He had experimented with new farming practices on his vast estates and established nascent industries on his properties. In 1789 he published *Finances, crédit national, intérêt politique et de commerce* and served on the Comité des finances in the Assemblée constituante. Talleyrand was a disciple of the Anglo-Swiss financier Panchaud, who had speculated actively in the Paris *bourse* in the 1780s and founded the Caisse d'escompte, a precursor of the Bank of France; his family had long-standing connections with French Atlantic commerce through the port city of Nantes. As former *agent général du clergé,* he had managed the Catholic Church's finances in France. So extensive was his experience and talent in public finance and trade, he might well have become a finance minister like his friend Alexander Hamilton had he not turned his attention to diplomacy instead—that, at least, is what Gouverneur Morris thought when he got to know Talleyrand in Paris.[10]

Their social networks, which stretched across the French nobility and among liberal aristocrats in various European capitals, provided them with privileged access on both sides of the Atlantic, and made them ideally positioned to channel flows of capital into the United States. "I knew them in Paris in the days of their splendor," wrote Cazenove to his Dutch investors when he found them in Philadelphia. Cazenove introduced Talleyrand to his brother's merchant house in London, J. H. Cazenove, Nephew, and Company: "It is to the friendship which binds you to Mr. Theophile Cazenove that we owe your correspondence," J. H. Cazenove wrote to Talleyrand. "Such auspices, combined with the consideration due you, assures of the reciprocity of our confidence." Even as their backgrounds opened doors in financial centers in Europe, the friendships they forged in the United States created investment opportunities in America. Carrying "the best letters of recommendation," Talleyrand wrote, gave him easy access to the highest circles of local society. By 1795 he, Liancourt, and Noailles were firmly ensconced in the nation's most elite networks. And Cazenove continued to help as the émigrés roamed the country. He put Talleyrand in touch with Stephen Higginson, a leading Boston merchant, as well as the French firm of LeRoy and Bayard in New York, with which he also connected Liancourt. Within months, Talleyrand was purchasing $20,000 to $25,000 of "American funds" from LeRoy and Bayard, the amount guaranteed from loss by Cazenove. These well-connected noblemen were hardly naive about the commercial value of their experiences and their contacts. Not just any refugee had access to such credit lines. "Forty years of age, having passed twenty years of my life in the handling of the most important affairs, in the exercise of several important magisterial offices," Talleyrand described himself in a memoir to Cazenove as someone "in the habit of dealing and living with the first men of France and England." Who could be better placed than he to funnel capital into the United States?[11]

Because of who they were, the émigrés had access to that most precious of things, so difficult for American merchants to gain: credit. "There are many ways here of making money without a great deal of trouble," Talleyrand mused, "but these ways depend on one thing, which is refused to all American merchants, that is a solid credit." Having forged too quickly, perhaps, into speculative investments after American independence, many European financiers had become wary. "We have experienced so many examples of dishonesty on the part of Americans," wrote the firm of Bourdieu, Chollet, and Bourdieu to Talleyrand, "that we would not wish to deliver ourselves to connections which would acquire unlimited confidence in that country." Given the concerns of such firms, Talleyrand and his friends were ideally positioned to serve as trusted intermediaries. "The fairly uncertain reputations of American merchants are such that European traders are always hesitant to appoint someone with their business," Talleyrand wrote to Madame de Staël from the United States several months after his arrival. "That is why I am proposing myself with certain advantages. . . . If some of your father's friends sent ships to America," he added, referring to Staël's father, Jacques Necker, the Swiss financier and former minister of French finance, "I am in a position to take good care of the affairs of those who address themselves directly to me." Thus could the *constituants* help link surplus capital in Europe looking for safe havens with investment opportunities in the United States. The émigrés' well-established political and financial connections would help repair still-damaged networks of transatlantic trade, and facilitate the movement of European capital from major financial centers in London, Amsterdam, Hamburg, Geneva, Genoa, and Paris into the United States.[12]

For Americans hungry for capital, meanwhile, the sudden arrival of a group of well-connected émigrés was a gift. Since the Revolution, which had severed commercial ties with British merchants, the United States had experienced chronic shortages of capital. French merchants might have jumped into the breach, but the trade relationship got off to a rocky start, with accusations of dishonesty and double dealing on both sides. Dutch financiers had extended loans to the public sector during and after the Revolution, and Benjamin Franklin had proved more than adept at wheedling government loans from wily French diplomats; by the late 1780s, however, that source, too, had largely dried up. The lack of credit was severely damaging the U.S. economy, particularly in specie-short regions of the backcountry already rife with social unrest. Many of the most sophisticated economic thinkers of the period desperately sought an influx of foreign capital, which was seen as the motor of economic development. Hamilton wrote in his "Report on Manufactures" that foreign capital "ought to be Considered as a most valuable auxiliary; conducing to put in Motion a greater Quantity of productive labour, and a greater portion of useful enterprise than could exist without it. It is at least evident, that in a Country situated like the United States, with an infinite fund of resources yet to be unfolded, every farthing of foreign capital, which is laid out in internal ameliorations, and in industrious establishments of a permanent nature, is a precious acquisition." Perhaps because they had spent those long summer nights together in conversation, Talleyrand agreed with Hamilton's assessment. "What America lacks is capital," he succinctly observed. "It has room to absorb an immense quantity."[13]

It is in this fragile context—this transitional moment from the nadir of American finance in the 1780s to the fuller faith and credit that would emerge in the 1800s—that the French émigré *constituants* entered the picture. All of them recognized that "to European Capitalists," as William Bingham put it, "the Field of Profit is immensely great in this country." And so they spent their first years working to rebuild their fortunes. Although the émigrés dabbled in government debt and other financial instruments, it was land that drew their particular focus. Arriving just as one of the greatest land bubbles of American history was heating up, and socializing at the salons, dinner parties, and teas of some of the greatest real estate speculators of the age, like Robert Morris and William Bingham, they all turned their energies, perhaps inevitably, in that direction. Every single one of the aristocratic French émigrés got pulled into American land speculation, helping to channel vast amounts of European capital into the northern and western backcountry.[14]

THE STORY of Asylum is a story of French émigrés guiding flows of capital from Europe to the United States. The key players were Noailles and Omer Talon—another French aristocratic émigré and former *constituant*.[15]

Several features shaped the contours of the Asylum Company investment: the French émigrés' personal networks; the favorable reports on Susquehanna valley lands and on the opportunities for getting rich quick on land; and Philadelphia's dense connections to foreign trade and migration. Noailles' social networks in Philadelphia were particularly important. Immediately upon his arrival Noailles directed correspondents to write to him at Robert Morris's. Morris was a logical choice of partner for Noailles. The two had probably met during the Revolution, when Morris ran U.S. finance. As the country's most famous merchant, he was a known quantity; he had traded extensively while supplying the French Farmers General with tobacco in the 1780s. By the 1790s Morris was speculating heavily on millions of acres of backcountry lands running from Georgia to the Canadian border in western New York. Perhaps it was Morris who first provoked Noailles' interest. What is certain is that within a month he was seriously exploring opportunities. "The acquisition of uncultivated land is of a very great advantage," Noailles wrote to a friend in England. "The settlement of few families doubles directly the capital sum and two years after the first cultivation one receive four times what he has expended." He was planning a trip to investigate. "I shall make a journey in the country, with several of my friends able to judge the value of land." He soon plunged in. In an undated letter from 1793, he reported to a Rhode Island friend he'd known during the American Revolution that he would have to delay a planned visit: "Since my arrival in this country I have made a purchase of five hundred thousand acres of land." This was the Asylum purchase.[16]

Morris was not the only person guiding Noailles' investment. Having established himself in the Binghams' residence, Noailles lived at the very center of Philadelphia's social life, and came under the more general influence of the city's merchants and financiers who had heedlessly launched themselves into some very ambitious land speculations. "Land speculation," Liancourt remarked, "is a common form of international currency exchange throughout the United States." But it was most intense in Philadelphia—"the avidity of the wealthy *habitants* of Philadelphia make it a characteristic distinctive to Pennsylvania." Noailles' selection of lands in the upper Susquehanna valley mirrored the choices of his friends. The Asylum lands were located just west and slightly downriver from the 800,000 acres William Bingham owned. Bingham's father-in-law, Thomas Willing, had also bought lands in the area, as had Théophile Cazenove: 1.4 million acres purchased on behalf of a consortium of Dutch financiers. Many others tried to get in on the action. Aside from Coleridge and Southey with their pantisocracy idea, Joseph Priestley, the radical scientist, theologian, and honorary French citizen—and Lansdowne's former librarian—purchased a large tract of land for refugees between the two branches of the Susquehanna in Northumberland, Pennsylvania. Priestley's friend Benjamin Vaughan, the diplomat and politician who helped negotiate the 1783 Treaty of Paris, also explored investment possibilities. "Dear John," he

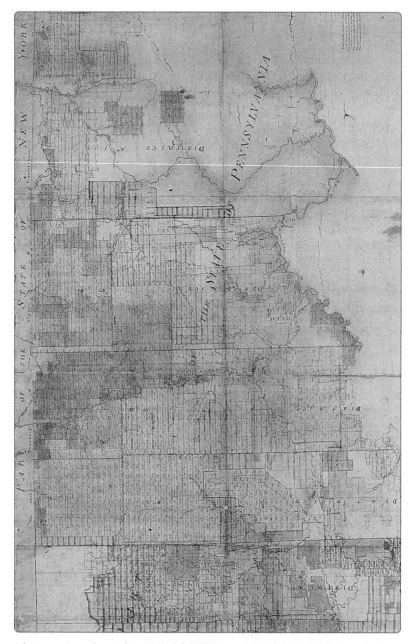

This map, now located in Philadelphia's American Philosophical Society, shows the location of various land purchases in the upper Susquehanna valley in the late eighteenth century. The names of Philadelphia merchants and politicians figure prominently among the purchasers.

wrote to his brother in Philadelphia, "I wish to know whether you cannot procure an establishment for some of the French refugee clergy on the lands belonging to my father in Pennsylvania, or on any of your own, or friends. Pray consult our excellent friend Mr Bingham;—& still more Mr Jefferson or Mr Jay."[17]

Pennsylvania lands drew foreigners like Noailles and Cazenove for a variety of reasons. In the first place, they were in the region that Europeans had most likely heard about. Promotional literature on Pennsylvania had circulated for nearly one hundred years in Europe, drawing settlers from Scotland, England, Scandinavia, and Germany. "More pains have been taken to impress favourable sentiments of that state than any other," wrote William Jackson while serving in Europe as William Bingham's land agent. "The opinions of its climate, soil, productions, situation, and even its state of society are higher in Europe than I was aware they could have been in relation to other parts of the United States." During the Revolution, Benjamin Franklin had mobilized the myth of the Pennsylvania Quaker to great effect, further popularizing the state in the eyes of Enlightened Europe, an image that J. Hector St. John de Crèvecoeur's *Lettres d'un cultivateur américain* (*Letters from an American Farmer*) polished to an even brighter sheen. This fame made it easier to sell its lands in Europe "because," as Cazenove remarked to his partners in Holland, "Pennsylvania is known so generally." Pennsylvania's economy was also booming in the 1790s, thanks to the demand for wheat and other goods shipped out of the Susquehanna valley through Baltimore and Philadelphia. Pennsylvania had the added appeal of being the only state that allowed noncitizens to purchase land. "There is one Advantage of a peculiar Nature, connected with Lands in this State," crowed William Bingham, "which is that they may be Sold to Foreigners, who may possess them in their own Names on the same Terms as Native Citizens." Many foreigners, moreover, testified to the region's natural beauty. "There is no river in America that abounds with such a variety and number of picturesque views," wrote one British traveler of the Susquehanna's eastern branch, where Asylum was located. "There is scarcely a spot . . . where the painter would not find a subject well worthy of his pencil." Talleyrand agreed: "There is nothing altogether so beautiful in Pennsylvania," he remarked. And then, of course, there were the thousands of refugees pouring into Philadelphia, the nation's largest port. "Philadelphia is full of colonists, and particularly of *habitants* of St. Domingue," Talleyrand remarked shortly after he arrived, an observation not lost on his compatriots. "This new arrival . . . has reanimated the hopes of speculators in land who are here in such great number." As prominent Frenchmen, Noailles and Talon seemed well placed to recruit refugees streaming into the United States and looking for places to settle.[18]

Despite these advantages, Asylum land did not sell as hoped, and Noailles and Talon—who had arrived, according to Liancourt, "richer in hopes than in cash"—were unable to meet their obligations to Morris and Nicholson. Despite that, the two former *constituants* retained an important asset: their privileged access to European sources of capital. They were well known among European liberals: from the moment he landed, Noailles was corresponding with his friend William Windham, soon to be the British secretary at war. Noailles also socialized regularly with the British minister in Philadelphia. It was almost certainly through the influence of Noailles and Talon, too, that the London banker John Cazenove became connected with the venture, probably through the agency of his brother Théophile. Such connections were too valuable for Morris and Nicholson to lose.[19]

Thus, on April 22, 1794, less than a year after the original purchase, Morris and Nicholson annulled the original sale and restructured the venture under the name of the Asylum Company, a corporation with shareholders. Instead of owners, Talon and Noailles became partners in the venture, retaining six thousand acres on their own accounts, and Nicholson became president of the newly formed Asylum Company, which grew to one million acres. Noailles was grateful: "You have compatized with my misfortunes," he wrote to Nicholson a few months later. "You have been serviceable to me and to my children." They were part of a distinguished group. Other shareholders of the Asylum Company included Thomas Mifflin, then governor of Pennsylvania; Thomas Willing, president of the Bank of the United States; Bishop William White, who was Mary Morris's brother; William Jackson, who would soon marry Willing's daughter; Peter

Stephen Du Ponceau; and John Vaughan. This was the *crème de la crème* of Philadelphia society, the most central nodes of the city's social networks, now financially connected, thanks to Noailles and Talon, to Europe. Their first objective was to attract enough capital to develop the region, draw settlers, drive land values up, and thereby attract more investment.[20]

To this end, the company began to pour money into the region. Noailles took charge of the business operations in Philadelphia, while Talon managed the land on-site, welcoming new arrivals, moving into the house supposedly built for Marie-Antoinette, and earning a salary of $3,000 to "live in the settlement with women, horses, a French cook, and everything that could persuade purchasers that they are not arriving at a wild place," as Talleyrand described the arrangement. The company issued five thousand shares, priced at $500 per share, each representing two hundred acres and paying a dividend of 6 percent per year, and deployed the money on "great expenditures." "The funds coming from the sale of the shares will be used to improve the lands by the construction of roads, canals, and public buildings." Soon the investors were planning a rural bank in central Pennsylvania, which they believed would "encourage and bring settlers rapidly at that settlement." It was widely recognized that, as Liancourt observed on his way to Asylum, "one of the causes of this increase in land values is the growing number of banks; by increasing the amount of money and credit, they increase the ease of acquisitions." Noailles and Talon also commissioned more than a dozen agents in Europe to attract refugees to Asylum, as well as agents in the United States who aggressively courted French and Saint Domingue refugees. "This company of rural commerce had agents placed in vigil for passengers coming from Europe, as if lying in wait for game," noted one émigré who refused to be lured. "The *factionnaire factotum* of these men extended a protective hand to the shipwrecked survivors who seemed to have saved a few suitcases, and offered them, with the eagerness of compassion, the means to restore their losses by buying, on hospitable land, a second *patrie* of a dimension proportionate to the means of each new arrival. Six francs per acre, it was nothing; it went unmentioned that the acre had been purchased for 15 cents by the speculators."[21]

Noailles and Talon were operating according to the best advice of land developers. They had an agent with authority to manage the lands on-site. They extended credit to settlers. They invested in features designed to attract settlers: roads for access to market and institutions like churches and schools. They aggressively advertised the lands. And their investments paid off, at least for a time. When Liancourt visited in the early summer of 1795, he thought the town had "attained an uncommon degree of perfection, considering its infant state." He even bought eight hundred acres "to give to my children in case they should have no resources." Refugees from Saint Domingue and France, and even some Americans, had moved into the thirty houses that made up the town. It had a distinguished and growing population. Talon was not the only former member of the French Constituent Assembly living there; the marquis de Blacons had also settled in town with his wife, where they ran a haberdashery. The continued turmoil in the Caribbean and Europe, which showed no signs of abating, suggested a continuing flow of refugees into the foreseeable future. Asylum's location on the Susquehanna promised residents with easy access to international markets: all they had to do was float their goods downriver, where they would make their way to the Chesapeake Bay and from there to the Caribbean or Europe. As the company sold land, raising even more funds to pay back investors and invest in new development—flour mills, canals— the virtuous circle would continue. "There can hardly remain a doubt," Liancourt concluded, "but that Asylum will speedily become a place of importance."[22]

Unfortunately, Noailles and Talon had missed several key aspects of a successful speculation. One problem was the local agent: Talon didn't speak English. Nor did he have any experience in the practical matters of backcountry settlement—surveying, deciding where to build roads, managing flour mills, and so forth. One settler arrived on his land, built a house, and cleared twenty-five acres of woodlands—only to learn that the Asylum Company didn't own the title to that plot. The colonists, moreover, were not suited to the Susquehanna country. Many had been aristocrats in France or wealthy planters in Saint Domingue; they had not labored in the earth but had lived off those who did. They lacked any "great inclination or ability to cultivate," according to Isaac Weld, an Englishman who visited the town in 1796. "They live entirely to themselves; they hate the Americans, and the Americans in the neighbourhood hate [them], and accuse them of being an idle and dissipated set." The settlement also faced heavy competition. As Weld traveled down the Susquehanna, he found that the region "abounded" with speculators. Just upriver from Asylum, Weld visited a settlement established on the holdings of the Pulteney Associates, a group of English investors offering exceedingly generous terms of credit to prospective settlers. Joseph Priestley's settlement was a bit farther downriver.[23]

But the most serious flaw faced by the Asylum Company was the quality of its land: mountainous, thin-soiled, and infertile. Land "more rugged and mountainous," one observer reported, "could hardly be found." Another dismissed the tracts in Asylum as "plots of sand covered with pine trees," while a third later recounted "the most comical stories about this forest clearing *manqué*." When Weld toured the area near Asylum, along the upper Susquehanna, he found locals barely scraping by amid hardship. Descending the river, he continually had difficulty procuring provisions. One impoverished resident dug into a pantry that could barely support a family and gave Weld's traveling party two little flour cakes, "scarcely as big as a man's hand each." Another provided them with enough cornmeal to make a loaf of bread, and a third with a few potatoes. At each house he visited Weld found the same: inhabitants "still more destitute." These were the lands that one refugee from Saint Domingue had purchased, after selling the stock of a clothing store she'd established in Philadelphia. "The poor dupe was forced to abandon her property," wrote one embittered refugee, "after contemplating the spot where she'd been sold the right to build, farm, and live."[24]

Noailles gave up and sold his shares in 1795, shortly before Liancourt's visit. Talon followed six months later. When Morris eventually abandoned the project, Nicholson was left as the sole owner. By then, however, Nicholson was already on his way to bankruptcy, and it was clear that the venture was destined for failure. Talleyrand, for one, was never taken in. "When one has a good scheme to propose," he noted tartly, "it is not necessary to have three or four agents in England, as many in France, eight in Holland, and several in American ports to keep watch for arrivals."[25]

ALTHOUGH LOST deep in the pine forests of central Pennsylvania—on poor land that took days of hard travel along bumpy routes to access—Asylum was not merely, as it may appear, some isolated frontier outpost. It was linked to Philadelphia by important capital flows, and from there to European financial centers like London, Amsterdam, and Hamburg, and to the revolutionary islands of the French Caribbean. All those distant places shaped the small failed settlement in the American backcountry as surely as did frontier settlers, Native Americans, and Eastern politicians. And Asylum was hardly alone—as Volney would discover on his travels even farther west a year later.

Night was already falling when Volney reached the village of Gallipolis on the banks of the Scioto River in the Ohio valley, and made his way to "a log-house, bearing the name of an inn." His trip there had been facilitated by a relative of "General Ouachinton," as Volney spelled the name of the country's president in "the true pronunciation frenchified." When he woke up the next morning he could see what he'd traveled all that way to find: two rows of huts built from tree trunks, plastered with clay, and covered over with shingles, a few ragged gardens behind with hedges of thorns. A cover of whitewash failed to hide the dampness of the cabins' interiors or the speed with which a fire would wipe out such closely spaced houses. The settlement ran along the banks of a small creek: a muddy brook when the waters were low, a noxious marsh when the Ohio overflowed, as it did from July through November, breeding all sorts of diseases. But it was the residents' appearance that most unsettled Volney: their "wild aspect and sallow complexions, thin faces, their ill and suffering appearance." This was all a far cry from the paeans to life in the American backcountry that Volney and his friends had read back in Paris, the idyllic world described in Crèvecoeur's *Letters from an American Farmer*. "The silence, the monotony, soil in some places parched up, in others marshy; and most all the trees fallen from dilapidation or blown down by storms, rotting on the ground; the tormenting swarm of flies, mosquitoes and gnats": put together, Volney concluded, they "do not possess all the charms that our romance-writers dream of amid the smoke of a city in Europe."[26]

Volney had stumbled on the sad remnant of a project that began with much grander ambitions. It was born in 1787, at the same time that many of the nation's most prominent political figures were locked in a room in Philadelphia debating the merits of a new constitution that might shore up the nation's credit. That is when the rump of the U.S. Congress that remained allocated several million acres of federal land to an international consortium of investors. By all logic, that should not have been possible; the Northwest Ordinance, after all, was designed to prevent large-scale speculation. But by the late 1780s, Congress was desperate. Its land auction in 1787 sold just 72,934 acres, netting the government a mere $117,108.22. Perhaps not surprisingly, settlers were reluctant to purchase lands in the Ohio valley: it was then the most active war zone in North America. Even as late as 1794, President Washington was issuing private warnings about the region. "In the present stage of our disputes with the Indians," he wrote to a friend who had asked his opinion about settling northwest of the Ohio, "no settlement is thought safe from the scalping knife, that is not under the protection of some fort." Making matters worse, congressional policies mandated that, in order to risk their lives settling in the area, settlers purchase a minimum of 640 acres at a dollar per acre, shoulder the cost of a $36 survey, and pay one-third of the total down with the remainder due in three months. No wonder public land sales met little success: what settler willing to risk everything to cross the Appalachians had that kind of capital? Even for the banker Alexander Baring "Congress lands" were "out of the question from their absurd high price." Sales did not improve over the course of the 1790s: from 1792 to 1796, federal land sales accounted for just one-tenth of 1 percent of federal revenue. More than three times that amount was generated through the sale of postage stamps! With debts still looming, public surveys dragging on endlessly, and Congress growing impatient for revenue, the government began to consider offers from outside purchasers with deeper pockets and more extensive connections. Thus the United States agreed to sell 5 million acres of Ohio

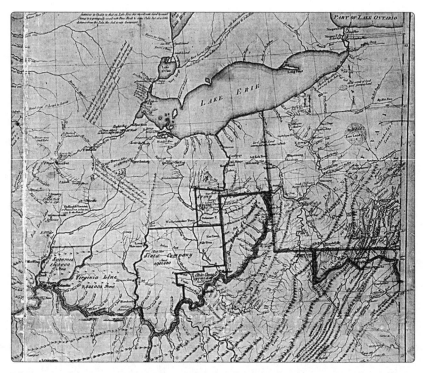

This map of the trans-Appalachian West details major land company sales made by Congress to well-connected speculators totaling most of the southern half of what is now Ohio. "A new map of the western parts of Virginia, Pennsylvania, Maryland and North Carolina" (London, 1778).

land to a consortium of investors, 3.5 million of which went to the Scioto Company.[27]

The Scioto Company had an extensive network of connections in London, Paris, and Amsterdam. The person who shepherded the purchase through Congress was William Duer, an ambitious and unscrupulous businessman who was then secretary to the Board of Treasury, the office in charge of selling western lands. Duer had extensive connections in Europe from his days as a lumber contractor supplying the French navy during the American Revolution. The most prominent associate of the Scioto Company abroad was the Van Staphorst firm, the Dutch bankers who had helped float the first loan to the newly recognized United States. The company also drew the interest of Jacques-Pierre Brissot de Warville, the journalist and future Girondin leader, along with his mentor, the Swiss financier and future French minister of finance Étienne Clavière. Brissot had traveled to the United States in 1788 with instructions to determine whether, "among the lands which Congress disposes, there still exist easily accessible regions." Brissot believed that France, with its large population, and America, with its large landholdings, made a perfect match. ("There are too many men in France," he once wrote in a memo to Lafayette; "there are not enough in America.") When he returned to Paris in 1789, however, he left no firm commitments behind. To solicit European investors, the company therefore sent the Connecticut poet Joel Barlow to France. And thus it was that in 1789 a shadowy group of speculators set out to accomplish what American colonists had fought a war to prevent three decades earlier: to lure French settlers into the Ohio valley.[28]

Barlow was not, it must be said, the best choice of agent. True, he had developed some of the requisite skills when he solicited subscribers for his 1787 poem about Christopher Columbus—skills that could now be deployed on behalf of a new and even more epic fiction about the Ohio valley. His financial experience, however, was wanting. In Paris, Barlow formed the French Compagnie du Scioto, which purchased three million acres from the American Scioto Company. Subtracting the roughly 15 percent of expenses paid in "douceurs [bribes] to public & private persons," Barlow estimated the American company's profits would exceed $1.2 million. Barlow's spirit was not the only one soaring in these early days of the French Revolution. A colony on the banks of the Ohio River captured the imaginations of discontented Parisians, mobilizing the fascination with the United States that had gripped Enlightenment France since the outbreak of the American Revolution. "I consider them as fathers and founders of a nation," Barlow wrote of the Scioto adventurers. "Their names will not only be carved on the bark of trees along the banks of the Ohio, engraved on the stones that shall form the walls of the future city—but they shall be written in the hearts of their posterity and not one of them shall be forgotten."[29]

Fed by the revolutionary press and the pamphlet literature, a veritable *sciotomanie* broke out among Paris's noble and bourgeois classes. Barlow settled himself in a small apartment above a gambling den in the *Palais*

Royal—not nearly as swanky as the apartments the Binghams had rented a few years earlier—and made the most of the revolutionary fervor then sweeping Paris. Barlow was soon reporting purchases of shares by many "respectable and wealthy families" in Paris, including noblemen and members of the National Assembly. Barlow believed that quick sales, even at a discount, would drive up the land prices; his objective, Barlow explained, was "an immediate settlement, by the sale of portions to individuals & by sending cultivators in the service of the company." Getting the colony up and running "will raise the reputation of the lands to such a degree that they will sell them all off in the course of one year at a great profit."[30]

Alas, Barlow's plan had a crucial flaw. The Scioto Company did not actually own the lands it sold to the Compagnie du Scioto; it owned only preemption rights, or rights to acquire the land at a future date. As if that were not bad enough, Barlow was selling lands the Compagnie du Scioto had not even bought from the Scioto Company! "I have proceeded as though it [the purchase] were already done, by givin[g] the company here power to resell portions of it before they make their first payment on the contract." French customers were, in short, buying doubly unowned land: purchasing tracts the French company did not yet own, which it had purchased in turn from the Scioto Company, which did not yet own the lands either. Barlow urged Duer to get around the problem by directly buying a few thousand acres for the first settlers. "Should the people not be put in possession of their small purchases on their arrival," Barlow warned, "we are ruined." But, he added, "do not let the European settlers know this manner of proceeding."[31]

Still, Barlow remained optimistic. "The affair goes extremely well," he wrote to Duer in early 1790. "It is true the payments are not made," he admitted, but he remained confident that "they will be certainly." Everything rested on the secure possession of the first titles. "Don't for God's sake fail to raise money enough to put the people in possession," he warned. "If it fails, we are ruined." As Barlow saw matters, it was not merely the Scioto Company's future that hung in the balance. He believed that the very solvency of the U.S. government—which rested at this point largely on the value of western lands—would be assured if the Scioto sale went as planned,

and urged Duer to tell Hamilton "that 20 millions of acres may be sold here
in 2 years, after it is known that these people are quietly in possession of
these lands." By early March, however, payments still were not forthcoming
and the company's financial situation was becoming increasingly dire.
Duer was miserable. "You have placed me on the Brink of Ruin," he wrote
to Barlow in November of that year.[32]

Meanwhile, roughly five hundred French settlers—"all of them mechanics, artists, or tradesmen"—had left for the Ohio valley, believing they
had purchased 120,000 acres of land there. They arrived in New York, Philadelphia, and Baltimore only to discover that their land titles might be in-
valid; one ship of émigrés heard the bad news in Alexandria, Virginia, after
a seventy-two-day journey across the Atlantic. Undaunted, they proceeded
west from their various locations to Pittsburgh, on the other side of the Appalachian Mountains, at the Ohio River's confluence. When they finally
arrived at the Scioto lands, they did their best, but "it was hard for people
brought up in the ease of a Parisian life," as Volney put it, "to sow, to weed,
to reap their wheat, to make it up into sheaves, to carry it home, to cultivate
corn, oats, tobacco, and watermelon, in a heat of 24 to 28 degrees [Celsius]."
These were not people with vast experience in frontier agriculture: "wigmakers, hat makers, carriage drivers, artists, dance and music teachers, all
lost in the American desert." All these difficulties paled in comparison
with the one that the Scioto agents had failed to mention, however: the
United States was then engaged in a losing war with the Miami and Shaw-
nee nations, which had dealt General Arthur St. Clair a devastating defeat in November 1791, just about the time the French settlers arrived.
During their first years of settlement, through 1792 and 1793, Native warriors captured four settlers and scalped one, "who survived this horrible
operation."[33]

Back in Paris, Barlow was not faring much better. He was running
short on cash and had already missed his first payment to the Scioto Company. One investor in the Compagnie du Scioto had paid for his shares with
thirty thousand bottles of champagne, leaving it to Barlow to figure out
how to turn them into cash. Realizing, perhaps, the limitations of his business acumen, Barlow had partnered with William Playfair, a fast-talking

Scottish scientist and economist—and future inventor of the pie chart. Unfortunately for Barlow, however, Playfair did not; in 1791 he absconded with the proceeds of the land sales, leaving Barlow with nothing to offer outraged shareholders in the now bankrupt Compagnie du Scioto. But their fate was not as hard as that of the hundreds of French settlers stranded in the Ohio wilderness, under attack by Native Americans, without legal title to any land. "Such is the situation of the colony planned on the Scioto," Volney ruefully concluded, "which is far from the poetic felicity sung by the *cultivateur américain,* and the delights of the future capital of the *Empire of the Ohio* prophesied by another writer." All that romantic poetry, and it "destroyed the comfort of five hundred families."[34]

ALL TRANSATLANTIC land schemes in the 1790s operated in the shadow of Scioto's spectacular failure. It sprinkled the conversations at dinner tables and in parlors when Noailles, Talleyrand, Liancourt, and Volney arrived in Philadelphia. And it stimulated a growing wariness of American land ventures in Europe, leading to books like *Look Before You Leap; or, A Few Hints to Such Artizans, Mechanics, Labourers, Farmers and Husbandmen as Are Desirous of Emigrating to America,* published in 1796. Land in the United States was so copious, and so much of it was for sale, that many Europeans had come to see buying it as blindly throwing away their money. "No speculations have been more completely injudicious than all those of Europeans in American lands," Alexander Baring reported when he came to the United States. "They have been complete leaps in the dark and they are now so perfectly aware of it that they reject all proposals indiscriminately without really understanding any." What had been the most attractive features of American lands—their price—had become a giant red flag. "The extreme cheapness of the lands contributes also to frighten," Talleyrand noted in a long memorandum on land speculation, "and recalls too much the banks of the Ohio."[35]

Talleyrand's initial skepticism about the wisdom of speculating in land pushed him toward investments in debt or stock. With Hamilton having proved the new U.S. government's commitment to paying public debts and protecting the rights of creditors, Talleyrand believed that government finance was the most promising object of speculation. His early efforts focused on bills of exchange, government bonds, bank stocks, and some commodity speculation. Talleyrand could also foresee that a resolution of the diplomatic crisis between the United States and Great Britain, and the signing of the Jay Treaty, would cause government bonds to rise on the London exchanges: bets that paid off for Talleyrand. As for land, coming in the wake of the Scioto and Asylum failures, Talleyrand wondered if the speculation was as sure as many investors imagined. "It is true that these lands increase in value by the sole effect of the passage of time," he admitted, but could they increase fast enough? He noticed how excessively leveraged so many speculators were, "bound by engagements which make it necessary to resell soon." Given the consistently tight credit in the United States, the conditions seemed too risky. Robert Morris was already encountering liquidity problems, and William Bingham was in only slightly better shape.[36]

Despite these early concerns, Talleyrand and the other *constituants* all gradually turned their attention to land. By 1795 it was the center of their interest. Perhaps the length of their exile was beginning to wear them down, along with the realities of their new lives marked by continuous instability. "Of all the scourges which rapidly destroy great properties," mused Talleyrand, "there is none more active, more devouring, nor of greater extent than revolutions, and it is with reason that all men who are friends of the social order and are interested in its maintenance fear these political convulsions as much as hurricanes and earthquakes." The realization may have been late in coming: after all, Talleyrand and Liancourt and their friends had helped bring about the very revolution and expropriations of property that they now bemoaned. No one knew better than they did that governments rise and fall. War could ravage nations—and disrupt their customs revenue and leave their debt unfunded. "Time indifferently destroys good as well as evil," Talleyrand mused. Only land was an exception to this universal rule. For French aristocrats, in particular, whose wealth had for centuries been founded on the revenues from their vast estates, backcountry land stood out like a bulwark. Talleyrand continued:

A single form of property resists this trial and emerges victorious not only without losing anything of great value, but without having delayed the progress of its natural increase in value. That is uncultivated lands in America. While commerce was interrupted, settled lands depreciating from lack of cultivation, buildings prey of fire, movables and animals given over to pillage, bonds of state loans depreciating and disappearing in the hands of the lender, uncultivated lands which could not deteriorate passed through without alteration the general crisis and received from time and the effects of the revolution an increase in price which their owners scarcely suspected. All that was necessary was to keep the titles.

Amid the political hurricanes and social earthquakes rocking the Atlantic world, only land remained solid and real. Only land could ensure a truly secure form of wealth, and "convert it into indestructible assets which time will increase daily, which require no supervision and of which not all the power of the Emperor . . . can ever deprive them."[37]

By the time he left the United States, Talleyrand had even developed the beginnings of a theory relating land to social revolution. Why, he wondered in an address delivered upon his return to a Paris still recovering from the Terror, did the American Revolution play out so differently from the French? "Without doubt this revolution, like others, has left in people's minds a tendency to excite or receive new turbulence." Few knew better than Talleyrand that such turbulence, once unleashed, might be impossible to tame. And yet his American friends had stood firm through these revolutionary forces while he and his French friends had succumbed. "This need for agitation has been able to satisfy itself in other ways in a vast new country," he explained, "where adventurous projects stimulate the mind, where an immense quantity of uncultivated land makes it easy for people to go and find a new activity, far from the scene of their first conflicts, to put their hopes in distant speculations, to throw themselves at the same time in the midst of a variety of new schemes, and finally to tire themselves out by travel and to thus soften revolutionary passions." Here, for Talleyrand, lay the difference between American elites' success in controlling their revolution and the failure of French elites to do the same: land was the answer. In America it provided a safety valve and "made it easy" for people to exhaust their revolutionary passions. France, by contrast, lacked a reservoir of land; its revolution had turned in on itself. The only way to tame such passions, perhaps, would be to find a new space to colonize.[38]

In the meantime, the émigrés could at least profit from the turmoil. By the mid-1790s, many of France's greatest aristocrats had fled, while wealthy planters were pouring out of the French Caribbean into the United States. "It is more than probable," a Dutch investor predicted in 1792, "that many French both from Europe & from the French West Indies will follow." Investors believed these refugees' demands for land would drive up values, as would the growing demand for wheat and corn stimulated by Atlantic warfare. Could all this turmoil be harnessed to generate stability? French minister Fauchet thought so. "The Émigrés," he wrote in a diplomatic report, "are using this method [speculation] to transfer their funds here and realize them. . . . They hope that the absence of good laws and the impossibility of ever establishing peace in the heart of the Republic will lead a considerable part of the French population to desert." Even George Washington thought the turmoil across the Atlantic might drive up land prices in America. "There are reasons to believe that in the course of this winter, and the ensuing Spring and Summer," he wrote to a friend in November 1794, "many men of property from Europe will remove to this country, or send over their property, with a view to invest it, either in our funds, or in lands."[39]

This was a new world, a world of continuous movement in which people and goods and especially capital never stopped circulating. The French armies smashing their way across northern Europe had unleashed a tidal wave of mobile capital. If French aristocrats escaped with a relatively modest trickle of silver, coin, or jewels, Dutch financiers were a different story. Henry Hope was one of the most prosperous bankers in Europe. Jefferson had called his firm "the first house in Amsterdam." So significant a figure was he that Adam Smith had dedicated the fourth edition of the *Wealth of Nations* to him, acknowledging "my very great obligations to Mr. Henry Hope of Amsterdam." When the Hopes fled from Amsterdam to London in 1795, they brought so much gold that the Royal Navy sent a frigate to escort them. Investors in the United States waited to see where all this capital would wash up. The triumphant French armies would oblige "a quantity of *riches Capitalistes hollandois* to quit their homes," Théophile Cazenove wrote to Alexander Hamilton in January 1795, just before French forces entered the city. "These émigré Capitalists will probably have taken a large amount of various debt instruments issued in Amsterdam." Even the considerable financial demands of the British state were unable to absorb the deluge. As interest rates in Europe declined—keeping British borrowing costs low and helping fund its war against France—this itinerant capital began searching further afield for more profitable outlets. "Given the political state of Europe," commented Talleyrand, "there is surely some capital looking to escape." It was a remarkably modern way of thinking about the circulation of capital: as Talleyrand put it, of "funds which seek new employment." And what better haven existed than America? "In a state which is approaching prosperity as rapidly as America," he wrote, "the most liquid and extensive capital is strongly attracted." As Talleyrand toured the American backcountry in 1794 he found himself "wishing that a part of the considerable capital that was coming to shelter itself in America would be used in clearing the land and for large-scale agriculture."[40]

As for Liancourt, the more he traveled, the more persuaded he was of the potential profits from land speculation. Everywhere, it seemed, farm values were steadily rising: "New lands, cleared under his own supervision, is still perhaps the most profitable investment for the father of a family." The same was true of uncultivated tracts. "The increase of the price of land is uncommonly great," Liancourt marveled. "It has more than doubled within the last three or four years." Everyone seemed to be making money. "Every step we take in America, either in towns or in the country, shows that a fortune is available for one who takes the trouble to seek it." It was not long before he decided on land investments as the pillar of his financial strategy, writing to his wife that he would invest "in well chosen lands of America, which will double in value, increase ten-fold, perhaps, in the space of eight to ten years. It is a capital idea. It is the one that is, for future events, the possible foundation of the comfort of our family."[41]

All this mobile capital needed guidance. It needed careful, intelligent, and, most of all, trustworthy intermediaries. If the Scioto Company scandal had shown anything, it was that unscrupulous men on the make played too central a role in international speculation. This had no doubt been true since the earliest days of long-distance finance, but how to distinguish between the unscrupulous and the visionary became an acute problem in times of revolution. Were they two sides of the same coin? Those who speculated were almost by definition risk takers. They were the audacious ones who looked down into the abyss—and took the plunge. Sometimes they landed safely and sometimes they didn't. William Duer had seemed like a safe bet—until he wasn't and sought refuge from his many creditors in debtors' prison. Robert Morris, much more famous and successful than Duer ever was, had seemed like a far safer bet—until he wasn't, either. In the fall of 1798 he watched the progress of another outbreak of yellow fever from a cell in debtors' prison. "Death will soon enter the door opposite mine," he wrote to his former partner John Nicholson, another prominent financier about to join Morris in prison. Whom were Europeans supposed to trust? Perhaps there might be a role after all for men like Talleyrand and Liancourt, Noailles and Cazenove—intermediaries who could more wisely channel mobile capital into the United States.[42]

IN JUNE 1796, while Volney was traveling through the Ohio valley, an unusually distinguished traveling party left Philadelphia. Among them were William and Anne Bingham with their two daughters, who after nearly a year of private lessons with Volney were growing increasingly fluent in French; Anne's sister Elizabeth Willing, now married to William Jackson; the vicomte de Noailles, described by this time as "a necessary family appendage and also an agreeable travelling companion"; Mr. Richards, a Briton being groomed to become a land agent; and Alexander Baring, the future Lord Ashburton. From Philadelphia the party traveled overland to New York, along the road that had become so familiar to Talleyrand and the other émigrés who shuttled back and forth between the country's two principal commercial cities. From there, they boarded a ship on the southern tip of Manhattan and headed north along the East River, through the Hell Gate, which opens into Long Island Sound, passing the remnants of a British frigate that had been cast on the rocks during the Revolution by the dangerous mix of currents and tides. They arrived in Newport, Rhode Island, and traveled from there by land to Providence and Boston. After spending several days socializing in the salons of Boston's elite, they sailed for Maine in mid-July. Finally they arrived at their destination: Henry and Lucy Knox's four-story, 3,025-square-foot-per-floor mansion named Montpelier, in Thomaston—"very fine," Baring described it, "bordering on magnificence." This was the centerpiece of Baring's newest American investment on behalf of his family's firm and the Hope firm: £100,000 placed in two million acres of Maine land.[43]

The travel party was just that—a public relations stunt as much as a business trip. "The projected excursion makes a deal of noise here & will do all over the country where we pass," Alexander Baring wrote to Henry Hope. With "such fine ladies in traveling . . . every lady's curiosity is raised to the highest. The Ladies' company & presence on the lands will be of infinite benefit." Even President Washington had heard about the expedition, writing to William Bingham and "wishing him, Mrs. Bingham and the Party, a pleasant journey, and Safe return." Learning about the trip from London, the Hopes and Alexander's father, Sir Francis Baring, offered publicity tips from across the Atlantic. "I am aware, that your purchases, the journey, and various circumstances," wrote Sir Francis somewhat cryptically, "may occasion an éclat, and perhaps excite a degree of enthusiasm which must be siez'd and promoted at the moment." With the public's eyes on Maine, it would be a good time to sell land. Anything that might drum up attention was encouraged. "You will with your ladies have ample scope to exercise your ingenuity in finding names for our districts and townships," wrote Hope. Even Sir Francis chimed in with suggestions: "What do they think of the following as additions to their list—Henry, I leave to themselves, but there remains Adrianople—Philip-ville or Phillipsburg—Williamstown in the North as a counterpart to the Williamsburg in the South."[44]

The deal had been a long time in the making, and included many of the characters who frequented Anne Bingham's salon in Philadelphia, including not just Noailles but also Liancourt, Talleyrand, and Cazenove. It began with Henry Knox, another pillar of Federalist high society, the founder of the Society of the Cincinnati, who began his career as a Boston bookseller but got his real launch by marrying into a wealthy family with extensive interests in Maine lands. During the Revolution, Knox rose in rank to become the youngest major general in the U.S. Army. The defeat of the British Empire pushed out the Loyalists who had laid claim to much of Maine—then still part of Massachusetts—creating opportunities for ambitious Americans eager to get their hands on backcountry lands. But the war ended with land rights in Maine hopelessly confused, forcing Knox to the Massachusetts courts, which, thanks in large part to his political connections, obligingly cleared the title to various legally dubious patents in 1785. It was a good time to buy. The country was in the midst of a postrevolutionary depression, with the circulation of specie at a nadir; few legislators wanted to risk raising taxes and fomenting popular discontent. It was much easier to pay off the wartime debt by selling off huge tracts of land to wealthy merchants and financiers.[45]

Teaming up with the ever-resourceful William Duer, Henry Knox laid claim to huge tracts of land in a series of secret purchases; by 1792 they owned nearly 3.5 million acres in Maine, with payments to be forthcoming. The next step was to raise the funds to pay the initial installment. Knox and Duer turned first to some French emigrants—hapless former investors in the Scioto Company. Forming an outfit called "The French Company of the Union, planned for a colony of exiles," they traveled to Maine in 1791 to negotiate with Duer and Knox, with Aaron Burr apparently providing legal advice. They could not agree on terms, however.[46]

When Duer fell into bankruptcy in 1792, the entire venture verged on collapse, and Knox searched desperately for a savior. Théophile Cazenove sent an agent to Maine to assess the quality of the lands but decided against purchasing on behalf of his Dutch investors. It was then that William Bingham stepped in, agreeing to acquire Duer's stake. (He later vowed that he would never again buy a million acres of land without seeing it first.) The holdings consisted of two large tracts, one along the coast, and the other, the "Kennebec tract," in the remote inland reaches of Maine. Even with Bingham's considerable support, however, the investors needed more capital in order to meet the payments promised to the Massachusetts legislature. "It will not be long," Talleyrand predicted, before Bingham himself would become overextended, "if he does not dispose of several million acres which he has acquired in the north of America." None of this, moreover, counted the infrastructure improvements that would be necessary to unlock the value of undeveloped land. "American capital," Bingham wrote to Knox in 1795, getting increasingly desperate, "is not sufficiently extensive to embrace all these vast objects. . . . We must have recourse to European capitals and engage them in our concerns."[47]

Bingham and Knox first courted Talleyrand, who was then planning to tour the backcountry. Armed with a letter of introduction from Knox to prominent Bostonians, Talleyrand traveled in August and September of 1794 with his friend Beaumetz to investigate the Maine lands, spending several days at Knox's home, Montpelier (it "would even be beautiful in Europe," commented Talleyrand). Talleyrand was always a shrewd observer, but in this case he paid particularly close attention. "We were on the property of the people to whom we were the most attached in America," Talleyrand reported, "and we looked at the territories of Mr. Bingham and the General Knox with the greatest care and interest." Cazenove was evidently still pondering some sort of investment, since he gave Talleyrand a list of printed questions about the lands before he left Philadelphia, and sent a Dutch companion to accompany him and Beaumetz through Maine. In addition to the long report he prepared in response to Cazenove's questions, Talleyrand also forwarded a brief account of the lands to Alexander Baring.[48]

Overall, Talleyrand was favorably impressed with Maine, its health, its fertility, and its extensive water system. Talleyrand noted in particular the deep harbors, excellent for shipping, shipbuilding, and naval support; the network of rivers that allowed for easy communication and transportation; and the forests and trees, which offered rich resources for commerce and navies. Indeed, it was Maine's prodigious lumber supplies that would entice Baring two years later: "The Southern states, as well as the West In-

THE MAINE LAND PURCHASE

William Bingham and Henry Knox owned two large tracts of Maine near the contested U.S./Canada border. They spent several years soliciting purchasers, hosting potential investors in Knox's mansion in Thomaston—Talleyrand and Liancourt among them—and sending agents to London and Paris to lure foreign capital into Maine's forested lands.

dies are supplied entirely from Maine, the old countries being exhausted." Given an adequate financial commitment, Talleyrand believed, the region would take off. The more he traveled, the more convinced Talleyrand became that the key to this new society was capital investment. "Agriculture," he decided, "could very usefully absorb much more capital than it currently uses."[49]

The émigrés had long studied the relationship among commerce, agriculture, and economic development. "Agriculture is the basis on which all States are founded," Talleyrand wrote in his memoirs. "It is agriculture, and I say this with the *économistes* [Physiocrats], that forms the chief wealth of the State, that teaches respect for property, and signals that our interest is always blind when it interferes with the interests of others; it is agriculture that points out to us, in the most immediate way, the indispensable relationship between the duties and the rights of men; it is agriculture that, by binding the tiller of the soil to his field, binds men to their country." No wonder he and Liancourt were friends. The influence of French liberal thought could not have been clearer. "We saw society at its origin," Talleyrand wrote to Cazenove with wonder. "We have witnessed the birth of a people arriving on the theater of the world . . . destined by nature to play an important role in the American federation."[50]

In the end, though, Talleyrand concluded that the region, for all its potential, had too many flaws. He was unimpressed with Maine's residents, whom he called lazy and avaricious. He worried about their loyalty to the state. If those who tilled the soil were bound to their country, what about the many fishermen who populated Maine, sending salted cod to Europe and the Caribbean? "To which country does a resident of the sea belong?" Add to its residents' general predisposition their distance from the federal government and their persistent dislike of taxes, and Talleyrand wondered about the future of the province of Maine. Would it even remain part of the United States? Ultimately, he concluded, Maine wasn't agricultural enough, and its economy not diversified enough. And so he chose not to invest, and gave the same recommendation to Cazenove. Though Talleyrand's Maine travels did not result in an agreement, they did produce at least one enduring anecdote. While he and Beaumetz wandered the Maine woods, Talleyrand met some local inhabitants who thought they "recognized in him an illegitimate son of the pretty daughter of a fisherman and the captain of a French national ship which had been there about the year 1758." Thus was born the rumor that Talleyrand, scion of one of France's noblest families, was in fact the illegitimate child of a Mount Desert, Maine, fisherman's daughter.[51]

Having failed to entice Talleyrand and Cazenove, Knox and Bingham began to court Liancourt. Not long after Talleyrand's return to Philadelphia, Noailles made Liancourt a proposal on Bingham's behalf. Within days, Liancourt had made a short excursion outside the city to visit some lands that Bingham wanted to sell. A month later, Liancourt dined at Noailles' with Bingham. "Spoke about the lands in the province of Maine," he noted in his diary. Liancourt did not specify the nature of the proposal, but it probably involved sending him to London or Hamburg to find investors. Months later, Bingham was still hoping that Liancourt might "be disposed to undertake some part of the business relative to the sale of the Maine Lands in Europe." It was a common practice, one the Scioto associates had employed by sending Barlow to Paris. "In general there are few rich people in America & Opportunities for investing Money very numerous," noted a Dutch investor with close ties to the United States. "Many therefore bought more than they were able to pay for & thus often dispatched Emissaries to Europe to dispose of part again by the Lump with some advance." Liancourt had all the right qualities for such a mission. "His intelligence, his activity and his private character all favorable," Bingham observed. But most of all, he was well connected: "a person of credibility," benefiting from the "weight of personal character, to support the recommendation," of the lands, someone who would be trusted by "the great capitalists of Europe." Knox agreed. "No man would be more industrious or impressive" as their representative in Europe, he wrote, evidently thrilled by the possibility. "He is really a man of business and perfectly calculated for this country. Unassuming and persevering, and at the same time he would be delighted with such a work of creation, as would be in his power." Liancourt's qualities, his connections, and most of all his reputation would surely lure foreign buyers. "A man of his character being an active member of a company," Knox added with no little relish, "would do much to elevate the reputation of the lands." But Liancourt refused the offer; he had arrived less than a year earlier and war was still ravaging Europe.[52]

In September 1795, a year after Talleyrand visited, Liancourt was able to see Maine with his own eyes. He had been traveling since May, when he first visited Asylum, Pennsylvania, with his friends and his dog, Cartouche. He had since traveled across upstate New York, where he visited Madame de La Tour du Pin, and into New England. He, too, made the ritual stop at Montpelier ("a handsome, though not a magnificent structure"), and then spent several days touring the countryside with Knox. Like Talleyrand and the others, Liancourt saw potential. "In this territory," he wrote, "it seems to me that no person can fail to thrive, who possesses so eminently, the qualities of intelligence, prudence, and activity, together with a sufficient capital, to lay out in improvements." The region abounded with lumber, salted fish for export to Europe and the Caribbean, an extensive coastline, and many navigable rivers. "In general," he decided, "this region is very suitable for acquiring a great fortune to any company or person who will contribute a substantial capital." Like Talleyrand, however, Liancourt was unimpressed by the residents—their "carelessness, the neglect that they showed in the cultivation of their lands." This issue was close to Liancourt's heart. He had long focused his attentions on agricultural improvement, having discussed the issue with his friend Arthur Young, and had tried to apply the most modern farming techniques to his estates north of Paris. Now, while traveling through Maine, Liancourt deplored what he perceived as shoddy farming practices: the land "so badly and poorly cultivated." Proper agriculture, he insisted, required "a good preparation of the soil, thoughtful labor, and"—perhaps the thing most lacking in Maine—"capital to sustain the work." Only with these could the region begin to generate "profitable farms."[53]

As it happened, Liancourt did have access to capital. According to Noailles, a friend had authorized Liancourt to invest £30,000 in whatever lands he thought most appropriate. Knox similarly believed that Liancourt's "command of funds are considerable." Unfortunately for them, Liancourt remained skeptical about the potential for immigration to these lands—so necessary to drive up land values—which he thought turned more naturally toward New York, Pennsylvania, or Ohio. He further concluded that the capital investments necessary to unlock the land's potential were greater in Maine than in regions like the Genesee tracts in New York or Pennsylvania's Susquehanna valley. And so, like Talleyrand and Cazenove, Liancourt decided not to invest.[54]

IN THE meantime, Bingham and Knox had sent William Jackson to London to seek out investors. Jackson was a logical choice. An elegant South Carolinian of refined manners but unimposing fortune, he had been one of Washington's aides-de-camp during the Revolution before accompanying John Laurens on a diplomatic mission to France. While in Europe, Jackson worked as a military contractor, buying supplies for the U.S. Army with French loans—a job that produced a network of European contacts for his future career. Although a disastrous experience outfitting privateers in Amsterdam did nothing to endear him to Dutch merchants, Jackson had better luck elsewhere, and went on to serve as Robert Morris's agent in London. Jackson must have been either incompetent or scrupulous—then again, perhaps they were the same thing—since despite these two potentially lucrative posts, his personal financial situation remained modest. It was probably for the money that Jackson agreed to serve as secretary of the Constitutional Convention in 1787—making him the person responsible for destroying the records of the convention. After a stint as secretary to the president during George Washington's first term, Jackson again retired from public service. In 1795 he would marry Elizabeth Willing, Thomas Willing's daughter.[55]

Arriving in Europe in July 1793, Jackson looked high and low for buyers of the Maine lands. When it came to selling land, however, timing was everything and Jackson's, alas, was not fortuitous. War between France and England had just broken out; although it drove up demand for wheat and lumber and other American exports, its immediate effect was to draw capital away from the United States. The fiscal needs of the state were, for the time being, attracting much of Britain's surplus capital. "All the monied men were waiting [for] the opening of Parliament, and every shilling was reserved to speculate in the expected loan," Jackson reported. Why, after all, invest in a speculative land venture in the United States when the British government was offering less risk and high returns on capital? ("Crowding out" is the term economists use today.) Striking out in England, Jackson decided in late 1793 on an audacious plan: to sell the Maine lands to the French government. If French money wasn't going to come into American lands, Jackson figured, he would bring American lands to France.[56]

Thus, in December 1793, a little over a month after Marie-Antoinette's execution at the guillotine along with twenty-one Girondin deputies, just as Robespierre was gaining power and war between Europe's two greatest empires was reaching a violent frenzy, Jackson crossed the English Channel with a prospectus for Knox and Bingham's Maine lands. Armed with a letter of introduction from Jefferson, he planned to travel to Paris, meet with the leaders of the Committee of Public Safety, and sell France a big chunk of Maine. Jackson explained his pitch in a letter to Bingham. The Maine lands, he proposed to argue, are "so peculiarly situated and circumstanced as to be capable of furnishing to France such quantities of masts and timber for her navy, and such supplies of lumber to her Colonies, now so much wanted, as no other country could afford." Maine could provide military supplies to help France wage war on British colonies in the Caribbean, and furnish the fuel necessary to keep its invaluable sugar mills going. The Maine lands, he observed, "must certainly on account of the timber, and at this particular juncture, be an object of great importance." As for the problem of surplus capital, the Catholic Church, Jackson pointed out, had just "yielded up *all* their furniture, and the silver Apostles have become the Agents of Freedom." The French government, unlike other European countries, therefore had considerable amounts of capital ready for such a project. And in the event that government officials decided against the purchase, Jackson had little doubt they would grant him "permission to treat with individuals for the sale or exchange of these lands for property in France." December 1793 was, after all, the month that antirepublican forces in the Vendée were defeated, and six thousand prisoners executed. The guillotine was exacting its bloody toll on the Place de la Concorde in Paris. "There are many persons in France who earnestly desire to remove their property and to invest it elsewhere," Jackson drily remarked. "These people, if sanctioned by an act of the Government, would not, I think, hesitate to embrace such an occasion." Here was a pool of motivated buyers, as Jackson read the situation—the Scioto experience be damned.[57]

Unfortunately, matters did not quite go as planned. When Jackson landed in Boulogne, he was promptly arrested. Or rather, as he put it, "so unfortunate as to be involved in the arrestation" of a fellow American passenger who had been carrying counterfeit currency—*assignats*, to be specific, the currency based on confiscated Church lands that had been devised by Étienne Clavière, the former investor in American debt and funder of Brissot's mission to America, who was executed shortly before Jackson's arrival in France. Jackson fell under suspicion. After spending eleven days in a prison in Boulogne, he was sent to the capital, where he languished in a Parisian jail. Eventually he was allowed to plead his case and was released. Undaunted, Jackson then made his pitch to the Committee of Public Safety:

> Being charged with the disposal of certain valuable lands, in quantity about 2000000 acres, situated in the Commonwealth of Massachusetts, and lying on the Atlantic Ocean, abounding in the best masts and an inexhaustible quantity of naval and other timber, and capable of furnishing immense supplies of lumber and provisions to the Colonies, I had conceived that the acquisition of these lands (which might be made through the medium of Trustees) would, at this moment, be an object of high importance to the Republic—and I had therefore, in consonance with the wishes of the Proprietors determined to place the purchase of them in the offer of the Committee.

Jackson added that he was willing to accept an assignment of the debt due from the United States to France as half the payment. In other words, Jackson was proposing to transfer two million acres of Maine to France—land co-owned by the U.S. secretary of war and son-in-law of the president of the Bank of the United States, a prominent public servant of Pennsylvania soon to be elected to the U.S. Senate—and further suggesting that the U.S. government provide France with the money to pay half the cost. It made Genet's antics in the United States seem like the height of diplomatic reserve.[58]

In the end, though, it was all for naught. The French government was not interested, nor would it grant permission for Jackson to sell land to French residents.

BUT STILL the intrepid Jackson did not give up. Back in London, he mobilized the contacts Bingham had forged with British Whigs during his stay ten years earlier. Bingham provided Jackson with letters of introduction to Sir Francis Baring and Lord Lansdowne. The former prime minister responded by extending "two pressing invitations to visit him at Bowood," his country seat; the influential banker was one of the first people Jackson called on when he arrived in London. Jackson now asked Sir Francis to furnish him with introductions to other European financiers. "I have mentioned my intention of going to Holland to Sir Francis Baring," Jackson reported. "He says he will give me letters to all his friends there, particularly to Mr. Hope." By the summer of 1794, Jackson was "perfectly convinced that no possible plan" could offer so many rewards to Bingham and Knox than "prevailing on the Houses of Hope and Baring" to get involved. Though Jackson did not succeed in persuading the Barings and Hopes to invest during his trip, he did spark enough interest to have them send Alexander Baring, Sir Francis's son, then only twenty-one years old and working for the Hopes in Amsterdam, to the United States to further explore the opportunity.[59]

Baring would leave quite a mark. A young American merchant described him as "an extraordinary young man, of great mercantile talents & possessed of much information. . . . He is respected by all the old characters who know him; and was so much esteemed by the House of Hope & Co. of Amsterdam, that after being some time in their compting-house, he was received into their firm, and at the time the French entered Holland, he staid behind & sent nearly 2 millions of property to England." Knox and

*Alexander Baring in a portrait by Sir Thomas Law-
rence painted a few years after his return to England.*

Bingham were waiting anxiously when Baring arrived in the United States
and immediately jumped to action, making sure that he slid right into their
network of friends and business associates. Baring even moved into the
Binghams' mansion; he became an intimate in their circle and a fixture at
their dinner parties and salons. Visitors of any standing who passed
through Philadelphia reported on his presence at the Bingham *soirées*—
where the discussions seemed often to focus on one subject. "Land speculations are now the rage of conversation everywhere," Baring reported soon
after his arrival.[60]

It was probably at the Binghams' that he met the émigré *constituants*,
befriending them and gaining insight into their characters. "I saw a good
deal of Talleyrand when he was here," Baring wrote to his father after
nearly a year of mingling with Philadelphia's Society Hill set. Alexander

developed a high regard for Talleyrand's judgment ("He has been all over the country with a very observant eye and seen deeper than any of his countrymen") and for his prospects ("He is an intriguant du premier ordre and must play a great part shortly"). Baring also discerned some of the qualities that would make Talleyrand one of the greatest diplomats of the following century: "His character is the reverse of his countrymen's in general being very reserved." But he was less impressed with the former bishop's motives. "Talleyrand's object on whatever theatre he is to act is to make money and perhaps he would not be very delicate about the means," Baring warned his father. "I should have some scruples in trusting to his integrity." All in all, it was a remarkably perspicacious assessment by the twenty-three-year-old Baring. As for Noailles, the French émigré with whom Baring probably socialized the most, the young banker called him "a singular character here." Baring enjoyed his company: "He is perfectly a man of honor and a bon compagnon." But he found little to admire in his financial talents: "[He is] no merchant and has no ideas of business beyond what you would suppose a metamorphosis from a French Viscount who has passed all his time in the army would produce." For all that Noailles lacked in mercantile experience, he nevertheless exercised a powerful influence in the Bingham family, particularly among the Bingham women; thus, Baring reported, "He is a man I found it desirable to concilliate. . . . He was of service to me in my negotiations. Every thing done there passes through his scrutiny." Eventually, after much anxiety on Bingham's part, some hard negotiating on Baring's—and, it appears, a little help from Noailles—the deal was done. The Barings and the Hopes launched themselves in the Maine lands.[61]

And so it was that Baring traveled through Maine that summer of 1796, having invested in hundreds of thousands of acres of land. The glamorous trip with Noailles and the "fine" Bingham ladies persuaded him that he'd made a good choice. He had already received positive reports from Talleyrand and Liancourt: "Both speak very highly of their advantages." Everything he saw on-site convinced him of those advantages. "It really has the appearance of a magic creation of a new world," he wrote to the Hopes.

"The same wonderfull increase in value of property strikes you every where." Baring was also drawn by the stature and political influence of his partners in the deal. "We have the first characters in the country both as to property influence and management," he reported. "Knox is to have no share in the management of this business, but merely in the eventual profits when ascertained. . . . Major Jackson for his trouble in Europe and Genl. Jackson and Royal Flint for their agency in the original purchase are also to have each the eventual proffit. . . . This arrangement," he crowed, "insures us the exertions and good will of all these people of the first influence." A final influence may have been Alexander's evident interest in Bingham's daughter: Baring long delayed his return, ostensibly to ensure the satisfactory outcome of his investment, though the true reason became clear to all when he married Ann Louisa Bingham in 1798, thus joining the Willing-Bingham clan with the Baring family in the newest and most powerful Anglo-American merchant network.[62]

Backed by the Barings and the Hopes—deeper pockets than these did not exist—capital flowed freely into New England's northern hinterland: lands not far from the Saint Lawrence watershed that French, British, and Native Americans had contested for nearly two centuries. For committed investors like the Barings and the Hopes, the purchase price was just the first of many capital outlays. Everyone recognized that further investments were required to unlock the land's value; it was the reason Liancourt shied away from investing there. Of these investments, roads came first. "The prime necessity of any habitation is the means of reaching it," Talleyrand had written when he toured Maine. "The attraction of a better road supersedes that of a better land, that is the general calculation." On this issue, the owners all agreed. "Rely upon it with confidence that in two years, this country will be highly popular," Knox predicted in October 1795. "But every thing depends upon *settlement* and *roads.*" Bingham was no less enthusiastic. "Cutting roads," he concluded, was "essentially connected with the prosperity of the settlement." Baring agreed: "The importance of roads is immense and cannot be too much attended to," he wrote to the Hopes in 1796.[63]

But roads were only the beginning. "Maine wants Inhabitants, & Capital to put those Inhabitants in Motion," Bingham would later muse. It was the job of the Barings, the Hopes, and Bingham to furnish the capital; to recruit the inhabitants, they hired David Cobb, another one of George Washington's former aides-de-camp. Cobb would prove himself an insistent advocate for all variety of capital expenditures. "I cannot but observe to you," he wrote shortly after arriving on-site, "the necessity of having a surveyor and chainmen attach'd to the concern, boats procur'd for passing to the different parts of the purchase, roads to be cut, let them cost what they may, and on certain places on these roads, houses should be built for entertainment." For years, Cobb badgered the landowners for "a chart blanch," as he spelled it, to "cut roads, build a few little houses, purchase mills, run out the lots." Every new town, Baring believed, "should come with some houses, a store, and if necessary a mill." Cobb also sought to recruit artisans to the settlement: "house wrights, blacksmiths, shoemakers, tanners and brick makers." They worked to extend credit to settlers, and establish a regular packet boat between Boston and Gouldsboro, Maine. Armed with his European capital, Knox launched a huge array of businesses in Maine: barrel works, saw- and gristmills, wharves, coasting and West India vessels, stores, lime quarries, kilns, brickworks, fisheries, gardens, orchards, grain fields, canals, and breeding farms.[64]

These capital improvements corresponded to Baring's ideas of economic development. "No idea can be more erroneous than that money expended on improvements is thrown away," he wrote in 1798. "I am on the contrary persuaded that the price of land is lost unless a sum is devoted to assist the settlement of it." In a long memo, Baring went on to chart his vision for unlocking the land's value: cutting roads; planning towns; building lumber mills, a tavern, and a store for residents to buy and sell their goods; establishing a land office to formalize land sales; and hiring a surveyor resident, along with workers to cut the roads and carpenters to build the infrastructure. And, of course, extending credit—this last "a very important point for consideration." None of these businesses were expected to make money; their purpose was to increase the value of the adjacent lands. "We do not want the profits of the store keeper or the miller," Baring specified. "Our object is solely to enhance the value of our lands by procuring these advantages to settlers."[65]

TALLEYRAND, LIANCOURT, Noailles, and the other émigré *constituants* came to America in the wake of a collapsed revolution. Flung to the farthest reaches of European settlement, they found themselves, quite against anyone's expectations, channeling capital across the Atlantic Ocean. Transactions like these had begun amid the social and political networks forged in salons in Paris, London, and Philadelphia; they now extended deep into the American hinterland.

The capital funneled through these channels served critical functions. It surveyed the land, developed towns and villages, built roads, dug canals, raised flour mills and sawmills, drained swamps, dredged streams, and, most of all, recruited settlers to sparsely populated frontier regions. All of this was hard and expensive work—well beyond the resources of either state or federal governments in the late eighteenth century. Surveying land was a long process, rife with conflicts of interest and fraud. Parceling out and selling land to thousands of individuals was a monumental bureaucratic task, requiring land offices around the country and administrative staff to run auctions and keep meticulous and voluminous records. Building roads took vast amounts of labor and capital, the two things most missing in the American backcountry. By funding these tasks and more, European capital, in the 1790s, essentially served the function of a state in a stateless place.[66]

All of this did more than consolidate U.S. state power in regions where it was exceedingly fragile. It also brought transatlantic capitalism to distant borderland areas. "Settling lands is a subject so much better understood in America, that it is almost ridiculous in me to offer an hint or suggestion of any kind," Sir Francis Baring wrote to his son with some diffidence, before proceeding to offer hints and suggestions. Capital investments in the Maine lands, Sir Francis argued, should have as their ultimate objective the transformation of the very nature of rural life. The goal was to change the society and culture that Liancourt and Talleyrand had deplored among Maine's residents. "We must consider them as the means of establishing markets for the sale of what those Settlers may produce, and some establishment may become necessary for that purpose," Baring urged his son. "On the first View, the chief articles are, Fish, Timber of every description, and salt meat. . . . The export for a few Years will probably be confined to America and the West Indies. Europe must come in by degrees."[67]

But this was more than an economic transformation; it was also a cognitive one. Traveling into the backcountry, the émigrés had a sense of moving not just through space but also through time. "It is a novel sight to the traveller," Talleyrand marveled, "who, setting out from a principal city, where society is in perfection, passes in succession through all the degrees of civilization and industry, which he finds constantly growing weaker and weaker, until in a few days he arrives at a mis-shapen and rude cabin, formed of the trunks of trees lately cut down." Drawing on the stadial theories of eighteenth-century thinkers, Talleyrand flirted with a line of thought that would come to its full fruition in Frederick Jackson Turner's thesis of frontier development a century later: "Such a journey is a sort of practical and living analysis of the origin of people and states: we set out from the most compounded mixture, to arrive at the most simple ingredients." Perhaps there was something to learn here, not just about the United States but about more general social processes. "It appears as if we travelled backwards in the history of the progress of the human mind," Talleyrand concluded. "We please ourselves by finding in the succession of space what appears to belong only in the succession of time."[68]

The émigré *constituants* had launched a revolution and watched it spin out of control. Did the idea of beginning anew appeal to them? Thrown across the Atlantic by the forces they helped unleash, did they imagine they could somehow go back to the origins of time itself and start over? Surely that was part of the appeal of the Susquehanna valley for all those alienated revolutionaries in Europe. Having failed at a political revolution in Europe, here they were, launching an economic revolution in America. Talleyrand had once proposed the nationalization of Church lands in France as a means of "populating the country with property owners." Here he was now, attempting the same for the United States. With nothing more than confidence on their side—the confidence of wealthy men in places like London, Amsterdam, Hamburg, and Geneva—the capital the émigrés channeled would transform the landscape itself. The flimsiest of things, nothing more than a promise written on a piece of paper, could be transmogrified into the most material of things: a road, a flour mill, a canal. Here was a revolution as profound, perhaps, as the one he had left behind. As he made his way through the dense forests in upstate New York, Talleyrand fantasized about the region's future. "Our imagination ran wild along this vast expanse," he recalled in his *Mémoires*. "We placed towns, villages, hamlets; the forests remained on the mountain peaks, the sides covered with harvests, and already herds came to graze in the pastures of the valleys that we saw beneath our eyes." These men who had sought to transform France in the image of their liberal, commercial ideal now traveled America and did that very thing. They would raise cities in the wilderness, bring commercial agriculture to rugged mountainsides, and extend the nation into the continental interior. And they would do it all with promises.[69]

OF ALL the late-eighteenth-century speculations, the Holland Land Company in western New York was surely the most consequential. This vast purchase along the borders of Lakes Erie and Ontario began with Théophile Cazenove, the Dutch banker who employed Philadelphia's best French chef and regularly hosted the *constituants* for dinner.

Sent to the United States by a group of Dutch investors, Cazenove was focused on land acquisition by the mid-1790s. By all rights, those lands in western New York should not have been for sale: they were far to the west of the boundary the Six Nations of the Iroquois and the British had established at the 1768 Treaty of Fort Stanwix. When the American Revolution broke out, the Senecas who lived in the region allied with the British, further cementing their claims to the land. To their surprise and outrage, however, when the terms of the 1783 peace treaty were made public, they discovered that Great Britain had recognized U.S. sovereignty to their homeland—generous terms made courtesy of Lord Lansdowne, then the British prime minister. U.S. negotiators browbeat the Senecas into a formal

Detail from a map printed in 1784 in London highlighting the boundaries of the United States. This map—unlike the Treaty of Paris negotiated between the United States and Great Britain—clearly recognizes the Seneca lands as unceded, drawing a line roughly along that determined by the 1768 Treaty of Fort Stanwix, though it includes lands of the Oneidas, who had allied with the United States during the Revolution.

cession of those lands at the 1784 Treaty of Fort Stanwix—a cession whose validity the Senecas never ceased to dispute until occupancy rights to much of this land were restored to them by the 1794 Treaty of Canandaigua. In 1791 Robert Morris (whom the Senecas called "the great Eater, with the big Belly," putting their finger on Morris's fatal flaw, his unquenchable land hunger) purchased the preemption rights to 4 million acres of the land— rights to purchase the land once the Senecas agreed to cede them. Cazenove bought 3.3 million of those acres from Morris, and later helped facilitate the Seneca cession at the 1797 Treaty of Big Tree by bribing the Seneca negotiators and interpreters.[70]

Cazenove had not in fact intended to buy so much of western New York. But such were the vagaries of business in the Age of Sail: in December 1792, Cazenove bought 1.5 million acres from Morris in Philadelphia, while his Dutch backers almost simultaneously bought 1.8 million from Morris's son, then in Amsterdam, before word crossed the Atlantic. Together, the two tracts formed the Holland Land Company, which sold shares to eager investors in Amsterdam. Cazenove sent Talleyrand to visit the lands in 1794, soliciting a report from him. After Hamilton retired as treasury secretary, the Holland Land Company retained him to provide legal advice and help lobby New York State to liberalize the laws restricting foreign ownership of lands.[71]

Bordering Lakes Erie and Ontario, this particularly well-situated territory provided access to the Montreal *entrepôt* via the Saint Lawrence River and to the New Orleans *entrepôt* via the Allegheny River; it also practically abutted the Susquehanna with its outlet through Baltimore. Best of all, perhaps, it lay along the western edge of the Mohawk River throughway, by which nearly all travelers west from New England were destined to pass. If the myriad canal schemes floating around ever got off the ground, it would one day connect the Great Lakes to New York City. As he followed the Mohawk River on his travels shortly before Cazenove made his purchase, Talleyrand was already writing about the trade that would one day transit through "the place to be opened by the canal."[72]

The Holland Land Company was a major player. Including the 3.5 million acres in western New York, 100,000 acres in central New York, and 1.4 million acres in north-central and northwestern Pennsylvania, its holdings totaled more than 5 million acres, making it the nation's largest private developer until the age of the American railroads. As in other land developments, the purchase price was only the beginning of the Holland Land Company's investment; massive infusions of capital were required to unlock the profits lying fallow. "A road running across good lands," Talleyrand observed to Cazenove, "is equal to the discovery of buried treasure." Building roads took labor and capital—two of the scarcest things in America; the average cost of a turnpike was $1,000 per mile. Without these investments, however, farmers could not sell their crops and pay the company

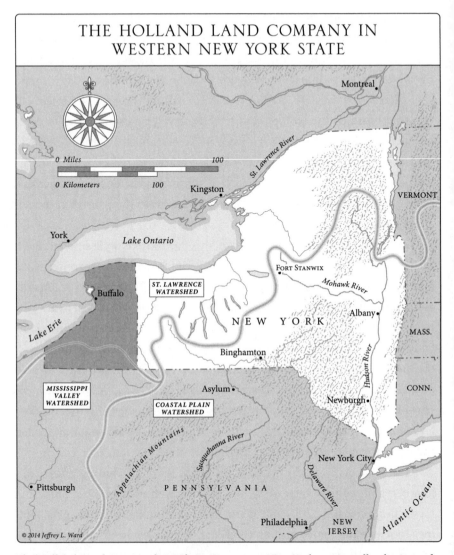

THE HOLLAND LAND COMPANY IN WESTERN NEW YORK STATE

The Holland Land Company's purchases in western New York were excellently situated. They bordered Lakes Erie and Ontario, lay at the nexus of two of North America's most important watersheds, and covered key transportation routes for goods and travelers passing through the Mohawk Valley corridor. With the formidable resources of its Dutch investors, the Holland Land Company would play an important role in the development of western New York.

for lands sold on credit. Talleyrand estimated that $20,000 to $25,000 of investment was required per 100,000 acres of land. But given an adequate commitment, he predicted, "your lands will find themselves truly watered and fertilized by the capital which . . . has come to seek them."[73]

At the time, New York State possessed neither the means nor the will to shower such sums on its hinterland. Surveying the company's lands alone took the better part of three years, during which Cazenove deployed parties of 150 men at a time—surveyors, draftsmen, cooks, axmen, and camp keepers—at a cost of over $70,000. To encourage settlement from New England, he even built a tavern in Utica, New York, along the Mohawk River, modeled on Philadelphia's City Tavern—the one where Liancourt had slept on his first night in Philadelphia, and where Philadelphia's merchants met to share news and information. These and many more outlays continued long before revenue began to trickle in. And when it did, the trickle was tiny: in 1801 the Holland Land Company sold just $26,343.54 worth of land, virtually all of it on credit, and cash revenues totaled a mere $625.14½! From 1801 to 1809, the Holland Land Company sold only five hundred thousand acres of land, collecting a tiny fraction of the proceeds in cash. Meanwhile, its tax bill continued growing, and by 1809 was approaching $10,000 per year. (The same held true in Maine: the Barings began paying Massachusetts state taxes a few years after their purchase and continued even during the War of 1812—thus helping to fund a government with which their own country was at war.) From the perspective of the fragile New York State finances, this was an excellent deal.[74]

A willingness to extend credit to cash-poor settlers was key; it distinguished land sold by speculators from that sold by the government. The Holland Land Company required only 5 percent down payments for its sales, repeatedly forgave accrued interest, and agreed to receive payment in labor for road building or in grain, hogs, and cattle. Meanwhile, massive infusions of capital were deployed not just for roads but also for schools, stores, sawmills and gristmills, land clearance, potash works, distilleries, breweries, and importing blacksmiths and other artisans. So great were the demands of settlers, they continually exceeded the patience of Joseph Ellicott, the company's indispensable land agent. "The numerous applications of this nature made to me daily," he complained in 1810, "would require the Capital of the Bank of the United States to supply."[75]

BY THE end of the eighteenth century, broad swaths of the U.S. backcountry were owned by foreign investors or reliant on foreign investment. European capital had stretched its long fingers from the coast of Maine, across northern and western New York to the Great Lakes, along river routes through central and western Pennsylvania, and deep into the Ohio valley. It had begun to penetrate distant borderland areas—where the United States pushed into the Saint Lawrence and Mississippi watersheds—which were bitterly contested by Native American nations to the west and European empires to the north and south. The capital moving into these areas performed a critical function, helping to orient the economy of these westward- and northward-facing regions toward the East Coast's port cities. Indeed, one might say that it imposed its own geography on the continent's natural geography.

No project proved more critical to the development of western New York than the Erie Canal, eventually completed in 1825, which famously connected the Great Lakes to the Atlantic coast, pulling trade away from the Mississippi and Saint Lawrence Rivers and to New York. Less known is the key role played by the Holland Land Company in its development. As early as 1797, Alexander Hamilton's father-in-law and major New York landowner Philip Schuyler floated a plan to extend the title of lands owned by foreigners on the condition that Holland Land Company stockholders offer a low-interest loan of $250,000 to the Western Inland Lock Navigation Company. Although the company refused, seeing the offer as a form of extortion, the connection between the Holland Land Company and the Erie Canal persisted. Joseph Ellicott, the company's agent, started lobbying for the canal in 1808. In 1816 he was named as a commissioner to the Erie Canal board, which gave him a perch from which to route the canal through company lands. Ellicott, in turn, appointed his niece's husband, also an employee of the Holland Land Company, as the engineer to select the canal's western terminus. After a long fight, the Erie Canal board chose

Buffalo—also on company lands. In 1817 the Holland Land Company donated one hundred thousand acres to provide a route for the canal and to
support its financing. When the canal route was finalized, Ellicott raised
the price of company land by $1.50 per acre, and estimated the increase in
land values at $1.2 million. But that was not all: when the first loan to fund
the Erie Canal was floated in 1817, more than a third of it was taken by two
London investors, and there is some evidence that the director of the Holland Land Company helped secure the European market for canal loans.
By 1829 more than half of New York's outstanding Erie Canal debt was held
abroad.[76]

The Holland Land Company was not the only European outfit to play
an important role in the growing American economy. Soon after they
launched themselves in Maine, the Barings emerged as the most central
player in U.S. government finance. Securing that connection may well have
been one of Francis Baring's motivations for sending his son to the Binghams' mansion in the first place; it was certainly its most important result.
In 1795, before Alexander left for America, Bingham tried to lure the Barings with promises of lucrative government contracts. "From my present
Situation [as U.S. senator] & more immediate relationship with the Administration of the Executive Department of the Government"—Bingham had
just recently been elected to the Senate and referred here to his father-in-
law, Thomas Willing, the president of the Bank of the United States—"I
have had an opportunity of recommending your House to the Secretary of
the Treasury, for the Agency of a Business which the Bank of the United
States has already made known to you. I shall be happy in finding new Opportunities of rendering you Service," he promised. Two days later, Bingham wrote another letter to the Barings "informally, as it relates to the
Bank Direction, but with the Privity of some of the Directors, & of the
Secretary of the Treasury, with whose Department the Bank of the United
States is intimately connected."[77]

This was, as Bingham intimated, the beginning of a long and mutually
beneficial relationship between the United States and the Baring Bank. No
doubt the United States benefited. A few years later, the Barings raised
money for U.S. negotiations with the Barbary States and funded the Quasi-

War with France, buying 11,000 muskets and 330 cannons from the British government on behalf of the United States. From the Barings' perspective, the growing value of American securities on London capital markets was due at least in part to their relationship. "I will venture to assert," Sir Francis Baring bragged in 1804 to Albert Gallatin, Thomas Jefferson's Swiss-born treasury secretary, "that the estimation in which the American funds are now held in this Country, may be attributed in some measure to the accommodation and facilities of every description which my House has constantly furnished." By that time, the Barings were acting as London agents for the U.S. government—a function they would perform until 1835—even as they continued to finance major government projects as well as individual states' debt.[78]

This was the long-term legacy of young Alexander Baring's travels to the United States in the 1790s: not his investment in Maine, but rather his marriage into the Bingham-Willing family and the establishment of secure channels of British capital into the United States. Soon after he arrived in 1795 and became acquainted with American merchants and their credit networks, he remarked to his father that "we may through the same channel creep into other very respectable connections here." They certainly did. The years following Alexander's trip to the United States correspond exactly with the shift in the Barings' North American business. "So marked was the geographical re-alignment of the house's business," the Baring Bank historian John Orbell has written, "that, in 1808–13, 70 to 80 per cent of the commission income was derived from 'American and Colonial Account.'" The Barings' American work continued to grow in the years that followed. By the end of the 1830s, the firm had funded the debt of Ohio, Indiana, Illinois, New York, Louisiana, Florida, Kentucky, and Maryland, among others.[79]

Meanwhile, the Hope firm of Amsterdam expanded its American business to become the most important issuer of U.S. federal and state securities to clients in Holland and throughout Europe, marketing Pennsylvania, Ohio, Indiana, Illinois, and Louisiana bonds, as well as those of various municipalities. All of it was traceable to Alexander Baring's trip in the 1790s and to the growing partnership between the Barings and the Hopes forged in the cauldron of the French Revolution. Looking back on that period some years later, John Williams Hope recalled the significance of Alexander's trip to the firm's business: "A very few years after his first passage to A[merica]," he wrote to Henry Hope, "our confidence became fixed as to the gov^t & funds of that country; and that our intercourse with him ever since has effectually Confirmed & riveted it." By the time he wrote those words, in 1804, one year after the Louisiana Purchase, John Williams Hope could claim, "We have an unlimited credit for A[merica] certainly more than for any Gov^t in E[urope]."[80]

By the time state capital began aggressively funding internal improvements, in other words, it followed the path that men like Talleyrand, Noailles, Cazenove, and Liancourt had already cleared for private capital. The growing capital flows from Europe would go on to fund U.S. expansion into the Mississippi valley and lay the groundwork for the industrial development of the Old Northwest—from canals to railroads to mining to construction, and more—all of it built on the channels of capital first established after the American and French Revolutions. It was very much what Hamilton had predicted in his 1791 "Report on Manufactures." Within a few decades, the Holland Land Company tracts became an industrial center. Large stretches of the Ohio valley, including the area surrounding Lake Erie and future cities like Cleveland, evolved into the heartland of American industry. Indeed, William Bingham may well have stated a grand truth about American history when he observed to his future son-in-law Alexander Baring that "foreign Capital . . . has been uniformly, from the first Establishment of this Country, the operative and influential Cause of its Prosperity."[81]

IN EARLY November 1795, Liancourt returned from his travels through Pennsylvania, New York, and Maine. He'd been gone for six months, covered thousands of miles, seen millions of acres of land, invested in some and turned down most, and learned enough about the United States to fill three of the eight volumes of his travelogue. As he crossed the Delaware River from New Jersey into Pennsylvania, he was surprised at the emotions that washed over him when he saw Philadelphia in the distance: "As the sight of its steeples came into view, I felt the pleasure that bears some relation to that which one feels upon returning home after a long absence." The loneliness of exile still weighed heavily: he could not bear to call Philadelphia home. But it had become something akin to home. With its French businesses, its French population, and its French manners, the city offered him solace from the pain he felt at being so far from his family, his country, and his life. "It was here I first landed from Europe, here I spent more time than anywhere else in America, here that were my most intimate acquaintances, who, though but new, are the oldest I have on this continent."[82]

Noailles had been in the country the longest—more than two and a half years by the end of 1795. He had become a citizen and made Philadelphia his home, spending summers at the country houses of his new friends. Moreau could not afford the luxury of leaving Philadelphia for the summer. He continued his work selling books, and in 1795 began printing them as well. As for Talleyrand, Philadelphia had become, if not his home, at least his home base, the place where he had made his new life in exile. As they converged on Philadelphia, the old friends reunited. Liancourt dined at Moreau's house on November 30, enjoying the company of Moreau's son, of whom he'd grown so fond. Talleyrand returned from New York a few days later, on December 5, with his friend and fellow *constituant* Beaumetz still in tow. They had just learned some happy news: Talleyrand had been taken off the list of émigrés in France—the list of those who had willingly alienated themselves from the country, whose property could be legally confiscated, and who were subject to imprisonment or worse upon return. But he didn't want to rush things. He would wait another six months before leaving, to avoid a dangerous winter crossing, get confirmation that he would not be imprisoned upon arrival, and finalize his business dealings.

It would be their last winter together in Philadelphia. By the middle of 1796, Talleyrand and Beaumetz would be gone, with Talleyrand sailing to Hamburg, where he would try to sell some of Robert Morris's lands, and

Beaumetz traveling to India, where he would try to sell some of Cazenove's. But for now, the friends still had a few months together, and they would make the most of them. And so the year 1795 ended with the émigrés celebrating: Talleyrand, Liancourt, and Moreau dining and drinking at a friend's house on December 31.[83]

Chapter 5

FRANCE IN THE
MISSISSIPPI VALLEY

T HE YEAR 1796 BEGAN AS THE PREVIOUS YEAR HAD, WITH THE
French émigré *constituants* together in Philadelphia's Society Hill
neighborhood. In January Moreau published Liancourt's small
book on Philadelphia's prison in both French and English. Liancourt's
friends among the scientific and political elite seem to have taken notice: it
may be what got him elected to the American Philosophical Society on
January 15. Moreau had been a member since 1789, on the strength of his
earlier writings on the laws and constitutions of the French Caribbean colonies; Talleyrand was elected, like Liancourt, in 1796, and Volney the following year. They joined dozens of other French members, including
Ambroise-Marie-François-Joseph Palisot de Beauvois, a French botanist
and naturalist who had been a member since 1792. They would learn more
about Palisot in the months to come.[1]

At the end of January, Beaumetz and Talleyrand finally parted ways,
when Beaumetz left Philadelphia to marry Henry Knox's sister-in-law. It

was evidently an alliance of love, not convenience. His friends tried to talk him out of what they deemed an unwise match, but Beaumetz went ahead. He was, Moreau reported, "in no mood to listen to our arguments." A few months later the economic pressures entailed by his new family pushed him out of the United States entirely. He left for Bombay on the ship *Asia*, planning to sell Cazenove's American land to British nabobs—employees of the British East India Company. It was a project Talleyrand had been promoting for years, and one he had thought of pursuing a year earlier, when his chances of returning to France seemed remote. "I had a vivid regret upon seeing Beaumetz leave," Moreau wrote the night of his friend's departure. "I could foresee all that could result from this voyage, born of necessity, which his unfortunate situation made necessary."[2]

Despite Philadelphia's quietude, the epic events sweeping the globe continued to intrude. As the evening gloom was descending on the first Saturday of February, General Anthony Wayne marched triumphantly into the capital. The troops of the Philadelphia Light Horse met him four miles outside the city and accompanied him across the Schuylkill as cannon fire and bells rang out amid "demonstrations of joy." "Thousands of citizens crowded to see and welcome the return of their brave General, whom they attended to the City Tavern, where he alighted," one newspaper reported. It was, Moreau wrote in his diary, "a great parade."[3]

Wayne had won a decisive victory in 1794 against the Western Confederacy of Indians at Fallen Timbers, not far from Lake Erie, on the other side of Ohio from Gallipolis. It was the greatest military triumph of Washington's presidency and set the stage for the Treaty of Greenville, in which the Western Confederacy finally ceded the viciously contested Northwest to the United States. Wayne had spent the months since mopping up the lingering resistance of the weakened Indian villages and was now returning in triumph. But Philadelphians were not just celebrating Wayne's victory; they were coming together "in celebration of the Peace lately concluded with the Western Indians, and the Algerines; and also, on account of the Peace concluded by France with several European Powers." As Liancourt, Talleyrand, Volney, and the others would soon learn, events in Ohio and

Europe were inseparable. Perhaps the thought had already crossed their minds as they watched the "brilliant display of fireworks" that lit up Philadelphia's sky that night.[4]

And so life as they had come to know it in Philadelphia continued. "Here is the veritable state of Philadelphia society," Liancourt wrote: "grand dinners, grand teas, for arrivals from Europe, English, French, foreigners of all countries, of all classes, of all characters." The Bingham girls were getting still better at French under Volney's tutelage. And their dance steps kept improving under Noailles'. The émigrés' intellectual pursuits roamed broadly. Talleyrand helped Moreau with the proofs of an anthropological article on dancing. But Liancourt was still too restless to remain satisfied. He had achieved some financial security; getting courted by Knox, Bingham, Noailles, and Cazenove to purchase their land did not hurt and certainly kept the dinner invitations coming. Still, there was something too self-interested about all this socializing. "There is no one in this country for whom making money is not the dominant idea," Liancourt wrote in disgust. Philadelphians barely deigned to recognize a foreigner after one or two parties, "unless they suppose him rich, particularly in disposable money; in that case the civilities continue as long as they think he wants to buy land, and even longer, for the homage to wealth is the religion around which all sects unite." His financial stability, it seemed, had come at a cost. "This mercantile spirit, so generally widespread, necessarily produces egoism, isolates him who is touched by it, and leaves neither the taste nor the time for society."[5]

Liancourt's improving economic condition had ironically led him to a greater, almost existential isolation. Liancourt blamed his apathy on the "egoism" of the Americans he frequented and their obsession with money. He was laying the groundwork here for another French traveler, also from one of the most distinguished lineages the French nobility had produced, and also a reformer with a particular interest in prisons, who would follow in Liancourt's footsteps some three decades later as he, too, fled a France wracked by political upheaval. "Individualism is a recent expression," Alexis de Tocqueville would write in 1840. "Our fathers knew only egoism."

But Tocqueville had a kinder view of this individualism. Admitting it produced a heightened sense of isolation, he thought it was also a "thoughtful and peaceful sentiment." Inseparable from democracy itself, it would only grow along with the equality of conditions. But that line of reflection was not yet thinkable in the 1790s. It would have to await the further development of a certain understanding of modernity.[6]

As the months wore on, Liancourt grew increasingly critical of his second home. "That which we call *society* does not exist in this city. The vanity of luxury is very common here; they like to show the new European arrival their handsome furniture, their elegant English glasses, their beautiful porcelain. But once that guest has seen the parade of a ceremonial dinner, they prefer the newer arrival, who doesn't yet know the magnificence of their house, and who has not yet praised their old Madeira wine that has made two or three trips to India; and a new face is always better than an old for one who has little to say." Liancourt certainly was getting sour. Perhaps it was time to go traveling again.[7]

In mid-March 1796, Liancourt saw an advertisement in the local newspaper for a ship sailing to Charleston, "with elegant accommodations." Strolling down to the docks from his home just off Fourth Street, he applied for passage. "I leave to take another very long voyage in the part of the United States that I haven't yet visited," Liancourt wrote to his wife on

For CHARLESTON,
(To fail the 22d inft.)
THE Ship South-Carolina,
John Garman, commander,—
a regular Packet, with elegant accommodations.
For freight or paffage apply to the Capt. on board,
at Smith's wharf, or to
GUSTAVUS & HUGH COLHOUN.
Who have for fale, the cargo of faid fhip, con-
fifting of New Rice in whole and half tierces.
March 14

Advertisement from Claypoole's American Daily Advertiser *for March 16 to March 23, 1796, published in Philadelphia for the ship on which Liancourt sailed.*

March 20. "It's a very tiresome trip, but it prevents me from vegetating in the same place, living without interest." He was falling into a depression again. "Movement, curiosity, even fatigue are happy distractions." As Liancourt finalized his preparations, Moreau gave him several crates of books from his press for a bookseller in Charleston, including copies of his own *Description topographique,* which dealt with the Spanish part of Saint Domingue, as well as Liancourt's recent book on the Philadelphia prison. On the twenty-fourth, Liancourt boarded the *South-Carolina* along with a new traveling companion, Palisot de Beauvois. Palisot had worked in Africa and Saint Domingue before fleeing the Revolution; he was now a refugee in Philadelphia. The two would spend the next six weeks traveling through South Carolina and Georgia before splitting up, with Palisot heading off to the western frontier regions of Georgia and Liancourt returning to Philadelphia overland, by way of Virginia's Shenandoah valley.[8]

But Liancourt and Palisot were not the only Frenchmen to leave Philadelphia during the spring of 1796. Three days before Liancourt departed,

Advertisement that began to appear in the Charleston City Gazette and Daily Advertiser *shortly after Liancourt's arrival, selling books in French and in English published by Moreau in Philadelphia.*

the French general Georges-Henri-Victor Collot—a military engineer, geographer, and former governor of Guadeloupe who had been paroled to Philadelphia after surrendering the French Caribbean island to the British—quietly slipped out of town. As Liancourt and Palisot sailed south along the American coastline, gliding past the Chesapeake Bay and the outer banks of the Carolinas, Collot was heading west toward the rugged Appalachian Mountain passes that divided the East Coast from the Ohio valley, right into the territory that General Wayne had just conquered from the Western Confederacy. Volney left Philadelphia some six weeks later, traveling along a parallel route, first crossing south to Virginia to meet with Jefferson before plunging into the Ohio valley. Noailles, meanwhile, was sailing up the Atlantic coast to Maine that summer along with the Bingham family, Alexander Baring, and others.

French people were traveling all over the country, in areas where U.S. authority was still very fragile, as well as in regions where it was bitterly contested, just as the diplomatic situation between France and the United States was rapidly degenerating. Some of these Frenchmen were up to no good. Liancourt had begun discreetly passing information gleaned from his travels to the new French ambassador in Philadelphia, Pierre-Auguste Adet. It was Adet who sent Liancourt's traveling companion Palisot to the South on a sensitive diplomatic mission. He had sent Collot, too. Within two months, Secretary of War James McHenry was writing to the governor of the Northwest Territory about Collot, warning that "there are certain persons employed and paid to visit the Western country for the purpose of encouraging the people of those parts to secede from the Union, and form a separate connection with a foreign power," and ordering him to find a way to seize their papers. Volney would be implicated as a spy soon after. As relations broke down between France and the United States during these last years of the decade, the John Adams administration would threaten both Volney and Collot with deportation under the Alien and Sedition Acts. But even they were only the tip of the iceberg. Traveling on their shadowy adventures, Liancourt, Volney, and Collot were all playing bit parts in a grand drama that would determine the future of the United States.[9]

LIANCOURT SAILED out of Philadelphia on the *South-Carolina,* a packet boat traveling the route between Philadelphia and Charleston, carrying rice, indigo, and cotton up the coast and returning with flour from the Delaware valley, and with brandy, books, coffee, and other imported goods from the Philadelphia *entrepôt.* Liancourt's experience belied the "elegant accommodations" promised by the ship captain. The ship was full—overloaded, really—with nearly thirty passengers on a boat built to accommodate a dozen. Five or six were refugees from Saint Domingue, several of whom still had not come to terms with their collapsed fortunes. Four passengers of African descent were also aboard, sailing from Pennsylvania, a state where slavery was gradually disappearing and from which it was illegal to remove slaves, to South Carolina, where the institution was about to enter its most explosive period of expansion. Who they were—whether slave or free, American or French—and why they were going to Charleston, Liancourt did not say.[10]

It took only six days for their ship to pass the sandbar that divides Charleston Harbor from the Atlantic and sail into port. Charleston was hot and dusty, smaller than Philadelphia, and even dirtier: Liancourt could smell the foul odor of dead animals rotting in the streets. Closer to the Caribbean, the city was awash with French people: colonists from Saint Domingue as well as French privateers headed toward or away from the Caribbean warfare against the British navy, monarchical and British-leaning French planters mingling freely with the pro-revolutionary French sailors. "Love of gambling levels all," Liancourt ruefully concluded, "and the French gaming houses, of which Charleston is full, gather around their tables frenzied aristocrats and Sans-Culottes." Liancourt even ran into a childhood friend who had escaped France and was taking shelter from the revolutionary storms in South Carolina. Some refugees, the more radical ones, attended the local Democratic-Republican club, which had been founded three years earlier in the wake of Genet's arrival in Charleston, at the peak of Franco-American comity and enthusiasm. But that was practically a different era; now it was 1796 and Americans had deserted the club. Only Frenchmen remained.[11]

Soon after their arrival, Liancourt and Palisot made their way just beyond the city limits to call on André Michaux, yet another Frenchman living in America, but not one who had fled the Revolution. He was a botanist
by training, a student of the great Bernard de Jussieu at Paris's Jardin du
Roi, the premier global center for botanical research. Michaux had conducted scientific expeditions for the French crown in Persia before King
Louis XVI sent him to the United States in 1785, as royal botanist to the new
French ally. He was instructed to travel throughout the American continent and send trees, plants, fruits, and seeds back to France, helping the
imperial power secure a reliable supply of natural resources for its navy and
colonies. It was the impetus for the 111-acre garden he established in 1786
outside Charleston, the United States' closest major port to the French Caribbean. From a larger perspective, Michaux was a cog in a vast colonial
machine of the French state that reached across much of the globe, mobilizing scientific expertise to advance France's colonial enterprises and link
French colonies across three oceans to the imperial center in Paris. It was a
model of eighteenth-century Enlightened administration. By the time Liancourt met Michaux, the tireless naturalist had "botanized" through
three-quarters of the United States, Quebec, the Bahamas, and Spanish
Florida.[12]

In his published travelogue, Liancourt was coy about this visit to South
Carolina's "French Garden," leaving just a one-page description in an eight-
volume work of more than eighteen hundred pages. He mentioned only
that Michaux had recently traveled the Illinois country, discovered a new
species of tree in Tennessee, and placed seeds in the possession of General
William Blount, a major land speculator and the former territorial governor of Tennessee. Whether those seeds were botanical or of a political nature neither Michaux nor Liancourt said. Of all the things Liancourt might
have written about Michaux, this was a curious one to mention; Michaux
and Blount both had some dubious connections with foreign powers going
back several years that both would surely have preferred to avoid publiciz-
ing in 1796. Indeed, Blount would soon face impeachment charges in the
U.S. Senate for plotting with the English to detach portions of the West
from the United States. Liancourt did not even say how much time he spent

with Michaux. But there is little doubt that he and Palisot paid careful attention to what the naturalist had to say. The French minister Adet had sent Palisot down to South Carolina to find Michaux, after all. Having heard that Michaux was traveling through western Virginia and the Carolinas, Adet hoped to "procure some information on the fate of this man so precious to the Sciences." There was a good deal Adet could not say here. But, as he wrote to the French foreign minister, he would have to "limit myself again merely to informing you that two other people are at this very moment executing Voyages for research and for the greatest interest of Commerce and Politics." Indeed. Palisot would travel with Liancourt overland to Beaufort, South Carolina, and sail on to Savannah. He and Liancourt would part ways there, with Liancourt heading north to Virginia and Palisot west into Cherokee territory, to live among those whom Adet called "les Sauvages" and travel deeper in the region than Michaux had ever gone.[13]

It was probably from Michaux that Liancourt got his information on the Southwest and the Mississippi valley. Michaux was among the most well-informed men on the region's geopolitics. He was certainly in a position to impart much of what Liancourt learned on his trip south about the absence of state power along Georgia's western frontier, a region contested among European empires, U.S. settlers, and Indian peoples. "Vexations, theft, assassination, treachery" were the norm on the frontier, he reported. American settlers committed "all the crimes against the Indians who often take furious revenge." Liancourt did not mince words. "Like Savages," he wrote of the frontier settlers, they carried out depredations of all sorts against Chickasaw, Cherokee, and Creek peoples in the Southwest: they "scalp the Indians they kill, and carry their scalps in triumph."[14]

But Liancourt discovered that frontier settlers were not aggressive just toward Native Americans: "The avidity of Georgians and their ambition are not limited to coveting the lands of the Indians; they extend to Florida, and there is more than one American settler who views this part of the Spanish possessions as their prerogative." In 1796 Spain hung on to its North American possessions of Florida and Louisiana by a thread. "Should Spain keep it much longer," Liancourt mused, "England will soon obtain it." He continued:

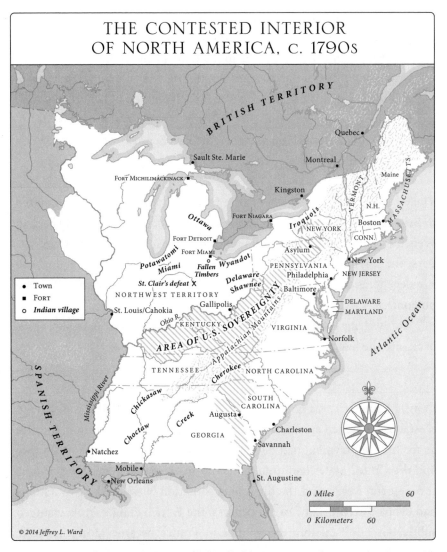

THE CONTESTED INTERIOR
OF NORTH AMERICA, c. 1790s

Throughout the 1790s the trans-Appalachian West remained bitterly contested among Native Americans, the British and Spanish empires, and the new nation rising up along the coast. U.S. sovereignty barely stretched across the Appalachian Mountains. As warfare in Europe and the Caribbean altered the geopolitical balance of the Atlantic world, a new French threat to the United States began to loom in the Mississippi Valley.

In fact, she partly possesses it already, there being several English garrisons stationed upon the Spanish territories along the Missisippi; and the numerous inhabitants of the Indian territory throughout this immense district, so rich in skins, are unacquainted with any but English traders. When the English have established themselves still more firmly in this trade, they will become more important, and then the rich Spanish settlements in Mexico will not be long secure.[15]

The weakness of Spanish power in the area; the trading concessions granted to British firms in the region; the presence of French settlers, dating back to French colonization of the Mississippi valley; the aggressiveness of U.S. settlers; the fraying loyalties of Native American nations in the region; and the degeneration of Franco-American diplomatic relations all led to one outcome.

"It is well past time," Liancourt concluded, "that these possessions pass back into the hands of France."[16]

———

BY 1796 Liancourt was not the only person to conclude that it was time to reestablish a French empire in North America. But the conclusion, for him as for his countrymen, had been long in coming. Politics in both France and the United States had undergone dramatic changes over the previous three stormy years, and the diplomatic situation between the two nations had evolved accordingly. In the process, the French émigrés' role changed subtly but unmistakably. As politics in France became more moderate while those in the United States became more heated, the *constituants'* correspondence grew more influential. Increasingly, the reports in their letters and conversations were informing policy in the metropolitan center. It was a dramatic turnaround.

When Genet had landed in Charleston in early April 1793, almost three years to the day before Liancourt and Palisot sailed on that March afternoon in 1796, war between France and Great Britain had just broken out. Genet was charged with shoring up the American alliance, to reap the benefits French diplomats expected in return for their intervention in the American Revolution fifteen years earlier. Three long years later, however, those benefits had failed to materialize. The United States was not the client state French diplomats had thought to establish. Quite the contrary: so long as their Caribbean colonies needed provisions, as the French minister Fauchet put it in 1795, "we will find ourselves at the mercy of America." Meanwhile, he exclaimed, "all the goods produced by our Colonies have been abandoned to the United States and have furnished immense and lucrative exports to *Holland* and *Hamburg!*" It was precisely the reverse of what should have resulted from the costly French intervention in the American Revolution. Instead of a dependent United States benefiting France's colonies, France's dependent colonies were benefiting the United States![17]

The Jay Treaty was the final straw. The United States, to all appearances, had turned its back on its ally to embrace its former enemy. "If we are not careful," French authorities concluded in 1796, "the United States and England will soon form an alliance, toward which habits, language and a treacherous government invisibly lead the former." The Anglo-American rapprochement clarified matters for French diplomats: it was obvious that France would need an alternative base in the New World to protect its Caribbean interests. As Liancourt traveled south during the summer of 1796, a new geopolitical dynamic had emerged. France and the United States were now set on diverging paths. Hanging in the balance were the most significant diplomatic issues of the age: the preservation of neutrality in the face of war between the great powers and the consolidation of U.S. power in the trans-Appalachian West. "Louisiana is holding its arms out to us," Fauchet had written to his superiors in Paris the year before. France had only to reach back for its former colony to fall into its embrace.[18]

"HE MUST BE A FOOL," Alexander Hamilton once remarked, "who can be credulous enough to believe that a despotic Court aided a popular revolution from regard to Liberty." Whatever motivated dreamy French liberals to support the cause, French intervention in the American Revolution had not been based primarily on ideology; it was driven by the strategic aims of hardheaded, farseeing men like the French foreign minister Charles Gravier, comte de Vergennes.[19]

By detaching Great Britain's mainland colonies from its empire, French diplomats and naval planners had hoped to weaken their traditional enemy, the dominant European power since the Seven Years' War. More important, they sought to turn mainland North America to their commercial and strategic advantage. From the perspective of the imperial center in Paris, the United States was valuable insofar as it could help France's immensely profitable Caribbean interests. Through its new ally, France had secured a base to provide resources for its navy, provisions for its slaves, and logistical support for its operations in the almost inevitable event of another war with Britain. Three aspects of the alliance stand out as particularly critical for advancing French imperial objectives, all of them enshrined in the 1778 Treaty of Amity and Commerce between France and the United States: first, access to the continent's abundant natural resources, particularly lumber; second, the use of America's strategic harbors to support French military aims in the Caribbean; and third, the growth of commerce between the United States and the French Empire through the establishment of mutual commercial privileges and the creation of free ports.

After securing U.S. independence from the British Empire, French imperial administrators began to integrate the thirteen mainland colonies into what historians have called the French "colonial machine": a highly centralized and sophisticated scientific bureaucracy under the supervision of the French Ministère de la marine (Ministry of the Navy), whose agents spanned the globe from the Indian Ocean to the Caribbean gathering medical, cartographical, and botanical knowledge to further imperial aims. Wood may have been their foremost objective; it was the eighteenth century's oil and coal. Wood provided the raw material for houses, tools, wagons, and ships, and the fuel to power industry and provide heat. It was the most essential requirement for naval power—and thus for state power at a time when Britain and France were engaged in a bitter naval arms race. Without access to reliable supplies of wood—France had lacked them during the Seven Years' War—a navy had no masts, tar, pitch, turpentine, or virtually any other material necessary for ships to conduct trade and make war. A single ship of the line of first rank required 120,000 cubic feet of oak, as well as rare pine or fir trees that furnished ships' masts. Supplying these onerous requirements had decimated European forests; indeed, they had declined at such alarming rates that by the late eighteenth century conservation laws were in place across the Continent.[20]

French naval planners looked to the untapped American forests with great hopes. Lumber from American forests, as one naval ministry report put it, would make France "less dependent on northern Europe for its naval munitions." The continent's vast forests would help maintain French control of its all-important Caribbean islands. (For the owners of those forested lands in New York and Maine, among other places, that demand promised lucrative and reliable exports.) Thus, the 1778 Treaty of Amity and Commerce specifically named "Ships Masts, Planks, Boards and Beams of what Trees soever" among the goods granted the rights of liberty of commerce and navigation. Indeed, one of the primary purposes of André Michaux's mission to the United States in 1785 was to survey American forests and identify new sources of timber for the French navy. Michaux would eventually publish a history of American oak trees, and his son, also a botanist, would publish a broad survey of American forests and their uses for European trade and statecraft. But Michaux was hardly alone. Other well-connected Frenchmen, like J. Hector St. John de Crèvecoeur, sent detailed reports on American forests and samples of different American woods to the French Royal Academy of Sciences, while French engineers scoured the continent assessing the quality of different woods.[21]

France's second principal interest was in the fine harbors and ports of the American coast. In a future war, a 1788 navy report exulted, "their utility will be even greater for the French flotillas than they were for the English" in the last. The Treaty of Amity and Commerce guaranteed French ships access to American harbors, "whether publick and of War or private and of Merchants." Looking forward to a future war with Britain, the French consul in New York predicted "great advantages": "French fleets . . . will repair there, provision themselves at good prices, reestablish their crew, find arms, naval munitions, masts and lumber of all kinds. The cooperation of the United States will keep England checked in Canada . . . and put the English Antilles in the greatest danger." Such advantages explained why France had sacrificed "blood and treasure," as one ministerial report put it, to achieve American independence.[22]

But the Franco-American alliance was more than military; it would be knit together by an expanded trade network among France, the United States, and the French Caribbean. "It has to be established that in principle, by snatching the United States from Great Britain," one naval report affirmed, "it was above all their commerce that we wanted to take away." It is in this specific respect that France revenged itself for the catastrophic defeat in the Seven Years' War: the colonial trade that had so enriched Great Britain would now reorient itself toward France. "The loss of this possession," read another report, referring to Canada, "is more than compensated for by the American revolution which it certainly influenced greatly." Whereas defending Canada had cost the French government dearly, the United States would contribute far more in trade while costing nothing to defend. Considered from this perspective, "the King gained a new domain infinitely more useful and less onerous than Canada ever was." The 1778 Treaty of Amity and Commerce sought to enshrine these commercial objectives by offering a mutual grant of most favored nation status, creating a Franco-American trade zone that French liberals hoped would permanently tie France to the United States through the power of *doux commerce* and "reciprocal interest." To further that goal, various pro-American institutions sprouted up in France, most notably the Société gallo-américaine, founded by Jacques-Pierre Brissot de Warville and others in 1787 with the objective of tying French and American interests together and establishing "perpetual Communication between the two nations."[23]

The French Revolution seemed to bring the two nations closer than ever, realizing the dreams of French liberals and Francophile Americans alike. Americans thrilled to the spectacle of their great ally throwing off the bonds of tyranny. When the French monarchy was abolished in 1792, the United States and France were no longer just military allies and commercial partners; they became sister republics. "How cordially we desire the closest union with them," Secretary of State Thomas Jefferson wrote that year. "Mutual good offices, mutual affection and similar principles of government seemed to have designed the two people for the most intimate communion, and even for a complete exchange of citizenship among the individuals composing them."[24]

GENET'S ARRIVAL in the United States in 1793 was imbued with all the good intentions and happy feelings of these early years of the French Revolution. His primary objective was to shore up the Franco-American alliance, ensuring that the promises the United States made to France fifteen years earlier were fulfilled. Genet's instructions ordered him to "ensure the religious observation of the articles [of the 1778 treaty] . . . by which the contracting parties are committed to freely admit prizes taken by one of the parties on their enemies." Genet began outfitting privateers to attack British shipping in the Caribbean upon his arrival in Charleston. His instructions also ordered him to attend to the commercial and matériel aspects of the treaty: to "ensure the execution of the articles that are favorable to the commerce and navigation of the [French] Republic." Here, too, Genet moved vigorously. Within a year, 1,845 large masts and 1,200 small masts were floating down the Connecticut River from New Hampshire on their way to France, while several ships in New York had been loaded with all sorts of masts and were ready to sail. In nearly all his endeavors, Genet read his instructions broadly but not unreasonably; even Talleyrand would later admit that Genet acted with "measures perhaps unconsidered, but which his instructions commanded."[25]

It is probably not surprising that Genet's instructions went further to promote Franco-American cooperation than anything envisioned under the *ancien régime;* what is curious, at least in retrospect, is that it is precisely the ways in which his mission represented a rupture with monarchical French policy that got Genet in the most trouble in the republican United States. Genet had come not just to secure the U.S. alliance with France; he also came with a burning fervor to expand the republican project begun in 1776 and advanced in 1789, ready to light a fuse that extended deep into the Mississippi and Saint Lawrence valleys. Genet's instructions called for him to convert the Treaty of Amity and Commerce between the United States and France into "a national pact in which the two countries would amalgamate their commercial and political interests to favor in all its aspects an expansion of the Empire of liberty." With Genet's help, the two nations would spread liberty throughout the continent. His instructions ordered the new ambassador, "while waiting for the American government to decide to make common cause with us, to take all the measures that his position entails in order to sow principles of liberty and independence in Louisiana and the other American provinces neighboring the United States." Genet was to liberate settlers across the trans-Appalachian West in the name of France, just as French forces were liberating peoples across Europe and the Caribbean.[26]

When Genet landed in Charleston, he immediately began organizing an invasion of Spanish Florida in collaboration with Michel-Ange-Bernard Mangourit, the French consul, and William Moultrie, the governor of South Carolina and former Revolutionary War general. The mission was to be manned by discontented frontiersmen along the South Carolina and Georgia backcountry in alliance with Creeks and Cherokees in the Southwest. Drawing on the deep well of sympathy for the French Revolution in the southern backcountry, they recruited a former officer who had led Patriot forces in the brutal Georgia warfare against the British. The plan hinged on renewing French alliances with Native Americans in the backcountry, particularly the Creeks, with whom the French planned to forge "an eternal alliance founded on friendship, fraternity, and the reciprocity of Services." By late April 1793, Mangourit was plotting to detach the Spanish loyalties of the Creek leader Alexander McGillivray and attach them to France. Another officer was sent off to negotiate with the Cherokees, Choctaws, and Chickasaws. Mangourit instructed them to appeal to the lingering memories of the French regime in America.

Indians,

Ask your fathers. They will tell you that the French formerly drank of the same waters with them.

> What is the cause of your hospitable treatment of the French
> who travel on your lands? It is the memory of this gentle Nation
> that was once your friend and never betrayed you.

If the French under the Old Regime had been so friendly, how much more
devoted would the new, regenerated French be! "The liberty that the French
have achieved," Mangourit added, "commands them to love the Indians,
because they are men and free."[27]

Governor Moultrie gave these French plans his full support. He was
motivated in part by his political sympathies, in part by his desire to have
an Indian buffer against the Spanish and British presence in the Mississippi valley, and in part by his own interests in backcountry lands: like so
many others who joined these military adventures, Moultrie was a major
land speculator. The invasion of Louisiana "seems all the more so superb to
him," Consul Mangourit wrote, "as he has interest in some thousands of
acres next to the river." But large landowners were hardly the only ones
interested in pushing the Spanish out of the Mississippi valley; here was an
ambition that could unite land speculators and settlers alike. By October
Mangourit reported that the recruitment was "taking place with an ardor
so great that instead of 1500 men, we have almost 4000."[28]

Audacious as it was, this French invasion of the southern backcountry
was only the first part of an even more ambitious plan to "emancipate
Spanish America, open the navigation of the Mississippi to the settlers of
Kentucky, deliver our former brothers of Louisiana from the tyrannical
yoke of Spain, and reunite, perhaps, the American constellation to the
beautiful star of Canada." Advancing this global republican project was
one of the principal objectives of Genet's mission: "It is to convince" Americans of its utility, read his instructions, "that the Citizen Genet must direct
all his efforts." The new French minister was further authorized to "maintain agents in Kentucky and to send agents to Louisiana." Which is where
Michaux came in.[29]

While Genet was slowly making his way overland from Charleston to
Philadelphia during April and May 1793, André Michaux was in Philadelphia planning a scientific expedition into the Mississippi valley sponsored

by the American Philosophical Society. Secretary of State Thomas Jefferson had a long-standing interest in exploring the West; it would eventually come to fruition with the Lewis and Clark expedition under his presidency. As a member of the APS, he took the lead in raising the funds for Michaux's mission, drafting a subscription paper to raise money and pledging $50. In addition to George Washington, who pledged $100, and John Adams, who pledged $20, Jefferson persuaded three other cabinet officers, twelve senators, and thirteen representatives in the House to subscribe. Genet arrived in Philadelphia just as the final preparations were getting under way. From his perspective, it was a ready-made opportunity to carry out his instructions. And so, after explaining the details to Michaux, Genet enlisted the naturalist to the cause of spreading the French Revolution deep into the continent.[30]

Probably it is the only instance in U.S. history in which most of the government's top officers funded the mission of a foreign agent in its own territory.

———————

THE STRATEGY behind the Genet-Michaux mission in the backcountry had been developed in Paris in late 1792 in a series of memoirs, letters, and conversations among members of the foreign ministry, notably Brissot, foreign minister Pierre Lebrun, several Americans in Paris, including Joel Barlow, and some French liberals who fancied themselves experts on the United States. They believed that a few boats, batteries, and munitions, along with several thousand pro-French settlers sailing down the Mississippi, could easily capture New Orleans and thus hold the entire Louisiana territory. Several factors were expected to facilitate the mission.[31]

First, the settlers of Kentucky—described in French ministerial reports as "robust, entrepreneurial, good hunters, and friends of liberty, and by the way all of them armed"—were believed to favor an invasion. "Kentuckians have burned for a long time with the legitimate desire to profit from the free navigation of the Mississippi," read Genet's instructions. During his travels to the United States in the 1780s, Brissot had noted the "defiance that the residents of the West showed" toward Congress. He saw how easily

Subscription agreement to sponsor Michaux's mission west, initially a scientific mission on behalf of the American Philosophical Society, but which became a mission on behalf of the French government to detach Louisiana from Spain and, perhaps, pieces of the trans-Appalachian West from the United States. It was signed by President George Washington, Vice President John Adams, Secretary of State Thomas Jefferson, Secretary of the Treasury Alexander Hamilton, Secretary of War Henry Knox, and Representative James Madison, along with twenty-four other members of Congress. It is the only document known to have been signed by all of the country's first four presidents.

westerners, desperate for Mississippi River navigation, could seize New Or-leans: "If ever Americans march towards New Orleans, it will fall under their power." What was more, western settlers were known to be almost universally pro-Republican and pro-French. "The news of a revolution in France has left the liveliest sensations among them," a government report affirmed after Brissot had returned to France. Second, the Indian nations in the continental interior were also said to be pro-French. Brissot himself had been impressed by "the attachment" of Native American villages in the Mississippi valley to the French. "A man of this nation [France] can travel in safety, without arms, from Canada to Illinois," he insisted. "The savages celebrate him as a brother." Genet received much the same information when he arrived. "They call the French their father," wrote one partisan of French plans in the interior. "Several of their chiefs carry the medal of Louis XIV and refuse to carry the medal of Charles IV [of Spain] out of respect for France." This opinion was not just French bluster; British offi-cers widely agreed about the residual loyalties of Native American nations. The French, warned one, could easily "resume their former influence over the Indians." And finally, the French *habitants* who had settled the West under the French regime from New Orleans up to the Great Lakes were expected to enthusiastically welcome their liberators. "The French people established on the Scioto and in other parts of the interior of the United States," noted one minister, would be "excellent for lending a hand" to the mission. Another letter similarly assured Genet that he could muster "a great number [of troops] at gallipolis an establishment on the ohio." French land ventures could even serve as a decoy for Genet: it was suggested that concern about the fate of those poor French emigrants at Scioto would fur-nish an excellent pretext to send agents west in the first place.[32]

As if by fortunate coincidence, the former Revolutionary War general George Rogers Clark, in Louisville, Kentucky, had already expressed in-terest in sponsoring an expedition to seize Louisiana. French authorities responded warmly; Thomas Paine, then in Paris and a close associate of Brissot's, even sounded out Jefferson about Clark's suitability for such an enterprise. Clark certainly seemed like an ideal candidate. He had fought the British during the American Revolution with a band of Kentuckians in close alliance with French *habitants* in the country—so close, in fact, he claimed at the time to be fighting in the name of the king of France. A large Kentucky landowner, he had, like so many others in the region, become alienated by the U.S. government's inattention to western interests. He had since fallen onto hard times, battling alcoholism and fighting for large land claims he believed the federal government owed him for his wartime service. He was, in short, ready to shift his loyalties to France. "The contest in which the Republic of the French is actually involved, against almost all the Despots of Europe," Clark wrote to French authorities before Genet had even left Europe, "is among the most awful, interesting and solemn, in all its consequences, that has ever arisen in the world." Whether Clark was genuinely inspired by the French Revolution or just looking for an opportunity to advance his own interests will never be exactly clear. Perhaps it does not matter. What did matter was his promise to "raise an abundance of men in this western country—men as well American as French," vowing that he and his army "will instantly expatriate ourselves (as the Law directs), and are ready to become citizens of the French: Republic." Clark also pledged support among "the Indian tribes, from New Mexico to the Allegany mountains," who, he assured French diplomats, "are my friends and could be brought to march under my banners." A revolution along the Mississippi River promised great advantages to France: "The possession of New Orleans will secure to France the whole Fur, Tobacco and Flour trade of this western world, and a great consumption of her manufactures." With a mere fifteen hundred men, Clark promised, he could "take the whole of Louisiana for France," and asked only for "some *small* resources by Letters of credit or cash" to assist in the venture.[33]

On May 18, 1793, just fifteen days after Noailles arrived in Philadelphia, Michaux met with Genet to deliver several intelligence reports on the former French colonies in North America. By late June French plans were in motion. Genet appointed Michaux "Agent of the French Republic to the People of Kentucky, Louisiana and Illinois" and authorized him to "conclude alliances with the French people of Louisiana and with the Indians founded on the genuine interest of People and on the liberal principles adopted by the French Republic." Michaux was instructed to appoint Clark as the head of the mission and Benjamin Logan, another former Revolutionary War officer, as the second in command; he carried a commission for Clark with the title of "Commander in Chief of the Independent and Revolutionary Legion of the Mississippi," endowing Clark with the "exclusive command of the Independent and Revolutionary region of the Mississippi," and with a promise of promotion to *maréchal de camp* of the French Republic. Genet further authorized Michaux to advance up to £3,000 to finance the mission, and ordered him to help with logistical preparations. "You will find in Kentucky," he wrote, "many veteran officers unhappy with the conduct of the federal government, and who wish for no more than to enlist under the banner of liberty." Although he was confident that enough Kentuckians would volunteer to man the mission, Genet added, "There are here [in Philadelphia] other officers and under-officers that I could send to you along with the Supplements of Help and munitions when it is time." In addition, Genet expected his western army to find support among the Native American nations: "You will also give all your attention to cultivating the friendship of the Indians, to win it by some presents, and to commit them to make common cause with us to give liberty to our brothers of Louisiana." To that end Michaux carried commissions for American or Indian officers or others Clark would choose to appoint. And finally, Genet counted on the French *habitants* still scattered throughout the territory. "We cannot doubt the good intentions of the French people of Louisiana," Genet wrote. "All we ask of them is to amalgamate their political and commercial interests with ours and with those of the United States."[34]

Perhaps the mission's most striking feature is the support Genet and Michaux obtained from prominent American politicians. The Kentucky senator John Brown offered his support by writing letters of introduction for Michaux to George Rogers Clark and Governor Isaac Shelby of Kentucky. "Any assistance you may be so good as to afford him in accomplishing his view," wrote the senator to Clark, "will lay me under obligations which I shall at all times be happy to acknowledge." Brown wrote to Shelby, "Mr Michaux is a Citizen of France and stands high in the confidence of the Minister of that Republic," and requested "any civilities you may be pleased to shew him." Brown also offered suggestions for planning the attack and gave Genet "the address of many certain men, and promised me to use all his influence toward the success of our projects."[35]

Thomas Jefferson went even further. Jefferson was aware of French designs on Spanish America as early as February 1793, when an American land agent just back from Paris warned him that the French "propose to emancipate S. America, and will send 45. ships of the line there in the spring." That vague warning came into focus when Genet arrived in Philadelphia that summer and shared his plans with Jefferson. "Mr. Genet called on me and read to me very rapidly instructions he had prepared for Michaud who is going to Kentuckey," Jefferson recorded in his notes of their meeting. "In these papers it appears that besides encouraging those inhabitants to insurrection, he will furnish the expense about £3000. sterl." Jefferson then added this tantalizing detail: "He said he communicated these things to me, not as Secy. of state, but as Mr. Jeff." In either capacity—whether as secretary of state or as "Mr. Jefferson"—Jefferson well knew that Genet's western plans violated the Washington administration's neutrality policy, and did so in a far more serious way than arming a few privateers in some East Coast ports. According to his notes, Jefferson warned Genet that any Kentucky residents would be hanged if they committed hostilities against a nation at peace with the United States. But, he added, a little too clever by half, "I did not care what insurrections would be excited in Louisiana." Genet's reports on the meeting suggest, however, that Jefferson did not even raise this mild objection. According to some notes Genet took of their meeting, Jefferson told him that he believed a war with Spain was inevitable, and although he was not in a position officially to tolerate an insurrection against Louisiana at the moment, "the *Kentukois* can always take it [Louisiana], even if it meant returning it to Spain when they consent to free navigation. He agrees that this expedition will be very easy." Genet further reported, in a letter to the minister of foreign relations in Paris, that Jefferson would not look with disfavor on "a small spontaneous eruption by the settlers of *Kentukey*." This was odd behavior on Jefferson's part, to say the least—this meeting with a foreign diplomat who shared his plans to foment insurrection within the borders of the United States, at the very moment the Washington cabinet was formulating its demand for Genet's recall. Jefferson chose to share none of these details with the other members of the cabinet, including the president.[36]

The only concrete result of Jefferson's meeting with Genet was a letter from Jefferson introducing Michaux to Kentucky governor Isaac Shelby. This was no casual missive dashed off as an afterthought, but a carefully crafted document; the editors of Jefferson's papers call it "a subtle exercise in calculated ambiguity." Jefferson wrote two drafts of the letter—the second, at Genet's request, clarifying the connection between Michaux and the French ministry. Michaux, wrote Jefferson, "is a man of science and merit, and goes to Kentuckey in pursuit of objects of Natural history and botany, to augment the literary acquirements of the two republicks. Mr. Genet the Minister of France here, having expressed to me his esteem for M. Michaud and good opinion of him, and his wish that he should be made known to you, I take the liberty of recommending him to your notice, your counsels, and good offices." Not surprisingly, all of this later became embarrassing for Jefferson, who would try to cover his tracks.[37]

Jefferson's history here helps explain why he would later be so sensitive about his close friendship with Volney, who arrived in the United States two years later, in 1795. It also shines a different light on their contact. In 1796—just as Liancourt and Palisot were conferring with Michaux outside of Charleston, as Collot was traveling across the Appalachians into the Ohio valley, and as Noailles was sailing up the coast of Maine—Volney traveled south to Charlottesville, where he spent three weeks visiting Jefferson before heading west across the Appalachians. During that visit, Jefferson drafted at least six letters of recommendation for Volney, including one to the very same Isaac Shelby, who had left the governor's office three weeks earlier. "This will be delivered to you by Mr. Volney," Jefferson wrote, in an echo of the letter he'd written for Michaux three years earlier. "As he proposes to take Kentucky in his route Westward, I take the liberty of recommending him to your attentions and friendly offices. The esteem in which he is held both here and in Europe as well as his great personal merit and talents render him worthy of any services which his character as a stranger and a traveller may call for in the places where he shall pass. Your

Excellency will therefore I hope pardon the liberty I take in giving him an opportunity of paying his respects to you and of solliciting your patronage of him while within your state."[38]

Whether Volney was in fact engaged in a mission like Michaux's remains unclear, as we shall see, but the precedent was hardly reassuring.

MICHAUX LEFT for Kentucky, Jefferson's letter in hand, in the late summer of 1793. In October four French agents followed, setting out by stagecoach with authorizations from Genet to recruit Americans along the way for the planned expedition. That same month, Genet formed a second army, the "Revolutionary Legion of America," to lead an attack on Florida, and named William Tate, a South Carolina speculator in frontier lands, as commander in chief. By January 1794 plans were well under way. Newspapers in Kentucky were running announcements that Clark, now identified as a "Major General in the armies of France, and commander in chief of the French revolutionary Legions on the Mississippi River," was recruiting volunteers and promising free land for those who enlisted under the French banner. "All lawful plunder to be equally divided agreeable to the custom of War," one report added. Several hundred miles away in western Georgia, Tate's army was enlisting soldiers for the attack on Florida. "A spirit of recruiting prevails here to a great de-

> CINCINNATI, January 25.
> GEORGE R. CLARK, Esq.
> Major General in the armies of France, and commander in chief of the French revolutionary Legions on the Mississippi River.
> PROPOSALS,
> For raising volunteers for the reduction of the Spanish posts on the Mississippi, for opening the trade of the said River, and giving freedom to its inhabitants, &c.
> All persons serving the expedition, to be entitled to one thousand acres of land; those that engage for one year, will be entitled to 2000 acres; if they serve two years or during the present war with France, they will have three thousand acres of any unappropriated land that may be conquered—The officers in proportion, pay, &c. as other French troops.—All lawful plunder to be equally divided agreeable to the custom of War. All necessaries will be provided for the enterprize, and every precaution taken to cause the return of those who wish to quit the service as comfortable as possible, and a reasonable number of days allowed them to return; at the expiration of which time their pay will cease. All persons will be commissioned agreeable to the number of men they bring into the field.—Those that serve the expedition will have their choice of receiving their lands or one Dollar per day.
> A Copy.   G. R. CLARK.

Proposal for volunteers to serve under George Rogers Clark, as reprinted in the Carlisle Gazette, March 19, 1794.

gree, for an expedition, under French authority, against Augustine, West-Florida, and New-Orleans," newspapers reported from the frontier. "The people here have got recruiting mad, for the French service. . . . They have enlisted upwards of 30 of the militia troop of horse, now in service, in Green county."[39]

Back in Kentucky, Clark wrote Genet that "upwards of two thousand men have been waiting With impatiance to penetrate into that Country Declare them selves Citizens of France and Give freedom to their neibours on the Mississipi." The soldiers in the Mississippi Legion had, according to Clark, switched their allegiance from the United States to France. "The Great intrest that France have In this Country I think is worth their attention. the People in General yet Look up to them for something To be Done as they are out of all hopes of Congress eaven Favouring them in their negociations with Spain respecting the Mississippi." Other reports warned about the risks of the mission for U.S. interests in the West. "General Logan has, I am told, embarked in the enterprize as second in command, and will unless prevented by the *Federal Arm*, proceed down the River before the last of February, at the head of two thousand men," wrote Kentucky senator John Brown, who had by now changed his mind about the wisdom of the project. "Clark it is said has resumed his sobriety, and attention, & yet promises to renew his fame." Plans were afoot to blockade the mouth of the Cumberland River, at the Ohio, near its confluence with the Mississippi. It would take a powerful show of force, Brown predicted, to stop the mission. But was that even possible? "So popular is the undertaking here that I fear Government will want power, either to prevent it, or to punish the adventurers." Local Democratic-Republican societies had given the mission their full support, Clark reported, going so far as to lend ammunition for the invasion.[40]

After checking in on the preparations in Kentucky, Michaux headed south to assist the expedition against Florida. "I am expecting Michaux from one day to the next, with great details on the execution" of the plans, Mangourit, the Charleston consul, wrote to Genet at the end of January. "I will prepare everything needed to put them into action. Rifles, Cannons, cannonballs, bayonets, sabers, gun carriages . . . send all this if you can."

Everything was ready; all he needed was the naval forces and the funds promised by Genet. "The *habitants* of the backcountry are impatient to leave," Mangourit wrote on February 24, urging Genet to set the plans in motion before the "killing heat" set in. "Hasten therefore everything: the season is favorable." The consul could barely contain his excitement. He broke out into song midletter:

Allons enfans de la patrie!

But still there was no sign of Michaux. Finally, on March 14, Michaux arrived in Charleston, where Mangourit immediately assigned him to the Louisiana expedition, probably to serve as a liaison with the forces descending from Kentucky. A former president of the French Patriotic Society in Charleston was made an adjutant; other Frenchmen in South Carolina were enlisted to provide supplies. By this time, fifteen hundred men were said to be ready to march on Florida, and Mangourit settled on April 10 to begin the invasion.[41]

Panicked letters were trickling back from the frontier. "We have been for a long time held in suspense by the different reports which have circulated, relative to certain persons being employed in this State to recruit a corps of troops for the service of France," wrote a federal agent in Georgia to Secretary of War Henry Knox in April 1794. "There cannot now be any doubts remaining upon this subject." Some of the troops were to descend on Florida, while "large detachments" were marching from South Carolina and Kentucky to invade Louisiana. A commander of federal troops in Georgia informed Knox that warships were congregating at Saint Marys, Georgia, right on the Florida border (site of a U.S. Navy base today), along with a French infantry company and more than eighty American recruits. "This armament and land force," he warned, "will be sufficient, they say, to take the Floridas as soon as they please." By now the news had made it to Philadelphia newspapers and was generating considerable alarm. "It is said," reported the *Gazette of the United States* in late May, "that an expedition is actually undertaking against New Orleans from Kentuckey, and that 6000 men are employed on it. It is also surmised, that some of the French frigates which lately arrived in the Chesapeake are to co operate in this enterprise, and may daily be expected to make their appearance at the mouth of the Missisippi."[42]

The Spanish governor of Louisiana, Luis Héctor, baron de Carondelet, was frantic. "It is whispered by some," he wrote to his superiors in Spain, "that within a few months the French will be here." He was miserable at "the critical state in which Louisiana is left." Carondelet had few illusions about the loyalties of the French population in New Orleans. "If some four frigates were to present themselves here with 1200 French troops, there would arise a faction in this city in favor of the Convention which would cause great havoc and perhaps the loss of the province." Two Spanish commissioners in Philadelphia agreed, warning the Louisiana governor to take precautions, "since the perversity of the French, scattered through the whole continent, gives much ground for apprehension."[43]

FROM THE perspective of the early twenty-first century, when the United States stands astride the globe as a preeminent power, these plans to spread revolution in the American backcountry may seem quixotic. Surely the Mississippi valley was destined to become part of the United States, and the United States destined to span the continent. How could a few French missions in the Mississippi valley have posed any threat to the inevitable emergence of U.S. sovereignty over the territory?

"Hindsight," the eminent historian David Potter once wrote, is "the historian's chief asset and his main liability." In our age of American power and hegemony, it is easy to forget how fragile the U.S. Republic was in the mid-1790s. In fact, Michaux's mission posed monumental risks to U.S. interests in the West, to the authority of the federal government over its citizens, to U.S. military expeditions against the Western Confederacy, and to broader diplomatic relations between the United States and European powers. Many believed that an attack on Spanish territory would unleash a wider war in the region. Spain would ally with Great Britain, which was still waiting in the Great Lakes poised to sail down the Mississippi. Both empires would mobilize their robust alliances with Native American villages in a war for all the western territories. "It must be remembered that Spain is in a strict alliance with Great Britain," the *Boston Gazette* warned in January 1794, "and that if we raise troops, or suffer them to be raised from among ourselves with a view to carry war into the dominions of Spain, we may rest assured the arms of both kingdoms will be turned against us"—along with, the author might have added, the arms of the powerful Native American nations in the Ohio valley and the Southwest. The United States, still at war with the Western Confederacy, was in no position to resist such an alliance. On the other hand, if the French succeeded in mobilizing their Native alliances and ended up in control of the Mississippi River and New Orleans, one American officer predicted that "the State of Kentucky *must* unite with France as the Mississippi is the only communication that fine country has with the Sea." Either way it did not bode well for U.S. power in the West.[44]

By this time, however, matters were beginning to fall apart for the impetuous Genet, who possessed neither the organizational nor the diplomatic skills to carry out a mission of such ambition. He was wildly overextended, "provisioning the Antilles, exciting the Canadians, arming the Kentuckians and preparing an expedition by sea to second their descent upon New Orleans." He had also managed to offend both friends and allies by continuing to arm privateers in violation of Washington's neutrality proclamation. Thinking he could go over the president's head to appeal to the pro-French population, Genet had become the de facto head of a domestic political party. It was, as a Spanish diplomat in Philadelphia archly remarked, "most extraordinary conduct"—a spectacular violation of all reasonable norms of diplomatic protocol, something possible only during those heady years of Girondin ascendancy. Even Jefferson had been forced to distance himself. By 1794, Washington's cabinet had submitted a request for the French ambassador's recall and taken forceful steps to prevent further trouble on the frontier. Secretary of War Henry Knox had already written to Kentucky governor Isaac Shelby instructing him to "use effectual military force to prevent the execution of the plan of the said Frenchmen" in the event that more peaceable means were not sufficient.[45]

When the French government received the request for Genet's recall along with the supporting documentation, it took only three days for its leadership—by then in the hands of the Girondins' foes, the Montagnards—to agree. To replace Genet, the French government sent Jean-Antoine Joseph Fauchet, who arrived in February 1794. "Twas a Meteor following a Comet," Hamilton wryly remarked. Although Hamilton discerned "the same general spirit in him which governed his predecessor," Fauchet was more diplomatically sure-footed and recognized the recklessness of the Genet-Michaux plans for the Mississippi valley. Shortly after Fauchet's arrival, Washington issued a Proclamation on Expeditions against Spanish Territory. Having "received information that certain persons in violation of the laws, presumed under colour of a foreign authority to enlist citizens of the United States and others within the state of Kentucky, and have there assembled an armed force for the purpose of invading and plundering the territories of a nation at peace with the said United States," he reminded Americans that the United States was a neutral power and that it was illegal to enlist in a foreign army. "All lawful means," he warned, "will be strictly put in execution for securing obedience to the laws, and for punishing such dangerous and daring violations thereof." While this notice was published in the newspapers, Edmund Randolph, who had replaced Jefferson as secretary of state at the beginning of the year, wrote to Shelby urging him to suppress any military activities, and warning him that any military efforts against Louisiana "must be repressed by law, or they will terminate in anarchy." Perhaps most significantly of all, Fauchet added his voice to those of Washington and Randolph. On March 6, just as Michaux was arriving in Charleston to help with the invasion of Florida, Fauchet published announcements in the Philadelphia newspapers warning, "EVERY Frenchman is forbid to violate the Neutrality of the United States. All commissions or authorizations tending to infringe that neutrality are revoked and are to be returned to the agents of the French Republic." The announcement came just in time to prevent war along the frontier.[46]

And so the whole affair ended with a whimper. Though it turned out to have been so much sound and fury, Genet's attempt to foment revolution in the Mississippi valley from 1793 to 1794 had "at least served to show that we have many friends in the [Spanish and British] possessions," Fauchet mused somewhat philosophically—"even among the savages." The thought would linger tantalizingly in the minds of French military planners and go on to shape their strategic thinking about the American West for another decade. Before closing the book on the episode, however, Fauchet made one final effort to prove his good faith to the Washington administration, and the depth of French friendship for the United States, by demanding Genet's arrest and deportation back to France. It was an ominous request indeed, coming from the Montagnard government that had executed Genet's patrons, Brissot and Clavière, just a few months earlier. But Washington took pity on the now-disgraced minister, and refused to carry out the arrest warrant, granting him refugee status in the United States.[47]

EVEN AS the Washington administration was mopping up the remnants of the Genet-Michaux expedition, relations between the United States and Great Britain continued to degenerate. Genet had upset diplomatic sensibilities by using American ports and even American citizens to equip and man French privateers in flagrant contravention of American law. Alas, Great Britain was proving no more respectful of Washington's policy of neutrality.

French officials were not the only ones to recognize the strategic value of the United States to the French Caribbean; as much as the French intended to benefit from the U.S. alliance, the British aimed to isolate France's Caribbean islands. Taking advantage of its naval superiority, the British government issued a new Order in Council in late 1793, an executive policy imposing a total blockade of France and French Caribbean colonies. By its terms, British ships were authorized to "stop and detain all ships laden with goods[,] the produce of any colony belonging to France, or carrying provisions or other supplies for the use of any such colony." Before Americans had even been informed of the new policy, armed British privateers began seizing American ships trading with French islands, harassing their captains, impounding their cargoes, and impressing their sailors. More than 250 American ships were detained. The public was outraged. In response, Congress passed an embargo on all trade with Great Britain and its Caribbean possessions. These measures hit the U.S. economy hard; exports plummeted, declining some 27 percent in 1794 alone.[48]

As if that were not trouble enough, British officials in Canada were busy supporting their Native American allies in the Ohio valley and along the Great Lakes. In February 1794 Guy Carleton, 1st Baron Dorchester—the official who had overseen the British evacuation of New York at the end of the American Revolution and had since become the governor of British North America—delivered a fiery speech urging Native villages of Lower Canada to prepare for war against the United States. Dorchester had long believed that the United States would break into pieces, and he watched the growing tensions between Great Britain and her former colony with a conviction that war was inevitable—even desirable. Denouncing the American expansion in the Northwest as an aggression against "the King's Rights in the Indian Country," he insisted that "what belongs to the Indians will of course be confirmed and secured to them." Newspapers throughout the United States reprinted the speech; by the British foreign ministry's own account, it aggravated "the spirit of hostility to Great Britain" among the population. For Secretary of State Randolph, the speech constituted a clear attempt to "foster and encourage in the Indians hostile dispositions towards the United States."[49]

But Dorchester did not limit himself to oratory. In preparation for war with the United States, he directed John Graves Simcoe, the governor of Upper Canada, to rally Indians in the Ohio valley, arm British vessels on the Great Lakes, and build a new fort among the Miami in Ohio. This last act was particularly provocative, since it involved marching British forces into territory ostensibly recognized as American, at least according to the 1783 peace treaty. When Randolph received word that Simcoe had marched to the foot of the Miami River rapids, near present-day Toledo, with three companies of British soldiers, tensions became fevered. Then reports began trickling into Philadelphia of British attacks on western New York, along Lake Oswego, not far from the Holland Land Company's tracts. As a further insult, British officers around the Great Lakes and in the Ohio valley declared that any U.S. incursions into Indian territory—land that the U.S. government claimed as its own—would be considered by them "as a direct violation of His Majesty's rights." Taking this flurry of activity as a sign of British support for Native rights to land in the Northwest, Wyandot chiefs during the summer of 1794 urged Detroit's commander: "We hope you will now fulfill your promise; rise up and stand by us." Simcoe, meanwhile, had developed even more grandiose plans: first an invasion of the Ohio valley, then the destruction of American forts in Ohio and Pennsylvania, the neutralization of Kentucky, and finally a grand sweep across Pennsylvania, ending with the conquest of Philadelphia.[50]

Public opinion was aghast. "It was not enough, for ten years, to deny us the use of our own territory, line our frontiers with an armed force, and instigate the Indians to cut our throats," the *Pittsburgh Gazette* lamented. If the country failed to respond to these provocations, it warned, "our independence must be destroyed, and we must again become a colony of Great Britain." Anti-British feelings ran hot. In New York, the audience at one theater rioted when an actor playing a British officer had the temerity to wear a red coat on stage. "The People are French and they want war," the new French ministers concluded.[51]

It was not just popular sentiment that erupted. When Washington learned of the British maneuvers, he, too, was outraged. "This may be considered as the most open & daring act of the British agents in America," he wrote of Simcoe's fort-building activities. "There does not remain a doubt in the mind of any well informed person in this country (not shut against conviction[)] that all the difficulties we encounter with the Indians; their hostilities—the murders of helpless women & innocent children along our frontiers, results from the conduct of the Agents of Great Britain in this Country." It was, according to Washington, the British who were "instigating" tribes in the West "to unite in the War against us; and whilst it is an undeniable fact that they are furnishing the whole with Arms, Ammunition, cloathing—& even provisions, to carry on the War." Washington was as openly angry as he ever got in his missive to John Jay. "Can it be expected I ask, so long as these things are known in the United States . . . that there ever will, or can be any cordiality between the two Countries. I answer NO!" Washington warned that peace would be impossible so long as Great Britain held the Great Lakes forts. "I will undertake, without the gift of prophecy, to predict, that it will be impossible to keep this Country in a state of amity with G. Britain long, if the Posts are not surrendered."[52]

Washington may have blamed the British here, but there were good reasons to think that Americans instigated many of the provocations. When Liancourt began his travels northwest across Pennsylvania in 1795, he witnessed the tensions along the frontier firsthand. "Everything I hear about the Indians, interests me on their behalf," he wrote, describing a common frontier dynamic. "The Americans make war on them, in order to chase them from their lands, and the Americans of the frontiers are more pillaging, more cruel than the Indians, to whom one makes a crime out of the reprisals they take." But there was little doubt that the British were arming Native Americans. According to the reports Liancourt gathered, Americans were finding British soldiers among the dead Indians. "The Indian army," he added, "was supplied by the help of English garrisons." He also recorded descriptions of the rich lands along the Miami River—the very spot where Simcoe had just erected a British fort—where the soil was fertile to a depth of twenty to twenty-five feet, "the fields, planted by the Indians, in corn and beans, presented a well-maintained cultivation, and the harvests of an abundance that surpassed everything that had ever been seen" by Liancourt's informants. It was never clear whether Liancourt was reporting on geopolitical conditions along the frontier or on opportunities for land speculation. Then again, perhaps the two could not be disconnected. When Liancourt crossed into Upper Canada in late June, he met Simcoe in person and learned more about the governor's strategic thinking. "In a time of war, strong parties can be diligently sent, by means of navigation, from Upper Canada to all parts of the United States, even Georgia." According to Simcoe, "Upper Canada is the key to the Indian Country." Simcoe was evidently itching for a fight, which he believed Britain and its Native American allies could still win. No wonder Simcoe was considered, "even by soldiers," of harboring "excessive indisposition against the Americans."[53]

In a last-ditch effort to preserve peace, Washington appointed John Jay, the chief justice of the United States and a former diplomat, as a special envoy to England. But it wasn't clear that the American public wanted peace with England any more than Simcoe did. Indeed, so reviled was Jay, and the cause of peace with England, that on the day he left, the Friends of Liberty in Philadelphia hung Jay in effigy and, as if that were not enough, guillotined the effigy—and then blew it up with gunpowder for good measure. As Jay sailed down the Delaware that day in May 1794, he could hear the crowds on the quay who had turned out to jeer him.[54]

WHEN TALLEYRAND arrived in 1794, the U.S. embargo meant that virtually no ships were traveling between the United States and England. The only way for Talleyrand to get a letter across the Atlantic was to send it aboard the *Ohio*, the very ship carrying Jay to London. It was a telling coincidence. From the moment they arrived, the émigré *constituants'* networks of information, correspondence, friendship, and business overlapped with the networks of transatlantic diplomacy shaping the future of the United States.[55]

Noailles had landed in 1793, just as the rift with Great Britain was growing. Before he left England, Noailles had "made some offers of service here," according to the British foreign minister Lord Grenville. Although Grenville refused the offer of formal service, when Noailles arrived in the United States he began to socialize regularly with George Hammond, the British ambassador, as well as with prominent pro-British Federalist politicians like William Bingham. Before long, he sent some observations to Hamilton on America's military readiness. "I have prepared a small work relative to your state of defense and to the particular means to protect your country from all foreign insults," he wrote in October 1793. "I will send you the *mémoire* relating to this object if you indicate the means or, in case you don't have safe means, I'll await your return to Philadelphia, or I will seal it sous enveloppe to Mr. Willing if I leave for the Susquehanna."[56]

It is hard to know exactly what Noailles' relationship to British officials was at this stage, in the heat of Genet's mission in the United States and the Girondin-Montagnard ascendancy in France. Noailles lived in the Bingham mansion, which was also the site of the first political caucus in American history, where pro-British Federalist senators gathered to decide how to vote. The French minister Fauchet thought Noailles had become a veritable leader of the Federalist Party and of Federalist policy. "General Knox,

Secretary of War, a vain man without manners and without character, low lackey & servile to the President," Fauchet reported in May 1794, "is very linked to Noailles, who frequently directs his choices and his operations." Consul Mangourit in Charleston shared the same opinion about Noailles. Mangourit urged Genet in a dispatch to "hold firm against Tal[on], Noail[les], and Hamilton." When Talleyrand arrived in the United States, Fauchet believed that he and his friend Beaumetz would also promote Federalist policy. He knew, for one thing, about their letters of introduction to Hamilton. "It is to him that the ex-*constituant* beaumetz and the former Archbishop of Autun [Talleyrand] were addressed from England."[57]

However ominous these signs, Fauchet, Genet, and Mangourit were almost certainly exaggerating the émigrés' involvement in pro-British machinations. It is true that Noailles was intimate with Hamilton, whom he'd known and admired since their service together in the American Revolution: "a man of great understanding, fine talents, a communicative genius, an untainted probity, an absolute disinterestedness." And it is true that Liancourt traveled to Upper Canada at a particularly sensitive time with a passport from the British minister Hammond, and spent several days with Governor Simcoe, whom he evidently respected. At the same time, however, Liancourt was refused entry to Lower Canada (present-day Quebec) by Lord Dorchester on the ground that he might foment trouble among the French Canadian population. What is more, notwithstanding Fauchet's suspicions, there is no evidence that Noailles was directing Federalist war policy in any way. Indeed, most of the émigrés sought to establish connections among both Federalists and Republicans. As even the arch-Federalist-cum-Tory William Cobbett would later admit, Liancourt "was, while here, intimate with Adet, Talleyrand, Moreau, Volney, Collot, Jefferson, &c. &c. and he was at the same time, equally intimate with Knox, Hamilton, General Washington, and even the British Embassador." Nor is there evidence that Talleyrand and Hamilton collaborated diplomatically during their long summer nights together.[58]

The émigrés were tremendously knowledgeable about the state of international affairs and tremendously well connected. But insofar as they promoted any policy, it was to defend U.S. neutrality. As soon as he arrived, for instance, Noailles began urging restraint to his friends in London. "The Americain privateers would do great injury to the trade of England," he wrote to William Windham, who would become the British secretary at war the following year. He also warned about British activities in the Northwest. The "People of America think that England encourages the Indian war," he reported, and offered some advice about the best British policy. "It is . . . the interest of England not to quarrel with America, as it is the interest of America to keep not only the most exact neutrality but a perfect harmony." Talleyrand agreed. In June 1794, shortly after his arrival, he insisted on the importance of Jay's mission. "I cannot urge you too much to keep informed on this negotiation," he wrote to a correspondent in London. "On the maintenance of peace depends the whole political existence of this country." (He added that a successful negotiation would cause the prices of American funds and bank stocks to rise.) The *constituants'* connections to transatlantic diplomacy, then, at least in the period before 1795, do not boil down to a clear pro-British or pro-French position. But that does not mean they had no links to diplomacy; in fact, their connections were more subtle and far more interesting than the plots that Genet and Fauchet supposed the émigrés were hatching. Those connections had less to do with the content and more with the infrastructure of transatlantic diplomacy.[59]

Much as elite American social and economic networks facilitated the émigrés' arrival in the United States, so did the émigrés' social and economic networks facilitate John Jay's arrival in London. When he landed on June 15—a fast summer crossing of only one month—Jay carried, along with his diplomatic papers, a letter of introduction from Hamilton to his sister-in-law Angelica Church, the same correspondent who wrote letters on behalf of Talleyrand and Liancourt. The introduction helped lubricate his arrival in London society. "We are much indebted to their Civilities and friendly attentions," Jay wrote to Hamilton the following month. "She looks as well as when you saw her, and thinks as much about America and her Friends in it as ever." By the time he wrote those words, Jay had received a letter that Hamilton sent through Charles de Cadignan, a Frenchman who had sailed from America to London to sell lands for the Asylum Company, the French land company in the Susquehanna valley managed by Noailles. Given that connection, Cadignan probably carried letters from Noailles to his friends and correspondents in London as well. In late September Jay would send a letter of introduction to Washington on behalf of Liancourt, who was then preparing to leave London for Philadelphia.[60]

As JAY was in London trying to make peace with England during the summer of 1794, rebellion broke out along the Appalachian frontier.

Discontent had been simmering for years. Although war in Europe and the Caribbean had stimulated the demand for American exports along the East Coast, the growing wealth did not extend very far west. The ever-growing population of trans-Appalachian settlers was cut off from eastern markets by the absence of roads to the waterways feeding into the Atlantic. They felt abandoned by the federal government, which, from their perspective, never did enough to defend them against Native Americans. Nor did officials in Philadelphia seem interested in securing their navigation rights on the Mississippi; American diplomats had even offered to give up those rights in exchange for trading concessions from Spain. Perhaps the lack of interest in securing trading privileges through New Orleans had to do with the powerful landed interests at the highest levels of government. With the "opening of the Mississippi," Alexander Baring would observe, "the back countries . . . will monopolize the supplying of the West India market with Lumber and provisions." It was a worrisome possibility for owners of East Coast lands. "Their inland navigation and the communication between New Orleans and the West India islands is so easy and complete that it is impossible the Eastern country can enter into competition in this trade." Nor, possibly for analogous reasons, did Eastern politicians seem particularly concerned about the shortage of specie that so hampered economic development along the frontier; their policies just made matters worse with onerous taxes. Indeed, the only measures coming out of Philadelphia seemed to be repressive ones, and the whiskey tax was just the last straw. Western Pennsylvania finally rose up in armed rebellion against the federal government in 1794.[61]

During that hot and momentous July, Talleyrand, Beaumetz, and Moreau were all in New York: Moreau at his grueling and humiliating first job hauling barrels from ship holds, Talleyrand and Beaumetz learning about European and American politics, exploring opportunities to speculate in backcountry lands, and planning their trip to investigate Knox and Bingham's holdings in Maine. It was on July 4 that they watched from Talleyrand's lodgings as Genet paraded below them with other French radicals and launched invectives back up at them. Talleyrand and Beaumetz left New York on a packet boat to New Haven on July 15, stopping in Connecticut and Boston on the way to Maine. The very same day, some four hundred miles to the west, U.S. Marshal David Lenox and the Treasury Department inspector Colonel John Neville served legal documents to several distillers in Westmoreland, Pennsylvania, who had not registered their stills under federal tax laws. Armed resistance began that night. By the next day, five hundred men had attacked the two officials and burned Neville's house; Lenox fled to Pittsburgh. On August 1, while Talleyrand was handing out his letters of introduction in the parlors of elite Bostonians, six thousand men converged at Braddock's Field, a few miles outside of Pittsburgh, preparing to mount a rebellion against the U.S. government. Settlers across the Ohio valley responded to the insurgents' call to join the uprising as "citizen[s] of the western country." "We are too distant from the grand seat of information," wrote one angry Kentuckian. As the frontier disturbances spread from Pennsylvania, Maryland, and Virginia across the Ohio valley to Kentucky and Ohio, the events began to look a lot like those of 1776. Many westerners were ready to declare their independence and ally themselves to a foreign power; some even affirmed their willingness to "renounc[e] the allegiance to the United States and annex themselves to the British."[62]

By this time, word had leaked back to Philadelphia about the insurrection, and Washington's cabinet met in emergency sessions to formulate a response. Federalists in Philadelphia were convinced that this revolt, like the one Genet had fomented in Kentucky the year before, was directly linked to the French Revolution, and to the Democratic-Republican clubs that had sprouted up around the country. Although the French minister

Fauchet had shut down the Genet-Michaux Kentucky insurrection, rumors circulated that he was now lending his support to the whiskey rebels. "He pretended to think it was a duty of patriotism to second the Western Insurrection," Hamilton later wrote. "He knew and approved of a conspiracy which was destined to overthrow the administration of our Government even by the most irregular means." Federalists referred to the uprising as a "Jacobin" movement, accusing it of being led by the "sans-culottes of Pittsburgh." John Adams would later tell Liancourt that the Whiskey Rebellion, just like the formation of Democratic-Republican Societies, was "due to émigrés and not nationals." What is more, Liancourt added, "that is the opinion of many reasonable men of the country." In the eyes of wary Federalists, western Pennsylvania had become "a center of terrorism under the guiding hand of Albert Gallatin," the French-speaking, Swiss-born Jeffersonian politician.[63]

But Federalists were not the only ones to see the events along the Appalachian frontier through the prism of the French Revolution; Republican leaders in western Pennsylvania did, too. David Bradford, one of the movement's leaders, compared himself to Robespierre, while his followers talked about setting up a guillotine in the upper reaches of the Ohio valley. "My imagination presented the evils" of the French Revolution "so strongly to my view, and brought them so close to probable experience at home," the moderate Republican Hugh Henry Brackenridge later wrote, "that, during the whole period of the insurrection, I could scarcely bear to cast my eye upon a paragraph of French news."[64]

Given these associations, it was probably inevitable that the émigré *constituants,* erstwhile French revolutionaries traveling through the backcountry, would raise suspicions the summer after Genet had sought to organize an insurrection in the West. Americans had good reasons to worry. In preparing for Genet's mission, one French military plan had described the ideal agent to send into the American backcountry:

When landed in Philadelphia, the commissioners will declare themselves as assigned with making purchases of land in Kentucky and elsewhere. They would put themselves in relations with

merchants who would give them letters of recommendations for
the interior, as well as letters of credit. They would even have a bit
of an aristocratic air to better trick the public's watchfulness.

It's hard to think of a better description of Noailles, Talleyrand, Liancourt,
and the others. Indeed, when Liancourt explored the backcountry the following summer, people refused to believe that he would travel for his own
curiosity. "We were asked, there as elsewhere, if we were going to purchase
land," he reported. "In America, it cannot be imagined that any other intention could determine a man to travel, and those to whom we respond
that we are travelling for our own curiosity think us very stupid, when they
do us the favor of not thinking us liars." It is not surprising that many
people wondered, in this summer of insurrection, whether darker motives
were at work in these backcountry travels.[65]

On August 4, while he was in Boston preparing to leave for Maine, Talleyrand sent his friend Madame de Staël a letter. "I am traveling to the best
of my ability," he wrote. "I can see how I could usefully give work to those
who, after the current campaign, would like to remove all fantasies from
their minds and no longer believe in a France, nor in foreign powers." That
same day, in Philadelphia, Supreme Court justice James Wilson—himself
an aggressive buyer of backcountry lands whose reckless speculations
would soon bring him low—certified that Washington and Allegheny
Counties in western Pennsylvania were formally in a state of insurrection.
Also that day, Secretary of War Henry Knox assessed the number of insurgents "in the Counties West of the Mountains" at ten thousand, of which
seven or eight thousand were probably armed. Putting down such a force,
he estimated, would require 12,400 men. Three days later, on August 7,
Washington issued a proclamation calling up the militia. Washington had
determined to muster an overwhelming force to crush the insurrection.
"The essential interests of the Union demand it," Washington declared.
"The very existence of Government and the fundamental principles of social order are materially involved in the issue."[66]

For poor Knox, this was a trying time. He was planning to leave for
Maine to join Talleyrand, Beaumetz, and the Dutch agent whom Théo-

phile Cazenove had sent along. He would show them the territory and—if fortune smiled down—persuade them to invest in his massive land speculation. But the president had just scheduled an emergency cabinet meeting to discuss the federal response to the Whiskey Rebellion. Could the secretary of war leave Philadelphia to sell lands to French investors on the northern frontier when the western frontier was in a state of full-blown insurrection? "Accustomed to consider even your desires, much less your orders, as paramount to every other consideration," Knox wrote to Washington when he learned of the meeting, "I shall certainly defer my journey,

Henry Knox *by Gilbert Stuart. Knox began his career as an apprentice bookseller and learned military engineering and artillery by reading the wide selection in Boston's London Book-Store. During the American Revolution he rose to become chief of artillery for the Continental army under George Washington, brigadier general, and then, later, Washington's first secretary of war.*

or even renounce it altogether, if your view of the subject should render my continuance here of public importance although," he added somewhat plaintively, "permanent pecuniary ruin or something very like it attends either one or the other." Knox was wavering—weighing his public responsibilities against his private financial exigencies—and needed to decide quickly. "I had made arrangements for departing at nine this evening in order that by riding all night I might arrive at New York tomorrow noon so as to sail in a packet which waits to take me to Providence but your answer shall regulate my conduct."[67]

Washington and Knox were old friends. The two had fought in the Revolution together, as the erstwhile Boston bookseller became one of Washington's most trusted generals. Perhaps, too, as a fellow landowner, Washington sympathized with Knox's plight. He was far more conservative than Knox with his investments, and far less strapped for cash; but Washington owned tens of thousands of acres in the Ohio valley, including sixty-three thousand acres in western Pennsylvania, land continually beset by squatters and now threatened with insurrection. Although he "could see no propriety in the absence of the Officers of the government" at such a time, Washington nonetheless let Knox off the hook: "I consent to your pursuing your plan—& wish you a good journey & a safe & speedy return." In Knox's absence, Hamilton would serve as Washington's acting secretary of war. And so it was that when Washington set out as commander in chief at the head of thirteen thousand troops to put down the Whiskey Rebellion in late September, in the only time in American history that a sitting president has led troops in the field, it was Hamilton and not Knox who rode at his side.[68]

The insurrection had just been quashed when Liancourt arrived in Philadelphia in November 1794, carrying a letter of introduction to Washington from John Jay; it was all the merchants at the City Tavern were talking about as he went to let a room. "I am terrified by the beginnings of Jacobinism that appear in this country," he wrote in his diary. A week later, Liancourt watched the troops march back into town. "*Grand ordre, décence, bonne mine,*" wrote the former French officer, reassured, perhaps: great order, decency, and good appearance. "Arrived at city hall, touching spectacle." Washington was even more impressed. "The spirit with which the Militia turned out, in support of the Constitution," he wrote, "is the most conclusive refutation that could have been given to the assertions of Lord Sheffield, and the prediction of others of his cast, that without the protection of G. Britain, we should be unable to govern ourselves; and would soon be involved in anarchy and confusion." Sheffield had evidently hit a nerve: the pamphlet had been written ten years earlier. It was in response to Lord Sheffield's writings on the United States that William Bingham had penned his 1784 pamphlet promoting Anglo-American trade and cooperation, which had first gotten him noticed by Lord Lansdowne back when he and Anne were living in London after John Jay had signed the peace treaty with Great Britain.[69]

But had Sheffield's predictions really been proved wrong?

EXACTLY ONE week before Liancourt arrived in Philadelphia, John Jay put his signature on the second treaty he had negotiated with Great Britain in eleven years. With British troops building forts in the Northwest and disaffected backcountry settlers on the edge of rebellion, the United States could hardly risk a new war with its former colonial master. In sending Jay to London, Washington had set aside innumerable humiliations on land and on sea to make peace with England. But at what cost? On what terms? The country was on edge.

Winter travel across the Atlantic was notoriously dangerous. A year earlier, Moreau had left France in November: his trip had taken over four months and nearly cost him and his family their lives. Jay refused to take the risk. "Not being fit for a winters voyage," he scribbled in a quick note to Hamilton, "I shall stay here 'till Spring." And so the treaty went ahead, carried along its uncertain voyage aboard a British mail packet, the *Tankerville*. Jay was wise to have stayed in London. In December a French privateer attacked the *Tankerville* and both copies of the treaty were lost in the frigid waters of the North Atlantic.[70]

By February, other ships from England had arrived in Philadelphia. They confirmed that a treaty had been signed but lacked any information about its contents: the text was already supposed to have been delivered. "A ship has just arrived from London, from which it left on December 4, and brings positive news that a treaty was signed on November 19," the French minister Pierre-Auguste Adet wrote to the Foreign Ministry in Paris. "The American Government gives its assurances that it has not yet received any official notice on the subject." No one knew what the two countries had agreed to. "Altho' nearly three months have passed since the signing of the Treaty by Jay," Madison reported in the middle of February, "the official account of it has not been received, and the public have no other knowledge of its articles than are to be gleaned from the imperfect scraps of private letters." It is, he added a few weeks later, "a circumstance very singular." It hardly seemed auspicious, however, to find reports in late February in the *Aurora General Advertiser,* Philadelphia's most outspokenly Republican newspaper, that a group of London merchants had thrown Jay a "splendid entertainment," with a variety of public figures attending, including the British foreign minister Lord Grenville and the banker Henry Hope. The group toasted King George III. "May Britons and Americans never forget that they are of one family," the assembled guests heard as they finished their glasses. It was a proposition a great many Americans rejected. Finally, on March 7, a copy of the treaty arrived in Philadelphia. President Washington and Secretary of State Randolph read its provisions and immediately put the treaty under lock and key. Its contents would remain hidden, even from the other members of Washington's cabinet, until the Senate could reconvene in June. "What its contents are," Madison wrote, "the Executive alone as yet know the most impenetrable secrecy being observed. You will easily guess the curiosity and disappointment of the public."[71]

Speculation was rampant. Would the British abandon their forts in the Great Lakes? Would they stop harassing America's commerce and impressing its sailors? Would the new treaty abrogate the Treaty of Amity and Commerce between France and the United States? "Its contents have produced conjectural comments without number," Madison wrote to his friend James Monroe, then the American minister in Paris. For all of Genet's machinations, pro-French sentiment remained overwhelming among Americans. "I should hope it to be impossible that any stipulation, if any should be attempted, inconsistent with the Treaties with France, can ever be pursued into effect," Madison added. "I cannot even believe that any such stipulation would be hazarded. The President, to say nothing of the people, would so certainly revolt at it." This was Liancourt's impression as he began his travels into the Pennsylvania backcountry in May, with the treaty's provisions still a closely guarded secret. "Political opinions are for liberty," he observed. "They are, as a consequence, always for the success of the French against their current enemies. . . . The hostility to England is great; it is so among all the classes; it has received renewed force from the grievances that America reproached England for last year." Liancourt presciently concluded: "I think that the negotiations of M. Jay will not extinguish this *germe*."[72]

In June senators from the fifteen U.S. states returned to Philadelphia for the momentous debate. Behind closed doors, they argued the merits of the treaty. It was almost a repeat of the convention that had gathered in Philadelphia eight years earlier, holding its secret meetings through the hot summer while Philadelphians could only wonder at the proceedings. Everything was on the line for Washington. A Senate rejection of the treaty meant certain war with Britain, crippling American shipping in the Caribbean and resurrecting the frayed British alliance with Native Americans in the Ohio valley in an all-out assault on the Northwest Territory. It would ravage American trade—on which government revenues almost entirely depended—and, as Hamilton warned Washington, "would cut up credit by the roots." Foreign capital flows might halt. The United States might lose its tenuous grip on the territory north of the Ohio River. Ratification, on the other hand, would threaten the already fragile Franco-American alliance, enrage the powerful pro-French sentiment in the United States, and risk inciting such civil unrest as would make the Genet affair and the Whiskey Rebellion seem like minor eruptions. "This government in relation to France and England may be compared to a ship between the rocks of Sylla and charibdas," George Washington mused. "If the Treaty is ratified the partisans of the French (or rather of War and confusion) will excite them to hostile measures, or at least to unfriendly Sentiments; if it is not, there is no foreseeing all the consequences which may follow, as it respts. G. B." Finally, after three long weeks of debate, the vote was cast: the Senate ratified the treaty by a margin of twenty to ten: the bare two-thirds minimum required under the Constitution.[73]

On July 1, just days before the celebration of national independence from Britain, the treaty's provisions leaked out when the Republican printer Benjamin Franklin Bache obtained a copy. At last the public learned why Washington had gone to such lengths to keep it hidden. Everyone's worst fears were realized. Jay had secured one vital objective for the United States: the evacuation of the forts along the Great Lakes by which British forces supplied the Western Confederacy of Native Americans. But by the terms of the treaty, even this, his greatest success, was mitigated: Great Britain would hold the forts for another year before evacuating. The rest of the treaty went from bad to worse. Britain had agreed to open its Caribbean islands to American trade, but on terms so restrictive that the Senate ultimately struck out the provision as a condition of ratification. Jay failed, however, to secure a British recognition of American neutrality, and of the essential principle of free ships, free goods: indeed, the treaty explicitly renounced those principles as established in the U.S. Treaty of Amity and Commerce with France. American shipping to the Caribbean would still be subject to harassment, American cargoes still subject to seizure, and American sailors still subject to impressment. Jay further promised that the United States would not interfere with British trade for ten years, thus giving up the only weapon in the U.S. diplomatic arsenal: commercial retaliation. Suddenly, and with almost no concessions on the British side, save those they had already agreed to at the close of the Revolution in 1783, Great Britain was on the same commercial footing as France, which had won those terms by rescuing the United States in the Revolution. The United States had become a de facto ally of Great Britain, its former enemy and a monarchy, against France, its former ally and a republic. Although American merchants would profit—gaining greater access to British credit and seeing land values in backcountry regions rise—almost everyone else would be hurt. The treaty may have kept the United States from a war with

Great Britain in the 1790s, but it was a diplomatic humiliation, "a monument of weakness," as Liancourt put it.[74]

Washington left Philadelphia for Mount Vernon in the middle of July, as the public outcry was just beginning. He knew the response would be bad, but he had no idea how bad, nor how powerful and enduring the consequences would be. "The outpouring of popular feeling over the Jay Treaty," conclude the historians Stanley Elkins and Eric McKitrick in their meticulous study of the Federalist period, "was more directly responsible than anything else for the full emergence of political parties in America." Opponents of the treaty began immediately to "impress on the minds of the people," as Washington wrote to his secretary of state, "that their rights have not only been *neglected,* but absolutely *sold.* That there are *no* reciprocal advantages in the treaty; that the benefits are all on the side of G. Britain; and, what seems to have had more weight with them than all the rest and most pressed is that the treaty is made with design to oppress the French, in open violation of our treaty with that nation, and contrary too to every principle of gratitude and sound policy."[75]

The country erupted. From the second week of July to the end of August, hardly a day passed without some public protest. According to Bache's Republican *Aurora General Advertiser,* some six thousand people gathered in the yard of the Pennsylvania State House on July 26 to denounce the treaty's terms. "The greatest order prevailed at the meeting," it reported, adding, as if by way of postscript: "In the evening the treaty was burnt in several public places of the city." The Federalist *Gazette of the United States,* on the other hand, put the number assembled at fifteen hundred, of which "five or six hundred were spectators, and two or three hundred Frenchmen." And according to them, it was less a meeting than a mob. The Federalist treasury secretary Oliver Wolcott recorded his account: "The treaty was thrown to the populace, who placed it on a pole; a company of about three hundred then proceeded to the French minister's house before which some ceremony was performed. The mob then went before Mr. Hammond's house and burned the treaty with huzzahs and acclamations." They continued to the Binghams' house and burnt another copy of the treaty there, and then began to throw stones through the windows. Noailles, watching the scene from inside the Bingham property, mounted a horse, headed out the gates to disperse the furious crowd—and was "somewhat hurt by attempting to ride over the mob," according to Wolcott, who did not record whether anyone in the crowd was hurt by being ridden over. But it wasn't only crowds in Philadelphia that exploded in anger. In Charleston, a public hangman burned copies of the treaty, while a mob gathered at Federalist senator Jacob Read's house, where, according to his brother, they "burnt the Treaty and groan'd thrice," before returning later to beat his door with sticks. Further inland, in Pendleton, South Carolina, a group of militiamen assembled and erected a liberty tree, with a liberty cap "and an inscription on its base expressive of the general detestation of the Treaty." In Boston, Republicans organized a group of boys to parade around town with lighted lanterns carved out of watermelons. Petitions from several states threatened secession. Jay was burned in effigy in Boston, Philadelphia, New York, and even as far west as Lexington, Kentucky; he joked that he could travel from one end of the seaboard to the other by the light of his burning effigies. "Damn John Jay," read some graffiti on the side of one New York building. "Damn everyone that won't damn John Jay. Damn everyone that won't put up lights in the windows and sit up all night damning John Jay."[76]

Madame de La Tour du Pin, the émigrée who had settled on a farm near Albany, was in New York at the time the news of the treaty reached the city. Like the other émigrés, she was friends with Hamilton, having been introduced by Angelica Church in London to his wife's family. She watched the former treasury secretary debate the treaty's merits against a Republican opponent in public:

> We were assembled on the squares. The two leaders harangued their partisans. I was seated, in the company of other women, on the steps of a front stoop, from which Hamilton was speaking to people pressed into the square. A stone was thrown that hit him in the head, but without hurting him very much. He nonetheless con-

tinued his speech, which excited a prodigious enthusiasm. Then everyone went home, and he very calmly offered me his arm to take me home.

Angry crowds on this scale hadn't been seen in the country since the American Revolution. Hamilton feared that the local militias "cannot be depended on," and wondered if it would be possible to call the army back from the West to restore order. For refugees who had fled their country in the face of violent mobs—who had watched angry Parisian crowds take over the National Assembly, imprison aristocrats, and in some cases kill them in the streets—the sight of vast protests through the streets of New York and Philadelphia must have been terrifying. Liancourt's cousin, the pro-American duc de La Rochefoucauld, had been stoned to death by a Paris mob. It was how Liancourt had become the duc de La Rochefoucauld-Liancourt.[77]

Arguments about the Jay Treaty continued through the summer and fall of 1795 and into 1796, bitterly dividing Americans. "It is scarcely possible for a dozen Americans to sit together without quarrelling about politics and the British treaty," the English traveler Isaac Weld remarked as he trekked through the Susquehanna valley, leaving an inimitable description of one such debate:

> The farmers were of one opinion, and gabbled away for a long time; the lawyers and the judge were of another, and in turns they rose to answer their opponents with all the power of rhetoric which they possessed. Neither party could say any thing to change the sentiments of the other one; the noisy contest lasted till late at night, when getting heartily tired they withdrew, not to their respective chambers but, to the general one that held five or six beds, and in which they laid down in pairs. Here the conversation was again revived, and pursued with as much noise as below, till at last sleep closed their eyes, and happily their mouths at the same time; for could they have talked in their sleep, I verily believe they would have prated on until morning.

Liancourt experienced much the same when he arrived in Boston in the fall of 1795. "The treaty with England is spoken of everywhere, and spoken of continually." If anything, the pro-English treaty persuaded Liancourt of the overwhelming popularity of pro-French opinion. "We encounter in Virginia this same language of affection for France, of hatred and above all suspicion of the English, and of attachment for M. de la Fayette, that one encounters in all the parts of America that are not too close to the great cities and places of speculation." Liancourt found Republican opinion more dominant in the southern states in general. But even in the northern back-country opinion ran considerably in favor of France. Only the port cities with their merchant classes stood apart, suggesting to Liancourt that parts of the backcountry might well be ripe for the plucking. "The people of the country and those of the big cities, those who live at some distance from the coast and those who cling to the areas of commerce are two distinct people by their manners and their opinions," Liancourt concluded by the end of his travels. Although he admired Washington and Hamilton, Liancourt decided that the Jay Treaty was bad for America. The country had "put itself in a state of dependence on England; where it voluntarily renounces its duty, its obligation to assist its ally France in its wartime needs." He predicted it would prove to be a "great misfortune for the tranquillity of America."[78]

In short, between April 1793, when Genet sailed into Charleston aboard the *Embuscade,* and the end of March 1796, when Liancourt sailed in aboard the *South Carolina,* relations between France and the United States had changed dramatically.

THE JAY TREATY was a key turning point. The rapprochement of Great Britain and the United States had two major effects on North American geopolitics: one on Native Americans and the second on Franco-American relations. Both would fundamentally reshape sovereignty in the Mississippi valley.

The Jay Treaty secured the British evacuation of the long-disputed western posts, thereby isolating the Ohio valley Indians and crippling their resistance to U.S. expansion. For Great Britain's steadfast allies—some of whom had fought alongside the British through wars against the French in the 1750s and 1760s and against the rebellious Americans in the 1770s and 1780s—it was an appalling betrayal. The groundwork had already been set even as Jay was in London negotiating the terms of his treaty. In August 1794 the Western Confederacy fought a pitched battle at Fallen Timbers, within sight of Fort Miami—the very fort Simcoe had built along the Miami River in Ohio. British forces refused to intervene, however; they just looked on as their Native American allies fought below and lost the most significant battle in their long war, now nearly half a century long, to retain control of their traditional lands. British officers even locked the gates to the fort when the defeated Native warriors sought refuge after the battle. "In spite of a decade of promises and encouragement, the inflammatory Dorchester speech, the building and reinforcing of Fort Miami, the tons of supplies and powder sent from Detroit, and the continual assurances of assistance," writes the historian Robert Allen, "the British in the moment of crisis were abandoning the tribes. The events at Fallen Timbers and Fort Miami in August of 1794 destroyed the British-Indian alliance." The British had decided that they would deliver the land northwest of the Ohio River as the price for peace between the United States and Great Britain. "Thou hast given them our land in order to have peace from them," said a Delaware chief to the British.[79]

The loss at Fallen Timbers set the stage for the Treaty of Greenville, signed the following year between the Western Confederacy and General Anthony Wayne, in which Native leaders abandoned their long-standing demand for an Ohio River boundary between Indian country and the United States. Native Americans did now what they had never done before, neither after the Seven Years' War nor after the American Revolution: they recognized American sovereignty in the Ohio valley. Despite the Indians' attempt to reassert their claims during the War of 1812, Fallen Timbers and the Jay Treaty together signaled the end of the Indian barrier state in the Ohio valley. After those decisive military and diplomatic triumphs, General Wayne began his long march back to Philadelphia, where Liancourt, Talleyrand, Moreau, and the others watched him arrive that first Saturday in February 1796, to be *fêted* at the City Tavern under a sky lit up by fireworks.[80]

If the Jay Treaty reduced British and Native threats to U.S. control of the West, however, setting the stage for the extension of U.S. sovereignty into Native American territory, it created an ominous new French menace. For diplomats in France, as for Native Americans in the West, the treaty was an appalling betrayal. France had established what was meant to be a permanent alliance in the Revolutionary War—one desperately sought by the Americans—and with the fall of the monarchy French republicans hoped to expand the alliance into an "intimate liaison," a "family pact between free peoples." But at the very moment that France opened its arms to the United States, its sister republic, "the royalist party was preparing it [an alliance] with our enemies," as the French minister Adet put it to his superiors. Apprised of the situation in the United States by reports filtering back to Paris from agents and observers—including information from Talleyrand, Liancourt, Noailles, Volney, and others—French authorities now concluded that they could no longer depend on their fickle ally. "I have observed, studied the Americans; I believe I have seen them," Adet wrote in early 1796. "And every day convinces me more and more that if ever France opens a negotiation with them, it is no longer principles of loyalty, disinterest, and frankness that must guide our *démarches;* it will be necessary to oppose dissimulation with reserve, the language of unspoken ambition with force, ambiguous and obnoxious forms with precision, and finally the greedy pretensions of a speculating people with mercantile calculations."[81]

The fecklessness of France's erstwhile ally, now back in the arms of its great enemy, led to a dramatic shift in French policy. No longer able to rely on the United States for military support or supplies for their Caribbean colonies, French naval planners began to look for a more secure continental foothold. They did not need to look far. "Louisiana abundantly produces all the goods that the United States furnish," read one government report: "tobacco, indigo, furs, masts, skirting boards, naval stores, rice, pears, beans, corn, horses and mules, cattle, salted beef, candle wax, hemp, wool, cotton, tallow, hides, butter, iron and lead." These products and more, French authorities were assured, would provide "all that is necessary for the subsistence of our colonies." Upon extensive travel and discussion with his informants, Liancourt quite independently drew the same conclusion. "The commercial advantages, which Louisiana holds out," he concluded, "are uncommonly great. It might furnish the most durable wood of every sort for ship-building and masts. . . . Louisiana could supply the French colonies with entire houses in frame." And, he added, no doubt thinking of his travels with Knox the previous year, they "might be had at an easier and cheaper rate from that country than from the Province of Maine."[82]

As a strategic site without equal, New Orleans secured control of the entire Mississippi River valley: "The master of New Orleans," affirmed one French government report, "holds the key to continental America." Not only would the occupation of New Orleans guarantee French dominance in Louisiana and a reliable source of supplies for the Caribbean colonies, it would ensure U.S. obedience to French interests. "It gives us the means to balance the marked predilection of the federal government for our enemy," the French Directory concluded in early 1796, "and to retain it in the line of duty by the fear of dismemberment which we can bring about." The carrot had failed; it was time to use a stick. A few months later, Liancourt agreed that a French Louisiana would keep the United States in check. "The possession of Louisiana," he wrote, "would have the further advantage of posing a barrier to this childish rapacity that the Americans have to extend themselves everywhere and which, stemming more from an inconsistency of character than to any political view, would prevent them from forcefully establishing themselves in any of their new States."[83]

In developing this new line of thought, French planners counted on their former Native American alliances. With the British having betrayed Native peoples in the Ohio valley, the time seemed ripe for French officers to cultivate their erstwhile allies. Choctaws, Chickasaws, and Creeks of the Southwest "are much more attached to the French than to any other nation," one French diplomatic document affirmed. "They love the French, esteem the English and fear the Americans." Liancourt had discovered much the same from his travels. "All these [Indians], who have had any dealings with the French, prefer them to any other people," he wrote. "The Indians still say to the English—'*You are our brothers, but the French were our fathers.*'" And so, Liancourt concluded of the Creeks and Cherokees, "upon the slightest favorable occurrence, they might easily be gained over to France." Meanwhile, French people who had long resided across the Mississippi valley, in Kentucky, Indiana, Illinois, and the Northwest Territory, would provide critical support to French ambitions in the Mississippi valley.[84]

A variety of reports urging a Franco-Native invasion of Louisiana now began to draw the notice of French officials. The one that received the most attention was a plan hatched by Louis LeClerc de Milford, a brash former French soldier adopted into the Creek nation, who married the sister of the Creek leader Alexander McGillivray and was renamed "Tastanegy," or Great War Chief. Milford sailed to Philadelphia in 1795, where the French minister Fauchet, impressed with his zeal, sent him on to France to submit his proposal to the Committee of Public Safety. Over the course of the next several years he sought to persuade French authorities to ally with the Creeks in an invasion of Louisiana. "If we don't have any continental settlement in America," he insisted, with a keen sense of the priorities of French diplomats, "our islands will be lost to us and will be shared between England and its old Colony." Milford assured the French government of the Creeks' "friendship for the French, their fathers," and of the interest both of them had "to restrain and frighten the United States." Nor could he help commenting on "the audacity of the Americans whose independence is due to France and who today, far from repaying their sacred debt, seem desirous of throwing themselves into the arms of their former tyrants." Louisiana, he concluded, would provide France with "the base of a power more than sufficient to restrain the ambition of the United States and punish them for their ingratitude." No wonder that Talleyrand, when he returned to France and became foreign minister, wrote of Milford's reports that he "found the subject worthy of the most serious consideration."[85]

As THE United States and France grew apart after 1795, the émigré *constituants* grew closer to their *patrie*. They had traveled a long way since the days in 1793 and 1794, when Genet and Fauchet suspected them of advancing an Anglo-American alliance. The change was due as much to the new politics in France as it was to the altered political configuration in the United States.

After the émigrés took refuge in America, politics in France shifted back toward the center. The Girondins who had sent Genet to America had fallen at the hands of the *Montagne;* the Montagnards who had sent Fauchet to replace Genet had in turn fallen to the Directory. The new government was proving itself less hostile to the *constituants,* whose centrist politics were gradually coming back into vogue. To replace Fauchet, the Directory sent Pierre-Auguste Adet, who was, like his superiors in Paris, more moderate in both temperament and politics. Adet was also an old friend of Moreau's: he had served as *chef de l'administration des colonies* in Saint Domingue. A chemist and a student of Antoine Lavoisier, in 1796 he was elected to the American Philosophical Society, the same year as Talleyrand and Liancourt. The growing moderation of French politics helped rekindle the *constituants'* attachment to France. "I knew," charged the arch-Federalist William Cobbett, referring to Talleyrand, "that, notwithstanding his being proscribed at Paris, he was extremely intimate with Adet." And although the intemperate Cobbett's accusations should always be taken with some skepticism, in this case he does seem to have been right. "Nothing would make me live in a country at war with France," Talleyrand wrote to his friend Madame de Genlis in May 1795, a year after he arrived from London. "I have a horror for England," he added. By early 1796 Moreau and Talleyrand were visiting Adet at his home.[86]

The growing political moderation in France did not change the Washington administration's attitude, however. Quite the contrary: as French politics became more moderate, American politics became more pro-English. In February 1796 rumors even began circulating that the Federalist William Bingham might replace the pro-French James Monroe as ambassador to France. "It has been whispered that you are to be recalled and Bingham to replace you," Madison wrote to Monroe. "I entirely disbelieve it but the whisper marks the wishes of those who propagate it." The rumors were enough to provoke a censorious response from Adet, who wrote to his superiors in Paris describing Bingham as a "very rich man, playing the Frenchman in Philadelphia, for taste and spending; a sort of political zero, but nevertheless an *anglomane*." By the time John Adams took office in early 1797, U.S. diplomacy had shifted decisively in favor of Britain. The growing anti-French sentiment alienated Liancourt, who found himself disenchanted with his Federalist friends and began complaining about the "political intolerance" in Philadelphia society. "The English influence prevails in the first circles," he wrote. "This great *personage* who caressed the envoys of Robespierre, when that monster and his accomplices assassinated all honest men, is openly against France today now that its principles are inclined toward *douceur* and humanity." What a strange turn of events. Even the tenor of Philadelphia's street politics changed. The working-class festive culture that had long bent ardently toward France shifted toward the end of the decade. Where French songs had long reigned supreme in theaters and public performances, now Federalist political songs like "The President's March" began to replace them. "It is to be hoped," the Federalist *Gazette of the United States* would write in 1798, that "no more attempts will be made to grate and torture the public ear with those shouts Ca Ira and the Marseilles Hymn."[87]

On November 4, 1796, Moreau noted a single sentence in his diary entry for the day: "I put on the *Cocarde*." It was a highly symbolic gesture. The cockade was the most visible sign of fidelity to the French Revolution; it had once symbolized the radicalism of the Girondin and Montagnard enemies of the *constituants,* and was now being reappropriated. "We only admit those who carry the *cocarde* into the Chancelleries," reported the consul general of Philadelphia in 1797. By that time, Moreau had assumed an official connection to the French legation in Philadelphia as a precaution. "As relations between France and America were darkening," he wrote in his diary, "acts might occur that would make the sojourn of French people in the United States very disagreeable, my friend Letombe [the consul

Revolutionary poster in Paris.
BY LAW: it is forbidden to enter WITHOUT A COCARDE and to
employ here any qualifications other than that of CITIZEN.
We carry shredded tobacco.

Liberty cap with a cocarde (cockade): the great symbol of the French
Revolution. A hot-air balloon in the background drops bombs on a
fortified city in an early depiction of aerial warfare.

general in Philadelphia] proposed to attach me to the French Legation as a measure of protection for my family and myself." Indeed, as early as August 1796, the secretary of the French legation in Philadelphia was referring to him as the "consul Moreau St.-Merry."[88]

It was roughly at this time that Liancourt began to collaborate more closely with the French minister. Adet would later write to Paris in praise of Liancourt: "I have to tell you that since my arrival here I've received only favorable reports about him. I would even add that I've learned by indirect means that some precious information I've received, and of which I didn't know the source, was furnished by him." Meanwhile, Liancourt was distancing himself from his American friends. "Liancourt has become very violent" against the United States, Anne Bingham reported to John Adams at a dinner in late 1796. But Liancourt was not the only émigré with angry words about the United States. One American who spoke excellent French recalled a conversation that almost certainly took place during the winter of 1795 to 1796 among La Tour du Pin's husband, Talleyrand, Volney, and two French investors developing a large tract of land in western New York. Liancourt may well have been present, too. They "appeared to forget that I was an American" and allowed themselves to speak freely. "Speculating upon the posture of European affairs, Desjardins at length turning to me, exclaimed, 'Yes, my friend, before this war'—the war waged by despotism against republican principles—'shall end, your frontier will be lined with French bayonets.' To this sentiment they all seemed to respond in acquiescence."[89]

That conversation took place just a few months before Liancourt sailed out of Philadelphia with Palisot, whom Adet had sent to meet Michaux, and Collot and Volney left on their respective trips out west, also on behalf of the French government. All these expeditions—at precisely the time that France's leadership had decided to rebuild its North American empire.

BACK IN the summer of 1795, Talleyrand had approached Adet with a petition to the French government asking that his name be struck from the list of proscribed émigrés so that he might return to France. Talleyrand argued that he had originally left France in 1792 on an official mission to Great Britain and had therefore never, strictly speaking, been an émigré. Back in Paris, Madame de Staël launched her own campaign to drum up support for Talleyrand's return, persuading her friend Eugénie de La Bouchardie to convince her lover Marie-Joseph Chénier, the poet and politician, to present Talleyrand's petition to the National Assembly. On September 4, they succeeded, and the National Assembly voted to remove his name from the list of proscribed émigrés.[90]

Talleyrand was in New York when he learned in a letter from Moreau— ever a conduit of information from France to the United States—that his petition had succeeded. By that time, however, winter was setting in and Talleyrand didn't want to risk the transatlantic voyage. He also wanted official confirmation that he could, indeed, return safely. And so he'd settled into one final social season in Philadelphia with his friends and fellow *constituants*.

In the late spring of 1796, Liancourt—to whom Talleyrand was by now "strongly attached"—had left for his travels south and Volney for his travels west, while Noailles planned his glamorous trip to Maine. It was time for Talleyrand to go, and he began to look for a safe conveyance across the Atlantic. He would have to choose carefully. Sailing aboard a French boat was too risky. "The ships that go from America to France carry provisions, like flour, rice, and salted meats," Talleyrand remarked—tempting targets for British privateers. "Of three ships loaded in this way, two are led to Bermuda, Halifax, or some English port." Nor were American ships much safer now that the French had authorized the seizure of U.S. vessels bound for enemy ports. Perhaps Talleyrand also recalled Moreau's unhappy experience with an American captain on his grueling journey across the Atlantic. In late April advertisements began to appear in the Philadelphia papers for *Den Nye Prøve*, a Danish ship sailing for Hamburg, "a fine stout vessel" captained by Peter Hansen. Talleyrand applied for passage. "This will allow me to avoid all the English piracies to which I will be subject," he wrote. "From here to Hamburg is sent sugar, coffee, or other colonial goods, and this type of shipment ordinarily arrives at its destination without worries." It is possible, too, that Talleyrand just liked the ship's name.[91]

Time was now beginning to press on Talleyrand to wrap up his business affairs. In mid-May he finalized an agreement with Robert Morris to serve as a European agent for one hundred thousand acres of land. He chatted with the Spanish ambassador about the latest diplomatic news, including rumors that a French commissioner was sailing over to demand an explanation from the American government about the Jay Treaty. Just before Talleyrand's departure, Noailles left Philadelphia for his trip to Maine with Alexander Baring and the Bingham women. Seven years earlier, Noailles and Talleyrand had struggled together in the Assemblée constituante to reform French life; together, on the fateful night of August 4, 1789, they had dismantled the *ancien régime.* Already it seemed like a different era. Noailles was not planning to return to France, while Talleyrand had no intention of coming back to America. It was the last time the old friends would ever see each other. On June 11, Moreau ate at Samuel Richardet's tavern with Talleyrand, and the two worked through the night. The next day, Talleyrand dined at Moreau's. On the morning of June 13, Talleyrand left Moreau's house to board his ship for Hamburg.[92]

Moreau was losing his closest friend in Philadelphia and keenly felt the blow. Every night that he was in Philadelphia, according to Moreau, Talleyrand would stop by for a visit, during which they shared many "delightful confidences," discussing, without exception, "France's past fate, its present state, and finally what we thought of its future." So close had Talleyrand

Advertisement from Finlay's American Naval and Commercial Register, *Philadelphia, June 7, 1796.* Den Nye Prøve *was the ship on which Talleyrand sailed back to Europe.*

become to the family that he asked whether Moreau's son could accompany him back to Europe, where he would take him "under his wing." But Moreau's wife, taking stock of her husband's friend, refused, fearing that Talleyrand "would cultivate tastes which we would be unable to gratify, and which might turn him against us." Though he didn't leave with Moreau's son, Talleyrand did take one hundred copies of Moreau's recent book on the Spanish part of Saint Domingue and two hundred copies of Liancourt's book on the Philadelphia prison. Moreau's wife also gave him a cask of fresh drinking water for the voyage. Perhaps she remembered her painful trip over and how it had nearly killed the family. The bookstore where they had spent so many nights was only a block from the docks, so Moreau and his son accompanied Talleyrand to his ship and watched as he limped up the gangway. The two of them looked on forlornly as *Den Nye Prøve* sailed down the Delaware River, waiting until it slipped out of sight.[93]

Given what was about to ensue, it is hard to imagine a more appropriate conveyance for Talleyrand's voyage back to Europe than *The New Challenge,* its holds loaded with rich stores of Caribbean sugar and coffee.

THE ÉMIGRÉS RETURN TO FRANCE; FRANCE RETURNS TO AMERICA

TALLEYRAND'S TRIP BACK ACROSS THE ATLANTIC WAS UNEVENTFUL, a short forty days of easy sailing. He left Philadelphia on Monday, June 13, 1796. On Wednesday, he wrote from Newcastle, Delaware, to tell Moreau: "We are well." Happy as he was to be returning home, Talleyrand could not help but feel nostalgic for those he'd left behind: "Adieu, my friend, a thousand greetings to all of yours." What a change in outlook! As he sailed down the Delaware he likely thought of his first view of the river, some two years earlier, when he'd been so reluctant to land in America that he sought to jump aboard a ship heading to India.[1]

Captain Hansen had chosen a circuitous route to Europe—no doubt to avoid privateers. By Saturday, *Den Nye Prøve* had made it to Cape Henry, at the southern entrance to the Chesapeake Bay, the very spot where the French admiral De Grasse had successfully fought off the British navy some fifteen years earlier, closing the bay and isolating General Cornwallis at Yorktown. "The wind is light but fair," Talleyrand wrote to Moreau, handing his letter off to an inbound ship. "There has been no sight of a privateer on the coast for several days. Adieu. In forty-five days I will write you from Elbe."[2]

As he crossed the Atlantic, Talleyrand had time to ponder the previous two years, and all he'd learned about the United States from his travels through the backcountry, from his investments in lands, and from his personal contact with men like Alexander Hamilton, Henry Knox, and William Bingham. Perhaps he thought about a meal he'd shared with Hamilton, at which Hamilton "drank freely" and, becoming a bit too voluble, lashed out at his former coauthor of the *Federalist Papers,* who had negotiated the recent treaty with England: "Jay was an old woman for making it." After further discussion, the two had agreed that Washington would almost surely ratify it. "Tho' the treaty is a most execrable one," Hamilton concluded, sobering up, perhaps, "yet when once we have come to a determination on it, we must carry it through thick and thin, right or wrong." Talleyrand had reported the story to Volney, who told Jefferson. The Jay Treaty had shaken up both Franco-American relations and the émigrés' feelings about the United States. Right or wrong, Hamilton would stand by his country—and Talleyrand would stand by his. Perhaps, too, on his journey home, Talleyrand's thoughts turned to the long evening talks he'd had with Moreau, and their fantasy of moving to Louisiana. "We found many reasons to make us wish to have a home there for ourselves," Moreau had recalled in his diary. "Then we determined to devote all our thoughts and energies in this direction, and Talleyrand decided that we would wind up becoming its administrators."[3]

When Talleyrand arrived in Hamburg in late July, he found the city, like Philadelphia, full of French people. "The émigrés," Talleyrand reported, "are *doux.*" Among them was Liancourt's twenty-nine-year-old son, Alexandre, who had fought under Lafayette before taking refuge in Hamburg. Alexandre then lived in the borough of Altona with his wife, the daughter of a wealthy Saint Domingue planter and a relative of Joséphine de Beauharnais, the future empress of France. Talleyrand spent some time getting his bearings: gathering recent information on French politics and the state of the European wars, learning more about the young and brilliant Corsican general who was just then marching through Italy smashing the Austrian army to pieces. Talleyrand had already heard Volney's opinion: "It will be the head of Caesar on the shoulders of Alexander," Volney exclaimed in the presence of other refugees when he heard that Napoleon, whom he had met years earlier, had taken command of France's Italian army.[4]

Talleyrand was busy in Hamburg. He succeeded in consigning the one hundred copies of Moreau's *Description topographique* of the Spanish part of Saint Domingue that he'd brought with him. He also solicited enough interest in Liancourt's essay on the Philadelphia prisons that a local bookseller translated it and published a German edition. He delivered a letter of introduction from Alexander Baring to Caspar Voght, one of Hamburg's premier merchants, trying, perhaps, to interest him in a speculation in which he also wanted the Barings to participate. Or perhaps he just wanted to sell Voght some American land. Before Talleyrand left Philadelphia, he'd drafted an agreement to sell some of Robert Morris's Pennsylvania lands. He later sent Morris $142,500.42 for 106,875.5 acres. Finally, after a month in Hamburg, Talleyrand began the trip home, arriving in Paris on September 20. He'd been gone four years.[5]

Only three days after his arrival, Talleyrand attended a meeting of the Institut national des sciences et des arts, the new organization created from the ashes of the royal academies, which had incorporated the venerable Académie française. Talleyrand had been elected to the institute the previous December; Napoleon Bonaparte would be elected the following December. It would serve as the launching pad for the next stage of Talleyrand's career.

The following April, Talleyrand read a report to the institute on U.S. trade with England—"Mémoire sur les relations commerciales des États-Unis avec l'Angleterre"—in which he recalled the growing alienation he'd felt in the United States as a Frenchman. "In every part of America through which I traveled, I did not find a single Englishman who did not feel himself American, not a single Frenchman who did not feel himself a foreigner." The ties that bound Americans to England, Talleyrand concluded, were not just linguistic, constitutional, cultural, and religious; they were also economic. "The ever growing energy of the commercial relations between the United States and England," he believed, rested in large part on the credit granted by English firms, and on the trust that existed between British and American merchants. "The great capital of English merchants allows them to extend longer credit than merchants from any other nation could do." To be sure, Americans did not deny that they owed their independence to France. "But unfortunately," he added, "they think that the services of nations are founded on mere calculations, and not on attachment: they even say that the former government of France, when it made sacrifices in their favor, acted much more for their independence than for their liberty."[6]

In almost every respect, this analysis reflected Hamiltonian thought: about the natural economic and constitutional ties between the United States and Great Britain, about the importance of capital to economic development, and about the self-interested motivation of states in international relations. Indeed, given Talleyrand's status today as an archetypal "realist," his complaint about American ingratitude is curious. Is it possible that Talleyrand's views about the conduct of foreign relations were influenced by Hamilton, the person who had worked harder than anyone to resurrect trade relations between the United States and Great Britain? The one who had insisted that by intervening on behalf of the United States during the Revolution, France "was and ought to have been influenced by considerations relative to its own interest"? The politician who had only contempt for those who claimed that gratitude or "attachment" were proper motivations in foreign policy? No doubt Talleyrand and Hamilton had discussed these issues during their long evening talks together in Philadelphia and New York. And no doubt Talleyrand had heard similar views in his conversations at dinners and balls with other Federalists in his social circle.[7]

Perhaps it was time to abandon sentimentality when it came to the Franco-American alliance. The fact was, Talleyrand concluded in his "Mémoire," France's American policy had failed. It had failed to pull the Americans more than briefly out of the British trade orbit, it had failed to create a permanent alliance between France and the United States, and it had failed to benefit France's Caribbean colonies either commercially or militarily. "Whoever has well observed America," he concluded, "cannot doubt, that still she remains altogether English in the greater part of her habits; that her ancient commerce with England has increased, rather than declined in activity . . . and that, consequently, that independence, far from being of disadvantage to England, has benefited her in many respects." There could be only one solution to counteract this powerful English influence, Talleyrand mused: "It would require, perhaps, a French settlement in America to resist their influence with any hopes of success."[8]

Louisiana was still on his mind. Given Talleyrand's views about the importance of shared language—that "in the calculations of the various relations that can exist among men, identity of language is one of the most binding"—it would be a great advantage to establish a new colony in a region with a significant French-speaking population. But Talleyrand had just returned to Paris. He had no official position and little influence. Despite his efforts, the French Directory was focusing its attention elsewhere: on Napoleon overcoming Austrian resistance in Italy. And so, with some despondency, Talleyrand wrote to Moreau in February 1797, several weeks before he delivered his "Mémoire" on Anglo-American trade:

> I have made so little progress in getting support for our excellent ideas relative to the colonies that I have given up everything we planned together about that. Present-day diplomats are not at all impressed with the possibilities of Louisiana.

Perhaps it would require a change in the government to implement these "excellent ideas."[9]

Talleyrand did not give up. In July, three months after his first address to the institute, he gave another one, entitled "Essay on the Advantages to Be Derived from New Colonies, in the Present Circumstances": "My goal is to arouse public attention" on the subject of colonization, "and to call forth the deepest meditations and knowledge on this subject." Upon extensive travel and reflection about the effects of revolutions on social order, Talleyrand had concluded that new colonies could overcome the social and political tensions unleashed by the French Revolution. "While I was in America," he observed, "I was struck to see that after a revolution, in truth very different from ours, there remained so few traces of ancient hatreds, so little agitation, or worry." The relative peace in America—so different from the continued turbulence in France—stemmed, according to Talleyrand, from the existence of "immense quantities of uncultivated lands." The availability of all this land served as a safety valve, calming tempers and "softening revolutionary passions." Thus, Talleyrand concluded, France would be well served to launch such settlements "immediately upon the first days of peace."[10]

But these new settlements should be founded on principles very different from those of France's Caribbean colonies. The migrants who populated these new colonies should be free, not enslaved. The relationship between colony and *métropole* should be one of mutuality rather than exploitation; colonists should be voluntary migrants rather than criminals and vagrants. "There should be no domination; no monopoly," Talleyrand insisted, only "justice, benevolence." This formulation was not so distant from the postcolonial relationship he described between the United States and Great Britain. Perhaps the same could be accomplished for France with colonies along the Mississippi and Saint Lawrence valleys? After all, the enduring cultural bonds that linked colony and *métropole* "may be easily perceived in Louisiana, which remains French, although it has been under Spanish domination for more than thirty years; and in Canada, although in English power for the same length of time: the colonists of these two countries were Frenchmen; they are so still, and an obvious bias inclines them always towards us."[11]

Less than two weeks after his speech, Talleyrand was appointed France's minister of foreign relations. It was July 1797, and he had left America only thirteen months earlier.

––––––––––

TALLEYRAND WAS not the only French émigré elected to the Institut national. In late September 1796, a few days before Talleyrand arrived in Paris, a colleague there wrote to Moreau: "Volney is in Philadelphia. Does he know he is a member of the Legislative Corps and a member of the Institut national?" Once again, Moreau was serving as the node for transmission of political and scientific information from France to the United States.

"What convinces me that he is in high favour with the Directory," his friend continued, "is that the Directory has declared that even though Volney is not in residence, the Institut should consider him as one of their resident members."[12]

Moreau's correspondent was right: Volney was back in favor. But it had not always been so. Back in 1793, Volney was planning what he called a *"Voyage philosophique"* on behalf of the French government. "Considering that the French Republic can only have a great interest in knowing this country, which mostly professes the same principles as us, and with which, due to this similarity, we cannot too closely tie ourselves in union," the Ministry of Foreign Affairs appointed Volney to the United States "in the capacity of Naturalist." His mission was to "crisscross the United States, gain an in-depth knowledge of its governance, observe the manners of the residents, the production of its soil, the nature of its commerce, and the types of relations that could exist and be strengthened between that people and France." This resembled the missions of André Michaux and Joseph Palisot de Beauvois: to gather scientific and political intelligence on behalf of French colonial interests. Volney was hoping his mission might even lead to an appointment as consul or ambassador. To facilitate his travels, Volney received support from well-connected Americans like Gouverneur Morris—then in Paris to sell lands for Robert Morris—who wrote two letters of introduction. "My friend Colo. Hamilton will thank me for procuring him the acquaintance of Mr. DeVolney," Morris wrote to Alexander Hamilton. "A Splendid reputation in the literary world will command his ready admittance to all good Company his agreeable qualities will render him a desireable guest and a valuable acquaintance." Morris wrote a similar letter to Washington. But Volney did not make it out of France in time to deliver the letters: with the ascension of Robespierre, Volney, still in Paris, was thrown in jail.[13]

Volney regained his freedom in 1794 after the fall of the *Montagne*, and left for the United States in 1795—but this time without any official assignment. He arrived in Philadelphia in October, time enough to spend the winter with Moreau, Talleyrand, and Liancourt. In June 1796 Volney started his travels through the American backcountry. Liancourt was in

South Carolina with Palisot, while General George-Henri Victor Collot was heading west on his mission for Adet, and Talleyrand was sailing home to Europe. Volney traveled first to Virginia, where he visited Thomas Jefferson at Monticello. The two had been friends for years; they had known each other intimately in Paris, back when Jefferson had served as the American minister to France in the 1780s. Volney spent several weeks with Jefferson and collected a series of introductory letters to Jefferson's friends and correspondents in the Ohio valley. From Monticello, Volney plunged west through the Shenandoah Mountain pass into the Ohio valley. By July, after fourteen days of travel, he made it to Gallipolis, where he recorded his grim observations of the French settlement. He continued down the Ohio to Louisville and then up the Wabash to Vincennes. "In this visit I had inclinations more specific than to observe well," he recalled. "Other than the general interest, I had a *particular* and *personal* interest to know what kind of asylum the much-extolled soil of the Mississippi and Upper Louisiana could, if the need arise, offer to Frenchmen from Europe." Volney then trekked north to Lake Erie and then back across the Mohawk valley corridor to Albany, sailing from there down the Hudson to New York—a trip, he said, of nine hundred leagues, "more tiring and as dangerous as what I tried in Turkey." By this time the Directory had come to power in France and Volney had come back in favor; he was old friends with Louis-Marie de La Révellière-Lépeaux, one of the Directory's five members. Whether that was enough to get him appointed by the institute on a paid mission, however, was unclear. "Will I be chosen?" he asked. "I am living in uncertainty." After a second winter in Philadelphia, Volney continued his travels during the spring of 1797, still unsure whether the institute had hired him. "I recently saw Boston," he wrote to La Révellière in May. "To see everything, it would be necessary to see Québec and New Orleans, but I am worn out and losing interest. If I'm working only for myself, I've had enough. If it's for you, Government or *Institut,* at least say something. My finances are getting worn out too."[14]

Word of Volney's finances and fatigue evidently filtered back to Jefferson. Later that summer, the two were reunited in Philadelphia, and Jefferson wrote to his old friend: "I am really uneasy at your stay here, dur-

*Engraving of Volney by John James Barralet.
When he received a copy, Jefferson wrote the artist: "I received safely the portrait of mr Volney,
which I find to be a perfect resemblance, & I pray
you to accept my thanks for it."*

ing the heats of the present season, and in your weak state." It was July. The
summer heat was wearing everyone down, and the annual yellow fever
scare was looming. Jefferson wanted to know if he could help his friend:
"You mentioned that you were detained by business. Perhaps it may be
some retardation of funds, or some other matter in which I can be serviceable to you. I am rarely rich in money, but probably can command such
sums as might accommodate wants as moderate as yours." It was a generous offer; Jefferson was not lying when he said that he rarely had money at
his disposal. Volney wrote back the same day. "I am as touched by Your
offer, considered in its content and its form, as a heart can be that Knows
the Sentiment of Friendship and the price of generosity," he replied. "I
would not Hesitate to accept it, if I were in the situation." The state of his
finances had improved; it was not a lack of funds that was keeping Volney

in Philadelphia. Had Volney finally received a response from La Révellière about his status with the French government? Clearly something had intervened in the previous months to ease those concerns. He had, he told Jefferson, "nothing to desire as far as money is concerned." As for the real reasons, Volney's reply was somewhat elliptical; he thought it prudent not to commit them to paper: "My motive for staying here relates to other causes, which it would probably be good for us to discuss before Your departure: for it is possible that Our separation will be a long one. Will You Assign me an hour in the evening after 6 o'clock."[15]

Alas, we will never know what they talked about—whether they discussed Volney's status with the institute, the political conditions on the frontier, the letters of introduction Jefferson had once written for Michaux, or the letters he now wrote for Volney.

Perhaps they talked about the growing anti-French sentiment in the United States. Volney, like Talleyrand, worried about the shifting political climate in America and its growing attachment to England: "I say it with regret, but my research has not led me to find in the Americans that fraternal and benevolent disposition about which some writers have flattered us; on the contrary, I have thought that they retain a strong tinge of the national prejudice of their mother country against us." It is hardly surprising that Volney and Talleyrand should have drawn such similar conclusions: after all, the two shared the same circle of American friends and associates. Despite his friendship with Jefferson and his reputation as an atheist, Volney, like Talleyrand, was well acquainted with Federalist Philadelphia and New York. "I see federalists," Volney wrote, "and I dine in New York with Alexander Hamilton and governor [John] Jay." Given what he was hearing at dinner tables in Philadelphia, and given what he'd learned from his travels out west, few Frenchmen were better informed about American conditions. "There are very few people here who are devoted to England," he reported to La Révellière in early May 1797, "but there are a great number who have a taste for its constitution and M. Adams is at the head." Like Talleyrand and Liancourt before him, Volney agreed that "the *habitants* of the country are for us." But, he added with considerable insight, "the more I study the general spirit, the more I realize that almost nobody wants the

English or the French for masters." He warned that French assaults on American shipping would inevitably alienate Republican farmers as they had already alienated Federalist merchants. "Everywhere in my travels I noticed that you are beginning to be feared. . . . The idea of your expedition to Canada has alarmed all the *East;* the cession of Louisiana holds all spirits in a state of anxiety," he reported. "When the merchants cease buying their [the farmers'] wheat, they will feel that their cause is common."[16]

Genet and his Girondin patrons had thought to rouse pro-French sentiment and mobilize American gratitude for French intervention in the Revolutionary War. But they had miscalculated. Gratitude to France had proved too fickle, British commercial and linguistic ties too enduring. "Let's consider it even; let us speak of interests," Volney wrote to La Révellière. "It is the compass of this country which listens to its own. Listen to our own and follow them. Friendship has been ruinous for us." Ultimately, Volney concluded that the United States had "fallen from its founding principles." There could be only one sure way to counter the British influence on the United States and preserve France's lucrative Caribbean possessions. "If you want to keep the island colonies," he told La Révellière in May 1797, "give yourselves continental colonies that will supply them."[17]

WHILE TALLEYRAND was making his way back across the Atlantic, and Volney was keeping the French Directory informed about political and social conditions in the United States, General George-Henri Victor Collot was conducting his mission for France through the Mississippi valley. If Volney was unsure about his official connection to the French government, far less ambiguity clouds Collot's travels. A former officer in the French army, six feet tall and fluent in English, Collot was a specialist in military geography and cartography. And he was a spy.

This was not Collot's first time in the United States. Like Noailles, he had fought in the American Revolution under the comte de Rochambeau. After the French Revolution broke out, Collot joined with the Girondins and served as governor of Guadeloupe before it fell to the British in 1794. Taken prisoner by the British navy, he had been paroled to the United

States, where he expected to find a welcome refuge among republicans; instead, he watched as the country signed a humiliating peace treaty with Great Britain. Like the émigré *constituants*, Collot was disgusted by "the formation, in the midst of a bloody war, of [American] ties of friendship and mutual advantage with our cruelest enemies," and became convinced of "the impossibility of being able any longer to delude ourselves concerning the prodigious influence exercised by the English over the American government." (Like the émigrés, too, he speculated in lands around Asylum, Pennsylvania.) The French ambassador Adet agreed with Collot's assessment and sent him west to scout out American and Spanish military fortifications, assess their troops' strength, explore their strategic flaws and advantages, and analyze river currents, soils, and agriculture. By the time Collot finished, he had produced the most accurate and detailed map of the Ohio and Mississippi Rivers ever drawn. But his mission was not just a military one; it had an important political aspect as well. Collot was instructed to determine the extent of Republican sympathies among western settlers and to "try by every possible means to bring about Jef—'s election as President." Looking ahead to a future split between the trans-Appalachian West and the East, he would assess "what would be the best way to support the Southern states in case they break with those of the East, without giving them cause for concern about their own independence." And, for the purposes of future colonization, he would suggest "what types of settlers are best for populating Louisiana." In short, he was to plan for a French reacquisition of the Mississippi valley.[18]

In the spring of 1796, Collot left Philadelphia with Joseph Warin, a young French military engineer who had previously served in the U.S. Army. They were following the route Michaux had taken in 1793: west across Pennsylvania and then down the Ohio River. From the beginning, Collot cast a practiced eye on his surroundings. He was particularly impressed with the Alleghenies, which could be crossed through only a limited number of mountain passes: "If the leaders of the 1794 insurrection had been men of war, and had known these mountains in their military *rapport*, they could, with the forces that they commanded, have prevented the federal troops from crossing the Alléganies." Given the rumors of

French involvement in the Whiskey Rebellion, these were risky comments indeed. Arriving in Pittsburgh, Collot quickly concluded that it was among the most important strategic sites in the North American interior. An army that controlled it controlled the Ohio-Mississippi River system, and could hold the passes against a military force coming from the Eastern Seaboard. If Louisiana were to return to French control, he believed the Allegheny Mountains would be its eastern border: settlers in Kentucky and Tennessee would inevitably be won over to the French side. They would have no choice but to ally with whatever power controlled Mississippi navigation.[19]

Proceeding west, Collot examined fort after fort at each strategic point, from Pittsburgh to Marietta, Ohio, to Lexington, Kentucky. One evening in Lexington, according to his account, he and Warin found a crowd in the central square gathered around something stretched out on the ground and

This map, drawn by Collot during his travels through the United States, portrays the Appalachians as a barrier—almost a wall—and suggests how the French understood the continent's geography. The course of all waterways to the west of the mountains fed into the Gulf of Mexico, rather than the Atlantic, creating significant challenges to U.S. sovereignty in the trans-Appalachian West.

covered with a blanket. Going in for a closer look, they discovered that it was the erstwhile French general George Rogers Clark, so drunk he'd passed out in the street. Whether Collot exaggerated the scene is impossible to know; he may just have wanted to undermine Clark's political standing in France, whose support Clark still courted. On they continued: to Saint Louis, up the Mississippi and Missouri Rivers, and then all the way down the Mississippi to New Orleans. He was traveling along the former line of French fortifications by which New France had established itself in North America—an alliance among the French military, a few European settlers, and the much larger population of Native American nations in the Great Lakes and Mississippi valley. Could the rusting infrastructure of that empire be reforged?[20]

Collot roamed through various French settlements in the Northwest, including Gallipolis, as well as various towns like Sainte Geneviève, Saint Louis, and Saint Charles, all of them on the western bank of the Missis-

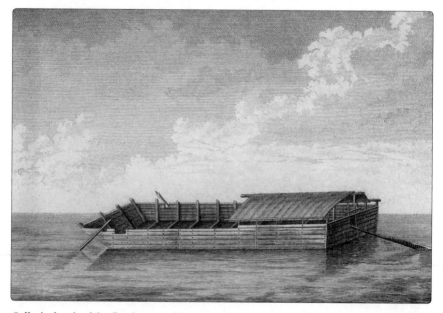

Collot's sketch of the flat-bottomed boat that he used to descend the Ohio and Mississippi Rivers. These boats, built from lumber in the upper Ohio valley, shipped goods all the way down the Mississippi to New Orleans, where they were taken apart and the lumber used for other purposes.

sippi. On the American side, he noted the many French people who still resided in Kaskaskia, Prairie du Rocher, Saint Philippe, and Prairie du Chien, among other settlements. "The majority of these people are composed of traders, adventurers, *coureurs de bois, rameurs,* and warriors," he concluded. "Of French virtues, they have conserved only courage." Collot also remarked on the "*bonne disposition* that the Indians of the entire [Ohio] country retain for the French." In the upper Mississippi valley, Collot gave details on the various Native peoples he encountered, on the numbers of their warriors, and the state of their villages. In the lower Mississippi, Collot mentioned the qualities of the Osages—"the most *doux* and hospitable people of all the nations living west of the Mississippi River, who idolize the whites and particularly the French." Collot emphasized what many Frenchmen had noticed before him: the weakness of Spanish power in the region. Spanish authorities had hastily built a fort just below Saint Louis when Genet's expedition loomed ("so impolitic and so badly managed," Collot snorted). It took only a glance for Collot to realize that the fort could not resist an invasion: "A bad square redoubt was constructed, flanked by four bastions, of which the flanks are precisely two and a half feet, surrounded by a ditch two feet deep and six feet wide, and enclosed by an *entourage* of serrated planks." It sounds unimpressive even now. Making matters worse, "the garrison, composed of seventeen men, and the *habitants* all devoted to France, were charged with defending the post." Collot was contemptuous. "The commander's instructions were the only reasonable thing in this extraordinary defense," he added: "to evacuate *sur-le-champ,* the moment the enemy appeared, and to retreat to the garrison at New Madrid." The same chaotic military position prevailed lower down the Mississippi near New Orleans: "Eighty men and a captain are charged with the defense of these different forts, which would require at least a thousand."[21]

On the other hand, the strategic value of Saint Louis greatly impressed Collot. It was located across the river from the former Native American city of Cahokia, at the confluence of the Missouri and Mississippi Rivers; few towns on the continent were better situated. "This place will be, *en grand,* relative to New Orleans, what Albany is relative to New York." Just as Al-

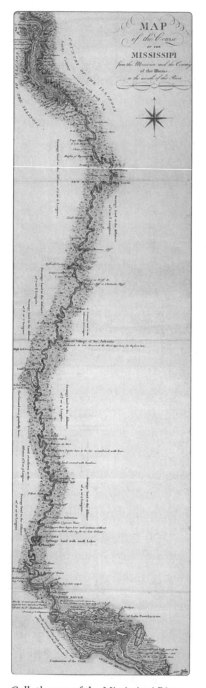

Collot's map of the Mississippi River.

bany served as the transit point for goods coming in from the Great Lakes across the Mohawk River corridor and down to New York City, so would Saint Louis be the great *entrepôt* for goods from the Great Lakes and the Missouri River valley: all the agriculture and the furs from the upper Northwest would pass through Saint Louis before being shipped to New Orleans. But the military advantages of the site most impressed him. Saint Louis itself, "considered from its military perspective, is one of the best [strategic sites] that exists on the Mississippi River; put in a respectable state of defense, it would cover all of upper Louisiana, and stop all that would descend from the upper Mississippi, the Illinois, and the Missouri." It could also threaten British possessions along Upper Canada's western edge. And it benefited from a population of French *habitants*. Of its six hundred residents, two hundred were in a state to carry arms, "all of them French," including "excellent patriots whose life and fortune belong to France." Collot went on to explain, in elaborate detail, how France could control the entire upper Mississippi valley with a mere fifteen hundred men. By the time Collot made it back to Saint Louis after an extended excursion up the Mississippi and Missouri

Rivers, he learned that both the Spanish governor of Louisiana and the U.S. secretary of state had issued orders for his arrest, while the English—or so he claimed—had sent several Indian warriors to assassinate him. "My voyage," he observed with no little understatement, "has already made a lot of noise."[22]

In late October, after more than six months of travels, Collot and his party made it to New Orleans, where Governor Carondelet had them arrested. Poor Warin died from wounds he'd sustained a few weeks earlier, when two Native Americans—sent, perhaps, by the British government—struck him down with a hard blow to the chest. After letting Collot languish in jail for two months, Carondelet finally sent him back to Philadelphia. When he arrived in late December 1796, Adet was beside himself with excitement at the intelligence Collot had gathered. "You have, I must tell you, exceeded my expectations," he exclaimed. "Instead of a few useful pieces of information, which I had flattered myself I could present to the Government, I believe I will present it with a collection of observations of the greatest importance." By this time, news of the mission had become public, and U.S. officials were once again in a state approaching panic about French intentions in the West.[23]

VOLNEY WAS still in Philadelphia when Collot returned. Hoping a total break between France and the United States could be avoided, Volney was buckling under the diplomatic pressure.[24]

In March 1797 the French government ratcheted up the tensions, authorizing the seizure of American ships carrying British goods as well as the execution of American crewmen found aboard British ships—even those who had been impressed, or forced to serve. This was as great a violation of American neutrality as anything the British had attempted in the dark year of 1794. As if that were not bad enough, French agents continued to foment discontent among backcountry settlers, while credible rumors circulated that the French government was actively involving itself in congressional business. Adet had become so politically toxic that his Republican allies in Congress said "they could not communicate with him, Adet, even secretly"—a strong intimation that such clandestine communications had existed in the past. In response, the French consul in Philadelphia proposed using a different official to send messages to France's congressional allies. Another official suggested sending a "Consular agent to follow the *mouvemens* of our Enemies, and to take part, either officially or privately, in all the measures of the French party." Needless to say, none of this was apt to promote a rapprochement. Having "spies and inflammatory agents" flitting about the country "like the locusts of Egypt," as the Federalist congressman Harrison Gray Otis so colorfully put it, "fomenting hostilities against this country and alienating the affections of our own citizens": it was not conducive to Franco-American comity.[25]

By then, news of Collot's mission in the Mississippi valley had trickled all the way to Paris. In 1796 an old associate of George Rogers Clark's by the name of Samuel Fulton had traveled to France, and rumors about his activities were running through diplomatic circles. According to James Monroe, the American ambassador, Fulton was alleged to be plotting with the French government to detach the trans-Appalachian West from the United States. "The English faction with us will endeavor to impose on the publick the belief of an intrigue between some men in America [and] this government to prevail on the latter to interfere in our interior," the ambassador warned Madison. Monroe worked to squash the rumors. "Nothing is more false," he insisted. "Besides the man is not a fit agent for such a business. He appears to be a worthy well tempered person, but well satisfied I am he has no trust unless it is to sell land."[26]

Monroe was an avid Republican, however, and his political sympathies may have clouded his judgment, for he was quite wrong. In fact, Fulton had succeeded in securing another commission for Clark from the French government. "I received your letter of December Last with which you accompany a Copy of a Commission Granted Me by the Directory," Clark wrote to Fulton in early March 1797 from Louisville. "Assure them that I shall do every thing in my power to promote their intrest in this Country *which has always been considerable*." According to Clark, the geopolitical wrangling in the Mississippi valley had reached another critical stage. British officials were raising an army of two thousand frontiersmen to invade Spanish possessions along the Mississippi, with the governor of Canada's full support: "There are Sundry British agents in this State from Canada indevouring to raise volunteers to go against Louisiana." Clark resisted these plans by telling his contacts that they would "in a Short time be call^d into service" by the French government for war against the British. "You may assure the Directory," he added, "that we are no Less the friends of France than we were in 93—and are proud to say we had the honour of being officers under the French Republic."[27]

With tensions between the United States and France growing, President Adams became convinced that Volney was a spy like Collot, and was laying the groundwork for a French reoccupation of the Mississippi valley. Louisiana remained a Spanish possession for the time being, but it was well-known that French diplomats were pressuring Spain to cede them the territory. Whatever his personal feelings toward France, however, Adams did not want a war. He opposed the very idea of standing armies: he worried that the United States could not win such a conflict, he predicted it would drive the country into the arms of Great Britain, and he feared the uncontrollable consequences a war might entail, both on the republican form of government at home and on U.S. power abroad. So in May 1797 he sent three special envoys to France in a last-ditch effort to make peace. "Ministers will be sent to you," Volney warned the Directory. "Whoever they may be, treat them with politeness."[28]

Those were wise words, but they would not be heeded.

BY THE time Adams's three envoys arrived in Paris, Talleyrand was France's minister of foreign relations. Two years earlier, while he was still in the United States, Talleyrand had watched with some bemusement as his friend Alexander Hamilton resigned as secretary of the treasury. "He found it quite singular that a man of his value, endowed with such superior talents, would leave a ministry to return to the law, giving as a motive for his decision that his position as minister did not provide him with the means to raise his family of eight children," Madame de La Tour du Pin recalled. "Such an excuse appeared to M. de Talleyrand utterly singular and, to be blunt, even a little jejune." Talleyrand was not about to make the same mistake.[29]

When the American ministers arrived in Paris in October 1797, Talleyrand refused to meet with them. He humiliated them for days, shunting them from one antechamber in Paris to another while he decided whether to even recognize their diplomatic credentials. Eventually Talleyrand sent three agents of his own—later named X, Y, and Z in public dispatches—to explain to the Americans that if the United States wanted to make peace with France, they would need to provide a $250,000 bribe to Talleyrand, as well as a loan of $12 million to the French government. The Americans were outraged.

Talleyrand's strategy here remains mysterious; the XYZ Affair was a rare misstep in a legendary diplomatic career. He appears to have wanted to drag out the negotiations as long as possible, while focusing his attention on European warfare and French domestic politics. At the time, many people thought France was on the verge of defeating Great Britain, and that an imminent French invasion of England would bring a swift end to the war. "Volney is convinced France will not make peace with England, because it is such an opportunity for sinking her as she never had & may not have again," Jefferson wrote to Madison in June 1797, passing along rumors that Napoleon would soon march his armies to the English Channel. "It is imagined the armies of the Rhine will be destined for England." All the French needed was more time to finish the job. Perhaps that explains why Talleyrand sought to divide the three American envoys from one another, wooing the Republican Elbridge Gerry, whom he'd known from his stay in the United States, while spurning the Federalists John Marshall and Charles Cotesworth Pinckney. Certainly the little-traveled and naive Gerry was a rich target. He spent his first months in Paris "seeing the curiosities of Paris, Versailles, &c., in dining parties of Americans, & in attending the operas & theaters," as he wrote in one letter home, "for not the least notice has been taken of us by the directory or any officer of the Government, except by Mr Talleyrand, who has sent me a billet to dine with him tomorrow." Talleyrand's time in the United States may have taught him the wrong lessons: apparently he believed that party divisions in the United States were so deep that he could split the mission and isolate the Federalist Party. Ironically, he was acting not unlike Genet in this regard. Like Genet, too, he would later blame his diplomatic failure on British machinations in the United States.[30]

Talleyrand mobilized the social networks he'd developed in the United States to advance his diplomacy. Gerry's fellow American diplomats "expressed their opinions, that not being acquainted with Mr Talleyrand, they could not with propriety call on him; but that according to the custom of France, *he might expect this of Mr Gerry,* from a previous *acquaintance in America.*" And so Gerry attended various social events with Talleyrand, who, he reported, "has been very civil & friendly to me. he dined with me a few days ago & sent me an invitation to a superb supper made for General & Madam Buonaparte: at which will be the Directory, all the foreign ministers, except the american Envoys, and the finest selection of ladies in paris. one of my colleagues urged me to accept the invitation. but it is impossible." Finally, after several frustrating months, Marshall and Pinckney left France while Gerry—somewhat blinded by the attention, perhaps—remained, hoping against hope to settle the diplomatic differences with Talleyrand. After the Federalist ministers left Paris, they sent a complete account of the experience to John Adams.[31]

When the news broke in the spring of 1798, U.S. public opinion exploded. "Millions for defense, not one cent for tribute" became the slogan of the day. As public feeling toward France reached a new low, war came to seem inevitable. For those who had known Talleyrand during his stay in the United States, the insult was personal: there he was, blackmailing the country that had given him refuge. "What think you," wrote Eleanor (Nelly) Parke Custis, Washington's step-granddaughter, "of the delectable Apostate Bishop of Autun, what an intolerable wretch he is, I could positively hang *him,* the five Directors, & *Monsieur* le *Philosophe* Chasseboeuf de Volney." Custis had met the two Frenchmen at social events in Philadelphia and Washington; her husband, Lawrence Lewis, was probably the person who "facilitated" Volney's trip to Ohio in 1796. Her brother-in-law, Thomas Law, had traveled through the backcountry with Liancourt and Talleyrand, and done business with Talleyrand. As her description of Talleyrand's "delectable" nature suggested, she found his repellent behavior curiously attractive and seemed even more exasperated for having been charmed: "Does not your wrath often kindle at the recollection of Talleyrand & Volney, when with their smooth tongues & woe begone faces, they excited the sympathy of Americans, & were treated with so much kindness—that they were both Spy's, and are doing all in their power to injure those who befriended them." President Adams, along with other Federalists, now began to look on the émigré *constituants* as agents of the Republican Party. "I have reason to remember," he later wrote, that "all other Frenchmen in America, even . . . Talleyrand and the Duke de Liancourt . . . exerted their influence and all their praises to exalt Mr. Jefferson over my shoulders, and to run me down as an aristocrat and a monarchist." It seemed to Federalists that rather than furnishing an asylum for persecuted refugees from Europe, the United States had instead opened its doors to agents of Europe's most aggressive power collaborating with pro-French elements.[32]

Similar accusations made it into the public press. "Our country has been the resort of abominably seditious foreigners of every distinction," wrote the reactionary English pamphleteer William Cobbett, who had moved to the United States in late 1792 and become something of a seditious foreigner himself. "It is a matter of serious consideration in times so alarming: what is to be done with these miscreants, who, beyond the possibility of doubt, did not come here solely for *Repose*." In a pamphlet entitled *Remarks on the Insidious Letter of the Gallic Despots*, Cobbett further accused Talleyrand of having "insinuated himself, if not into the *best* at least into the *most fashionable* families," a perch from which he scrutinized the public and private affairs of the nation. "He pryed into all the concerns of merchants, into the strength and finances of the government, and in short followed most industriously and effectually his business as a Spy." What was worse, "he was continually closetted with ADET." Moreau responded to these attacks on his friend with similar vituperation, using his press to launch assaults on Cobbett.[33]

Federalists took advantage of the public hostility toward French refugees to pass the Alien and Sedition Acts. In April 1798 Congress began debating a law authorizing the president to arrest and deport any citizen of a hostile foreign nation, without a hearing or a trial, "as alien enemies." Along with the Naturalization Act, which extended the time of residence before an immigrant became eligible for citizenship to fourteen years (from five), the Alien and Sedition Acts challenged one of the country's most cherished myths. "Let us no longer pray," declared one Federalist, "that America may become an asylum to all nations." These laws have not fared well in the historical record; nativist overreactions in American history rarely do. Some historians have seen them as proto-McCarthyite Federalist paranoia. Most charitably, historians chalk them up to a partisan power grab. What such accounts overlook, however, is the very specific context in which the laws were passed: at the very moment when French émigrés traveled to a bitterly contested Mississippi valley barely attached to the United States. Government authorities believed Volney was involved in what he called "a *conspiracy* by which I (a lone Frenchman) would have plotted, in *Kentokey,* to deliver Louisiana to the Directory." Even as he ridiculed the charge, Volney admitted that those were indeed the objectives "of the majority of our diplomats." Whatever his intentions, Volney was at the center of the political storm far beyond his ability to control. The Alien Act, Jefferson wrote to Madison, "is understood to be meant for Volney & Collot," adding, "There is now only wanting, to accomplish the whole declaration beforementioned, a sedition bill which we shall certainly soon see proposed." Bemoaning the "deplorable state" of relations between France and the United States, Jefferson and his fellow Republicans thought the Federalists were wildly overreacting. But even they admitted, "No doubt there have been faults on both sides."[34]

With all this fury directed at him, and at France, Volney grew alienated from American politics and from Philadelphia's high society. He broke from his Federalist friends. One young Philadelphian at the time later recalled Volney's behavior during this period:

Volney affected to entertain republican opinions much more democratic than those of John Adams, the successor of Washington.
This caused him to cease to attend my father's soirées. He thought
he saw there none but Adamites, as he called the federalists of 1798.
Meeting him one day, my father asked the cause of his estrange-
ment? He cast at that worthy parent an angry look, and morosely
remarked, that he chose to keep aloof from the enemies of French
freedom!

Other French émigrés felt besieged as well. By the end of 1796, the poison-
ous diplomatic context had begun to contaminate Philadelphia's Franco-
American social networks; Anne Bingham had lost her formerly warm
feelings toward many of her French friends. Liancourt, now described as
"very violent" toward the United States, was "negotiating his return," she
told President Adams. "Volney she Says professes Friendship and a good
opinion, but is so proud a Man and has such Principles that she can have no
confidence. Cazenove from a high Government Man has become an inveterate Democrat. She considers them all as Spies upon Us, and wishes them
all away," Adams reported to his wife, Abigail. "I was highly pleased with
her Attachment to her Country," he added.[35]

Anne would get her wish. As Congress debated the Alien Act, Volney
confronted what he called "an epidemic of animosity against the French
and the threat of an immediate rupture," "violent public attacks directed
against me," and "the anger of the president." "The régime," he added, "became a real *terrorisme*." Strong words from someone who had lived through
the Terror in France. But Volney was right: the president was angry—and
exasperated with the French scientific and colonial establishment. "I shall
not be guilty of so much affectation of regard to science, as to be very willing to grant passports to . . . any other French philosophers, in the present
situation of our country," he wrote to his secretary of state, Timothy Pickering. "We have had too many French philosophers already, and I really
begin to think, or rather to suspect, that learned academies, not under the
immediate inspection and control of government, have disorganized the
world, and are incompatible with social order." Clearly it was time to go. By

this time, however, commerce between France and the United States had ground to a halt, and virtually no ships traveled between the two countries. Eventually, after some searching, the Frenchmen found a vessel willing to take them—flying a flag of truce. "The threatening appearances from the Alien bills have so alarmed the French who are among us that they are going off," Jefferson wrote to Madison in early May. "A ship chartered by themselves for this purpose will sail within about a fortnight for France with as many as she can carry. Among these I believe will be Volney, who has in truth been the principal object aimed at by the law."[36]

Liancourt, too, left the United States as the anti-French sentiment grew. With his name still on the list of émigrés—making him subject to arrest upon his return to France—in late 1797 he boarded a ship from New York to Hamburg, where his son still lived in exile. Stories in U.S. newspapers nevertheless linked him to the XYZ Affair. "The Duc de Liancourt, an agent and particular friend of Monsieur Talleyrand," one newspaper claimed, went to Copenhagen on a mission "which it is supposed was to obtain money." If Liancourt did make such a trip, it was no doubt to sell lands. But his association with Talleyrand—who was now deeply unpopular among Americans—stimulated more rumors. Newspaper reports in early 1799 claimed that France was about to send Liancourt to the United States as an envoy to make peace. These rumors were even more far-fetched, since Liancourt was still then on the list of proscribed émigrés. But that did not bother William Cobbett. "He is, perhaps, the only man, that the Despots of Paris could send out on a *coaxing* mission," wrote the vituperative journalist. What made the alleged appointment plausible, at least in Cobbett's eyes, was the extensive social network Liancourt had forged among French and Americans, Federalists and Republicans. "I often used to wonder at the conduct of those who seemed to have a just abhorrence of the French revolution, and yet admitted this man to their intimacy."[37]

Moreau remained in Philadelphia longer than Talleyrand, Volney, or Liancourt, and by 1798 was conspicuous for his French patriotism. Moreau had started wearing the cockade in 1796; by 1798 he reported that he was "the only person in Philadelphia who continued to wear a French *cocarde*." At around this time, he relocated his bookstore north to French-Town, away from the Society Hill neighborhood in which he had established it. Now worried about "acts of violence on the part of the Federalists," he and a number of Republicans met secretly to prepare to defend themselves: "Since I was a party to these meetings, I was given keys to two shelters in which I and my family could take refuge in case my own house should be attacked." Eventually Moreau was added to a list of French people to be deported. He asked some intermediaries to speak with the president—a former customer of his bookstore—and to find out the reason for his inclusion among the suspicious aliens. "Nothing in particular," Adams replied, "but he's too French."[38]

Moreau had finally had enough. In August he boarded a ship with his family and sailed to France. Once again, the Moreaus had a star-crossed voyage. The very day their pilot left the ship at Cape Henlopen, Moreau's son fell ill with the dreaded yellow fever. His parents were in terror. Thankfully, after a dose of ipecac, the boy recovered after only two days of fever. Several other passengers caught the fever and died, however. One French couple lost two daughters, leaving them childless. Another man fell ill and, despite the rain and his agony, was put on the aft forecastle. Moreau "would not swear that amidst the general terror afflicting everbody," the man was even dead before his body was thrown overboard. And still the deaths continued as the ship made its grim way across the Atlantic, leaving bodies to be buried in its wake. "What a scene!" Moreau exclaimed. "But where to flee?" The plague had at least one benefit, however. A month after their departure, an English frigate accosted the ship, but the crew quickly abandoned their hostile intentions: "As soon as yellow fever was mentioned, their officer threw himself back into his launch and made off." Eventually their ship arrived in Bordeaux with the Moreaus safely back in France.[39]

Noailles was the only one of the *constituants* left in Philadelphia. Having become an American citizen, he continued to live in the Bingham compound and participate in Philadelphia's mercantile life—sending shipments of Caribbean goods like sugar and cochineal to Europe. By 1799 Noailles had done well enough rebuilding his fortune that even Alexander Baring referred to him as "rich." Perhaps Baring's esteem for the vicomte's abilities in business had grown as well. Although Baring had once warned his father against extending Noailles too much credit, the Baring account books in London show that the firm was doing business with Noailles, sometimes in transactions of up to £15,000, until 1802.[40]

In an ironic twist, Collot did not leave the United States with Volney, Liancourt, Moreau, and so many other French citizens—although he was the chief target of the Alien Act, and Adams had already signed an order deporting him. "Having long possessed evidence the most satisfactory to my mind, that Collot is a pernicious and malicious intriguer," John Adams wrote to Secretary of State Timothy Pickering, "I have been always ready and willing to execute the alien law upon him." But then it dawned on Adams and Pickering that, of all the French émigrés, Collot, with the vast knowledge he'd gained on his travels, posed the greatest danger to the United States. Could they risk letting him return to France? They came up with an ingenious solution. Because Collot was on parole from the British, Pickering persuaded the British ambassador to drag out the negotiations over a prisoner exchange, thus keeping perhaps the country's most dangerous alien trapped in Philadelphia until 1800.[41]

By that time, Jefferson was gearing up for a heated presidential race marked by accusations that he was too partial to French interests. His friendship with Volney had become a political liability. In August 1800 Volney wrote to his old friend Noailles: "Mr. Jefferson must be happy with me: he prayed me upon my departure not to write to him: I have obeyed him."[42]

BY 1800 the French Directory was out of power. The coup of 18 Brumaire (November 9, 1799), orchestrated in part by Talleyrand, had established a three-person consulate to the head of the nation, with Napoleon as first consul. And so the wily Talleyrand became France's foreign minister under a new regime. "The good Maurice is not unlike the mannikins with which children play—dolls with heads of cork and legs of lead," Madame de Staël had once quipped. "Throw them up which way you please, they are sure to fall on their feet."[43]

The new regime was good to Volney as well. He was friends with Talleyrand and Napoleon, the latter having been introduced to him back in

1792, when Volney bought a Corsican plantation hoping to produce sugar, coffee, indigo, and cotton to replace the declining exports from the French Caribbean. Shortly after the coup he became a senator, and his influence grew accordingly. With Napoleon in power, Volney became a prominent figure. His previous writings had already shaped Napoleon's thinking, with the *Voyage en Syrie et en Egypte* leaving a particular mark; indeed, Volney may well have been the first to suggest an invasion of Egypt to the future general. Napoleon had hoped to take Volney to Egypt along with other members of the Institut national, but he was still in the United States when the campaign began; the Corsican general had to settle for his writings instead. One of Napoleon's generals in Egypt later wrote that Volney's *Voyage* served as "the guidebook of the French in Egypt; it's the only one that never misled them." Indeed, so high was his esteem for Volney's *Voyage*, Napoleon would bring the book with him to his exile on Saint Helena—annotated in his own hand. Perhaps Volney's *Tableau du climat et du sol des États-Unis,* which Volney was then compiling, would serve the same purpose for a future French army in Louisiana that his writings on Egypt had recently served in the Middle East.[44]

Having failed to conquer Egypt, French imperial officials had shifted their gaze to Louisiana. "No country is more worthy to fasten the attention of France than Louisiana," read one memorandum submitted to the Ministry of Foreign Affairs, calling the former French colony "the modern Egypt." A French campaign to Louisiana, like the one to Egypt, would provide a laboratory for new scientific discoveries. "There are improvements for which one has to wait a long time," read another government report promoting the French acquisition of Louisiana, "but there are others that must be accelerated: all that the First Consul obtained in work and enlightenment in Egypt in the space of two years is dazzling proof." Talleyrand, of course, had never lost interest in Louisiana; he had just failed to impress the French Directory of its significance. But now Napoleon was in charge and Talleyrand's influence was surging.[45]

The first step was to make peace with the United States. "We must return to the broad purpose that led to the war we made for their independence," Talleyrand wrote in a 1799 report. "It is time to end the dis-

In this satirical sketch about Napoleon's invasion of Egypt, James Gill-ray portrays a group of besieged French scientists defending themselves by throwing books and globes at their enemies. Among the books fall-ing from the column are the Encyclopédie *and, just below the punc-tured hot-air balloon,* Volney's Les Ruines.

agreements." In 1801 the U.S. Senate ratified the Convention of Mortefon-taine, which ended hostilities between France and the United States and also dissolved the 1778 Treaty of Amity and Commerce. (Not until the United States signed the NATO Treaty in 1949 would it enter into another permanent alliance with any nation.) The next step was to halt the naval warfare with England. To that end, the preliminaries of the Treaty of Amiens were signed in October 1801. For the first time in nearly a decade, war ceased to ravage the Atlantic world. But this peace was not founded on a particularly durable balance of power, and many people in the United

States, Great Britain, and France thought that the end of hostilities was just temporary, "a kind of armistice," as Napoleon ominously called it.[46]

Before the ink was even dry on the preliminaries of the Treaty of Amiens, Napoleon began to turn his attention to America. Rumors had already begun to circulate that Spain had at last yielded to French pressure and surrendered the vast territory of Louisiana. In late March 1801, an American in Paris wrote a breathless letter to Jefferson, who had just been elected president: "Spain has ceded Louisiana to France, & an expedition is preparing to take possession of New Orleans, & to plant a Colony in that country." According to his sources, "Genl. Collaud [Collot], who is to command it, sails in a few days for Philadelphia, & will proceed by land to the Missisippi." (Collot had been released from the United States in 1800.) The next day, another American in Paris—this one a speculator seeking to sell land in western New York—wrote to Hamilton with the same information.[47]

American diplomats were alarmed at the news. "I am apprehensive that this cession is intended to have, and may actually produce, effects injurious to the union and consequent happiness of the people of the United States," wrote the U.S. ambassador Rufus King from London. "Louisiana and the Floridas may be given to the French emigrants, as England once thought of giving them to the American tories." King had also heard, perhaps from the source who'd informed Jefferson, "that General Collot, who was a few years ago in America, and a traveler in the Western country . . . has been lately set at liberty." It was still unclear what his role in the new colony would be, but none of this news could bode well for the United States. British diplomats were equally concerned at the prospect of a French Louisiana. Suddenly, all their efforts over a century of war to push France out of North America seemed on the verge of collapse. "The acquisition might enable France to extend her influence, and perhaps her dominion up the Mississippi; and through the lakes even to Canada," King added. "This would be realizing the plan, to prevent the accomplishment of which, the seven years' war took place."[48]

At the end of 1801 the rumors were confirmed. "The exchange has actually been agreed upon," wrote Robert R. Livingston, the U.S. ambassador

Letterhead for official correspondence of the French "Colonie de la Louisiane," circa 1803, which was to have been led by General Claude Victor-Perrin, named governor of Louisiana.

to France. "The armament destined, in the first instance, for Hispaniola, is to proceed to Louisiana, provided Toussaint makes no opposition." Napoleon's plans were falling into place. With peace established between France and England, the French navy was free to cross the Atlantic. Napoleon would send an army to Saint Domingue; from there, it would sail on to Louisiana. "General Collot, whom you may have seen in America, was originally intended for Governor of that province, but he is, at present, out of favor," Livingston added. If that was a relief, it could not have been good news to hear that Collot would nevertheless accompany the mission and provide advice about conditions in the Mississippi valley as second in command—with Adet serving as prefect.[49]

ALL THE dreams that French imperial planners had harbored since the Franco-American rupture in the mid-1790s were now on the verge of being realized. The full implications of a French Louisiana were gradually dawning on American officials. Livingston was appalled.

Our own Western territory may be rendered so dependent upon them as to promote their political views, while the interest they have always nurtured with the Indians, and the national character of the peasantry of Canada, may render the possessions of Britain very precarious, to say nothing of the danger which must threaten her islands in case a respectable establishment should be made by France in Louisiana, which will not fail to be the case, as the territory is uncommonly fine, and produces sugar, and every article now cultivated in the islands.

These were precisely the factors that since the Jay Treaty had motivated France's interest in reconquering Louisiana. A French army in New Orleans posed existential threats to the United States, and to its sovereignty in the West. A French Louisiana, warned a New York newspaper in 1802, could "hold forth every allurement to the inhabitants of the Trans-Alleghany settlements . . . and inveigle them by degrees into the idea of forming a separate empire."[50]

Equally ominous was the impact that a French Louisiana might have on American slavery. Back in the days of the Genet expedition, Brissot had dreamed of sending "a corps of eight to ten thousand *mulâtres*" from Saint Domingue in alliance with American frontiersmen to attack Spanish American colonies in the name of the French Republic. In the years that followed, France had become a powerful emancipatory force in the Caribbean. After the uprising in Saint Domingue, the French government formally abolished slavery in its Caribbean colonies in 1794 and allied itself to the abolitionist cause. Over the four years that followed, former slaves fought valiantly to preserve French control of Saint Domingue against the combined forces of Spain and Great Britain. Meanwhile, Victor Hugues, the French commissioner in Guadeloupe, sent armies of sans-culottes and slaves-turned-citizens throughout the Caribbean to crush British shipping: events, as the historian Laurent Dubois has put it, that "rocked slave societies throughout the Americas." If such multiracial forces could defeat the greatest navies of the age, was there any doubt they could hold Louisiana against an American army that had barely succeeded in wresting the Ohio valley from the Western Confederacy? During the heat of the Quasi-War in 1798, rumors that France would invade the United States with a multiracial army of soldiers from Saint Domingue and foment slave rebellion had caused panic among slaveholders. "A few French Troops with . . . arms put into the hands of the Negroes," warned Mississippi's territorial governor, "would be to us formidable indeed." Rumors of collaboration between French radicals and the rebellion planned by the Virginia slave Gabriel in 1800 only stoked these fears. By 1802, the terror of slave rebellion was reaching a frenzy. "It is probable that this state of anxiety will last as long as the troubles in our Colonies," the French envoy in Washington remarked to Talleyrand in 1802. Other rumors circulated that Indians in the Northwest were awaiting France's return to America, and had been promised support in their struggle against the United States.[51]

Talleyrand sought to reassure Americans that France would prove solicitous toward the racial status quo in the United States. France, he insisted in 1803, "is not disposed to propagate around its colonies any principle that could damage the harmony and social order established in the other states." He urged the new French ambassador to emphasize France's desire to establish neighborly relations between itself and the United States. According to Talleyrand, Napoleon was possessed of a "very positive and pronounced desire to live with the American government," and to improve "the friendly relations that unite the two people."[52]

Americans were hardly reassured, however. Republicans and Federalists were united on the dangers a French Louisiana posed to U.S. national interests. "Since the question of Independence, none has occurred more deeply interesting to the United States than the cession of Louisiana to France," Alexander Hamilton warned in an article in the *New York Evening Post*. "This event threatens the early dismemberment of a large portion of our country: more immediately the safety of all the Southern States; and remotely the independence of the whole union." And so, he concluded, "the only question which now offers itself, is, how is the evil to be averted?" Here was one issue on which Jefferson and Hamilton agreed. "On the event of this mission," President Jefferson wrote to James Monroe, whom he was sending to France to negotiate American trading rights through the Mississippi, "depends the future destinies of this republic."[53]

REPORTS ABOUT these epic developments swirled through letters and newspapers in Philadelphia. Despite the repeated succession of astonishing events—European revolution, the execution of kings, armies sweeping across Europe, slave societies in revolt—daily life continued much as it had before. Marriages and annulments, births and deaths: such events beat to a different tempo, forming a contrapuntal rhythm to the tumultuous disruptions across the Atlantic world.[54]

In 1799 Ann Louisa Baring, Anne and William Bingham's daughter, gave birth to her first child, William Bingham Baring. His father, Alexander, was still in Philadelphia managing the Barings' growing financial and commercial ventures in the United States. If the Binghams' first grandchild provided an occasion for rejoicing, no one celebrated the scandalous marriage the same year of Ann's sister to the comte de Tilly, the French cad who eloped with fifteen-year-old Maria and then demanded an annual pension as his price to leave the country. "This circumstance which has been productive of more affliction & misery than I can express to you, has perfectly determined what was before almost so with Ann & myself," Alexander wrote to his father: "that we should renounce this Country." A year later, in March 1800, the Philadelphia newspapers announced that the Pennsylvania state legislature had passed an act declaring null and void the marriage of Maria Matilda and Alexandre de Tilly. It was a relief. Tilly had since written Maria a taunting letter insisting he would have the rights to her inheritance upon the death of her wealthy parents. Then, later that year or early the next, Anne Bingham, already a grandmother at age thirty-six, gave birth to her first son, also named William. "Mrs. Bingham is in her bed with a fine Boy," Alexander reported.[55]

The Federalist era was drawing to a close when young William Bingham was born. With the relocation of the nation's capital to the muddy banks of the Potomac River in November 1800, social life in Philadelphia quieted down. Anne Bingham's parlor was no longer the luminous site it had been when figures like President Washington, Secretary of State Jefferson, Secretary of the Treasury Hamilton, and Secretary of War Knox dined with senators and congressmen and visiting foreign dignitaries. With the diplomatic troubles of the late 1790s, Philadelphia had lost nearly all of its glamorous French aristocrats to more welcoming countries. Only Noailles remained, still living in his apartments across the splendid gardens in the Bingham compound. William Bingham now spent his time in Washington, where he remained through the new year, helping to secure the ratification of the Convention of Mortefontaine in the Senate. He returned to Philadelphia after Jefferson's inauguration as president on March 4, 1801.

That was the year that tragedy struck the family. Too soon after giving birth to her son, Anne went out on a sleighing party and caught a cold. It was just a cold, but in this age any sickness was cause for concern. Sure enough, Anne's health soon worsened. "Though her situation is by no means desperate it is highly critical," Alexander reported in late March, "so much so as to leave the hopes and fears of those about her . . . nearly ballanced." Inexorably, the balance began to tip; by the time William returned from Washington Anne was declining fast. "Her Disorder has been gaining Ground on her," William wrote in terror. Her doctors had "recommended an immediate Change of Climate & I Shall embark with her to morrow or the next Day for the Island of Madeira." By that time, according to Alexander, "her case was considered perfectly hopeless."[56]

Anne was carried from her mansion through the Philadelphia streets on a palanquin—a bed held up on four poles and carried by servants—to the ship *America*, which was then waiting by the docks for its hold to fill. Hundreds of people gathered to stare at the gloomy procession—a refracted portrait of the Philadelphia crowds that had gathered eight years earlier to see the French balloonist Jean-Pierre Blanchard carried up into the heavens, and then gathered again that year to watch Edmond Genet ride triumphantly into town. "As she is scarcely expected to live a week, her leaden coffin is part of the Cargo," one Philadelphian wrote. "What a melancholy set!" The couple left with Maria Matilda and one of Anne's sisters—and a consignment of Cuban sugar, Caribbean coffee, and Bohea tea from China.

They never made it to Madeira. Anne died in Bermuda on May 11. From there, the ship sailed on to Hamburg to deliver its cargo, while Anne's family returned home. "This business was made up hastily & not exactly in the manner I could have wished considering the value of the property," Alexander Baring wrote, with a certain lack of grace, "but it became necessary to decide without hesitation & I determined to let the whole cargo go."[57]

The sequence of events that led to Anne's death remains shrouded in some mystery. She whom the French had called *la belle Américaine* had always been drawn to their culture. She'd admired their conversation and their manners, their furniture and their clothing, and had imported them all to Philadelphia. She once told Alexandre Laujon, the French dancer who lived for some years in the American capital, that she loved the French for their "gallant manners," but that they "were, in general, all good or all bad." Laujon was startled. "Singular thought," he mused, "which was not without justice, and which later applied to her most painfully; she died of grief from it." It's an elliptical comment, to be sure. What could it mean? Perhaps it referred to her daughter's elopement with the comte de Tilly two years before her death. Anne never tried to hide the pain the event had caused her.[58]

Or could it have referred to another painful experience? Alexander Baring once mentioned to his father that Noailles' "very great influence in the Bingham family [stems] from certain female reasons you will easily understand." This comment, too, was elliptical—possibly even to Sir Francis Baring, certainly to posterity. One source was, however, more direct. That scoundrel, Alexandre de Tilly, recorded details that were perhaps best left unsaid. "The vicomte de Noailles who in America was called general Noailles was a friend of the house," he wrote in his *Mémoires*. "He was indeed, and even passed for the lover of Mme Bingham." Tilly is hardly a reliable witness, of course; and even if we grant them credence, the comments remain somewhat vague: he leaves unsaid whether Noailles was Anne's lover or merely "passed for" it. Probably the truth will never be known. What is known, however, is that Noailles put his apartment in the Bingham compound up for rent as Anne lay on her sickbed. Whether her illness was the cause of Noailles' move or, as Laujon may have been intimating, its consequence will remain a matter for speculation.[59]

Devastated, William returned to Philadelphia on May 26. But he could no longer stand his silent house, the great mansion he and Anne had built and furnished after their European trip. It was unbearably empty without the sounds of parties and Anne's joyous sociability. He had to flee. In August he put all of his properties up for rent, including the mansion with its spectacular gardens—"the elegance and convenience of this house are so generally known as to render a particular description of its advantages unnecessary," one advertisement read—along with Lansdown, his country house overlooking the Schuylkill, where his portrait of Washington, himself dead twenty months earlier, still hung. William also sold his coach, his chariot, and even the sleigh on which Anne had taken her fateful trip that chilly February night. The family was headed to London, and he instructed his correspondents to send his mail "to the Care of Sir Francis Baring."[60]

Bingham sailed with his two daughters, Alexander Baring, and his grandson. They arrived in London in October. But movement had not soothed William's pain. Without Anne, he couldn't see a way forward. "My Plan of Life must essentially vary as the Scenes which constituted my domestic Happiness have vanished," he wrote dully from England. "The ir-

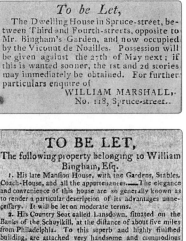

Advertisements that began to appear in Philadelphia newspapers shortly after Anne Bingham's death.

reparable loss I have sustained casts a gloom over all my pursuits and blunts the edge of every enjoyment of life," he lamented in a letter to Noailles. "Whether time will moderate my feelings is an experiment yet to be tried." William's son—the indirect cause of Anne's illness—remained in America with his grandfather Thomas Willing, the ever reliable Old Square Toes; William's feelings toward the boy were too complex for him to sort out. "I cannot express to you the degree of Tenderness & anxiety I feel of this Subject," he wrote to Anne's brother. "He has Claims upon me of a different & more endearing Nature than are usually attached to the Situation of Children. He will never know the extent of the irreparable loss he has Sustained, nor feel the Poignancy of Grief with which the remembrance of their Misfortune afflicts his Sisters."[61]

Where William had once consoled Noailles on the death of his wife, now it was Noailles' turn to console William. "I feel that in all times and in all places, my primary sentiment is one of regret for that which we have lost," he wrote mournfully after the family had sailed away. "We will never meet anything to which she can be compared." In the meantime, Noailles remained in Philadelphia, attending to a long and complicated arbitration on his own behalf as well as Bingham's. "It is impossible for me to predict the moment at which I will return to Europe." In October William wrote to give Noailles some personal and political news. Peace was on the way, he reported: a treaty between France and England. He could not help speculating on how it might affect American commerce: "It appears to me, that the Commercial Speculations of the Country were not founded on the Expectation of Such a Speedy Termination of the Hostilities—therefore those who have been too enterprizing will sustain corresponding . . . distress." But money could not fill the emptiness left by Anne's death. Not even in Philadelphia was anyone prepared to step into her empty shoes or fill her empty house. In November Noailles told Bingham that their grand mansion had not yet been rented. "Few people wish to live in a residence as vast as the one you own," he added. "It needs to be attended to by a man with many domestics on his account."[62]

Meanwhile, everyone's attention was turning toward the Caribbean. The upcoming peace treaty between France and Great Britain was sure to have a transformative effect on the French Caribbean. "The present State of St Domingo occupies their attention very Seriously," William wrote of Napoleon's administration, "& the government seems determined to reinstate that Colony—for this Purpose, a considerable number of Troops will be Sent out immediately—which will occasion a great demand on the United States—for their approvisionment."[63]

"BEFORE BONAPARTE could reach Louisiana," Henry Adams once observed, "he was obliged to crush the power of Toussaint. . . . If he and his blacks should succumb easily to their fate, the wave of French empire would roll on to Louisiana and sweep far up the Mississippi; if St. Domingo should resist, and succeed in resistance . . . America would be left to pursue her democratic destiny in peace."[64]

The road to Louisiana ran through Saint Domingue—not just metaphorically but also geographically. By giving France control of the Windward Passage between Cuba and Saint Domingue, which separates the Atlantic Ocean from the Caribbean Sea, the island secured French access into the Caribbean and to the Gulf of Mexico. With navigation dependent on winds and currents, ships headed to the region passed almost of necessity through the Windward Passage. Without that access, the Caribbean archipelago was not a beachhead but a thousand-mile barrier blocking France from the vast North American interior. Holding the choke point could not have been more critical: if Saint Domingue and Cuba "fall to English hands," fretted one navy report, the British would control commerce "from the mouth of the Orinoco to that of the Mississippi." (Even today, the Windward Passage remains of such importance that the Central Intelligence Agency considers it one of the Atlantic Ocean's five "strategic straits," one the United States secures from a nearby naval base in a Cuban bay that once served as a pirate stronghold.) The Atlantic economy and its imperial order rested on the ability of Europeans to freely export colonial goods from the Caribbean. No government—not the French, not the British, not the American—wanted to see this strategic channel controlled by a nation of former slaves.[65]

More distressing still—for slave owners at any rate—was the powerful symbolism of a republic of freed slaves for the millions of workers on plantations across the United States and the Caribbean, and for the system of racial oppression on which slave owners' wealth and power rested. "The erection of an independent Negro Government in the island of St. Domingo," read one report from London that circulated in American newspapers at the end of 1801, "was calculated to give much alarm to those in this country who are interested in West-India property. Toussaint's Republic was viewed as a formidable example, and its effects might have spread to the whole circle of islands where negroes are to be found." The essential problem, from the perspective of those interests, was that "Toussaint only

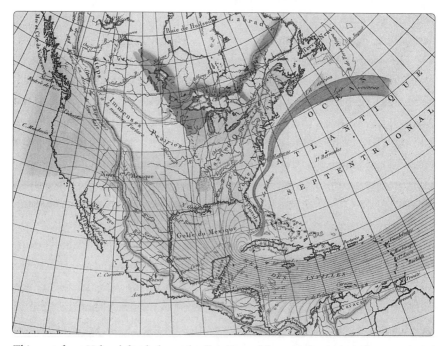

This map from Volney's book shows the directions of the oceanic winds and currents, and suggests how North America and the Caribbean were understood as two parts of a larger whole. The Windward Passage between Cuba and Saint Domingue served as France's doorway into the Caribbean Sea, the Gulf of Mexico, and the North American continent. In the eighteenth century, when winds and currents played such a determinant role in maritime travel, the Windward Passage was a strategically essential point—as it remains today.

recognises a nominal dependence on France." Toussaint-Louverture was the brilliant former slave turned general who had successfully defended both emancipation and French control of the colony over the previous seven years—and who had governed Saint Domingue as it engaged in a lucrative trade relationship with the United States. So long as he and his armies served French interests, his authority could be tolerated and even encouraged. The possibility that he might escape French control, on the other hand, was intolerable.[66]

So although France and Great Britain had just spent nearly a decade fighting each other across Europe and in the Caribbean; although they had engaged in diplomatic intrigue in capitals around the Atlantic world and deep in the American hinterland; although the British navy had spent four years trying to conquer Saint Domingue and lost tens of thousands of troops in the effort, the two bitter enemies could agree on one thing: a republic of freed slaves could not be allowed to control its own destiny. "A great many French troops are to be sent to St. Domingo to assert the interests of the French Republic," American newspapers reported in late 1801. "If necessary, the French government is to be allowed to charter 70 English vessels to carry out the troops without delay." Before the final peace treaty was even signed, two enemies had set aside their differences in the cause of a greater goal: reestablishing slavery in the Caribbean. Thus, with the consent of Great Britain, Napoleon sent his brother-in-law, General Charles-Victor-Emmanuel Leclerc, along with a force that would eventually total more than eighty thousand, to Saint Domingue. It was the largest expeditionary force ever to have sailed from France, and was soon followed by a motley mix of refugee planters and merchants eager to reestablish their former wealth and privilege. By the time it was all over, at the end of the ten years of warfare that began in 1793, both France and Great Britain lost more troops trying to conquer that single Caribbean colony than they would lose at Waterloo.[67]

If a commitment to preserving the plantation order explains why the British navy let Leclerc's force cross the Atlantic, American support for the French mission was more ambivalent. To be sure, the prospect of a republic of former slaves in the Caribbean had no appeal to President Jefferson, who was plagued by fear of "the Cannibals of the terrible republic" pulling into American ports, sending "black crews, supercargoes & missionaries thence into the Southern states," and fomenting insurrection throughout the nation. He was far from the only person to harbor such fears. As French forces were fighting in Saint Domingue, the governor of South Carolina wrote to Jefferson to report on rumors of a "landing of French negroes on the East coast of that state." It was enough to pray for a French victory against the former slaves of Saint Domingue. On the other hand, Jefferson had no desire to see a victorious France installed in Louisiana either. "There is on the globe one single spot, the possessor of which is our natural and habitual enemy," Jefferson wrote in 1801. "It is New Orleans." No amount of lingering attachment to France could soften this view. "France, placing herself in that door, assumes to us the attitude of defiance." William Cobbett was busy fomenting panic at the prospect. "There is not a river, a creek, a cove, an inlet, not a hill nor a dale, nor a rock nor a cave, of which they do not know the bearings and dimensions," he warned in 1802. "They have calculated, to a pound of gun-powder and to a drop of blood, the means of severing from your authority the states of Kentucky and Tennessee."[68]

Here was the terrible paradox for the planter-president: only an army of former slaves stood in the way of a French Louisiana. The dilemma was just as Henry Adams described it. If the French succeeded in conquering Saint Domingue, Louisiana was theirs, and the entire trans-Appalachian West might slip from U.S. control. If France failed, on the other hand, a republic of former slaves would arise in the heart of the Atlantic plantation complex, threatening its very existence. American officials had to thread a very narrow needle. "In general," wrote the French envoy in Washington to Talleyrand, Americans "hope that France, too occupied by the revolution in its former possessions, cannot hope to acquire a new. This disposition does not prevent, however, the desire in the South for France to succeed definitively in re-establishing order." For Americans, he concluded, the ideal outcome would be for France to reestablish slavery in Saint Domingue, "but in a moment distant enough to prevent the Government from carrying out its ambitions on Louisiana."[69]

Napoleon might easily have stepped around the trap. Some evidence suggests that in late 1801 the first consul considered simply "recogniz[ing] Toussaint" and granting Saint Domingue autonomy within the French Empire. "The government of the blacks recognized in Saint-Domingue and legitimized by France," Talleyrand warned the British in 1801, would be a "formidable base for the [French] Republic in the New World." The establishment of colonies connected to the *métropole* by bonds of mutual interest and commercial exchange was a vision that French imperial planners had once reserved for the United States, and which Talleyrand had outlined in his "Mémoire" on the advantages of new colonies. Had such an effort been pursued, it would have provided France not just with a strategic military base, but also with a highly motivated army of black soldiers to rebuild its colonial system in North America. Allied to France, Talleyrand warned, Saint Domingue would become "the scepter of the New World." Here were the outlines of a different French Empire: committed to the preservation of emancipation rather than the reestablishment of slavery, and manned by battalions of freed slaves who would be so formidable that neither the Americans nor the British nor even an alliance of the two could easily have dislodged them from the mainland.[70]

It is possible, even likely, that Talleyrand's warnings were just diplomatic bluster to persuade the British to open the Atlantic to the French fleet. If so, he was hitting a nerve. "France with an army of those black troops," Secretary of State Timothy Pickering warned, "might conquer all the British Isles and put in jeopardy our Southern States." It is tantalizing to ponder the implications of this road not taken. With a base of operations in the Caribbean, fifty thousand French soldiers not killed in the brutal attempt to reconquer Haiti, and a biracial army sent to hold Louisiana in alliance with Native Americans—still loyal to and nostalgic for their former ally—France might have permanently stalled U.S. expansion at the Mississippi River, perhaps even pushed it back to the Appalachians, finally establishing the region as the long-desired Native American buffer. France would have regained some of the territory it had lost forty years earlier and fulfilled the promise its diplomats were continually making to Spanish officials: that it would serve as a barrier against U.S. expansion and protect their American possessions. In which case not just the trans-Appalachian West, not just Louisiana, but all of the Spanish land left exposed by the Louisiana Purchase—Texas, New Mexico, Arizona, California—might have resisted the Americans' voracious appetite for land. As for the inner configuration of the American Republic, one can only imagine the consequences that a biracial French army would have had on the slave regime just then beginning its furious expansion through the cotton belts of Georgia, Alabama, and Mississippi.[71]

But none of this came to pass. Napoleon decided instead that Toussaint-Louverture's increasingly independent foreign policy, along with his unwillingness to recognize France's right to control the island's destiny, posed too great a threat to French Caribbean interests. And so his army sailed to Saint Domingue with the objective of crushing the Haitian Revolution before heading on to Louisiana.

———

NOAILLES FINALLY left Philadelphia shortly after Napoleon's army sailed to Saint Domingue. Years earlier he had told Anne Bingham "that he has renounced France forever, that he never will return . . . unless as a Traveller or Visiter and that if France Should make War on America he would take Arms in her Defence." But times had changed. His closest French friends had left the country. Anne Bingham was dead, her mansion empty. The U.S. capital had left for Washington. The United States—his naturalized country—had gone from ardently pro-French to rabidly anti. Life for a French aristocrat in Philadelphia was simply not as fun as it had been in the glory days of the 1790s.[72]

And so it was that Noailles left for the Caribbean sometime after the summer of 1802. His name by now removed from the list of émigrés, he was appointed brigadier general in the French army. "Count de Noailles," announced a New York newspaper in early January 1803, "who resided in Philadelphia a considerable period, is now in the French service in St. Domingo." The invasion was not going well. Yellow fever was proving more deadly to French troops than anyone had anticipated, and the Haitian resistance more determined. Noailles arrived around the time yellow fever took General Leclerc's life; he was replaced by Donatien-Marie-Joseph de Vimeur, vicomte de Rochambeau, the son of the general under whom Noailles had fought in the American Revolution. Alexandre Laujon, the young French dancer on whom Noailles had once placed a wager at a Philadelphia ball, ran into him on the streets of Cap-Français. "The family with which he'd been so intimately connected in Philadelphia had experienced great misfortune, and he had gone to Saint-Domingue to rejoin General Rochambeau to whom he was related," Laujon reported. "Hélas, Alfred," Noailles said, using Laujon's nickname as he reached out to shake his hand, "the *beau temps* when we knew each other is far behind us."[73]

Noailles was stationed at Fort Dauphin, just outside the town of Môle Saint-Nicolas, on the northwest tip of Haiti across from Cuba, guarding the Windward Passage: that critical shipping lane the French could not afford to give up. "I am penetrated by the importance of my mission," Noailles wrote to a correspondent in February 1803. "It will succeed wholly despite the momentary difficulties." He had also been charged with getting loans for the French forces. It was a task for which he was well suited, given his experience, his extensive mercantile contacts, his excellent English, and his friendship with key figures in the United States. At one point, he exchanged notes with Thomas Willing, drawing funds for the French campaign. His relationship with the Barings also helped: they had served as agents for the British army and navy in 1795, helping to supply British troops with munitions and supplies. The network he'd forged in Philadelphia was coming in handy. "I'll have occasion to pass your note to Mrs. Baring," Noailles added by way of a P.S. in one of his letters, referring, presumably, to Anne and William's daughter. By supplying French forces in the Caribbean with American provisions, Noailles was helping realize the role French diplomats had imagined for the United States many years earlier when they intervened in the American Revolution.[74]

In December 1802 Noailles traveled to Jamaica to try to solicit a loan from Alexander Lindo, a French-born merchant of Sephardic origin who had established one of the most important commercial houses in the British West Indies. While there, he paid a visit to Sir George Nugent, the governor of Jamaica, and told him that "the French plan was, to put to death every negro who had borne arms." Nugent asked him what the colony would be worth in that case, but Noailles had no answer to that question. He later went to Cuba to purchase supplies for the French troops. Some of his papers suggest that he was selling African slaves in Cuba to raise money for the French campaign. That was at the time that the Barings, too, began to investigate opportunities in the trade, exploring ways to most lucratively import slaves to Havana. Whether those explorations had any connection with Noailles' trips to Cuba can only be a matter for speculation. What was obvious even then, however, was that the mission was going badly; and French officers began peering down a dark abyss.[75]

In May 1803 the Peace of Amiens broke down, and war between France and Great Britain began again. Toussaint had been kidnapped during diplomatic discussions and sent to a French prison, but that was not enough for French forces to turn the tide of the war. Napoleon's army—confined to a few port cities, decimated by yellow fever, and facing the determined resistance of the Haitian troops under Generals Henri Christophe and Jean-Jacques Dessalines—now found itself in even worse straits. The British navy cut off French transatlantic supply lines and began a blockade of the island. As French military leaders in Saint Domingue watched one of the greatest armies their country had ever mobilized gradually and inexorably destroyed, they began resorting to increasingly vicious measures. May found Noailles in Cuba, where he purchased three hundred bloodhounds for the French army in Saint Domingue at $20 to $50 per head—by their size and weight, they looked more like wolves than dogs, witnesses reported. Americans had already heard the rumors about the animals. "A French frigate" had recently sailed, "bound to Cape-François with 200 blood hounds," one New York newspaper reported, "*to hunt the negroes!*" When the dogs arrived, Rochambeau immediately set them to their appointed work. "I send you, my dear commandant," Rochambeau wrote an adjutant, "28 *boule dogues*. . . . I don't need to tell you that no rations or expenses are authorized for the dogs' food; *you must only give them negroes to eat.* I salute you affectionately."[76]

It would be Noailles' most infamous contribution to the war. When they arrived, crowds of colonists under siege in Cap-Français lined the streets to throw flowers on the dogs. They constructed an amphitheater outside the former government palace, in the courtyard of an old Jesuit monastery. A young boy was tied to a post in the center. The dogs were let loose. Amid the cries of the victim and the applause of the spectators, the dogs "devoured his entrails and didn't abandon their prey until they had gorged themselves on the twitching flesh. Nothing was left on the post but bloody bones." What a way for Noailles to cap off his career. Fourteen years earlier he had led the Assemblée constituante in abolishing the feudal order in France; now he was supplying bloodhounds to hunt down and disembowel former slaves fighting for their freedom.[77]

By the middle of 1803, the French army was down to its last troops. A letter received at Bryden's coffeehouse in Baltimore reported "that the blood hounds lately imported in St. Domingo, from Cuba, have spread great terror among the negroes. Several black prisoners, who would have expiated their guilt upon the gallows, have been turned defenceless and naked upon the plains, and torn to pieces by those dogs!" The fighting in Saint Domingue had turned genocidal. "The war is carried on between the French and brigands"—as the newspapers called the former slaves fighting for their liberty—"with every species of barbarity their savage minds can invent."

> When the brigands take a prisoner they put him between two planks and fasten him with cords so that he cannot move, and then take a cross cut saw and saw him nearly asunder in different places so as to terminate his existence in the most barbarous manner—and the French in their turn when they take prisoners tie them neck and heels, and throw them into a place where they have a parcel of half starved blood-hounds to be torn to pieces by them.

The lurid details seemed to fascinate and repel Americans. Perhaps they were finding reassurance that their own system of plantation slavery was somehow more humane. Perhaps they were taking pride in the lesser violence of their revolution, so different—or so they liked to believe—from the bloodstained war in Haiti. Or perhaps they focused so unremittingly on the violence to deny that the struggle of former slaves fighting for their freedom against Europe's most powerful empires might bear any relation to their recent revolution. Whatever the reason, the U.S. reading public— at least to judge by the attention the newspapers devoted to the "HORRORS OF SAINT DOMINGO"—could not get enough of the events. The extensive coverage in newspapers and in the burgeoning American print culture would have long-term consequences, inspiring an enduring fear of slave insurrection among American slave owners, and creating a lasting symbol among slaves of the liberating possibilities embedded in violent resistance.[78]

Before he died, General Leclerc had written to Napoleon about the horrors of a campaign that he had, by then, begun calling a "war of extermination." "My soul is tainted," he lamented. "No pleasant idea can make me forget these hideous scenes." Staring down into the abyss, the French leaped. "General Rochambeau seems to have spread terror among the negroes," wrote Leonora Sansay, an American who traveled to the island and left a vivid portrait of these last days of French Saint Domingue in the form of a fictionalized autobiography. "I wish they were reduced to order that I might see the so much vaunted habitations where I should repose beneath the shades of orange groves; walk on carpets of rose leaves and fenchipone; be fanned to sleep by silent slaves, or have my feet tickled into extacy by the soft hand of a female attendant." These months of 1803, juxtaposing unspeakable horror and fevered colonial fantasy, almost seem, as one scholar has written, "blasted out of the continuum of history." Perhaps that continuum needed to be blasted open to make way for the creation of something "truly new to the world," as the distinguished historian David Brion Davis has written: "not simply a revolution, but a nation of former slaves who had achieved independence."[79]

IN EARLY 1803, Vincent Gray, the American consul at Havana, had reported that Noailles spoke "with great respect" about U.S. relations with France. By then the retrocession of Louisiana from Spain to France was open knowledge, and Noailles "expected troops for the transfer of Louisiana to arrive soon at Cap-Français." His linguistic skills, as well as his connections to American merchants and politicians—Noailles "is well acquainted with the temper and disposition" of Americans, Gray reported—would prove useful for the French authorities. Thus, the consul wrote that Noailles "might be ordered from Havana to Louisiana." That, at any rate, was the original plan: but it had been rendered impossible by the depleted state of French forces in Saint Domingue. "Since the number would not be so great as generally supposed," Gray wrote, "the commander in chief at Cap-Français would need to detain all the troops there in order to recover the entire island before the commencement of the 'unhealthy season'; 'therefore it was uncertain, when they would have it in their power to take possession of Louisiana.'" After all this time, only to get so close, Louisiana was slipping from France's fingers.[80]

In the end, it was the determination of the Haitian forces not to be reenslaved that bequeathed Louisiana to the United States. "The fate of *St. Domingo* appears to be nearly determined," one American newspaper reported in 1803. "A *Black Republic* is rapidly rising on the ruins of the French colonial regimen. 'This immense galley, worked for so many years by the slaves of AFRICA bound in thousands to its oars,' is about to be formed into a new NATION, which must excite the attention of the commercial world, & particularly that of the U States." By the end of that year, Rochambeau's remaining forces were stuck in Cap-Français, trapped between the British blockade at sea and Dessalines's army on land. Finally, on November 30, Rochambeau surrendered to the British, and the remnants of his army were evacuated to Jamaica. Dessalines marched into the thrice-burned city at the head of eight thousand men, renaming it Cap-Haïtien.[81]

Only Noailles refused to give up. His transfer to New Orleans with a French army was now aborted, but Noailles still defended the fort of Môle Saint-Nicolas against the Haitian troops and the British navy. For five long months they held out; Noailles' forces would be the last to leave the island. Late one December night, taking advantage of the distraction created as the defeated French forces sailed under British supervision past the fort and through the Windward Passage on their way to Jamaica, Noailles loaded his troops and the remaining inhabitants of the town on seven ships. They slipped quietly past the British blockade. "The Commander at the Mole, Genl. Noailles, has been more fortunate than Genl. Rochambeau and has arrived Safe to windward in this Island with his officers &c," Vincent Gray reported from Cuba.[82]

Noailles dropped the French inhabitants and most of his soldiers on the Cuban coast, promptly outfitted a privateer, the *Courrier,* and sailed it toward Havana. As the sun was setting on New Year's Eve, with 1804 about to dawn—at the very moment that the victorious forces on Saint Domingue were preparing to declare the independence of Haiti—Noailles encountered the *Hazard,* a British privateer. He raised a British flag and approached the *Hazard,* addressing the captain in his excellent English. After a few questions, Noailles learned that the *Hazard* was patrolling the waterways between Cuba and Haiti on the lookout for a general named Noailles who had

This epic painting by Jean Antoine Théodore Gudin, exhibited at the Paris salon of 1842, portrays Noailles' daring attack on the British cruiser sent to hunt him down on the night of December 31 to January 1, 1804. Noailles stands at the head of the French privateer as it rams the British cruiser. The man who looks at the action from the back of the ship, dressed in a tuxedo, is Noailles' grandson, who commissioned the painting.

recently managed to elude the British navy. What an opportunity! Noailles explained that he was on the same mission and suggested they join forces. Later, under the cover of night, he sprang his audacious trap. Ramming the British ship from the side, he stormed the deck at the head of thirty grenadiers and surprised its crew. After a fierce battle they captured their prize, and Noailles, although wounded, sailed into Havana victorious.[83]

NOAILLES' LAST battle may have been valiant, but it meant nothing. The game was up. Louisiana and Saint Domingue constituted the twin pillars of France's American strategy; together they would stand or fall. "Louisiana had been destined to supply this other colony," recalled François Barbé-Marbois, Napoleon's finance minister, who had once served in the French legation in the United States. "And since Saint Domingue was lost to France, Louisiana also lost a part of its importance." France's last gateway into the North American continent was gone, and Napoleon had squandered the army meant to occupy Louisiana. He had no choice but to stem the hemorrhaging. "I already consider this colony entirely lost," he told Barbé-Marbois on April 10, 1803.[84]

Napoleon wanted the matter resolved quickly. He and his minister of foreign relations both fretted about Spain's fragile hold on Louisiana. They had been emphasizing the precarious state of the Spanish defenses for years in their negotiations over the retrocession. Perhaps Collot's reports on the Mississippi valley had persuaded Napoleon that the British could effortlessly seize the province were they to launch an assault: "The conquest of Louisiana would be easy if they only took the trouble to descend it," Napoleon proclaimed. "I don't have a moment to lose if I want to take it out of their reach. . . . If I was in their place, I would not have waited." Some of these ex post facto reports may well be exaggerated—French officials, including Napoleon himself, may have later regretted selling Louisiana so quickly and cheaply to the Americans. And yet those expressions are entirely consistent with the reports that French naval and diplomatic officials had been submitting for years. As far back as Genet's 1793 antics, French authorities had insisted that a few thousand troops sailing down the Mississippi River could take New Orleans and hold the entire valley. It had been a central and continuous theme of their military assessments for more than a decade.[85]

American ministers knew that French leaders feared a British conquest of the territory, and emphasized that danger. "If you occupy Louisiana you won't have time to establish yourselves," Robert Livingston warned the French minister of the navy. English forces had only to "descend from *Canada by the Mississippi*," and Louisiana would "fall into the power of the English." A British Louisiana joined to Canada would make Great Britain the "exclusive master of the fur and skins," according to one French report. Allied to the United States by habits, language, tastes, and opinions, Britain would then be in a position to "monopolize South America." On the other hand, ceding Louisiana to the United States might create a long-term counterweight to British influence. "To liberate people from the commercial tyranny of England," Napoleon presciently argued, "it must be *counterposed* . . . by a maritime power that might one day become its rival: it is the United States." Certainly an American Louisiana, by eliminating the greatest cause of dissension between the two nations, would dramatically improve Franco-American relations: "It appears to me that in the hands of this growing power, it will be more useful to the policy and even to the commerce of France," he predicted. A generous cession by France might thus strengthen Franco-American comity and long-term trade. It was a parallel to the thinking that had led Lansdowne to offer those generous concessions in the Ohio valley to the American negotiators back in 1783. Then, British officials offered an expansive territory to the United States that was not even theirs to give in order to disrupt the Franco-American alliance; twenty years later, French officials employed the same strategy to disrupt the Anglo-American alliance.[86]

And so at last, French dreams of an empire in America came to a close. On April 10, Talleyrand met with the American ambassador Robert Livingston and asked him—whimsically, as though the thought had just crossed his mind—"whether we wished to have the whole of Louisiana." There he was: once again selling American lands. But they still had to agree on a price. "I need a lot of money," Napoleon warned his negotiators. "Lou-

isiana will give me the initial funds for war on the English scoundrels."
After haggling for several days, with Barbé-Marbois leading the negotiations and Talleyrand helping them along, the two countries agreed on a
purchase price of $15 million, $12 million for France and $3 million to settle
the claims of American merchants against France.[87]

But where was the money to come from? French borrowing costs were
nearing their peak; no French banks were willing to engage in such a risky
loan when they had safer and more lucrative places to allocate their capital
at home. Certainly the United States did not have the money. The government's annual revenue amounted to a mere $10 million. It was in no posi-
tion to make such a huge payment. When Livingston expressed his concerns
to Barbé-Marbois, he was told that Napoleon thought the United States
should just borrow the money. And so the two countries turned to a group
of bankers with extensive experience in transatlantic finance. With Théophile Cazenove in Paris advising Talleyrand, the sale was financed by a
consortium made up of the Barings, the Hopes, and William Bingham.[88]

How the group managed to secure the Louisiana deal remains unclear.
Perhaps it was Alexander Baring who set the stage when he toured Paris in
1802 and, according to a diary he kept of the trip, dined several times with
Talleyrand. According to Senator Volney, who dined with Talleyrand in
November, Bingham was also in Paris and had already stopped in on Volney for a visit; in December, Livingston reported having introduced Bingham to Napoleon. Or perhaps it was Pierre-César Labouchère, that
enterprising French partner in the Hope bank and Alexander Baring's
brother-in-law, who laid the groundwork. In 1801 Labouchère wrote to Sir
Francis asking him to "procure me a letter for Mr Livingston from M
King." Or perhaps it was, as Barbé-Marbois recalled, the American negotiators who insisted that the Barings and the Hopes get involved. Did Talleyrand secure a bribe from the bankers he'd known back in Philadelphia,
cashing in at last on American lands? A clue might have been found in
Théophile Cazenove's papers, but Talleyrand confiscated these when his
friend died, despite vain appeals by Cazenove's son. Only traces of their
collaboration were later discovered, in the form of a few letters from Talleyrand to Cazenove found in a bookseller's stall on the Paris quays many

years later. There is some indication that Sir Francis Baring cut Rufus King in on the deal; if so, that would not be surprising: the American ambassador to London had done business with Robert Morris and Talleyrand in the United States some years earlier.[89]

As for the terms, Alexander Baring took charge of the negotiations. Sir Francis even claimed that it was his son who persuaded the French government to lower their initial price. "The demand of france was originally 100 million of Livres," he wrote, "& I believe that M. Livingston & M. Monroe will allow, that merit was due to my son for reducing the price & facilitating the arrangement." It would be the most significant deal the Barings had yet negotiated: "of the utmost magnitude and importance," it "might stagger us in ordinary times," Labouchère wrote to Alexander Baring. Sir Francis, in London, was anxious, and urged total secrecy. Once negotiations began, he wrote to Labouchère, "further *correspondence* must be dropt altogether. . . . My nerves are equal to the operation, but not so, to the imprudencies which I see committed to paper, knowing that the paper is carefully preserved. I can say not more." During the stressful internal conversations between Paris and London, the Barings resorted to a cipher to protect the privacy of their correspondence. They used the term "Maine Lands" to stand in for "American Loan."[90]

In the end, the French government signed a treaty with the Hope and Baring firms alongside its treaty with the United States. France received an immediate credit of 2 million francs for its Caribbean operations from Thomas Willing, William Bingham's father-in-law, Old Square Toes. Meanwhile, the Hopes and Barings raised the rest of the money on the British capital markets, turning the desperately needed funds over to France . . . so it could wage war against Britain. Although the purchase price was fixed at $15 million, the actual cost to the United States was far higher after the $11 million (59,140,000 francs) in interest was factored in. When Alexander Baring sailed to the United States to deliver the contract and arrange the financing, it was Talleyrand—his former dinner partner in Philadelphia and consultant on Bingham's Maine lands—who drafted the passport.[91]

British authorities seemed happy at first to let the transaction go forward; they had long dreaded the prospect of a French Louisiana. "It would have been wise for this country to pay a million sterling for the transfer of Louisiana from France to America," Henry Addington, the British prime minister, told Francis Baring, and allegedly "saw nothing in our conduct but to approve." Addington—not, by some accounts, the brightest bulb ever to grace the British prime minister's office—would later change his mind. The U.S. government would also have qualms about how much the Barings and Hopes earned from the transaction, which Secretary of the Treasury Albert Gallatin estimated at $3 million. Even Francis Baring worried that the profits might appear excessive. "I think it moreover important," he wrote to Labouchère, his son-in-law, "that the Americans should not think we obtained too large a profit."[92]

These were familiar networks of capital, founded on the connections first forged by a group of French émigrés stranded in America and further strengthened by British and Dutch financiers looking to shelter their mobile capital: all of it coming together to execute the greatest land deal in American history.

EMPTY HOUSES:
A CONCLUSION

F IRST THERE WAS SUGAR. THEN COFFEE. AND INDIGO. DEEP IN THE
continent there were furs and out in the ocean there were fishing
banks. There was tobacco, lumber, and cotton; wheat, rice, and salted
beef; hemp, tar, pitch, and potash. On and on it went: candles, codfish, flax,
ginseng, iron, linseed oil, molasses, turpentine, even beeswax and snake-
root. First there were the commodities.

Then came the labor and the rush for land to grow it all: the settlers
scurrying across, grabbing the most fertile lands by the coast, irrigating the
fields, sowing the crops, and pushing ever outward to grab more land.
There were enslaved Indians and then millions upon millions of enslaved
Africans—for centuries they were the vast majority of those who crossed
the Atlantic—captured and chained and dragged across an ocean to live
grueling lives producing the crops. And boats to carry the workers over
and their harvests back. First hundreds of boats and then thousands: huge
ships crossing the ocean, smaller ones plying the coastal trade, and smaller
ones still pushing up rivers and floating down creeks into international

markets. Then came the merchants: traders and financiers in Genoa, Amsterdam, Paris, Nantes, London, and Liverpool, primitively accumulating the capital to clear the land and buy the labor and build the mills and dig the canals and make the roads to expand their trade and get rich off more commodities. Empires grew: aggressive, ever-expanding empires to protect the commodities and police the trade and finance their governments and fund their navies. And, inevitably, war to acquire them followed: continual, recurring war, beating to the rhythm of diplomatic time.

Intellectuals and aristocrats grew rich off the trade, gathering in mahogany-paneled rooms in Europe to drink coffee (with sugar) and talk about rights and reason and progress. Settlers resisted the empires with their demands for taxation and control over trade. Indians made war on the murderous settlers; slaves resisted masters and rose up in revolution. And all of them—settlers, Indians, slaves, merchants, and philosophers—all of them cried out for liberty. Finally, as the eighteenth century drew to a close, there came more wars: global, apocalyptic wars on a scale the world had never seen.

———

BY 1804 a decade had passed since the outbreak of global war that flung the émigrés to America.

A typical list of commodities prices in an eighteenth-century newspaper. This one appeared in January 1793, the month that Blanchard flew over Philadelphia.

Eleven years since Jean-Pierre Blanchard had floated blissfully through the skies over Philadelphia, marking the wondrous new age launched by the French Republic. They had been some of the most consequential years for American history, French history, and Atlantic history. The United States had gone from a small group of states huddled between the Appalachians and the Atlantic coast to a continental power stretching across the Mississippi valley to the Rocky Mountains. Saint Domingue had gone from a colony of slaves to one of insurgents and, finally, to a nation of free Haitian citizens. France had gone from a monarchy to a republic and then, in December 1804, to an empire. And the Atlantic basin had gone from peace to war to peace and back again. By the time it was all over, the map of Europe and its colonies had been redrawn and the ideological and political struggles of the nineteenth century had begun.

The émigrés did not bring about these extraordinary transformations, but they witnessed them, they participated in them, and their lives were bound up in nearly every part of them. Their travels connected glamorous salons in Paris to nail-biting diplomatic negotiations in London, bloody slave rebellion in Cap-Français to heated political debates in Philadelphia, daring espionage missions in New Orleans to nascent lumber mills in Maine. They connected European capital to abundant American land and delicate silverware at glittering dinner parties in Philadelphia to brute commodities grown by violently exploited slave labor in the Caribbean. These things are not always seen in relation to one another. Diplomatic history is not generally a history of sociability, economic history is not often a history of portraiture, and the history of material culture is not ordinarily a history of politics. But the lives of the émigré *constituants* brought all those spheres and more into contact.

If the changes the émigré *constituants* experienced seemed more dramatic than most, that was only because the heights from which they had fallen were more exalted. It was never entirely clear why the sight of former aristocrats living for several years on a few *livres* per day evoked so much pathos, while the existence of millions of peasants and slaves living lifetimes on much less evoked so little. In the end, location on the social and economic scale didn't matter; the reverberations shook everyone: from the pinnacle of the European aristocracy to the depths of Caribbean slavery, from the richest transatlantic merchants to the poorest settlers scratching out their lives in the rugged backcountry, from the Indian villages of the Ohio valley to the Jacobin clubs on the streets of Paris. No one was left untouched by the momentous events of the age. So although the émigrés did not make this new world, their lives poke through the accumulated detritus that makes up the historical archive with greater clarity and sharpness than most; and in that regard, they help us see how the processes that occurred on the vast time scales of geographic, political, economic, and diplomatic history became entangled with the events that transpired on the more minute time scale of an individual life.

From the émigrés' perspectives, the United States was a distant place. It was less a nation in emergence than a remote borderland on the fringes of European civilization; insofar as it mattered, it was as a useful accessory to the heart of the Atlantic world beating just to its south. To an extent that many people today forget, that was also the perspective of the people with whom the émigrés socialized during their travels in the United States: men like Washington, Hamilton, Jefferson, and Adams. None of those founding fathers could afford to ignore the diplomatic, economic, or political hierarchies of the Atlantic world, or the relatively powerless place they occupied in it. None of them could avoid looking outward: away from Philadelphia, New York, and Mount Vernon to Saint Domingue, New Orleans, Montreal, London, Amsterdam, and Paris. To say this is not to criticize the national outlines that too often configure our histories; it is, rather, to sketch them differently. How the United States emerged from the distant periphery of that world to occupy its center in a mere century and a half—just the briefest of moments on most historical time scales—is surely one of the more fascinating puzzles for our age of increasingly internationalized history.

After the émigrés' American experiences were over, and they and their friends and business associates had gone home, all of them continued to wrestle in one way or another with the changes they had experienced. All of them sought to make those changes intelligible—as, indeed, we still seek to do today.

No one could forget that these had been watershed years, Henry Hope least of all. In 1794 the illustrious banker wrote an unusually introspective letter to his friend and associate Sir Francis Baring. French armies had just driven Hope and his family out of Amsterdam with ships full of gold, all the way to London, where they had joined the Barings. Probably no single event better symbolizes the tectonic shift just then taking place in the history of global finance, as its center shifted from Amsterdam to London, where it would remain for the long nineteenth century, as British economic and naval power dominated the globe.

To people living through these changes, the unrelenting wars and revolutions felt like a rupture in the fabric of historical time. Sir Francis Baring and Henry Hope stood on one side of that rupture, their descendants on the other. "It may be happy for our Successors," Hope mused, "that they are by the agitated times in which they are brought up as it were initiated & their Minds are gradually prepared & their feelings be less effected than ours." Unlike their children, who knew only a world of perpetual change, the patriarchs could look back and remember what life had been like before, and recall those times when "the whole enlightened polished part of Europe" had reached a "Summit of perfection & refinement." Unlike their children, they were "alive to the Contrast between the past & present State of things." They could see that one historical era had ended and a new one had dawned. This new age would be marked, Hope thought, by a constant awareness of "the Vicissitude to which all human Affairs are subject." "This," he concluded, "seems to be the inevitable consequence of the great event in France."[1]

Hope was still in London in 1802, when he sat for a family portrait by Benjamin West, the American-born artist who had moved to England after the Seven Years' War and established himself at the pinnacle of the British art world. With its neoclassical touches, the portrait reflects Hope's yearning for the nobler, more refined times of the eighteenth century, when slaves and peasants knew their place. Up in the left, on top of an armoire, sits a model of Welgelegen, the grand mansion Hope built outside the Dutch town of Haarlem, where he hosted many of Europe's great politicians and financiers. Thomas Jefferson visited the house in 1788, the year it was completed, on the eve of "the great event in France" that Hope would bemoan six years later. He drew a sketch. "It is said this house will cost 4 tons of silver, [or] 40,000. £ sterl.," he commented laconically.[2]

Hope never returned to the Netherlands after French armies drove him out. He turned the Dutch branch of the bank over to John Williams Hope, the son of a Welsh clergyman who had started as a clerk in the Hope bank, married Henry Hope's niece, and taken his name. In the Hope family portrait, he stands to the right of the family, looking across to a distant spot outside the frame. John took over the firm's Dutch operations while his partner, Pierre-César Labouchère—who had also started as a clerk and married well—took over the French. In 1808 John Williams Hope sold Welgelegen to Louis Bonaparte, Napoleon's brother, whom the emperor had made king of Holland. It was in Welgelegen that Louis Bonaparte signed his abdication two years later, having failed to support his brother's plans

Henry Hope and Family *by Benjamin West.*

to invade Russia. Alexandre, Liancourt's son, was then Napoleon's ambassador to Holland. After Napoleon's defeat in 1815, the house became the property of the Dutch state. Today it is a museum.[3]

IN OCTOBER 1804, after Haiti achieved its heroic independence and Louisiana tumbled into American hands, Julian Ursyn Niemcewicz, a Polish nobleman, poet, and revolutionary-in-exile, visited Philadelphia. He'd last seen the city in the 1790s, when it was still the nation's capital, and Anne Bingham hosted her glittering parties. But now the Bingham mansion was silent and empty, echoing only with the distant memories of laughter and conversation.

"The house of Mr. Bingham filled me with sadness," Niemcewicz wrote. "Five years ago it was the most resplendent and attractive house in Philadelphia: the host, rich and hospitable, his wife beautiful and flirtatious and the daughters full of charm. . . . Today the parents have found a grave in a foreign land; the children are scattered; the house stands empty, offered for occupancy to whomsoever would wish to pay the taxes due. And so even in this new country there are awful examples of changes in fortune."[4]

William, brokenhearted, had left for Europe with his two daughters, Ann Louisa and Maria Matilda, along with his son in-law Alexander Baring. They traveled first to England, where Alexander saw his father for the first time in six years. Some of William's old instincts evidently persisted, since in late May 1802, the *Gazette of the United States* reported that "Miss Bingham, daughter of William, was presented to the Queen at the last drawing room by Mrs. King, lady of the American Minister." William and Alexander traveled to Paris later that year, where they visited their old friends from Philadelphia: Volney, Talleyrand, and Cazenove. Bingham's daughters joined them soon after. They planned to "spend the winter running in our circles and our balls," Volney reported. Perhaps Bingham wanted to recreate the glamorous trip he'd taken with Anne some twenty years earlier. "I had before my Departure from America made a Promise to my Daughters, to accompany them on a Visit to the Continent," he wrote to

Sir Francis Baring in January 1803. Perhaps it could allay the family's grief. And if, at the same time, "the Mind could be embellished, & the Taste improved, by a Short Residence in this Capital, the Sacrifice of Time might be viewed as a Consideration of less weight."[5]

It didn't work. William never recovered from Anne's death. After having done his part to finance the Louisiana Purchase, he traveled back to London; late in 1803 he fell ill. He left for Bath—presumably to take some of the mineral waters said to be so beneficial to the sick. But that didn't work either. He died in February 1804, surrounded by his two daughters and their families, Sir Francis Baring, and the marquess of Lansdowne. A large plaque on the southwest corner of Bath Abbey commemorates him today.[6]

Both his daughters stayed in England. Maria Matilda, the ex-wife of the comte de Tilly, had married Alexander's brother Henry in 1802. With this second marriage, Sir Francis's retirement, and the ascension of Alexander to the firm's leadership, the bonds between the first families in British and American finance had been cemented. Maria Matilda had greater success with her second marriage than her first—the couple had three sons and two daughters—but it eventually failed, too; she and Henry divorced in 1824. Maria Matilda moved to France, where she married the French marquis de Blaisel; one of her granddaughters married a comte de Noailles. As for William, the boy born to Anne Bingham just before her death, he eventually joined his sisters in London. He married into the French aristocracy and split his time between London, Paris, and Montreal. None of the Bingham children moved back to the United States; a very large number of their descendants became members of the British and French nobility.[7]

Alexander Baring kept rising in the British financial world. When he left America with Ann Louisa, Maria Matilda, and William, he had given up on both Maine and the United States. "We must certainly abandon our hopes of realizing an early profit," he admitted to his father. But he still held out some hope for a decent return in the future. "Though your original object in undertaking the speculation is thereby foiled I have never for a moment entertained a doubt that the capital invested is amply represented by the lands & will be ultimately profitable." If Alexander's investment in Maine had not worked out as he wished, he did not return empty-handed. He had a new family in tow, through which he would forge immensely lucrative connections in the future. So in a sense he had accomplished what he set out to do in America, and as he left he hoped, "I may never be obliged by my affairs to return." He had enough money for a comfortable life back in London. "I do not wish to succeed Benfield in his house in Grosvenor Square but I confess I am ambitious of living in a society more worth living for & living with than what America generally affords."[8]

Of course, Alexander's affairs did oblige him to return to America just two years later. It was a flurry of activity: meeting with Secretary of State James Madison and Secretary of the Treasury Albert Gallatin, signing documents, notarizing bills. For a brief moment, while Alexander crossed the ocean, it was neither France nor the United States that owned Louisiana but the Barings and the Hopes. But they gave it up soon and with less fuss, and suddenly the United States had doubled in size. The new purchase secured the country's access to the Mississippi River, and a flood of settlement across the Appalachians ensued, with the new settlers shipping their lumber and wheat down to New Orleans and into the Caribbean. Surely Baring wondered whether the opening of Louisiana would hurt the value of his holdings in Maine. If so, he doubtless found consolation in the magnificent profits his purchase and sale of Louisiana showered on him and his family. When Baring returned to England, he led the transformation of the Baring Brothers bank. Prime Minister Benjamin Disraeli called him "the greatest merchant banker England perhaps ever had." By 1818, the firm had become so dominant that the duc de Richelieu would famously remark: "There are six great powers in Europe: England, France, Prussia, Austria, Russia and the Baring Brothers."[9]

Alexander Baring ascended to the peerage in 1835. That was the year he sold most of the Maine lands: 835,000 acres for £230,000. It had not, in the end, been a very good investment. But for all that, Baring had not finished with American lands; he returned to the United States in 1842 for one last negotiation. Perhaps, as he sailed again to America, his mind turned to his father's friend Lord Lansdowne, who almost sixty years earlier had negotiated the first, bitterly contested border between the United States and Canada. Now he was finishing the job, and doing it in an area he knew well.

When Baring, now known as Lord Ashburton, returned to England a few months later, the border between Canada and the United States—including the line that separates Maine from New Brunswick in a particularly generous concession—had been settled by the Webster-Ashburton Treaty.[10]

UPON WILLIAM Bingham's death, Lansdown, his mansion on the banks of the Schuylkill—where his copy of Gilbert Stuart's Lansdowne portrait of George Washington had hung, where the Binghams had spent summers in refuge from yellow fever, where Noailles and Volney had been regular guests—passed down to the Baring family. Joseph Bonaparte, Napoleon's brother who became king of Spain in 1808 and then fled to America, lived there for a year, from 1816 to 1817. (Napoleon himself had planned to come to America before he was captured by the British and sent to Saint Helena.) Joseph later bought an estate near Bordentown, New Jersey, where he "lived like a true philosopher, doing good; receiving, as a father, all the unfortunates who were banished from France."[11]

For decades after, the Lansdown mansion remained empty, cared for by a tenant who lived in a modest house on the property. It burned down in 1854, when some boys lighting off fireworks on July 4 let their celebration get out of hand. In 1866 the Baring family ceded the land to the city of Philadelphia on the express stipulation that it be used "not for purposes of speculation, but for public use." Today the Horticultural Center at Philadelphia's Fairmount Park sits on the site. The only trace of the Bingham-Baring-Lansdowne connection is a curving road carrying the name of a former British lord who had proved so generous with his territorial concessions in 1783.[12]

The other Lansdowne House in London's Berkeley Square, where the Binghams first met Sir Francis Baring, fell into the possession of the 3rd Marquess of Lansdowne, who turned it into one of the centers of London society in the nineteenth century. On one memorable evening two thousand guests attended a concert at the house, including several members of the royal family. During the 1920s, the family rented the house to Gordon Selfridge, the American-born department store magnate, who threw lavish parties where Jazz Age guests danced to the Charleston. It remained in the family's possession until the fateful year of 1929, when capitalism underwent one of its periodic crises, this one signaling the decline of Britain's global dominance. "There is nobody in this country wealthy enough to take over the responsibility of buying Lansdowne House and keeping its present magnificent condition," the London *Evening News* complained. "An American multi-millionaire might be ambitious enough to try it," it added hopefully. But none did.

In 1933, the house was partially demolished to make way for an extension of Curzon Street. Just as Henry Hope had once shipped his fortune from Amsterdam to London, so were pieces of the Lansdowne House dismantled and put into crates and shipped to the United States. The dining room sat in those crates for twenty-five years before being reassembled in New York's Metropolitan Museum of Art. The Lansdowne portrait hangs today at the Smithsonian's National Portrait Gallery in Washington, D.C., purchased from the 8th Earl of Roseberry in 2001 for $30 million thanks to a donation from the foundation of an American media mogul. As for Lansdowne's drawing room, which had served as the model for the Binghams', it ended up at the Philadelphia Museum of Art. Lansdowne's mansion had finally made it to Philadelphia.[13]

ONE FRENCHMAN in the United States never did return. Having been granted asylum in the United States, Edmond-Charles Genet married Cornelia Tappen Clinton, the daughter of New York's Republican governor, in November 1794. It was by all accounts a blissfully happy marriage. With her dowry and the earnings from his ambassadorship they bought a 325-acre farm on Long Island, where their first four children were born. Genet established himself as a farmer, with all the duties it entailed. One receipt from 1795 reveals him receiving shipment for "two boat Loads of good York manure at the rate of four shillings the Cart Load." It was a far cry from his previous diplomatic pursuits. Or perhaps it wasn't.[14]

Genet mostly retired from active political life, although he continued to participate in the occasional Fourth of July celebration hosted by the

New York Democratic-Republican Society. In 1799, thanks in large part to lobbying by his well-connected sister, Madame Campan, Genet was removed from the list of émigrés. Talleyrand had helped as well. "I have the great pleasure, Citizen, to inform you that the executive directory has issued a decree by which, after having permanently struck your name from the list of émigrés, it urges you to return to the territory of the Republic," Talleyrand wrote to Genet. Behind the scenes, Talleyrand had proved himself generous to the man who once shouted invectives at him from the New York streets. "The reasons for his destitution are well known," Talleyrand wrote to the Directory: "He irritated the English faction in the United States, and embittered the American minister by a zeal too ardent, perhaps, but which proved his sincere attachment to France." Perhaps by then Talleyrand had more sympathy for Genet, given his own slips on American diplomacy.[15]

But Genet did not return to France. Life in the United States as a gentleman farmer under the Clinton family umbrella was a comfortable one. In 1802 the Genets moved up the Hudson valley to a large estate called Greenbush, overlooking the river just a few miles from Albany, closer to Cornelia's family. Two more children were born to the happy couple. Then, in 1810, Cornelia died. Genet was crushed; he said that only the need to care for six children kept him going. He eventually climbed back onto his feet, remarried, and renewed his activities. He was a strong advocate for canal development along the Hudson valley, including a canal running through Greenbush that would no doubt have caused his land to grow in value. He invested in turnpike companies and manufacturing, and wrote articles promoting the abolition of prison for debtors. He was a gentleman scientist, albeit not a very successful one. A system for pulling canal barges up inclined planes was one of his projects; another was the subject of his essay "On the Use of Milk to Regenerate Decayd Sheep and Other Purposes." He tried to devise ways to use hot-air balloons for transportation. On July 4, 1826, Genet participated in the Great Jubilee celebrations in Greenbush, offering some toasts on the fiftieth anniversary of Declaration of Independence, which also happened to be the day that both Thomas Jefferson and John Adams died. Genet outlived them both, but, in a similarly eerie coin-

WHEN THE UNITED STATES SPOKE FRENCH

cidence, died on July 14, 1834, forty-five years to the day after the fall of the Bastille.[16]

Genet lies buried in a small cemetery behind the Old Dutch Reformed Church in East Greenbush, beneath a gravestone that reads:

> Under this humble stone
> Are interred
> The remains of Edmond Charles Genet
> Late Adjutant General
> and Consul General
> From the French Republic
> To the United States of America.

MOREAU DE Saint-Méry retuned to Europe after most of his friends, arriving in Bordeaux in September 1798. With Talleyrand's patronage, he secured an appointment as historiographer of the Ministry of the Navy, where he helped write a new maritime penal code. He was also elected to several learned societies, including the Société libre des sciences, des lettres et des arts, the Société libre d'agriculture, and the Lycée des arts et des sciences. In December he presented a paper on yellow fever at the Institut national des sciences et des arts—there is no record of whether his comembers Talleyrand or Volney attended that day—and published papers on a variety of subjects, including agriculture, technology, finance, and legislation.

Talleyrand was not Moreau's only well-placed friend; like Liancourt's daughter-in-law, Moreau was also related to Napoleon's wife, Joséphine Beauharnais. That connection got him appointed as a *conseiller d'état* in 1800 and then named to the French Legion of Honor. In 1801 he became the ambassador to Parma and the following year administrator general of Parma, Piacenza, and Guastalla, all Italian states then controlled by France. Perhaps he had exaggerated when he bragged, back in Philadelphia, of having been "king of Paris for three days," while bemoaning his fate selling paper, ink, and quills. No matter; now the wheel had spun once more: his powers as administrator general were nearly unlimited. But still the wheel had not stopped turning. In 1806 Napoleon recalled Moreau and revoked his positions. As he skirted indigence, Moreau was awarded a small pension from the French state. From his fall in 1806 to his death in 1819 he threw himself into his intellectual pursuits; he edited the many manuscripts and documents he'd compiled to write his multivolume legal and anthropological histories of the French colonies, as well as the crates of papers he'd shipped home with him from the United States.

Today, those papers, known as the Collection Moreau de Saint-Méry, form the basis for the colonial archives of the French state. If you ever go to Aix-en-Provence to conduct research on a subject related to the French colonies, you are working in the archive Moreau began.

UPON HIS return to France, Volney also contacted Talleyrand with the hope of securing a diplomatic post to the United States, as Adet's replacement. It is too bad he did not get the job; it would have been interesting to see how he would have managed, as French ambassador, to navigate France's acquisition and subsequent sale of Louisiana.[17]

Instead, Volney threw himself into the work of the Institut national des sciences et des arts. He was appointed senator after the coup of 18 Brumaire in 1799; in 1803 he was made a *chevalier* of the Legion of Honor and in 1804, a *commandant*. It was in 1803, the year Talleyrand sold Louisiana to the United States, that he published his two-volume work, *Tableau du climat et du sol des États-Unis,* a work he had begun in part to help France better understand the American West. It thus had the distinction of being obsolete by the time it was published. It was a curiously dry account, mostly focused, as its title promised, on the continent's natural features. He continued his intellectual pursuits in the years that followed, publishing a book on ancient history in 1813, *Recherches nouvelles sur l'histoire ancienne,* and founding a prize to encourage the study of languages in 1820. In 1814 he ascended to the French peerage. He died on April 26, 1820, in Paris. The edition of his collected works published in 1826 identified Volney on the title page as count and peer of France, member of the French Academy, and honorary member of the Society of Calcutta. His Orientalist credentials remained strong.

PERHAPS IT is appropriate that Noailles did not long survive France's failed reconquest of Saint Domingue. Indeed, he lived only a few days into that historic year of 1804, his death as bound up with the birth of Haiti as were the last months of his life. Noailles had sustained wounds during his audacious attack on the British privateer sent to capture him off the coast of Cuba, after he evacuated with the last French troops on Haitian soil. He died six days later in Havana. His soldiers enclosed his heart in a silver box, wrapped in the regimental flag, and sent it back to France for burial. At the request of his son Alexis, the heart was laid to rest—if that is the appropriate term—in a small church in Poix, in the Somme, in 1816.[18]

Noailles would mostly be remembered for the great role he played in the French Assemblée constituante on the night of August 4, 1789. The story of his final, daring attack on the British corsair lived on, too. Perhaps it helped overshadow, in the memory of the French military at least, the horrors with which he'd been associated before that final battle, and the utter defeat to which Napoleon's forces had been subjected at the hands of France's former slaves. Noailles' name was engraved on the Arc de Triomphe in Paris, a monument to Napoleonic conquest. A bust of him, carved in 1839, sits in the Galerie des Batailles at Versailles. A few years later, the French artist Jean Antoine Théodore Gudin painted Noailles' final battle for the Salon de Paris of 1842. Today, it belongs to the current vicomte de Noailles, who lives in Argentina.

WHEN LIANCOURT sailed back to Europe, fleeing the hostile political environment in the United States, he remained on the list of émigrés. France was still closed to him. He arrived in Hamburg in late 1797 and spent the next year with his son and daughter-in-law. According to one person who saw him during that period, he was "devoured" by the desire to see France again. By September 1798 he was in Amsterdam; his request to be removed from the list of émigrés had been refused. He nonetheless seems to have spent some time in Paris, though in hiding; Talleyrand, who regularly visited him, kept him under his protection. Finally, on April 21, 1800, with Talleyrand's help, he was removed from the list of émigrés.[19]

Liancourt had taken advantage of the time to complete and publish his eight volumes of travels in the United States. "It is possible that it could have been better," Liancourt wrote to his old friend Arthur Young. But "my book is my work, as it is." He was neither the first nor the last author to console himself with such words. Perhaps predictably, given the state of Franco-American relations at the dawn of the nineteenth century, his book was not well received in the United States. "This poor French philosopher, half royalist, half Jacobin, has published a quarto volume of lies, nonsense, and trifles," wrote a reviewer in the *New York Commercial Advertiser*. "It would be difficult to find, in the world, a book so completely made of trash and tittle-tattle as this. It is not to be wondered that Europeans conceive the Americans, as little more civilized than savages: and particularly the French, who swallow down such histories of them as this of Liancourt." But even this hostile reviewer conceded that Liancourt's books were not entirely devoid of merit: "He now and then stumbles upon a fact, and sometimes makes a shrewd remark upon character." Fortunately, one might add, for posterity.[20]

The duc moved back to his former, if reduced, estate at Liancourt the following year, rejoicing in the quiet life it seemed to offer him. "I have once again become a *farmer*," he wrote to Young in 1802, "and even an *english farmer*." It was in his spectacular château, that, according to his son, he would occasionally dine with the fisherman who had ferried him across the English Channel in 1792; after their meal, the two would sit together on Liancourt's porch, surrounded by his vast gardens, smoking cigars.[21]

Liancourt recommitted himself to his philanthropy and reform efforts, which were the focus of the rest of his life. His particular interest remained agricultural reform, but he also threw himself into poor relief, education, prisons, manufacturing, hospitals, and vaccination campaigns. From 1806 to 1823 he served as the inspector general of the École nationale supérieure

François-Alexandre-Frédéric, duc de La Rochefoucauld-Liancourt, long after his return to France, as depicted in an 1836 portrait.

d'arts et métiers, the engineering school he had founded in 1780 at Liancourt for the children of poor soldiers. He died in his *hôtel particulier* on the rue Royal in Paris in 1827, at the age of eighty, having fallen back out of favor with the government for his liberalism, "one of the most virtuous, philanthropic, honored and honorable men of France," as the writer Alexandre Dumas pronounced at his funeral.[22]

IN 1812 Napoleon sent his Grande Armée of six hundred thousand troops into Russia. He clashed with his brother Louis, king of Holland, over furnishing that army with soldiers, forcing Louis to abdicate and give up Welgelegen, his home. But even as the emperor's brother lost a palace outside Amsterdam, Talleyrand gained one back in Paris.

Located in the heart of the city, on the corner of rue de Rivoli at rue Saint-Florentin, flanking the Place de la Concorde, it was only a three-minute walk from Liancourt's Paris home. Talleyrand's palace had once been called the Hôtel de Saint-Florentin and the Hôtel de l'Infantado, but soon it became known as the Hôtel Talleyrand. "For thirty years, from the depths of his palace, from the depths of his thought, he more or less led Europe," wrote Victor Hugo.

> In this palace, like a spider in his web, he lured and caught in succession heroes, thinkers, great men, conquerors, kings, princes, emperors, Bonaparte, Sieyès, Madame de Staël, Châteaubriand, Benjamin Constant, Alexander of Russia, William of Prussia, Francis of Austria, Louis XVIII, Louis Philippe, all the gilded and glittering flies who buzz through the history of the last forty years. All this glistening throng, fascinated by the penetrating eye of this man, passed in turn under that gloomy entrance, which, on the ornamental moulding above, carries the inscription: Hotel Talleyrand.

There he lived for more than a quarter century, at the center of that vast web, that panorama of nineteenth-century history, until he died in his palace, overlooking the cobblestones onto which so much revolutionary blood had spilled. According to Hugo, Talleyrand's body was embalmed and his brain, removed from his skull, was thrown into the sewer under the palace. But Hugo was writing satire, not history.[23]

In 1838 the hotel was purchased from Talleyrand's estate by James Mayer de Rothschild, one of Europe's preeminent bankers, who along with his four brothers financed French kings and French railroads and French industry throughout the nineteenth century, exceeding in wealth and power the Hopes and Barings alike. James and his brothers served as bankers to Europe and beyond, sending capital coursing from Europe's principal financial centers through the world's commercial arteries to the most distant parts of the globe. Few places were left untouched by their wealth, which helped shape the Victorian and belle epoque eras. To walk through Paris or London, New York or Buenos Aires today is to walk through cities their capital built.

Talleyrand's palace remained in the possession of the Rothschild family for over one hundred years. When the Rothschilds fled Paris in 1940, the Nazis occupied the *hôtel particulier* on the Place de la Concorde. They installed bunkers in the basement to protect them from American bombs. After Allied forces liberated Paris in 1944, the French government lent the palace to the triumphant American authorities; in 1950, the U.S. government purchased it from the Rothschilds. From Talleyrand's palace in the heart of Paris, American officials administered a later diplomat's plan to reconstruct postwar Europe, as capital began surging east across the Atlantic and a continent once again ravaged by war now rebuilt itself with American capital.

France and the United States had by then come full circle.

NOTE ON QUOTATIONS AND TRANSLATIONS

A s many readers will know, spelling, punctuation, capital-ization, and grammar were a good deal more flexible in the eighteenth century than they are today. When quoting material in the text, I tried to be as rigorously faithful as possible to the original, and avoided cluttering up the book with the distracting "[*sic*]." When quoting from a French-language document, I most often translated directly from the original French. When an English-language translation was available, I generally referred to it for help in maintaining the eighteenth-century flavor of the language but often adapted the wording when greater precision seemed necessary. When a grammatical or spelling "mistake" existed in the original French, on the other hand, I generally translated the original into more grammatically correct English prose rather than try to invent an English equivalent. Some French I left in the original, as it was often hard to know what to translate. The line between French and English gets somewhat blurry when you look too closely. Proper names of people and organizations have been left in roman text, while other French words were italicized.

ACKNOWLEDGMENTS

I owe an impossibly large debt to the rich community of friends and scholars of which I am privileged to be a part.

First and foremost, this book could not have been written without the generous material support from a variety of institutions. I wish everyone were lucky enough to work in a place as supportive of the humanities and social sciences as Canada and Quebec still are. The majority of the research support for this book was provided by two grants from the Social Science and Humanities Research of Canada and one from the Fonds de recherche du Québec—Société et culture. They made it possible for me to conduct research in far-flung archives, to present my ideas at many conferences, workshops, and seminars, and to support students along the way. *Merci infiniment!*

I am grateful to the New-York Historical Society for a short-term research fellowship. Two longer-term residential fellowships proved particularly helpful at critical stages of the project. One semester at the Library Company through the Program in Early American Society and Economy in the fall of 2004 got the research started. I will long be grateful to Cathy Matson for her warm and continuing support through the years and to Jim Green for, well, many things. That fellowship also gave me access to the unparalleled McNeil Center for Early American Studies, which I finally joined in an official capacity after many years as an unofficial hanger-on. Thanks to Dan Richter for shepherding such a wonderful community. My second residential fellowship took place at the New York Public Library's Dorothy and Lewis B. Cullman Center for Scholars and Writers, where I spent the Best Year of My Life.™ That fellowship gave me more than I could ever have hoped, personally and intellectually. I am grateful to my fellow Cullmanites for their comradeship and to Jean Strouse and Marie d'Origny for their inspired leadership. Alas, it's all downhill from there.

At the Université de Montréal, it was my pleasure to work with a group of wonderful students who helped my research and thinking: the many undergraduates who enriched my life in ways too numerous to mention, as well as the many graduate students who contributed so much. I am particularly grateful to: David Austin, Marie-Ève Beausoleil, Charles Brochu-Blain, Tamara Corriveau, François Dansereau, Julie de Chantal, Jonathan Harmon, Ariane Jacques-Côté, Laurie Laplanche, François Dominic Laramée, Guillaume Simard, Sarah Templier, Catherine Tourangeau, and Alexandre Trépanier. Élizabeth Grou deserves special mention for her heroic efforts with the images. I will miss them all greatly but look forward to staying in touch. My thanks to the department of history for its support and to the SGPUM for standing up for me. I would be remiss if I did not also acknowledge here the warmth with which Gérard Boismenu encouraged my move to Baltimore.

My return to Johns Hopkins came at the very end of writing this book, and what a privilege it is. I am first and foremost grateful to Mike Johnson and Dorothy Ross, who were my mentors years ago and who continue to serve as readers, interlocutors, and models of intellectual rigor and integrity. Thanks also to Phil Morgan, who has been a champion. Last but not least, I'm grateful to the History Seminar for feedback at several stages of the research and writing. I am thrilled to return to a group of colleagues and students with such a rich intellectual life, which I can now call home.

I presented parts of my research at seminars, conferences, and other venues too numerous to name. My apologies to all those who provided helpful comments and feedback along the way, and whom I have failed to acknowledge here. I am truly fortunate to be a part of such a generous community of scholars. I owe important debts to David Bell, Tom Bender, Elizabeth Blackmar, Richard Bushman, Drew Cayton, Joan DeJean, Eric Hinderaker, Jim Kloppenberg, Guy Lazure, Neil Safier, Pierre-Yves Saunier, and Anders Stephanson. A special thanks to Marie-Jeanne Rossignol, incomparable colleague and friend, who invited me twice to the Centre Charles V at the Université Paris Diderot–Paris 7, enabled two wonderful summers of fruitful research, and introduced me to the outstanding group of American and Atlantic historians in Paris, including Marcel Dorigny and Allan Potofsky. My debt to her is enormous. Zara Anishanslin, Susan Dalton, Evan Haefeli, Eric Hinderaker, Cathy Matson, Ellen Miles, Gary Nash, Andy Shankman, Billy Smith, David Steinberg, Karim Tiro, and Ashli White all read pieces of the manuscript and saved me from many glaring errors even as they offered wonderfully rich insight. David Bell, Robin Blackburn, Drew Cayton, Mike Johnson, Katherine Smoak, and David Waldstreicher went even further, reading the entire manuscript and offering many penetrating comments. None can be blamed for any errors that remain.

Many thanks to Andrew Wylie for his gracious support, as well as to everyone at Penguin: Scott Moyers, who has shepherded the book through while wearing many hats; Laura Stickney, who first saw promise in the manuscript; Mally Anderson, who picked up an orphan and raised it to maturity; Bruce Giffords; Yamil Anglada; and Tessa Meischeid. Thanks also to Maureen Clark for her truly outstanding copyediting.

This book was written while I lived in Montreal—in my humble opinion, the world's greatest city. My colleagues in the Groupe d' histoire de l'Atlantique français provided me with an intellectual home and continually stimulating conversations and activities. I am especially grateful to the friends in Montreal who provided me with a rich social and intellectual life: Sarah Bartok, Rui Castro, Susan Dalton, James Delbourgo, Mylène Desautels, Kate Desbarats, Nick Dew, Carolyn Fick, Silvia Gonçalves, Allan Greer, Ollivier Hubert, Laura Kopp, Jean-Pierre Le Glaunec, Laurence Monnais, David Meren, Cynthia Milton, Omri Moses, Andrew Piper, Tinka Markham Piper, Bruno Ramirez, Greg Robinson, Bob Rutledge, Emmanuelle Simoni, Daviken Studnicki-Gizbert, Anoush Terjanian, Till Van Rahden, Tom Wien, and Anya Zilberstein. *Merci à vous tous.*

Finally, I am most grateful to my family who have supported me along the way: many Codaccionis and derivatives thereof; Gilberte Furstenberg, Mark Furstenberg, Philippe Furstenberg, and all the other Furstenbergs; all the various *Ghjunchitacci*; the Guzmans; Alan Long; the Patels; and, above all, Yliette Guzman.

APPENDIX: FRENCH RESIDENTS ON SOUTH SECOND STREET, PHILADELPHIA

STREET NO.	LAST NAME	FIRST NAME	OCCUPATION	PLACE OF ORIGIN	DATES AT RESIDENCE
19	Berniaud	Claude	China merchant		1795–99
19	Dumas		China merchant		1794–98
19	Jacques	Toussaint	China merchant		1794–98
43	Nicholas	Michael	Shopkeeper		1795–97
43	Nicholas	[Mrs.]	Toy shop		1798
53	Moret	Anthony Lewis	Merchant	Hispaniola	1794–95
53	Marechaux	John	Merchant		1794–95
53	Mauranges	John Baptist	Merchant		1797–98
54	Marechaux	John	Merchant	French	1795
57	Dumoutet		Goldsmith and jeweler		1794–97
57	Bourgeois	Francis	Engraver and enameler	Paris and London	1797
61	Dorfeuille	[Sir] Martin Godfrey	Shopkeeper, schoolmaster, circulating library	Cap-Français	1794–95
61	Morel	John	Hairdresser and perfumer		1795
61	Lacave	John	Hairdresser	Paris	1797–98
61	Quesnet	B.	Dancing master		1794
63	Gouin du Fief		Schoolmaster	Nantes	
63	De Sauque	Louis	Confectioner and distiller		1798–99
67	Dubasque	Lewis	Merchant		1795
71	Chat	Claudius	Jeweler, goldsmith	Paris	1798
71	Chardon	Antoine	Paper manufacturer	Paris	1795–98

STREET NO.	LAST NAME	FIRST NAME	OCCUPATION	PLACE OF ORIGIN	DATES AT RESIDENCE
75	Chardon	Antoine	Paper manufacturer	Paris	1794
86	Richardet	Samuel	City Tavern and Merchant's Coffee House		1796–99
	Linion	Philip	Brewer	Québec	1792
91	Pasquier		China merchant	France	1796–97
91	Decamps	B.	Glass engraver and china merchant		1797–99
112	Descuret	Louis	Goldsmith and jeweler	Saint Domingue	
122	Duport	Pierre Landrin	Dancing master	Paris	1790
124	Brugniens	Bernard	Baker	France	1795–97
135	Rousset	Joseph	Hatter		1795–1800
135	Malambré	Jacob	Shoemaker		1799
164	Dutilh	Étienne	Merchant		1799
166	Collet	Charles	Confectioner		1797
167	Lafette	Peter	Gentleman, French boardinghouse		1795–98
169	Blondel	Antoine	Goldsmith and jeweler	Saint Domingue	1794–99
169	Descuret	Louis	Goldsmith and jeweler	Saint-Domingue	1794–99
	Palmer	John	Watchmaker		1795
178	Bugniard	Charles	Hairdresser		1798
185	Heraud	Joseph	Cook and caterer	France	1792–93
185	Imbert	Félix	Merchant	French Caribbean	1794–95
189	Chemerinot		Pastry cook		1799
193	Serre		Habit maker	France	1792–93
193	Dumoutet				1799
196	Bouvier	John Baptist	Umbrella maker		1798–99
Corner of Pine St.	Breuil	Francis	Merchant, slave trade	Saint Domingue	1803
Between Pine St. and Lombard St.	Dozel		Dancing master	Paris	1792
204	Tarascon	Lewis A.	Merchant	France	1798
204	Jounel	John Victor	Merchant	France	1798

STREET NO.	LAST NAME	FIRST NAME	OCCUPATION	PLACE OF ORIGIN	DATES AT RESIDENCE
208	Bonnaud	Cadet	Merchant		1798–99
211	Tarascon	Lewis A.	Merchant	France	1799
Between 211 and 221	Constance	[Miss]	Shopkeeper and hairdresser	Paris	1795
215	Bastide	Anthony	Umbrella maker	Paris	1794
215	Clastrie	John	Sugar maker		1798
220	Le Boutilier		Merchant		1795–97
228	Massane	Catharine	Shopkeeper, widow		1795
245	Munier	Nicholas	Hairdresser		1798
251	Thibault		Goldsmith and jeweler		1798
252	Boullance	Madame			1797
254	Jaymond		Pastry cook		1797
254 (245?)	Simonet	Chrétien	Pastry cook and confectioner		1795–98
259	Rossett	Francis	Hatter		1797
266	Bouché	Gabriel	Merchant	Saint Domingue	1793
266	Rodrigue	Victor	Merchant	Saint Domingue	1793
270	Treillé	Joseph	Hairdresser		
280	Morel	Alexander	Silk dyer	Lyon	1790
319	Bordeaux	Augustine	Jeweler		1799

NOTES

ABBREVIATIONS

Archives and archival collections

APS American Philosophical Society, Philadelphia, Pennsylvania
AN Archives nationales, Paris
BaP Baring Archives, London
CML-BaP Correspondence in Regard to Maine Lands (typescript), 3 vols., Baring Archives, London
CPÉU Correspondance politique, États-Unis
HSP Historical Society of Pennsylvania, Philadelphia
LoC Library of Congress, Washington, DC
MAÉ Archives du ministère des affaires étrangères, Paris
MHS Massachusetts Historical Society, Boston
NYHS New-York Historical Society

Published works

AFPEA Adams Family Papers: An Electronic Archive, Massachusetts Historical Society, http://www.masshist.org/digitaladams
ANB American National Biography Online, Feb. 2000, http://www.anb.org/
APDE Adams Papers Digital Editions, v. 1.0, Massachusetts Historical Society, http://www.masshist.org/publications/apde/index.php
ASPFRS American State Papers: Foreign Relations Series, http://memory.loc.gov/ammem/amlaw/lwsp.html
CFM Frederick Jackson Turner, ed., *Annual Report of the American Historical Association for the Year 1903*, vol. 2, *Correspondence of the French Ministers to the United States, 1791–1797* (Washington, DC: Government Printing Office, 1904)
MCGPA Frederick Jackson Turner, ed., "The Mangourit Correspondence in Respect to Genet's Projected Attack upon the Floridas, 1793–94," in *Annual Report of the American Historical Association for the Year 1897*, vol. 1 (Washington, DC: Government Printing Office, 1898)
PAH Harold Syrett, ed., *The Papers of Alexander Hamilton*, 17 vols. (New York: Columbia University Press, 1961–1987)
PGWPS Dorothy Twohig, et al., eds., *The Papers of George Washington: Presidential Series*, 17 vols. to date (Charlottesville: University of Virginia Press, 1987–)
PJM William T. Hutchinson, et al., eds., *The Papers of James Madison*, 17 vols. to date (Chicago: University of Chicago Press, 1962–)
PJMSS Robert J. Brugger, et al., eds., *The Papers of James Madison: Secretary of State Series*, 9 vols. to date (Charlottesville: University of Virginia Press, 1986–)

PTJ Julian P. Boyd, et al., eds., *The Papers of Thomas Jefferson*, 39 vols. to date (Princeton: Princeton University Press, 1950–)

SFDC "Selections from the Draper Collection in the Possession of the State Historical Society of Wisconsin, to Elucidate the Proposed French Expedition under George Rogers Clark against Louisiana, in the Years 1793–94," in *Annual Report of the American Historical Association for the Year 1896*, vol. 1 (Washington, DC: Government Printing Office, 1897)

TAFP Hans Huth and Wilma J. Pugh, eds., *Talleyrand in America as a Financial Promoter, 1794–96: Unpublished Letters and Memoirs* (Washington, DC: Government Printing Office, 1942)

WBML Frederick S. Allis, *William Bingham's Maine Lands, 1790–1820*, vols. 26 and 27 (Boston: Colonial Society of Massachusetts, 1954); continuous pagination

Journals

AHR American Historical Review
JAH Journal of American History
PMHB Pennsylvania Magazine of History and Biography
WMQ William and Mary Quarterly, 3rd. series

People

AA Abigail Adams
AA2 Abigail Adams Smith
AB Alexander Baring
AH Alexander Hamilton
FB Francis Baring
GW George Washington
JA John Adams
JM James Madison
JQA John Quincy Adams
TJ Thomas Jefferson
WB William Bingham

STRANGE REUNIONS: AN INTRODUCTION

1. M. L. E. Moreau de Saint-Méry, *Moreau de St. Méry's American Journey, 1793–1798*, ed. Kenneth Lewis Roberts and Anna M. Roberts (Garden City, NY: Doubleday, 1947), 91–92.

2. François-Alexandre-Frédéric La Rochefoucauld-Liancourt, *Journal de voyage en Amérique et d'un séjour à Philadelphie*, ed. Jean Marchand (Paris: Librairie R. Clavreuil, 1940), 58, 60–61. Liancourt's ship—which had also transported Noailles the year before—was alternately called the *Pigou* (by most newspapers), *Pigow* (by Liancourt), and *Pigeon* (by Moreau): ibid., 25n4.

3. Volney scene: Charles Alexandre Geoffroy de Grandmaison, ed., *Mémoires du comte de Moré: 1758–1837* (Paris: A. Picard et fils, 1898), 162; Orléans living with brothers: Samuel Breck to John McAllister, Dec. 15, 1854, Society Small Collection, HSP; Liancourt's "grand dinner" and dinners at the Tuileries and Volney's participation: Arthur Young, *Travels in France during the Years 1787, 1788, and 1789*, ed. Jeffry Kaplow (Garden City, NY: Anchor Books, 1969), 220, 226.

4. Moreau, *American Journey*, 214–15.

5. Condorcet to TJ, Dec. 21, 1792, *PTJ*, 24:761.

6. Mirabeau quoted in Duff Cooper, *Talleyrand* (1932; repr., New York: Grove Press, 2001), 28.

7. Liancourt, *Journal*, 101, 87. Additional biographical information for Liancourt comes from Frédéric Gaëtan de La Rochefoucauld-Liancourt, *Vie du duc de La Rochefoucauld-Liancourt (François-Alexandre-Frédéric), par Frédéric-Gaëtan, comte de La Rochefoucauld, son fils* (Paris: A. Henry, 1831); René Mantel, "La Rochefoucauld-Liancourt: Un novateur français dans la pratique agricole du XVIIIe siècle," in *Études d'histoire économique rurale au XVIIIe siècle*, ed. Albert Rigaudière, Evelyne Zilberman, and René Mantel (Paris: Presses univer-

sitaires de France, 1965), 151–68; Jean Dominique de La Rochefoucauld, Claudine Wolikow, Guy Ikni, *Le duc de La Rochefoucauld-Liancourt: 1747–1827: de Louis XV à Charles X, un grand seigneur patriote et le mouvement populaire* (Paris: Perrin, 1980); and "La Rochefoucauld-Liancourt, François-Alexandre-Frédéric, duc de," in *Dictionnaire des constituants: 1789–1791,* ed. Edna Hindie Lemay, Christine Favre-Lejeune, Yann Fauchois, and Alison Patrick (Paris: Universitas, 1991), 2:534–37.

8. Samuel Breck, "Recollections of My Acquaintance and Association with Deceased Members of the American Philosophical Society" (ms bound copy), APS. See also Gilbert Chinard, *Volney et l'Amérique d'après des documents inédits et sa correspondance avec Jefferson* (Baltimore: Johns Hopkins Press; Paris: Les presses universitaires de France, 1923), 7–27.

9. M. L. E. Moreau de Saint-Méry, *Description topographique, physique, civile, politique et historique de la partie française de l'isle Saint-Domingue. . . . ,* 2 vols. (Philadelphie: [Moreau], 1797); Liancourt, *Journal,* 78, 112; the duel: Moreau, *American Journey,* 183–84.

10. Noailles to Windham, June 1, 1793, *The Windham Papers: The Life and Correspondence of the Rt. Hon. William Windham, 1750–1810. . . . ,* 2 vols. (London: Herbert Jenkins, 1913), 1:122.

11. My ideas and research on these five men and their experiences in the United States have benefited tremendously from the excellent scholarship on them specifically, and on the French and Saint Domingue émigrés in Philadelphia and the United States more generally. See Fernand Baldensperger, "Le séjour de Talleyrand aux États-Unis," *Revue de Paris* 6 (1924): 364–87; Paul D. Evans, "Deux émigrés en Amérique: Talleyrand et Beaumez," *La Révolution française* 79 (1926): 51–61; Frances Sergeant Childs, *French Refugee Life in the United States, 1790–1800: An American Chapter of the French Revolution* (Baltimore: Johns Hopkins Press, 1940); Durand Echeverria, *Mirage in the West: A History of the French Image of American Society to 1815* (New York: Octagon Books, 1966); John L. Earl III, "Talleyrand in Philadelphia, 1794–1796," *PMHB* 91, no. 3 (1967): 282–98; Arnold Whitridge, "French Émigrés in Philadelphia," *Virginia Quarterly Review* 44, no. 2 (1968): 285–301; Michel Poniatowski, *Talleyrand aux États-Unis, 1794–1796* ([Paris?]: Librairie académique Perrin, 1976); Anne Catherine Bieri Hébert, "The Pennsylvania French in the 1790's: The Story of Their Survival" (Ph.D. diss., University of Texas at Austin, 1981); Catherine A. Hebert, "The French Element in Pennsylvania in the 1790s: The Francophone Immigrants' Impact," *PMHB* 108, no. 4 (1984): 451–69; La Rochefoucauld, Wolikow, and Ikni, *Le duc de La Rochefoucauld-Liancourt,* 221–78; Catherine Therese Spaeth, "Purgatory or Promised Land?: French Emigrés in Philadelphia and Their Perceptions of America during the 1790s" (Ph.D. diss., University of Minnesota, 1992); Thomas C. Sosnowski, "Bitter Farewells: Francophobia and the French Émigrés in America," *Consortium on Revolutionary Europe 1750–1850: Proceedings* 21 (1992): 276–83; Gary Nash, "Reverberations of Haiti in the American North: Black Saint Dominguans in Philadelphia," *Explorations in Early American Culture: A Special Supplemental Issue of Pennsylvania History* 65 (1998): 44–73; Thomas C. Sosnowski, "French Émigrés in the United States," in *The French Émigrés in Europe and the Struggle against Revolution, 1789–1814,* ed. Kirsty Carpenter and Mansel Philip (New York: St. Martin's Press, 1999); Darrell R. Meadows, "Engineering Exile: Social Networks and the French Atlantic Community, 1789–1809," *French Historical Studies* 23, no. 1 (2000): 128–50; Susan Branson and Leslie Patrick, "French Refugees from Saint Domingue to the Southern United States," in *The Impact of the Haitian Revolution on the Atlantic World,* ed. David P. Geggus (Columbia: University of South Carolina Press, 2001), 193–208; Paul Lachance, "Repercussions of the Haitian Revolution in Louisiana," in *The Impact of the Haitian Revolution in the Atlantic World,* 209–30; Allan Potofsky, "Émigrés et réfugiés de la Révolution française aux Etats-Unis," in *Exilés et réfugiés politiques aux États-Unis, 1789–2000,* ed. Catherine Collomp and Mario Menendez (Paris: CNRS éditions, 2003), 33–50; Nathalie Dessens, *From Saint-Domingue to New Orleans: Migration and Influences* (Gainesville: University Press of Florida, 2007); John Davies, "Class, Culture, and Color: Black Saint-Dominguan Refugees and African-American Communities in the Early Republic" (Ph.D. diss., University of Delaware, 2008); Ashli White, *Encountering Revo-*

lution: Haiti and the Making of the Early Republic (Baltimore: Johns Hopkins University Press, 2010); John Davies, "Saint-Dominguan Refugees of African Descent and the Forging of Ethnic Identity in Early National Philadelphia," *PMHB* 134, no. 2 (2010): 109–26. The book that comes closest to mine in its focus is the excellent study by Doina Pasca Harsanyi, *Lessons from America: Liberal French Nobles in Exile, 1793–1798* (University Park: Pennsylvania State Press, 2010), which deserves a special mention.

For recent work that connects the United States to the French Caribbean, see, in addition to the works mentioned above, Sibylle Fischer, *Modernity Disavowed: Haiti and the Cultures of Slavery in the Age of Revolution* (Durham, NC: Duke University Press, 2004); Sean X. Goudie, *Creole America: The West Indies and the Formation of Literature and Culture in the New Republic* (Philadelphia: University of Pennsylvania Press, 2006); Robin Blackburn, "Haiti, Slavery, and the Age of Democratic Revolution," *WMQ* 63, no. 4 (2006): 643–74; Christopher P. Iannini, *Fatal Revolutions: Natural History, West Indian Slavery, and the Routes of American Literature* (Chapel Hill: University of North Carolina Press, 2012); Sara E. Johnson, *The Fear of French Negroes: Transcolonial Collaboration in the Revolutionary Americas* (Berkeley: University of California Press, 2012). See also Christopher Hodson, *The Acadian Diaspora: An Eighteenth-Century History* (New York: Oxford University Press, 2012).

12. A vast literature has emphasized the importance of the French Revolution and Franco-British warfare to the development of domestic U.S. politics and political culture in the 1790s. It would be impossible to cite all that scholarship. Among the works that have most helped my analysis—and in addition to those cited above—see John Chester Miller, *The Federalist Era, 1789–1801* (New York: Harper, 1960), 126–82; Richard Buel, *Securing the Revolution: Ideology in American Politics, 1789–1815* (Ithaca, NY: Cornell University Press, 1972), 28–71; Ruth H. Bloch, *Visionary Republic: Millennial Themes in American Thought, 1756–1800* (Cambridge: Cambridge University Press, 1985), 150–86; David Brion Davis, *Revolutions: Reflections on American Equality and Foreign Liberations* (Cambridge, MA: Harvard University Press, 1990); Rachel N. Klein, *Unification of a Slave State: The Rise of the Planter Class in the South Carolina Backcountry, 1760–1808* (Chapel Hill: University of North Carolina Press, 1990), 203–37; Stanley M. Elkins and Eric L. McKitrick, *The Age of Federalism* (New York: Oxford University Press, 1993), 303–449; Marie-Jeanne Rossignol, *Le ferment nationaliste: Aux origines de la politique extérieure des Etats-Unis, 1789–1812* (Paris: Belin, 1994) (*The Nationalist Ferment: The Origins of U.S. Foreign Policy, 1789–1812*, trans. Lillian A. Parrott [Columbus: Ohio State University Press, 2004]); David Waldstreicher, *In the Midst of Perpetual Fetes: The Making of American Nationalism, 1776–1820* (Chapel Hill: University of North Carolina Press, 1997), 126–41; Simon P. Newman, *Parades and Politics of the Street: Festive Culture in the Early American Republic* (Philadelphia: University of Pennsylvania Press, 1997), 120–51; Susan Branson, *These Fiery Frenchified Dames: Women and Political Culture in Early National Philadelphia* (Philadelphia: University of Pennsylvania Press, 2001); Matthew Rainbow Hale, "Neither Britons nor Frenchmen: The French Revolution and American National Identity" (Ph.D. diss, Brandeis University, 2002); Matthew Rainbow Hale, "'Many Who Wandered in Darkness': The Contest over American National Identity, 1795–1798," *Early American Studies* 1, no. 1 (Spring 2003): 127–75; Rachel Hope Cleves, *The Reign of Terror in America: Visions of Violence from Anti-Jacobinism to Antislavery* (New York: Cambridge University Press, 2009), 58–103; Gordon S. Wood, *Empire of Liberty: A History of the Early Republic, 1789–1815* (New York: Oxford University Press, 2009), 174–208.

13. The attempt to transnationalize U.S. history largely gained momentum during the 1990s, with important works by Ian Tyrrell and Thomas Bender: Ian Tyrrell, "American Exceptionalism in an Age of International History," *AHR* 96, no. 4 (1991): 1031–55; Organization of American Historians, *La Pietra Report: Project on Internationalizing the Study of American History* ([New York?]: Organization of American Historians, 2000); Thomas Bender, *Rethinking American History in a Global Age* (Berkeley: University of California Press, 2002);

Thomas Bender, *A Nation among Nations: America's Place in World History* (New York: Hill & Wang, 2006); and Ian R. Tyrrell, *Transnational Nation: United States History in Global Perspective since 1789* (Basingstoke: Palgrave Macmillan, 2007). They all drew on an early statement by Akira Iriye, "The Internationalization of History," *AHR* 94, no. 1 (1989): 1–10. For an even broader perspective and general historiographical survey, see Pierre-Yves Saunier, *Transnational History* (New York: Palgrave Macmillan, 2013).

It was also in the 1990s that Bernard Bailyn began to organize his seminars in Atlantic history, an approach that grew out of his previous scholarship on migration to the British American colonies. His early thinking was summarized in Bernard Bailyn, *The Peopling of British North America: An Introduction* (New York: Alfred A. Knopf, 1986). Bailyn summed up his later conception of Atlantic history in *Atlantic History: Concept and Contours* (Cambridge, MA: Harvard University Press, 2005), and published an important collection of work that grew out of his seminar in Bernard Bailyn and Patricia L. Denault, *Soundings in Atlantic History: Latent Structures and Intellectual Currents, 1500–1830* (Cambridge, MA: Harvard University Press, 2009). Much of the theoretical underpinning for Atlantic history had been built by the work of Jack P. Greene and his students in the previous decades. For a synthesis of Greene's approach, see especially Jack P. Greene and Philip D. Morgan, *Atlantic History: A Critical Appraisal* (New York: Oxford University Press, 2009). I have cited more works on Atlantic history that have particularly influenced my thinking in François Furstenberg, "The Significance of the Trans-Appalachian Frontier in Atlantic History," *AHR* 113, no. 3 (2008): 647–77.

Both these trends accelerated in the 2000s. For historiographical assessments of Atlantic and international approaches, see Joyce E. Chaplin, "Expansion and Exceptionalism in Early American History," *JAH* 89, no. 4 (2003): 1431–55, and Rosemarie Zagarri, "The Significance of the 'Global Turn' for the Early American Republic: Globalization in the Age of Nation-Building," *Journal of the Early Republic* 31, no. 1 (2011): 1–37. Some critical responses to the moves to Atlanticize and internationalize U.S. history that have particularly influenced my thinking are Silvia Marzagalli, "Sur les origines de l'Atlantic History," *Dix-huitième siècle* 33 (2001): 17–31; Ian K. Steele, "Bernard Bailyn's American Atlantic," *History and Theory* 46 (2007): 48–58; Louis A. Perez Jr., "We Are the World: Internationalizing the National, Nationalizing the International," *JAH* 89, no. 2 (2002): 558–66; and, more recently, Johann N. Neem, "American History in a Global Age," *History & Theory* 50, no. 1 (2011). Finally, I have found myself increasingly influenced by geographical space and geographical approaches to historical narrative. For a fine essay on the subject, see Robert J. Mayhew, "Historical Geography, 2009–2010: Geohistoriography, the Forgotten Braudel and the Place of Nominalism," *Progress in Human Geography* 35, no. 3 (2011): 409–21.

14. Among the works of the Progressive school that can still speak to contemporary historians are Frederick Jackson Turner, "The Problem of the West," *Atlantic Monthly* 78, no. 468 (1896); Frederick Jackson Turner, "Contributions of the West to American Democracy," *Atlantic Monthly* 91, no. 543 (Jan. 1903); Frederick J. Turner, "The Middle West," *International Monthly* 4 (July 1901); Frederick Jackson Turner, "The Policy of France toward the Mississippi Valley in the Period of Washington and Adams," *AHR* 10, no. 2 (1905); Charles Austin Beard, *An Economic Interpretation of the Constitution of the United States* (1913; New York: Free Press, 1986); Vernon Louis Parrington, *Main Currents in American Thought: An Interpretation of American Literature from the Beginnings to 1920*, 3 vols. (New York: Harcourt, 1927); Arthur Preston Whitaker, *The Spanish-American Frontier: 1783–1795; The Westward Movement and the Spanish Retreat in the Mississippi Valley* (Boston: Houghton Mifflin, 1927); Thomas Perkins Abernethy, *From Frontier to Plantation in Tennessee: A Study in Frontier Democracy* (Chapel Hill: University of North Carolina Press, 1932); Thomas Perkins Abernethy, *Western Lands and the American Revolution* (New York: D. Appleton-Century, 1937); and Arthur Preston Whitaker, *The Mississippi Question, 1795–1803* (1934; Gloucester, MA: Peter Smith, 1962).

Notes

PART 1: THE UNITED STATES SPEAKS FRENCH

1 Details on the balloon trip have been drawn from Carroll Frey, ed., *The First Air Voyage in America: The Times, the Place, and the People of the Blanchard Balloon Voyage of January 9, 1793, Philadelphia to Woodbury, Together with a Fac Simile Reprinting of the Journal of My Forty-Fifth Ascension and the First in America* (Philadelphia: Penn Mutual Life Insurance Company, 1943); Lewis Leary, "Phaeton in Philadelphia: Jean Pierre Blanchard and the First Balloon Ascension in America, 1793," *PMHB* 67, no. 1 (1943): 52; "Blanchard" file, Francis Dallett Papers, box 2, folder 14, HSP. Quotations are from *Gazette of the United States* (Philadelphia), Jan. 5, 1793, and *Daily Advertiser* (New York), Jan. 9, 1793. See also *Dunlap's American Daily Advertiser* (Philadelphia), Jan. 11, 1793. A friend wrote to Madison about the flight, but Madison himself does not mention it: Richard Peters to JM, Feb. 26, 1793, *PJM*, 14:453–54.
2. *Federal Gazette* (Philadelphia), Jan. 9, 1793. For the text of the Washington letter: "Pass for Jean-Pierre Blanchard," *PGWPS*, 11:602–4.
3. "Admiration was painted": *Federal Gazette* (Philadelphia), Jan. 9, 1793; "could not help": Jean-Pierre Blanchard, *Journal of My Forty-Fifth Ascension, Being the First Performed in America, on the Ninth of January, 1793* (Philadelphia: Charles Cist, 1793), 15. Additional information was gleaned from *Dunlap's American Daily Advertiser* (Philadelphia), Jan. 10, 1793; *General Advertiser* (Philadelphia), Jan. 10, 1793.
4. Blanchard, *Journal*, 15. On the chimney sweep, see Julian Ursyn Niemcewicz, *Under Their Vine and Fig Tree: Travels through America in 1797–1799*, trans. Metchie J. E. Budka (Elizabeth, NJ: Grassmann, 1965), 38.
5. François-Alexandre-Frédéric La Rochefoucauld-Liancourt, *Voyage dans les États-Unis d'Amérique, fait en 1795, 1796 et 1797*, 8 vols. (Paris: Du Pont, 1799), 4:329–30.
6. Philadelphia housing prices: Carole Shammas, "The Housing Stock of the Early United States: Refinement Meets Migration," *WMQ* 64, no. 3 (2007): 566.
7. Carole Shammas, "The Space Problem in Early United States Cities," *WMQ* 57, no. 3 (2000): 520; Joseph J. Kelley, *Life and Times in Colonial Philadelphia* (Harrisburg, PA: Stackpole Books, 1973), 54; Amy Hudson Henderson, "Furnishing the Republican Court: Building and Decorating Philadelphia Homes, 1790–1800" (Ph.D. diss., University of Delaware, 2008), 88. See also Elizabeth Gray Kogen Spera, "Building for Business: The Impact of Commerce on the City Plan and Architecture of the City of Philadelphia, 1750–1800" (Ph.D. diss., University of Pennsylvania, 1980), 146–50; Thomas M. Doerflinger, *A Vigorous Spirit of Enterprise: Merchants and Economic Development in Revolutionary Philadelphia* (Chapel Hill: University of North Carolina Press, 1986), 37–45; Sam Bass Warner, *The Private City: Philadelphia in Three Periods of Its Growth*, 2nd ed. (Philadelphia: University of Pennsylvania Press, 1987), 11–12.
8. "striking odor": quoted in Jean Gaulmier, *L'idéologue Volney, 1757–1820: Contribution à l'histoire de l'orientalisme en France* (Genève: Slatkine, 1980), 358. The details about Philadelphia are drawn largely from Moreau de Saint-Méry, *Voyage aux États-Unis de l'Amérique, 1793–1798*, ed. Stewart L. Mims (New Haven, CT: Yale University Press, 1913); Susan E. Klepp, *Philadelphia in Transition: A Demographic History of the City and Its Occupational Groups, 1720–1830* (New York: Garland, 1989), 225–32; Billy Gordon Smith, *The "Lower Sort": Philadelphia's Laboring People, 1750–1800* (Ithaca, NY: Cornell University Press, 1990); Mary M. Schweitzer, "The Spatial Organization of Federalist Philadelphia, 1790," *Journal of Interdisciplinary History* 24, no. 1 (1993); Shammas, "Space Problem," 525; Gary B. Nash, *First City: Philadelphia and the Forging of Historical Memory* (Philadelphia: University of Pennsylvania Press, 2002); Simon P. Newman, *Embodied History: The Lives of the Poor in Early Philadelphia* (Philadelphia: University of Pennsylvania Press, 2003); and Ryan K. Smith, *Robert Morris's Folly: The Architectural and Financial Failures of an American Founder* (New Haven: Yale University Press, 2014) chap. 4. The juxtaposition between the Birch images and my own photographs in this section are offered here not, I hope, in the spirit of naïve realism, but rather in the spirit of furthering their effect of providing an embodied, spectatorial experi-

ence of 1790s Philadelphia. See Wendy Bellion, *Citizen Spectator: Art, Illusion, and Visual Perception in Early National America* (Chapel Hill: University of North Carolina Press, 2011), 113–69. The map in this section, "The Occupational Geography of Philadelphia, c. 1790," is based on painstaking research by Mary Schweitzer, who graciously gave me permission to draw on her conclusions presented in the article cited above. It is the best data we currently have on Philadelphia's social geography, although it is likely to be surpassed by the work being done by Paul Sivitz and Billy Smith. For the current state of their research, see "Philadelphia and Its People in Maps: The 1790s," http://philadelphiaencyclopedia.org/ archive/philadelphia-and-its-people-in-maps-the-1790s/, accessed Apr. 8, 2014.

9. One is reminded of a line from the great French historian Fernand Braudel, who has done so much to inspire my thinking about history and geography: "In truth the historian is a little like this traveler." Fernand Braudel, *La Méditerranée et le monde méditerranéen à l'époque de Philippe II*, 3 vols. (Paris: Armand Colin, 1990), 1:34.

CHAPTER 1: FRANCE COMES TO AMERICA

1. "love for war": Amblard-Marie-Raymond-Amédée Noailles, *Marins et soldats français en Amérique pendant la guerre de l'indépendance des États-Unis: 1778–1783* (Paris: Librairie académique Didier Perrin et cie, 1903), 103; dancing in Philadelphia: François Jean, marquis de Chastellux, *Voyages de M. le Marquis de Chastellux dans l'Amérique septentrionale*, 2 vols. (Paris: Prault, 1788), 1:239; "Vive le roi!" and "universal silence": Jerome A. Greene, *The Guns of Independence: The Siege of Yorktown, 1781* (New York: Savas Beatie, 2005), 263, 290–97; the scene: Douglas Southall Freeman, John Alexander Carroll, and Mary Wells Ashworth, *George Washington: A Biography*, 7 vols. (New York: Scribner, 1948), 4:383.

2. Noailles' connection with Franklin: Maréchal-Duc de Mouchy to Franklin [before Feb. 7, 1782], *Papers of Benjamin Franklin*, http://franklinpapers.org/franklin//intro.jsp, accessed Sept. 3, 2013; the Société des Trente: Timothy Tackett, *Becoming a Revolutionary: The Deputies of the French National Assembly and the Emergence of a Revolutionary Culture, 1789–1790* (Princeton, NJ: Princeton University Press, 1996), 89–90; "sketched": Jean Michel Pellerin, *Correspondance inédite de J.-M. Pellerin, député du tiers-état de la Senechaussée de Guérande aux États généraux....* (Paris: A. Sauton, 1883), 109; "patriotic drunkenness": Simon Schama, *Citizens: A Chronicle of the French Revolution* (New York: Alfred A. Knopf, 1989), 439; "let us only regret": Tackett, *Becoming a Revolutionary*, 172. On the liberal nobility's role in these events, see especially Harsanyi, *Lessons from America*, 3–21.

3. Chaos in the French armies after the declaration of war in 1792: David Avrom Bell, *The First Total War: Napoleon's Europe and the Birth of Warfare as We Know It* (Boston: Houghton Mifflin, 2007), 126–31; Noailles' resignation: Louis-Marie de Noailles, *Pièces relatives à la démission du Maréchal de camp Louis de Noailles* (Paris: Impr. de Du Pont, n.d.); Harsanyi, *Lessons from America*, 33–34; Burges's report: William Eden Baron Auckland, *The Journal and Correspondence of William, Lord Auckland*, 2 vols. (London: R. Bentley, 1861), 2:440–41.

4. Lord Auckland to Lord Grenville, Dec. 14, 1792, *The Manuscripts of J. B. Fortescue ... Preserved at Dropmore [Being Correspondence and Papers of Lord Grenville 1698–1820]*, 10 vols., Historical Manuscripts Commission (London: HMSO, 1892), 2:357.

5. Rochambeau's regiments: James Breck Perkins, *France in the American Revolution* (Williamstown, MA: Corner House Publishers, 1970), 302–4; "He dreamed" and "sanctioned": Louis-Philippe comte de Ségur, *Memoirs and Recollections of Count Segur ... Written by Himself ... Translated from the French*, 3 vols. (London: H. Colburn, 1825), 1:124, 102.

6. Noailles to Windham, June 1, 1793, *Windham Papers*, 1:121.

7. The description of the ship sailing in is from Niemcewicz, *Under Their Vine and Fig Tree*, 49.

8. *New Jersey State Gazette* (Trenton), May 8, 1793; TJ to Monroe, May 5, 1793, *PTJ*, 25:661.

9. "It is a tribute": Lafayette to GW, Mar. 17, 1790, *PGWPS*, 5:241; "Since the commencement": GW to Lafayette, June 10, 1792, *PGWPS*, 10:447; on this period of exultation: Echeverria, *Mirage in the West*, 116–74.

10. Philip Sheldon Foner, *The Democratic-Republican Societies, 1790–1800: A Documentary Sourcebook of Constitutions, Declarations, Addresses, Resolutions, and Toasts* (Westport, CT: Greenwood Press, 1976), 258, 22; Davis, *Revolutions,* 30; Bertrand Van Ruymbeke, "Fêtes républicaines et clubs Jacobins: Vivre la Révolution à Charleston en Caroline du Sud, 1792–1797," in *Cosmopolitismes, patriotismes, Europe et Amériques, 1773–1802,* ed. Marc Belissa and Barnard Cottret (Rennes: Perséides, 2005), 134–36; Eugene P. Link, *Democratic-Republican Societies, 1790–1800* (1942; repr., New York: Octagon Books, 1965), 87–88; Andrew Shankman, *Crucible of American Democracy: The Struggle to Fuse Egalitarianism & Capitalism in Jeffersonian Pennsylvania* (Lawrence: University Press of Kansas, 2004), 45–47; Michelle Orihel, "Political Fever: The Democratic Societies and the Crisis of Republican Governance in 1790s America" (Ph.D. diss., Syracuse University, 2010), 57–58. On American street culture in the age of the French Revolution, see especially Newman, *Parades and Politics of the Street;* Waldstreicher, *Perpetual Fetes;* Len Travers, *Celebrating the Fourth: Independence Day and the Rites of Nationalism in the Early Republic* (Amherst: University of Massachusetts Press, 1997); Mary P. Ryan, *Civic Wars: Democracy and Public Life in the American City during the Nineteenth Century* (Berkeley: University of California Press, 1997); Albrecht Koschnik, *"Let a Common Interest Bind Us Together": Associations, Partisanship, and Culture in Philadelphia, 1775–1840* (Charlottesville: University of Virginia Press, 2007). Good introductions to French revolutionary politics include William Doyle, *The Oxford History of the French Revolution* (Oxford: Oxford University Press, 2002), and Schama, *Citizens.*

11. "the liberty": TJ to Short, Jan. 3, 1793, *PTJ,* 25:14; see also William Hogeland, *The Whiskey Rebellion: George Washington, Alexander Hamilton, and the Frontier Rebels Who Challenged America's Newfound Sovereignty* (New York: Scribner, 2006), 138. The best treatment of the impact of French revolutionary violence on American political culture is Cleves, *Reign of Terror in America,* esp. 58–103. On the connection between the formation of political parties and the responses to the French Revolution, see the classic works of Joseph Charles, *The Origins of the American Party System: Three Essays* (Williamsburg, VA: Institute of Early American History and Culture, 1956), and Richard Hofstadter, *The Idea of a Party System: The Rise of Legitimate Opposition in the United States, 1780–1840* (Berkeley: University of California Press, 1969).

12. "The first cannons": Voltaire, *Fragmens sur l'Inde, sur le général Lalli, sur le procès du comte de Morangiès et sur plusieurs autres sujets* ([Londres?], 1774), 4; treaty with France: Samuel Flagg Bemis, *Jay's Treaty: A Study in Commerce and Diplomacy,* rev. ed. (New Haven, CT: Yale University Press, 1962), 187.

13. Genet's physical description: Passport for E. C. Genet, Edmond Charles Genet MMS, Oversize 1, Genet Papers, LoC. On the Genet mission and its implications for Franco-American relations, see, in addition to the works cited above, Meade Minnigerode, *Jefferson, Friend of France, 1793: The Career of Edmond Charles Genet, Minister Plenipotentiary from the French Republic to the United States, as Revealed by His Private Papers, 1763–1834* (New York: G. P. Putnam's Sons, 1928); Harry Ammon, *The Genet Mission* (New York: Norton, 1973); Marco Sioli, "Citizen Genet and Political Struggle in the Early American Republic," *Revue française d'études américaines* 64 (1995); Tamara Corriveau, "Jacques-Pierre Brissot, Étienne Clavière et la libre Amérique: Du Gallo-Américanisme à la mission Genet" (master's thesis, Université de Montréal, 2008); Christopher J. Young, "Connecting the President and the People: Washington's Neutrality, Genet's Challenge, and Hamilton's Fight for Public Support," *Journal of the Early Republic* 31, no. 3 (2011). For more general accounts, see Miller, *Federalist Era,* 126–39; Elkins and McKitrick, *Age of Federalism,* 303–74; Waldstreicher, *Perpetual Fetes,* 126–41; Wood, *Empire of Liberty,* 174–208.

14. "long swells": Braudel, *La Méditerranée,* 1:271; *Embuscade* cleared the shoals: *City Gazette* (Charleston), Apr. 9, 1793; on the Gulf Stream and seaweed and water: Thomas Twining, *Travels in America 100 Years Ago. . . .* (New York: Harper & Brothers, 1894), 21; "drawn by": Genet to Minister of Foreign Affairs, Apr. 16, 1793, *CFM,* 212.

15. Genet to Lebrun, Apr. 16, 1793, *CFM*, 212–13; "Memorandum from Alexander Hamilton," *PAH*, 14:455. On the French Revolution in South Carolina, see also Klein, *Unification of a Slave State*, 203–37.
16. GW to TJ, Apr. 12, 1793, *PGWPS*, 12:448–49.
17. *Argus* (Boston), May 2, 1793.
18. *City Gazette* (Charleston), May 4, 1793.
19. Quotations and scene are drawn from *City Gazette* (Charleston), May 4, 1793; *General Advertiser* (Philadelphia), May 16, 17, and 20, 1793; *Federal Gazette* (Philadelphia), May 18 and 22, 1793; *Dunlap's American Daily Advertiser* (Philadelphia), May 23, 1793; James S. Biddle, ed., *Autobiography of Charles Biddle, Vice-President of the Supreme Executive Council of Pennsylvania, 1745–1821* (Philadelphia: E. Claxton, 1883), 253; Genet to Lebrun, May 18, 1793, *CFM*, 214; Miller, *Federalist Era*, 133; Liam Riordan, "'O Dear, What Can the Matter Be?': The Urban Early Republic and the Politics of Popular Song in Benjamin Carr's Federal Overture," *Journal of the Early Republic* 31, no. 2 (2011): 209, 75–76; Ammon, *Genet Mission*, 54–59; Orihel, "Political Fever," 63–66, 73; Jeffrey L. Pasley, *The First Presidential Contest: 1796 and the Founding of American Democracy* (Lawrence: University Press of Kansas, 2013).
20. Genet to Lebrun, May 31, 1793, *CFM*, 216.
21. Genet suggesting the name "democratic": Link, *Democratic-Republican Societies*, 16; Elkins and McKitrick, *Age of Federalism*, 456; Minnigerode, *Jefferson, Friend of France*, 220; Sioli, "Citizen Genet and Political Struggle," 261; Sean Wilentz, *The Rise of American Democracy: Jefferson to Lincoln* (New York: Norton, 2005), 54; tavern name: Branson, *Fiery Frenchified Dames*, 64; "very interesting" guillotine: *General Advertiser* (Philadelphia), Mar. 5, 1794, and Branson, *Fiery Frenchified Dames*, 67; Southwark Theatre: Robert C. Alberts, *The Golden Voyage: The Life and Times of William Bingham, 1752–1804* (Boston: Houghton Mifflin, 1969), 241.
22. Genet to Lebrun, June 19, 1793, *CFM*, 217–18; "Philadelphia, August, 1793. All Able Bodied Seamen Who Are Willing to Engage in the Cause of Liberty, and in the Service of the French Republic, Will Please to Apply to the French Consul, at No. 132, North Second-Street" (n.p., n.d.).
23. Theater manager reminiscences: William Dunlap, *A History of the American Theatre*, 2 vols. (London: Richard Bentley, 1833), 1:204–5; Riordan, "'O Dear, What Can the Matter Be?'" 206; "It will require": JA to AA, Dec. 5, 1793, *AFPEA*.
24. "had secret": François Barbé-Marbois, *Histoire de la Louisiane et de la cession de cette colonie par la France aux États-Unis de l'Amérique septentrionale. . . .* (Paris: Impr. de Firmin Didot, 1829), 167; "terrorism": JA to TJ, June 30, 1813, Lester Jesse Cappon, ed., *The Adams-Jefferson Letters*, 2 vols. (Chapel Hill: University of North Carolina Press, 1959), 2:346–47.
25. Marcel Dorigny, "Sonthonax et Brissot: Le cheminement d'une filiation politique assumée," *Revue française de l'histoire d'outre-mer* 84 (1997): 29–40; Marcel Dorigny, "Brissot et Miranda en 1792: Ou comment révolutionner l'Amérique espagnol," in *La France et les Amériques au temps de Jefferson et de Miranda*, ed. Marcel Dorigny and Marie-Jeanne Rossignol (Paris: Société des études robespierristes, 2001), 95; Corriveau, "Jacques-Pierre Brissot." On the Genet mission's links to the Girondins, see also Eugene R. Sheridan, "The Recall of Edmond Charles Genet: A Study in Transatlantic Politics and Diplomacy," *Diplomatic History* 18, no. 4 (1994), and Wesley J. Campbell, "The Origin of Citizen Genet's Projected Attack on Spanish Louisiana: A Case Study in Girondin Politics," *French Historical Studies* 33, no. 4 (2010).
26. Carolyn E. Fick, *The Making of Haiti: The Saint Domingue Revolution from Below* (Knoxville: University of Tennessee Press, 1990), 22–23; Bernard Gainot and Marcel Dorigny, *Atlas des esclavages* (Paris: Autrement, 2006), 22–23; David Brion Davis, "Impact of the French and Haitian Revolutions," in *The Impact of the Haitian Revolution in the Atlantic World*, 4; Laurent Dubois, *Avengers of the New World: The Story of the Haitian Revolution* (Cambridge, MA: Belknap Press of Harvard University Press, 2004), 21, 22, 30. If the township of Northern Liberties is included in the Philadelphia population figures, the total is 38,435. On Sonthonax,

see Robert Louis Stein, *Léger Félicité Sonthonax: The Lost Sentinel of the Republic* (Ruther-ford, NJ: Fairleigh Dickinson University Press; London: Associated University Presses, 1985), 20, and Marcel Dorigny, *Léger-Félicité Sonthonax: La première abolition de l'esclavage: La Révolution française et la Révolution de Saint-Domingue* (Saint-Denis: Société française d'histoire d'outre-mer; Association pour l'étude de la colonisation européenne, 1997).

27. Bryan Edwards, *Historical Survey of the French Colony in the Island of St. Domingo* (1797), quoted in Joan Dayan, *Haiti, History, and the Gods* (Berkeley: University of California Press, 1995), 147; Fick, *Making of Haiti,* 106.

28. Dubois, *Avengers,* 153–54.

29. Some of the correspondence between Genet in Philadelphia and Sonthonax in Saint Domingue can be found in a folder in D/XXV/6, AN. On his use of the American debt, see "Lettre des ministres et membres du Conseil exécutif provisoire de la République française au Citoyen Président," Jan. 8, 1793, AF/III/64/259, AN.

30. three hundred ships: Meadows, "Engineering Exile," 73.

31. C. L. R. James, *The Black Jacobins: Toussaint L'Ouverture and the San Domingo Revolution,* 2nd ed. (New York: Vintage Books, 1963), 127. On these events, see David Patrick Geggus, *Slavery, War, and Revolution: The British Occupation of Saint Domingue, 1793–1798* (Oxford: Clarendon Press, 1982), 33–45; Fick, *Making of Haiti,* 91–182; Dubois, *Avengers,* 91–170; David Geggus, "The Arming of Slaves in the Haitian Revolution," in *Arming Slaves: From Classical Times to the Modern Age,* ed. Christopher Leslie Brown and Philip D. Morgan (New Haven, CT: Yale University Press, 2006), 209–32.

32. J. H. Powell, *Bring Out Your Dead: The Great Plague of Yellow Fever in Philadelphia in 1793* (Philadelphia: University of Pennsylvania Press, 1993), 1.

33. *General Advertiser* (Philadelphia), May 8, 1793; *Federal Gazette* (Philadelphia), May 8, 1793.

34. Anna Wharton Wood, "The Robinson Family and Their Correspondence with the Vicomte and Vicomtesse de Noailles," *Bulletin of the Newport Historical Society* 42 (1922): 30–31.

35. For discussion about the letter of introduction, which is cited below in chapter 3, see GW to AH, May 5, 1793, *PAH,* 14:414–15, or *PGWPS,* 12:515–16.

36. *Impartial Herald,* June 15, 1793. The letter was published in at least five different newspapers in early June. See also *PAH,* 15:120–21.

37. "The artifices": *Columbian Centinel* (Boston), June 29, 1793; *Massachusetts Mercury,* June 5, 1793; *Mirrour* (Concord, NH), June 24, 1793; *General Advertiser* (Philadelphia), July 24, 1793.

38. "Noailles and Talon": Genet to Lebrun, June 19, 1793, *CFM,* 218; "Before M. Noailles": Gren-ville to Hammond, July 25, 1793, *Manuscripts of J. B. Fortescue,* 2:408.

39. Physical description: A. Spielman and Michael D'Antonio, *Mosquito: A Natural History of Our Most Persistent and Deadly Foe* (New York: Hyperion, 2001), xv; Michael Specter, "The Mosquito Solution," *New Yorker* 88, no. 20 (2012). See also William Hardy McNeill, *Plagues and Peoples* (Garden City, NY: Anchor Press, 1976); Christopher Wills, *Yellow Fever, Black Goddess: The Coevolution of People and Plagues* (Reading, MA: Addison-Wesley, 1996); John Robert McNeill, *Mosquito Empires: Ecology and War in the Greater Caribbean, 1620–1914* (New York: Cambridge University Press, 2010); Billy G. Smith, *Ship of Death: A Voyage That Changed the Atlantic World* (New Haven, CT: Yale University Press, 2013), 162–68.

40. I am grateful to Billy Smith for allowing me an early peek at his new and brilliant book, *Ship of Death.* These details and many more are found there. For more on the yellow fever epi-demic, Powell, *Bring Out Your Dead,* remains the best introduction, supplemented by the essays in J. Worth Estes and Billy G. Smith, *A Melancholy Scene of Devastation: The Public Response to the 1793 Philadelphia Yellow Fever Epidemic* (Canton, MA: Science History Pub-lications, 1997).

41. William Currie, *A Description of the Malignant, Infectious Fever Prevailing at Present in Philadelphia.* . . . (Philadelphia: printed by T. Dobson 1793), 26–27. Mathew Carey identifies the first death on August 6 or 7 in *A Short Account of the Malignant Fever, Lately Prevalent*

in Philadelphia. . . . (Philadelphia: printed by the author, 1793), 16–17. Smith, *Ship of Death*, 188, identifies the boardinghouse as a brothel.

42. Carey, *Short Account*, 20–21, 94; Smith, *Ship of Death*, 196, 212.

43. "Fly": quoted in Horace Elisha Scudder, *Recollections of Samuel Breck, with Passages from His Notebooks, 1771–1862* (Philadelphia: Porter & Coates, 1877), 193–94, and Alberts, *Golden Voyage*, 247; "The disorder": Hammond to Grenville, Oct. 12, 1793, *Manuscripts of J. B. Fortescue*, 2:443–44; "The epidemic causes": Noailles to AH, Oct. 9, 1793, *PAH*, 15:358–59.

44. Currie, *Description*, 3–4; Dubois, *Avengers*, 280; Spielman and D'Antonio, *Mosquito*, 58. For a more modern explanation of the fever, see J. Worth Estes, "Introduction: The Yellow Fever Syndrome and Its Treatment in Philadelphia, 1793," in *Melancholy Scene of Devastation*.

45. "scenes of distress": Carey, *Short Account*, 31; handkerchiefs, tar, camphor: ibid., 22, 93; Currie, *Description*, 10; Smith, *Ship of Death*, 200; "Every body": TJ to Thomas Mann Randolph Jr., Sept. 2, 1793, *PTJ*, 17:20; "The governor": Noailles to AH, Oct. 9, 1793, *PAH*, 15:358.

46. Carey, *Short Account*, 30–32, 34–54, 79; Susan E. Klepp, "Appendix I: 'How Many Precious Souls Are Fled?': The Magnitude of the 1793 Yellow Fever Epidemic," in Estes and Smith, eds., *A Melancholy Scene of Devastation*, 166; Smith, *Ship of Death*, 216, 215, 211; Noailles to AH, Oct. 9, 1793, *PAH*, 15:359.

47. "Long-absent": Carey, *Short Account*, 68; mortality estimates: Klepp, "Appendix I: 'How Many Precious Souls Are Fled?,'" 164–65.

48. Smith, *Ship of Death*, 235; Currie, *Description*, 16, 7; Carey, *Short Account*, 20.

49. The physical description is from a 1793 police report, quoted in Poniatowski, *Talleyrand aux États-Unis*, 281n1. On Talleyrand's American travels, see especially Charles-Maurice de Talleyrand-Périgord, *Mémoires du prince de Talleyrand*, ed. Albert de Broglie, 5 vols. (Paris: Calmann Lévy, 1891), 1:230–47; Baldensperger, "Le séjour de Talleyrand aux États-Unis"; Poniatowski, *Talleyrand aux États-Unis*; and *TAFP*.

50. Sorel, Carnot, and Morris quoted in Alan Sked, "Talleyrand and England, 1792–1838: A Reinterpretation," *Diplomacy and Statecraft* 17, no. 4 (2006): 648. See also Cooper, *Talleyrand*.

51. Michel Poniatowski, *Talleyrand: Les années occultées, 1789–1792* (Paris: Perrin, 1995), 177–81; *Talleyrand et l'ancienne France: 1754–1789* (Paris: Libr. académique Perrin, 1988), 230, 274–78, 295, 315; Herbert Lüthy, *La Banque protestante en France, de la révocation de l'Édit de Nantes à la Révolution* (Paris: SEVPEN, 1959), 2:420. Paris bourse: George V. Taylor, "The Paris Bourse on the Eve of the Revolution, 1781–1789," *AHR* 67, no. 4 (1962).

52. "no credence": King George III to Grenville, Apr. 28, 1792, *Manuscripts of J. B. Fortescue*, 2:266–67; Talleyrand's trip to London: Sked, "Talleyrand and England"; Georges Pallain, ed., *Correspondance diplomatique de Talleyrand: La mission de Talleyrand à Londres, en 1792. . . . ,* 2 vols. (Paris: E. Plon, Nourrit et cie, 1891); F. L. Nussbaum, "L'Arrière-plan de la mission de Talleyrand à Londres en 1792: Documents inédits publiés avec une introduction et les notes," in *Assemblée générale de la commission centrale et des comités départementaux 1939*, ed. Commission de recherche et de publication des documents relatifs à la vie économique de la Révolution France (Paris: Tépac, 1945). See also Gouverneur Morris to GW, Feb. 4, 1792, *PGWPS*, 9:531–40; Benjamin Vaughan to John Vaughan, Feb. 27, 1794, Madeira-Vaughan Collection, APS. On Talleyrand's reception in London, see Albert Sorel, *L'Europe et la Révolution française* (Paris: E. Plon, Nourrit et cie, 1885), 2:387–93.

53. Staël's and Paris's salons: Antoine Lilti, *Le monde des salons: Sociabilité et mondanité à Paris au XVIIIe siècle* (Paris: Fayard, 2005), 239–40; Juniper Hall: Charlotte Barrett, ed., *Diary and Letters of Madame d'Arblay* (London: H. Colburn, 1842); Constance Hill, *Juniper Hall: A Rendezvous of Certain Illustrious Personages During the French Revolution* (London: J. Lane, 1904); Linda Kelly, *Juniper Hall: An English Refuge from the French Revolution* (London: Weidenfeld and Nicolson, 1991). For the London emigration, see Kirsty Carpenter, "London: Capital of the Emigration," in *The French Émigrés in Europe and the Struggle against Revolution, 1789–1814*, ed. Kirsty Carpenter and Mansel Philip (New York: St. Martin's Press, 1999).

54. Kelly, *Juniper Hall*, 40; Fanny Burney, *Diary and Letters of Madame d'Arblay*, ed. Charlotte Barrett (Philadelphia: Carey and Hart, 1842), 388.

55. Staël, "De l'esprit de conversation," in *Oeuvres complètes de Mme. la Baronne de Staël*, 17 vols. (Paris: Treuttel et Würtz, 1820), 10:102, 105–6, with help translating from O. W. Wight, ed., *Germany*, 2 vols. (New York: H. W. Derby, 1861), 1:81–82. See also Dena Goodman, *The Republic of Letters* (Ithaca, NY: Cornell University Press, 1994), 125–35.

56. "I'm going to leave": Mrs. Phillips to Miss Burney, May 14, 1793, Burney, *Diary and Letters*, 417; "What is," "Our role," and "I'll linger": Talleyrand to Staël, Nov. 1, Sept. 28, and Nov. 8, 1793, "Lettres de M. de Talleyrand à Madame de Staël, tirées des archives du Château de Broglie," *Revue d'histoire diplomatique* 90, no. 4 (1890): 89, 82, and 90.

57. Talleyrand as Guy Fawkes: Kelly, *Juniper Hall*, 45; letter to Staël, undated, "Lettres de M. de Talleyrand à Madame de Staël," 91.

58. Talleyrand, *Mémoires*, 1:232; Talleyrand to Staël, May 12, 1794, "Lettres de M. de Talleyrand à Madame de Staël," 209.

59. Talleyrand, *Mémoires*, 1:232; Baldensperger, "Le séjour de Talleyrand aux États-Unis," 364.

60. Volney quoted in Gaulmier, *L'idéologue Volney*, 358. For this description, in addition to Talleyrand's memoirs, I have drawn on Isaac Weld, *Travels through the States of North America and the Provinces of Upper and Lower Canada, during the Years 1795, 1796, and 1797*, 2nd ed., 2 vols. (London: John Stockdale, 1799), 1:8; Twining, *Travels in America*, 28; John A. Gallucci, ed., *Castorland Journal: An Account of the Exploration and Settlement of Northern New York State by French Émigrés in the Years 1793 to 1797* (Ithaca, NY: Cornell University Press, 2010), 69; Niemcewicz, *Under Their Vine and Fig Tree*, 207.

61. Memoir to Cazenove, June 23, 1794, *TAFP*, 38; Talleyrand to Staël, May 12, 1794, "Lettres de M. de Talleyrand à Madame de Staël," 209; Fauchet to Minister of Foreign Affairs, May 5, 1794, *CFM*, 333; *Manuscripts of J. B. Fortescue*, 3:524; Miller, *Federalist Era*, 141; Elkins and McKitrick, *Age of Federalism*, 391.

62. Alan Taylor, *The Divided Ground: Indians, Settlers and the Northern Borderland of the American Revolution* (New York: Alfred A. Knopf, 2006), 283; Elkins and McKitrick, *Age of Federalism*, 392; Richard White, *The Middle Ground: Indians, Empires, and Republics in the Great Lakes Region, 1650–1815* (Cambridge: Cambridge University Press, 1991), 464–65; Maya Jasanoff, *Liberty's Exiles: American Loyalists in the Revolutionary World* (New York: Alfred A. Knopf, 2011), 200.

63. Moreau, *American Journey*, 34.

64. These biographic details are mostly taken from Stewart L. Mims, "Introduction," in Moreau, *Voyage*, xiii–xxix; the warrant detail is from p. 2 of the diary; the witnessing of La Rochefoucauld's death from Harsanyi, *Lessons from America*, 39. See also James E. McClellan, *Colonialism and Science: Saint Domingue in the Old Regime* (Baltimore: Johns Hopkins University Press, 1992), 19–20.

65. Moreau, *American Journey*, 13.

66. Ibid., 40, 126, 34.

67. Ibid., 59, 42.

68. Ibid., 96. Trip from Baltimore to Philadelphia: Weld, *Travels*, 1:31–43; Twining, *Travels in America*, 59–80; oyster vendors in the evening: Niemcewicz, *Under Their Vine and Fig Tree*, 38.

69. Moreau, *American Journey*, 92, 127–28.

70. Ibid., 125. The scene would have been even more curious than suggested here, given the rumors that Beaumetz had been Madame Campan's lover. See Harsanyi, *Lessons from America*, 34.

71. Thomas P. Slaughter, *The Whiskey Rebellion: Frontier Epilogue to the American Revolution* (New York: Oxford University Press, 1986), 156.

72. "the expedition": Liancourt, *Journal*, 60; "His face": Burney, *Diary and Letters*, 365–66.

73. Income data is from Tackett, *Becoming a Revolutionary*, 319–20; also Lemay et al., *Dictionnaire des constituants*, 535.

74. Ferdinand Dreyfus, *Un philanthrope d'autrefois: La Rochefoucauld-Liancourt, 1747–1827* (Paris: Plon, 1903), 21.
75. La Rochefoucauld-Liancourt, *Vie du duc de La Rochefoucauld-Liancourt,* 99; Dreyfus, *Un philanthrope d'autrefois,* 13.
76. Young, *Travels in France,* 240; La Rochefoucauld-Liancourt, *Vie du duc de La Rochefoucauld-Liancourt,* 104, 103.
77. "Vive le roi!": Burney, *Diary and Letters,* 362–63; "less confident": La Rochefoucauld-Liancourt, *Vie du duc de La Rochefoucauld-Liancourt,* 38. This paragraph and the next are based on Liancourt's son's recollections, written much later, as well as on Burney's contemporary but second- or third-hand account, recounted in a letter to her sister. Each of these accounts seems equally problematic and I've tried my best to reconcile them, despite their inconsistencies.
78. Burney, *Diary and Letters,* 364.
79. La Rochefoucauld-Liancourt, *Vie du duc de La Rochefoucauld-Liancourt,* 44; Burney, *Diary and Letters,* 367.
80. Liancourt, *Journal,* 25–59. On the appearance of the Delaware River in November, I have drawn on the lovely description in Weld, *Travels,* 1:3, and Twining, *Travels in America,* 24–25.
81. Memoir to Cazenove, June 23, 1794, and June 10, 1794, *TAFP,* 39; La Rochefoucauld-Liancourt, *Vie du duc de La Rochefoucauld-Liancourt,* 44.
82. La Rochefoucauld-Liancourt, *Vie du duc de la Rochefoucauld-Liancourt,* 45.

CHAPTER 2: SETTLING IN AMERICA: PHILADELPHIA SPEAKS FRENCH

1. John Adams quoted in Peter Thompson, *Rum Punch & Revolution: Taverngoing & Public Life in Eighteenth Century Philadelphia* (Philadelphia: University of Pennsylvania Press, 1999), 151, and George W. Boudreau, *Independence: A Guide to Historic Philadelphia* (Yardley, PA: Westholme Publishing, 2012), 126. The poem is found in *The Philadelphiad; or New Pictures of the City. . . .* (Philadelphia: printed for the editor by Kline & Reynolds, 1784), 66; also see Henderson, "Furnishing the Republican Court," 192n67. Genet's residing in Philadelphia: Biddle, *Autobiography of Charles Biddle,* 251; City Tavern: J. Thomas Scharf and Thompson Westcott, *History of Philadelphia, 1609–1884,* 3 vols. (Philadelphia: L. H. Everts, 1884), 2:982; W. A. Newman Dorland, "The Second Troop Philadelphia City Cavalry (Continued)," *PMHB* 46, no. 1 (1922): 66, 75n162; John David Ronalds Platt, *The City Tavern: Independence National Historical Park, Philadelphia, Pennsylvania* (Denver: Denver Service Center, National Park Service, 1973), 45–55, 204–7, 220; Richard L. Bushman, *The Refinement of America: Persons, Houses, Cities* (New York: Vintage Books, 1992), 162–64; David S. Shields, *Civil Tongues & Polite Letters in British America* (Chapel Hill: University of North Carolina Press, 1997), 55–63; Michelle L. Craig, "Grounds for Debate? The Place of the Caribbean Provisions Trade in Philadelphia's Prerevolutionary Economy," *PMHB* 128, no. 2 (2004): 169; Boudreau, *Independence,* 125–33.
2. "excessive, suffocating heat": Talleyrand to Staël, Aug. 4, 1794, "Lettres de M. de Talleyrand à Madame de Staël," 214; Richardet at Cazenove's: Henry Scheaff, Mar. 18, 1801, *PTJ,* 33:360; Richardet to TJ, Oct. 12, 1802, *PTJ,* 38:485; Richardet at the City Tavern: Platt, *City Tavern,* 224–30.
3. Liancourt, *Journal,* 61–62; "boringly vain": ibid., 78.
4. Stewart Mitchell, ed., *New Letters of Abigail Adams, 1788–1801* (Boston: Houghton Mifflin, 1991), 133; Weld, *Travels,* 1:21.
5. Louis-Auguste Félix Beaujour, *Aperçu des États-Unis: Au commencement du XIXe siècle* (Paris: L. G. Michaud, 1814), 81.
6. Cooper, *Talleyrand,* 19.
7. General works on Philadelphia and on its French population that I have found useful for this chapter include Childs, *French Refugee Life;* Spera, "Building for Business"; Doerflinger, *Vig-*

orous Spirit; Spaeth, "Purgatory or Promised Land?"; Thompson, *Rum Punch;* Andrew J. Brunk, "'To Fix the Taste of Our Country Properly': The French Style in Philadelphia Interiors, 1788–1800" (Ph.D. diss., University of Delaware, 2000); Meadows, "Engineering Exile"; Branson, *Fiery Frenchified Dames;* White, *Encountering Revolution,* 10–50.

8. Meadows, "Engineering Exile"; White, *Encountering Revolution;* Nash, "Reverberations of Haiti"; Klepp, "Appendix I: 'How Many Precious Souls Are Fled?,'" 164. The numbers in this paragraph are compiled from Nash, "Reverberations of Haiti," 49–50; Smith, *"Lower Sort,"* 61n73; Klepp, *Philadelphia in Transition,* 336, 338.

9. This paragraph has drawn largely from Klepp, *Philadelphia in Transition;* Doerflinger, *Vigorous Spirit;* and E. Digby Baltzell, *Philadelphia Gentlemen: The Making of a National Upper Class* (Glencoe, IL: Free Press, 1958).

10. Nantucket cheese: Gilbert Chinard, ed., *The Letters of Lafayette and Jefferson* (Baltimore: Johns Hopkins Press, 1929), 61; "French money": Peter Stephen Du Ponceau to Anna, July 10, 1839, James L. Whitehead, "Notes and Documents: The Autobiography of Peter Stephen Du Ponceau," *PMHB* 63, no. 4 (1939): 436. On Franco-American trade in this period, see especially Marcel Dorigny, "La *Libre Amérique* selon Brissot et Clavière: Modèle politique, utopie libérale et réalisme économique," in *De la France et des États-Unis: Étienne Clavière et J.-P. Brissot de Warville,* ed. Marcel Dorigny (Paris: Éditions du CTHS, 1996); Paul Cheney, "A False Dawn for Enlightenment Cosmopolitanism? Franco-American Trade during the American War of Independence," *WMQ* 63, no. 3 (2006); and Allan Potofsky, "The Political Economy of the French-American Debt Debate: The Ideological Uses of Atlantic Commerce, 1787 to 1800," *WMQ* 63, no. 3 (2006). See also Roger G. Kennedy, *Orders from France: The Americans and the French in a Revolutionary World, 1780–1820* (New York: Alfred A. Knopf, 1989), 27–29.

11. Fonds Brissot, 446/AP/5/2/31-88, AN; Michelle Craig McDonald, "The Chance of the Moment: Coffee and the New West Indies Commodities Trade," *WMQ* 62, no. 3 (2005): 442, 458; Doerflinger, *Vigorous Spirit,* 242–50, 261–67, 335–56; James Alexander Dun, "'What Avenues of Commerce, Will You, Americans, Not Explore!': Commercial Philadelphia's Vantage onto the Early Haitian Revolution," *WMQ* 62, no. 3 (2005): 477–78; John H. Coatsworth, "American Trade with European Colonies in the Caribbean and South America, 1790–1812," *WMQ* 24, no. 2 (1967): 248; Julius Sherrard Scott, "The Common Wind: Currents of Afro-American Communication in the Era of the Haitian Revolution" (Ph.D. diss., Duke University, 1986), 84; Kennedy, *Orders from France,* 26–45.

12. Elkins and McKitrick, *Age of Federalism,* 382; Dun, "'What Avenues,'" 502; "Résumé de la lettre de Le Bas et Victor Hugues," 19 Messidor, an 3, AF/III/64/1/289, AN; Ashli White, "'A Flood of Impure Lava': Saint Dominguan Refugees in the United States, 1791–1820" (Ph.D. diss., Columbia University, 2003), 53–55; C. F. Volney, *Tableau du climat et du sol des États-Unis d'Amérique. . . . ,* 2 vols. (Paris: Courcier, Dentu 1803), 1:vii.

13. Smith, *Ship of Death,* 194; Doerflinger, *Vigorous Spirit,* 344.

14. Burke quotation, Francophobia/Francophilia, and number of English travelers to Europe are from Gerald G. Newman, *The Rise of English Nationalism: A Cultural History, 1740–1830* (New York: St. Martin's Press, 1987), 14, 35–38, 43; Young, *Travels in France,* 236; Marc Fumaroli, *Trois institutions littéraires* (Paris: Gallimard, 1994), xxxiv–xxxv; Kant quotation: ibid., 117; the French as models of refinement: Kennedy, *Orders from France,* 27–28; Bushman, *Refinement of America,* 36–37; Joan E. DeJean, *The Essence of Style: How the French Invented High Fashion, Fine Food, Chic Cafés, Style, Sophistication, and Glamour* (New York: Free Press, 2005); a sense of cultural inferiority among elite Americans: T. H. Breen, "Ideology and Nationalism on the Eve of the American Revolution: Revisions *Once More* in Need of Revising," *JAH* 84, no. 1 (1997); Shields, *Civil Tongues,* 308–28; and, most recently, Kariann Yokota, *Unbecoming British: How Revolutionary America Became a Postcolonial Nation* (New York: Oxford University Press, 2011).

15. Beatrice B. Garvan, *Federal Philadelphia, 1785–1825: The Athens of the Western World. . . .*

(Philadelphia: The Museum, 1987), 11; Moreau, *Voyage,* 193–94, 347; Faures quoted in White, "'Flood of Impure Lava,'" 141; ice cream: Alexandre Paul Marie de Laujon, *Souvenirs et voyages de A. de Laujon,* 2 vols. (Paris: A. Veret, 1835), 2:131; Brillat-Savarin: Jean Anthelme Brillat-Savarin, *The Physiology of Taste; or, Transcendental Gastronomy. Illustrated by Anecdotes of Distinguished Artists and Statesmen of Both Continents,* trans. Fayette Robinson (Philadelphia: Lindsay & Blakiston, 1854), 327, 114; Caroline Moorehead, *Dancing to the Precipice: Lucie de La Tour du Pin and the French Revolution* (London: Chatto & Windus, 2009), 218; Sosnowski, "French Émigrés in the United States," 142; Fernand Baldensperger, "Le séjour de Brillat-Savarin aux États-Unis," *Revue de littérature comparée* 2 (1922). On the invention of French gastronomy: DeJean, *Essence of Style,* 105–32.

16. *Aurora General Advertiser* (Philadelphia), Nov. 8, 1794; *Federal Gazette and Philadelphia Evening Post,* Nov. 4, 1791, and many others. On the invention of the profession of coiffeuse, or hairdresser, see DeJean, *Essence of Style,* 21–33.

17. Chestnut Street Theatre: Moreau, *American Journey,* 348; White, *Encountering Revolution,* 19; music: Riordan, "'O Dear, What Can the Matter Be?'" 196, 216, 209–11; Kelley, *Life and Times in Colonial Philadelphia,* 118; and J. A. Leo Lemay, "The American Origins of 'Yankee Doodle,'" *WMQ* 33, no. 3 (1976): 464; Pillet: *Aurora General Advertiser* (Philadelphia), Nov. 17, 1794; dancing: Laujon, *Souvenirs et voyages,* 2:121.

18. Moreau, *American Journey,* 309; Oeller's: Robert Earle Graham, "The Taverns of Colonial Philadelphia," *Transactions of the American Philosophical Society* 43, no. 1 (1953): 324; Kelley, *Life and Times in Colonial Philadelphia,* 170–71; Oeller's and refinement: Thompson, *Rum Punch,* 190–91; on the pineapple-laced punch: Mary Anne Hines et al., *The Larder Invaded: Reflections on Three Centuries of Philadelphia Food and Drink. . . .* (Philadelphia: Library Company of Philadelphia, 1987); on Liber: *General Advertiser* (Philadelphia), Aug. 3, 1793; on Blanchard: Leary, "Phaeton in Philadelphia," 52, and Frey, *First Air Voyage in America,* 60; Genet banquet: Graham, "The Taverns of Colonial Philadelphia," 324; *General Advertiser,* May 27, 1793; Oeller's naturalizations: "Frances and Emily André" file, Dallett Papers, HSP.

19. Richardet at Louth Hall: W. A. Newman Dorland et al., "The Second Troop Philadelphia City Cavalry (Continued)," *PMHB* 47, no. 2 (1923): 176n309; Richardet at City Tavern: quoted in Platt, *City Tavern,* 224; De La Grange: "La Barthe" file, Dallett Papers, HSP.

20. P. S. Du Ponceau to Citoyen Arcambat, Vice Consul of France in New York, July 9, 1794, Letterbook, 1792–1797, Du Ponceau Papers, HSP; McShane connection: Rufus Wilmot Griswold, *The Republican Court; or American Society in the Days of Washington* (New York: D. Appleton, 1856), 292; Loge Française: *Extrait des régistres de la loge française l'aménité, no. 73, séante à Philadelphie* (Philadelphia: par Jacques Carey, 1800); Etienne Taillemite, "Moreau de Saint Méry: Une biographie," in *Des constitutions à la description de Saint-Domingue: La colonie française en Haïti vue par Moreau de Saint-Méry. . . . ,* ed. Marcel Dorigny, Roger Dominique, Étienne Taillemite, et Dominique Taffin (Fort-de-France: Archives Départementales de la Martinique, 2004). Moreau's Masonic connections: McClellan, *Colonialism and Science,* 187.

21. White, *Encountering Revolution,* 29; Sosnowski, "French Émigrés in the United States," 145.

22. Ambrose-Marie-François-Joseph Palisot de Beauvois, *Catalogue raisonné du museum, de Mr. C.W. Peale, membre de la société philosophique de Pensylvanie* (Philadelphia: De l'imprimerie de Parent, 1800). Beauvois is listed under "Palisot" in the APS catalog; his election year is drawn from the APS Web site, http://www.amphilsoc.org/memhist/search, accessed Nov. 17, 2013, which is also where the numbers of foreign and domestic members were assessed. On his friendship with Moreau, see Moreau, *Voyage,* 401. On the Cercle des Philadelphes, see McClellan, *Colonialism and Science.*

23. On French newspapers in Philadelphia in this period: Childs, *French Refugee Life,* 122–40; Clarence S. Brigham, *History and Bibliography of American Newspapers, 1690–1820* (Worcester, MA: American Antiquarian Society, 1947), 890–949; Branson, *Fiery Frenchified Dames,* 60–61; White, *Encountering Revolution,* 31; subscription books: *General Advertiser,* May 27,

1793. On Bache, see especially James Tagg, *Benjamin Franklin Bache and the "Philadelphia Aurora"* (Philadelphia: University of Pennsylvania Press, 1991), and Jeffrey L. Pasley, *"The Tyranny of Printers": Newspaper Politics in the Early American Republic* (Charlottesville: University of Virginia Press, 2001); on the importance of his French education: Marie-Jeanne Rossignol, "Benjamin Franklin Bache, Bilingualism, Racialized Republican Order, and the French Abolition of Slavery in 1794," unpublished paper in author's possession. Moreau reports that he printed Gatereau's paper from 1795 until March 1796.

24. Gary B. Nash, *Forging Freedom: The Formation of Philadelphia's Black Community, 1720–1840* (Cambridge, MA: Harvard University Press, 1988), 141, 142.

25. Volney to La Réveillière, Jan. 14, 1797, Albert Mathiez, "Lettres de Volney à La Révellière-Lépeaux, 1795–1798," *Annales révolutionnaires* 3, no. 2 (1910): 174; also quoted in Gaulmier, *L'idéologue Volney*, 382; Laujon, *Souvenirs et voyages*, 2:116.

26. Moreau, *Voyage*, 101; Edmund Hogan, *The Prospect of Philadelphia, and Check on the Next Directory*. . . . (Philadelphia: printed by Francis & Robert Bailey, 1795), 180; Smith, *"Lower Sort,"* 21–25; Thompson, *Rum Punch*, 42; Branson, *Fiery Frenchified Dames*, 57–58; Grant Miles Simon, "Houses and Early Life in Philadelphia," *Transactions of the American Philosophical Society* 43, no. 1 (1953): 285; White, *Encountering Revolution*, 28.

27. "Nobody lives": quoted in Balzell, *Philadelphia Gentlemen*, 191; "I was surprised": Laujon, *Souvenirs et voyages*, 2:110. The sources used for the table were composed of the following. City Directories: James Hardie, *The Philadelphia Directory and Register*. . . . (Philadelphia: Jacob Johnson & Co., 1794); Edmund Hogan, *The Prospect of Philadelphia, and Check on the Next Directory*. . . . (Philadelphia: Francis & Robert Bailey, 1795); Cornelius William Stafford, *The Philadelphia Directory for 1797*. . . . (Philadelphia: William W. Woodward, 1797); Cornelius William Stafford, *The Philadelphia Directory for 1798*. . . . (Philadelphia: William W. Woodward, 1798); James Robinson, *Robinson's Philadelphia Register and City Directory, for 1799* (Philadelphia: John Bioren, 1799). Tax list: Wilbur J. McElwain, *United States Direct Tax of 1798*. . . . (Bowie, MD: Heritage Books, 1999). Principal newspapers consulted: *American Star, Aurora General Advertiser, Claypoole's Daily Advertiser, Dunlap's American Daily Advertiser, Federal Gazette, General Advertiser, Philadelphia Gazette*. Newspapers used to supplement the data: *Carey's United States Recorder, Courier de l'Amérique, Finlay's American Naval and Commercial Register, Gazette of the United States, Independent Gazetteer, Level of Europe, National Gazette, Pennsylvania Packet, Porcupine's Gazette, Poulson's American Daily Advertiser, Universal Daily Advertiser, Universal Gazette*.

28. List of goods: Moreau de Saint Mery, & Co., *Catalogue of Books, Stationery, Engravings, Mathematical Instruments, Maps, Charts, and Other Goods*. . . . (Philadelphia: printed by M. L. E. Moreau de Saint-Méry, 1795); Moreau, *Voyage*, 204, 210. Example of scientific works: Joseph Priestley, *Réflexions sur la doctrine du phlogistique et la décomposition de l'eau* (Philadelphia: De l'imprimerie de Moreau de Saint-Méry, 1797), and François-Alexandre-Frédéric La Rochefoucauld-Liancourt, *Des prisons de Philadelphie* (Philadelphia: Imprimé & se trouve chez Moreau de St-Méry, 1796). On Moreau's connection to the international scientific community: McClellan, *Colonialism and Science*, 227; Iannini, *Fatal Revolutions*, 244–46.

29. "Noah's ark": Grandmaison, *Mémoires*, 148; Moreau's store and son: Moreau, *Voyage*, 223–24, 210, 225.

30. Liancourt, *Journal*, 71; Moreau, *American Journey*, 178; Poniatowski, *Talleyrand aux États-Unis*, 210. On Cazenove, see David Kynaston, *Cazenove & Co.: A History* (London: B. T. Bastford, 1991), 11; Rayner Wickersham Kelsey, ed., *Cazenove Journal, 1794: A Record of the Journey of Theophile Cazenove through New Jersey and Pennsylvania* (Haverford: Pennsylvania History Press, 1922), vii–viii; Childs, *French Refugee Life*, 47; Paul Demund Evans, *The Holland Land Company* (1924; repr., Clifton, NJ: A. M. Kelley, 1975), 4–5; Poniatowski, *Talleyrand aux États-Unis*, 388; and *ANB*, s.v. "Cazenove, Théophile." On Talleyrand as epicure, see Ian Kelly, *Cooking for Kings: The Life of Antonin Carême, the First Celebrity Chef* (New

York: Walker, 2003), 46–47, and Cooper, *Talleyrand*, 31. On the likelihood of Liancourt's meaning Cazenove's house when referring to dining "*chez les Français*": Childs, *French Refugee Life*, 103.

31. "Les commissaires du conseil exécutif provisoire près les Etats Unis au Ministre des affaires étrangères," Mar. 21, 1794, *CFM*, 317; Fauchet to Minister of Foreign Relations, May 5, 1794, *CFM*, 332; *Gazette of the United States*, May 23, 1794; Newman, *Parades and Politics*, 120–51; Waldstreicher, *Perpetual Fetes*, 126–41; Ghislain de Diesbach, *Histoire de l'émigration: 1789–1814*, rev. ed. (Paris: Libr. académique Perrin, 1988), 513–14; Childs, *French Refugee Life*, 134.

32. Liancourt, *Journal*, 88; Liancourt, *Voyage*, 1:39, 1:19; Henriette Lucie La Tour du Pin Gouvernet, *Journal d'une femme de cinquante ans, 1778–1815*, ed. Aymar Marie Ferdinand de Liedekerke-Beaufort, 15th ed., 2 vols. (Paris: Librairie Chapelot, 1914), 2:3–4; Biddle, *Autobiography of Charles Biddle*, 253; Moreau, *American Journey*, 125.

33. White, "'Flood of Impure Lava,'" 130.

34. Liancourt, *Voyage*, 1:36; Liancourt, *Journal*, 98, 89.

35. James Fred Marshall, ed., *De Staël–Du Pont Letters; Correspondence of Madame de Staël and Pierre Samuel du Pont de Nemours and of Other Members of the Necker and du Pont Families* (Madison: University of Wisconsin Press, 1968), 34.

36. Liancourt to Madame de Liancourt, Mar. 20, 1796, Liancourt, *Journal*, 127; Memoir to Cazenove, June 23, 1794, and June 10, 1794, *TAFP*, 38; Liancourt, *Voyage*, 1:vii; Liancourt, *Journal*, 105, 99, 101–2.

37. Liancourt, *Des prisons*, 22, 21, 25, 9, 18, 31. On the reverse, see http://www.nytimes.com/2008/04/23/world/americas/23iht-23prison.12253738.html.

38. Liancourt, *Des prisons*, 30, 32, 35.

39. Breck, "Recollections" (ms bound copy), APS; Grandmaison, *Mémoires*, 148; Echeverria, *Mirage in the West*, 185.

40. Moreau, *Voyage*, 203.

41. "He Seems to despair": JA to AA, Dec. 5, 1793, *AFPEA*; "the depth": Wood, "Robinson Family and Their Correspondence," 33; "I am touched": Noailles to WB, n.d., Gratz Autograph Collection, box 205, folder 40, HSP; "Noailles declares": JA to AA, Dec. 20, 1796, *AFPEA*. The full name of Louise de Noailles, as she was informally known, was: Anne Jeanne Baptiste Pauline Adrienne Louise Catherine Dominique de Noailles.

42. Liancourt, *Journal*, 63; Liancourt to Madame de Liancourt, Mar. 20, 1796, ibid., 127, 130; Charles Maurice de Talleyrand-Périgord, "Essai sur les avantages à retirer de colonies nouvelles dans les circonstances présentes," in *Mémoires de l'Institut national des sciences et arts. Tome second* (Paris: Baudouin, 1798), 290. On expatriation: *Oxford English Dictionary*, s.v. "expatriation," and especially Fernand Baldensperger, *Le mouvement des idées dans l'émigration française, 1789–1815*, 2 vols. (Paris: Plon, 1924).

43. Liancourt, *Journal*, 83; Grandmaison, *Mémoires*, 147; Echeverria, *Mirage in the West*, 186; Charles Nisbet to Charles Wallace, May 18, 1797, quoted in Childs, *French Refugee Life*, 32; Robert Gilmor, *Memorandums Made in a Tour to the Eastern States in the Year 1797* (Boston: Trustees of the Boston Public Library, 1892), 7.

44. Liancourt, *Voyage*, 1:xi; *Le Courier de l'Amérique* (Philadelphia), Dec. 4, 1792; Talleyrand, "Essai sur les avantages," 289–91.

45. Cazenove to Moreau, Moreau, *American Journey*, 220; Talleyrand to Madame de Genlis, quoted in Poniatowski, *Talleyrand aux États-Unis*, 157; "rather dull": Joseph Priestley, *Letters to the Inhabitants of Northumberland and Its Neighbourhood on Subjects Interesting to the Author and to Them to Which Is Added a Letter to a Friend in Paris, Relating to Mr. Liancourt's Travels in the North American States* (Philadelphia: printed by John Bioren for John Conrad, 1801), 93; "very plain": Breck, "Recollections" (ms bound copy), APS; Liancourt, *Voyage*, 4:146. The reference to Sterne is an allusion to Laurence Sterne's *A Sentimental Journey through France and Italy* (London: printed for T. Becket and P. A. De Hondt, 1768), an influential travelogue that served as the model for much later travel writing. It may have

served, in a very indirect way, as a model for Anne and William Bingham's journey through France and England.

46. Talleyrand, *Mémoires*, 1:232, 233, 234, 239.

47. "toy[s]": Laujon, *Souvenirs et voyages*, 2:126; "In the days": George Washington Parke Custis, *Recollections and Private Memoirs of Washington* (New York: Derby & Jackson, 1860), 448, and Mary Caroline Crawford, *Romantic Days in the Early Republic* (Boston: Little, Brown, 1912), 356. My thinking about the subject of the changes in temporal consciousness has been especially influenced by Reinhart Koselleck, *Futures Past: On the Semantics of Historical Time* (Cambridge, MA: MIT Press, 1985); Reinhart Koselleck and Todd Samuel Presner, *The Practice of Conceptual History: Timing History, Spacing Concepts* (Stanford, CA: Stanford University Press, 2002); Giorgio Agamben, *Homo Sacer: Sovereign Power and Bare Life* (Stanford, CA: Stanford University Press, 1998); and Benedict Anderson, *Imagined Communities: Reflections on the Origin and Spread of Nationalism*, rev. and extended ed. (New York: Verso, 1991). See also the fine article by Matthew Rainbow Hale, "On Their Tiptoes: Political Time and Newspapers during the Advent of the Radicalized French Revolution, circa 1792–1793," *Journal of the Early Republic* 29, no. 2 (2009).

48. Grandmaison, *Mémoires*, 148.

49. Griswold, *Republican Court*, 271.

50. Alberts, *Golden Voyage*, 313; Twining, *Travels in America*, 30.

51. Doerflinger, *Vigorous Spirit*, 63; Baltzell, *Philadelphia Gentlemen*, 81; Schweitzer, "Spatial Organization of Federalist Philadelphia," 45–46; Henderson, "Furnishing the Republican Court," 83–89. On Philadelphia's nouveaux riches, see also the biting commentary in François Jean de Chastellux, *Voyages dans l'Amérique septentrionale dans les années 1780, 1781 et 1782* (Paris: J. Tallandier, 1980).

52. Griswold, *Republican Court*, 260; Hogan, *Prospect of Philadelphia*, 129; James Hardie, *The Philadelphia Directory and Register: Containing the Names, Occupations, and Places of Abode of the Citizens. . . .*, 2d ed. (Philadelphia: printed for the author by Jacob Johnson, 1794), 63.

53. Volney to TJ, Mar. 28, 1796, *PTJ*, 29:53; Chinard, *Volney et l'Amérique*, 36; Talleyrand quip quoted in Poniatowski, *Talleyrand aux États-Unis*, 312; Orléans: Grant Miles Simon, "Part of Old Philadelphia, a Map Showing Historic Buildings & Sites from the Founding until the Early Nineteenth Century" ([Philadelphia?]: American Philosophical Society, 1952); Talleyrand/Beaumetz: Scudder, *Recollections of Samuel Breck*, 247; Liancourt: Breck, "Recollections" (ms bound copy), APS; Liancourt, *Journal*, Nov. 28, 1794, 62; Cornelius William Stafford, *The Philadelphia Directory, for 1797: Containing the Names, Occupations, and Places of Abode of the Citizens. . . .* (Philadelphia: printed for the editor by William W. Woodward, 1797), 152; Moreau: Hogan, *Prospect of Philadelphia*, 116; Dennis C. Kurjack, "St. Joseph's and St. Mary's Churches," in *Historic Philadelphia: From the Founding until the Early Nineteenth Century* (Philadelphia: American Philosophical Society, 1980), 205.

54. Du Ponceau to his niece Anna, July 9, 1839, and July 12, 1839, Peter Stephen Du Ponceau, "Notes and Documents: The Autobiography of Peter Stephen Du Ponceau III," *PMHB* 63, no. 4 (1939): 434, 440; "For the first time": Chastellux, *Voyages*, 1:251–52; "Nothing can be": Joseph Williams to his brother Jeremiah Williams, Aug. 21, 1782, United States Revolution Collection, oversized material, folder 9, American Antiquarian Society, Worcester, MA. My thanks to Zara Anishanslin for passing along the Williams reference. On French influence in fashion and the Republican Court, see also Kate Haulman, *The Politics of Fashion in Eighteenth-Century America* (Chapel Hill: University of North Carolina Press, 2011), 181–215.

55. Laujon, *Souvenirs et voyages*, 2:114–15.

56. "superb Gobelin": Henderson, "Furnishing the Republican Court," 261; "24 small coffee cups": Margaret L. Brown, "Mr. and Mrs. William Bingham of Philadelphia: Rulers of the Republican Court," *PMHB* 61, no. 3 (1937): 309; Garvan, *Federal Philadelphia*, 58; "sopha's covered" and Droze clock: Henderson, "Furnishing the Republican Court," 265, 182–83; exchange rate: Lawrence H. Officer, "Dollar-Sterling Mint Parity and Exchange Rates, 1791–

1834," *Journal of Economic History* 43, no. 3 (1983): 592; Morrises' hiring fencing and dancing masters: J. E. Ross, ed., *Radical Adventurer: The Diaries of Robert Morris, 1772–1774* (Bath: Adams & Dart, 1971), 60, 80, 117; Talleyrand's recollection: Talleyrand, *Mémoires*, 1:239.

57. Susan Gray Detweiler, *George Washington's Chinaware* (New York: Abrams, 1982), 108.

58. Wainwright, *Colonial Grandeur in Philadelphia: The House and Furniture of General John Cadwalader* (Philadelphia: Historical Society of Pennsylvania, 1964), 16, 19, 20–22, 25; Garvan, *Federal Philadelphia*, 57–58, 65.

59. Kennedy, *Orders from France*, 11; Newman, *Rise of English Nationalism*, 2–3; Riordan, "'O Dear, What Can the Matter Be?'" 214; Young, *Travels in France*, 63. On French views of the English, see also David Avrom Bell, *The Cult of the Nation in France: Inventing Nationalism, 1680–1800* (Cambridge, MA: Harvard Univeristy Press, 2001), 43–49, 78–106; Julie Allard, "'Nous faisons chaque jour quelques pas vers le beau simple': transformations de la mode française, 1770–1790" (master's thesis, McGill University, 2002), 73–91; Josephine Grieder, *Anglomania in France 1740–1789: Fact, Fiction, and Political Discourse* (Genève: Droz, 1985); Ian Buruma, *Anglomania: A European Love Affair* (New York: Random House, 1998), 21–49.

60. Morris quoted in Carol Borchert Cadou, *The George Washington Collection: Fine and Decorative Arts at Mount Vernon* (Manchester, VT: Hudson Hills Press, 2006), 131; Washington's errands quoted in Detweiler, *George Washington's Chinaware*, 108; Moustier-Washington furnishings: ibid., 119–35; Nelly signing off letters: Patricia Brady, ed., *George Washington's Beautiful Nelly: The Letters of Eleanor Parke Custis Lewis to Elizabeth Bordley Gibson, 1794–1851* (Columbia: University of South Carolina Press, 1991), 3, 23; "*Sunny* moments": Eleanor Parke Custis to Elizabeth Bordley, Nov. 6, 1821, ibid., 114. See also Henderson, "Furnishing the Republican Court," 128–30, 256, and Detweiler, *George Washington's Chinaware*, 106.

61. Hemings as chef: Annette Gordon-Reed, *The Hemingses of Monticello: An American Family* (New York: W. W. Norton, 2008), 164–65; Richardet's job search: Richardet to TJ, Oct. 12, 1802, *PTJ*, 38:485.

CHAPTER 3: FRANCO-AMERICAN NETWORKS AND POLITE ATLANTIC SPACES

1. Lansdowne to Washington, Mar. 2, 1794, Lansdowne folder, case 9, box 33, Gratz Autograph Collection, HSP.

2. J. Cuthbert Jun. to Benjamin Rush, Feb. 19, 1794, and Benjamin Vaughan to Benjamin Rush, Feb. 20, 1794, Rush Papers, HSP; Benjamin Vaughan to John Vaughan, Feb. 20, 1794, and Feb. 27, 1794, Madeira-Vaughan Collection, APS (photostat copy in Gratz Autograph Collection, case 8, box 19, HSP); Angelica Church to Elizabeth Hamilton, Feb. 4, 1794, *PAH*, 16:380n3. The second Church letter, which I have not seen in its original, is quoted in Griswold, *Republican Court*, 324.

3. "spoke our language": La Tour du Pin Gouvernet, *Journal d'une femme*, 2:82; "intimate relationship": Pierre Auguste Caron de Beaumarchais to AH, Oct. 29, 1796, *PAH*, 20:356; frequent socializing: "Notes on Alexander Hamilton," Aug. 24, 1797, *PTJ*, 29:517, and Ron Chernow, *Alexander Hamilton* (New York: Penguin Press, 2004), 465–67; long summer nights: La Tour du Pin Gouvernet, *Journal d'une femme*, 2:83; the content of their discussions: Talleyrand, *Mémoires*, 1:240–46; "greatest advantage": Talleyrand to Messrs. Bourdieu, Chollet and Bourdieu, June 10, 1794, *TAFP*, 28; Talleyrand watching Hamilton at the Supreme Court: Samuel Breck to John McAllister, Dec. 19, 1854, Society Small Collection, HSP, and Breck, "Recollections" (ms bound copy), APS; "in raptures": ALS, Hamilton Papers, LoC; "most distinguished": Talleyrand, *Mémoires*, 1:241; "Napoleon, Fox, and Hamilton": quoted in Chernow, *Alexander Hamilton*, 466; Spaeth, "Purgatory or Promised Land?," 154; and Poniatowski, *Talleyrand aux États-Unis*, 105; Burr in Paris: Cooper, *Talleyrand*, 73–74, and Poniatowski, *Talleyrand aux États-Unis*, 153. Moreau also praised Hamilton as "one of the most outstanding statesmen the United States of America had." He reported, however, that Hamilton spoke French "in a very incorrect manner." He is the only French person I found to criticize Hamilton's French. See Moreau, *Voyage*, 149.

4. Talleyrand, *Mémoires*, 1:231.

5. Liancourt, *Journal*, 63; Angelica Church to AH, Sept. 19, 1794, *PAH*, 17:251–52.

6. Liancourt, *Journal*, 84, 91; Liancourt, *Voyage*, 3:260, 7:149.

7. "Esteem for": AH to Noailles, April–June 1782, *PAH*, 3:83–84; "My dear brother": Church to AH, Feb. 17, 1793, *PAH*, 14:89; Monsr. de TJ to Church, June 7, 1793, *PTJ*, 26:215; "a man of": Noailles to William Windham, June 1, 1793, *Windham Papers*, 1:125. On Hamilton's friendship with Noailles: AH to Lafayette, Nov. 3, 1782, *PAH*, 3:191–94; and AH to Noailles, n.d., but evidently shortly before April 1782, *PAH*, 26:420–23.

8. "whom I entertain": WB to Jasper Yeats, May 1, 1795, Ferdinand J. Dreer Autograph Collection, HSP; "and cannot speak": Liancourt, *Voyage*, 1:50–51; "My respect": Alexander Graydon, *Memoirs of a Life, Chiefly Passed in Pennsylvania, within the Last Sixty Years, with Occasional Remarks Upon the General Occurrences, Character and Spirit of That Eventful Period* (Harrisburgh [sic]: John Wyeth, 1811), 346–47. Not all French travelers, it must be said, found letters so effective in the United States. "In France, with letters of recommendation for the leading persons of station in each town, a foreigner would be welcomed, fêted, etc. In this country, they take your letter; they have you sit down; they bring a glass of Madeira wine and then, everything is over. Most of them not only do not return your visits; still less, any dinners, offering a place to stay, etc.: but if you wish to invite the people to whom you have been recommended to a Tavern, they will come most willingly" (Gallucci, *Castorland Journal*, 11). It's unclear, based on this testimony, whether the chilly reception was due to American manners or to this Frenchman's character.

9. "Mr. Volney": TJ to Harry Innes, June 21, 1796, *PTJ*, 29:131; "Dear Sir": GW to Tobias Lear, May 6, 1796, John Clement Fitzpatrick, ed., *The Writings of George Washington from the Original Manuscript Sources, 1745–1799*, 39 vols. (Washington, DC: Government Printing Office, 1931), 35:36; "considered to be": Breck, "Recollections" (ms bound copy), APS, 15; Paul Leicester Ford, *The True George Washington* (Philadelphia: J. B. Lippincott, 1896), 195–96. The other five letters by Jefferson on Volney's behalf were all of the same date: to John Breckinridge, Jean Baptiste Ducoigne, Henri Peyroux de la Coudrèniere, Isaac Shelby, and Archibald Stuart. For letters of travelers through the backcountry, see also Édouard Charles Victurnien Colbert-Maulevrier, *Voyage dans l'intérieur des États-Unis et au Canada*, ed. Gilbert Chinard (Baltimore: Johns Hopkins Press, 1935). The anecdote about Washington's letter for Volney appears to have originated with Samuel Breck. It was picked up by Griswold, *Republican Court*, 333, who almost certainly made it infamous. A search today will find dozens of references to this letter.

10. Moorehead, *Dancing to the Precipice*; see also Childs, *French Refugee Life*, 25.

11. La Tour du Pin Gouvernet, *Journal d'une femme*, 2:3.

12. Ibid., 2:9–10, 19; Childs, *French Refugee Life*, 94.

13. La Tour du Pin Gouvernet, *Journal d'une femme*, 2:31; Talleyrand's clothing during his backwoods trip: Scudder, *Recollections of Samuel Breck*, 197–98.

14. Moorehead, *Dancing to the Precipice*, 214; Childs, *French Refugee Life*, 25; La Tour du Pin Gouvernet, *Journal d'une femme*, 2:52; Liancourt, *Voyage*, 2:316–19.

15. On the romantic association of La Tour du Pin's life, see Baldensperger, "Le séjour de Talleyrand aux États-Unis," 376–77.

16. Revolutionary sailors' Atlantic networks: Peter Linebaugh and Marcus Rediker, *The Many-Headed Hydra: Sailors, Slaves, Commoners, and the Hidden History of the Revolutionary Atlantic* (Boston: Beacon Press, 2000); radical political networks: Seth Cotlar, *Tom Paine's America: The Rise and Fall of Transatlantic Radicalism in the Early Republic* (Charlottesville: University of Virginia Press, 2011); slave networks: Scott, "Common Wind"; merchant networks: Peter Mathias, "Risk, Credit and Kinship in Early Modern Enterprise," in *The Early Modern Atlantic Economy*, ed. John J. McCusker and Kenneth Morgan (Cambridge: Cambridge University Press, 2000); Kenneth Morgan, "Business Networks in the British Export Trade to North America, 1750–1800," in ibid.; David Hancock, "The Trouble with Networks:

Managing the Scots' Early-Modern Madeira Trade," *Business History Review* 79, no. 3 (2005); Pierre Gervais, "Neither Imperial, nor Atlantic: A Merchant Perspective on International Trade in the Eighteenth Century," *History of European Ideas* 34 (2008). On harder sociological network theory and its applicability to history, a good introduction is Charles Wetherell, "Historical Social Network Analysis," *International Review of Social History* 43 (1998).

17. Noailles to Knox, May 10, 1782, Knox Papers, MHS. The description of Washington's levees is from Griswold, *Republican Court*, 269–70; see also Henderson, "Furnishing the Republican Court," 75–77. For an early statement on the importance of the Republican Court to Philadelphia politics and society, see also David S. Shields and Fredrika J. Teute, "The Republican Court and the Historiography of a Woman's Domain in the Public Sphere," paper presented at the annual conference of the Society for Historians of the Early American Republic, Boston, July 15, 1994, in the author's possession. For the diplomatic and political consequences of the Republican Court under Jefferson's administration, see Fredrika J. Teute and David S. Shields, "Jefferson in Washington: Domesticating Manners in the Republican Court," paper presented at the Institute of Early American History and Culture, Third Annual Conference, Old Salem, NC, June 7, 1997.

18. GW to the Secretary of the Treasury, May 5, 1793, Fitzpatrick, *Writings*, 32:37–38; [Noailles] to Windham, June 1, 1793, *Windham Papers*, 122. For the message from the French foreign minister to GW passed by William Stephens Smith, see "Notes on Conversation with William Stephens Smith and George Washington, dated Feb. 20, 1793," *PTJ*, 25:243.

19. Fauchet to Minister of Foreign Affairs, 16 Floréal, an 2 (May 5, 1794), and Fauchet to Minister of Foreign Affairs, 17 Prairial, an 2 (June 5, 1794), *CFM*, 332, 379.

20. Fauchet to Minister of Foreign Affairs, 17 Prairial, an 2 (June 5, 1794), ibid., 2:379–80; Liancourt, *Journal*, 103.

21. "principles should be adopted": GW to AH, May 6, 1794, Fitzpatrick, *Writings*, 33:352–53; "When he came": Niemcewicz, *Under Their Vine and Fig Tree*, 86–87. On Talleyrand's disappointment, see Baldensperger, "Le séjour de Talleyrand aux États-Unis," 369–72. In the passage quoted here, Washington goes on in a similar vein to attribute Liancourt's critical comments toward the United States to Washington's rebuff.

22. Liancourt, *Journal*, 69, 66. The literature on these larger questions is far too vast to cite here. On the French and European contexts most relevant to discussion here, see especially Jürgen Habermas, *The Structural Transformation of the Public Sphere: An Inquiry into a Category of Bourgeois Society* (Cambridge, MA: MIT Press, 1989); Goodman, *Republic of Letters*; and Susan Dalton, *Engendering the Republic of Letters: Reconnecting Public and Private Spheres in Eighteenth-Century Europe* (Montreal: McGill-Queen's University Press, 2003). On the U.S. context, see especially Bushman, *Refinement of America*; Shields, *Civil Tongues*; Catherine Allgor, *Parlor Politics: In Which the Ladies of Washington Help Build a City and a Government* (Charlottesville: University of Virginia Press, 2000); Branson, *Fiery Frenchified Dames*; Joanne B. Freeman, *Affairs of Honor: National Politics in the New Republic* (New Haven, CT: Yale University Press, 2001); and Henderson, "Furnishing the Republican Court."

23. "Have here": Volney to La Réveillière, Jan. 14, 1797, Mathiez, "Lettres de Volney à La Réveillière," 174; also quoted in Gaulmier, *L'idéologue Volney*, 382; "with two or three dishes": Moreau, *Journey*, 275. On the influence of French and U.S. republicanism in the Age of Revolutions: Susan Dunn, *Sister Revolutions: French Lightning, American Light* (New York: Faber and Faber, 1999), and Patrice L. R. Higonnet, *Sister Republics: The Origins of French and American Republicanism* (Cambridge, MA: Harvard University Press, 1988). On a later period, see Mark Hulliung, *Citizens and Citoyens: Republicans and Liberals in America and France* (Cambridge, MA: Harvard University Press, 2002).

24. "Caught between their aristocratic backgrounds and their liberal ideas," writes Catherine Spaeth, "most exiles seem to have found the perfect republicans in the Federalists." See Spaeth, "Purgatory or Promised Land?," 155. On Jacobinism in the United States, see especially Cleves, *Reign of Terror in America*.

25. The development of political parties as a framework for institutionalizing dissent: Hofstadter, *Idea of a Party System;* Jefferson's political sociability: Teute and Shields, "Jefferson in Washington"; Dolley Madison's political sociability: Allgor, *Parlor Politics,* 48–101.

26. Breck, "Recollections" (ms bound volume), APS; *ANB,* s.v. "Bingham, William." See also Brown, "Mr. and Mrs. William Bingham."

27. On Willing, see Thomas Balch and Edward Shippen, eds., *Letters and Papers Relating Chiefly to the Provincial History of Pennsylvania: With Some Notices of the Writers* (Philadelphia: Crissy and Markley, Printers, 1855); Eugene R. Slaski, "Thomas Willing: A Study in Moderation, 1774–1778," *PMHB* 100, no. 4 (1976); and William Weisberger, *ANB,* s.v. "Willing, Thomas." Willing, his father, and his mother's grandfather had all been mayor of Philadelphia.

28. Hoping for a diplomatic post: AA to Eliz. Cranch, Dec. 3, 1784, *APDE;* Liancourt, *Journal,* 62.

29. Lansdowne was also a patron of literature: Joseph Priestley, the famous radical, had worked as his librarian. On his London house: Sherry Babbitt, *Handbook of the Collections* (Philadelphia: Philadelphia Museum of Art, 1995), 143–44.

30. TJ to JH, Jan. 30, 1787, *PTJ,* 11:95; JA to JQA, June 21, 1784, *APDE;* Abigail Adams Smith, *Journal and Correspondence of Miss Adams, Daughter of John Adams, Second President of the United States. . . . ,* ed. Caroline Amelia Smith De Windt (New York: Wiley and Putnam, 1841), 27–28, 34–35. The emphasis has been changed from the original.

31. TJ to JM, Jan. 30, 1787, *PTJ,* 11:95; Alberts, *Golden Voyage,* 138–39.

32. "If the world" and "delicately attentive": quoted in Alberts, *Golden Voyage,* 128, 143; "It was very natural": Thomas Willing Balch, ed., *Willing Letters and Papers: Edited with a Biographical Essay of Thomas Willing of Philadelphia (1631–1821)* (Philadelphia: Allen, Lane and Scott, 1922), 111.

33. Voltaire, *Siècle de Louis XIV,* quoted in Goodman, *Republic of Letters,* 114. "Grand Tour": Jeremy Black, *The British and the Grand Tour* (1985; London: Routledge, 2010).

34. AA to Mercy Otis Warren, Sept. 5, 1784, *APDE;* standard complaint: Goodman, *Republic of Letters,* 77; French as frivolous: ibid., 53–73; American complaints about leisure more generally: Shields, *Civil Tongues,* 308–28; Elizabeth Powel's sociability: Sarah Templier, "Under the Roof and the Pen of Elizabeth Willing Powel: Material Culture, Sociability, and Letters in Revolutionary and Early Republican Philadelphia" (master's thesis, Université de Montréal, 2013).

35. Smith, *Journal and Correspondence,* 32, 37, 61, 34.

36. Anne Willing Bingham to TJ, June 1, 1787, *PTJ,* 11:393; TJ to GW, Dec. 4, 1788 [incorrectly dated Nov. 4], *PTJ,* 14:330. See also Brown, "Mr. and Mrs. William Bingham," 296. Bingham's paean to Frenchwomen was written in response to an extraordinary condemnation of them by Jefferson. See TJ to Anne Bingham, Feb. 7, 1787, *PTJ,* 11:122–23.

37. Laujon, *Souvenirs et voyages,* 116; Arthur Lee to James Warren, Dec. 12, 1782, quoted in Alberts, *Golden Voyage,* 120; Smith, *Journal and Correspondence,* 19–20, 29.

38. Guidebook and "Countless shops": quoted in Darrin M. McMahon, "The Birthplace of the Revolution: Public Space and Political Community in the Palais-Royal of Louis-Philippe-Joseph d'Orléans, 1781–1789," *French History* 10, no. 1 (1996): 15, 16; details about the Palais Royal: David Andress, "The Micro-Physics of Öffentlichkeit? Habermas, Foucault, and the Administration of Democratic Space in the Palais-Royal, 1789–1790," *Cultural & Social History* 3, no. 2 (2006), and Maurice Garçon, "Les métamorphoses du Palais-Royal," *Miroir de l'histoire* 11, no. 126 (1960): 715; Talleyrand's participation in the Club de Valois: Poniatowski, *Talleyrand: Les années occultées,* 178.

39. Laujon, *Souvenirs et voyages,* 2:116; Smith, *Journal and Correspondence,* 44.

40. Smith, *Journal and Correspondence,* 47, 15, 47, 52; "very unwell": JQA, Mar. 5, 1785, *APDE.*

41. Alberts, *Golden Voyage,* 138–39; Morris to William Bingham, Jan. 19, 1784, E. James Ferguson and John Catanzariti, eds., *The Papers of Robert Morris, 1781–1784,* 9 vols. (Pittsburgh: University of Pittsburgh Press, 1973), 9:39–40; AA2 to JQA, Jan 22, 1786, *APDE.*

42. Diary of JA, June 22, 1784, *AFPEA.*

43. AA to Mary Cranch, London, Sept. 30, 1785, *APDE;* AA2 to JQA, Feb. 9, 1786, and Feb. 1, 1786, ibid.

44. AA to JQA, Feb. 9, 1786, ibid.

45. AA to JQA, Feb. 16, 1786, ibid. For the scene, see also Alberts, *Golden Voyage,* 152–55.

46. Henderson, "Furnishing the Republican Court," 92–93, 89, 95–97; examining mansions: Thompson Westcott, *The Historic Mansions and Buildings of Philadelphia: With Some Notice of Their Owners and Occupants* (Philadelphia: Porter & Coates, 1877), 343–44; "somewhat enlarged": Griswold, *Republican Court,* 259. This may be the place to express my great debt to Amy Henderson's outstanding dissertation for her many insights that have powerfully shaped my own thinking.

47. "best English style": quoted in Westcott, *Historic Mansions,* 344; "abounds with," "green-house contains," and "building is": Henderson, "Furnishing the Republican Court," 92; Hogan, *Prospect of Philadelphia,* 127; "considerable numbers": Twining, *Travels in America,* 36; wooden fence: Kelley, *Life and Times in Colonial Philadelphia,* 71.

48. "brought from Europe": quoted in Brown, "Mr. and Mrs. William Bingham," 297; "elegant and even superb": quoted in Alberts, *Golden Voyage,* 163; upstairs rooms: Garvan, *Federal Philadelphia,* 37–38, 62; "In a word," Niemcewicz, *Under Their Vine and Fig Tree,* 37.

49. TJ to Anne Bingham, Feb. 7, 1787, *PTJ,* 11:122–24; TJ to William Bingham, Sept. 25, 1789, *PTJ,* 15:467–77.

50. "I have never seen": quoted in Brown, "Mr. and Mrs. William Bingham," 297; "into saloons": Griswold, *Republican Court,* 259; Breck, "Recollections" (ms bound copy), APS; "papered in": quoted in Alberts, *Golden Voyage,* 163; Parisian salons: Goodman, *Republic of Letters,* 84–89; Adam on dining rooms: Robert Oresko, ed., *The Works in Architecture of Robert and James Adam* (London: Academy Editions; New York: St. Martin's Press, 1975), 48; "food is served": Niemcewicz, *Under Their Vine and Fig Tree,* 37; "meeting point": Alexandre Tilly, comte de, *Mémoires du comte Alexandre de Tilly, pour servir à l'histoire des moeurs de la fin du 18e siècle,* 3 vols. (Paris: Chez les Marchands de Nouveautes, 1828), 3:245

51. Liancourt, *Voyage,* 6:331; Warder quoted in Henderson, "Furnishing the Republican Court," 96; J. P. Brissot de Warville, *Nouveau voyage dans les États-Unis de l'Amérique septentrionale, fait en 1788,* 3 vols. (Paris: Buisson, 1791), 2:92; Arthur Lee quoted in Branson, *Fiery French-ified Dames,* 136; "spirit of equality": Niemcewicz, *Under Their Vine and Fig Tree,* 37; "There is a propriety": Kenneth R. Veit and Helen E. Bowling, eds., *The Diary of William Maclay and Other Notes on Senate Debates* (Baltimore: Johns Hopkins University Press, 1988), 357.

52. Peter Markoe, "The Times of 1788," as quoted in John Frederick Lewis, *The History of an Old Philadelphia Land Title, 208 South Fourth Street* (Philadelphia: Patterson & White, 1934), 202–3.

53. Price of portrait: Carrie Rebora Barratt and Ellen Gross Miles, *Gilbert Stuart* (New York: Metropolitan Museum of Art, 2004), 206. I am enormously grateful to Zara Anishanslin for suggesting this exploration of the Stuart portraiture in the culture of the Republican Court, and for informing the pages that follow with her sharp insight. I am equally grateful to David Steinberg, who gave this section his incomparably close and deeply informed reading, and saved me from innumerable embarrassing errors of fact and interpretation. And finally to Ellen Miles, who graciously read this section and corrected several mistakes. None of them is responsible for any errors that remain.

54. Jay's unfinished portait: Barratt and Miles, *Gilbert Stuart,* 121; Stuart quoted in Margaret C. S. Christman, "The Story of the Lansdowne Washington," in *George Washington: A National Treasure* (Washington, DC: National Portrait Gallery, Smithsonian Institution, in association with the University of Washington Press, Seattle, 2002), 48.

55. Edgar P. Richardson, *American Paintings and Related Pictures in the Henry Francis du Pont Winterthur Museum* (Charlottesville: University of Virginia Press, 1986), 92–94.

56. AB to FB, Nov. 1796, BaP; GW to Gilbert Stuart, Apr. 11, 1796, George C. Mason, *The Life and Works of Gilbert Stuart* (New York: C. Scribner's Sons, 1879), 88; "notorious": Custis, *Recol-*

lections, 526. On Washington's fatigue with sitting for portraits, see Barratt and Miles, *Gilbert Stuart,* 166–68, who also quote the letter from Washington to Stuart.

57. AB to FB, Nov. 1796, BaP. On the correspondence between Washington's dress in the portrait and at his public events, see Ellen Gross Miles, *George and Martha Washington: Portraits from the Presidential Years* (Washington, DC: Smithsonian Institution, National Portrait Gallery, 1999), 46.

58. Lansdowne to William Jackson, Mar. 5, 1797, Balch and Shippen, *Letters and Papers,* 306; "exquisite statues" and Lansdowne portrait hanging in library: "Diary of a Lover of Literature," June 28, 1804, *Gentleman's Magazine* (Mar. 1834), 252; Lansdowne to Anne Bingham, quoted in Barratt and Miles, *Gilbert Stuart,* 170; "General Washington's conduct": Balch and Shippen, *Letters and Papers,* 307. On the library, which was originally designed as a gallery, see Arthur T. Bolton, *The Architecture of Robert and James Adam, 1758–1794,* 2 vols. (1922; repr. Woodbridge, Eng.: Antique Collectors' Club, 1984), 2:14–17, who suggests that pictures rather than statues were likely hung in the room. Damie Stillman, "The Gallery for Lansdowne House: International Neoclassical Architecture and Decoration in Microcosm," *The Art Bulletin* 52, no. 1 (1970), 75–80, in the most careful examination of the evolution of Lansdowne's gallery, seems to indicate that the room remained a shell until 1819. That is hard to reconcile, however, with the description of the room by the visitor quoted in the paragraph, which can only correspond to the gallery. Having explored this issue carefully, I have tentatively concluded that the portrait was most likely displayed in the unfinished gallery, although further research may clarify this issue. See also Peter Meadows, *Joseph Bonomi, Architect: 1739–1808: An Exhibition of Drawings from Private Collections* (London: Royal Institute of British Architects, 1988).

59. Lansdowne to Anne Bingham, quoted in Barratt and Miles, *Gilbert Stuart,* 170.

60. "who was intimate": Gilmor, *Memorandums Made in a Tour,* 6; also quoted in Barratt and Miles, *Gilbert Stuart,* 175; on Noailles and Stuart's friendship: Mason, *Life and Works,* 55; on Lansdown: Westcott, *Historic Mansions,* 335; Kelley, *Life and Times in Colonial Philadelphia,* 71; on Bingham's hanging the Washington portrait at Lansdown: Charles Henry Hart, "Stuart's Lansdowne Portrait of Washington," *Harper's New Monthly Magazine,* 93, no. 555 (Aug. 1896), 379, and Barratt and Miles, *Gilbert Stuart,* 176.

61. "the inviolable union": quoted in Barratt and Miles, *Gilbert Stuart,* 171; see also Dorinda Stuart Gilbert Evans, *The Genius of Gilbert Stuart* (Princeton, NJ: Princeton University Press, 1999), 67–69; Lansdowne to GW, July 4, 1791, and GW to Lansdowne, Nov. 7, 1791, *PGWPS,* 9:150 and note. On portraiture and diplomatic exchange, see Barratt and Miles, *Gilbert Stuart,* 172–73.

62. Mason, *Life and Works,* 92; Gilmor, *Memorandums Made in a Tour,* 6; Barratt and Miles, *Gilbert Stuart,* 208; Gustavus A. Eisen, *Portraits of Washington,* 3 vols. (New York: R. Hamilton & Associates, 1932), 1:78.

63. "failed entirely": Barratt and Miles, *Gilbert Stuart,* 169; George Washington Parke Custis to Thomas Carberry, April 7, 1839, contributed by Horatio King, in *The Magazine of American History with Notes and Queries,* 13 (1885): 583; Eisen, *Portraits of Washington,* 1:72; "conclusive": quoted in Mason, *Life and Works,* 92; Noailles as model: John K. Howat, "'A Young Man Impatient to Distinguish Himself'": The Vicomte de Noailles as Portrayed by Gilbert Stuart," *Metropolitan Museum of Art Bulletin* 29, no. 7 (1971); Barratt and Miles, *Gilbert Stuart,* 208. Eisen further notes the similarities in background and pose that unite the Lenox portrait of Washington and the portrait of William Bingham. Eisen, *Portraits of Washington,* 1:83.

64. Quoted in Barratt and Miles, *Gilbert Stuart,* 220.

65. Laujon, *Souvenirs et voyages,* 116; Goodman, *Republic of Letters,* 130, 124 (Hume quotation), 6 (Voltaire). This interpretation of Anne Bingham largely corresponds to Branson, *Fiery Frenchified Dames,* and Henderson, "Furnishing the Republican Court." For an insightful analysis of the Progressive historians' erasure of elite women's role in the early Republic's politics, see Shields and Teute, "Republican Court."

66. Griswold, *Republican Court*, 263, 254 ("manners were a gift"); "tone and carriage": Niemce-wicz, *Under Their Vine and Fig Tree*, 37; "conversational cleverness": Breck, "Recollections" (ms bound copy), APS; "combination of expression": quoted in Alberts, *Golden Voyage*, 214; "She joins": Smith, *Journal and Correspondence*, 29; Alberts, *Golden Voyage*, 143; Branson, *Fiery Frenchified Dames*, 134; "[Mrs.] Bingham stood above": Samuel Breck to John McAl-lister, July 29, 1858, Society Small Collection, HSP; Adams quoted in Brown, "Mr. and Mrs. William Bingham," 308. On Bingham's qualities as a *salonnière*: Teute and Shields, "Jefferson in Washington," 12–14; on the importance of "attention" as a primary feature of French *sa-lonnières*: Goodman, *Republic of Letters*, 79–84.

67. JA to AA, Dec. 20, 1796, *AFPEA*; Laujon, *Souvenirs et voyages*, 120.

68. "She blaz'd": quoted in Garvan, *Federal Philadelphia*, 23; Marshall quoted in Barratt and Miles, *Gilbert Stuart*, 196. For other readings of Stuart's portrait of Bingham, see ibid., 195–98, and Henderson, "Furnishing the Republican Court," 365–69.

69. Marion Rust, *Prodigal Daughters: Susanna Rowson's Early American Women* (Chapel Hill: University of North Carolina Press, 2008), esp. 160–94; Susanna Rowson, *Trials of the Human Heart: A Novel. In Four Volumes* (Philadelphia: Printed for the author, 1795), 1:ix–x. On Elizabeth Willing Powel and Rush: Templier, "Under the Roof and the Pen," 86–92.

70. Lowndes Stoddert quoted in Brown, "Mr. and Mrs. William Bingham," 317–18; table: Louise Conway Belden, *The Festive Tradition, Table Decoration and Desserts in America, 1650–1900*, A Winterthur Book (New York: W. W. Norton, 1983), 4–5; doleful watchmen: Niemcewicz, *Under Their Vine and Fig Tree*, 38.

71. Clarence L. Ver Steeg, *ANB*, s.v. "Morris, Robert."

72. Scudder, *Recollections of Samuel Breck*, 203; Liancourt, *Journal*, Feb. 24, 1795, 102.

73. Chastellux, *Voyages*, 1:173–74; see also 1:190 and George B. Tatum and Cortlandt Van Dyke Hubbard, *Philadelphia Georgian: The City House of Samuel Powel and Some of Its Eighteenth-Century Neighbors* (Middletown, CT: Wesleyan University Press, 1976), 16. On links between Powel and Bingham: Branson, *Fiery Frenchified Dames*, 133. On the Philadelphia aristocracy: Griswold, *Republican Court*; on the Virginia aristocracy: Charles Royster, *The Fabulous His-tory of the Dismal Swamp Company: A Story of George Washington's Times* (New York: Alfred A. Knopf, 1999).

74. Bushman, *Refinement of America*, 37. On Talleyrand's quip: Lilti, *Le monde des salons*, 41.

75. Lucy Breck to unidentified recipient, Oct. 24, 1796, quoted in letter by Samuel Breck, Apr. 24, 1848, Society Small Collection, HSP; Liancourt, *Journal*, 73; "fêted . . . *comme il faut*": Fauchet to Minister of Foreign Affairs, June 5, 1794, *CFM*, 378; "fêted, caressed": Fauchet to Minister of Foreign Affairs, Dec. 1, 1794, ibid., 493; "assembled": Samuel Breck to John McAllister, Dec. 19, 1854, Society Small Collection, HSP. On the desire of Americans to have French émigrés at their houses and parties: Diesbach, *Histoire de l'émigration*, 502–3. The comte de Moré leaves a different impression: "Malgré toute son amabilité, monseigneur n'obtint pas dans la société de Philadelphie autant de succès qu'en méritait la légèreté de son ton et de ses manières. En effet, les Anglo-Américains ont des mœurs simples et positives, et le mépris cynique de leur hôte pour le respect humain d'Amérique les scandalisa très fortement" (Grandmaison, *Mémoires*, 155). Every other source I have found belies Moré's claim, however.

76. "liberal pay": Breck, "Recollections" (ms bound copy), APS; "used to walk": quoted in Barratt and Miles, *Gilbert Stuart*, 198; "French is almost": Gilmor, *Memorandums Made in a Tour*, 5.

77. Twining, *Travels in America*, 30, 40–41; Laujon, *Souvenirs et voyages*, 2:119.

78. "Attempts to arm": quoted in Moorehead, *Dancing to the Precipice*, 342; "no amateur": Scud-der, *Recollections of Samuel Breck*, 165.

79. "I have seldom seen": Graydon, *Memoirs*, 348; "remarkable": Laujon, *Souvenirs et voyages*, 2:112; "form was perfect": Scudder, *Recollections of Samuel Breck*, 199; "extremely disap-pointed": letter of Lucy Breck, dated Oct. 1796, Breck Family Papers, 1796, box 2, HSP.

80. Whitehead, "Autobiography of Peter Stephen Du Ponceau," 434–35; Smith, *Journal and Cor-respondence*, 34; Henderson, "Furnishing the Republican Court," 81.

81. Dinner: Arnold Palmer, *Movable Feasts; a Reconnaissance of the Origins and Consequences of Fluctuations in Meal-Times, with Special Attention to the Introduction of Luncheon and Afternoon Tea* (London: Oxford University Press, 1952), 12–15; Belden, *Festive Tradition*, 16–20; "with much form": Weld, *Travels*, 1:22; Martha Washington's salons: Branson, *Fiery Frenchified Dames*, 128–29; British ambassador's wife: Henderson, "Furnishing the Republican Court," 76, 79; lottery: Gilmor, *Memorandums Made in a Tour*, 22; conversation was "serious or lively": Whitehead, "Autobiography of Peter Stephen Du Ponceau," 434–35; Parisian salons: Goodman, *Republic of Letters*, 78–79, 91. The most vivid description of salon life in New York, before the capital moved to Philadelphia, is AA to Mary Smith Cranch, Jan. 24, 1789, L. H. Butterfield, Marc Friedlaender, and Richard Alan Ryerson, eds., *Adams Family Correspondence*, 11 vols. to date (Cambridge, MA: Belknap Press of Harvard University Press, 1963), 9:8.

82. Liancourt, *Journal*, 93, 118; *Voyage*, 6:327–29. See, however, Liancourt's more ambivalent comments in *Journal*, 90, 105–6.

83. Shields and Teute, "Republican Court," 5; Teute and Shields, "Jefferson in Washington," 14.

84. Moreau, *Voyage*, 219; "fine miniature": quoted in Brown, "Mr. and Mrs. William Bingham," 311; Willing's refusal: Balch, *Willing Letters and Papers*, lix. The first reference to this possibly apocryphal story appears to come from Benjamin Perley Poore, *The Rise and Fall of Louis Philippe, Ex-King of the French. . . .* (Boston: William D. Ticknor, 1848), 82. On the romance, see also Breck, "Recollections" (ms bound copy), APS.

85. "very great influence": AB to FB, Nov. 1796, CML-BaP; "very ill" and "lost his senses": quoted in Brown, "Mr. and Mrs. William Bingham," 319; Tilly, *Mémoires*, 243–46; Robert Morris to Maria Morris, June 26, 1799, Society Miscellaneous Collection, folder 14, HSP. On this affair, see Matilda Bingham de Tilly letters, 1799, Collection 661, HSP.

86. AB to J. Williams Hope, Dec. 8, 1795, CML-BaP. On the importance of marriage in constituting business networks, see Hancock, "Trouble with Networks," 474–75; David Hancock, *Citizens of the World: London Merchants and the Integration of the British Atlantic Community, 1735–1785* (New York: Cambridge University Press, 1995), 42–43, 139–42, 245–47.

87. Algar Labouchere Thorold, *The Life of Henry Labouchere* (London: G. P. Putnam's Sons, 1913), 21–22.

88. Talleyrand to Staël, Nov. 14, 1795, "Lettres de M. de Talleyrand à Madame de Staël, tirées des archives du Château de Broglie," *Revue d'histoire diplomatique* 4, no. 3 (1890): 216. On the emergence of capitalism in the trade of Italian city-states, I have been particularly influenced by Fernand Braudel, *Civilization and Capitalism, 15th–18th Century*, trans. Sian Reynolds, 3 vols. (London: Collins, 1985); Giovanni Arrighi, *The Long Twentieth Century: Money, Power, and the Origins of Our Times* (New York: Verso, 1994).

89. "I have been introduced": AB to J. Williams Hope, Dec. 8, 1795, CML-BaP; "Nothing can be done": P. C. Labouchère to FB, Dec. 5, 1801, Northbrook Papers, 1 A13.3.1, BaP. On reputation, risk, and bankruptcy, see Toby L. Ditz, "Shipwrecked; or, Masculinity Imperiled: Mercantile Representations of Failure and the Gendered Self in Eighteenth-Century Philadelphia," *JAH* 81, no. 1 (1994).

90. AB to FB, Nov. 22, 1796, CML-BaP.

91. Roland M. Baumann, "John Swanwick: Spokesman for 'Merchant Republicanism' in Philadelphia, 1790–1798," *PMHB* 47, no. 2 (1973): 136, 143; AB to FB, May 5, 1796, Nov. 1796, and Nov. 22, 1796, CML-BaP.

92. "secret rejection": Roland M. Baumann, *ANB*, s.v. "Swanwick, John"; "broken heart": quoted in ibid.

93. Cazenove's connection to the Brissot, Duer, Clavière consortium: Max M. Mintz, *Gouverneur Morris and the American Revolution* (Norman: University of Oklahoma Press, 1970), 206; his brother: Poniatowski, *Talleyrand aux États-Unis*, 77, 94–95; his cousin: Arthur Quirin Maurice de Cazenove, *Quatre siècles* (Nîmes, 1908), 130–32; his move to Philadelphia:

Kelsey, *Cazenove Journal,* ix; his help raising money for Moreau's store: Moreau, *Voyage,* 140; Taillemite, "Moreau de Saint Méry: Une Biographie."

94. Talleyrand's links to Panchaud: Wilma J. Pugh, "Introduction," in *TAFP,* 4–5; discussions with G. Morris and link to Flahut: Poniatowski, *Talleyrand aux États-Unis,* 357; Ghislain de Diesbach, *Madame de Staël* (Paris: Perrin, 1983), 102; "There are many ways": Talleyrand to Mr. Goring of London, June 10, 1794, *TAFP,* 27; "In a short time": Talleyrand to Madame de Staël, Aug. 4, 1794, "Lettres de M. de Talleyrand à Madame de Staël," 213; choice of Cazenove: Poniatowski, *Talleyrand aux États-Unis,* 388.

95. Liancourt, *Journal,* 66, 71, 72; Moreau, *American Journey,* 178; Chinard, *Volney et l'Amérique,* 31–32.

PART 2: THE FRENCH REVOLUTION IN THE WEST

1. Braudel, *La Méditerranée,* 1:17.

2. I am grateful to Heather Short for tipping me off to these matters, and for kindly mitigating the geological ignorance displayed in the above paragraph. See also the U.S. Geological Survey Appalachian Highlands Province Web site, http://geomaps.wr.usgs.gov/parks/province/appalach.html, accessed Oct. 18, 2013, and its "A Tapestry of Time and Terrain" page: http://tapestry.usgs.gov/Default.html, accessed Nov. 5, 2013.

3. John Wesley Powell, *Physiographic Regions of the United States* (New York: American Book, 1895), 73–75; Albert Perry Brigham, *Geographic Influences in American History* (Boston: Ginn, 1903), 4.

4. The previous three paragraphs are based on Ellen Churchill Semple, *American History and Its Geographic Conditions* (Boston: Houghton, Mifflin, 1903), 4; ec.gc.ca/stl, accessed Apr. 8, 2014; Donald Grant Creighton, *The Empire of the St. Lawrence* (Toronto: Macmillan, 1956), 6; William Cronon, *Nature's Metropolis: Chicago and the Great West* (New York: W. W. Norton, 1991), 23–24; Frederick Jackson Turner, *The Character and Influence of the Indian Trade in Wisconsin: A Study of the Trading Post as an Institution* (Baltimore: Johns Hopkins Press, 1891), 20–21.

5. White, *Middle Ground,* 1; Turner, *Character and Influence of the Indian Trade,* 14–15, 25.

6. Henry Adams, *History of the United States of America during the Administrations of James Madison* (New York: Library of America, 1986), 6. The two other roads that crossed the Appalachians were Forbes Road, connecting the Susquehanna to the Ohio valley, and Braddock's Road, connecting the Potomac to the Monongahela valley; see Fred Anderson, *The Crucible of War: The Seven Years' War and the Fate of Empire in British North America, 1754–1766* (New York: Alfred A. Knopf, 2000), 94–97, 272–73; Albert Perry Brigham, "The Great Roads across the Appalachians," *Bulletin of the American Geographical Society* 37 (1905); Turner, *Character and Influence of the Indian Trade,* 73.

7. "Plan proposé pour faire une révolution dans la Louisiane," *SFDC,* 951; "In the style": Malcolm J. Rohrbough, *The Trans-Appalachian Frontier: People, Societies, and Institutions, 1775–1850* (New York: Oxford University Press, 1978), 113; "the key": "Extrait d'un mémoire sur les rapports commerciaux de l'Amérique septentrionnale avec l'Europe," AF/IV/1211/58, AN.

8. "nursing mother": "Mémoire sur la Nouvelle-Orléans," AF/IV/1211/156, AN; Liancourt, *Voyage,* 6:195–96; ships from Marietta: Pichon à Talleyrand, 14 Prairial, an 9, CPÉU, 53, p. 140, MAÉ; Andrew R. L. Cayton, *The Frontier Republic: Ideology and Politics in the Ohio Country, 1780–1825* (Kent, OH: Kent State University Press, 1986), 30.

9. Turner, *Character and Influence of the Indian Trade,* 44–45; Hammond to Grenville, Feb. 2, 1792, *Manuscripts of J. B. Fortescue,* 2:254; Lawrence Hatter, "Channeling the Spirit of Enterprise: Commercial Interests and State Formation in the Early American West, 1763–1825" (Ph.D. diss., University of Virginia, 2011), 7–8.

10. The literature here is vast; I have cited the work that has most influenced me in Furstenberg, "Significance of the Trans-Appalachian Frontier."

11. Ojibwa chief quoted in Robert S. Allen, *His Majesty's Indian Allies: British Indian Policy in the Defence of Canada, 1774–1815* (Toronto: Dundurn Press, 1992), 32. On the Royal Proclamation and its aftermath, see especially Colin G. Calloway, *The Scratch of a Pen: 1763 and the Transformation of North America* (Oxford: Oxford University Press, 2006), 92–111, and William J. Campbell, *Speculators in Empire: Iroquoia and the 1768 Treaty of Fort Stanwix* (Norman: University of Oklahoma Press, 2012). On Lansdowne and the Proclamation, see R. A. Humphreys, "Lord Shelburne and the Proclamation of 1763," *English Historical Review* 49, no. 194 (1934).

12. "never could": quoted in Taylor, *Divided Ground*, 112; "Infamous treaty": White, *Middle Ground*, 408; "The Indians": quoted in Turner, *Character and Influence of the Indian Trade*, 49; Native village resistance: White, *Middle Ground*, 467; "As long as": quoted in Julius William Pratt, *Expansionists of 1812* (1925; repr., Gloucester, MA: P. Smith, 1957), 20.

13. "Mountains, as a rule": Braudel, *La Méditerranée*, 1:37, 44; "The Western settlers": GW to Benjamin Harrison, Oct. 10, 1784, *PGWPS*, 2:92. On tenuous settler loyalties, see the citations in Furstenberg, "Significance of the Trans-Appalachian Frontier." On imperial disintegration, see especially John M. Murrin, "1776: The Countercyclical Revolution," in *Revolutionary Currents: Nation Building in the Transatlantic World*, ed. Michael A. Morrison and Melinda S. Zook (Lanham, MD: Rowman & Littlefield, 2004), 65–90.

14. "The inhabitants": Constantin-François Volney, *Tableau du climat et du sol des États-Unis d'Amérique* (Paris: Parmentier, 1825), 19; "Their sole": "Cursory Observations on the Province of Louisiana," CPÉU, supp. 28, p. 67, MAÉ; "Choose lands": *Salem Mercury*, May 19, 1789; Patrick Griffin, *American Leviathan: Empire, Nation, and Revolutionary Frontier* (New York: Hill & Wang, 2007), 224 (who quotes this same text from the *Pennsylvania Gazette*); "separation": TJ to JM, June 10, 1787, quoted in Cayton, *Frontier Republic*, 23.

15. "The inhabitants": J. C. Mountflorence, "Mémoire," Oct. 26, 1792, http://oieahc.wm.edu/wmq/Oct08/campbell.pdf, accessed Dec. 17, 2012; Dorchester: quoted in Slaughter, *Whiskey Rebellion*, 57; Noailles to Windham, June 1, 1793, *Windham Papers*, 1:124; "nature has traced: "Plan proposé pour faire une révolution dans la Louisiane," *SFDC*, 951.

16. "parcel of banditti": quoted in Cayton, *Frontier Republic*, 7; "neglect" quoted in Patrick Griffin, "Reconsidering the Ideological Origins of Indian Removal," in *The Center of a Great Empire: The Ohio Country in the Early American Republic*, ed. Andrew R. L. Cayton and Stuart D. Hobbs (Athens: Ohio University Press, 2005), 28; Republican club quoted in Jon Kukla, *A Wilderness So Immense: The Louisiana Purchase and the Destiny of America* (New York: Alfred A. Knopf, 2003), 169; Blount: Frederick Jackson Turner, "Documents on the Blount Conspiracy, 1795–1797," *AHR* 10, no. 3 (1905); Thomas H. Winn, *ANB*, s.v. "Blount, William." See also Eric Hinderaker, *Elusive Empires: Constructing Colonialism in the Ohio Valley, 1673–1800* (New York: Cambridge University Press, 1997), 239, 246, and Eric Hinderaker and Peter C. Mancall, *At the Edge of Empire: The Backcountry in British North America* (Baltimore: Johns Hopkins University Press, 2003), 133–40.

17. John Holroyd, Earl of Sheffield, *Observations on the Commerce of the American States* (Dublin: Luke White, 1784). Excellent accounts of the diplomatic context are Lawrence S. Kaplan, *Colonies into Nation: American Diplomacy, 1763–1801* (New York: Macmillan, 1972), esp. 157–81; Rossignol, *Le ferment nationaliste*.

CHAPTER 4: TRANSATLANTIC LAND SPECULATION

1. La Tour du Pin Gouvernet, *Journal d'une femme*, 2:72.

2. Liancourt, *Journal*, 120; Talleyrand quoted in Moreau, *Voyage*, 348.

3. Details on the falls are drawn from Twining, *Travels in America*, 60, and Weld, *Travels*, 1:32. Guillemard would be chosen as the fifth commissioner—chosen by the other four—to settle pre–Revolutionary War debts under the provisions of the Jay Treaty. In 1797 he was elected to the American Philosophical Society. *PAH*, 26:88n1; *PTJ*, 29:154n.

4. Nicholson landholdings: Peter C. Mancall, *Valley of Opportunity: Economic Culture Along the Upper Susquehanna, 1700–1800* (Ithaca, NY: Cornell University Press, 1991), 167.

5. Wood, "Robinson Family and Their Correspondence," 30–31; Liancourt, *Voyage*, 1:153. Details on Asylum have also been drawn from Rob Mann and Diana DiPaolo Loren, "Keeping Up Appearances: Dress, Architecture, Furniture, and Status at French Azilum," *International Journal of Historical Archaeology* 5, no. 4 (2001): 286, 288, 292, 298, 301; Norman B. Wilkinson, "A French Asylum on the Susquehanna River," *Historic Pennsylvania Leaflet No. 11* (Harrisburg: Pennsylvania Historical and Museum Commission, 1991), online at the Pennsylvania Historical and Museum Commission, http://www.phmc.state.pa.us/, accessed Aug. 20, 2012; Kennedy, *Orders from France*, 93.

6. "When Coleridge and I": Daniel White, "Introduction to the Fall of Robespierre," http://www.rc.umd.edu/editions/robespierre/intro.html, accessed Nov. 5, 2011, n2; Staël dreamed: Poniatowski, *Talleyrand aux États-Unis*, 126–27. On Southey's pantisocracy, see also Andrew R. L. Cayton, *Love in the Time of Revolution: Transatlantic Literary Radicalism and Historical Change, 1793–1818* (Chapel Hill: University of North Carolina Press, 2013), 78, 203–4.

7. "I suffer": Liancourt to wife, Mar. 20, 1796, Liancourt, *Journal*, 128, 126; "in the end": Liancourt, *Voyage*, 1:3; "only enough": Théophile Cazenove to the Six Houses, *TAFP*, 57; "a man of": Talleyrand, *Mémoires*, 1:232.

8 "This country offers": Noailles to William Windham, June 1, 1793, *Windham Papers*, 1:136; "It was amusing": Scudder, *Recollections of Samuel Breck*, 199–200; "He had nothing": Liancourt, *Voyage*, 3:212; "I promise myself": Memoir to Cazenove, June 23, 1794, *TAFP*, 55.

9. Liancourt to his wife, Mar. 20, 1796, Liancourt, *Journal*, 127; Talleyrand to Staël, May 12, 1794, "Lettres de M. de Talleyrand à Madame de Staël," 211.

10. "There is a lot": Talleyrand to Staël, May 12, 1794, "Lettres de M. de Talleyrand à Madame de Staël," 211; Liancourt's book: *Finances, crédit national, intérêt politique et de commerce; forces militaires de la France* (n.p., 1789); Liancourt's service on the *Comité des finances*: La Rochefoucauld, Wolidow, and Ikni, *Le duc de La Rochefoucauld-Liancourt*, 141–98; Talleyrand's family's connection to the Atlantic trade: Jean Meyer, *L'armement nantais dans la deuxième moitié du XVIIIe siècle* (Paris: SEVPEN, 1969), 92; Gouverneur Morris on Talleyrand: Pugh, "Introduction," 4.

11. "I knew them": Théophile Cazenove to the Six Houses, *TAFP*, 57; "It is to the friendship": ibid., 109; "the best letters": ibid., 54; Talleyrand and LeRoy: ibid., 97; Liancourt and LeRoy: La Rochefoucauld Liancourt to LeRoy et Bayard, Dec. 20, 1794, Gratz Autograph Collection, case 11, box 27, HSP; Talleyrand purchases funds guaranteed by Cazenove: Talleyrand to Le Roy & Bayard, Jan. 14, 1795, Gratz Autograph Collection, HSP, case 10, box 6; "forty years": *TAFP*, 54.

12. "There are many ways": Talleyrand to Goring, June 10, 1794, *TAFP*, 27; "We have experienced": ibid., 69; "fairly uncertain reputations": Talleyrand to Staël, Aug. 4, 1794, "Lettres de M. de Talleyrand à Madame de Staël," 213–14. Bourdieu, Chollet, and Bourdieu in London had been longtime agents for the *fermiers généraux de France* in French purchases of American tobacco, and had extensive connections with Jacques Necker. Herbert Luthy, "Necker et la Compagnie des Indes," *Annales: Économies, Sociétés, Civilisations* 15, no. 5 (1960): 865.

13. "Alexander Hamilton's Final Version of the Report on the Subject of Manufactures," *PAH*, 10:276; "What American lacks": *TAFP*, 56. On the more general financial context of postrevolutionary America, I have drawn particularly on E. James Ferguson, *The Power of the Purse; a History of American Public Finance, 1776–1790* (Chapel Hill: University of North Carolina Press, 1961), 179–288; Mira Wilkins, *The History of Foreign Investment in the United States to 1914* (Cambridge, MA: Harvard University Press, 1989), who quotes Hamilton's report on 45; Max M. Edling and Mark D. Kaplanoff, "Alexander Hamilton's Fiscal Reform: Transforming the Structure of Taxation in the Early Republic," *WMQ* 61, no. 4 (2004): 713–

44; Robert E. Wright, *The First Wall Street: Chestnut Street, Philadelphia, and the Birth of American Finance* (Chicago: University of Chicago Press, 2005), 45–85.

14. Bingham to J. & F. Baring, May 12, 1795, CML-BaP.

15. Details about the Asylum Company have been drawn from Liancourt, *Voyage*, 1:151–70, and J. G. Rosengarten, *French Colonists and Exiles in the United States* (Philadelphia: J. B. Lippincott, 1907), 140–50.

16. "The acquisition": Noailles to William Windham, June 1, 1793, *Windham Papers*, 1:135–36; "Since my arrival": Noailles to Mary Robinson, 1793, Wood, "Robinson Family and Their Correspondence," 30.

17. "Land speculation": Liancourt, *Voyage*, 6:291; lands' location: *A General Draft of the 6 Districts, Situate on the Eastern Side of Allegany River, in the State of Pennsylvania . . . May 1796*, APS; "Dear John": Benjamin Vaughan to John Vaughan, Dec. 6, 1792, Benjamin Vaughan Papers, APS.

18. "More pains": William Jackson to WB, Sept. 27, 1793, *WBML*, 309; "known so generally": Théophile Cazenove to the Six Houses, July 22, 1794, *TAFP*, 60; booming economy and allowing noncitizens to purchase land: Mancall, *Valley of Opportunity*, 167, 176–80; Evans, *Holland Land Company*, 203–12; "There is one Advantage": William Bingham to J. & F. Baring & Co., Mar. 30, 1795, CML-BaP; "There is no river": Weld, *Travels*, 2:349; "There is nothing": *TAFP*, 113; "Philadelphia is full": Talleyrand to unidentified recipient, May 8, 1793, MHS. For more comments on the advantages of Pennsylvania's liberal laws regarding foreign landownership, see William Jackson to William Bingham, August 1793, *WBML*, 291, and Liancourt, *Voyage*, 6:287. Some investors made efforts to alter New York State law to legalize landownership by foreigners, see AH to Cazenove, Jan. 22, 1796, *PAH*, 20:45–47, n1, 2, and 3, and Cazenove to Egbert Bensen and AH, May 29, 1797, *PAH*, 21:91–93.

19. "richer in hopes": Liancourt, *Voyage*, 1:151–52; John Cazenove's connection to Asylum: John Nicholson to Omer Talon, June 30, 1795, John Nicholson folder, Society Collection, HSP.

20. new corporate structure: *Plan of Association of the Asylum Company: As Established April 22d, 1794. And Improved April 25th, 1795* (Philadelphia: R. Aitken and Son, 1795); George Livermore, *The Origin, History and Character of the New England Primer* (New York: C. F. Heartman, 1915), 172; Liancourt, *Voyage*, 1:152; "You have compatized": Noailles to Nicholson, Nov. 4, 1794, Misc. Manuscript Collection, LoC; shareholders: Asylum Company Papers, box 1, folder 5, HSP; Asylum Company Minutebook, 1794–1804, HSP.

21. "live in the settlement": Talleyrand to Bourdieu, Chollet, and Bourdieu, June 10, 1794, *TAFP*, 29; issued shares: Asylum Company Papers, box 1, folder 5, HSP; "great expenditures": Liancourt, *Voyage*, 1:153; "The funds coming": Talleyrand to Bourdieu, Chollet, and Bourdieu, June 10, 1794, *TAFP*, 29; "encourage and bring settlers": C. B. Boulogne to John Nicholson, Mar. 15, 1795, folder 3, Asylum Company, Gratz Autograph Collection, HSP; "one of the causes": Liancourt, *Voyage*, 1:118; "This company": Grandmaison, *Mémoires*, 150–52; see also Poniatowski, *Talleyrand aux États-Unis*, 384.

22. The importance of local agents: Liancourt, *Voyage*, 3:43, and especially Alan Taylor, *William Cooper's Town: Power and Persuasion on the Frontier of the Early American Republic* (New York: Vintage, 1995); "uncommon degree of perfection": quoted in Childs, *French Refugee Life*, 71; "to give to my": Liancourt, *Journal*, 109; the people in Asylum: Liancourt, *Voyage*, 1:157–61; "There can hardly": ibid., 1:156. I never found evidence that the land that Liancourt bought for his children was in Asylum, but that is the contention of Childs and Kennedy, and I have no reason to think they are wrong; Childs, *French Refugee Life*, 98, and Kennedy, *Orders from France*, 93.

23. no land title: Mr. Le Fevre to John Keating, July 12, 1799, Asylum Company Papers, box 1, folder 9, HSP; "no great inclination": Weld, *Travels*, 2:351; Weld on Pulteney: 2:333–36.

24. description of land quality: Paul Wallace Gates, *The Farmer's Age: Agriculture, 1815–1860* (New York: Holt, Rinehart and Winston, 1960), 42; "more rugged": reported in Graydon, *Memoirs*, 349; "plots of sand": Grandmaison, *Mémoires*, 152; "most comical stories": La Tour

du Pin Gouvernet, *Journal d'une femme*, 2:72; "destitute": Weld, *Travels*, 2:344–45; "poor dupe": Grandmaison, *Mémoires*, 151.

25. Talleyrand to Bourdieu, Chollet, and Bourdieu, June 10, 1794, *TAFP*, 29.

26. Volney, *Tableau du climat et du sol*, 385, 384, xvi ("frenchified"), 385, 8. On the health of the Ohio valley: Conevery Bolton Valencius, *The Health of the Country: How American Settlers Understood Themselves and Their Land* (New York: Basic Books, 2002).

27. first land auction: Peter S. Onuf, *Statehood and Union: A History of the Northwest Ordinance* (Bloomington: Indiana University Press, 1987), 42; "In the present stage": GW to Alexander Spotswood, Nov. 23, 1794, Fitzpatrick, *Writings*, 34:47; congressional terms: Malcolm J. Rohrbough, *The Land Office Business: The Settlement and Administration of American Public Lands, 1789–1837* (New York: Oxford University Press, 1968), 10–13; "Congress lands": AB to Hope & Co., May 26, 1796, CML-BaP; more than postage stamps: Alan Taylor, "Land and Liberty on the Post-Revolutionary Frontier," in *Devising Liberty: Preserving and Creating Freedom in the New American Republic*, ed. David Konig (Stanford, CA: Stanford University Press, 1995). The details of the Scioto transaction are complicated, involving the fusion of two separate purchasers: the Ohio Company of Associates and William Duer's Scioto Company. For more details and context on Scioto, see Archer Butler Hulbert, "The Methods and Operations of the Scioto Group of Speculators," *Mississippi Valley Historical Review* 1, no. 4 (1915); Rosengarten, *French Colonists and Exiles*, 125–40; Robert F. Durden, "Joel Barlow in the French Revolution," *WMQ* 8, no. 3 (1951); Jean Vidalenc, *Les émigrés français, 1789–1825* (Caen: Association des publications de la Faculté des lettres et sciences humaines de l'Université de Caen, 1963), 258–61; Echeverria, *Mirage in the West*, 134–36; Robert Francis Jones, *The King of the Alley: William Duer, Politician, Entrepreneur, and Speculator, 1768–1799* (Philadelphia: American Philosophical Society, 1992); Suzanne Desan, "Transatlantic Spaces of Revolution: The French Revolution, Sciotomanie, and American Lands," *Journal of Early Modern History* 12 (2008): 467–505; Richard Buel, *Joel Barlow: American Citizen in a Revolutionary World* (Baltimore: Johns Hopkins University Press, 2011), 96–139; and "Observations on Behalf of the French Settlers at Gallipolis," Feb. 2, 1795, Letterbook 1792–1797, Du Ponceau Papers, HSP.

28. biographical information on Duer: Jones, *King of the Alley*, and Jonathan J. Bean, *ANB*, s.v. "Duer, William"; Staphorst and the first Dutch loan: Evans, *Holland Land Company*, 3; Brissot's connection to Scioto: Eloise Ellery, *Brissot de Warville: A Study in the History of the French Revolution* (1915; New York: Burt Franklin, 1970), 73; Hulbert, "Methods and Operations of the Scioto Group," 507–10; Fonds Brissot, 446/AP/5, dossier 4, AN; "among the lands": Brissot de Warville, *Nouveau voyage*, 1:18; "too many men": Mémoire à LaFayette, 446/AP/5, dossier 2, doc. 25, AN.

29. "douceurs": Barlow to [probably Duer], Paris, Nov. 29, 1789, Scioto and Ohio Land Company Papers, NYHS; "I consider them": quoted in Durden, "Joel Barlow in the French Revolution," 330.

30. Barlow's apartment in Paris: Buel, *Securing the Revolution*, 134; and Scudder, *Recollections of Samuel Breck*, 171–72; "respectable and wealthy": quoted in Durden, "Joel Barlow in the French Revolution," 329; Barlow to [probably Duer], Nov. 29, 1789, Scioto and Ohio Land Company Papers, NYHS.

31. Barlow to [probably Duer], Nov. 29, 1789, Scioto and Ohio Land Company Papers, NYHS.

32. "20 millions": Barlow to Duer, Jan. 25, 1790, Scioto and Ohio Land Company Papers, NYHS; "You have placed me": Duer to Barlow, Nov. 4, 1790, Scioto and Ohio Land Company Papers, NYHS.

33. "all of them": Volney, *Tableau du climat et du sol*, 387; "wigmakers, hat makers": Chinard, *Volney et l'Amérique*, 42; Volney, *Tableau du climat et du sol*, 388. Twenty-four to twenty-eight degrees Celsius translates to 75 to 82 degrees Fahrenheit; the contemporary English translation of Volney's text, however, puts it at 85 degrees or 95 degrees: *View of the Climate and Soil of the United States of America: To Which Are Annexed Some Accounts of Florida, the*

French Colony on the Scioto, Certain Canadian Colonies, and the Savages or Natives (London: J. Johnson, 1804), 363.

34. Payment in champagne: Buel, *Joel Barlow* 124; "Such is the situation": Volney, *Tableau du climat et du sol*, 391.

35. *Look Before You Leap; or, A Few Hints to Such Artizans, Mechanics, Labourers, Farmers and Husbandmen as Are Desirous of Emigrating to America, Being a Genuine Collection of Letters, from Persons Who Have Emigrated* (London: W. Row, 1796); "No speculations": "Remarks of A.B. on Land Speculations Particularly Applicable to Bingham's Maine Lands . . . Dated c. Jan–Feb 1796," CML-BaP; "extreme cheapness": Memoir to Cazenove, June 23, 1794, *TAFP*, 37.

36. Talleyrand to Goring, June 10, 1794, *TAFP*, 25.

37. "Of all the scourges": "Observations on Speculation in Lands in the United States of America," *TAFP*, 151–52; "Time indifferently destroys": Talleyrand, "Essai sur les avantages à retirer," 290; "A single form of property": "Observations on Speculation," *TAFP*, 151–52; "convert it into": Memoir to Cazenove, ibid., 52 (Talleyrand is referring here to his plan to sell American lands to Indian nabobs, but the analogy with French émigrés is obvious).

38. Talleyrand, "Essai sur les avantages," 290–91.

39. "more than probable": Peter Stadnitski, "Preliminary Information respecting a Negotiation on Lands in America," 1792 (typescript), BaP; Fauchet to Commissioner of Foreign Relations, dispatch 12, *CFM*, 465–66; "There are reasons": GW to Alexander Spotswood, Fitzpatrick, *Writings*, 34:47.

40. "the first house": "Notes of a Tour through Holland and the Rhine Valley," *PTJ*, 13:10; dedication: Adam Smith, *An Inquiry into the Nature and Causes of the Wealth of Nations, with a Life of the Author. . . .* 3 vols. (Edinburgh: Creech, 1806), 1:4; naval frigate for Hopes: Philip Ziegler, *The Sixth Great Power: A History of One of the Greatest of All Banking Families, the House of Baring, 1762–1929* (New York: Alfred A. Knopf, 1988), 54; capital flight from Amsterdam and its impact on U.S. merchants: Fauchet to Minister of Foreign Relations, Dec. 1, 1794, Turner, *CFM*, 491; "a quantity of" and "These émigré Capitalists": Théophile Cazenove to AH, Jan. 13, 1795, *PAH*, 18:38; declining interest rates and British borrowing costs: Larry Neal, *The Rise of Financial Capitalism: International Capital Markets in the Age of Reason* (Cambridge: Cambridge University Press, 1990); "Given the political state": Talleyrand to Cazenove, Sept. 24, 1794, Poniatowski, *Talleyrand aux États-Unis*, 128; "funds which seek": Talleyrand to Bourdieu, Chollet, and Bourdieu, June 10, 1794, *TAFP*, 29; "In a state": Memoir to Cazenove, June 23, 1794, *TAFP*, 34; see also Bourdieu, Chollet, and Bourdieu to Talleyrand, June 10, 1794, ibid., 68; "wishing that a part": Talleyrand, *Mémoires*, 1:236. On the importance of financial centers and financial surpluses to the history of global capitalism, see Arrighi, *Long Twentieth Century*.

41. "New lands": Liancourt, *Voyage*, 1:117; "Every step we take": ibid., 1:79; "well-chosen lands": Liancourt to his wife, Mar. 20, 1796, *Journal*, 128.

42. "Death will soon enter": quoted in Bruce H. Mann, *Republic of Debtors: Bankruptcy in the Age of American Independence* (Cambridge, MA: Harvard University Press, 2002), 98.

43. "necessary family appendage": AB to Hope & Co., Philadelphia, Dec. 3/28, 1796, BaP; also in *WBML*, 766; measurements from Alan Taylor, *Liberty Men and Great Proprietors: The Revolutionary Settlement on the Maine Frontier, 1760–1820* (Chapel Hill: University of North Carolina Press), 43; British frigate at Hell Gate: Gilmor, *Memorandums Made in a Tour*, 10; "very fine": AB to Hope & Co., Dec. 3, 1796, *WBML*, 770.

44. "The projected excursion": AB to Hope & Co., May 26, 1796 (typescript), BaP; "wishing him": GW to WB, June 9, 1796, Fitzpatrick, *Writings*, 35:87; "I am aware": FB to AB, London, July 22, 1796, CML-BaP.

45. Land titles: Taylor, *Liberty Men*, 18–19.

46. secret land purchases: ibid., 41; "French Company of the Union": Childs, *French Refugee Life*, 67–68; Joseph Stancliffe Davis, *Essays in the Earlier History of American Corporations*, 2 vols.

(Cambridge, MA: Harvard University Press, 1917), 1:270; Burr's involvement: Aaron Burr to William Duer, July 19, 1792, Bingham Papers, box 16, HSP.

47. Cazenove sends agent: Evans, *Holland Land Company*, 22–23; Alberts, *Golden Voyage*, 231; "It will not be long": Talleyrand to Goring, June 10, 1793, *TAFP*, 25; "American capital": WB to Knox, Sept. 12, 1795, *WBML*, 580.

48. Letter of introduction: Henry Knox to Christopher Gore, June 24, 1794, Knox Papers, vol. 35, p. 141, MHS; "would even be beautiful": Talleyrand to Cazenove, Sept. 24, 1794, Poniatowski, *Talleyrand aux États-Unis*, 119; "on the property": ibid., 108; Cazenove's questions: ibid., 117; Talleyrand's report to Cazenove: ibid., 131–58; his report to AB: AB to FB, May 5, 1796, CML-BaP.

49. "The Southern states": AB to Hope & Co., Dec. 3, 1796, *WBML*, 785; "Agriculture could": Poniatowski, *Talleyrand aux États-Unis*, 128.

50. "Agriculture is the basis": Talleyrand, *Mémoires*, 1:236; "We saw society": Talleyrand to Cazenove, Sept. 24, 1794, Poniatowski, *Talleyrand aux États-Unis*, 109.

51. Criticism of Maine residents: Talleyrand to Cazenove, Sept. 24, 1794, Poniatowski, *Talleyrand aux États-Unis*, 125; "To which country": ibid., 126–27; fisherman's daughter anecdote: Griswold, *Republican Court*, 325.

52. Noailles made a proposal, an excursion, "Spoke about": Liancourt, *Journal*, 71, 83; "disposed to undertake": WB to Knox, Sept. 19, 1795, *WBML*, 582; "In general": Stadnitski, "Negotiation on Lands in America"; "His intelligence": WB to Knox, Sept. 12, 1795, *WBML*, 580; *TAFP*, 19; "person of credibility," WB to Knox, Sept. 19, 1795, *WBML*, 582; "weight of personal character": WB to Knox, Sept. 26, 1795, ibid., 584; "the great capitalists of Europe": WB to Knox, Sept. 19, 1795, ibid., 582; "He is really": Knox to WB, Oct. 7, 1795, ibid., 585; "A man of his character": Knox to WB, Nov. 11, 1795, ibid., 587.

53. "In this territory": Liancourt, *Voyage*, 3:42; "In general": ibid., 3:74; "carelessness": ibid., 3:67; "badly and poorly cultivated": ibid., 3:114–15.

54. Noailles authorized to invest: WB to Knox, Sept. 12, 1795, *WBML*, 581; "command of funds": Knox to WB, Oct. 7, 1795, ibid., 585.

55. Harry M. Ward, *ANB*, s.v. "Jackson, William"; on Jackson's experience in Amsterdam: Pieter Jan van Winter, *American Finance and Dutch Investment, 1780–1805: With an Epilogue to 1840*, ed. James C. Riley, 2 vols. (New York: Arno Press, 1977), 1:40–43.

56. "All the monied men": Jackson to WB, Apr. 30, 1794, Bingham Papers, box 16, HSP; *WBML*, 323.

57. All the quotations are from William Jackson to WB, November 8 to Dec. 1, 1793, Bingham Papers, box 16, HSP.

58. Jackson to WB, Apr. 30, 1794, Bingham Papers, box 16, HSP; *WBML*, 321.

59. Baring one of first people: Jackson to WB, Aug. 1793, *WBML*, 288–89; "I have mentioned": Jackson to WB, Apr. 30, 1794, Bingham Papers, box 16, HSP; *WBML*, 325; "perfectly convinced," June 24, 1794, *WBML*, 335. Sending the young son of a merchant family abroad for training seems to have been standard practice; see also Hancock, *Citizens of the World*, 110–14, 140–42.

60. "an extraordinary young man": Gilmor, *Memorandums Made in a Tour*, 22; "Land speculations": AB to J. Williams Hope, Dec. 8, 1795, CML-BaP; see also Twining, *Travels in America*, 54: "speculation, the object of almost every American at this period."

61. AB on Talleyrand and Noailles: AB to FB, Nov. 1796, CML-BaP.

62. "Both speak very highly": AB to FB, May 5, 1796, CML-BaP; "It really has" and all subsequent quotations: AB to Hope & Co., May 26, 1796, *WBML*, 662. Royal Flint (1754–1797) was a New York businessman and land speculator who frequently collaborated with William Duer; Henry Jackson (1747–1809) was a native of Boston, a general during the American Revolution, and an investor in Knox's lands in Maine.

63. "The prime necessity" and "The attraction": *TAFP*, 72, 75; "Rely upon it": Knox to WB, Oct. 7, 1795, *WBML*, 586; "Cutting roads": "Bingham's Answers to Questions," Apr. 19, 1796, *WBML*, 741; "The importance": AB to Hope & Co., Dec. 3, 1796, *WBML*, 792. On roads, see also Hancock, *Citizens of the World*, 301–7.

64. "Maine wants": WB to John Vaughan, Feb. 8, 1801, Gratz Autograph Collection, HSP; "I cannot but": Cobb to WB, Oct. 30, 1796, *WBML*, 808; "chart blanch": Cobb to WB, Feb. 10, 1797, *WBML*, 836–37; "should come with": "Baring's Project for the Settlement of Maine Lands," Feb. 1798, *WBML*, 922; "house wrights": Cobb to WB, Apr. 9, 1797, *WBML*, 862; range of ventures: Taylor, *Liberty Men*, 41.

65. The memo is in *WBML*, 919–35, quotations on 921 and 926. "Our object": "Baring's Project," 931–32. For some of the expenses reflected in the Baring accounts, see "Lands in the District of Maine," Baring Account Books, Jan. 1797 to Dec. 1798, BaP.

66. On the mechanics of state power in developing the frontier, see Rohrbough, *Land Office Business*.

67. FB to AB, July 22, 1796, CML-BaP.

68. Talleyrand, "Mémoire sur les relations commerciales des États-Unis avec l'Angleterre," in *Mémoires de l'Institut national des sciences et arts. Tome second* (Paris: Baudouin, 1798), 100–101.

69. "populating the country": quoted in Harsanyi, 23; "Our imagination": Talleyrand, *Mémoires*, 234; Poniatowski, *Talleyrand aux États-Unis*, 142.

70. Taylor, *Divided Ground*, 313–17; Evans, *Holland Land Company*, 3–35; William Wyckoff, *The Developer's Frontier: The Making of the Western New York Landscape* (New Haven, CT: Yale University Press, 1988); Charles E. Brooks, *Frontier Settlement and Market Revolution: The Holland Land Purchase* (Ithaca, NY: Cornell University Press, 1996), 4, 14, 18–21. My thanks to Karim Tiro for saving me from several mistakes in this section; any that remain are wholly my fault.

71. Evans, *Holland Land Company*, 206.

72. Poniatowski, *Talleyrand aux États-Unis*, 140.

73. Largest private land developer: Brooks, *Frontier Settlement*, 13; total acreage: Evans, *Holland Land Company*, xii; Wyckoff, *Developer's Frontier*, 17–18; railroads: Richard White, *Railroaded: The Transcontinentals and the Making of Modern America* (New York: W. W. Norton, 2011), 23–25; "A road running": Talleyrand to Cazenove, "Observations on Speculation," *TAFP*, 168; Wyckoff, *Developer's Frontier*, 44; average cost of turnpike: Evans, *Holland Land Company*, 282; "watered and fertilized by capital": Talleyrand to Cazenove, Sept. 24, 1794, Poniatowski, *Talleyrand aux États-Unis*, 129.

74. Surveying the company's lands: William Chazanof, *Joseph Ellicott and the Holland Land Company: The Opening of Western New York* (Syracuse, NY: Syracuse University Press, 1970), 23–28; modeled on City Tavern: Platt, *City Tavern*, 52; Holland Company revenue: Chazanof, *Joseph Ellicott*, 41, 39, 30; land sold from 1801 to 1809 and tax bill: ibid., 44–45, 88–93; Baring tax bill in Maine: *WBML*, 1248–49. On private developers and credit to settlers, see also Paul D. Evans, "The Pulteney Purchase," *New York State Historical Association Quarterly Journal* 3, no. 2 (1922): 93–94.

75. Extending credit to settlers: Evans, *Holland Land Company*, 286, 306–25; Chazanof, *Joseph Ellicott*, 30; "numerous applications": Evans, *Holland Land Company*, 298.

76. Evans, *Holland Land Company*, 207–9, 287–94; Chazanof, *Joseph Ellicott*, 160–74; Gerard T. Koeppel, *Bond of Union: Building the Erie Canal and the American Empire* (Cambridge, MA: Da Capo Press, 2009), 211; Wilkins, *History of Foreign Investment*, 55.

77. WB to J. & F. Baring & Co., Mar. 30 and June 1, 1795, CML-BaP.

78. Quasi-War purchases: Ralph Willard Hidy, *The House of Baring in American Trade and Finance: English Merchant Bankers at Work, 1763–1861* (Cambridge, MA: Harvard University Press, 1949), 32; "I will venture": FB to Albert Gallatin, Apr. 20, 1804, Northbrook Papers, 1 A17.7, BaP.

79. "we may through": AB to FB, Dec. 11, 1795, CML-BaP; "so marked": John Orbell, *Baring Brothers & Co., Limited: A History to 1939* (London: Baring Brothers, 1985), 14–15; by the end of the 1830s: Hidy, *House of Baring*, 69–70; Orbell, *Baring Brothers*, 33; Wilkins, *History of Foreign Investment*, 34–35; van Winter, *American Finance and Dutch Investment*, 2:914–16. See also "Proceedings of the Commissioners of the Sinking Fund," June 7, 1802, *PJMSS*, 3:285–87.

80. Hope firm as most significant issuer of U.S. securities: Wilkins, *History of Foreign Investment*, 57–58; "A very few years": J. W. Hope to H. Hope, June 13, 1804, Northbrook Papers, 1 A4.52, BaP.
81. WB to AB, Philadelphia, Feb. 1, 1796, CML-BaP.
82. Liancourt, *Voyage*, 3:271–72.
83. Moreau, *Voyage*, 216–18.

CHAPTER 5: FRANCE IN THE MISSISSIPPI VALLEY

1. Palisot: McClellan, *Colonialism and Science*, 160–61; Liancourt's admission to the APS: Liancourt, *Journal*, 84–85.
2. "in no mood": Moreau, *American Journey*, 210–11; "vivid regret": Moreau, *Voyage*, 222.
3. *Claypoole's American Daily Advertiser* (Philadelphia), Feb. 8, 1796; Moreau, *Diary*, 211.
4. *Claypoole's American Daily Advertiser* (Philadelphia), Feb. 8, 1796; *Aurora General Advertiser* (Philadelphia), Feb. 8, 1796.
5. All quotations from Liancourt, *Voyage*, 6:326–27. Article on dancing: M. L. E. Moreau de Saint-Méry, *Danse: Article extrait d'un ouvrage de M. L. E. Moreau de St-Méry*. . . . (Philadelphia: Imprimé par l'auteur, 1796); Talleyrand helping with proofs: Moreau, *American Journey*, 216.
6. Alexis de Tocqueville, *De la démocratie en Amérique*, 2 vols. (Paris: Gallimard, 1961), 2:143–44.
7. Liancourt, *Voyage*, 6:327.
8. Liancourt to his wife, Mar. 20, 1796, *Journal*, 131.
9. Liancourt providing information: Adet to Minister of Foreign Relations, Mar. 26, 1797, *CFM*, 1003; "there are certain persons": James McHenry to Gov. St. Clair, May 1796, Arthur St. Clair and William Henry Smith, *The St. Clair Papers: The Life and Public Services of Arthur St. Clair*. . . . 2 vols. (Cincinnati: R. Clarke, 1882), 2:395. See Poniatowski, *Talleyrand aux États-Unis*, 313.
10. Liancourt, *Voyage*, 4:1–4.
11. Charleston: ibid., 4:70–72; the ship's arrival: *Charleston City Gazette*, Mar. 31, 1796.
12. Information on Michaux in this paragraph and elsewhere has been gleaned from Charlie Williams, "André Michaux, a Biographical Sketch," *Castanea: Occasional Papers in Eastern Botany*, no. 2, Proceedings of the André Michaux International Symposium 69, no. 2 (2006); James E. McClellan, "André Michaux and French Botanical Networks at the End of the Old Regime," ibid.; William S. Bryant, "Botanical Explorations of André Michaux in Kentucky: Observations of Vegetation in the 1790s," ibid. On the colonial machine, see James E. McClellan and François Regourd, *The Colonial Machine: French Science and Overseas Expansion in the Old Regime* (Turnhout: Brepols, 2011). On Michaux's garden outside Charleston, see Clifton F. Lord and Martha Jane K. Zachert, "The Botanical Garden of André Michaux near Charleston, 1786–1802," paper presented at the American Pharmaceutical Association Convention, Las Vegas, NV, 1962. For the British context, a nice survey can be found in Richard Drayton, "Knowledge and Empire," in *The Oxford History of the British Empire*, vol. 2, *The Eighteenth Century*, ed. P. G. Marshall (Oxford: Oxford University Press, 1998).
13. Adet to Minister of Foreign Relations, Oct. 28, 1796, *CFM*, 959–61.
14. Liancourt, *Voyage*, 6:179–80.
15. Ibid., 4:195–96.
16. Ibid., 6:195.
17. "we will find ourselves," "all the goods produced," and "Louisiana is holding": Fauchet to Commissioner of Foreign Relations, Feb. 4, 1795, *CFM*, 567.
18. "If we are not careful": Instructions to Général Pérignon, 26 Ventôse, an 4 (Mar. 16, 1796), *MCGPA*, 667.
19. "He must be a fool": Hamilton, "Relations with France," *PAH*, 19:521.
20. Colonial machine: McClellan and Regourd, *Colonial Machine*; forests: Robert Greenhalgh

Albion, *Forests and Sea Power: The Timber Problem of the Royal Navy, 1652–1862* (Hamden, CT: Archon Books, 1965); Paul W. Bamford, *Forests and French Sea Power, 1660–1789* (Toronto: University of Toronto Press, 1956), 11–12, 63–65, 184–95; Frederick L. Nussbaum, *A History of the Economic Institutions of Modern Europe: An Introduction to "Der Moderne Kapitalismus" of Werner Sombart* (New York: Augustus M. Kelley, 1968), 251–54; William R. Carlton, "New England Masts and the King's Navy," *New England Quarterly* 12, no. 1 (1939); William Cronon, *Changes in the Land: Indians, Colonists, and the Ecology of New England* (New York: Hill & Wang, 1983), 20–21, 27, 30, 108–26. See also the observations by Georges-Henri-Victor Collot, *Voyage en Amérique septentrionale ou description des pays arrosés par le Mississippi, l'Ohio, le Missouri et autres rivières affluentes.* . . . (Paris: Chez, 1804), 2 vols., 2:198–204. On the naval arms race: Michael Duffy, "World-Wide War and British Expansion," in *The Oxford History of the British Empire*, vol. 2, *The Eighteenth Century*, ed. P. J. Marshall (Oxford: Oxford University Press, 1998), 185.

21. "less dependent": M. Demoustier, "Considérations sur quelques objets qui intéressent particulièrement la Marine du Roi., par une suite des nouveaux rapports qui dérivent de la Souveraineté des États Unis de l'Amérique," Dec. 12, 1788, Marine B/7/461, AN; "Ships Masts": Article 26, "Treaty of Amity and Commerce between the United States and France; February 6, 1778," Avalon Project at Yale Law School, http://avalon.law.yale.edu/-18th_century-fr17 88=1.asp, accessed Oct. 20, 2013; Michaux and oak trees: McClellan, "André Michaux and French Botanical Networks," 72; Crèvecoeur report: Julia Post Mitchell, *St. Jean de Crèvecoeur* (New York: Columbia University Press, 1916), 132–33; other lumber reports: "Compte rendu par M. Rolland sous-ingénieur constructeur sur des bois de l'Amérique septentrionale," Dec. 23, 1785, Marine B/7/460, AN; "Suite des observations déjà adressées par M. Rolland, sous-ingénieur constructeur. . . . ," Mar. 31, 1786, ibid.

22. "their utility": M. Demoustier, "Considérations sur quelques objets qui intéressent particulièrement la Marine du Roi. . . ," Dec. 12, 1788, Marine B/7/461, AN; "whether publick": Article 21, "Treaty of Amity and Commerce," Avalon Project at Yale Law School; "great advantages" and "French fleets": [Antoine René Charles Mathurin] de la Forest, "Mémoire sur la situation actuelle des États Unis relativement [*sic*] à l'industrie américaine et au commerce étranger," New York, Feb. 18, 1789, Marine B/7/461, AN; "blood and treasure": "Mémoire sur l'État Politique des affaires de la République française dans les Etats-Unis de l'Amérique, 1er Ventôse, l'An 2ème de la République française une & indivisible," Mémoires et documents, États-Unis, vol. 10, MAÉ.

23. "It has to be established": "Mémoire sur le Commerce de France, avec les États-Unis en France," 1786, Marine B/7/460, AN; "The loss of this possession" and "reciprocal interest": Demoustier, "Considérations sur quelques objets"; "perpetual Communication": "Esquisse d'un Club ou assemblée, ou meeting Gallo-américain," Fonds Brissot, 446/AP/5/1/152, AN. On commerce and the Franco-American relationship, see Dorigny, "La *Libre Amérique* selon Brissot et Clavière." On the pro-American, antimercantilist circles in Paris, see Echeverria, *Mirage in the West*, esp. 24–31, 41–42, 130–32, and Marc Belissa, "'Agrandir le cercle de la civilisation': Le débat sur les conséquences de la Révolution Américaine," *Revue d'histoire moderne et contemporaine* 46, no. 3 (1999).

24. "How cordially": TJ to Gouverneur Morris, Dec. 30, 1792, *PTJ*, 24:801; on the good intentions and happy feelings: Echeverria, *Mirage in the West*, 116–74.

25. "ensure the religious": "Supplément aux instructions," *CFM*, 208; "ensure the execution": ibid., 207; masts: Commissioners to Minister of the Marine, Mar. 15, 1794, *CFM*, 302–3; "measures perhaps": Pallain, *Correspondance diplomatique de Talleyrand*, 429n1. For the organization of French consular affairs in the United States under Genet's supervision, see "Instructions concernant les affaires consulaires générales. . . . ," AF/III/64/1, AN, as well as Stéphane Bégaud, Marc Belissa, and Joseph Visser, *Aux origines d'une alliance improbable: Le réseau consulaire français aux États-Unis, 1776–1815* (Bruxelles: Direction des archives, Ministère des affaires étrangères, 2005).

26. All quotations are from "Mémoire pour servir d'instruction au citoyen Genet. . . . ," *CFM*, 204–5.

27. Genet's organization after arriving in Charleston: Frederick Jackson Turner, "The Origin of Genet's Projected Attack on Louisiana and the Floridas," *AHR* 3, no. 4 (1898): 664; R. R. Palmer, "A Revolutionary Republican: M. A. B. Mangourit," *WMQ* 9, no. 4 (1952): 486–89; sympathy for the French Revolution in the Carolina backcountry: Klein, *Unification of a Slave State*, 205–6; the officer was Elijah Clarke, who resigned his commission as major general in the Georgia militia to take charge: Samuel Willard Crompton, *ANB*, s.v. "Clarke, Elijah"; "an eternal alliance": *MCGPA*, 591; Mangourit's plan to ally with McGillivray: Mangourit to Genet, Apr. 28, 1793, ibid., 578. To lead the mission to the Creeks, Mangourit sent Colonel Samuel Hammond, an old-time frontier veteran who had fought in the American Revolution and would later be appointed surveyor general of Georgia in 1796, before going on to a political career at the state and federal level: ibid., 571–72, 591; negotiating with Chickasaws: ibid., 593, 623; "Ask your fathers": "Instructions to Colonels Tate and Hammond," ibid., 623–24. For Mangourit's spirited defense of his actions, see M. A. B. Mangourit, *Mémoire de Mangourit. . . .* (Paris: Impr. de Gueffier, 1794).

28. "seems all the more": quoted in Robert J. Alderson, *This Bright Era of Happy Revolutions: French Consul Michel-Ange-Bernard Mangourit and International Republicanism in Charleston, 1792–1794* (Columbia: University of South Carolina Press, 2008), 101, 138–39; "taking place with": quoted in Klein, *Unification of a Slave State*, 208.

29. Quotations in this paragraph are from "Mémoire pour servir d'instruction au citoyen Genet," *CFM*, 204–5. Ambitious as they were, Genet's western plans were only one piece of an even grander scheme to bring republican liberty to the entire Western Hemisphere, a project to be led by the Venezuelan patriot Francisco de Miranda. Miranda had traveled to Philadelphia in the 1780s, trying unsuccessfully to peddle his plans to "revolutionize" Spanish America, and then moved on to London. Unable to persuade authorities there, he eventually went to France to offer his services in the cause of republicanism, where he at last met with a positive response. Now a general in the French armies, he was to meet George Rogers Clark's force in New Orleans once the Mississippi valley had been liberated, and move south from there to liberate all of Spanish America. When this plan failed to materialize, Miranda would later move back to London and get the support of Federalists like the Connecticut painter John Trumbull—who, like Arthur St. Clair, the governor of the Northwest Territory, had served on Washington's staff during the Revolution—along with Rufus King, soon to be sent to London as the American ambassador, and William Stephens Smith. All of them believed that U.S. support of Miranda would prevent France from implanting itself in the Mississippi valley. See Marshall Smelser, "George Washington Declines the Part of El Libertador," *WMQ* 11, no. 1 (1954); Whitaker, *Mississippi Question*, 103; Karen Racine, *Francisco de Miranda: A Transatlantic Life in the Age of Revolution* (Wilmington, DE: Scholarly Resources, 2003); Wesley J. Campbell, "The French Intrigue of James Cole Mountflorence," *WMQ* 65, no. 4 (2008); Dorigny, "Brissot et Miranda en 1792," 95; and Campbell, "Origin of Citizen Genet's Projected Attack."

30. "Jefferson and André Michaux's Proposed Western Expedition: Editorial Note," *PTJ*, 25:75–81; "American Philosophical Society's Subscription Agreement for André Michaux's Western Expedition" [ca. Jan. 22, 1793], *PTJ*, 25:81–84.

31. Early planning in Paris: "Plan proposé pour faire une révolution dans la Louisiane," *SFDC*, 947, 952; Turner, "Origin of Genet's Projected Attack," 659; the Paris circles that developed the plan: Cayton, *Love in the Time of Revolution*, 75–77; could easily capture New Orleans: "Unsigned and Unaddressed Memoir," *SFDC*, 974. Campbell, "Origin of Genet's Projected Attack," downplays Brissot's role in the Genet mission more than I do, although I suspect the two of us agree more than we differ on its objectives.

32. "robust, entrepreneurial": "Plan proposé pour faire une révolution dans la Louisiane," *SFDC*, 947; "Kentuckians have": "Instructions," *CFM*, 205; "defiance" and "If ever": Brissot de

Warville, *Nouveau voyage*, 2:433, 435; "The news of a revolution": "Plan proposé pour faire une révolution dans la Louisiane," *SFDC*, 947; "the attachment" and "A man of": Brissot de Warville, *Nouveau voyage*, 2:430; "They call the French": De Pauw to Genet, June 12, 1793, *SFDC*, 980; "resume their former": Hugh C. Bailey and Bernerd C. Weber, "A British Reaction to the Treaty of San Ildefonso," *WMQ* 17, no. 2 (1960): 245; supportive French population in the West: "Plan proposé pour faire une révolution dans la Louisiane," *SFDC*, 949; "The French people established": ibid., 946n; "a great number": De Pauw to Genet, June 12, 1793, ibid., 981; Scioto as pretext: "Plan proposé pour faire une révolution dans la Louisiane," ibid., 951.

33. Clark's overtures and planning: James O'Fallon to Capt. Herron, Oct. 18, 1793, as quoted in Edmund Randolph to GW, Feb. 27, 1794, *PGWPS*, 15:289; Paine, Jefferson, and Clark: Louise Phelps Kellogg, "Letter of Thomas Paine, 1793," *AHR* 29, no. 3 (1924); W. M. Verhoeven, *Gilbert Imlay: Citizen of the World* (London: Pickering & Chatto, 2008), 150–57; Clark's early involvement and his revolutionary activities: Gilles Havard and Cécile Vidal, *Histoire de l'Amérique française*, rev. ed. (Paris: Flammarion, 2006), 688; Clark quotations: Clark to [French Minister], Feb. 5, 1793, *SFDC*, 967–71. On Clark and the Genet mission, see Turner, "Origin of Genet's Projected Attack," 532; "Jefferson and André Michaux's Proposed Western Expedition," Editorial Note, *PTJ*, 25:75–81; Kukla, *Wilderness So Immense*, 156–78; Havard and Vidal, *Histoire de l'Amérique française*, 701–3.

34. Michaux meets with Genet: Charlie Williams, "Explorer, Botanist, Courier, or Spy? André Michaux and the Genet Affair of 1793," *Castanea* 69, no. 2 (2006): 101; Genet appoints Michaux agent: ibid.; "Copie de l'autorisation donnée au Citoyen André Michaux. . . ." *SFDC*, 995; the commission for Clark: "Autorisation donnée par le Ministre Plénipotentiaire de la République française au Général Clarke [*sic*]," ibid., 996; "exclusive command": CPÉU, supp. 28, p. 47, MAÉ; "Mémoire pour servir d'instructions au Citoyen André Michaux, agent de la République française dans l'état de Kentuckey [*sic*] et sur le Mississipi [*sic*]," ibid., 993; "You will find in Kentucky" and subsequent quotations: ibid., 994–95.

35. Brown to Clark and Brown to Shelby, both June 24, 1793, *SFDC*, 982; Genet to Minister of Foreign Affairs, July 25, 1793, *CFM*, 221.

36. "propose to emancipate": "Notes on Conversation with William Stephens Smith and George Washington," Feb. 20, 1793, *PTJ*, 25:243; TJ to William Carmichael and William Short, Mar. 23, 1793, *PTJ*, 25:430; "Genet called on me" and subsequent TJ quotations from meeting with Genet: "Notes on a Cabinet Meeting and Conversations with Edmond Charles Genet," July 5, 1793, *PTJ*, 26:437–39; "the *Kentukois*": "Entretient avec M. Jefferson le 26 Juin," *PTJ*, 26:375n; "small spontaneous eruption": Genet to Minister of Foreign Relations, July 25, 1793, *CFM*, 221. On Jefferson's association with Genet's western plans, see Ammon, *Genet Mission*, 83–85; Bemis, *Jay's Treaty*, 142–149; Alexander DeConde, *Entangling Alliance: Politics & Diplomacy under George Washington* (Durham, NC: Duke University Press, 1958), 235–251; "Jefferson and André Michaux's Proposed Western Expedition," "Editorial Note," *PTJ*, 25:75–81.

37. "a subtle exercise": *PTJ*, 26:394n; TJ to Shelby, June 28, 1793, *PTJ*, 26:393–94.

38. Volney's visit to Jefferson: "Editorial Note," *PTJ*, at Volney to TJ, Nov. 16, 1793, 27:390–391; Chinard, *Volney et l'Amérique*, 37–41; "This will be": TJ to Shelby, June 21, 1796, *PTJ*, 29:134. For the other letters of introduction—TJ to John Breckinridge, Jean Baptiste Ducoigne, Harry Innes, Henri Peyroux de la Coudrenière, and Archibald Stuart—all dated June 21, 1796, see *PTJ*, 29:131–34. Volney also visited Madison and "borrowed" one of Madison's slaves as a guide. See Volney to Madison, Sept. 12, 1797[?], *PJM*, 17:45–46.

39. Four French agents followed: Randolph to Shelby, Mar. 29, 1794, *ASPFRS*, 1:456; "Revolutionary Legion of America": "Genet's Commission to William Tate," Oct. 15, 1793, *MCGPA*, 599; Tate as land speculator: Alderson, *Bright Era of Happy Revolutions*, 51; Clark identified in newspapers as "Major General": Kukla, *Wilderness So Immense*, 176; "All lawful plunder": *Carlisle Gazette* (PA), Mar. 19, 1794; "A spirit of recruiting": Jan. 3, 1794, also quoted in part in Alderson, *Bright Era of Happy Revolutions*, 145; "The people have got": *Columbian Herald, or, the Southern Star*, Jan. 3, 1794, also quoted in part in Alderson, *Bright Era of Happy Revolutions*, 145.

40. "upwards of two thousand": George Rogers Clark, "George Rogers Clark to Genet, 1794," *AHR* 18, no. 4 (1913); "General Logan has," "Clark it is said," and "So popular": "Extract of a Letter from Kentucky," Jan. 25, 1794, *PGWPS*, 15:291; support of local Democratic-Republican societies: E. Merton Coulter, "The Efforts of the Democratic Societies of the West to Open the Navigation of the Mississippi," *Mississippi Valley Historical Review* 11, no. 3 (1924): 379; Orihel, "Political Fever," 342–43.

41. "I am expecting Michaux": Mangourit to Genet, Jan. 31, 1794, *MCGPA*, 610; forces and funds promised by Genet: Commissioners to the Minister of Foreign Affairs, May 20, 1794, in *MCGPA*, 659; "The *habitants* of the backcountry" and subsequent Mangourit quotations: Mangourit to Genet, Feb. 24, 1794, *MCGPA*, 620–21; Michaux arrives in Charleston, assigned to the expedition: *MCGPA*, 573, 617; Alderson, *Bright Era of Happy Revolutions*, 143 (I noted the fourteenth because that was a Friday); fifteen hundred men ready and April 10 set as date: Hammond to Mangourit, Mar. 19, 1794; Mangourit to Genet, Mar. 5, 1794, *MCGPA*, 635–36, 625.

42. "We have been": Extract of a letter from Constant Freeman, Agent for the Department of War in Georgia, to the Secretary of War, Apr. 18, 1794, *ASPFRS* 1:459; "This armament": Extract of a letter from Major Henry Gaither to the Secretary of War, Apr. 13, 1794, in *ASPFRS*, 1:460; "It is said": *Gazette of the United States* (Philadelphia), May 23, 1794.

43. "It is whispered" and "If some four frigates": Carondelet to Alcudia, *SFDC*, 996, 998; "since the perversity": Viar and Jaudenes to Carondelet, ibid., 1000.

44. "Hindsight": David Morris Potter and Don Edward Fehrenbacher, *The Impending Crisis, 1848–1861* (New York: Harper & Row, 1976), 145; "It must be remembered": *Boston Gazette*, quoted in Hale, "Neither Britons nor Frenchmen," 107; "the State of Kentucky": Bailey Weber, "A British Reaction to the Treaty of San Ildefonso," 244.

45. "provisioning the Antilles": Turner, "Origin of Genet's Projected Attack," 666; "most extraordinary conduct": Viar and Jaudenes to Carondelet, *SFDC*, 999; "use effectual military force": Knox to Shelby, Nov. 9, 1793, *ASPFRS*, 1:458.

46. "Twas a Meteor": Hamilton, "Relations with France," *PAH*, 19:526; Proclamation on Expeditions against Spanish Territory, Mar. 24, 1794, *PGWPS*, 15:446; "must be repressed": quoted in *PGWPS*, 15:416n5; "Every Frenchman": *Philadelphia General Advertiser*, Mar. 7, 1794; *PGWPS*, 15:342n11; announcement came just in time: *MCGPA*, 574.

47. "at least served": Commissioners to Minister of Foreign Affairs, May 20, 1794, *CFM*, 347. The best account I've found of these proceedings is "The Recall of Edmond Charles Genet," Editorial Note, *PTJ*, 26:685–92.

48. Order in Council: *ASPFRS*, 1:430; 250 American ships detained, harassment, outrage: *PAH*, 16:382n4; Miller, *Federalist Era*, 141; Elkins and McKitrick, *Age of Federalism*, 389, 391; 27 percent decline: Coatsworth, "American Trade," 47.

49. Dorchester's view of the United States: Jasanoff, *Liberty's Exiles*, 200; "the King's Rights": Taylor, *Divided Ground*, 283; "what belongs": Elkins and McKitrick, *Age of Federalism*, 392; White, *Middle Ground*, 464–65; "spirit of hostility": *Manuscripts of J. B. Fortescue*, 3:527; "foster and encourage" Randolph to Hammond, May 20, 1794, *ASPFRS*, 1:461.

50. Randolph receives word of Simcoe's activities: Randolph to Hammond, May 20, 1794, *ASPFRS*, 1:461; reports of attacks along Lake Oswego: *Manuscripts of J. B. Fortescue*, 3:530; "as a direct violation": ibid., 3:530; "We hope you will now fulfill": Taylor, *Divided Ground*, 287.

51. "From the Pittsburgh Gazette," *New-Jersey Journal* (Elizabethtown, NJ), May 7, 1794, quoted in Pasley, *First Presidential Contest*, 102; riot in New York theater: Riordan, "'O Dear, What Can the Matter Be?'" 195–96; "The people are French": "Les commissaires du conseil exécutif provisoire près les États Unis au ministre des affaires étrangères," Mar. 21, 1794, *CFM*, 317.

52. "This may be considered" and subsequent GW quotations: GW to Jay, Aug. 30, 1794, in *PGWPS*, 16:614–15.

53. "Everything I hear" to "ever been seen": Liancourt, *Voyage*, 1:78; "time of war": ibid., 2:126; "excessive indisposition": 2:130.

54. Jeering Jay, hanging him in effigy, and then killing the effigy some more: Shankman, *Crucible of American Democracy*, 53.
55. The *Ohio*: *PGWPS*, 15:620n2; Talleyrand sends letter on the ship: Talleyrand to Staël, May 12, 1794, "Lettres de M. de Talleyrand à Mme de Staël," 210.
56. "made some offers": *Manuscripts of J. B. Fortescue*, 2:408; "I have prepared": Noailles to AH, Oct. 9, 1793, *PAH*, 15:359.
57. Bingham mansion as site of first caucus: Alberts, *Golden Voyage*, 263; "General Knox": Fauchet to Minister of Foreign Relations, May 5, 1794, *CFM*, 332; "hold firm": Mangourit to Genet, Feb. 10, 1794, *MCGPA*, 609; "It is to him": Fauchet to Minister of Foreign Relations, May 5, 1794, *CFM*, 331.
58. "a man of great understanding": Noailles to Windham, June 1, 1793, *Windham Papers*, 1:125; "was, while here": *Porcupine's Gazette* (Philadelphia), Jan. 11, 1799.
59. "The Americain privateers," "People of America," and "It is": Noailles to Windham, June 1, 1793, *Windham Papers*, 1:133; "I cannot urge": *TAFP*, 30.
60. "We are much indebted": Jay to AH, July 18 [–August 5], 1794, *PAH*, 16:608; sending letters through Cadignan: Jay to GW, Sept. 22, 1794, *PGWPS*, 16:699.
61. "the back countries": "Remarks of A.B. on Land Speculations Particularly Applicable to Bingham's Maine Lands," c. Jan–Feb 1796, CML-BaP.
62. "citizen[s] of the western country" and "We are too distant": quoted in Griffin, *American Leviathan*, 233–34. See also Gregory H. Nobles, *American Frontiers: Cultural Encounters and Continental Conquest* (New York: Hill & Wang, 1997), 99–103.
63. "He pretended to think": *PAH*, 19:527; "Jacobin" and "sans-culottes": Liancourt, *Journal*, 73–74; "a center of terrorism": quoted in Slaughter, *Whiskey Rebellion*, 194–95. Despite these accusations by Federalist politicians, and although Fauchet may have "cherished" the revolt, I have found no evidence that he provided any material or logistical support to the movement. On Fauchet's noninvolvement, see also Graydon, *Memoirs*, 345, and Collot, *Voyage*, 47–48. For more on the French connotations of the Whiskey Rebellion, see Cleves, *Reign of Terror in America*, 64–67, and Elkins and McKitrick, *Age of Federalism*, 461–85.
64. David Bradford as Robespierre and guillotine: Hogeland, *Whiskey Rebellion*, 137–38, 163, 169, 173; "My imagination presented": H. H. Brackenridge, *Incidents of the Insurrection in the Western Parts of Pennsylvania, in the Year 1794* (Philadelphia: John McCulloch, 1795), 85–86.
65. "When landed": "Plan proposé pour faire une révolution dans la Louisiane," *SFDC*, 948; "We were asked": Liancourt, *Voyage*, 1:108.
66. "I am traveling": Talleyrand to Staël, Aug. 4, 1794, "Lettres de M. de Talleyrand à Madame de Staël," 212; James Wilson certifies insurrection: "Editorial Note," Donald Dean Jackson and Dorothy Twohig, eds., *The Diaries of George Washington*, 6 vols. (Charlottesville: University of Virginia Press, 1976), 6:173; "in the Counties": Knox to GW, Aug. 4, 1794, in *PGWPS*, 16:468; "The essential interests": "Proclamation," Aug. 7, 1794, *PGWPS*, 16:534.
67. Knox to GW, Aug. 8, 1794, *PGWPS*, 16:539.
68. GW owns sixty-three thousand acres: Shankman, *Crucible of American Democracy*, 56; "could see no propriety": GW to Knox, Aug. 8, 1794, *PGWPS*, 16:540. On GW's landholdings in the West, see also Hugh Cleland, *George Washington in the Ohio Valley* (Pittsburgh: University of Pittsburgh Press, 1955); Royster, *Dismal Swamp Company*; Slaughter, *Whiskey Rebellion*, 79–84.
69. "I am terrified," "*Grand ordre*" et seq.: Liancourt, *Journal*, 65, 70; "The spirit with which": GW to Edmund Pendleton, Jan. 22, 1795, Fitzpatrick, *Writings*, 34:98–99.
70. "Not being fit": Jay to AH, Nov. 19, 1794, *PAH*, 17:390.
71. "A ship has just arrived": Commissioners to Commissioner of Foreign Relations, Feb. 2, 1795, *CFM*, 552; "Altho' nearly": JM to TJ, Feb. 15, 1795, *PTJ*, 28:265; "a circumstance": JM to Monroe, Mar. 11, 1795, *PJM*, 15:487; "splendid entertainment" and "May Britons": *Aurora General Advertiser* (Philadelphia), Feb. 21, 1795; Pasley, *First Presidential Contest*, 108; "What its contents": JM to Monroe, Mar. 11, 1795, *PJM*, 15:487.

72. "Its contents": JM to Monroe, Mar. 26, 1795, *PJM*, 15:496 ; "political opinions" and "I think": Liancourt, *Voyage*, 1:113–14.

73. "would cut up": AH to GW, Apr. 14, 1794, *PGWPS*, 15:589; "Sylla and charibdas": GW to John Randolph, July 31, 1795, Fitzpatrick, *Writings*, 34:266.

74. Bache obtains a copy: Elkins and McKitrick, *Age of Federalism*, 420; "monument of weakness": Liancourt, *Voyage*, 3:14–16.

75. "The outpouring": Elkins and McKitrick, *Age of Federalism*, 415; "impress on the minds": Fitzpatrick, *Writings*, 34:266.

76. hardly a day passed: Elkins and McKitrick, *Age of Federalism*, 420; "The greatest order": *Aurora General Advertiser* (Philadelphia), July 27, 1795; "five or six hundred": *Gazette of the United States* (Philadelphia), July 27, 1795; "The treaty was thrown": Wolcott to GW, July 27, 1795, George Gibbs, *Memoirs of the Administrations of Washington and John Adams, Edited from the Papers of Oliver Wolcott. . . .*, 2 vols. (New York: Printed for the Subscribers, 1846), 217; "somewhat hurt": Oliver Wolcott to Mrs. Wolcott, July 26, 1795, ibid, 218; "burnt the Treaty and groan'd": Wood, *Empire of Liberty*, 198; Klein, *Unification of a Slave State*, 219; liberty cap "and an inscription": ibid., 220; watermelons in Boston: Alfred Fabian Young, *The Shoemaker and the Tea Party: Memory and the American Revolution* (Boston: Beacon Press, 1999), 113; "Damn John Jay": quoted in Chernow, *Alexander Hamilton*, 486.

77. La Tour du Pin Gouvernet, *Journal d'une femme*, 2:84; no angry crowds on this scale: Pasley, *First Presidential Contest*, 124; "cannot be depended on": AH to Wolcott, July 28, 1795, *PAH*, 18:512.

78. "The farmers": Weld, *Travels*, 1:102–3; "The treaty with England": Liancourt, *Voyage*, 3:14–16; "We encounter in Virginia": ibid., 5:8–9; republican opinion more dominant in South: ibid., 4:144; "The people of the country": ibid., 5:8; "put itself": ibid., 3:14–16.

79. British forces locked the gates: Taylor, *Divided Ground*, 278–88; "In spite of": Allen, *His Majesty's Indian Allies*, 83; Bemis, *Jay's Treaty*, 360–62; "thou hast": quoted in Taylor, *Divided Ground*, 288. For the broader context, see Hinderaker, *Elusive Empires*, 226–67.

80. On the long war: John J. Bukowczyk, "Trade, War, Migration, and Empire in the Great Lakes Basin, 1650–1815," in *Permeable Border: The Great Lakes Basin as Transnational Region, 1650–1990* (Pittsburgh: University of Pittsburgh Press, 2005).

81. appalling betrayal: Joseph Fauchet, *Coup d'oeil sur l'état actuel de nos rapports politiques avec les États-Unis de l'Amérique septentrionale* (Paris: Pougin, Laran, 1797), 35–36; "intimate liaison" and subsequent Adet quotations: Adet to Minister of Foreign Relations, Mar. 21, 1796, *CFM*, 877–78.

82. "Louisiana abundantly": AF/IV/1211/59, AN; "Mémoire du C. Laudieu ou Landieu . . . 1796," AF/IV/1211/57, AN; J. A. James, "Louisiana as a Factor in American Diplomacy, 1795–1800," *Mississippi Valley Historical Review* 1, no. 1 (1914): 45; "The commercial advantages" and "might be had": Liancourt, *Voyage*, 4:196–97.

83. "The master": "Louisiana," AF/IV/1211/59, AN; "It gives us": quoted in Turner, "Policy of France toward the Mississippi Valley," 269; "The possession of": Liancourt, *Voyage*, 4:199–200.

84. "are much more": "Mémoires et Nottes [*sic*] sur la Louisiane et les Florides," AF/IV/1211/55, AN; "All these": Liancourt, *Voyage*, 4:201; enduring French loyalties to Native Americans: Havard and Vidal, *Histoire de l'Amérique française*, 671–719; French in Mississippi valley will provide support: Bryant, "Botanical Explorations of André Michaux in Kentucky," 214.

85. "If we don't": "Mémoire Présenté par François Tastanegy, Grand Chef de guerre de la Nation Crik Au Directoire-Exécutif de la République française, en L'an Cinq," AF/IV/1211/61, AN; all other quotations in this paragraph: E. Wilson Lyon, "Milfort's Plan for a Franco-Creek Alliance and the Retrocession of Louisiana," *Journal of Southern History* 4, no. 1 (1938), 79, 80, 83. The most complete treatment of the Tastanegy document is Gilbert C. Din, "Louis Leclerc de Milford, aka General François Tastanegy: An Eighteenth-Century French Adventurer among the Creeks," in *Nexus of Empire: Negotiating Loyalty and Identity in the Revolutionary Borderlands, 1760s–1820s*, eds. Gene A. Smith and Sylvia L. Hilton (Gainesville: University

Press of Florida, 2010); see also Barbara H. Stein and Stanley J. Stein, *Edge of Crisis War and Trade in the Spanish Atlantic, 1789–1808* (Baltimore: Johns Hopkins University Press, 2009), 49–50. The most useful file I found for understanding French interest in Louisiana is AF/IV/1211 at AN. See also AF/IV/1213, dossier 9; Château de Vincennes, Ministère de la Terre; CPÉU, supp. 5, MAÉ.

86. Adet in Saint Domingue: Turner, "Policy of France toward the Mississippi Valley," 268n1; Cobbett: *Porcupine's Gazette* (Philadelphia), May 6, 1797; "Nothing would": Talleyrand to Madame de Genlis, May 1, 1795, quoted in Poniatowski, *Talleyrand aux États-Unis,* 291; Moreau and Talleyrand dining at Adet's: Moreau, *American Journey,* 213.

87. "It has been whispered": JM to Monroe, Feb. 26, 1796, *PJM,* 16:233–34; Adet response: "Sommaires des dépêches du Citoyen Adet du 15 Prairial au 3 Messidor," AF/IV/1213/9, AN; "political intolerance": Liancourt, *Voyage,* 6:327–28; French songs replaced by "The President's March" and the quotation from the *Gazette:* Riordan, "'O Dear, What Can the Matter Be?'" 221–22; change in street culture: Waldstreicher, *Perpetual Fetes,* 141–73.

88. "I put on the *Cocarde*" and "as relations": Moreau, *American Journey,* 225, 240; "We only admit": "Extrait d'une dépêche du Cit. Létombe, consul général," 12 Germinal, an 5 (Apr. 1, 1797), AF/III/64/2, AN; reference to Moreau as consul: "Extrait d'une dépêche du Consul Brunet secrétaire de légation chargé de la correspondance en absence du ministre plénipotentiaire," Philadelphie, 2 Fructidor, an 4 (Aug. 19, 1796), AF/III/64/260.

89. "I have to tell you": Adet to Minister of Foreign Relations, Mar. 26, 1797, *CFM,* 1003; "Liancourt has become": JA to AA, Dec. 20, 1796, *AFPEA;* "appeared to forget": Elkanah Watson, *Men and Times of the Revolution; or, Memoirs of Elkanah Watson. . . . ,* ed. Winslow C. Watson (New York: Dana, 1856), 888. The timing of the conversation was almost certainly the winter of 1795 to 1796, because that is the only one during which Talleyrand and Volney overlapped. Liancourt was not mentioned in Watson's recollections, but he referred to Desjardins as "a former Chamberlain of Louix XVI," presumably confusing him with Liancourt; if that is the case, it was Liancourt who predicted French bayonets across the American frontier. On Desjardins, see the very fine *Castorland Journal,* edited by John A. Gallucci.

90. The details of the machinations in Paris to get Talleyrand struck from the list of émigrés are recounted in Poniatowski, *Talleyrand aux États-Unis,* 291–300 (for the text of the petition, see 293–94).

91. "strongly attached": Talleyrand, *Mémoires,* 1:347; "The ships that go": Talleyrand to Staël, Mar. 8, 1796, quoted in Poniatowski, *Talleyrand aux États-Unis,* 327. On seizures of American ships carrying grain, see Elkins and McKitrick, *Age of Federalism,* 421.

92. Agreement with Robert Morris: Talleyrand to Robert Morris, May 15, 1796; Washburn Papers, 10:10, MHS. Talleyrand chats with Spanish ambassador: Don Carlos to Victor Collot, June 10, 1796, Wayne Papers, 44:67 HSP; details on Talleyrand's final days: Moreau, *Voyage,* 223–25.

93. "delightful confidences" and subsequent quotations: Moreau, *American Journey,* 214–15, 217.

CHAPTER 6: THE ÉMIGRÉS RETURN TO FRANCE; FRANCE RETURNS TO AMERICA

1. Talleyrand to Moreau, June 15, 1796, Moreau, *Voyage,* 226.
2. Ibid., June 18, 1796.
3. "drank freely" and subsequent AH quotations: "Notes on Alexander Hamilton," *PTJ,* 29:517; "We found many": Moreau,*Voyage,* 224.
4. "*doux*": Talleyrand to Moreau, July 31, 1796, Moreau, *Voyage,* 232; Alexandre and his wife: C. Mullié, *Biographie des célébrités militaires des armées de terre et de mer de 1789 à 1850,* 2 vols. (Paris: Poignavant, 1851), 2:177–78; "It will be": quoted in Constantin-François de Chasseboeuf Volney, *Oeuvres de C.-F. Volney,* ed. Adolphe Bossange, 8 vols. (Paris: Parmentier, 1826), 1:xxviii.
5. Consigning the book: Moreau, *American Journey,* 226; German translation of Liancourt's

essay: *Aurora General Advertiser* (Philadelphia), Jan. 28, 1798; *Universal Gazette* (Philadelphia), Mar. 1, 1798; Talleyrand delivered a letter to Voght: AB to FB, Nov. 1796, CML-BaP; agreement to sell Morris's land: "An Inventory of Lands, Proposed to Be Committed by Robert Moris to Mr Talleyrand for Sale in Europe," Robert Morris Business Papers, folder C, HSP; sent Morris money: Pugh, "Introduction," 22.

6. Talleyrand, "Mémoire sur les relations commerciales," 92, 88, 97, 93.
7. Hamilton, "Defense of the President's Neutrality Proclamation," *PAH*, 14:503.
8. Talleyrand, "Mémoire sur les relations commerciales," 89, 103.
9. "in the calculations": ibid., 106; "I have made": Talleyrand to Moreau, Feb. 17, 1797, Moreau, *Journey*, 239.
10. Talleyrand, "Essai sur les avantages à retirer," 296, 290–91, 294.
11. Ibid., 2:298.
12. François Urban Domergue to Moreau, Sept. 22, 1796, Moreau, *American Journey*, 221–22.
13. "*Voyage philosophique*": Volney to TJ, Nov. 16, 1793, *PTJ*, 27:390–91; "Considering that": "Extrait des registres des délibérations du Conseil Exécutif provisoire du 3ème jour du 2è mois de la 2 année de la République une et indivisible," 3 Brumaire, an 2, AF/III/64/1/259, AN; hoping for appointment: Gaulmier, *L'idéologue Volney*, 350–51; "My friend": Morris to AH, Oct. 29, 1793, *PAH* 15:380; letter to Washington: Morris to GW, Oct. 29, 1793, *PGWPS* 14:300.
14. "In this visit": quoted in Gaulmier, *L'idéologue Volney*, 353; "more tiring" and "Will I be": Volney to La Révellière, Jan. 14, 1797, Mathiez, "Lettres de Volney à La Révellière," 171–72; "To see": Volney to [La Révellière], May 2, 1797, Jean François Bodin, *Recherches historiques sur la ville d'Angers, ses monumens et ceux du Bas-Anjou*, 2 vols. (Saumur: Dubosse [et] P. Godet, 1846), 2:535; Gaulmier, *L'idéologue Volney*, 350. Volney also had contact with Adet: Volney to TJ, Nov. 13, 1795, *PTJ*, 28:525–26.
15. TJ to Volney, July 5, 1797, *PTJ*, 29:474; Volney to TJ, July 5, 1797, ibid., 29:474.
16. "I say it with regret": Volney, *Tableau du climat et du sol*, 1:xii; "I see federalists": Volney to [La Révellière], Jan. 14, 1797, Bodin, *Recherches historiques*, 2:532; "There are very few": Volney to La Révellière, 12 Floréal, an 5 (May 2, 1797), Mathiez, "Lettres de Volney à La Révellière," 183. See also Chinard, *Volney et l'Amérique*, 82. "Everywhere in my travels" and "The idea of your expedition": Volney to [La Révellière], Jan. 14, 1797, Bodin, *Recherches historiques*, 2:531, and Mathiez, "Lettres de Volney à La Révellière," 173; "When the merchants": Volney to [La Révellière], Jan. 23, 1797, Bodin, *Recherches historiques*, 2:533, and Mathiez, "Lettres de Volney à La Révellière," 177.
17. "Let's consider it": Volney to [La Révellière], 12 Floréal, an 5 (May 2, 1797), Bodin, *Recherches historiques*, 2:534; "fallen from its": Volney, *Tableau du climat et du sol*, 1:x; "If you want to keep": Volney to [La Révellière], 12 Floréal, an 5 (May 2, 1797), Bodin, *Recherches historiques*, 2:535. See also Chinard, *Volney et l'Amérique*, 81.
18. For background information on Collot, see George W. Kyte, "A Spy on the Western Waters: The Military Intelligence Mission of General Collot in 1796," *Mississippi Valley Historical Review* 34, no. 3 (1947); Robert S. Weddle, *Changing Tides: Twilight and Dawn in the Spanish Sea, 1763–1803* (College Station: Texas A & M University Press, 1995), 223–27; Anne Perotin-Dumon, *Être patriote sous les tropiques: La Guadeloupe, la colonisation et la Révolution, 1789–1794* (Basse-Terre: Société d'histoire de la Guadeloupe, 1985), 179–82; and James Morton Smith, *Freedom's Fetters: The Alien and Sedition Laws and American Civil Liberties* (Ithaca, NY: Cornell University Press, 1956), 164–69. "the formation": Durand Echeverria, "General Collot's Plan for a Reconnaissance of the Ohio and Mississippi Valleys, 1796," *WMQ* 9, no. 4 (1952): 516; Collot's land speculation: David Karel, *Dictionnaire des artistes de langue française en Amérique du Nord: Peintres, sculpteurs, dessinateurs, graveurs, photographes, et orfèvres* (Québec: Presses de l'Université Laval, 1992), s.v. "Collot," 187; most detailed map: Kyte, "Spy on the Western Waters," 434; "try by every possible means," "what would be," and "what types": Echeverria, "General Collot's Plan," 516, 520.
19. "If the leaders": Collot, *Voyage*, 1:46–47; importance of Pittsburgh, Alleghenies as Louisiana's

eastern border: Kyte, "Spy on the Western Waters," 432; see also CPÉU, supp. 19, pp. 341–42, MAÉ.

20. Clark on the street: Collot, *Voyage*, 1:215–17.

21. "The majority": ibid., 1:317–18; "*bonne disposition*": ibid., 1:103; observations on Native Americans: ibid., 1:384–403; "the most *doux*": ibid., 2:51; Collot on the Saint Louis fort: ibid., 1:340–41; "Eighty men": ibid., 2:72.

22. "This place will be": ibid., 1:343; "considered under its military": ibid., 1:341; "all of them French," ibid., 1:339; "My voyage": ibid., 2:2–3. On the strategic and political significance of the area, see Stephen Aron, *American Confluence: The Missouri Frontier from Borderland to Border State* (Bloomington: Indiana University Press, 2006).

23. Adet to Collot, 20 Nivôse, an 5, CPÉU, supp. 28, doc. 35, MAÉ.

24. Volney hopes break between France and the United States can be avoided: TJ to JM, May 31, 1798, *PTJ*, 30:380.

25. "they could not": "Extrait d'une dépêche du C^en Le Tombe [Letombe]," 16 Floréal, an 5 (May 5, 1797), AF/III/64/2, AN; see also "Extrait d'une dépêche du C^en Adet, au ministre des relations extérieures," 11 Germinal, an 5 (Mar. 31, 1797), ibid; "Consular agent": "Extrait d'une lettre du Cit. Ferdinand Bayard," 25 Ventôse, an 5 (Mar. 15, 1797), AF/III/64/2, AN; "spies and inflammatory agents": quoted in Echeverria, "General Collot's Plan," 512.

26. Monroe to JM, Sept. 19, 1796, *PJM*, 16:397–98.

27. Clark to Fulton, Mar. 2, 1797, Archives Vincennes, Ministère de la Terre, B9, 1.

28. Volney to ?, 12 Floréal, an 5 (May 1, 1797?), Bodin, *Recherches historiques*, 535. The date is confusing because he refers to opening of Congress on May 15 in the past tense.

29. La Tour du Pin Gouvernet, *Journal d'une femme*, 2:37.

30. "Volney is convinced": TJ to JM, June 15, 1797, *PJM* 17:24; "seeing the curiosities": Russell W. Knight, ed., *Elbridge Gerry's Letterbook: Paris, 1797–1798* (Salem, MA: Essex Institute, 1966), 23; Talleyrand blaming English machinations for his failure: "Rapport aux consuls de la République du 9 Frimaire an 8," AF/IV/1681/A, AN.

31. Knight, ed., *Elbridge Gerry's Letterbook*, 45, 30.

32. "What think you" and subsequent Nelly Custis quotations: Eleanor Parke Custis to Elizabeth Bordley, July 1, 1798, in Brady, *George Washington's Beautiful Nelly*, 57; Lewis facilitating Volney's trip: Volney, *Tableau du climat et du sol*, 384. Volney identified Washington's relative as a "Colonel *Lewis*"—probably he meant Washington's nephew Lawrence Lewis, who was not a colonel but became a captain of the light dragoons in 1799, and who was married to Washington's stepgranddaughter Nelly: Frank E. Grizzard, "Lewis, Lawrence," in *George Washington: A Biographical Companion* (Santa Barbara, CA: ABC-CLIO, 2002), 198–99. "I have reason": JA to Benjamin Rush, Oct. 10, 1808, John A. Schutz and Douglass Adair, eds., *The Spur of Fame: Dialogues of John Adams and Benjamin Rush, 1805–1813* (Indianapolis: Liberty Fund, 2000), 133.

33. "Our country": Chinard, *Volney et l'Amérique*, 97–99; "insinuated himself": William Cobbett, *Remarks on the Insidious Letter of the Gallic Despots* (Philadelphia: printed by William Cobbett, 1798); Moreau's response: M. L. E. Moreau de Saint-Méry, *See Porcupine, in Colours Just Portray'd* (Philadelphia: printed by M. L. E. Moreau de Saint-Méry, 1796?); [James Philip Puglia], *The Political Massacre* (Philadelphia: printed by Moreau de Saint-Méry, 1796); [James Philip Puglia], *The Blue Shop; or, Impartial and Humorous Observations on the Life and Adventures of Peter Porcupine. . . .* (Philadelphia: printed by Moreau de Saint-Méry, 1796).

34. "Let us no longer": quoted in Wood, *Empire of Liberty*, 249; "a *conspiracy*": Volney, *Tableau du climat et du sol*, 1:iiin1; "is understood": TJ to JM, Apr. 26, 1798, *PTJ*, 30:300; "deplorable state" and "No doubt": TJ to William Short, May 1, 1798, *PTJ*, 30:319. For further evidence that the French were on the minds of lawmakers when they debated the Alien Act, see *Annals of Congress*, House of Representatives, 5th Cong., 3d sess., 1798–1799, 2429–37, 2785–3017.

35. "Volney affected": Breck, "Recollections" (ms bound volume), 15; Liancourt "very violent": JA to AA, Dec. 20, 1796, *AFPEA*.

36. "an epidemic" and subsequent Volney quotations: Volney, *Tableau du climat et du sol*, 1:ii–iii, and Volney to La Révellière, July 7, 1798, Mathiez, "Lettres de Volney à La Révellière," 186; "I shall not": JA to Pickering, Sept. 16, 1798, *The Works of John Adams, Second President of the United States. . . .* , ed. Charles Francis Adams, 8 vols. (Boston: Little, Brown, 1850), 8:596; flying flag of truce: Pickering to GW, Oct. 3, 1798, *PGWPS*, 3:75; "The threatening appearances": TJ to JM, May 3, 1798, *PTJ*, 30:323; see also TJ to Thomas Randolph, May 3, 1798; *PTJ*, 30:326.

37. "The Duc de Liancourt": *Amherst Village Messenger*, Sept. 15, 1798; "He is, perhaps" and subsequent Cobbett quotations: *Porcupine's Gazette*, Jan. 11, 1799.

38. All quotations are from Moreau, *American Journey*, 253. On the violence (or threat thereof) associated with the political contests of the late 1790s, see especially Michael A. Bellesiles, "'The Soil Will Be Soaked with Blood': Taking the Revolution of 1800 Seriously," in *The Revolution of 1800: Democracy, Race, and the New Republic*, ed. James Horn, Jan Lewis, and Peter S. Onuf (Charlottesville: University of Virginia Press, 2002), 59–86.

39. Moreau, *Voyage*, 392–94.

40. "rich": AB to FB, Jan. 20/Feb. 5, 1799, CML-BaP; Noailles' involvement in sugar and cochineal trade, and his transactions with the Barings: "Jan. 1799 to 1800," Baring Account Books, BaP.

41. "Having long possessed": JA to Pickering, Aug. 13, 1799, *Works*, ed. Adams, 9:14; Pickering's negotiations and Collot: George W. Kyte, "The Detention of General Collot: A Sidelight on Anglo-American Relations, 1798–1800," *WMQ* 6, no. 4 (1949).

42. Volney to Noailles, Aug. 11, 1800, Ferdinand J. Dreer Autograph Collection, French Prose Writers, 2:59 HSP.

43. Madame de Staël is quoted in Breck, "Recollections" (ms bound copy). I have also found this quotation in William Hood Thomas Jerdan, *The Autobiography of William Jerdan with His Literary, Political and Social Reminiscences and Correspondence during the Last Fifty Years* (London: Arthur Hall, Virtue, 1852), 4:278.

44. "the guidebook" and Napoleon's bringing Volney's *Voyage* to Saint Helena: A. J. O'Connor, "Volney and the Egyptian Expedition," *French Studies* 4, no. 3 (1950): 253. On Volney's influence on Napoleon's campaign in Egypt, see Paul Strathern, *Napoleon in Egypt* (New York: Bantam Books, 2008), 14–15; Philip G. Dwyer, *Napoleon: The Path to Power* (New Haven, CT: Yale University Press, 2008), 347, 378; Vincent Cronin, *Napoleon Bonaparte: An Intimate Biography* (New York: Morrow, 1972), 144, 149. In *Orientalism* (New York: Pantheon Books, 1978), Edward W. Said called Volney's work a "handbook" and one of the "texts to be used by any European wishing to win the Orient," 81.

45. "No country": Valentin de Cullion, "Mémoire sur l'approvisionnement de l'armée de St. Domingue," AF/IV/1212/51, AN; "There are improvements": "Objets, relatifs à la Louisiane, sur lesquels il importe d'appeler l'attention particulière du gouvernment," AF/IV/1211/52, AN.

46. "We must return": "Rapport aux consuls de la République du 9 Frimaire an 8," AF/IV/1681/A, AN; "a kind of armistice": quoted in G. Labouchère, "L'annexion de la Louisiane aux États-Unis et les Maisons Hope et Baring," *Revue d'histoire diplomatique* 30 (1916), 424.

47. Napoleon orders report on colonial possessions: Elijah Wilson Lyon, *Louisiana in French Diplomacy, 1759–1804* (Norman: University of Oklahoma Press, 1934), 111; "Spain has ceeded": Joseph Allen Smith to TJ, Mar. 22, 1801, *PTJ*, 33:404; American writes to Hamilton: William Constable to AH, Mar. 23, 1801, *PAH*, 25:372.

48. "I am apprehensive," "Louisiana and the Floridas," and "that General Collot": King to JM, Mar. 28, 1801, *ASPFRS* 2:509; "The acquisition might": ibid., June 1, 1801.

49. "The exchange has" and subsequent Livingston quotations: Livingston to King, Dec. 30, 1801, ibid., 2:512; Collot to accompany the mission: Livingston to JM, May 28, 1802, *PJMSS*, 2:518.

50. "Our own Western territory": Livingston to King, Dec. 30, 1801, *ASPFRS*, 2:512; "hold forth": *New York Daily Advertiser*, Feb. 12, 1802. On these concerns see also Madison's instructions to Livingston, Mar. 2, 1803, *ASPFRS*, 2:540–41.

51. "a corps": Brissot quoted in Dorigny, "Brissot et Miranda en 1792," 99; "rocked slave societies": Laurent Dubois, *A Colony of Citizens: Revolution & Slave Emancipation in the French*

Caribbean, 1787–1804 (Chapel Hill: University of North Carolina Press, 2004), 190–91; "A few French Troops": Governor Winthrop Sargent quoted in Adam Rothman, *Slave Country: American Expansion and the Origins of the Deep South* (Cambridge, MA: Harvard University Press, 2005); "state of anxiety": Pichon to Talleyrand, dispatch dated 2 Frimaire, an 11 (Nov. 23, 1802), ibid., 77; for similar fears, see also Klein, *Unification of a Slave State,* 210–18, and Link, *Democratic-Republican Societies,* 185–86; other rumors about Indians: Pichon to Talleyrand, CPÉU, 55, 361, MAÉ.

52. "is not disposed": Talleyrand to Citoyen Bernadotte, 20 Nivôse, an 11 (Jan. 10, 1803), CPÉU, 55, MAÉ; Talleyrand and neighborly relations: Talleyrand to Bernadotte, n.d., ibid; "very positive" Talleyrand to Bernadotte, 24 Nivôse, an 11 (Jan. 14, 1803), ibid; see also Talleyrand to Bernadotte, 1 Pluviôse, an 11 (Jan. 21, 1803).

53. "Since the question": Alexander Hamilton, "For the *Evening Post,*" Feb. 8, 1803, in *PAH,* 26:82–83; "On the event": quoted in Whitaker, *Mississippi Question,* v.

54. For the American context: esp. Hale, "On Their Tiptoes." For the more general context: Koselleck, *Futures Past;* M. H. Abrams, *Natural Supernaturalism: Tradition and Revolution in Romantic Literature* (New York: W. W. Norton, 1973).

55. "This circumstance": AB to FB, May 7, 1799, CML-BaP; annulment granted: *Universal Gazette* (Philadelphia), Mar. 27, 1800; Tilly's taunting letter: Tilly, *Mémoires,* 3:254; "Mrs. Bingham is in her bed": AB to FB, Jan. 22, 1801, CML-BaP. Robert Alberts indicates that young William Bingham was born in late 1800 (*Golden Voyage,* 394).

56. "Though her situation": AB to FB, Mar. 29, 1801, CML-BaP; "Her Disorder" and "recommended": quoted in Brown, "Mr. and Mrs. William Bingham," 321; "her case": AB to FB, May 12, 1801, CML-BaP.

57. carried in palanquin and crowds gathering: Griswold, *Republican Court,* 362n; "As she is": Brown, "Mr. and Mrs. William Bingham," 321; "This business": AB to FB, May 12, 1801, CML-BaP.

58. Laujon, *Souvenirs et voyages,* 116.

59. "very great influence": AB to FB, Nov. 1796, CML-BaP; "the vicomte": Tilly, *Mémoires,* 3:245.

60. Advertisement for Bingham mansion and goods: *Philadelphia Gazette,* Aug. 7, 1801; "to the Care of": WB to AH, July 21, 1801, *PAH,* 25:401.

61. "My Plan of Life" and "I cannot express": WB to Willing, May 22, 1802, quoted in Brown, "Mr. and Mrs. William Bingham," 322; "irreparable loss": WB to Noailles, Nov. 27, 1801, quoted in Alberts, *Golden Voyage,* 426.

62. "I feel that": Noailles to WB, Sept. 12, 1801, box 1, folder 23, Bingham, W., mss., Lilly Library, Indiana University, Bloomington; "It appears to me": WB to Noailles, Oct. 24, 1801, Ferdinand J. Dreer Autograph Collection, American Statesmen, 1:57, HSP; "Few people": Noailles to WB, Nov. 9, 1801, box 1, folder 23, Bingham, W., mss., Lilly Library, Indiana University, Bloomington, Indiana.

63. WB to Noailles, Oct. 24, 1801, Ferdinand J. Dreer Autograph Collection, American Statesmen, 1:57, HSP.

64. Adams, *History of the United States,* 256, 264.

65. "fall to English hands": "Mémoire secret: Iles d'Amériques," AF/IV/1211/32, AN; "strategic straits": Central Intelligence Agency, *The World Factbook,* https://www.cia.gov/library/publications/the-world-factbook/geos/zh.html, accessed Nov. 16, 2013; pirate stronghold: Marion Emerson Murphy, *The History of Guantanamo Bay,* 2nd ed. (Guantánamo Bay, Cuba: United States Naval Base, 1953).

66. *Spectator* (New York), Dec. 5, 1801.

67. "A great many": ibid; force of eighty thousand: Dubois, *Avengers,* 251; largest expeditionary force: Dayan, *Haiti,* 150; lost more troops than at Waterloo: Robin Blackburn, *The Overthrow of Colonial Slavery, 1776–1848* (London: Verso, 1988), 263n51.

68. "the Cannibals": TJ to Aaron Burr, Feb. 11, 1799, *PTJ,* 21:22; "black crews": TJ to JM, Feb. 12, 1799, *PTJ,* 21:29–30; "landing of French negroes": Pichon to Talleyrand, dispatch dated 6 Brumaire, an 11 (Nov. 1, 1802), CPÉU, 55, 52, MAÉ; "There is on the globe": quoted in Kyte,

"Spy on the Western Waters," 433, and in D. W. Meinig, *The Shaping of America: A Geographical Perspective on 500 Years of History,* 4 vols. (New Haven, CT: Yale University Press, 1986), 2:10; "There is not": William Cobbett, *Cobbett's Annual Register,* Mar. 2, 1802, 202, and *Greenfield Gazette* (Massachusetts), Feb. 21, 1803.

69. "In general": Pichon to Talleyrand, 3 Frimaire, an 11 (Nov. 24, 1802), CPÉU, 55, pp. 83–84, MAÉ.
70. Talleyrand quotations are from Dubois, *Avengers,* 260.
71. "France with an army": quoted in Donald Hickey, "America's Response to the Slave Revolt in Haiti, 1791–1806," *Journal of the Early Republic* 2, no. 4 (1982): 365; Fifty thousand French soldiers: Dubois, *Avengers,* 298.
72. "that he has renounced France": JA to AA, Dec. 20, 1796, *AFPEA.*
73. "Count de Noailles": *New York Daily Advertiser,* Jan. 3, 1803; "The family" and subsequent quotations: Laujon, *Souvenirs et voyages,* 2:254.
74. "I am penetrated": Noailles to d'Aure, 23 Pluviôse, an 11 (Feb. 1803), Papiers Hector d'Aure, 416/AP/1, AN; getting loans for French mission: Gray to JM, Feb. 7, 1803; exchanging notes with Willing: "Traités et correspondance entre M. de Noailles, MM Willing et [?] à Philadelphie. . . . ," ibid.; Barings supplying British forces: "From Sept. 1794 to Dec. 1796," Baring Account Books, BaP; "I'll have occasion": Noailles to d'Aure, 23 Pluviôse, an 11 (Feb. 1803), Papiers Hector d'Aure, 416/AP/1, AN.
75. "the French plan": Philip Wright, ed., *Lady Nugent's Journal of Her Residence in Jamaica from 1801 to 1805* (Mona, Jamaica: University of the West Indies, 2002), 137–38; suggestions of selling African slaves: Papiers Hector d'Aure, 416/AP/1, AN; Barings explore opportunities in the trade: Thomas and William Earl & Co. to FB, Oct. 19, 1802, CML-BaP.
76. Noailles purchases bloodhounds: Gray to JM, May 26, 1803, and Nov. 19, 1803, *PJMSS,* 5:35, 6:76; look like wolves: Thomas Madiou, *Histoire d'Haiti,* 3 vols. (Port-au-Prince: Impr. de J. Courtois, 1847), 2:411; "French frigate": *New York Morning Chronicle,* Mar. 3, 1803; "I send you": Madiou, *Histoire d'Haïti,* quoted in Johnson, *Fear of French Negroes,* 26.
77. Throwing flowers on the dogs: Dubois, *Avengers,* 292; "devoured his entrails": Madiou, *Histoire d'Haïti,* quoted in Johnson, *Fear of French Negroes,* 26; Dayan, *Haiti,* 155.
78. "that the blood hounds": *Olio* (Georgetown, DC), Apr. 29, 1803; "The war is carried on" and subsequent quotations: *New-York Gazette and General Advertiser,* July 23, 1803.
79. "war of extermination": quoted in Dubois, *Avengers,* 290; "My soul is tainted": quoted in Dayan, *Haiti,* 152; "General Rochambeau": Mary Hassal, *Secret History; or, the Horrors of St. Domingo, in a Series of Letters* (Philadelphia: Bradford & Inskeep, 1971), 25; on the violence from 1802 to 1804: Dubois, *Avengers,* 289–98; Robin Blackburn, *The American Crucible: Slavery, Emancipation and Human Rights* (London: Verso, 2011), 210–19; "blasted": Dayan, *Haiti,* 166; "truly new" and "not simply": David Brion Davis, *The Problem of Slavery in the Age of Revolution, 1770–1823* (Ithaca, NY: Cornell University Press, 1975), 562–63. On Haiti and history, see also Susan Buck-Morss, *Hegel, Haiti and Universal History* (Pittsburgh: University of Pittsburgh Press, 2009).
80. All quotations are from Vincent Gray to JM, Feb. 4 and Mar. 15, 1803, *PJMSS,* 4:301, 424.
81. All quotations are from *Herald* (Rutland, VT), Jan 7, 1803.
82 Vincent Gray to JM, Dec. 20, 1803, *PJMSS,* 6:193.
83. Details on Noailles' escape from Môle Saint-Nicolas and his last battle are drawn from Alfred Fierro, André Palluel-Guillard, and Jean Tulard, eds., *Histoire et dictionnaire du consulat et de l'empire* (Paris: Robert Laffont, 1995), s.v. "Noailles," 985–86; *Pennsylvania Biographical Dictionary,* 3rd ed. (St. Clair Shores, MI: Somerset Publishers, 1999), 296; John C. Fredriksen, ed., *Revolutionary War Almanac* (New York: Facts on File, 2006), 545; Madiou, *Histoire d'Haiti,* 3:104; and Laujon, *Souvenirs et voyages,* 281–82.
84. All quotations are from Barbé-Marbois, *Histoire de la Louisiane,* 219. Jefferson's diplomacy vis-à-vis Haiti: Blackburn, "Haiti, Slavery, and the Age of Democratic Revolution"; Guillaume Simard, "Les relations diplomatiques franco-américaines lors de l'expédition du général Leclerc: Le commerce, le territoire, la race et l'opinion, 1800–1804" (master's thesis, Université de Mon-

tréal, 2007); French worries about losing access to the Gulf of Mexico: Mémoire secret, dossier: "Iles d'Amérique," AF/IV/1211/32, AN; more general strategic issues: Yves Bénot, *La démence coloniale sous Napoléon: Essai* (Paris: Éditions La Découverte, 1992), 102; reorientation of Napoleon's foreign policy after Haiti: Yves Bénot and Marcel Dorigny, *Rétablissement de l'esclavage dans les colonies françaises, 1802: Ruptures et continuités de la politique coloniale française.* . . . (Paris: Maisonneuve et Larose, 2003); importance of the Haitian Revolution to this reorientation: Robert L. Paquette, "Revolutionary Saint Domingue in the Making of Territorial Louisiana," in *A Turbulent Time: The French Revolution and the Greater Caribbean*, ed. David Barry Gaspar and David Patrick Geggus (Bloomington: Indiana University Press, 1997), 204–25.

85. "The conquest": quoted in Labouchère, "L'annexion de la Louisiane," 427.

86. "If you occupy": Ministre de la Marine et des Colones au Premier Consul, Dec. 20, 1802, AF/IV/1190/39, AN; "exclusive master" and "monopolize": "Memoires et Nottes [*sic*] sur la Louisiane et les Florides," AF/IV/1211/55, AN; "To liberate": quoted in Labouchère, "L'annexion de la Louisiane," 426; "It appears": quoted in Barbé-Marbois, *Histoire de la Louisiane*, 287.

87. "whether we wished": Lyon, *Louisiana in French Diplomacy*, 216; "I need a lot of money": quoted in Labouchère, "L'annexion de la Louisiane," 429, 431.

88. French borrowing costs: Michael D. Bordo and Eugene N. White, "Tale of Two Currencies: British and French Finance during the Napoleonic Wars," *Journal of Economic History* 51, no. 2 (1991): 306, 314; Livingston's concern and Napoleon's response: Lyon, *Louisiana in French Diplomacy*, 218.

89. Baring in Paris: "Baring Notes and Diary on Trip to Paris, Sept 1802," Northbrook Papers, 1 A9.8, BaP; Volney dines with Talleyrand and sees Bingham: Volney to Mme L'Espinasse-Dangirand, Nov. 29, 1802, J. Dresch, "Quatre lettres inédites de Volney," *Revue de littérature comparée* 2 (1922): 91; Livingston presents Bingham to Napoleon: Livingston to Talleyrand, 20 Frimaire, an 11 (Dec. 11, 1802), CPÉU, 55, MAÉ; "procure me a letter": Labouchère to FB, Dec. 5, 1801, Northbrook Papers, 1 A13.3.1, BaP; Labouchère's role: Barbé-Marbois au Premier Consul, 6 Floréal, an 16 [12?], AF/IV/1681, AN; as Barbé-Marbois recalled: Barbé-Marbois, *Histoire de la Louisiane*, 330–32; Talleyrand-Cazenove letters: Arthur de Cazenove, *Quatre Siècles* (Nîmes: Imprimerie Coopérative La Laborieuse, 1908), 171–72; Rufus King may get a cut: FB to Rufus King, Mar. 1, 1804, NP1 A4.70, BaP; King's previous association with the gang: Talleyrand to Richard Morris, May 15, 1796, Washburn Papers, 10:10, MHS, which was witnessed by Rufus King.

90. "The demand": FB to Henry Addington, Nov. 12, 1803, Northbrook Papers, 1 A4.7, BaP; "of the utmost": PC Labouchère to AB, Jan. 30, [1803], ibid; "further *correspondence*": FB to PCL, Feb. 15, 1803, ibid.; Maine lands as cipher: FB to P. C. Labouchère, Apr. 21, 1803, ibid.

91. French government signs treaty with the Hopes and Barings: Ministère du trésor public, "Rapport au gouvernement de la République," 22 Frimaire, an 12, AN; "Négociation du fonds américain crée pour prix de la cession de la Louisiane," 27 Nivôse, an 12, signed Barbé-Marbois, ibid.; France receives immediate credit: Ministère du trésor public, "Rapport au Gouvernement de la République," 20 Thermidor, an 11, ibid.; Talleyrand drafts passport for Baring: Labouchère, "L'annexion de la Louisiane," 444.

92. "It would have been wise": "Memorandum, Account of Week's Events by Sir F. Baring," n.d., Northbrook Papers, 1 A4.13, BaP; Addington: Leslie Stephen, *Dictionary of National Biography* (London: Smith, Elder, 1885), s.v. "Addington"; Addington changes his mind: H. Addington to FB, Dec. 16, 1803, Northbrook Papers, 1 A4.28, BaP; Gallatin's estimate of the profits: Alberts, *Golden Voyage*, 423; "I think it": FB to P. C. Labouchère, Oct. 9, 1804, Northbrook Papers, 1 A4.67, BaP.

EMPTY HOUSES: A CONCLUSION

1. H. Hope to FB, Apr. 25, 1794, Northbrook Papers, 1 A3.6, BaP. The parallels to György Lukács, *The Historical Novel* (Lincoln: University of Nebraska Press, 1983), 23, are striking. See also Koselleck, *Futures Past*.

2. David Watkin, "'The Hope Family' by Benjamin West," *Burlington Magazine* 106, no. 741 (1964); "It is said": *PTJ*, 13:11.

3. *PTJ*, 13:xvii.

4. Niemcewicz, *Under Their Vine and Fig Tree*, 277.

5. "Miss Bingham": *Gazette of the United States* (Philadelphia), May 26, 1802; "spend the winter": Volney to Mme L'Espinasse-Dangirand, Nov. 29, 1802, Dresch, "Quatre lettres," 91; "I had before": WB to FB, Jan. 19, 1803, Northbrook Papers, 1.B3.1 BaP.

6. Details from Alberts, *Golden Voyage*, 426–27.

7. Brown, "Mr. and Mrs. William Bingham," 324; Alberts, *Golden Voyage*, 432.

8. "We must certainly" and subsequent quotaions: AB to FB, June 26, 1801, CML-BaP.

9. "the greatest merchant banker": Alberts, *Golden Voyage*, 435; "six great powers": Philip Ziegler, *Sixth Great Power*, 10. See also Herbert H. Kaplan, "Commerce, Consumption, and Culture: Hope & Co. and Baring Brothers & Co. and Russia," *Proceedings of the American Philosophical Society* 142, no. 2 (1998): 258–62.

10. Profits on Maine lands: "Documents Relating to the Purchase of Land in the District of Maine," DEeP 3, BaP.

11. Louis Belmontet, *Biographical Sketch of Joseph Napoleon Bonaparte, Count de Survilliers*, 2nd ed. (London: J. Ridgway, 1833), vi.

12. Ibid.; Westcott, *Historic Mansions*, 349–50; Scudder, *Recollections of Samuel Breck*, 248; Kelley, *Life and Times in Colonial Philadelphia*, 71.

13. Maria Perry, *The House in Berkeley Square: A History of the Lansdowne Club* (London: The Lansdowne Club, 2003), 111–16, 119, 124; William Rieder, "The Lansdowne Dining Room, London," in *Period Rooms in the Metropolitan Museum of Art*, ed. Amelia Peck (New York: Metropolitan Museum of Art, 1996), 147–56; Margaret C. S. Christman, "The Story of the Lansdowne Washington," in *George Washington: A National Treasure* (Washington, DC: National Portrait Gallery, 2002), 42–75. The house today is owned by the Lansdowne Club, which maintains several Adam-designed rooms in pristine condition.

14. "two boat Loads of good York manure": Genet—Misc. Papers, Genet Papers, NYHS.

15. Fourth of July festivities: Link, *Democratic-Republican Societies*, 151; sister's lobbying: Ammon, *Genet Mission*, 173; "I have the great pleasure" and "The reasons for": Pallain, *Correspondance diplomatique de Talleyrand*, 429n1.

16. Genet moves up the Hudson valley: "Accounts of Edmund Charles Genet with the Children of Cornelia Tappen Genet as Their Legal Guardian," BV "Genet," Genet Papers, NYHS; Ammon, *Genet Mission*, 172; sadness at Cornelia's death: ibid., 176; canal plans: "Printed Papers Relating to Navigation of Hudson River," Genet—Misc. Papers, Genet Papers, NYHS; system for pulling barges: Ammon, *Genet Mission*, 178; "On the Use of Milk": "Notes and Papers on Various Subjects," Genet—Misc. Papers, Genet Papers, NYHS.

17. Volney hopes to get diplomatic appointment: Mathiez, "Lettres de Volney à La Révellière," 188.

18. Personal communication from Antoine de Noailles to the author, Nov. 11, 2013.

19. Liancourt's departure: Moreau, *Voyage*, 236; "devoured": quoted in Dreyfus, *Un philanthrope d'autrefois*, 240; under Talleyrand's protection: La Rochefoucauld-Liancourt, *Vie du duc de La Rochefoucauld-Liancourt*, 50; struck from the list of émigrés: Dreyfus, *Un philanthrope d'autrefois*, 247.

20. "It is possible": quoted in Dreyfus, *Un philanthrope d'autrefois*, 214; "This poor French": *New York Commercial Advertiser*, June 23, 1800.

21. "English farmer": Dreyful, *Un philanthrope d'autrefois*, 270, quoted in Mantel, "La Rochefoucauld-Liancourt: Un novateur français dans la pratique agricole du XVIIIe siècle," 158.

22. Dumas: La Rochefoucauld, Wolikow, and Ikni, *Le duc de La Rochefoucauld*, 439.

23. "For thirty years": Hugo, "Talleyrand," in *Choses vues* (Paris: G. Charpentier et cie, 1888), 2–3.

ILLUSTRATION CREDITS

Page 3: The Library Company of Philadelphia

Page 7: Gilbert Stuart (1755–1828). *Louis-Marie, Vicomte de Noailles.* 1798. Oil on canvas, 50 x 40 in. (127 x 101.6 cm). Purchase, Henry R. Luce Gift, Elihu Root Jr. Bequest, Rogers Fund, Maria DeWitt Jesup Fund, Morris K. Jesup Fund and Charles and Anita Blatt Gift, 1970 (1970.262). The Metropolitan Museum of Art, NY, U.S.A. Image copyright © The Metropolitan Museum of Art. Image source: Art Resource, NY

Page 8: François Gerard (1770–1837). *Charles-Maurice de Talleyrand Périgord (1754–1838), Prince de Bénévent.* 1808. Oil on canvas, 83⅞ x 57⅞ in. (213 x 147 cm). Purchase, Mrs. Charles Wrightsman Gift, 2012 (2012.348). The Metropolitan Museum of Art, New York, NY, U.S.A. Image copyright © The Metropolitan Museum of Art. Image source: Art Resource, NY

Page 9: Smithsonian American Art Museum, Washington, DC / Art Resource, NY

Page 10: Pennsylvania Academy of the Fine Arts. Gift of Mrs. Thomas Bayard

Page 12: James Sharples (the Elder) (1751–1811). *Médéric-Louis-Élie Moreau de Saint-Méry.* 1798. Pastel and black chalk (or black pastel) on toned (now oxidized) wove paper: 9⁷⁄₁₆ x 7¼ in. (24 x 18.4 cm). Bequest of Charles Allen Munn, 1924 (24.109.89). The Metropolitan Museum of Art, New York, NY, U.S.A. Image copyright © The Metropolitan Museum of Art. Image source: Art Resource, NY

Page 21: The Library Company of Philadelphia

Page 23: The Library Company of Philadelphia

Page 25: Amsterdam City Archives

Page 27, left: The Library Company of Philadelphia; right: Photograph by the author

Page 28, above left: The Library Company of Philadelphia; above right: Photograph by the author; below left: The Library Company of Philadelphia; below right: Photograph by the author

Page 29: The Library Company of Philadelphia

Page 32: The Library Company of Philadelphia

Page 37: Bibliothèque nationale de France

Page 44: Print Collection, Miriam and Ira D. Wallach Division of Art, Prints and Photographs, The New York Public Library, Astor, Lenox and Tilden Foundations

Page 45: Albany Institute of History & Art, bequest of Nancy Fuller Genet

Page 51: Rare Book and Special Collections Division, Library of Congress

Page 58: Bibliothèque nationale de France

Page 71: The British Library

Page 79: Eno Collection, Miriam and Ira D. Wallach Division of Art, Prints and Photographs, The New York Public Library, Astor, Lenox and Tilden Foundations

Page 82 : Bibliothèque nationale de France

Page 83: Bibliothèque nationale de France

Page 89: The Library Company of Philadelphia

Page 93, above: Architect of the Capitol; below: Bibliothèque nationale de France

Page 95: The Library Company of Philadelphia

Page 100, left: The Library Company of Philadelphia; right: The Library Company of Philadelphia

Page 103: Maker: Simon Chaudron, 1758–1846. Punch Pot, 1805–10. Silver, Overall: 8¾ x 9⁵/₁₆ x 5¹³/₁₆ in. (22.2 x 23.7 x 14.8 cm); 47 oz. 15 dwt. (1485.6 g). Foot: Diam. 4¹/₁₆ in (10.3 cm). Purchase, Mr. and Mrs. Marshall P. Blankarn Gift, 1966 (66.103). Image copyright © The Metropolitan Museum of Art. Image source: Art Resource, NY

Page 104, above left: The Library Company of Philadelphia; above right: The Library Company of Philadelphia; below left: The Library Company of Philadelphia; below right: The Library Company of Philadelphia

Page 110: The Library Company of Philadelphia

Page 114: Charles B. J. Fevret de Saint Mémin, *Théophile Cazanove*, 1799, engraving (2⅜ x 2½ inches), Corcoran Gallery of Art, Washington, D.C. Gift of William Wilson Corcoran, 75.16.131

Page 128: Library of Congress, Geography and Map Division

Page 135, left: Courtesy of Mount Vernon Ladies' Association; right: Courtesy of Mount Vernon Ladies' Association

Page 136, left: Courtesy of Mount Vernon Ladies' Association; right: Courtesy of Mount Vernon Ladies' Association

Page 157: Charles Willson Peale (1741–1827). *Thomas Willing*. 1782. American. Oil on canvas: 49½ x 39¾ in. (125.7 x 101 cm). Gift of Dr. Ernest G. Stillman, by exchange, 1966 (66.46). The Metropolitan Museum of Art, New York, NY, U.S.A. Image copyright © The Metropolitan Museum of Art. Image source: Art Resource, NY

Page 160: Charles Willson Peale, American, 1741–1827, *Miniature Portrait of the Honorable William Bingham (1751–1804)*, c. 1780, watercolor on ivory; gilt metal frame, H: 1½ in. x W: 1⅛ in. (3.80 x 3.00 cm), Carnegie Museum of Art, Pittsburgh: Gift of Herbert DuPuy, 27.10.71. Photograph © 2013 Carnegie Museum of Art, Pittsburgh

Page 164: Bibliothèque nationale de France

Page 166: National Park Service, Adams National Historical Park

Page 169: Courtesy of the Frick Art Reference Library

Page 171, above: © By kind permission of the Trustees of the Wallace Collection; below: The Library Company of Philadelphia

Page 173: Reproduced courtesy of The Baring Archive

Page 175: Robert Adam (1728–1792), after a design by; plaster ceiling by Joseph Rose (1746–1799); woodwork carved by John Gilbert; marble chimneypiece supplied by John Devall & Co., London. Dining room from Lansdowne House. British. 1766–69. Wood, plaster, stone. Overall, room: H. 566 x W. 294 x D. 215 in. (1437.6 x 746.8 x 546.1 cm); overall, mantelpiece: H. 75 x W. 87⅜ in. (190.5 x 221.9 cm). Rogers Fund, 1931 (32.12). The Metropolitan Museum of Art, New York, NY, U.S.A. Image copyright © The Metropolitan Museum of Art. Image source: Art Resource, NY

Page 178: Winterthur Museum, Garden & Library. Gift of Henry Francis du Pont

Page 180: National Portrait Gallery, Smithsonian Institution / Art Resource, NY

Page 181: Reproduced by permission of English Heritage

Page 184, left: Wikimedia Commons; right: Wikimedia Commons

Page 185: Courtesy of Judy and Michael Steinhardt

Page 188, left: Library of Congress; right: William Russell Birch (1755–1834). *Mrs. William Bingham (Anne Willing)*. 1795. Enamel on copper, 4⅜ x 3⅜ in. (11 x 8.5 cm). Dale T. Johnson Fund, 2006 (2006.235.16). Image copyright © The Metropolitan Museum of Art. Image source: Art Resource, NY

Page 189: The Philadelphia Museum of Art / Art Resource, NY

Page 191: Beinecke Rare Book and Manuscript Library, Yale University

Page 192, left: Courtesy of Independence National Historical Park; right: Winterthur Museum, Garden & Library. Museum purchase with funds provided by Henry Francis du Pont

Page 193, image of William Jackson: Courtesy of Independence Historical National Park; image of Volney: Emmet Collection, Miriam and Ira D. Wallach Division of Art, Prints and Photographs, The New York Public Library, Astor, Lenox and Tilden Foundations

Page 197: The Library Company of Philadelphia

Page 220: Library of Congress, Geography and Map Division

Page 228: The Lionel Pincus and Princess Firyal Map Division, The New York Public Library, Astor, Lenox and Tilden Foundations

Page 230: De Sève, drawing, Moitte, gravure, *Le grand barbet*, in George-Louis Leclerc Buffon, *Histoire naturelle, générale et particulière* (Paris, 1755), 5:300, pl. 37

Page 231: Courtesy of Cornell University Library

Page 240: American Philosophical Society

Page 248: Library of Congress, Geography and Map Division

Page 269: Reproduced courtesy of The Baring Archive

Page 276: Library of Congress, Geography and Map Division

Page 289: The Library Company of Philadelphia

Page 290: The Library Company of Philadelphia

Page 305: American Philosophical Society

Page 311: Courtesy of the American Antiquarian Society

Page 328: Gilbert Stuart, American, 1755–1828. *General Henry Knox,* about 1805. Oil on panel, 121.6 x 98.11 cm (47⅞ x 38⅝ in.), Museum of Fine Arts, Boston. Deposited by the City of Boston, L-R 30.76b. Photograph © 2014 Museum of Fine Arts, Boston

Page 344, above: *Au nom de la loi.* © Coll. Musée de la Révolution française / Domaine de Vizille. MRF 2001.6; below: *Deux scènes avec des aérostats (souvenir du général Meusnier La Place).* © Coll. Musée de la Révolution française / Domaine de Vizille. MRF 1985-147

Page 347: The Library Company of Philadelphia

Page 357: Université de Montreal

Page 361: Courtesy of the John Carter Brown Library at Brown University

Page 362: Special Collections Research Center, University of Chicago Library

Page 364: Library of Congress, Geography and Map Division

Page 377: Courtesy of The Lewis Walpole Library, Yale University

Page 379: Document preserved by the National Archives of France, Pierrefitte-Sur-Seine, cliché Atelier Photographique des Archives Nationales

Page 385, above: The Library Company of Philadelphia; below: The Library Company of Philadelphia

Page 388: Courtesy of the John Carter Brown Library at Brown University

Page 398: Courtesy of Alexis and Diane de Noailles

Page 405: The Library Company of Philadelphia

Page 409: Benjamin West, American, 1738–1820, *The Hope Family of Sydenham, Kent,* 1802, oil on canvas, 183.2 x 258.44 cm (72⅛ x 101¾ in.), Museum of Fine Arts, Boston. Abbott Lawrence Fund, 06.2362, Museum of Fine Arts, Boston. Photograph © 2014 Museum of Fine Arts, Boston

Page 420: © RMN-Grand Palais / Art Resource, NY

INDEX

✑

Page numbers in *italics* refer to illustrations.
Page numbers beginning with 429 refer
to endnotes.